POLITICAL SCIENCE: AN INTRODUCTION

NINTH EDITION

Michael G. Roskin
Lycoming College

Robert L. Cord

James A. Medeiros

Walter S. Jones

PEARSON
Prentice Hall

UPPER SADDLE RIVER, NEW JERSEY 07458

Library of Congress Cataloging-in-Publication Data

Political science: an introduction/Michael G. Roskin . . . [et al.].—9th ed.
　　　p. cm.
　　Includes bibliographical references and index.
　　ISBN 0-13-193291-8
　　1. Political science.　I. Roskin, Michael.
　　JA71.P623 2006
　　320—dc22

2005010383

Editorial Director: Charlyce Jones Owen
Editorial Supervisor/Assistant: Maureen Diana
Marketing Manager: Kara Kindstrom
Marketing Assistant: Jennifer Lang
Prepress and Manufacturing Buyer: Sherry Lewis
Interior Design: John P. Mazzola
Cover Art Director: Jayne Conte
Cover Design: Bruce Kenselaar
Cover Photo: Michael G. Roskin
Composition/Full-Service Project Management: Kari Callaghan Mazzola and John P. Mazzola
Director, Image Resource Center: Melinda Reo
Manager, Rights and Permissions: Zina Arabia
Manager, Visual Research: Beth Brenzel
Manager, Cover Visual Research and Permissions: Karen Sanatar
Image Permission Coordinator: Cynthia Vincenti
Printer/Binder: Courier Companies, Inc.
Cover Printer: Phoenix Color Corp.

This book was set in 10/12 Meridien.

Pearson Education LTD.
Pearson Education Singapore, Pte. Ltd
Pearson Education, Canada, Ltd
Pearson Education–Japan
Pearson Education Australia PTY, Limited

Pearson Education North Asia Ltd
Pearson Educación de Mexico, S.A. de C.V.
Pearson Education Malaysia, Pte. Ltd
Pearson Education, Upper Saddle River, NJ

10 9 8 7 6 5 4 3 2 1
ISBN 0-13-193291-8

CONTENTS

PREFACE   xxiii

PART I   THE BASES OF POLITICS

CHAPTER 1
A SCIENCE OF POLITICS?   1

The Master Science   2
  History   3
  Human Geography   4
  Economics   4
  Sociology   4
  Anthropology   4
  Psychology   5
Political Power   5
  Biological   5
  Psychological   8
  Cultural   8
  Rational   9
  Irrational   10
  Power as a Composite   11

Is Politics a Science?   12
    The Struggle to See Clearly   *12*
    What Good Is Political Science?   *15*
Key Terms   16
Key Web Sites   17
Further Reference   17

CHAPTER 2

THEORIES: CLASSIC AND MODERN   18

Classic Theories   20
    The Contractualists   *22*
    Marxist Theories   *23*
    Institutional Theories   *25*
Contemporary Theories   26
    Behavioralism   *26*
    Systems Theory   *28*
    Modernization Theory   *31*
    Rational-Choice Theory   *32*
    New Institutionalism   *33*
Key Terms   34
Key Web Sites   34
Further Reference   35

CHAPTER 3

NATIONS, STATES, AND GOVERNMENTS   36

The Elements of Nationhood   37
    Territory   *37*
    Population   *39*
    Independence   *39*
    Government   *40*
The Crises of Nation Building   41
    Identity   *41*
    Legitimacy   *41*
    Penetration   *41*
    Participation   *42*
    Distribution   *42*

Government: What It Is and What It Does   44
  Classifying Governments   45
  The State as Agent of Modernization   47
Making Public Policy   50
  Public Policies: Material and Symbolic   51
Key Terms   52
Key Web Sites   53
Further Reference   53

CHAPTER 4

INDIVIDUALS AND CONSTITUTIONS   54

Constitutions in the Modern World   55
  The Highest Law of the Land   56
  The Purpose of a Constitution   59
The Adaptability of the U.S. Constitution   61
  Can the Constitution Ensure Rights?   62
Freedom of Expression in the United States   65
  Free Speech and Sedition   66
Key Terms   69
Key Web Sites   70
Further Reference   70

CHAPTER 5

DEMOCRACY, TOTALITARIANISM, AND AUTHORITARIANISM   71

Modern Democracy   73
  Representative Democracy   74
Democracy in Practice: Elitism or Pluralism?   78
Totalitarianism   82
  What Is Totalitarianism?   82
Authoritarianism   86
  Authoritarianism and the Developing Nations   87
The Democratization of Authoritarian Regimes   87
Key Terms   90
Key Web Sites   90
Further Reference   91

PART II   POLITICAL ATTITUDES

CHAPTER 6

POLITICAL IDEOLOGIES   92

What Is Ideology?   93
The Major Ideologies   93
   Classic Liberalism   93
   Classic Conservatism   96
   Modern Liberalism   97
   Modern Conservatism   98
   Marxist Socialism   99
   Social Democracy   101
   Communism   102
   Nationalism   105
   Fascism   106
Ideology in Our Day   107
   The Collapse of Communism   107
   Neoconservatism   108
   Libertarianism   109
   Feminism   109
   Environmentalism   110
Is Ideology Finished?   111
Key Terms   112
Key Web Sites   112
Further Reference   113

CHAPTER 7

POLITICAL CULTURE   114

What Is Political Culture?   115
   Political Culture and Public Opinion   115
   Participation in America   117
The Decay of Political Culture   119
   Elite and Mass Cultures   122
   Political Subcultures   123
Political Socialization   127
   The Agents of Socialization   127

Key Terms   131
Key Web Sites   131
Further Reference   132

CHAPTER 8

PUBLIC OPINION   **133**

The Shape of Public Opinion   135
   Social Class   136
   Education   137
   Region   137
   Religion   138
   Age   139
   Gender   139
   Ethnic Group   141
Public Opinion Polls   141
   Polling Techniques   143
   How Reliable Are the Polls?   144
American Opinion   145
   Presidential Ratings   145
   Liberals and Conservatives   146
   Who Pays Attention?   147
Is Polling Fair?   149
   Should America Be Governed by Polls?   149
Key Terms   150
Key Web Sites   150
Further Reference   151

PART III   POLITICAL INTERACTIONS

CHAPTER 9

POLITICAL COMMUNICATION AND THE MEDIA   **152**

Communication in Politics   153
   Modern Mass Media   154
The Giant: Television   157

Television News   *158*

Television and Politics   *160*

Television: Ownership and Control   *164*

Are We Poorly Served?   166

What Can Be Done?   *167*

The Adversaries: Media and Government   168

Key Terms   171

Key Web Sites   171

Further Reference   172

CHAPTER 10

INTEREST GROUPS   173

What Is an Interest Group?   173

Who Belongs to Interest Groups?   *175*

Interest Groups and Government   *175*

Bureaucrats as an Interest Group   *177*

Effective Interest Groups   178

Political Culture   *178*

The Rise of Big Money   *179*

The Rise of Single-Issue Groups   *181*

Size and Membership   *183*

Access   *183*

Strategies of Interest Groups   *185*

Interest Groups: An Evaluation   189

Stalemating Political Power   *190*

Key Terms   191

Key Web Sites   191

Further Reference   192

CHAPTER 11

POLITICAL PARTIES AND PARTY SYSTEMS   193

Functions of Parties   194

A Bridge between People and Government   *194*

Aggregation of Interests   *194*

Integration into the Political System   194
Political Socialization   195
Mobilization of Voters   196
Organization of Government   196
Parties in Democracies   196
Centralization   196
Setting Government Policy   199
Party Participation in Government   199
Financing the Party   200
Classifying Political Parties   201
The Party in Communist States   201
Party Systems   204
Classifying Party Systems   204
The Party System and the Electoral System   207
Are Parties Fading?   209
Key Terms   210
Key Web Sites   210
Further Reference   210

Chapter 12

Elections   212

Why Do People Vote?   212
Who Votes?   215
Income and Education   216
Race   216
Age   217
Gender   217
Place of Residence   218
How Do People Vote?   219
Party Identification   219
Who Votes How?   220
Class Voting   221
Regional Voting   223
Religious Blocs   223
Age Groups   223
Gender Gap   223

Marriage Gap   224
Racial Minorities   224
Urban Voting   224

Electoral Realignment   224
A Reagan Realignment?   225
What Wins Elections?   226
Retrospective Voting   229
Candidate Strategies and Voter Groups   230
Key Terms   231
Key Web Sites   231
Further Reference   232

PART IV   THE INSTITUTIONS OF POLITICS

CHAPTER 13

THE BASIC INSTITUTIONS OF GOVERNMENT   233

The Form of State   235
Electoral Systems   236
Single-Member Districts   236
Proportional Representation   239
Unitary or Federal Systems   240
Unitary Systems   241
Federal Systems   243
The United States: Balkanization of Government   248
The Unitary-Federal Mixture   250
Choosing Institutions   250
Key Terms   251
Key Web Sites   252
Further Reference   252

CHAPTER 14

LEGISLATURES   253

Presidential and Parliamentary Systems   255
Separation and Fusion of Powers   257
Advantages of Parliamentary Systems   259

What Legislatures Do   262
    The Committee System   262
    A Closer Look at Legislatures   265
The Decline of Legislatures   268
    Structural Disadvantages   268
    Lack of Expertise   268
    Psychological Disadvantages   270
    The Absentee Problem   270
    Lack of Turnover   271
    The Dilemma of Parliaments   271
Key Terms   272
Key Web Sites   272
Further Reference   273

CHAPTER 15

EXECUTIVES   274

Presidents and Prime Ministers   275
    "Forming a Government" in Britain   275
    "Constructive No Confidence" in Germany   276
    "Cohabitation" in France   276
    The "Presidentialization" of Prime Ministers   277
    Executive Terms   277
The Roles of the Executive   279
    Head of State   279
    Chief of Government   279
    Party Chief   280
    Commander in Chief   280
    Chief Diplomat   281
    Dispenser of Appointments   281
    Chief Legislator   281
Executive Leadership   281
Disabled Presidents   283
Cabinets   289
    Who Serves in a Cabinet?   289
    The Rise of Noncabinet Advisers   290
The Danger of Expecting Too Much   291
Key Terms   292

Key Web Sites   292
Further Reference   293

CHAPTER 16

ADMINISTRATION AND BUREAUCRACY   294

The U.S. Federal Bureaucracy   295
    The Cabinet Departments   295
    Federal Agencies   296
    Independent Regulatory Agencies   296
Bureaucracies in Other Nations   296
    Communist Countries   297
    France   297
    Germany   298
    Great Britain   299
Characteristics of Bureaucracies   300
Bureaucracy in Modern Governments   301
    Administration   301
    Services   304
    Regulation   304
    Licensing   305
    Information Gathering   306
The Trouble with Bureaucracy   306
    Administrator or Policymaker?   307
    Adjudication   307
    Discretionary Implementation   308
    Rule Making   308
    Advisory Roles   308
What to Do with Bureaucracy?   309
    Ombudsmen   310
    Legislative Checks   310
    Cutting   310
    Decentralization   311
    Politicize the Bureaucracy   311
Bureaucracy and Society   312
Key Terms   313
Key Web Sites   313
Further Reference   313

CHAPTER 17

LEGAL SYSTEMS AND THE COURTS   315

Types of Law   316
- *Criminal Law   316*
- *Civil Law   317*
- *Constitutional Law   317*
- *Administrative Law   317*
- *International Law   318*

The Courts, the Bench, and the Bar   320
- *The U.S. Court System   320*
- *Judges   321*
- *Comparing Courts   322*
- *The British Court System   323*
- *The European Court System   323*

The Role of the Courts   324
- *The U.S. Supreme Court   325*
- *The Supreme Court's Political Role   327*
- *The Views of Judges   327*
- *The Political Impact of the Court   328*

Key Terms   331
Key Web Sites   332
Further Reference   332

PART V   WHAT POLITICAL SYSTEMS DO

CHAPTER 18

POLITICAL ECONOMY   334

Government and the Economy   335
- *Inflation   337*
- *Tax Hike   337*
- *Balance of Payments   337*
- *Gold Standard   340*
- *Wage-Price Freeze   340*
- *Oil Shocks   340*
- *Stagflation   341*

Interest Rates   *341*

Tax Cut   *342*

Budget Deficits   *343*

Trade Deficits   *344*

Budget Balancing   *344*

Who Is Entitled to What?   345

The Costs of Welfare   *348*

How Big Should Government Be?   351

Key Terms   353

Key Web Sites   353

Further Reference   354

CHAPTER 19

VIOLENCE AND REVOLUTION   355

System Breakdown   356

Violence as a Symptom   *356*

Types of Violence   *357*

Change as a Cause of Violence   *362*

Revolutions   364

Intellectuals and Revolution   *364*

The Stages of Revolution   *366*

After the Revolution   368

The Waning of Revolution   *370*

Key Terms   373

Key Web Sites   374

Further Reference   374

CHAPTER 20

INTERNATIONAL RELATIONS   375

Power and National Interest   377

The Role of Elites   379

Keeping Peace   383

World Government   *383*

Collective Security   *383*

Functionalism   *384*

Third-Party Assistance   *384*

    Diplomacy   *385*

    Peacekeeping   *385*

  The Cold War   386

    Truman Doctrine   *386*

    Marshall Plan   *386*

    Containment   *387*

    Deterrence   *387*

  Beyond Sovereignty?   389

    The United Nations   *390*

    The North Atlantic Treaty Organization   *390*

  Key Terms   391

  Key Web Sites   391

  Further Reference   392

CHAPTER 21

THE GLOBAL SYSTEM   393

  Historical Systems   394

    The Nineteenth-Century Balance of Power System   *395*

    The Interwar System   *395*

    The Bipolar Cold War System   *395*

  What System Is Emerging?   396

    A Unipolar Model   *396*

    A Counterweight Model   *396*

    A Multipolar Model   *397*

    A Stratified Model   *398*

    A Zones-of-Chaos Model   *398*

    A Globalized Model   *398*

    A Resource-Wars Model   *401*

    A "Clash-of-Civilizations" Model   *401*

    A Proliferation Model   *402*

  Foreign Policy: Involved or Isolated?   404

    Cycles of U.S. Foreign Policy   *405*

    The United States in a Dangerous World   *409*

  Key Terms   410

  Key Web Sites   411

  Further Reference   411

INDEX   412

FEATURE BOXES

CHAPTER 1

KEY CONCEPTS   "Never Get Angry at a Fact"   3
KEY CONCEPTS   Legitimacy, Sovereignty, and Authority   6
HOW TO . . .   Study a Chapter   13
KEY CONCEPTS   Politics versus Political Science   15

CHAPTER 2

CLASSIC WORKS   Not Just Europeans   21
HOW TO . . .   Thesis Statements   27
KEY CONCEPTS   Models: Simplifying Reality   30
KEY CONCEPTS   Politics as a Game   33

CHAPTER 3

KEY CONCEPTS   The Notion of Nation   38
KEY CONCEPTS   War and Nation Building   43
CLASSIC WORKS   Aristotle's Six Types of Government   46
HOW TO . . .   Support Your Thesis   48
KEY CONCEPTS   Dahl's "Influence Terms"   49

CHAPTER 4

CASE STUDIES   The Dangers of Changing Constitutions   56
CASE STUDIES   Canada's New Constitution   60
CASE STUDIES   The Right to Bear Arms   62
KEY CONCEPTS   What Is a Right?   63
CASE STUDIES   The Internment of Japanese Americans   64
HOW TO . . .   Sources   67
CASE STUDIES   The Pentagon Papers   68

CHAPTER 5

KEY CONCEPTS   The "Two-Turnover Test"   75
HOW TO . . .   References   79
CASE STUDIES   Image and Reality of Total Control   85
KEY CONCEPTS   Why Democracies Fail   88
CASE STUDIES   Democracy in Iraq?   90

CHAPTER 6

CLASSIC WORKS   The Origins of Ideologies   94
KEY CONCEPTS   Classifying Ideologies   95
CASE STUDIES   Why Did Capitalism Not Collapse?   100
HOW TO . . .   Tight Writing   103
CASE STUDIES   Islamism: A New Ideology   111

CHAPTER 7

KEY CONCEPTS   Civil Society   116
CLASSIC WORKS   The Civic Culture   118
CASE STUDIES   America the Religious   121
HOW TO . . .   Quotations   122
CASE STUDIES   Quebec: "Maîtres Chez Nous"   125
KEY CONCEPTS   Culture and Development   128
CLASSIC WORKS   The Authoritarian Personality   130

CHAPTER 8

KEY CONCEPTS   What Public Opinion Is and Isn't   134
KEY CONCEPTS   Classic Opinion Curves   140
CASE STUDIES   A Short History of Polling   142
HOW TO . . .   Variables   144
CLASSIC WORKS   Almond's Three Publics   148

CHAPTER 9

CLASSIC WORKS   The Two-Step Flow of Mass Communications   154
KEY CONCEPTS   The Tendency to Media Monopoly   155
KEY CONCEPTS   The Elite Media   156
KEY CONCEPTS   The Web: Newest Mass Medium?   158
HOW TO . . .   Definitions   161
KEY CONCEPTS   The Television Wasteland   165
CASE STUDIES   The Media and Watergate   169
CASE STUDIES   The Media and the Iraq War   170

CHAPTER 10

KEY CONCEPTS   How Interest Groups Differ from Political Parties   174
CASE STUDIES   NDEA: How Government Created an Interest Group   176
KEY CONCEPTS   Countervailing Power   177
CASE STUDIES   French Antipluralism   178
CASE STUDIES   The Enron Scandal   179
CASE STUDIES   The Rise of Political Action Committees   180
CASE STUDIES   How Powerful Are U.S. Unions?   184
HOW TO . . .   Tables   186
CASE STUDIES   How the NAACP Used the Courts   187
CLASSIC WORKS   Olson's Theory of Interest Groups   190

CHAPTER 11

CASE STUDIES   FDR's Coalition Party   195
HOW TO . . .   Cross-Tabulation   197
KEY CONCEPTS   Parties That Ignore Voters   198

Classic Works   Duverger's Three Types of Parties   200
Classic Works   Kirchheimer's "Catchall" Party   203
Key Concepts   What Is a "Relevant" Party?   205
Case Studies   Multiparty Systems Are More Fun   206
Classic Works   Sartori's Types of Party Competition   208

Chapter 12

Case Studies   Is the U.S. Electoral System Defective?   214
Classic Works   Down's Theory of Voting   216
Case Studies   The Puzzle of Education and Voting   218
How to . . .   Tendency Statements   221
Key Concepts   Partisan Polarization   227
Case Studies   The 9/11 Election   229
Key Concepts   Changing Positions   230

Chapter 13

Key Concepts   Legitimacy and Monarchy   237
Case Studies   French and German Variations   238
Case Studies   The Shaky Lives of Confederations   240
How to . . .   Percentages   243
Key Concepts   Nationality and Citizenship   246
Key Concepts   Burden Shifting   249

Chapter 14

Key Concepts   Head of State versus Head of Government   257
Classic Works   Where Did the U.S. System Originate?   258
Key Concepts   Bicameral or Unicameral?   261
Key Concepts   Pork-Barrel Politics   264
How to . . .   Longitudinal Study   267
Case Studies   Congressional Overspending   269

CHAPTER 15

CASE STUDIES Israel's Directly Elected Prime Ministers 277

CASE STUDIES Authoritarianism Returns to Russia 278

CASE STUDIES Limiting the President's War Powers 280

KEY CONCEPTS An Imperial Presidency? 282

CLASSIC WORKS Barber's Presidential Character 284

HOW TO . . . Graphs 286

CLASSIC WORKS Lasswell's Psychology of Power 288

CHAPTER 16

CASE STUDIES Japan: Bureaucrats in Command 298

CLASSIC WORKS Weber's Characteristics of Bureaucracies 300

HOW TO . . . Scattergram 302

KEY CONCEPTS Bureaucratic Politics 305

CLASSIC WORKS Djilas's "New Class" 306

CASE STUDIES Bureaucrats and Smoking 309

CHAPTER 17

CLASSIC WORKS The Roots of Law 316

KEY CONCEPTS Common Law versus Code Law 318

CASE STUDIES Law in Russia 325

CASE STUDIES Marbury v. Madison 326

HOW TO . . . Fourfold Table 329

CHAPTER 18

CASE STUDIES Postwar U.S. Recessions 336

HOW TO . . . Maps 338

CASE STUDIES How High Are U.S. Taxes? 342

CASE STUDIES Up and Down Phases of the U.S. Boom 343

CASE STUDIES The Growth of Inequality 345

KEY CONCEPTS What Is Poverty? 346

KEY CONCEPTS Poverty and Ideology 348

Chapter 19

Key Concepts   Terrorism   358

How to . . .   Thinkpiece   360

Key Concepts   Rising Expectations   363

Case Studies   Revolutionary Political Warfare in Vietnam   365

Case Studies   The Iranian Revolutionary Cycle   367

Case Studies   Anti-Communist Revolutions   370

Chapter 20

Key Concepts   Types of National Interest   378

Key Concepts   Why War?   380

How to . . .   "They"   382

Key Concepts   The Democratic Peace   383

Key Concepts   The Soviet Union and "Overstretch"   388

Chapter 21

Key Concepts   International Systems and Models   394

How to . . .   Theories   399

Key Concepts   The Importance of Economics   403

Case Studies   Interventions without Risk?   406

Classic Works   Klingberg's Alternation Theory   408

Classic Works   Kennan's Dinosaur Analogy   409

Classic Works   Thucydides on War   410

PREFACE

It is indeed gratifying to see a book that one has worked on reach a ninth edition; it means one is doing something right. It also means that the editors at Prentice Hall recognize that the approach, used in the first edition of 1974, was sound and should not be greatly altered. The success of the book owes something to the fact that it is neither a U.S. government text nor a comparative politics text. Instead, it draws examples from the United States and from other lands to introduce the whole field of political science to new students. Fresh from high school, few students know much of other political systems, something this book attempts to correct.

The ninth edition continues an eclectic approach that avoids selling any single theory, conceptual framework, or paradigm as the key to political science. Attempts to impose a methodological grand design are both unwarranted by the nature of the discipline and unconducive to the broadening of students' intellectual horizons. Instructors with a wide variety of viewpoints have no trouble using this text. Above all, the ninth edition still views politics as exciting and tries to communicate that feeling to young people approaching the discipline for the first time.

Instructors familiar with earlier editions will see much continuity in the ninth edition. I have had positive instructor responses to introducing methodologies early in an undergraduate's career. We're not talking about high-level numbers crunching—which I neither engage in nor advocate—but about a reality-testing frame of mind that looks for empirical verifiability. Where you can, of course, use numbers. I often discuss methodologies in class in connection with student papers, and I decided to insert those methodologies as "How to" boxes. The "How to" boxes each make one methodological point per chapter, and they include thesis statements, endnotes, quotations, tables, cross-tabs, percentages, graphs, and other

standard fare, all at the introductory level. I hope that instructors find this useful, and I am open to suggestions for altering or adding to these points. I also
added some vocabulary words to the running glossaries throughout the chapters.
The definitions are in the context under discussion; change that context and you
may need another definition. There is a difference, for example, between the
governing elites discussed in Chapter 5 (a tiny fraction of 1 percent of a population) and public-opinion elites discussed in Chapter 8 (probably several percent).

Some material—such as Key Concepts, Case Studies, and Classic Works—
continues in boxed form, both to highlight the material and to break up pages,
making the text reader-friendly. Those who have used previous editions will
have no trouble using the ninth edition, as the overall structure of the text stays
the same. The impact of recent events—such as the Iraq War and the 2004 presidential election—is discussed throughout the text.

■ SUPPLEMENTS

COMPANION WEBSITE™

www.prenhall.com/roskin   This Website brings an online study guide to students and a valuable tool to instructors. When students log on, they will find a
wealth of study and research sources. Chapter outlines and summaries with special features from the book, true/false tests, fill-in-the-blank tests, and multiple-
choice tests, all with immediate feedback and chapter page numbers, give students
ample opportunity to review the information. The site also includes a large variety of links to sites pertaining to material covered in each chapter of the text.
For instructors, there is a faculty resource section that includes links to helpful
sites, graphics to download from the book, and textual PowerPoint slides to use
in presentations.

INSTRUCTOR'S MANUAL WITH TEST ITEM FILES

An instructor's manual with test item files is available to instructors from their
Prentice Hall representative.

■ ACKNOWLEDGMENTS

Several people reviewed this and earlier editions, and I sincerely considered most
of their comments. For this edition, I wish to thank Rob Alexander, Ohio Northern University; John Mercurio, San Diego State University; James T. McHugh,
Roosevelt University; and Joseph Marbach, Seton Hall University.

Are further changes needed in the book, or have I got it about right? Instructors' input on this matter—or indeed on anything else related to the text or supplementary materials—is highly valued. Instructors may contact me directly at Lycoming College, Department of Political Science, Williamsport, Pennsylvania 17701, or by e-mail at roskin@lycoming.edu.

Michael G. Roskin

A SCIENCE OF POLITICS?

CHAPTER 1

QUESTIONS TO CONSIDER

- Why is politics now out of favor?
- What does it mean to "never get angry at a fact"?
- Why did Aristotle call politics "the master science"?
- What did Machiavelli bring to the study of politics?
- How are legitimacy, sovereignty, and authority different but similar?
- Is the Iraqi government now legitimate? How can you tell?
- Is politics largely biological, psychological, cultural, rational, or irrational?
- How can something as messy as politics be a science?

Interest in politics in the United States has slumped. Not only students but also attentive and educated citizens have turned away from politics. People are more likely to talk about sports and real estate than politics. The mass media find the strongest viewer and reader interest in health and business news, lifestyles, and famous personalities. Except when jolted by war and terrorism, political news is less interesting; many ignore even election campaigns.

This depoliticization is a major topic of investigation by political scientists. Is it a disgust at politicians and their constant, empty struggle for partisan advantage? Is it a feeling of helplessness, a sense that individual citizens do not matter? Is it the perception that Washington is the playground of rich and powerful interest groups who simply buy whatever they want, including politicians? Or is it a healthy sign that in relatively good times people naturally turn to other concerns? If the economy is not bad and world problems seem distant, why follow politics? Perhaps terrorism and war are needed to renew interest in politics.

It is the thesis of this book that politics still matters. If you do not take an interest and participate, someone else will, and they will influence the decisions that govern your lives. Will they take us to war in a foreign land? Who might have to fight in that war? You. Will they alter the tax code to favor certain groups of citizens and corporations? Who will have to pay in taxes what others avoid paying? You. Will they set up federal programs whose costs escalate far beyond what anyone had foreseen? Who then will have to pay these costs? You. One of the tasks of this book is to make you aware of what politics is and how it works so that you can look after yourself and prevent others from using you. The ignorant are manipulated.

Many find politics distasteful, and perhaps they are right. Politics may be inherently immoral or, at any rate, amoral. Misuse of power, influence peddling, and outright corruption are prominent features of politics. But you need not like the thing you study. Biologists may behold a disease-causing bacterium under a microscope. They do not "like" the bacterium but are interested in how it grows, how it does its damage, and how it may be eradicated. Neither do they get angry at the bacterium and smash the glass slide with a hammer. Biologists first understand the forces of nature and then work with them to improve humankind's existence. Political scientists try to do the same with politics.

■ THE MASTER SCIENCE

Aristotle, the founder of the **discipline**, called politics "the master science." He meant that almost everything happens in a political context, that the decisions of the *polis* (the Greek city-state) governed most other things. Politics, in the words of Yale's Harold Lasswell, is the study of "who gets what." But, some object, the economic system determines who gets what in countries with free markets. True, but who determines if we shall have a free-market system? Who tells Bill Gates that he must split up his giant Microsoft, a decision worth billions of dollars? Politics is intimately connected to economics.

Suppose something utterly natural occurs, like a flood. It is the political system that decides whether and where to build dikes and whether and which of the flood victims to aid. The flood is natural, but its impact on society is controlled in large part by politics. How about science, our bacteriologists squinting through microscopes? That is not political. But who funds the scientists' education and their research institutes? It could be private charity (the donors of which get tax breaks), but chances are the government plays a major role. When the U.S. government decided that AIDS research deserved top priority, funding for other programs was cut. Bacteria and viruses may be natural, but studying them is often quite political. In this case, it pitted gays against women concerned with breast cancer. Who gets what: funding to find a cure for AIDS or for breast cancer? The choice is political.

---

discipline   A field of study, often represented by an academic department or major.

KEY CONCEPTS

"NEVER GET ANGRY AT A FACT"

This basic point of all serious study sounds commonsensical but is often ignored, even in college courses. It actually traces back to the extremely complex thought of the German philosopher Hegel, who argued that things happen not by caprice or accident but for good and sufficient reasons: "Whatever is real is rational." That means that we should be able, by the application of our reason, to figure out why things are so. We study politics in a "naturalistic" mode, not getting angry at what we see but trying to understand how it came to be.

For example, we hear of a politician who took money from an interest group. As political scientists, we push our anger to the side and ask questions like: Do most politicians in that country take money? Is it an old tradition and does the culture of this country accept it? Do the people even expect politicians to take money? How big are campaign expenses? Can the politician possibly run for office without taking money? In short, we see if extralegal exchanges of cash are part and parcel of the political system. If they are, it makes no sense to get angry at an individual politician. If we dislike it, we may then consider how the system might be reformed to discourage the taking of money on the side. And reforms may not work. Japan reformed its electoral laws in an attempt to stamp out its traditional "money politics," but little changed. Like bacteria, some things in politics have lives of their own.

Because almost everything is political, studying politics means studying nearly everything. Some students select "interdisciplinary majors." Political science already is one, borrowing from and overlapping with all of the other social sciences. At times, it is hard to tell where history, human geography, economics, sociology, anthropology, and psychology leave off and political science begins. Here, briefly, is how political science relates to the other social sciences.

HISTORY

History is one of the chief sources of data for political scientists. When we discuss the politics of the Third French Republic (1871–1940), the growth of presidential power under Franklin Roosevelt, and even something as recent as the Cold War, we are studying history. But historians and political scientists look for different things and handle data differently. Typically, historians study one episode in detail, digging up documents, archives, and news accounts on the topic. With masses of data focused on just one point, they venture few or no generalizations. Political scientists, on the other hand, begin by looking for generalizations. We often take the findings of historians and compare and contrast them. A historian might do a detailed study of Weimar Germany (1919–1933); a political scientist might put that study alongside studies of France, Italy, and Russia of the same period to see what similarities and dissimilarities can be found. To be sure, some historians do comparative studies; they become de facto political scientists.

HUMAN GEOGRAPHY

Human geography (as distinct from physical geography) has in recent decades been neglected by political scientists, although it influences politics more than many realize. The territorial component of human behavior—borders, ethnic areas, trade flows, centralization of power, and regions—have great political ramifications. Strife in Afghanistan, Chechnya, and Kosovo are heavily geographical problems, as is Canada's unsettled federalism, from which some Quebeckers wish to depart. French political scientist André Siegfried pioneered the use of maps to explain regional political variations, a technique of today's electoral studies. The "red" and "blue" states in U.S. presidential elections show the relevance of political geography.

ECONOMICS

Economics, proclaim some economists, is the subject matter of politics. (Political scientists are apt to claim the opposite.) True, many political quarrels are economic: Who gets what? Sufficient economic development may be the basis for democracy; few poor countries are democratic. A declining economy may doom democracy, as was the fate of the Weimar Republic and recently of Russia. What policies promote economic development? How big a role should government have? What is the new *euro* currency doing to European union? When economists get into questions of policy, they become "political economists." A relatively new school of political science, "rational-choice theory," shares the economic perspective that humans generally pursue their self-interests.

SOCIOLOGY

Parts of sociology and political science merge. Sociologist Seymour Martin Lipset is equally renowned as a political scientist. It was he who first demonstrated the close connection between democracy and level of wealth. As we shall consider in the next chapter, political science conventionally starts by looking at society to see "who thinks what" about politics. In demonstrating how political views vary among social classes, regions, religions, genders, and age groups, sociology gives an empirical basis to political-culture, public-opinion, and electoral studies.

ANTHROPOLOGY

Anthropology, which traditionally focused on primitive societies, may seem little relevant to political science. But the descriptive and interviewing techniques of anthropology have been heavily adopted by political scientists. The subfield of political culture could be viewed as a branch of anthropology.

Japanese deference patterns, which we still see today, were laid down more than a millennium ago. Some current political systems still reserve political power for traditionally influential families or clans. In Central Asia the families of *emirs* who ruled under the Persians did so under the Russian tsars, the Communists, and now the newly independent states. In Africa, voting and violence follow tribal lines.

PSYCHOLOGY

Psychology, particularly social psychology, contributes much to political science's understanding of which personalities are attracted to politics, why and under what circumstances people obey authority figures, and how people form national, group, and voting attachments. Studies of Hitler, Stalin, and Mao Zedong are heavily psychological. Psychologists are especially good with **methodology**; they devise ways to study things objectively and teach us to doubt claims that have holes in them. Asking questions in a "blind" manner and "controlling" for certain factors are techniques developed from psychology.

■ POLITICAL POWER

Political science often uses the findings of other social sciences, but one feature distinguishes it from the others—its focus on power. Our second founding father (after Aristotle) is the Renaissance Florentine philosopher Niccolò Machiavelli, who emphasized the role of power in politics. You can take all the factors and approaches mentioned above, but if you are not using them to study power—which is a very broad subject—you are probably not doing political science.

Some people dislike the concept of **political power**. It smacks of coercion, inequality, occasionally of brutality. Some speakers denounce "power politics," suggesting governance without power, a happy band of brothers and sisters regulating themselves on the basis of love and sharing. Communities formed on such a basis do not last; or if they do last it is only by transforming themselves into conventional structures of leaders and led, buttressed by obedience patterns that look suspiciously like nasty old power. Political power seems to be built into the human condition. But why do some people hold political power over others? There is no definitive explanation of political power. Biological, psychological, cultural, rational, and irrational explanations have been put forward.

BIOLOGICAL

Aristotle said it first and perhaps best: "Man is by nature a political animal." (Aristotle's words were *zoon politikon,* which can be translated as either "political animal" or "social animal." The Greeks lived in city-states in which the *polis* was the same as society.) Aristotle meant that humans live naturally in herds, like elephants or deer. Biologically, they need each other for sustenance and survival. It is also natural that they array themselves into ranks of leaders and led, like all herd animals. Taking a cue from Aristotle, a modern biological explanation would say that forming a political system and obeying its leaders is innate human behavior, passed on

---

methodology   The techniques for studying questions objectively.
political power   Ability of one person to get another to do something.

LEGITIMACY, SOVEREIGNTY, AND AUTHORITY

These three related concepts—**legitimacy**, **sovereignty**, and **authority**—are basic to political science. Legitimacy originally meant that the rightful king or queen was on the throne by reason of "legitimate" birth. Since the Middle Ages, the term has broadened to mean not only the "legal right to govern" but also the "psychological right to govern." Legitimacy now refers to an attitude in people's minds—in some countries strong, in others weak—that the government's rule is rightful. Legitimacy in the United States is fairly high. Even Americans who do not particularly like the government generally obey it. We even pay taxes. One quick test of legitimacy: How many police are there? Few police, as in Sweden and Norway, indicates that little coercion is needed; legitimacy is high. Many police, as in Franco's Spain or Saddam Hussein's Iraq, indicated that much coercion was needed; legitimacy was low.

Where legitimacy is weak, few people feel obliged to pay their taxes and obey the law because the government itself is perceived as dirty and dishonest. Eventually, massive civil disobedience can break out, as it did in Yugoslavia in 2000. Citizens rallied against the criminal misrule of President Slobodan Milosevic; police batons and electoral rigging could not prevent him from being voted out of office. The Iraqi Governing Council of 2003–2004 was composed of highly educated Iraqis representative of all Iraqi groups, but it had little legitimacy because it had been installed by the U.S. occupation. Arguably, the Council was the best government Iraq will ever have, but few valued it. Without legitimacy, governments are ineffective.

A government achieves legitimacy several ways. At the most elemental level, it must provide security, so that people feel reasonably safe. Many Iraqis complained that, bad as Saddam was, under him they could walk down the street. As Hobbes (see Chapter 2) saw, no security means no legitimacy. Related to security is "rule of law." Regimes that provide it gain legitimacy. Just existing a long time fosters legitimacy. Citizens generally respect long-established governments. The fact that the Constitution is more than two centuries old confers great legitimacy on the U.S. government. New governments, on the other hand, have shaky legitimacy; their citizens have little or no respect for them.

A government gains legitimacy by governing well. Ensuring economic growth and jobs so that people can feed their families builds legitimacy. The government of West Germany, founded in 1949 after defeat in World War II, had little legitimacy at first, but level-headed political leadership with sound economic policies gradually earned the Bonn government legitimacy. On the other hand, the German Weimar Republic that followed World War I faced a series of economic and political catastrophes that undermined its legitimacy and let Hitler take power.

The structure of government contributes to its legitimacy. If people feel they are fairly represented and have a say in the selection of their officials, they are more likely to obey. Finally, governments shore up their legitimacy by national symbols. The flag, historic monuments, patriotic parades, and ringing speeches aim at convincing people that the government is legitimate and should be obeyed. Although they ended centuries of monarchy in 1975, in 2002 the Laotian Communist regime kneeled before a new bronze statue of the king who founded Laos's monarchy 650 years earlier. The Communists were trying to prop up their fraying legitimacy by tying themselves to the old kings, a symbol of legitimacy most Laotians could understand. When legitimacy has collapsed, however, the manipulation of national symbols may appear to be a hollow joke. A gigantic statue of dictator Marcos of the Philippines became an object of ridicule and a symbol of what was wrong with his regime. Symbols by themselves do not create legitimacy.

Sovereignty (from the Old French "to rule over") originally meant the power of a monarch over his or her kingdom. Later the term broadened to mean national control over the country's territory, boss of one's own turf. Nations are jealous of their sovereignty, and governments safeguard it. They maintain armies to deter foreign invasion, they control their borders with passports and visas, and they hunt down terrorists. Disputes over sovereignty are among the nastiest: Palestine, Northern Ireland, and Bosnia are examples.

Sovereignty is sometimes a legal fiction. Iraq regained nominal sovereignty in 2004 but was still under U.S. influence. Sovereignty and legitimacy are connected. Lebanese Muslims, for example, saw the Christian-dominated government as illegitimate. In 1975, civil strife broke among a dozen politico-religious militias. Syria occupied eastern Lebanon from 1976 to 2005, and Israel occupied southern Lebanon from 1982 to 2000. Lebanon in effect lost its sovereignty, which it is now trying to regain. For decades it could neither control its own territory nor repel foreign invaders. A loss of legitimacy led to a loss of sovereignty.

Authority is the psychological ability of leaders to get others to obey them. It relies on a sense of obligation based on the legitimate power of office. A private obeys a captain; a motorist obeys a state trooper; a student obeys a professor. But not all people obey authority. Some privates are insubordinate, some motorists are speeders, and some students neglect the assigned reading. Still, most people obey what they perceive as legitimate authority most of the time.

Some authority comes with the office, but it must also be cultivated. An American president gets much authority just because he is president. Gerald Ford was respected and obeyed even though he was not elected president or vice-president. Minority leader of the House of Representatives, Ford became vice-president when Spiro T. Agnew resigned and president when Richard Nixon resigned. Nixon, implicated in the Watergate scandal of 1972, suffered an erosion of executive authority so acute that he could not effectively govern. A president cannot rule by decree but must obtain the willing consent of Congress, the courts, the civil service, and important interest groups. When Nixon lost this consent, his power as president eroded.

In short, legitimacy means respect for a government; sovereignty, respect for a country; and authority, respect for a leader. None are automatic; all must be earned. Where you find one, you find the others. Where one erodes, so usually do the others.

The Berlin Wall crumbled in 1989 because the East German regime had lost legitimacy. (Michael Roskin)

to future generations with one's genes. Some thinkers argue that human politics shows the same "dominance hierarchies" that other mammals set up.

The advantage of the biological approach is its simplicity, but it raises a number of questions. If we grant that humankind is naturally political, how do we explain the instances when political groups fall apart and people disobey authority? Perhaps we could improve the theory by modifying it: Humans are imperfectly political (or social) animals. Most of the time people form groups and obey authority, but sometimes, under certain circumstances, they do not. This begs the question of which circumstances promote or undermine the formation of political groups.

PSYCHOLOGICAL

Psychological explanations of politics and obedience are closely allied with biological theories. Both posit needs derived from centuries of evolution in the formation of political groups. The psychologists have refined their views with empirical research. One is the famous Milgram study, in which unwitting subjects were instructed by a professor to administer progressively larger electric shocks to a victim. The "victim," strapped in a chair, was actually an actor who only pretended to suffer. Most of the subjects were willing to administer potentially lethal doses of electricity simply because the "professor"—an authority figure in a white lab smock—told them to. Most of the subjects disliked hurting the victim, but they rationalized that they were just following orders and that any harm done to the victim was really the professor's responsibility. They surrendered their actions to an authority figure.

Psychological studies also show that most people are naturally conformist. Most members of a group see things the group's way. Psychologist Irving Janis found many foreign policy mistakes were made in a climate of "groupthink," in which a leadership team tells itself that all is well and that the present policy is working. Groups tend to ignore doubters who tell them, for instance, that the Japanese will attack Pearl Harbor in 1941 or that the 1961 Bay of Pigs landing of Cuban exiles will fail. Obedience to authority and groupthink suggest that humans have deep-seated needs—possibly innate—to fit into groups and to go along with their norms. Perhaps this is what makes human society possible, but it also makes possible horrors such as the Nazi Holocaust and the more recent Balkan massacres.

CULTURAL

How much of human behavior is learned as opposed to biologically inherited? This is a very old debate. For much of the twentieth century, the *cultural theorists*—those who believe behavior is learned—dominated. Anthropologists concluded that all

---

legitimacy   Mass feeling that the government's rule is rightful and should be obeyed (see page 6).

sovereignty   A national government's being boss on its own turf, the last word in law in that country (see page 6).

authority   Political leaders' ability to command respect and exercise power (see page 6).

differences in behavior were cultural. Cooperative and peaceful societies raise their children that way, they argued. Political communities are formed and hold together on the basis of cultural values transmitted by parents, schools, churches, and the mass media. Political science developed an interesting subfield called *political culture,* and its researchers found that a country's political culture was formed by many long-term factors: religion, child rearing, land tenure, and economic development.

The cultural school maintains that trouble comes when the political system gets out of touch with the cultural system, as when the shah of Iran attempted to modernize an Islamic society that did not like Western values and lifestyles. The Iranians threw the shah out and celebrated the return of a medieval-style religious leader, who voiced the values favored by traditional Iranians. Cultural theories can also be applied to U.S. politics. Republicans tend to win elections by articulating the values of religion, family, and self-reliance, which are deeply ingrained into American culture. Many thinkers believe economic and political development depend heavily on **culture**.

The cultural approach to political life holds some optimism. If all human behavior is learned, bad behavior can be unlearned and society improved. Educating young people to be tolerant, cooperative, and just will gradually change a society's culture for the better, according to this view. Changing culture, however, is extremely difficult, as the American occupiers of Iraq discovered.

Although most thinkers agree that culture contributes a lot to political behavior, the theory has some difficulties. First, where does culture come from? History? Economics? Religion? Second, if all behavior is cultural, various political systems should be as different from each other as their cultures. But, especially in the realm of politics, we see similar political attitudes and patterns in lands with very different cultures. Politicians everywhere tend to become corrupt, regardless of culture.

RATIONAL

Another school of thought approaches politics as a **rational** thing; that is, people know what they want most of the time, and they have good reasons for doing what they do. Classic political theorists, such as Hobbes and Locke, as we shall see in the next chapter, held that humans form "civil society" because their powers of reason tell them that it is much better than anarchy. To safeguard life and property, people form governments. If those governments become abusive, the people have the right to dissolve them and start anew. This Lockean notion greatly influenced the U.S. Founding Fathers.

The biological, psychological, and cultural schools downplay human reason, claiming that people are either born or conditioned to certain behavior, and individuals seldom think rationally. But how can we then explain cases in which people break away from group conformity and argue independently? How can we explain a change of mind? "I was for Jones until he came out with

---

culture   Human behavior that is learned as opposed to inherited.
rational   Based on the ability to reason.

The Declaration of Independence, here being signed in large bold letters by John Hancock, embodied a rational view of politics. (Library of Congress)

his terrible economic policy, so now I'm voting for Smith." People make rational judgments like that all the time. A political system based on the presumption of human reason stands a better chance of governing justly and humanely. If leaders believe that people obey out of biological inheritance or cultural conditioning, they will think they can get away with all manner of corruption and misrule. If, on the other hand, rulers fear that people are rational, they will respect the public's ability to discern wrongdoing. Accordingly, even if people are not completely rational, it is good that rulers think they are.

IRRATIONAL

Late in the nineteenth century, a group of thinkers expounded the view that people are basically **irrational**, especially when it comes to political power. They are emotional and dominated by myths and stereotypes, and politics is really the manipulation of symbols. A crowd is like a wild beast that can be whipped up by charismatic leaders to do their bidding. What people regard as rational is really just myth; just keep feeding them myths to control them. The first practitioner of this school was Mussolini, founder of fascism in Italy, followed by Hitler in Germany. A soft-spoken Muslim fundamentalist, Osama bin Laden, got an irrational hold on thousands of fanatical followers. Believing the myth that America was the enemy of Islam, some happily ended their lives in terrorist acts.

There may be a good deal of truth to the irrational view of human political behavior, but it has catastrophic consequences. Leaders who use irrationalist techniques start believing their own propaganda and lead their nations to war, economic ruin, or tyranny. Some detect irrationalism even in the most advanced societies, where much of politics consists of screaming crowds and leaders striking heroic poses.

irrational   Based on the power of fears and myth to cloud reason.

POWER AS A COMPOSITE

There are elements of truth in all these explanations of political power. At different times in different situations, any one of them can explain power. Tom Paine's pamphlet *Common Sense* rationally explained why America should separate from Britain. The drafters of both the U.S. Declaration of Independence and the Constitution were imbued with the rationalism of their age. Following the philosophers then popular, they framed their arguments as if human political activity were as logical as Newtonian physics. The late historian Henry Steele Commager referred to the Constitution as "the crown jewel of the enlightenment," the culmination of an age of reason.

But how truly rational were they? By the late eighteenth century, the thirteen American colonies had grown culturally separate from Britain. People thought of themselves as Americans rather than as English colonists. They increasingly read American newspapers and communicated among themselves rather than with Britain. Perhaps the separation was more cultural than rational.

Nor can we forget the psychological and irrational factors. Samuel Adams was a gifted firebrand, Thomas Jefferson a powerful writer, and George Washington a charismatic general. The American break with Britain and the founding of a new order was a complex mixture of all these factors. The same complex mixture of factors goes into any political system you can mention. To be sure, at times one factor seems more important than others, but we cannot exactly determine the weight to give any one factor. And notice how the various factors blend into one another. The biological factors lead to the psychological, which in turn lead to the cultural, the rational, and the irrational, forming a seamless web.

One common mistake made about political power is viewing it as a finite, measurable quantity. Power is a connection between people, the ability of one person to get another to do his or her bidding. Political power does not come in jars or megawatts. Revolutionaries in some lands speak of "seizing power," as if power were kept in the national treasury and they could sneak in and grab it at night. The Afghan Taliban "seized power" in 1995–1996, but they were a minority of the Afghan population. Many Afghans hated them, and some fought them. Revolutionaries think that they automatically get legitimacy and authority when they "seize power"; they do not. Power is earned, not seized.

Is power identical to politics? Some power-mad people (including more than a few politicians) see the two as the same, but this is an oversimplification. We might see politics as a combination of goals or policies and the power necessary to achieve them. Power, in this view, is a prime *ingredient* of politics. It would be difficult to imagine a political system without political power. Even a religious figure who ruled on the basis of love would be exercising power over followers. It might be "nice power," but it would still be power. Power, then, is a sort of *enabling device* to carry out or implement policies and decisions. You can have praiseworthy goals, but unless you have the power to implement them, they remain wishful thoughts.

Others see the essence of politics as a *struggle for power,* a sort of gigantic game in which power is the goal. What, for example, are elections all about? The getting of power. There is a danger here, however. If power becomes the goal of politics, devoid of other purposes, it becomes cynical, brutal, and self-destructive. The Hitler regime destroyed itself in the worship of power. Obsessed with retaining presidential power, President Nixon ruined his own administration. As nineteenth-century British historian and philosopher Lord Acton put it, "Power tends to corrupt; absolute power corrupts absolutely."

■ Is Politics a Science?

If we cannot pinpoint which factors contribute what weight to politics, how can politics be a science? Part of the problem here is the definition of *science*. The original meaning of science, from the French, is simply "knowledge." Later, the natural sciences, which rely on measurement and calculation, took over the term. Now most people think of science as precise and factual, supported by experiments and data. Some political scientists (as we will consider later) have attempted to become like natural scientists; they **quantify** data and manipulate them statistically to validate **hypotheses**. The quantifiers make some good contributions, but usually they focus on small questions of detail rather than on large questions of meaning. This is because they generally have to stick to areas that can be quantified—public opinion, election returns, and congressional voting.

But large areas of politics are not quantifiable. How and why do leaders make their decisions? Many decisions are made in secret, even in democracies. We do not know exactly how decisions are made in the White House in Washington, the Elysée in Paris, or the Kremlin in Moscow. When members of Congress vote on an issue, can we be certain why they voted that way? Was it constituents' desires, the good of the nation, or the campaign contributions of interest groups? What did the Supreme Court have in mind when it ruled that laying off schoolteachers based on race is unconstitutional but hiring them based on race is not? Try quantifying that. Much of politics—especially dealing with how and why decisions are made—is just too complex to be quantified.

Does that mean that politics can never be like a natural science? Political science is an **empirical** science that accumulates both quantified and qualitative data. With such data we can find persistent patterns, much like in biology. Gradually, we begin to generalize. When the generalizations become firmer, we call them theories. In a few cases the theories become so firm that we may call them *laws*. In this way, the study of politics accumulates knowledge, the original meaning of science.

THE STRUGGLE TO SEE CLEARLY

Political science also resembles a natural science when its researchers, if they are professional, study things as they are and not as they wish them to be. This is more difficult in the study of politics than in the study of stars and cells. Most political

---

quantify   To measure with numbers.
hypothesis   An initial theory a researcher starts with, to be proved by evidence.
empirical   Based on observable evidence.

HOW TO . . .

STUDY A CHAPTER

Read each chapter before class. And do not simply read the chapter; *learn* it by writing down the following:

A. Find what strikes you as the *three main points*. Do not outline; construct three complete sentences, each with subject, verb, and predicate. They may be long and complex sentences, but they must be complete declarative sentences. You may find two, four, or six main points, but by the time you split, combine, and discard what may or may not be the main points, you will know the chapter. Look for abstract generalizations; the specifics come under the third point below, examples or case studies. Do not simply copy three sentences from the chapter; synthesize several sentences.

Examples

1. Study politics as a scientist studies nature, trying to understand reality and not getting angry at it.
2. Political science combines many disciplines but focuses on power: who holds it and how they use it.
3. Politics can be studied objectively, provided claims are supported by empirical evidence.

B. List a *dozen vocabulary words* and be able to define them. These are words new to you or words used in a specialized way. This text makes it easier with the Key Terms at the base of pages; otherwise, read with a dictionary handy.

Examples

authority	methodology
culture	political power
discipline	quantify
empirical	rational
hypothesis	scholarship
irrational	sovereignty
legitimacy	

C. Note specific *examples* or *case studies* that illustrate the main points or vocabulary words. Most will contain proper nouns (that is, capitalized). Examples are not main points or definitions; rather, they are empirical evidence that support a main point. The examples need not be complete sentences.

Examples

Aristotle's "master science"

AIDS vs. breast-cancer research

West Germany's success story

Communist regimes in Eastern Europe

Lebanon's loss of legitimacy and sovereignty

shah's regime in Iran erodes

scientists have viewpoints on current issues, and it is easy to let these views contaminate their analyses of politics. Indeed, precisely because a given question interests us enough to study it indicates that we bring a certain passion with us. Can you imagine setting to work on a topic you cared nothing about? If you are interested enough to study a question, you probably start inclined to one side. Too much of this, however, renders the study biased; it becomes a partisan outcry rather than a scholarly search for the truth. How can you guard against this? The traditional hallmarks of **scholarship** give some guidance. A scholarly work should be *reasoned*, *balanced*, and supported with *evidence*.

Reasoned   You must spell out your reasoning, and it should make sense. If your perspective is colored by an underlying assumption, you should say so. You might say, "For the purpose of this study, we assume that people are rational," or "This is a study of the psychology of voters in a small town." Your basic assumptions influence what you study and how you study it, but you can minimize bias by honestly stating your assumptions. Early in the twentieth century, German sociologist Max Weber, who contributed vastly to all the social sciences, held that any of your findings that support your political views must be discarded as biased. Few attempt to be that pure, but Weber's point is well-taken: Beware of structuring the study so that it comes out to support a given view.

Balanced   You can also minimize bias by acknowledging that there are other ways of looking at your topic. You should mention the various approaches to your topic and what they have found. Instructors are impressed that you know the literature in a given area. They are even more impressed when you can then criticize the previous studies and explain why you think they are incomplete or faulty: "The Jones study of voters found them largely apathetic, but this was an off-year election in which turnout is always lower." By putting several approaches and studies side-by-side and stating what you think of them and why, you present a much more objective and convincing case. Do not totally commit yourself to a particular viewpoint or theory, but admit that your view is one among several.

Evidence   All scholarly studies require evidence, ranging from the quantified evidence of the natural sciences to the qualitative evidence of the humanities. Political science utilizes both. Ideally, any statement open to interpretation or controversy should be supported with evidence. Common knowledge does not have to be supported; you need not cite the U.S. Constitution to "prove" that presidents serve four-year terms.

But if you say presidents have gained more and more power over the decades, you need evidence. At a minimum, you would cite a scholar who has amassed evidence to demonstrate this point. That is called a "secondary source," evidence

---

scholarship   Intellectual arguments supported by reason and evidence.

KEY CONCEPTS

POLITICS VERSUS POLITICAL SCIENCE

Political science ain't politics. It is not necessarily training to become a practicing politician. Political science is training in the analysis of politics, which may or may not aid working politicians. Side-by-side, the two professions compare like this:

Politicians	Political Scientists
love power	are skeptical of power
seek popularity	seek accuracy
think practically	think abstractly
hold firm views	reach tentative conclusions
offer single causes	offer many causes
see short-term payoff	see long-term consequences
plan for next election	plan for next publication
respond to groups	seek the good of the whole
seek name recognition	seek professional prestige

The two professions of politician and political scientist bear approximately the same relation to each other as do bacteria and bacteriologists.

that has passed through the mind of someone else. Most student papers use only secondary sources, but instructors are impressed when you use a "primary source," the original gathering of data, as in your own tabulation of what counties in your state showed the strongest Nader vote. Anyone reading a study must be able to review its evidence and judge if it is valid. You cannot keep your evidence or sources secret.

WHAT GOOD IS POLITICAL SCIENCE?

Some students come to political science supposing it is just opinions; they write exams or papers that ignore all or some of the preceding points. Yes, we all have political views, but if we let them dominate our study we get invalid results, junk political science. Professional political scientists push their personal views well to one side while engaged in study and research. First-rate thinkers are able to come up with results that actually refute their previously held opinion. When that happens, we have real intellectual growth, an exciting experience that should be your aim.

Something else comes with such an experience: You start to conclude that you should not have been so partisan in the first place. You may back away from the strong views you held earlier and take them with a grain of salt. Accordingly, political science is not necessarily training to become a practicing politician. Political science is training in objective and often complex analysis, whereas the practice of politics requires fixed, popular, and simplified opinions.

Political science can contribute to good government, often by warning those in office that all is not well, "speaking Truth to Power," as the Quakers say. Sometimes this advice is useful to working politicians. Public-opinion polls, for example, showed an erosion of government legitimacy in the United States starting in the mid-1960s. The causes were Vietnam, Watergate, and inflation. Candidates for political office, knowing public opinion, could tailor their campaigns and policies to try to counteract this decline. Ronald Reagan, with his sunny disposition and upbeat views, utilized the discontent to win two presidential terms.

As far back as 1950, the American Political Science Association warned about the weaknesses of U.S. political parties; they were decentralized and uncontrolled. Political parties in the United States cannot force views on members, nor do the parties have control over who call themselves members. In 1989, David Duke, a former leader of the Ku Klux Klan with ties to Nazis, won a seat as a Republican in the Louisiana state legislature. The Republican National Committee tried to distance itself from Duke, but he continued to call himself a Republican, and there was no legal way to stop him. Parties in the United States are too weak even to control who uses their names.

Some political scientists warned for years of the weak basis of the shah's regime in Iran. Unfortunately, such warnings were unheeded. Washington's policy was to support the shah; only two months before the end of his reign did the U.S. embassy in Tehran start reporting how unstable Iran had become. State Department officials had let politics contaminate their political analyses; they could not see clearly. Journalists were not much better; few covered Iran until violence broke out. Years in advance, American political scientists specializing in Iran saw trouble coming. Political science can be useful.

KEY TERMS

authority (p. 8)	methodology (p. 5)
culture (p. 9)	political power (p. 5)
discipline (p. 2)	quantify (p. 12)
empirical (p. 12)	rational (p. 9)
hypothesis (p. 12)	scholarship (p. 14)
irrational (p. 10)	sovereignty (p. 8)
legitimacy (p. 8)	

Key Web Sites

American Political Science Association
www.apsanet.org

CIA World Factbook
www.odci.gov/cia/publications/factbook/index.html

John F. Kennedy School of Government at Harvard
ksgwww.harvard.edu/ksgpress/opin/index.html

Yahoo's political science section
dir.yahoo.com/Social_Science/Political_Science/

Further Reference

Almond, Gabriel A. *Ventures in Political Science: Narratives and Reflections.* Boulder, CO: Lynne Rienner, 2002.

Boulding, Kenneth E. *Three Faces of Power.* Newbury Park, CA: Sage, 1989.

Friedrich, Carl J., ed. *Authority.* Cambridge, MA: Harvard University Press, 1958.

Huysmans, Jeff. *What Is Politics? A Short Introduction.* New York: Columbia University Press, 2004.

Janis, Irving L. *Victims of Groupthink: A Psychological Study of Foreign-Policy Decisions and Fiascoes.* Boston, MA: Houghton Mifflin, 1972.

Kagan, Jerome. *Galen's Prophecy: Temperament and Human Nature.* New York: Basic Books, 1994.

Lasswell, Harold. *Politics: Who Gets What, When, How.* New York: McGraw-Hill, 1936.

Lewellen, Ted C. *Political Anthropology: An Introduction,* 3rd ed. Westport, CT: Praeger, 2003.

Milgram, Stanley. *Obedience to Authority: An Experimental View.* New York: Harper & Row, 1974.

Minogue, Kenneth. *Politics: A Very Short Introduction.* New York: Oxford University Press, 1995.

Shively, W. Phillips. *The Craft of Political Research,* 6th ed. Upper Saddle River, NJ: Prentice Hall, 2005.

Theodoulou, Stella, and Rory O'Brien, eds. *Methods for Political Inquiry: The Discipline, Philosophy, and Analysis of Politics.* Upper Saddle River, NJ: Prentice Hall, 1999.

Wilson, Edward O. *Sociobiology: The New Synthesis.* Cambridge, MA: Harvard University Press, 1975.

THEORIES:
CLASSIC AND MODERN

CHAPTER

2

QUESTIONS TO CONSIDER

- Who founded political science?
- What did Machiavelli, Confucius, Kautilya, and Ibn Khaldun have in common?
- How did Hobbes, Locke, and Rousseau differ?
- What is the crux of Marx's theory?
- What is "positivism" and how does it underlay much of social science?
- What is Easton's theory of the political system?
- How does modernization theory borrow from Marx?
- What is rational-choice theory?
- What is a "provable thesis"?

Why bother with theories at all, wonder many students new to political science. Why not just accumulate facts and let the facts structure themselves into a coherent whole? Because they won't. Gathering facts without a guiding principle leads only to large collections of meaningless facts. To be sure, theories can grow too complex and abstract and depart from the real world, but without at least some theoretical perspective, we do not even know what questions to ask. Even if you say you have no theories, you probably have some unspoken ones. The kind of questions you ask and which you ask first are the beginning of theorizing.

Take, for example, the structure of this book. We have adopted the view—widespread in political science for decades—that the proper starting point of political analysis is society. We assume that politics grows out of society. We start with people's values, attitudes, and opinions and see how they influence government. The subtitle of one influential book by a leading sociologist was *The Social Bases of Politics.* Its message: You start with society and see how it influences politics.

But that could stack the deck. If you assume that society is the basis of politics and that values and opinions are the important facts, you will gather much material on values and opinions and relatively little on the history, structure, and policies of government. Everything else will appear secondary to citizens' values and opinions. And indeed, political science went through a period in which it was essentially sociology, and many political scientists did survey research. This was part of the behavioral tide; survey research was seen as the only way to be "scientific" because it generated quantifiable data.

Most textbooks offered a "percolation up" model of politics. The first major bloc in most studies was concerned with the society and covered such things as how political views were distributed, how interest groups formed, who supported which political parties, and how people voted. That was the basis, the bottom part of the pyramid. The second major bloc was usually the institutions of government. They were assumed to be a reflection of the underlying social base. Legislatures and executives reacted to public opinion, interest groups, and political parties. The study of politics looked like Figure 2.1 below.

But just using the term *social base* assumes that society is the underlying element in the study of politics. Could it be the other way around? To use a coffee-making metaphor, instead of "percolating up," could politics "drip down"? A book titled *The Political Basis of Society* might posit society as largely the result of political institutions formed and decisions made over the decades. Maybe politics leads society, in which case our model would look like Figure 2.2 (at the top of page 20).

How can you prove which model is more nearly correct? It is possible (and very likely) that the flow is going both ways simultaneously and that both models are partly correct. Why, then, emphasize one model over the other? There is no good reason; it is simply the current fashion in political study, which began as a reaction against the emphasis on institutions that dominated political science before World War II. A seemingly simple matter of which topics to study first has theoretical implications. You cannot escape theory. We can only whet your appetite for political theories in our very brief discussion here. Consider further study of political theory; you will find that nothing is so practical as theory.

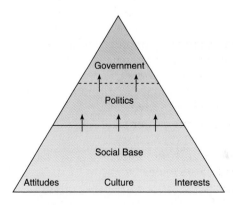

Figure 2.1

Pyramid with social base and political superstructure. (Flow is from bottom to top.)

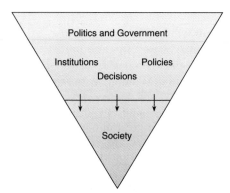

Figure 2.2
_____

Pyramid with political institutions forming the social base. (Flow is from top to bottom.)

■ Classic Theories

Some say Plato founded political science. His *Republic,* among other things, described an ideal *polis,* but his reasoning was largely speculative, and his ideal system ended up looking a bit like modern fascism or communism. Plato's student, Aristotle, on the other hand, was the first *empirical* political scientist. As noted in the previous chapter, he regarded politics as the "master science" and sent out his students to gather data from the dozens of Greek city-states. With these data, he constructed his great *Politics.* Both Plato and Aristotle saw Athens in decline; they attempted to understand why and to suggest how it could be avoided. They thus began a tradition that is still at the heart of political science: a search for the sources of the good, stable political system. Aristotle was not shy about defining what was politically "best," as in this passage:

> [T]he best political community is formed by citizens of the middle class, and those states are likely to be well administered in which the middle class is large . . . in which the citizens have moderate and sufficient property; for where some possess much and others nothing there may arise an extreme democracy or a pure oligarchy, or a tyranny may develop out of either extreme . . . [D]emocracies are safer and more permanent than oligarchies, because they have a middle class which is more numerous and has a greater share in government, for when there is no middle class, and the poor greatly exceed in number, troubles arise, and the state soon comes to an end.

Even though *Politics* was written in the fourth century B.C., Aristotle could be describing why democracy succeeds or fails today: Much depends on the size of the middle class, a point confirmed by modern research. Do Russia or Iraq have a middle class strong enough to sustain democracy? Ancient can still be relevant. Aristotle was both **descriptive** and **normative**: He used the facts he and his students

---

descriptive   Explaining what is.
normative   Explaining what ought to be.

CLASSIC WORKS

NOT JUST EUROPEANS

China, India, and North Africa produced brilliant political thinkers long before their European counterparts. Unknown in the West until relatively recently, it is unlikely that their ideas influenced the development of Western political theory. They do suggest that the political nature of humans is basically the same no matter what the cultural differences, and that great minds come to similar conclusions on how to deal with politics.

In China, Confucius, a sixth-century B.C. advisor to rulers, propounded his vision of good, stable government based on two things: the family, and correct, moral behavior instilled in rulers and ruled alike. At the apex, the emperor sets a moral example by purifying his spirit and perfecting his manners. He must think good thoughts in utter sincerity; if he does not, his empire crumbles. He is copied by his subjects, who are arrayed hierarchically below the emperor, down to the father of a family, who is like a miniature emperor to whom wives and children are subservient. The Confucian system bears some resemblance to Plato's ideal Republic; the difference is that the Chinese actually practiced Confucianism, which lasted two and a half millennia and through a dozen dynasties. Some claim it formed the cultural basis for East Asia's recent remarkable economic growth.

Two millennia before Machiavelli and Hobbes, the Indian writer Kautilya in the fourth century B.C. arrived at the same conclusions. Kautilya, a prime minister and adviser to an Indian monarch, wrote in *Arthasastra* (translated as *The Principles of Material Well-Being*) that well-being comes from living in a well-run kingdom. Like Hobbes, Kautilya posited a state of nature that meant anarchy. Monarchs arose to protect the land and people against anarchy and insure their prosperity. Like Machiavelli, Kautilya advised his prince to operate on the basis of pure expediency, doing whatever it takes to secure his kingdom domestically and against other kingdoms. Kautilya thus could be said to have founded both political economy and the realist school of statecraft.

In fourteenth century A.D. North Africa, Ibn Khaldun was a secretary, executive, and ambassador for several rulers. Sometimes out of favor and in jail, he reflected on what had gone wrong with the great Arab empires. He concluded, in his *Universal History,* that the character of the Arabs and their social cohesiveness was determined by climate and occupation. Ibn Khaldun was almost modern in his linking of underlying economic conditions to social and political change. Economic decline in North Africa, he found, had led to political instability and lawlessness. Anticipating Marx, Toynbee, and many other Western writers, Ibn Khaldun saw that civilizations pass through cycles of growth and decline.

Notice what all three of these thinkers had in common with Machiavelli: All were princely political advisors who turned their insights into general prescriptions for correct governance. Practice led to theory.

had collected to prescribe the most desirable political institutions. Political scientists have been doing the same ever since, both describing and prescribing.

Most European medieval and Renaissance political thinkers took a religious approach to the study of government and politics. They were almost strictly normative, seeking to discover the "ought" or "should," and were often rather casual about the "is," the real-world situation. Informed by religious, legal, and philosophical values, they tried to ascertain which system of government would bring humankind closest to what God wished.

Niccolò Machiavelli in the early sixteenth century brought what some believe is the crux of modern political science: the focus on power. His great work *The Prince* was about the getting and using of political power. Many philosophers peg Machiavelli as the first modern philosopher because his motivations and explanations had nothing to do with religion. Machiavelli was not as wicked as some people say. He was a **realist** who argued that to accomplish anything good—such as the unification of Italy and expulsion of the foreigners who ruined it—the Prince had to be rational and tough in the exercise of power.

Although long depreciated by American political thinkers, who sometimes shied away from "power" as inherently dirty, the approach took root in Europe and contributed to the elite analyses of Mosca, Pareto, and Michels. Americans became acquainted with the power approach through the writings of the refugee German scholar of international relations, Hans J. Morgenthau, who emphasized that "all politics is a struggle for power."

THE CONTRACTUALISTS

Not long after Machiavelli, the "contractualists"—Hobbes, Locke, and Rousseau—analyzed why political systems should exist at all. They differed in many points but agreed that humans, at least in principle, had joined in what Rousseau called a **social contract** that everyone now had to observe.

Thomas Hobbes lived through the upheavals of the English Civil War in the seventeenth century and opposed them for making individuals frightened and insecure. Hobbes imagined that life in "the **state of nature**," before **civil society** was founded, must have been terrible. Every man would have been the enemy of every other man, a "war of each against all." Humans would live in savage squalor with "no arts; no letters; no society; and which is worst of all, continual fear, and danger of violent death; and the life of man, solitary, poor, nasty, brutish, and short." To get out of this horror, people would—out of their profound self-interest—rationally join together to form civil society. Society thus arises naturally out of fear. People would also gladly submit to a king, even a bad one, for a monarch prevents anarchy. Notice how Hobbes's theory, that society is based on rational self-interest, is at odds with Aristotle's theory that humans are born "political animals." Which theory is right? (Hint: Have humans ever lived as solitary animals?) But also notice that Hobbesian situations appear from time to time, as in Iraq recently, where Sunni remnants of the Saddam regime, Al Qaeda suicide bombers, Shia religious militias, and separatist Kurds battled as if there were no government.

---

realism   Working with the world as it is and not as we wish it to be; usually focused on power.

social contract   Theory that individuals join and stay in civil society as if they had signed a contract.

state of nature   Humans before civilization.

civil society   Humans after becoming civilized. Modern usage: associations between family and government.

Another Englishman, John Locke, also saw the seventeenth-century upheavals but came to less harsh conclusions. Locke theorized that the original state of nature was not so bad; people lived in equality and tolerance with one another. But they could not secure their property: There was no money, title deeds, or courts of law, so their property was uncertain. To remedy this, they contractually formed civil society and thus secured "life, liberty, and property." Locke is to property rights as Hobbes is to fear of violent death. Some philosophers argue that Americans are the children of Locke. Notice the American emphasis on "the natural right to property."

Jean-Jacques Rousseau lived in eighteenth-century France and, some say, laid the philosophical groundwork for the French Revolution. He accepted the theories of Hobbes and Locke but gave them a twist. Life in the state of nature, Rousseau theorized, was downright good; people lived as "noble savages" without artifice or jealousy. (All the contractualists were influenced by not-very-accurate descriptions of American Indians.) What corrupted humans, said Rousseau, was society itself. The famous words at the beginning of his *Social Contract*: "Man is born free but everywhere is in chains."

But society can be drastically improved, argued Rousseau, leading to human freedom. A just society would be a voluntary community with a will of its own, the **general will**—what everyone wants over and above the "particular wills" of individuals and interest groups. In such communities humans gain dignity and freedom. Societies make people, not the other way around. If people are bad, it is because society made them that way (a view held by many today). A good society, on the other hand, can "force men to be free" if they misbehave. Many see the roots of totalitarianism in Rousseau: the imagined perfect society; the general will, which the dictator claims to know; and the breaking of those who do not cooperate. Happily, the U.S. Founding Fathers were uninfluenced by Rousseau, but the architects of the French Revolution believed passionately in him, which perhaps explains why it ended badly.

Most of the U.S. Founding Fathers had studied Hobbes and Locke, whose influence is obvious. What is the Constitution but a social contract? Much of the Declaration of Independence reads as if it had been cribbed from Locke, which it had, by Jefferson. Please do not say political theories have no influence.

MARXIST THEORIES

Another political theory that made a big difference was Marxism. A German living in London, Karl Marx, who was trained in Hegelian philosophy, produced an exceedingly complex theory consisting of at least three interrelated elements: a theory of economics, a theory of social class, and a theory of history. Like Hegel, Marx argued that things happen not by accident; everything has a cause. Hegel

---

general will   Rousseau's theory of what everybody in the community wants.

posited the underlying cause that moves history forward as spiritual, specifical-ly the **Zeitgeist**, the spirit of the times. Marx found the great underlying cause in economics.

Economics   Marx concentrated on the "surplus value"—what we call prof-it. Workers produce things but get paid only a fraction of the value of what they produce. The capitalist owners skim off the rest, the surplus value. The workers—what Marx called the **proletariat**—are paid too little to buy all the products they have made, resulting in repeated overproduction, which leads to depressions. Eventually, argued Marx, there will be a depression so big the capitalist system will collapse.

Social Class   Every society divides into two classes: a small class of those who own the means of production and a large class of those who work for the small class. Society is run according to the dictates of the upper class, which sets up the laws, arts, and styles needed to maintain itself in power. (Marx influenced the theory of elites, discussed in Chapter 5.) Most laws concern property rights, noted Marx, be-cause the **bourgeoisie** (the capitalists) are obsessed with hanging on to their prop-erty, which, according to Marx, is nothing but skimmed-off surplus value anyway. If the country goes to war, said Marx, it is not because of the wishes of the com-mon people but because the ruling bourgeoisie needs a war for economic gain. The proletariat, in fact, has no country; proletarians are international, all suffering under the heel of the capitalists.

History   Putting together his economic and social-class theories, Marx ex-plained historical changes. When the underlying economic basis of society gets out of kilter with the structure that the dominant class has established (its laws, insti-tutions, businesses, and so on), the system collapses, as in the French Revolution. Prior to 1789, France's ruling class was the feudal nobility. Their system was from the Middle Ages, based on hereditary ownership of great estates worked by peas-ants, on laws stressing the inheritance of these estates and the titles that went with them, and on chivalry and honor. All were part and parcel of a feudal society. But the economic basis changed. Ownership of land and feudal values eroded with the rise of manufacturing, which brought a new class, the urban capitalists (or bour-geoisie), whose way of life and economy were quite different. By the late eigh-teenth century, France had an economy based on manufacturing but was still dominated by feudal aristocrats with their minds in the past. The system was out

---

Zeitgeist   German for "spirit of the times"; Hegel's theory that each epoch has a distinctive spirit, which moves history along.

proletariat   Marx's name for the industrial working class.

bourgeois   Adjective, originally French for city dweller; later and current, middle class in general. Noun: *bourgeoisie*.

of kilter: The economic basis had moved ahead, but the class **superstructure** had stayed behind. In 1789, the superstructure came down with a crash, and the bourgeoisie took over with its new capitalist and liberal values of a free market, individual gain, and legal (but not material) equality.

The capitalists did a good job, Marx had to admit. They industrialized and modernized much of the globe. They put out incredible new products and inventions. But they too are doomed, Marx wrote, because the faster they transform the economy, the more it gets out of step with the capitalist superstructure, just as the previous feudal society was left behind by a changing economy. This leads us back to Marx's theory of surplus value and recurring economic depressions. Eventually, reasoned Marx, the economy will be so far out of kilter from the bourgeois setup that it too will collapse. Socialism, predicted Marx, will come next, and we should aid in its coming. Marx was partly a theorist and partly an ideologist. We will consider Marxism as ideology in Chapter 6.

Marxism, as applied in the Soviet Union and other Communist countries, led to tyranny and failure, but as a system of analysis, Marxism is still interesting and useful. Social class is important in structuring political views, but never uniformly. For example, many working-class people are conservative, and many middle-class intellectuals are liberals or **leftists**. Economic interest groups still ride high and, by means of freely spending on election campaigns, often get their way in Washington. They seldom get all they want, however, as they are opposed by other interest groups. Marx's enduring contributions are (1) his understanding that societies are never fully unified and peaceful but always riven with conflict and (2) that we must ask "Who benefits?" in any political controversy.

INSTITUTIONAL THEORIES

From the nineteenth century through the middle of the twentieth century, American thinkers focused on **institutions**, the formal structures of government. This showed the influence of law on the development of political science in the United States. Woodrow Wilson, for example, was a lawyer (albeit unsuccessful) before he became a political scientist; he concentrated on perfecting the institutions of government. Constitutions were a favorite subject for political scientists of this period, for they assumed that what was on paper was how the institutions worked in practice. The rise of the Soviet, Italian, and German dictatorships shook this belief. The constitution of Germany's Weimar Republic (1919–1933) looked fine on paper; experts had drafted it. Under stress it collapsed, for Germans of that time did not have the necessary experience with or commitment to democracy. Likewise,

---

superstructure   Marx's term for everything that is built on top of the economy (laws, art, politics, etc.).
leftist   In favor of radical social change to uplift poor.
institutions   The formal structures of government, such as the U.S. Congress.

the Stalin constitution of 1936 made the Soviet Union look like a perfect democracy, but obviously it did not work that way.

■ Contemporary Theories

Some thinkers of classic bent dismiss contemporary theories as trivial, obvious, superficial, or simply restatements of classic ideas. One such scholar sniffed that everything he learned from modern theories could be written on the inside of a matchbook cover. We need not be so harsh. Contemporary—meaning post–World War II—theories have made some contributions. Even when they ultimately fail and are abandoned, they leave a residue of interesting questions. True, compared to classic theories, most are pretty thin stuff.

BEHAVIORALISM

The Communist and Fascist dictatorships and World War II forced political scientists to reexamine their institutional focus, and many set to work to discover how politics really worked, not how it was supposed to work. Postwar American political scientists here followed in the tradition of the early nineteenth-century French philosopher Auguste Comte, who developed the doctrine of **positivism**, the application of natural science methods to the study of society. Comtean positivism was an optimistic philosophy, holding that as we accumulate valid data by means of scientific observation—without speculation or intuition—we will perfect a science of society and with it improve society. Psychologists were perhaps the most deeply imbued with this approach (and still are); many took the name **behavioralists** for their concentration on actual human behavior as opposed to thoughts or feelings.

Beginning in the 1950s, behaviorally inclined political scientists borrowed the natural scientists' approach and accumulated statistics from elections, public-opinion surveys, votes in legislatures, and anything else they could hang a number on. Behavioralists made some remarkable contributions to political science, shooting down some long-held but unexamined assumptions, and giving political theory an empirical basis. Behavioral studies were especially good in examining the "social bases" of politics, the attitudes and values of average citizens, which go a long way toward making the system function the way it does. Their best work has been on voting patterns, for it is here they can get lots of valid data.

During the 1960s, the behavioral school established itself and won over much of the field. In the late 1960s, however, behavioralism came under heavy attack, and not just by rear-guard traditionalists. Many younger political scientists, some of them influenced by the radicalism of the anti-Vietnam war movement, complained

---

positivism   Theory that society can be studied scientifically and incrementally improved with the knowledge gained.

behavioralism   The empirical study of actual human behavior rather than abstract or speculative theories.

HOW TO . . .

THESIS STATEMENTS

You are assigned a paper in political science. Begin it with a clear, punchy **thesis**, a first sentence giving your main idea or claim, the thing you are going to prove. If you cannot *prove* your thesis with empirical evidence, discard or change it. An initial attempt at a thesis is an *hypothesis* (discussed on page 144). If your evidence proves the opposite of your hypothesis, you may be able to save it by putting a "not" in front of it. Proving why something failed to happen is often as good as proving why it did. Your thesis paragraph should be about as long as this one.

The simplest thesis is that something is (or is not) happening: "More and more interest groups set up shop in Washington." Avoid trivial theses, anything well-known or established: "The president is inaugurated on January 20 following the election." An interesting thesis explains how one thing relates to another: "White Protestant males vote strongly Republican." Gathering examples or case studies (see page 13) is often the initial step to developing a thesis. If you take the six counties in your state with the highest Nader vote, what generalizations can you make about them? Do not gently introduce your thesis (save that for your English class); move directly into it. A thesis is more definite than what the paper is "about." You left that behind in high school.

Indirect	Direct
Television has a big impact on politics, and many critics feel it is not always a good impact.	U.S. television advertising makes viewers cynical and indifferent and leads to low voter turnout.
Unprovable	**Provable**
Democracy is government of the people, by the people, and for the people.	Better-off countries tend to be democracies, poor countries not.
Trivial	**Nontrivial**
Nader voters were unhappy with both of the main parties.	Nader voters were mostly urban and intellectual, often in university towns.
Vague	**Clear**
This paper is about U.S. policy toward Iran over three decades.	U.S. policy toward Iran was doomed by over-reliance on the shah.

that the behavioral approach was static, conservative, loaded with its practitioners' values, and irrelevant to the urgent tasks at hand. Far from being "scientific" and "value-free," behavioralists often defined the current situation in the United States as the norm and anything different as deviant. Almond and Verba found that Americans embody all the good, "participant" virtues of the civic culture. By examining only what exists at a given moment,

---

thesis   A main idea or claim, to be proved by evidence.

behavioralists neglected the possibility of change; their studies may be time-bound. Behavioralists have an unstated preference for the status quo; they like to examine settled, established systems, for that is where their methodological tools work best.

Perhaps the most damaging criticism, though, was that the behavioralists focused on relatively minor topics and steered clear of the big questions of politics. Behavioralists can tell us, for example, what percentage of Detroit blue-collar Catholics vote Democratic, but they tell us nothing about what this means for the quality of Detroit's governance or the kinds of decisions elected officials will make. There is no necessary connection between how citizens vote and what comes out of government. Critics charged that behavioral studies were often irrelevant.

By 1969, even a top political theorist like David Easton had to admit that there was something to the criticism of what had earlier been called the "behavioral revolution." Some called the newer movement **postbehavioral**, a synthesis of traditional and behavioral approaches. Postbehavioralists recognize that facts and values are tied together; they are willing to use both the qualitative data of the traditionalists and the quantitative data of the behavioralists. They look at history and institutions as well as public opinion and rational-choice theory. They are not afraid of numbers and happily use correlations, graphs, and percentages to make their cases. If you inquire around your political science department, you are apt to find traditional, behavioral, and postbehavioral viewpoints among the professors—or even within the same professor.

SYSTEMS THEORY

A major postwar invention was the "political systems" model devised by David Easton, which contributed to our understanding of politics by simplifying reality but in some cases departed from reality. The idea of looking at complex entities as systems originated in biology. Living entities are complex and highly integrated. The heart, lungs, blood, digestive tract, and brain perform their functions in such a way as to keep the animal alive. Take away one organ and the animal dies. Damage one organ and the other components of the system alter their function to compensate and keep the animal alive. The crux of systems thinking is this: You cannot change just one component, because a change in one component changes all the others.

In the political systems model, many argued that the politics of a given country worked the same way as a biological system. According to the Easton model (Figure 2.3, on page 29), citizens' demands, "inputs," are felt by the government decision makers, who process them into authoritative decisions and actions, "outputs." These outputs have an impact on the social, economic, and political environment that the citizens may or may not like. The citizens express their demands anew—this is the crucial "feedback" link of the system, which may modify the earlier decision. Precisely what goes on in the "conversion process" was left opaque, a "black box."

---

postbehavioral   Synthesis of traditional, behavioral, and other techniques in the study of politics.

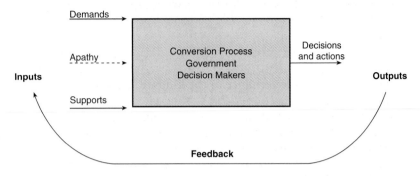

Figure 2.3

A model of the political system. (Adapted from David Easton, *A Systems Analysis of Political Life.* Chicago, IL: University of Chicago Press, 1965, p. 32.)

In some cases, the political systems approach fits reality. A weak economy in the United States worries voters. As the winning presidential candidate, Bill Clinton vowed to speed economic growth and create more jobs. Clinton enjoyed several years of a good economy, and the feedback was positive, supporting him even amid scandal and impeachment. During the Vietnam war, feedback on the military draft was very negative. The Nixon administration defused much youthful anger by ending the draft in 1971 and changing to an all-volunteer army. In yet another example, the socialist economics of French President François Mitterrand produced inflation and unemployment. The French people, especially the business community, complained loudly, and Mitterrand altered his policy away from socialism and back to capitalism. The feedback loop worked.

But in other cases, the systems model falls flat. Would Hitler's Germany or Stalin's Russia really fit the systems model? How much attention do dictatorships pay to citizens' demands? To be sure, there is always some citizen input and feedback. Hitler's generals tried to assassinate him—a type of feedback. Workers in Communist systems had an impact on government policy by not working much. They expected more consumer goods and, by not exerting themselves, communicated this desire to the regime. Sooner or later the regime had to reform. All over the Soviet bloc, workers used to chuckle: "They pretend to pay us and we pretend to work." In the USSR, (botched) reform came from the Gorbachev regime, and it led to system collapse.

How could the systems model explain the Vietnam war? Did the citizens of the United States demand that the administration send half-a-million troops to fight there? No, nearly the opposite: Lyndon Johnson won overwhelmingly in 1964 on an antiwar platform. The systems model does show how discontent with the war ruined Johnson's popularity so that he did not seek reelection in 1968. The feedback loop did go into effect but only long after the decision for war had been made. Could the systems model explain the Watergate scandal? Did U.S. citizens

MODELS: SIMPLIFYING REALITY

A model is a simplified picture of reality that social scientists develop to order data, to theorize, and to predict. A good model fits reality but simplifies it, because a model that is as complex as the real world would be of no help. In simplifying reality, however, models run the risk of oversimplifying. The real problem is the finite capacity of the human mind. We cannot factor in all the information available at once; we must select which points are important and ignore the rest. But when we do this, we may drain the blood out of the study of politics and overlook key points. Accordingly, as we encounter models of politics—and perhaps as we devise our own—pause a moment to ask if the model departs too much from reality. If it does, discard or alter the model. Attempts to disregard reality because it does not fit the model end in catastrophe.

demand that President Nixon's staff order the Democratic headquarters bugged? No, but once details about the cover-up started leaking out in 1973, the feedback loop went into effect, putting pressure on the House of Representatives to form an impeachment panel.

Plainly, there are some problems with the systems model, and they seem to be in the "black box" of the conversion process. Much happens in the mechanism of government that is not initiated by and has little to do with the wishes of citizens. The American people were little concerned about the health effects of smoking. Only the analyses of medical statisticians, which revealed a strong link between smoking and lung cancer, prodded Congress into requiring warning labels on cigarette packs and ending television advertising of cigarettes. It was a handful of specialists in the federal bureaucracy who got the anticigarette campaign going, not the masses of citizens.

The systems model is essentially static, biased toward the status quo, and unable to handle upheaval. This is one reason political scientists were surprised at the collapse of the Soviet Union. "Systems" are not supposed to collapse; they are supposed to continually self-correct.

We can modify the systems model to better reflect reality. By diagramming it as in Figure 2.4 (on page 31), we logically change little. We have the same feedback loop: outputs turning into inputs. But by putting the "conversion process" of government first, we suggested that it—rather than the citizenry—originates most decisions. The public reacts only later.

Next we add something that Easton himself later suggested. Inside the "black box" a lot more happens than simply the processing of outside demands. Pressures from the various parts of government—government talking mostly to itself and short-circuiting the feedback loop—are what Easton called "withinputs." These two alterations, of course, make our model more complicated, but this also reflects the complicated nature of reality. The systems model, like all models in political science, must be taken with a grain of salt.

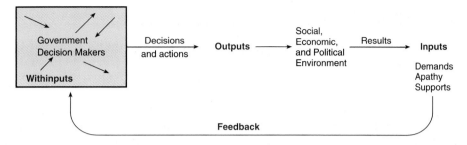

Figure 2.4

A modified model of the political system.

MODERNIZATION THEORY

Modernization theory, a broad-brush term, is rooted in Hegel, who argued two centuries ago that all facets of society—the economic, cultural, and political—hang together as a package, which changes and moves all societies in the same direction. Hegel thought the underlying cause of this process was spiritual, but Marx argued that it was economic: "Steam engines and dynamos bring their own philosophy with them." You cannot have a feudal society with a modern economy, at least not for long. Max Weber argued that the cause was cultural, specifically, the rise of Protestantism. Others have emphasized the growth of education, communications, and the middle class, but all agree it happens as a package. Today's modernization theorists see the process as complex, multicausal, and little amenable to outside guidance. We do not develop countries; they develop themselves, a point neglected in Iraq.

Most agree on the importance of industrialization. As a country industrializes, its economy, culture, communications, and politics also change. Giving new life to this theory was the remarkable Chapter 2 of Seymour Martin Lipset's 1960 *Political Man*. Lipset classified countries as either "stable democracies" (such as Canada and Norway) or "unstable democracies and dictatorships" (such as Spain and Yugoslavia). With few exceptions, the stable democracies had more wealth, industry, radios, doctors, cars, education, and urban dwellers than the unstable democracies and dictatorships. In a word, they were more industrialized. And Lipset supplied an explanation: Industrialized countries have large middle classes, and they are the basis of democracy. Lipset combined Marx with Aristotle (see the quote from Aristotle earlier in this chapter).

More recent research tends to confirm a relationship between level of economic development and democracy. There is a dividing line between poor and middle-income countries, but it is not air-tight. Lands with a per capita **Gross Domestic Product (GDP)** of less than $5,000 are rarely democracies. If they

Gross Domestic Product (GDP) Sum total of goods and services produced in a given country in one year, often expressed per capita (GDPpc), by dividing population into GDP.

attempt to found a democracy, it often fails, usually by military coup. Countries with a per capita GDP of more than $6,000, however, are mostly democracies. When they establish a democracy, it usually lasts. When South Korea and Taiwan were poor, they were dictatorships. As they industrialized, their middle classes and education levels grew, and by the 1990s both had turned into democracies. Much U.S. thinking on China is based on these hopeful examples. China's rapid economic growth suggests it could become a middle-income country in the first half of this century and hence be ripe for democracy. (Be skeptical here. Economic growth is rarely smooth, and China is a huge, complex nation ruled by a Communist party that refuses to relinquish power.) When Mexico topped $8,000 per cap, it was ready for its first democratic election, that of Vicente Fox in 2000. There is an interesting exception to this wealth-democracy connection: India, with a per capita GDP of still under $2,000, was founded and stayed democratic. (Any ideas why?)

Modernization theory also has some insights into the turmoil and instability that afflict many developing countries. It is because they modernize just one or two facets—often their economy and military—and leave the rest—such as religion and social structure—traditional. The two conflict; the traditional sectors resent and oppose the modern sectors. This helps explain the upsurge of Islamic fundamentalism in Iran, Egypt, Algeria, and Saudi Arabia. One must also note the high unemployment in these lands. If modernization theory is correct, if and when they reach middle-income levels they should stabilize and democratize.

RATIONAL-CHOICE THEORY

In the 1970s a new approach, initially invented by mathematicians, rapidly grew in political science—rational-choice theory. Little interested in culture or development, rational-choice theorists argue that one can generally predict political behavior by knowing the interests of the actors involved, because they rationally choose to maximize their interests. As U.S. presidential candidates take positions on issues, they calculate what will give them the best payoff. They might think, "Many people oppose the war in Iraq, but many also demand strong leadership on defense. I'd better criticize just 'mistakes' in the war but nothing that would make me look weak on national security." The waffle is not indecision but calculation, argue rational-choice theorists.

Rational-choice theorists enrage some other political scientists. One study of Japanese bureaucrats claimed you need not study Japan's language, culture, or history. All you need to know was what their career advantages were to predict how they would decide issues. A noted U.S. specialist on Japan blew his stack at such glib, superficial shortcuts and denounced rational-choice theory. More modest rational-choice theorists immersed themselves in Hungary's language and culture but still concluded that Hungarian political parties, in cobbling together an extremely complex voting system, were making rational choices to give themselves a presumed edge in parliamentary seats.

Many rational-choice theorists backed down from some of their more know-it-all positions. A few have even called themselves "neo-institutionalists" (see

KEY CONCEPTS

POLITICS AS A GAME

Some rational-choice thinkers subscribed to a branch of mathematics called game theory, setting up political decisions as if they were table games. A Cuban missile crisis "game" might have several people play President Kennedy, who must weigh the probable payoffs of bombing or not bombing Cuba. Others might play Khrushchev, who has to weigh toughing it out or backing down. Seeing how the players interact gives us insights and warnings of what can go wrong in crisis decision making. If you "game out" the 1962 Cuban missile crisis and find that three games out of ten end in World War III, you have the makings of an article of great interest.

Game theorists argue that constructing the proper game explains why policy outcomes are often unforeseen but not accidental. Games can show how decision makers think. We learn how their choices are never easy or simple. Games can even be mathematized and fed into computers. The great weakness of game theory is that it depends on correctly estimating the "payoffs" decision makers can expect, and these are only approximations arrived at by examining the historical record. We know how the Cuban missile crisis came out; therefore we adjust our game so it comes out the same way. In effect, game theory is only another way to systematize and clarify history (not a bad thing).

following section) because all their rational choices are made within one or another institutional context: the U.S. Congress, for example. Rational-choice theory did not establish itself as the dominant **paradigm**—no theory has and none is likely to—but it contributed a lot by reminding us that politicians are consummate opportunists, a point many other theories forgot.

NEW INSTITUTIONALISM

In the 1970s political science began to rediscover institutions and in the 1980s proclaimed the "New Institutionalism." Its crux is that government structures—legislatures, parties, bureaucracies, and so on—take on lives of their own and shape the behavior and attitudes of the people who live within and benefit from them. Institutions are not simply the reflections of social forces. (Our discussion at the beginning of this chapter, on the importance of structures, contains a neoinstitutionalist argument.) Legislators, for example, behave as they do largely because of rules laid down long ago and reinforced over the decades. Once you know these complex rules, some unwritten, you can see how politicians logically try to maximize their advantage under them, much as you can often predict when a baseball batter will bunt. It is not a mystery but the logic of the game they are playing. The preservation and enhancement of the institution becomes one of politicians' major goals. Thus, institutions, even if outmoded or ineffective, tend to rumble on. The Communist parties

paradigm   A model or way of doing research accepted by a discipline.

of the Soviet bloc were corrupt and ineffective, but they endured because they guaranteed the jobs and perquisites of their members.

The new institutionalism is a sound approach—and popular in current research—and with it political science comes full circle, back to where it was before World War II, with some interesting new insights, some borrowed from other disciplines. It is, however, likely not the last model we shall see, for we will never have a paradigm that can consistently explain and predict political actions. Every couple of decades political science comes up with a new paradigm—usually one borrowed from another discipline—that attracts much excitement and attention. Its proponents exaggerate its ability to explain or predict. Upon examination and criticism, the model usually fades and is replaced by another trend. Political science tends to get caught up in trends. After a few iterations of this cycle, we learn to expect no breakthrough theories. Politics is slippery and not easily confined to our mental constructs. By acknowledging this, we open our minds to the richness, complexity, and drama of political life.

KEY TERMS

behavioralism (p. 26)
bourgeois (p. 24)
civil society (p. 22)
descriptive (p. 20)
general will (p. 23)
Gross Domestic Product (GDP) (p. 31)
institution (p. 25)
leftist (p. 25)
normative (p. 20)
paradigm (p. 33)

positivism (p. 26)
postbehavioral (p. 28)
proletariat (p. 24)
realism (p. 22)
social contract (p. 22)
state of nature (p. 22)
superstructure (p. 25)
thesis (p. 27)
Zeitgeist (p. 24)

KEY WEB SITES

Political philosophy
www-personal.ksu.edu/~lauriej/index.html

Plato
www.rit.edu/~flwstv/plato.html

Aristotle
members.tripod.com/~batesca/aristotle.html

Confucius
www.albany.net/~geenius/kongfuzi/index.html

Machiavelli
www.sas.upenn.edu/~pgrose/mach/

Hobbes
www.rjgeib.com/thoughts/nature/hobbes-bio.html

Marx
www.anu.edu.au/polsci/marx/classics/manifesto.html

FURTHER REFERENCE

Almond, Gabriel A., and James S. Coleman. *Politics of Developing Areas.* Princeton, NJ: Princeton University Press, 1960.

Boesche, Roger. *The First Great Political Realist: Kautilya and his Arathashastra.* Lanham, MD: Lexington, 2003.

Easton, David. *A Framework for Political Analysis.* Englewood Cliffs, NJ: Prentice Hall, 1965.

Lane, Ruth. *Political Science in Theory and Practice: The "Politics" Model.* Armonk, NY: M. E. Sharpe, 1997.

Laver, Michael. *Private Desires, Political Action: An Invitation to the Politics of Rational Choice.* Thousand Oaks, CA: Sage, 1997.

Lipset, Seymour Martin. *Political Man: The Social Bases of Politics,* rev. ed. Baltimore, MD: Johns Hopkins University Press, 1981.

———, ed. *Political Philosophy: Theories, Thinkers, and Concepts.* Washington, D.C.: CQ Press, 2001.

Losco, Joseph, and Leonard Williams, eds. *Political Theory: Classic and Contemporary Readings,* 2nd ed., 2 vols. Los Angeles, CA: Roxbury, 2002.

Morgenthau, Hans J., David Clinton, and Kenneth W. Thompson. *Politics Among Nations: The Struggle for Power and Peace,* 7th ed. Burr Ridge, IL: McGraw-Hill, 2005.

Tannenbaum, Donald, and David Schultz. *Inventors of Ideas: An Introduction to Western Political Philosophy,* 2nd ed. Belmont, CA: Wadsworth, 2003.

Tinder, Glenn. *Political Thinking: The Perennial Questions,* 6th ed. Upper Saddle River, NJ: Pearson Longman, 2004.

White, Stephen K., and J. Donald Moon, eds. *What Is Political Theory?* Thousand Oaks, CA: Sage, 2004.

NATIONS, STATES, AND GOVERNMENTS

- What is the difference between a nation and a state?
- What is nationalism and where did it originate?
- Describe the "crises" of nation-building.
- What are "weak states" and "failed states"?
- What is the difference between socialism and statism?
- Are American attitudes on the role of government widely held?
- What were Aristotle's six types of government?
- What are Dahl's "influence terms"? Why are some better?
- Can or should the state modernize its society?
- What is "symbolic politics"?

Which came first, states or nations? A **nation** is a population with a certain sense of itself, a cohesiveness, a shared history and culture, and often (but not always) a common language. A **state** is a government structure, usually sovereign and powerful enough to enforce its writ. (Notice that here we use *state* in its original sense; the fifty U.S. states are not states in this sense of the word.) Many argue that nations must have developed before states. States are rather artificial creations; they come and go and change form through the centuries. Surely nations must be the underlying element: Groups of people with kindred feelings must antedate government structures.

---

nation   Population with a historic sense of self.

state   Government structures of a nation.

Historical research tends to refute this commonsense view. In most cases, it was states—government structures—that created their nations around them. The Zulus of South Africa, for example, are not a tribe but an artificially created nation put together from many clans and tribes less than two centuries ago by a powerful warrior, Shaka. Present-day people think of themselves as Zulus only because Shaka united them by conquest, forced them to speak his language, and made them great warriors.

France often comes to mind as a "natural" nation, a neat hexagon with a common history, language, and culture. But present-day France consists of several regions with very different languages and histories that were united—mostly by the sword— over the course of centuries. Paris inculcated a sense of Frenchness by means of education, language, and centralized administration. The French nation is an artificial creation developed by the French state for its own convenience.

The most artificial nation of all could well be the United States—put together through design by a group of men meeting in Philadelphia from thirteen distinct colonies. While assimilating tens of millions of immigrants of different languages and cultures, the United States developed a sense of nationhood over the years based largely on the ideals articulated in its founding documents. Nations do not fall from heaven; they are created by human craftsmanship of varying degrees of quality.

For many countries, the process of creation is not yet complete. The Spanish state coincides imperfectly with the Spanish nation. The kings of Toledo and Madrid tried to copy the French methods of centralization, but these Castilians were never able to impose a uniform sense of Spanishness on Catalans, Basques, Galicians, Andalucians, and Navarese. **Regionalism** bedevils Spanish politics to this day. India existed only as a concept before the British conquered the Indian subcontinent and turned it into the **Raj**. The English language, the railroad, and the telegraph stitched India together. It, too, is plagued by breakaway ethnic movements, such as that of the Sikhs in the Punjab.

■ THE ELEMENTS OF NATIONHOOD

Nations are commonly said to have several defining characteristics, such as territory, population, independence, and government. By each point, however, we could place a question mark, for the characteristics are sometimes strong and clear and sometimes weak or absent.

TERRITORY

In general, every nation occupies a specific geographical area. It is hard to have a nation without territory. But what about peoples without territory, who carry their "nation" around with them in their heads? Jews lost their territorial nation to

---

regionalism   Feeling of difference sometimes found among populations of a nation's regions.
Raj   British-ruled India.

KEY CONCEPTS

THE NOTION OF NATION

What are we to call this entity that dominates our lives, structures our politics, and brings forth our patriotism? Many terms are used, sometimes interchangeably. The terms have somewhat different meanings, though.

The colloquial expression is *country*, as in "Have you ever visited another country?" *Country*, of course, also means a rural or farming area, and centuries ago the two meanings were one. When people spoke of their "country" (French *pays*, Spanish *país*, Italian *paese*, German *Land*) they meant their native locality, perhaps not much bigger than a large U.S. county, where people shared the same traditions and dialect. Later the term broadened to mean a big, sovereign political entity, a nation.

The term *nation* has also been around for centuries, but not necessarily in its present sense. Far back in history, human groups called themselves nations, but originally this meant something like a big tribe, such as the "nation of Israel" or "Sioux nation." The Latin root of nation means "birth," so the word connoted the group you were born into and had some blood linkage with. The term *ethnic group*, from the Greek *ethnos*, meaning "nation," is in turn from the Greek for custom, *ethos*, indicating people with shared customs.

In the seventeenth century, the definition of nation changed to mean these large, powerful political entities that currently govern us. State power was merged with the notion of a people with much in common (history, culture, language) occupying a territory. This was the *nation-state*, a combination of people (nation) and government structure (state). It is usually just called *nation*.

The rise of the modern nation changed the face of the globe. Citizens—an old Roman concept that originated with the Latin for "city" and that revived with the idea of nation-states—transferred their ultimate loyalties from kings, churches, and localities to this new entity, the nation. Starting with the French Revolution in 1789 came the new force of **nationalism**, which quickly spread over Europe and then over the globe, unleashing the desire for peoples to govern themselves as independent nations. Vast empires, such as those of Austria-Hungary and Britain, fell apart as subject peoples demanded independence. As a result, many new countries were created, especially in Eastern Europe, the Americas, Asia, and Africa. Today, 193 entities call themselves nations.

Greek and Roman conquest some two millennia ago but, because many of them had a firm ideal of their peoplehood, were able to establish the modern state of Israel in 1948. Ironically, the people they displaced, the Palestinian Arabs, now also have a firm ideal of their peoplehood and strive to establish their own state. Should we count dispersed peoples, such as Jews or Palestinians, as a "nation"? Perhaps they are a potential nation, a people waiting or struggling to establish themselves on a territory.

And what occurs when territorial claims overlap? Wars often result. Most states and nations are rather artificial things; few have natural boundaries. Germany has fought France over Alsace; the United States has fought Mexico over Texas; and

---

nationalism   A people's heightened sense of cultural, historical, and territorial identity, unity, and sometimes greatness.

Argentina still claims what it calls the Malvinas Islands from Britain, which calls them the Falklands. Which claim is rightful? What criteria should be used to decide?

History is a poor guide, for there was almost always someone else there first. Israelis and Arabs quarrel endlessly about this. (If you go back far enough, neither of them was there first.) Language and ethnicity may also be poor guides in deciding which territory belongs to which state. The peoples of the earth, unfortunately, are not neatly arrayed into nations; rather there is a lot of spillover into neighboring states. Most Alsatians, for example, are or were originally German in language, culture, and family names. Most, however, also speak perfect French and think of themselves as French. To whom, then, does Alsace rightfully belong, Germany or France?

POPULATION

Every nation has people within its borders. Ideally, it should be a population with a sense of cohesion, of being a distinct nationality. Having a common language is a real help but is often not the case. For example, there has long been conflict between French-speaking and Flemish-speaking Belgians. Still, enough of both language groups "feel" Belgian to hold the country together. States with populations diverse in language, culture, or identification are called *multinational states.* Only half of the Soviet population was Russian; many other Soviet nationalities did not like being ruled by Moscow and broke away, producing fifteen countries where there used to be one.

What if part of a nation's population does not want to belong to that nation? Some Basques in Spain would like to form an independent nation; some Québécois in Canada and Sikhs in India would like to do the same. If a substantial portion of the population is unhappy, the nation could fall apart. Many Slovaks resented being governed by Czechs and in 1993 set up a separate Slovakia. Slovenes and Croats resented being governed by Serbs, and in 1991 they declared their independence from Yugoslavia. Eritreans fought a long guerrilla war with Ethiopia and won their independence in 1993. Just because people are living in a particular state does not necessarily mean they like it; the state may be ready to explode.

INDEPENDENCE

The nation should also be independent, meaning that it governs itself as a "sovereign" entity (see Chapter 1). Colonies, such as Algeria under the French, become nations only when they get formal independence, as Algeria did in 1962. Subdivisions of a nation, such as Quebec or Nevada, are also not considered nations since they lack sovereignty. Some Québécois would still like to become sovereign and independent.

There are some problems with the concept of independence, too. When a large, powerful country dominates a smaller, weaker country, is the latter fully independent and sovereign? Stalin set up obedient puppet governments in Eastern Europe—which is why these countries were known as Soviet "satellites"—and Soviet tanks crushed anti-Communist uprisings in Central Europe. Were these countries truly independent? For that matter, does not the United States supervise things in its own backyard, in the Caribbean and Central America? Is Haiti, which was briefly occupied by U.S. forces in 1994, truly sovereign? By definition, all nations are sovereign and independent, but some are more sovereign and independent than others.

Bolstering sovereign independence is **diplomatic recognition** by other countries, especially by the major powers. This may be followed by exchanges of ambassadors and the setting up of embassies. If most of the important nations recognize a new country, it automatically confers a certain legitimacy on it. If no one recognizes the country, its claim to exist is dubious. Under white rule, South Africa created nominally independent puppet states out of some of its "black homelands," but no one else recognized them; the fake little republics were re-merged into South Africa as soon as Nelson Mandela became president.

GOVERNMENT

A nation must obviously have some organizing hold over its population. The absence of such organization is **anarchy**, and it probably means that the territory will soon split apart or be conquered and absorbed by other nations. No government, no nation. Afghanistan is an example of the horrors of anarchy.

Government, however, can in certain circumstances exist independently of the nation. Underground governments or "governments-in-exile" struggle to expel occupiers or puppet governments. The Continental Congress was a **protogovernment** that preceded, conceived of, and fought for an independent United States. In 1940, General Charles de Gaulle declared a "Free French" government in London to expel the Germans, and many major powers recognized it as the government of France. With the liberation of Paris in 1944, it turned into a government with territory, population, and independence.

The existence of a legal government does not necessarily mean it is an effective government that controls its territory and population (discussed later). Where weak, governments may have trouble even staying alive in the face of domestic and foreign opposition. Bogota, for example, cannot control wide areas of Colombia, where drug dealers and guerrillas hold sway.

Older political theorists, influenced by legal abstractions, tended to take these characteristics of nations as givens. Wherever there was a nation, they reasoned, it must automatically have territory, population, independence, government, and other qualities. Modern political scientists discard purely legalistic notions and search for the empirical reality. Theoretically, country X is a nation, but does it really have a **cohesive** population and an effective, independent government that

---

diplomatic recognition   The official announcement by one state that it is prepared to have dealings with another state.

anarchy   The absence of government.

protogovernment   A beginning or trial-basis government.

cohesive   Holding together.

allows it to control its territory? Some that claim the title of nation are actually **weak states**, such as Colombia, or even **failed states**, such as the Congo. Many nations—perhaps all—are continually building and rebuilding themselves.

■ THE CRISES OF NATION BUILDING

Some social scientists hold that the process of constructing nations—if the process is to be successful—requires that countries go through the same five stages in approximately the same sequence. Each opportunity for further growth represents a "crisis" in the life of the nation, which the state structure must resolve with greater or lesser success.

IDENTITY

The "identity crisis" is the first hurdle in building a nation. People who previously identified with a tribe, region, or other subnational group must come to think of themselves first and foremost as citizens of the nation. This does not happen easily, quickly, or automatically. The American Civil War was fought over this point. France and Britain still contain regional groups that do not think of themselves as French or British but rather as Breton and Corsican (in France) or Scottish, Welsh, and Irish (in Britain). Swiss, except when traveling abroad, identify themselves as members of a canton (Bern, Geneva, Basel). Yugoslavia never established a national identity for its Serbs, Croats, Slovenes, Bosnians, Macedonians, and others. In this, Yugoslavia resembles many Third World countries, which have not yet solved their identity crisis. Many Africans still think of themselves as members of a tribe rather than as Sudanese or Nigerians.

LEGITIMACY

Legitimacy does not fall from heaven. As discussed in Chapter 1, a government must cultivate the respect and willing obedience of its citizens, the widespread feeling among the people that the regime's rule is rightful. Regimes with legitimacy problems can be overthrown by military coup, as in Latin America and Africa, or by revolution, as in Iran and Burma. Ultimately, as in the case of Yugoslavia, no legitimacy means no nation.

PENETRATION

Related to both identity and legitimacy, the "crisis of penetration" means that the nation must get substantially all the population, even in outlying or culturally distinct regions, to obey the government's writ. One quick check of penetration: Do

---

weak state   One unable to govern effectively, corrupt and penetrated by crime.
failed state   One incapable of even minimal governance, with essentially no national government.

all areas pay taxes? If not, there is a penetration problem. Typically, the regime establishes its rule first in the capital, then slowly extends its rule over the country, often encountering resistance that requires military strength to overcome. Lack of penetration means that a government can have a law on its books—against drug trafficking, for example—but much of the country, including some officials, disregard the law. Afghanistan is a prime example of a government that scarcely exists outside of the capital, Kabul. In the Afghan provinces, warlords and drug lords rule by the gun.

PARTICIPATION

As people become more educated, they demand to have a say in their governance. This feeling typically starts with the better-off and prominent people. The knights and wealthy burghers in effect tell the king or queen, "If you want taxes and military service from us, we demand a say in policy." The monarch, usually desperate for taxes, sets up a representative body to gain their compliance, such as the Parliament in England or Riksdag in Sweden. At first only the elite of society are thus represented, but gradually the desire for participation reaches all sectors of society—the common men and women—and they demand the right to vote. At a minimum, people need to *feel* they can participate in order for nationhood to evolve.

Regimes often resist expanding voting rights, fearing that the newly enfranchised will demand too much. Women got the right to vote in the United States only with the Nineteenth Amendment in 1920, Swiss women only in 1971. The danger is that unrepresented people will oppose the government, and regime legitimacy will erode. Eventually, the regime usually decides that expanding participation is better than breeding revolution. Said one British parliamentarian in the nineteenth century, "We count ballots rather than crack skulls." The white minority regime of South Africa was slow to realize this basic point.

The best way to solve the participation crisis is through slow and incremental steps, as Britain did in the nineteenth century. A series of Reform Acts expanded the British electoral franchise one step at a time, gradually giving more people the right to vote. This allowed both institutions and people time to adjust. Voting was meaningful and participation genuine. When suffrage is suddenly thrust on an unprepared people, however, the result is seldom democracy. On paper, Spain got universal male suffrage in 1874, well ahead of Britain, but in practice local bosses and the interior ministry controlled election results. In much of the Third World—where largely uneducated people got the franchise all at once—local political bosses or tribal leaders tell people how to vote.

DISTRIBUTION

The "crisis of distribution" is never fully settled. It concerns the classic question of "who gets what?" Once the broad masses of citizens are participating in elections, they often want to change the distribution of the nation's income in their favor. "Why should the rich have everything?" they ask. Much of the working class

KEY CONCEPTS

WAR AND NATION BUILDING

War clearly plays a role in the growth of states. Most nations were established and consolidated by conquest. Heresies, rebellions, and breakaway movements were put down with great bloodshed. In some lands this is still happening.

For any ruler, state survival is the top priority. Monarchs and presidents alike will do whatever they must to avoid foreign conquest or internal dismemberment. In the interest of survival they build their military power to counter any combination of threats. This means that they must also enlarge and modernize their political systems.

First, they must constantly increase taxes to provide for armies and equipment. Peter the Great of Russia ordered his officials "to collect money, as much as possible, for money is the artery of war." The French monarchs instituted the mercantilist economic system, with its protected industries, to raise revenues. The need to raise money for war persuaded kings to share some power with parliaments. The power to tax is the preeminent power of legislatures. James I and Charles I precipitated the English Civil War when they tried to bypass Parliament by decreeing their own taxes in order to pay for their wars in Europe. After winning the English Civil War, the Parliamentarians beheaded Charles I in 1649 and laid the groundwork for establishing the eventual predominance of the House of Commons.

The need for a larger and better military establishment forced monarchs to improve the organization and administration of their kingdoms. They needed to raise both taxes and soldiers. Prior to gunpowder and cannon in the fifteenth century, feudal lords in their castles could defy monarchs, but as kings could afford more cannons, they were able to crack castle walls and subdue lords. This power ended the feudal system and boosted the absolutism of monarchs. Failure to modernize one's administration and army could lead to loss of power. The map of Europe became much simpler as small states were conquered and absorbed by larger states. War was the great engine of modernization and consolidation.

When French revolutionaries in 1792 faced an invading army of professional soldiers, they mobilized the entire population, "the nation in arms," and beat the invaders. Harnessing this new nationalism and using the new idea of drafting all young males, Napoleon built the largest army in Europe and proceeded to conquer the entire continent. To resist Napoleon's legions, other European lands turned to nationalism and conscription as well.

By either the power or example of its arms, European nations spread their organization, technology, and nationalism over Asia, Africa, and the Middle East. One traditional country after another fell to Europeans and soon adopted their ways. Those who were not conquered, the Turks and the Japanese, modernized sufficiently to stave off the Europeans. Warfare gave countries little choice: Modernize or die.

Reflecting for a moment on U.S. history, we may ask which contributed more to modernization: the modest welfare measures of Roosevelt's New Deal or the gigantic industrial and manpower mobilization of World War II? Indeed, many welfare measures flowed as a result of the war. The G.I. Bill gave millions of veterans college educations. The National Defense Education Act of 1958, triggered by the launch of the Soviet *Sputnik* the year before, pumped millions of dollars into U.S. higher education. One of the largest federal "welfare" programs is the Department of Veterans Affairs, a new department that even conservatives support. War plays a major role in the foundation and growth of the powers of government.

throws its votes to the party that promises higher wages, increased educational opportunities, and more welfare benefits. This is how the Labor parties of Britain and Norway and the Social Democratic parties of Germany and Sweden grew until they won power and established extensive welfare states funded by taxes that fall more heavily on the rich. To a lesser degree, the American working class gave much of its vote to the Democrats under Franklin D. Roosevelt and Lyndon Johnson in order to carry out a redistribution of income.

The distribution question is never over, however, because the poorer sectors of society always want more welfare, whereas the better-off, represented by conservative parties, argue that the welfare state has gotten out of hand, that taxes are too high and benefits too generous. When conservatives win elections—as Margaret Thatcher did in Britain in 1979 and Ronald Reagan did in the United States in 1980—they try to cut welfare programs. This raises a hue and cry from some voters who fear for their benefits. This permanent tug-of-war is the story of most elections in advanced, industrialized democracies.

Few nations have had the luxury of being able to deal with these crises one at a time and with sufficient pauses in between crises. These circumstances would allow a country's institutions—its parties, parliament, executive departments, and so on—to become stronger each time they surmount a new crisis. But what if all five crises hit at the same time? This has especially been the situation in the Third World. Newly independent countries, many of them with serious identity and legitimacy problems, are expected to implement complex laws, to give all citizens the right to vote, and to provide rising and equitable living standards. This is often too much for their weak economies and institutions to bear all at once, and they collapse into revolution or military rule. The first item to go is usually participation, hence the many Third World dictatorships. Unfortunately, the Third World does not have the luxury of spreading out its crises in this world of rapid change.

■ GOVERNMENT: WHAT IT IS AND WHAT IT DOES

All but the most primitive societies have had well-defined government structures. As noted, Locke, from whom our Founding Fathers borrowed heavily, viewed government as a device to protect rights and property. "The great and chief end," wrote Locke in *Two Treatises of Civil Government*, "of men uniting . . . under government, is the preservation of their property [and so, their natural rights]." To Locke, government represented an agreement between the rulers and the ruled, who would support those in power as long as the government served in their interests. Governments have a monopoly on the legal use of coercion. Bandits and rebels, of course, may use coercion too, but outside the law.

One thing governments do is grow. Since World War I began in 1914, the governments of the advanced industrialized countries today eat on average five times as much of gross domestic product—from 9 percent of GDP to 45 percent. Even the United States, which preserves a healthy distrust of big government and has attempted several conservative cutbacks of federal spending, has seen government spending rise from 27 percent of GDP in 1960 to 33 percent in 1998. Other countries have generally grown more—Sweden, for example, from 31 percent in 1960 to 61 percent in 1998. Some argue that such growth of government is unstoppable, because citizens keep demanding more and more—such as prescription drugs for oldsters in the United States—that even conservative administrations cannot reject.

CLASSIFYING GOVERNMENTS

Most theorists agree that government should provide for the lives, stability, and economic and social well-being of citizens. This does not necessarily mean that government directly runs or supervises the economy or society. Nor does it mean that all governments pursue these tasks; corrupt and weak governments do not pursue them, but they risk being overthrown.

First, a nation must preserve itself as a state and ensure its national survival. It helps if the world community recognizes the nation's independence and the integrity of its boundaries—in a word, its sovereignty. Also important is a country's stability. A politically stable nation has an established system with the orderly transfer of power from one party or leader to another. It preserves domestic peace by delivering justice, maintaining law and order, and protecting property. A government can also enlist popular support by ensuring there are jobs, education, and health care for citizens, who then likely see the regime as legitimate.

How can government best advance the economic and social well-being of its citizens? States face two questions: (1) How much of the economy should the state own or supervise? (2) How much of the nation's wealth should be redistributed to help the poorer sectors of society? The answers produce four general approaches to promoting the general welfare: laissez-faire, statism, socialism, and the welfare state. These array themselves into a fourfold table (see Figure 3.1 below), much beloved of political scientists:

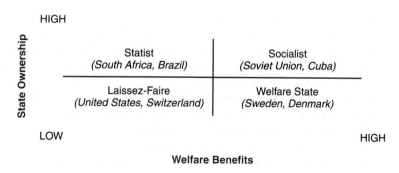

Figure 3.1

Statist, socialist, laissez-faire, and welfare-state approaches.

CLASSIC WORKS

ARISTOTLE'S SIX TYPES OF GOVERNMENT

The earliest and most famous classification of governments was Aristotle's in the fourth century B.C. He distinguished among three legitimate kinds of government—where the ruling authority acts in the interests of all—and three corrupt counterparts—where government acts only in the interests of self.

A monarchy, according to Aristotle, is one person ruling in the interest of all. But monarchy can degenerate into tyranny, the corrupt form, under which the single ruler exercises power for the benefit of self. Aristocracy, Greek for rule of the best (*aristos*), is several persons ruling in the interest of all. But this legitimate rule by an elite can decay into oligarchy, the corrupt form, in which several persons rule in the interest of themselves.

Aristotle saw the *polity* (what we might call constitutional democracy) as the rule of many in the interests of all and the best form of government. All citizens have a voice in selecting leaders and framing laws, but formal constitutional procedures protect rights. Aristotle warned that polity can decay into the corrupt form, democracy, the rule of many in the interests of themselves, the worst form of government. Deluded into thinking that one person is as good as another, the masses in a democracy follow the lead of corrupt and selfish demagogues and plunder the property of the hardworking and the capable. Aristotle's classification, which reigned for nearly twenty-five centuries, is still useful and can be summarized like this:

Who Governs	Legitimate Forms *Rule in the Interest of All*	Corrupt Forms *Rule in the Interest of Selves*
One	Monarchy	Tyranny
A few	Aristocracy	Oligarchy
Many	Polity	Democracy

In a **laissez-faire** system the government owns little or no industry and redistributes relatively little in the form of welfare programs. As we shall explore in Chapter 6 on ideologies, these countries are the followers of Adam Smith, who argued that government interference in the economy slows growth and decreases prosperity. As Thomas Jefferson summed it up, "That government is best that governs least." The theory here is that private enterprise and individual initiative make a nation both free and prosperous.

A **welfare state** owns little or no industry but does redistribute wealth to aid the less well-off. Sometimes also known as "social democracies," the welfare states of northwest Europe offer "cradle-to-grave" benefits in the form of health insurance,

---

laissez-faire   French for "let it be"; economic system of minimal government interference and supervision; capitalism.

welfarism   Economic system of major government redistribution of income to poorer citizens.

child care, job training, and retirement funds. To pay for this, they charge the world's highest taxes—in Sweden and Denmark more than 50 percent of the country's GDP. Industry, though, is private and oriented to capitalist moneymaking.

Statism is an old system that predates laissez-faire. A statist system is one in which the state (meaning the national government) is the number-one capitalist, owning and running much major industry, but is not interested in providing welfare benefits. Statism began when the French kings founded a powerful, centralized state that supervised industry for the sake of French wealth and power. Sometimes called by its French name *étatisme,* it typically includes state ownership of railroads, steel mills, banks, oil, and other big enterprises. Small and medium business is left in private hands. Statism caught on in much of Europe and Latin America. France, Brazil, and Mexico were statist systems but are now reforming. Some call the bureaucratic supervision of Japan's economy a form of statism. Many developing countries have followed statist models with the argument that only the government has the money, ideas, and talent to start up new industries. The economic results suggest state-owned firms are inefficient because they are run by bureaucrats and face no competition; often they operate at a loss and have to be subsidized by the national treasury. Statist Chile grew more prosperous after it privatized its state-owned firms.

A **socialist** system practices both state ownership and extensive welfare benefits. Exemplified by the former Soviet Union, government owns most of the means of production, claiming it runs the economy in the interests of the society as a whole. However, the collapse of Communist regimes (which called themselves "socialist"; we called them "Communist") throughout Europe indicates those governments ran things poorly. Today, only North Korea and Cuba remain as (negative) examples of socialism, and their systems seem ripe for change.

In actual practice, governments often combine elements of these four systems. Even the basically laissez-faire United States has some government supervision of the economy and welfare measures. Communist China and Vietnam, once strictly socialist, now have growing private, capitalistic sectors of their economy. The questions are never settled, and countries often change their combinations. In our day, we have seen a massive shift away from state-owned industry in the ex-Soviet Union, France, and Latin America. Welfare states like Sweden have felt the pinch of too-generous benefits and too-high taxes.

THE STATE AS AGENT OF MODERNIZATION

A basic American attitude is that government—known in other countries as "the state"—be kept small. In much of the rest of the world, however, state power is accepted as natural and good. In France, for example, a strong state was started by

---

statism   Economic system of state ownership of major industries to enhance power and prestige of state; a pre-capitalist system.

socialism   Economic system of government ownership of industry, allegedly for good of whole society; opposite of capitalism.

HOW TO . . .

SUPPORT YOUR THESIS

"Well, that's what I think" isn't good enough. Writing a paper is like a lawyer making a case. You must present enough evidence to convince a judge. Like a judge, your instructor decides if your evidence is valid and supports your point. In a short paper you might back up your thesis with three to five supporting elements. You may wish to use *subheads*, little titles in the middle of your paper, to separate your supporting arguments. Subheads help you structure your ideas and make the paper easier to read and understand. If you cannot support your thesis with facts, numbers, quotes, or just plain reasoning, abandon or change it. As they say in the news business: "Back it up or back off."

Boldfaced and Centered

You can boldface and center your subheads (like the above subhead) to make them stand out. A new subhead indicates you are moving on to another supporting element. A paragraph is one thought or point. Make about three of them per double-spaced page. A paragraph that rambles on for a whole page is hard to read. Have no more than one subhead per page. For example, if your thesis is that a sour economy hurts incumbent presidents in elections, you might make a subhead for each election: "The 1992 Elections," "The 1996 Elections," and so on. In a five-page paper, you may wish to have about three subheads, indicating you are supporting your thesis with three elements.

Louis XI in the fifteenth century, expanded under Louis XIII and Cardinal Richelieu in the seventeenth century, implanted itself into French consciousness, and later spread through most of Europe. It was taken for granted that the state should supervise the economy and education, collect taxes, build highways and canals, and field standing armies. A bureaucratic elite, trained in special schools, ran the country.

These attitudes lasted well into the twentieth century and are still present. Defeated by Germany in 1870–1871, the French elite used the state as an agent of modernization. Paris tried to build a unified and cohesive population, to turn "peasants into Frenchmen." A centralized school system stamped out local dialects, broke stagnant rural traditions, and recruited the best talent for universities. State-owned industries turned France into an economic power. Beaten by Germany again in World War II, the French elite again used state power to modernize France.

Did it work? France did modernize greatly, but was this the fastest or most efficient way? Britain and the United States advanced farther with minimal government supervision; the competitive spirit of the free-market economy did the job faster and cheaper. (The comparison is not quite fair; Britain and the United States faced no powerful, expansionist Germany on their borders. If they had, the role of government would have been much bigger.)

Japan is another example of state-led modernization. With the Meiji Restoration of 1868, Tokyo assigned various branches of industry to samurai clans, provided

KEY CONCEPTS

DAHL'S "INFLUENCE TERMS"

One of Yale's Robert Dahl's many contributions is his explication of the varieties of power, which Dahl defines as A getting B to do what A wants. Dahl prefers the more neutral "influence terms," which he arrayed on a scale from best to worst.

Rational persuasion, the nicest form of influence, means telling the truth and explaining why someone should do something, like your doctor convincing you to stop smoking.

Manipulative persuasion, a notch lower, means lying or misleading to get someone to do something, the way politicians do in elections.

Inducement, still lower, means offering rewards or punishments to get someone to do something, like bribery.

Power threatens severe punishment, such as jail or loss of job.

Coercion is power with no way out; you have to do it.

Physical force is backing up coercion with use or threat of bodily harm.

Thus we can tell which governments are best: the ones that use influence at the higher end of the scale. The worst use the unpleasant forms of influence at the lower end.

funds, and told them to copy the best of the West. In one generation, Japan went from handicrafts to heavy industry under the slogan "Rich nation, strong army!" After World War II, the Ministry of Finance and Ministry of International Trade and Industry (MITI) supervised Japan's rapid economic leap by aiming bank loans to growth industries, keeping out foreign competition, and penetrating the world market with Japanese products. Before we say government supervision of the economy does not work, we had better explain why it worked in Japan. The Japanese, of course, have an entirely different and more cooperative culture. An American MITI might not work in our economic and cultural context.

Does—or should—the state serve as an agent of modernization? Should government attempt to supervise the economy by providing plans, suggestions, industry-wide cooperation, and loans? The traditional American answer is "No, it'll just mess things up." Looking more closely, though, we notice that the federal government has repeatedly goaded American society forward by acquiring large territories, letting settlers homestead them, and giving railroads rights of way. In the 1930s, the Tennessee Valley Authority brought electricity and flood control to a backward part of America. Faced with murderous competition in computers, the U.S. government under conservative Ronald Reagan set up a consortium of private firms to plan and build the next generation of computers before our friends across the Pacific could. America, too, has used the state as an agent of modernization and still uses federal programs to promote industry. One of the great questions of modern politics is how much state intervention do we want?

Civil Society   One more recent approach identifies the strength of **civil society** or *pluralism* as a key feature that distinguishes one type of government from another. Every modern society contains many associations and organizations: religious denominations, colleges, labor unions, industrial corporations, civic associations, political parties, and the mass media. We can classify governments according to how much **autonomy** they allow these associations. In pluralistic systems, associations are largely free and can even influence government.

Totalitarian governments, such as Nazi Germany and the Soviet Union, permit little or no autonomy. As Carl J. Friedrich and Zbigniew Brzezinski pointed out, such countries have official and dogmatic ideologies to which all social institutions must adhere. Everything is organized—even churches and bicycle clubs—and supervised by the state. Civil society is either crushed or controlled. The reestablishment of civil society in ex-Communist countries—and in Iraq—is a difficult but crucial task if democracy is to flourish.

Centralization of Political Power within the State   Governments may also be classified as unitary or federal by their territorial distribution of power. Most nations are **unitary states**. A single national or central government drafts and administers most laws and allows little local autonomy. The national government in Beijing or Paris writes the rules for Fujian or Bordeaux. In the twenty or so **federal** nations such as the United States, Germany, Australia, Canada, and much of Latin America, power is divided between the national government and the state or provincial governments. Usually, the national government controls foreign affairs, defense, and currency, and state authorities handle education, welfare, and policing.

■ MAKING PUBLIC POLICY

All modern governments make public policy. Weak or corrupt governments are less involved in such matters. President Mobutu of Zaire (now Congo) was chiefly interested in enriching himself, a demonstration that Aristotle's classification is still applicable. In legitimate systems, public policies are created to meet perceived national needs. Policies include legislation, judicial rulings, executive decrees, and administrative decisions. Policies are implemented through programs aimed at influencing the direction of government activity and public life.

Although governments claim to pursue policies and programs consistent with the good of the nation, the programs often favor influential interest groups. Since money is always limited, everyone cannot get everything they want. Is it more important for

---

civil society   Associations bigger than family but smaller than government. (Not the same as Hobbes's definition on page 22.)

autonomy   The state leaving associations free and unsupervised.

unitary state   Centralization of power in a nation's capital with little autonomy for subdivisions.

federalism   Balancing of power between a nation's capital and autonomous subdivisions, such as U.S. states.

the United States to bring democracy to Iraq or fund seniors' drug prescriptions? Should we use federal funds to lift education standards or to put more police on our streets? Decision makers must make complex choices amid debate, lobbying, partisan bickering, and sometimes outright bribery. With almost every choice, some get helped and others hurt. Out of sight, money often changes hands. Conflict over public policy choices constitute what is conventionally called "politics." It can never be totally clean because it is tightly bound up with power and money. "Politics," as one politician said, "is like a delicate flower. It needs a little dirt to grow in."

PUBLIC POLICIES: MATERIAL AND SYMBOLIC

Material public-policy decisions require the expenditure of public funds, which are always scarce. Most acts of Congress have dollar signs attached. But symbolic public policies involve little money or personnel and often are not even passed as laws. They create sentimental attachments (patriotism, loyalty, or deference) or confer social status on certain groups. The proclamation of a new public holiday, such as for Martin Luther King, Jr., is a **symbolic** policy that does nothing in a material way to help African Americans. As Murray Edelman pointed out in *The Symbolic Uses of Politics,* governments often use symbolic policies to deflect public concern. Material, or **tangible**, policies can be expensive and may anger the groups that have to bear the burden. Thus it is easier to proclaim "National Clean Air Day" than to enforce emission standards that cost industry money. Notice how much of current politics, especially that which is covered in the mass media, are symbolic rather than material.

All governments are careful to support and foster symbols of national unity. Symbols are created and popularized to give people something they can identify with. Americans are moved by images of the Statue of Liberty, "Old Glory," and more recently the World Trade Center. Symbols can become a source of controversy. In 2000, South Carolinians—mostly white—voted to keep their state flag with its Confederate battle flag in one corner. Others—mostly black—opposed the flag as a symbol of slavery. For whites, the state flag was a symbol of heritage and pride; for blacks it was a symbol of oppression. In 2004 the U.S.–appointed Iraqi governing council brought out a new flag for Iraq, but Iraqis detested its colors and symbols, and it was dropped. Choose your symbols carefully and make sure they unite.

Moral symbols are often invoked by public officials to build support. In America, most candidates for public office like to be photographed in church, because it is a powerful moral symbol linked with family values and stability. No high public officials are seen smoking or drinking in public, and for many years it was taboo for elected officials to be divorced. (Conservative Ronald Reagan, ironically, was the first divorced person to win the presidency.) Symbolic issues can become politically divisive, as in the question of prayer in public schools.

---

symbolic Acts and statements calculated to make citizens content without costing much.
tangible Real benefits to complaining groups, usually dollars.

Left: A symbol of reunified Germany is the refurbished Brandenburg Gate at the heart of Berlin near the federal parliament, the Bundestag; right: A Polish symbol is the three giant steel crosses at the Gdansk shipyard that mark the spot where forty-five workers were gunned down as they demonstrated against the regime in December 1970. This powerful symbol helped launch the Solidarity movement and bring down the Communist regime in 1989. (Michael Roskin)

Symbols can even lead to war. When Croatia declared its independence from Yugoslavia in 1991, it restored the use of medieval Croatian currency, uniforms, and coat of arms. These old symbols made Croats feel good, but they alarmed the Serbian minority, for they were exactly the names and symbols used by the Croatian fascist regime of World War II, a regime that murdered some 350,000 Serbs. As a result, the Serbs of Croatia broke away in four years of bloody war. Symbols can be dynamite.

KEY TERMS

anarchy (p. 40)
autonomy (p. 50)
civil society (p. 50)
cohesive (p. 40)
diplomatic recognition (p. 40)
failed state (p. 41)
federalism (p. 50)
laissez-faire (p. 46)
nation (p. 36)
nationalism (p. 38)
protogovernment (p. 40)

Raj (p. 37)
regionalism (p. 37)
socialism (p. 47)
state (p. 36)
statism (p. 47)
symbolic (p. 51)
tangible (p. 51)
unitary state (p. 50)
weak state (p. 41)
welfarism (p. 46)

KEY WEB SITES

Nationalism (from Netherlands, critical)
web.inter.nl.net/users/Paul.Treanor

Nationalism (from Britain)
kennedy.soc.surrey.ac.uk/scoresonline/2/1/natlinks.html

Internationalism
www.oneworld.org

Elizabethtown College world-affairs links
www.etown.edu/vl/

Corruption in worldwide comparison
www.transparency.de

FURTHER REFERENCE

Dahl, Robert A., and Bruce Stinebrickner. *Modern Political Analysis,* 6th ed. Upper Saddle River, NJ: Prentice Hall, 2003.

Edelman, Murray. *The Symbolic Uses of Politics.* Urbana, IL: University of Illinois Press, 1964.

Emerson, Rupert. *From Empire to Nation: The Rise to Self-Assertion of Asian and African Peoples.* Cambridge, MA: Harvard University Press, 1960.

Finer, S. E. *The History of Government from the Earliest Times,* vols. I–III. New York: Oxford University Press, 1997.

Hutchinson, John, and Anthony D. Smith, eds. *Nationalism: Critical Concepts in Political Science.* New York: Routledge, 2000.

Lindblom, Charles E. *The Market System: What It Is, How It Works, and What to Make of It.* New Haven, CT: Yale University Press, 2001.

Lipset, Seymour Martin. *American Exceptionalism: A Double-Edged Sword.* New York: Norton, 1996.

Palmer, Monte. *Political Development: Dilemmas and Challenges.* Itasca, IL: F. E. Peacock, 1997.

Porter, Bruce D. *War and the Rise of the State: The Military Foundations of Modern Politics.* New York: Free Press, 1994.

Tilly, Charles, ed. *The Formation of National States in Western Europe.* Princeton, NJ: Princeton University Press, 1975.

Van Creveld, Martin. *The Rise and Decline of the State.* New York: Cambridge University Press, 1999.

Zijderveld, Anton C. *The Waning of the Welfare State: The End of Comprehensive State Succor.* Piscataway, NJ: Transaction, 1999.

INDIVIDUALS AND CONSTITUTIONS

CHAPTER

4

QUESTIONS TO CONSIDER

- What is a constitution?
- What is constitutionalism?
- What is wrong with constitutions specifying social and economic rights?
- How can the very short U.S. Constitution still work in the modern age?
- Do most constitutions have "checks and balances"?
- How has the U.S. Constitution changed over time?
- What, if any, limits can be placed on free speech?

Every political system has a problem establishing and limiting power. Government and the people must both have certain powers and rights, but these must also be limited to keep them from encroaching on the rights of others. Choices such as a fair balance between government powers and civil liberties, and between the wishes of the majority and the rights of the minority are not easy ones. For example, may states ban same-sex marriages, or does that deny gays and lesbians equal rights? And if one state allows such marriages, must other states recognize them as legal? If religious parents believe that children should pray in public schools, does this conflict with the separation of church and state?

These questions raise problems of rights and political power, and some of these problems are admittedly more difficult than others. Most of us would probably agree that a Supreme Court decision is law even if Congress dislikes it. We will probably disagree, though, over the right of air traffic controllers to strike. Some will argue that the controllers should not be denied the right to ask for higher wages simply because they perform a public service. Others will argue that no one, including overworked air traffic controllers, has the right to endanger public safety. Prayer in public school is also difficult. Which prayers would suit all religions? What about children who do not wish to pray? How do we determine the limits of political power and balance the needs of the majority with the rights of individuals and **minorities**? Some guidelines are provided by traditions, by **statutes**, and above all by national constitutions, which lay down the basic rules for governing.

■ CONSTITUTIONS IN THE MODERN WORLD

In common usage, a **constitution** is a written document outlining the structure of a political system. Most also specify individual rights and freedoms, although this is sometimes a more recent thing. Canada got its Charter of Rights and Freedoms only in 1982. Britain got the equivalent only in 2000, when it adopted the European Convention on Human Rights. Before that, British rights and freedoms were not so clear. Political scientists define "constitution" as that set of rules and customs, either written or unwritten, legally established or extralegal, by which a government conducts its affairs. By this definition, almost all nations have constitutions since they operate according to some set of rules. In chaotic, corrupt, or dictatorial systems, constitutions may not count for much. Afghanistan, divided by armed tribes and warlords, has not been able to implement its new constitution. In Congo (formerly Zaire), Mobutu allowed nothing to limit his stealing of the country's wealth. And Stalin in 1936—precisely when he began his bloody purges—set up a Soviet constitution that looked fine on paper but was just a trick to fool the gullible. A few countries like Britain and Israel have no single written document but still have constitutions. British customs, statues, precedents, and traditions are so strong that the British government considers itself bound by practices developed over the centuries. Thus Britain has a constitution.

In the modern world, nearly every nation has a written constitution, and it is supposed to establish the forms, institutions, and limits of government and balance minority and majority interests. Not all function that way. Political scientists study not only what is written but what is actually practiced. The Constitution of the United States, for example, is very short and leaves much unsaid. Its seven articles mostly define the powers of each branch of government; the subsequent twenty-seven amendments broadly define civil rights but leave much open for interpretation.

In contrast, most nations that have won independence since World War II have adopted constitutions of remarkable detail. The postwar Japanese constitution, which was drafted by the U.S. military government in five days in 1946, contains forty articles on the rights and duties of the people alone, among them the right

---

minority   Subgroup distinct by language, ethnicity, race, or religion within the larger society.

statute   An ordinary law passed by a legislature, not part of the constitution.

constitution   Basic rules that structure a government, usually written.

CASE STUDIES

THE DANGERS OF CHANGING CONSTITUTIONS

Beware the country that keeps changing its constitution; it is a sign of instability and indicates that no constitution has rooted itself into the hearts and minds of the people. France, since the Revolution, has had fifteen constitutions, not all of them put into practice. Brazil has had seven since independence in 1822. Yugoslavia, under Tito, came out with a new constitution every decade, each more dubious than the one before. The 1963 Yugoslav constitution provided for a legislature of *five* chambers. Such constant experimentation with the highest law of the land meant that no constitution was established and legitimate, one reason Yugoslavia fell apart in bloodshed in 1991. Constitutions are too important to experiment with.

to productive employment, a decent standard of living, and social welfare benefits—a sharp contrast to the general values of "justice . . . domestic tranquility . . . common defense . . . general welfare . . . liberty" outlined in the American Preamble. Article I of the postwar German constitution (the Basic Law) also has a long list of rights, including not only fundamental legal and political freedoms, but also social and economic safeguards, including state supervision of the educational system and public control of the economy.

The 1988 Brazilian constitution enumerates many rights—forty-hour work-week, medical and retirement plans, minimum wages, maximum interest rates, environmental protection, you name it—that Brazil's struggling economy cannot afford. These rights can block needed economic reforms. Many now believe that detailed social and economic rights should never have been put into the constitution; they belong to statutes or to the workings of the market. Rights that cannot be fulfilled are common in newer constitutions, whose drafters thought they could fix social and economic evils.

Britain may be able to get by with no written constitution, although the British government is thinking about drafting one. The United States manages to function with a very general constitution. In both Britain and the United States, the details are filled in by usage over time. But most recently established nations commit themselves to long written constitutions that try to spell out everything in detail.

THE HIGHEST LAW OF THE LAND

Nations adopt constitutions for the same reason that the ancient Mesopotamian lawgiver Hammurabi codified the laws of Babylon: to establish a supreme law of the land. Constitutions state the fundamental laws of society and are not meant to be easily revised. They stand as a yardstick by which activities of the government or the people are to be measured. A legislature can pass a law one year and repeal it the next, but amending the constitution is made deliberately much harder. In Sweden, constitutional amendments must be passed by two successive legislatures with a general election in between. Amending the U.S. Constitution is even more difficult. The most common procedure requires the approval of two-thirds of both the Senate and the House of Representatives, then ratification by three-fourths of the state legislatures. The fact that our Constitution has been amended only seventeen times since the adoption of the Bill of Rights in 1791 illustrates how difficult the amendment procedure is. (The last, the Twenty-Seventh Amendment of 1992, specified no congressional pay raises without an election in between.) The Equal Rights Amendment failed to pass in 1983 because fewer than three-fourths of the state legislatures voted to ratify it.

The General Nature of Constitutional Law   Since constitutions, no matter how detailed, cannot cover every legal or administrative problem that may arise, many provide for a constitutional court to interpret the highest law in specific cases. This concept of judicial interpretation of a constitution is a fairly new thing worldwide; it was pioneered by the United States and has spread only in recent decades. Accordingly, many of our examples are American.

The U.S. Constitution says that "Congress shall make no law respecting an establishment of religion, or prohibiting the free exercise thereof" in Amendment I of the Bill of Rights. This is a very general statement. The way it will be interpreted in a specific case (such as the question of prayer in school or a satanic cult that believes in animal sacrifice or illegal drugs) must depend on the decision makers in power at the time the case arises. Does it mean that prayer in public schools breaches the separation of church and state? Or that prayer in schools is part of the free exercise of religion? Or that prayer in schools is permissible if that is what most people in a given school district want?

Constitutional law must be interpreted for specific incidents. Who is given the immense authority to decide what the general wording of a constitution means? Starting with the United States, now over thirty nations give this responsibility to the highest national court. The procedure by which the court rules on the constitutionality of a government act and declares null and void those acts it considers unconstitutional is known as **judicial review**. The power of judicial review is a controversial one. Many critics have accused the Supreme Court (most notably when Earl Warren was chief justice from 1953 to 1969) of imposing personal philosophies as the laws of the land. To a large extent, a constitution is indeed what its interpreters say it is, but the possibility of too subjective an interpretation seems to be a necessary risk to the concept of judicial review.

The courts do not always interpret a constitution in a consistent fashion. In the United States, the Warren Court exemplified **judicial activism**, which does not necessarily mean "liberal." It refers to a judge's willingness to strike down certain laws and practices in order to guarantee citizens' rights. The opposite philosophy

---

judicial review   Ability of courts to decide if laws are constitutional; not present in all countries.

judicial activism   Willingness of some judges to override legislatures by declaring certain statutes unconstitutional.

is **judicial restraint**, when a Supreme Court sees its job not as legislating but as following the lead of Congress. Justices Oliver Wendell Holmes and Felix Frankfurter, who counseled the Court on judicial restraint, were regarded by many as great liberals.

Likewise, Germany's Federal Constitutional Court is no stranger to controversy. Modeled after the U.S. Supreme Court—except that it has sixteen justices—the German court is mandated to make sure all laws conform to the **Basic Law**. In 1975 the German court found that a law permitting abortions conflicted with the strong right-to-life provisions of the Basic Law—enacted to repudiate the horrors of the Nazi era—and declared abortion unconstitutional. After German unification in 1990, the court allowed some abortions in East Germany, because it had been the established law and usage there. In 1979 the court found there was nothing unconstitutional about "worker codetermination"—that is, employees having nearly the same rights as owners and managers in determining the long-term future of their corporations.

Not all nations give their highest court the power to rule on the constitutionality of laws. In nations that do not have a clearly established procedure of judicial review, this responsibility is often given to the legislature. The British Parliament alone determines what is constitutional.

Constitutions and Constitutional Government   A constitution depends largely on the way it is interpreted. Two separate nations could adopt very similar constitutions but have them work quite differently. Sweden and Italy have similar structures, but their **political cultures** (see Chapter 7) are quite different, so their written rules function differently. A constitution can be a fiction. The Soviet constitution set a government framework—a federal system with a bicameral legislature, with executive and administrative powers given to the cabinetlike Council of Ministers—and accorded to its citizens a long list of democratic rights. In actuality, the top command of the Communist party controlled nearly everything, including individual rights.

Constitutionalism means that the power of government is limited. We see the beginnings of it in the Magna Carta England's nobles forced King John to sign in 1215. The Great Charter does not mention democracy; it merely limits the king's power. Over the centuries, however, it was used to promote democracy and individual freedom in modern Britain, the United States, and Canada. In a constitutionally governed nation, laws and institutions limit government to make sure that the fundamental rights of citizens are not violated. In contrast, a totalitarian or authoritarian government (see Chapter 5) is not limited by its constitution; individuals and minority

---

judicial restraint   Unwillingness of some judges to overturn statutes passed by legislatures.

Basic Law   German *Grundgesetz*. Germany's constitution since 1949.

political culture   The psychology of the nation in regard to politics.

constitutionalism   Degree to which government limits its powers.

groups have little protection against arbitrary acts of government, in spite of what the constitution may say. In the 1970s, the military regimes of Argentina and Chile "disappeared" (meaning tortured and killed) thousands of suspected leftists even though their written constitutions promised human rights.

THE PURPOSE OF A CONSTITUTION

If some nations pay little heed to what is written in their constitutions, why do they bother to write a constitution at all? Constitutions fulfill a variety of roles: They provide the symbolic function of putting in writing a statement of national ideals, they formalize the structure of government, and they attempt to justify the government's right to govern.

A Statement of National Ideals   According to the Preamble of the U.S. Constitution, our nation is dedicated to six goals: to form a more perfect union, to establish justice, to ensure domestic tranquility, to provide for the common defense, to promote the general welfare, and to secure the blessings of liberty. The 1977 Soviet constitution proclaimed the Soviet Union to be a "developed socialist society" dedicated to building a classless utopia. The constitution of the Federal Republic of Germany, seeking to erase any traces of Nazi rule, states its determination to "serve the peace of the world" and expressly proclaims that no group of people can be stripped of their German citizenship—a reaction to Hitler's Nuremburg Laws, which declared hundreds of thousands of Germans to be noncitizens.

Preambles and lists of rights are symbolic statements: They indicate the values, ideals, and goals of those who draft the documents. Preambles are by nature very general and have dubious legal force. How are they interpreted? What does the U.S. Constitution mean by a "more perfect union," for example? Debate over this term led to the Civil War. What does the Constitution mean by "establishing justice"? What is justice, and is it the same for all citizens? If African Americans have been denied equal rights for two centuries, does this mean that it is just for them to be given an advantage now in admission to colleges or getting jobs and housing? And what does the Preamble mean by "promoting the general welfare"? The questions of what the general welfare is and how it is to be balanced against the rights of the individual or of a minority group are almost certain to be disputed. Do children who pray in school disrupt the general welfare? Does the availability of cheap handguns, not accurate enough for any use but robbery, harm the general welfare, even though the Bill of Rights gives citizens the right to bear arms? Constitutions state national ideals, but the interpretation of these goals and values requires some decisions.

Formalizes the Structure of Government   A constitution is also a blueprint, a written description of who does what in government, defining the authority and limiting the powers of each branch and providing for regularized channels through which conflict may be resolved. Articles I through III of the U.S. Constitution outline the duties of Congress, the president, and the judiciary. Congress may collect

CASE STUDIES

CANADA'S NEW CONSTITUTION

Canada was in a curious situation. The British North America Act of 1867, passed by the British Parliament, gave Canada its independence, but as the British Dominion of Canada it could amend its constitution only by approval of the House of Commons in London. Increasingly, this rankled Canadians, who demanded "patriation" of their constitution, that is, bringing it back to Canada. They got this only in 1982 along with something they had never had before, a Charter of Rights and Freedoms modeled on the U.S. Bill of Rights.

taxes and customs duties but is prohibited from taxing exports. The president is named commander in chief of the armed forces but must have the "advice and consent" of the Senate to conclude treaties. In a system in which there is **separation of powers**, the constitution divides authority and responsibilities among the various branches of government; it also limits the power of each branch.

No other constitution uses "checks and balances" like the American one; most, in fact, specify the unification of power, a point we will study in Chapter 14. Few other countries abhor the concentration of power the way the U.S. Founding Fathers did. By our lights, the 1993 Russian constitution gives the president far too much power and the parliament, the **State Duma**, too little, an imbalance that bothers few Russians, most of whom prefer a strong hand at the top to prevent anarchy and stabilize the economy. Again, political culture counts for a lot in how a constitution actually works.

A constitution also outlines the division of power between central and regional or local governments. In a federal system, powers and responsibilities are divided between one national government and several provincial or state governments. Germany and Australia, like the United States, are federal systems. Their constitutions give their central governments control over certain areas, such as foreign policy, defense, and money supply. The German *Land* of Bavaria may not practice its own foreign policy; neither may Texas mint its own currency. Certain powers are delegated to the central government and others left to the states. In the U.S. Constitution, this division is a general one; any powers not accorded to the central government are reserved for the states or the people. The states traditionally control education, police protection, health and welfare services, and local commerce. Of course, this division of power has become less clear-cut, especially in recent years, as the federal government has taken on a greater share of financing the operations of education, health, welfare, housing, and much else.

---

separation of powers   U.S. doctrine that branches of government should be distinct and should check and balance each other, found in few other governments.

State Duma   Russia's national legislature.

As we shall explore in Chapter 13, most nations are unitary systems; that is, they do not divide power territorially but concentrate it in the nation's capital. The constitutions of unitary systems, such as France's, specify some powers of regions and localities to raise taxes, engage in urban and economic planning, and elect regional assemblies. Unitary systems do not seek to "balance" powers between central and provincial, but they may give a little autonomy to local bodies. They may also remake and even erase existing states and localities; this is not true with federal systems, which cannot easily erase or alter their component states, each of which has a legal existence.

Establishes the Legitimacy of Government　A constitution may also give a government the stamp of legitimacy, something both symbolic and practical. Many nations will not recognize a new state until it has established a written constitution, which is a sign of permanence and responsibility. The U.S. Articles of Confederation and, subsequently, the U.S. Constitution symbolized American independence.

Most constitutions were written shortly after major changes of regime and try to establish the new regime's right to rule. Typically, a **constituent assembly** is a legislature meeting for the first time after the overthrow of one regime to write a new constitution. The Spanish parliament elected in 1977 turned itself into a constituent assembly to repudiate the Franco system with the new 1978 constitution. That job done, it turned itself back into the *Cortes,* the regular parliament. In 1990, Bulgaria elected a 400-member Grand National Assembly to write a new, post-Communist constitution. That done, in 1991 Bulgaria elected a regular parliament, the 240-member National Assembly. After ousting the Taliban regime, Afghan factions met in a *loya jirga,* a traditional constituent assembly, to produce a new constitution in 2004. The warlords who run most of Afghanistan, however, ignore it.

■ THE ADAPTABILITY OF THE U.S. CONSTITUTION

Constitutions are modified by traditions, new usages, and laws. For instance, the U.S. Constitution does not mention political parties, yet our party system has become an established part of the American political process. Judicial precedents and government traditions, too, make up the fundamental laws of a society. Constitutions need some flexibility to adapt over time. The way that the U.S. Constitution has adapted over two centuries and in two areas—the "right to bear arms" and the growth of "big government" in the twentieth century—demonstrates this.

---

constituent assembly　Legislature convened to draft new constitution.

CASE STUDIES

THE RIGHT TO BEAR ARMS

The Founding Fathers wanted to prevent any concentration of power that might flow from a standing national army. Accordingly, the Constitution's "militia clauses" envisioned the defense of the United States as largely in the hands of state "militias" (now the National Guard), which would disperse power among the states and citizen militia members. To bolster this, Amendment II of the Bill of Rights (adopted in 1791) says, "A well regulated Militia, being necessary to the security of a free State, the right of the people to keep and bear Arms, shall not be infringed." The militia concept of citizen-based defense never came to much (the states did not want to spend the money), and the federal government took over the leading defense role. Now even state National Guard units are federally funded and supervised.

Americans now own some 192 million firearms, and over 30,000 a year die from gunshots. Due in large part to handguns, the U.S. murder rate is four to five times higher than European murder rates and three times higher than the Canadian rate. President John F. Kennedy, Dr. Martin Luther King, Jr., and Senator Robert F. Kennedy were gunned down. President Ronald Reagan and Alabama Governor George Wallace were seriously wounded. Many now wish to restrict lethal weapons. Yet opponents of gun-control legislation argue that the Constitution ensures the right of every citizen to purchase and own firearms. Hunters, shopkeepers who have been robbed, and those who feel that police cannot protect them argue that their constitutional right to pursue a hobby or to protect their lives will be jeopardized by gun-control legislation.

The "right to bear arms" case illustrates that a two-century-old constitution—at least in its traditional interpretation—may not provide the right answer for all of the needs of modern society. If gun controls are necessary to limit violence in America (and there is no consensus on the issue), can the Constitution be interpreted to allow such legislation to be passed? Does Amendment II mean citizens can own whatever firearms they wish privately or only for the purpose of maintaining a militia? Can suspected terrorists purchase guns?

CAN THE CONSTITUTION ENSURE RIGHTS?

Civil Liberties and Civil Rights   During World War II, Nazi concentration camps exterminated millions, and the Japanese army raped and pillaged China. In reaction, the world took steps to prevent such horrors. In 1948, the UN General Assembly adopted the Universal Declaration on Human Rights, a symbolic statement (with no real power of sanction) that establishes fundamental precepts and norms that most nations are reluctant to violate openly. Countries that do— Mao had tens of millions of Chinese killed; Saddam Hussein used poison gas against fellow Iraqis; Laurent Kabila condoned and covered up tribal massacres in the Congo—risk being isolated from world aid and trade. Charges of human-rights violations may persuade Sudan to cease killing in its Darfur region. Although not directly enforceable, the setting of norms for human rights made us more likely to seek them.

The Universal Declaration, patterned on the French Declaration of the Rights of Man and Citizen and on the American Declaration of Independence and the

KEY CONCEPTS

WHAT IS A RIGHT?

Where do "rights" come from? Are they natural or artificial? Thinkers of a classic bent—including the U.S. Founding Fathers—took "natural rights" as a basis for **human rights**. Nature expresses God's intentions, which are not hard to discern. You know instantly and instinctively that it is wrong to crash a jetliner into a building. Life and liberty are natural, therefore government may deprive people of these basic rights only for good cause. Human rights can generally be formulated in the negative as "freedom from," namely, from various forms of tyranny, the great concern of Thomas Jefferson.

Civil rights are newer and at a higher level; they arrived with the birth of modern democracy, in which citizens need the freedom to speak and vote. They are not as self-evident as human rights. Press freedom is probably a civil rather than a human right, although the two overlap. Those deprived of civil rights—such as the right to organize an opposition party—may soon also find themselves locked up by the dictatorial regime. In the United States, equal opportunity became a major civil-rights issue.

Economic rights are the newest—appearing in the nineteenth century with the early socialists (see Chapter 6)—and shift rights into the material realm. Advanced by people like Franklin D. Roosevelt, they are usually formulated in the positive as "freedom to," namely, to live adequately, have a job, and get an education. Many of them cost lots of taxpayer money in government programs. Conservatives say these are not rights at all, merely desirable things demanded by various groups, such as oldsters demanding prescription drugs as a "right." Some fear a "rights industry" creating dubious rights without limit.

"Right" said English philosopher Jeremy Bentham, "is the child of law." Something becomes a right only when it is put into a constitution or statutes. Before the Medicare law, old people had no right to federally funded health insurance. Now they think it is one of the Ten Commandments. All rights are more or less artificial or "socially **constructed**." Is something good and desirable automatically a right? Is everything an interest group demands really its right? Beware of overusing the term "rights."

Bill of Rights, affirms the basic civil and human rights that government may not arbitrarily take away. These include the rights to life and freedom of assembly, expression, movement, religion, and political participation. The Universal Declaration also provides for many economic and cultural needs: the rights to work, to

human rights   Freedom from government mistreatment such as arrest, torture, jail, and death without due process.

civil rights   Ability to participate in politics and society, such as voting and free speech; sometimes confused with but at a higher level than *human rights.*

economic rights   Guarantees of adequate material standards of living; the newest and most controversial rights.

constructed   Something widely believed as old and hallowed but actually recent and artificial.

CASE STUDIES

THE INTERNMENT OF JAPANESE AMERICANS

One of the biggest U.S. violations of minority rights came in 1942, when some 120,000 Japanese Americans on the West Coast were interned under infamous Executive Order 9066, in the mistaken belief that they were enemy aliens (most were born in the United States). Robbed of their homes, businesses, and liberty without due process of law, they were sent to ramshackle, dusty camps surrounded by barbed wire and guard towers—in some ways similar to Nazi concentration camps. Not one case of disloyalty was ever demonstrated against a Japanese American; they were victims of racism and wartime hysteria.

Even Secretary of War Henry L. Stimson, who signed the order, feared it "would make a tremendous hole in our Constitution." It did, but not until 1983 did a federal court overturn the legality of internment. The incident shows that even a well-established democracy can throw out its civil liberties in a moment of exaggerated and groundless panic. (A similar reaction flared after 9/11, aimed at Muslims.) The 442nd Regimental Combat Team, recruited from Japanese Americans, was the most decorated U.S. unit of World War II.

an education, to marry, raise a family, and provide for that family; the right to live according to one's culture. These rights are almost impossible to enforce and few have tried. The fact is that rights and liberties are difficult to define, and all nations restrict civil liberties in some way. The problem of minority groups is worldwide. Europe's most serious civil-rights problem is with Gypsies, who are despised nearly everywhere.

Minority Groups and Civil Liberties   Few nations are homogeneous; most have citizens from several racial, ethnic, religious, cultural, or linguistic backgrounds, and their civil or cultural liberties are often compromised. Haitians living in Florida or Chicanos in California are at a disadvantage unless they speak English. Indians and Pakistanis in Great Britain, Algerians in France, and Turks in Germany are under pressure to conform to the dominant culture. But the Universal Declaration states that minorities have the right to preserve their cultural uniqueness. Can it—or should it—be enforced in these situations? The major U.S. debate over "multiculturalism" hinges on this question. Should the United States abandon *e pluribus unum* and instead preserve each ethnic group? Do the children of each group have the right to be schooled in their parents' language? In 1998 California voters—including a majority of Latinos—approved Proposition 227, ending bilingual education and making English the only and standard language of instruction. Were rights violated? Or were they improved? Most Spanish-speakers want their children to master English *para ganar más dinero.*

■ FREEDOM OF EXPRESSION IN THE UNITED STATES

"Congress shall make no law . . . abridging the freedom of speech, or of the press; or the right of the people peaceably to assemble, and to petition the government for a redress of grievances." So says Amendment I of the U.S. Bill of Rights. We think of freedom of expression as a hallmark of any democratic nation. Citizens who think the government is bad or wrong may say so publicly. An antigovernment or antireligion artwork should draw no interference or investigation from a government agency.

It sounds easy but is not. Does freedom of speech give a campus bigot the right to incite hatred of African American students? Does a newspaper have a right to publish information that might damage the security of the nation? Can a publicly funded museum reject art works that offend the religious sensibilities of citizens? We may all believe in the right of free expression, but most of us would agree that there are limits. As Justice Oliver Wendell Holmes argued, nobody should be permitted to yell "Fire!" in a crowded theater unless there really is a fire. Free speech does not include the right to spread dangerous or malicious falsehoods, for example, telling police there are drugs in a certain apartment when there are not.

According to Justice Holmes, freedom of expression must also be restricted in cases in which statements or publications present a "clear and present danger" of bringing about "substantive evils," which Congress has a right to prevent. The Supreme Court in its 1925 *Gitlow v. New York* decision upheld the conviction of a radical who called for the violent overthrow of the government on the grounds that his words had represented a "bad tendency," which could "corrupt morals, incite

Looking like an exercise in free speech, this decades-old peace vigil in Washington is likely staffed by the Secret Service. No other "vigils" are allowed across the street from the White House, which is tightly secured. (Michael Roskin)

crime, and disturb the public peace." That decision, during a "red scare," would likely have come out differently in tranquil times.

Controversies relating to free speech are never-ending. In 2001, in another First Amendment case, the Supreme Court ruled that a radio station could air an (illegally) intercepted cell phone conversation. Unknown sources had sent the station a tape of a heated conversation between two teachers' union leaders. The Court ruled that the public's right to know something of public importance overrode a federal law against wiretaps.

Recently, some have argued that free speech has gone too far, especially if it deals in racism and pornography or if it throttles others' speech in the name of "political correctness." Congress took a long time to pass a campaign-reform law to curb the influence of big money, partly because campaign contributions are seen by many (including the Supreme Court) as a form of free speech. Dollars, they argued, are like words; both should flow without restriction to support candidates and causes. The Internet has opened vast new areas in this debate, as the Net lends itself to all manner of hate-filled, extremist causes. Should there be no limit to racist or terrorist urgings on the Internet?

FREE SPEECH AND SEDITION

Sedition is defined as criticism of the government or officials designed to produce discontent or rebellion. The U.S. government has used sedition laws to suppress radical expression several times since the adoption of the Bill of Rights. Congress passed the first Sedition Act in 1798, after the XYZ affair. It was aimed at the "Jacobins," as American defenders of the French Revolution were called, at a time when the United States was in an undeclared naval war with France. The Sedition Act was supposed to expire the day that President John Adams left office (which indicates that its true purpose may have been to influence the election). The act aroused controversy, but it lapsed without any test of constitutionality in the Supreme Court. The next Sedition Act came during the Civil War, when President Lincoln used his war powers to suppress Northern opponents of the war. The matter came before the Supreme Court, which declined to judge the legality of his actions, which went untested. After the Civil War, all "political prisoners" were pardoned.

Twentieth-Century Sedition Acts   During World War I the Espionage Act of 1917 produced Justice Holmes's "clear and present danger" doctrine. At a time when socialists and pacifists were urging people to resist U.S. involvement in the war by refusing to serve in the army and to disrupt the war effort in other ways, this act prohibited any attempts to interfere with the military draft. Several were charged under the Espionage Act in 1919. In one case, the Supreme Court upheld the law on the grounds that free speech could be restricted if it created a "clear and

---

sedition   Incitement to public disorder or to overthrow the state.

HOW TO . . .

SOURCES

Sources—where you get your facts, data, quotes, and ideas—are very important, the first things an instructor checks. Good sources are from specialized books, scholarly articles, or respected periodicals. Bad sources are ones that appear commonplace or dubious, such as textbooks (never use your current textbook as a source), encyclopedias, dictionaries, and popular newsweeklies. To cite something, in parentheses and just before the period, put the author's last name followed (without comma) by the year (Smith 1996).

Web search engines are easy to use but seldom give a complete picture. Many Web sites are advertising or propaganda. Most are so current or narrow that they fail to mention what happened last year or in another country; they lack historical and comparative perspective. For that, you still need books and articles.

Scholars divide sources into two types: *primary* and *secondary*. A primary source is direct material unfiltered through the mind of another. It might be a 2004 quote from presidential candidate George W. Bush (Jones 2006). It might be a statistical tabulation in a report (World Bank 2004, 274–275). It might be your own survey of college students.

A secondary source is another's synthesis, ideas, or opinions. It might be an article on a Web site about the U.S. occupation of Iraq (Berry 2004). It might be a scholar's reading of the World Bank figures (Adams 2005). To use a football analogy, which is better—your personal observation of the game (primary source) or the sportscaster's description of it (secondary source)? Instructors usually like primary sources. An article may include as a primary source numbers from official documents, such as EPA budget cuts under Bush (Williams 2003). Williams's comments on the cuts, on the other hand, would be a secondary source (Williams). Just noting the same source twice does not make it two sources. A source means a *different* book or article.

Instructors are impressed if you have lots of good sources, say ten in a five-page paper. If you cite a specific fact or quote, include the page number (Thompson 1991, 247). In the library's reference section there are ways to get started fast, most on computer.

New York Times Index
Reader's Guide to Periodical Literature
Social Sciences Index
Public Affairs Information Service
CIA World Factbook
Facts on File
LexisNexis
Academic Index
First Search

For anything to do with executive-legislative relations (Congress, the White House, new laws, budgets), there's something so good it's almost cheating: *Congressional Quarterly,* which puts out a weekly, an annual, and best of all, a *Congress and the Nation* for each presidential term. For foreign countries, check the magazine *Current History* and the *Country Study* series of books published by the Library of Congress.

CASE STUDIES

THE PENTAGON PAPERS

In 1971 a multivolume, secret Defense Department study of the decisions that went into the Vietnam war was leaked to the *New York Times* and *Washington Post*, both of which started publishing a series of sensational articles based on them. The Nixon administration immediately got a court order blocking further publication on national security grounds. In what became known as the *Pentagon Papers* case, the Supreme Court quickly and unanimously rejected the government's claim that official secrets had been compromised. By that time, most Americans were fed up with the war. The reasoning of Justice Hugo Black:

> Only a free and unrestrained press can effectively expose deception in government. And paramount among the responsibilities of a free press is the duty to prevent any part of the Government from deceiving the people and sending them off to distant lands to die of foreign fevers and foreign shot and shell . . . [T]he newspapers nobly did precisely that which the founders hoped and trusted they would do.

present danger" to national security. Several hundred people, including Socialist party leader Eugene Debs, were imprisoned under the act, but most were pardoned as the war ended.

In the 1940s and 1950s, sedition acts were directed against Communists. The 1940 Smith Act, the most comprehensive sedition act ever passed, made it a crime to advocate the violent overthrow of the government, to distribute literature urging such, or to knowingly join any organization or group that advocated such actions. The Smith Act aroused much controversy but was not put to a constitutional test until 1951, when the Supreme Court upheld the convictions of the leaders of the American Communist party even though they had not been charged with any overt acts of force against the government. "It is the existence of the conspiracy which constitutes the danger," ruled Chief Justice Vinson, "not the presence or absence of overt action." Since then, there have been other court rulings on the constitutionality of the Smith Act, and they have fluctuated. In *Yates v. the United States* in 1957, the Warren Court reversed the conviction of the American Communist party leaders on the grounds that there was no overt action, only abstract advocacy of rebellion. Four years later, in *Scales v. the United States,* the Court upheld the section of the Smith Act that makes membership in the Communist party illegal—but this ruling also specified that it is active membership, involving the direct intent to bring about the violent overthrow of the government, that is criminal. The Court was careful to point out that membership per se was not made illegal by the Smith Act.

The most stringent legislation against Communist subversion was passed during the McCarthy era after World War II, another red scare. The McCarran Act of 1950 (the Internal Security Act) barred Communists from working for the federal government or in defense-related industries, established a Subversive Activities

Control Board (SACB) to enforce the act, and required SACB-designated organizations to register with the attorney general. Critics of the McCarran Act charged that the law not only encroached on the rights of free speech and free assembly but also violated the self-incrimination clause of the Fifth Amendment. Although the Internal Security Act in its entirety has never been declared unconstitutional, every action by the SACB demanding specific organizational or individual registration with the attorney general's office has been declared unconstitutional. Finally, with the realization on all sides that the SACB accomplished nothing, it was abolished in 1973. Interestingly, the U.S. government did essentially nothing to stop criticism of the Vietnam War; opposition was too widespread, and there was no declaration of war.

The history of government actions to curb speech or arrest suspicious persons in the United States indicates that the guarantees of the Bill of Rights have been interpreted to mean different things over time. When Congress, the president, and the courts perceive danger and threat, they tend to be more restrictive, in other times more permissive. Rights are highly context-dependent. After the 9/11 terrorist attacks of 2001, few Americans worried about detaining hundreds of suspicious people without due process. By 2004, with examples of panicked overreaction in mind, some worried that the Patriot Act, passed in haste, should be modified to make sure it does not infringe on the Constitution.

We should remember this context-dependency when we see legal restrictions on human and civil rights in other lands. Some regimes really are under siege; opponents want to overthrow them (often with good reason). And since elections are routinely rigged, the only way to overthrow such regimes is by extralegal means, which may include violence. In such situations, free speech may lead quickly to violent overthrow, which may be richly deserved. Governments of whatever stripe clamp down when they are scared, and they are scared because they know they may be overthrown. Myanmar (formerly Burma), South Korea, Indonesia, Egypt, Iran, South Africa, Argentina, and many other lands have imprisoned political opponents for speaking out. "Free speech" is not just a nice thing; it can be dynamite. Freedom of expression thrives best under long-established, legitimate governments in tranquil times. It is, in short, political.

KEY TERMS

Basic Law (p. 58)
civil rights (p. 63)
constituent assembly (p. 61)
constitution (p. 55)
constitutionalism (p. 58)
constructed (p. 63)
economic rights (p. 63)
human rights (p. 63)
judicial activism (p. 57)

judicial restraint (p. 58)
judicial review (p. 57)
minority (p. 55)
political culture (p. 58)
sedition (p. 66)
separation of powers (p. 60)
State Duma (p. 60)
statute (p. 55)

KEY WEB SITES

U.S. Constitution, annotated
www.law.emory.edu/FEDERAL/usconst.html

Federalist Papers
www.law.ou.edu/hist/federalist/

U.S. Constitution, conservative view
www.constitution.org

Constitutions of many countries
www.constitution.org/cons/natlcons.htm

Britain's Magna Carta
www.constitution.org/eng/magnacar.htm

FURTHER REFERENCE

Arkes, Hadley. *Natural Rights and the Right to Choose.* New York: Cambridge University Press, 2002.

Axelrod, Alan. *Minority Rights in America.* Washington, D.C., CQ Press, 2002.

Bezanson, Randall P. *Speech Stories: How Free Can Speech Be?* New York: New York University Press, 1998.

Dahl, Robert A. *How Democratic Is the American Constitution?,* 2nd ed. New Haven, CT: Yale University Press, 2002.

Eastland, Terry, ed. *Freedom of Expression in the Supreme Court: The Defining Cases.* Lanham, MD: Rowman & Littlefield, 2000.

Elazar, Daniel J. *Covenant and Civil Society: The Constitutional Matrix of Modern Democracy.* Piscataway, NJ: Transaction, 1998.

Epstein, Richard A. *Principles for a Free Society: Reconciling Individual Liberty with the Common Good.* New York: Perseus, 1998.

Falk, Richard. *Human Rights Horizons: The Pursuit of Justice in a Globalizing World.* New York: Routledge, 2000.

Giglio, Ernest. *Rights, Liberties and Public Policy.* Brookfield, VT: Avebury, 1995.

Maddex, Robert L., Jr. *Constitutions of the World,* 2nd ed. Washington, D.C.: CQ Press, 2001.

Moon, Richard. *The Constitutional Protection of Freedom of Expression.* Toronto: University of Toronto Press, 2000.

Ravitch, Frank S. *School Prayer and Discrimination: The Civil Rights of Religious Minorities and Dissenters.* Boston, MA: Northeastern University Press, 1999.

Spitzer, Robert J. *The Right to Bear Arms: Rights and Liberties under the Law.* Santa Barbara, CA: ABC-CLIO, 2001.

Stone, Geoffrey R. *Perilous Times: Free Speech in Wartime from the Sedition Act of 1798 to the War on Terrorism.* New York: Norton, 2004.

DEMOCRACY, TOTALITARIANISM, AND AUTHORITARIANISM

CHAPTER 5

QUESTIONS TO CONSIDER

- Why does modern democracy mean representative democracy?
- Which are the most crucial elements of democracy?
- What are the elite and pluralist theories of politics?
- Why is totalitarianism a twentieth-century phenomenon?
- What is the difference between totalitarian and authoritarian?
- Are totalitarian systems bound to fail? Why?
- Why have many countries recently turned democratic?
- Why does democracy sometimes fail? Will it work in Iraq?

In 1948 English writer George Orwell finished his *1984*, a projection into the future of life in the Soviet Union in particular and of totalitarian societies in general. In this nightmare, individuals have no rights; they are creatures of the state. The government brainwashes them, spies on them, controls every aspect of their lives, and breaks doubters psychologically. The media systematically lie.

At the extreme opposite is Athens in the fifth century B.C. All adult male citizens were equal and had the right and duty to attend the General Assembly, which met ten times a year, to enact laws, elect executives (who were accountable for their actions), all by simple majority votes. Thousands turned out for the General Assembly, for participation in politics was highly valued and gave Athenians dignity and human worth.

Orwell's picture of totalitarianism and the Athenian ideal of democracy are at opposite ends of the spectrum of government; in between are many variations. Table 5.1 (on page 72) shows the principal gradations from perfect democracy to perfect totalitarianism and lists some characteristics of each of the systems. Such tables have to be qualified in at least three ways: (1) Some countries have the

Table 5.1 The Spectrum of Government Power

Democratic Government			Nondemocratic Government		
Perfect Democracy (Power in Hands of the People)	*Democracy (USA, Great Britain, France)*	*Limited Democracy (Singapore, Russia, Zimbabwe)*	*Authoritarianism (Syria, Iraq, Burma)*	*Totalitarianism (Communist China, Fascist Italy, Nazi Germany)*	*Perfect Totalitarianism (All Power Held by Government)*
Nonpartisan politics	Two-party or multiparty politics	Dominant-party politics	Single-party or no-party politics	Single-party politics	Single-party politics
Full individual participation in government	Popular elections with universal franchise	Popular elections with limited slate	Self-determined or party-determined leadership	Self-determined or party-determined leadership	Absence of voting franchise
Virtually unlimited individual liberties	Carefully protected individual liberties	Limited individual liberties	Elections without choices	Voting franchise varies in scope, limited to approval of party candidates	Absence of individual liberties
Absolute social and economic equality	Vertical mobility with progress toward social and economic equality	Approximate freedom of the press	Irregular tolerance of individual liberties	Absence of constitutionalism	Government control of press
Free access to administrative office	Detailed constitutional restraints on government	Some social and economic equality	Little or no constitutional restraint on government	Extremely narrow political liberties	Enforced economic and social stratification
Absolute freedom of the press	Freedom of the press	Limited constitutional restraint on government	Intermittent martial law	Social structure determined by state	Total economic control by government
	Broad access to public office	Some access to public office	Direct military influence on government	Substantial economic control by government	Thought control and obliteration of individual conscience
	Unrestricted formation of political groups	Formation of some political groups	Government determination of economic system and structure	Government control of mass media	
			Government control of press		

trappings of democracy—elections, parliaments, and parties—but are not. Their elections are stacked, the parliaments tame, and the parties cowed. Russia and Egypt are like this. (2) Many countries are in flux, shifting between more and less democratic. Venezuela, Bolivia, and Peru have recently taken on authoritarian hues. (3) There are many intermediate positions, not just four. Singapore might be at the upper end of the "limited democracy" category, whereas Zimbabwe has slid into the authoritarian category. Freedom House annually ranks countries on a 1–7 scale and puts them into "free," "partly free," and "not free" categories to indicate their degree of democracy (see page 197). In general, democratic governments have limited powers; totalitarian ones have few limits on their power.

There is no "average" democratic state or "average" undemocratic state, much less "perfect" ones. There is much variation in how things work in practice. Athens had a limited democracy, for most of the population—women, resident aliens, and slaves—could not participate in politics, and an elite controlled things. The Soviet Union held elections with 99.9 percent turnout, but they were elections without choices. Similarly, democracies claim to protect civil liberties, but these are accorded unevenly—in high degree to middle-class whites and grudgingly to impoverished nonwhites. Political science looks to see how things actually work, not just what is written on paper.

■ MODERN DEMOCRACY

There is probably no single word with more meanings than **democracy**. Twentieth-century dictators misused the word to persuade subjects that they lived in a just system. The Soviet Union used to claim it was the most democratic system in the world, and the government of mainland China still calls itself the "People's Republic." Democracy does not always equal freedom. Parties and elections can be used to bring dictatorial regimes into power. Democracy needs thoughtful citizens, limits on power, rule of law, and human and civil rights. Not every country that calls itself a democracy is one.

Democracy (from the Greek *demokratía*; demos = "people" and kratía = "government") carried a negative connotation until the nineteenth century, as thinkers accepted the ancient Greeks' criticism of direct democracy as unrestrained mob rule. A "true" democracy, a system in which all citizens meet periodically to elect officials and personally enact laws, has been rare: Athens's General Assembly, New England town meetings, and Swiss *Landsgemeinde*. Some direct democracy continues in U.S. states through **referendums** on issues the legislature will not handle. Although referendums seem very democratic, their sponsors can oversimplify and manipulate issues, as Californians see with the scores of measures—some contradicting others—they face on every ballot. Pakistan's president—a general who

---

democracy   Political system of mass participation, competitive elections, and human and civil rights.
referendum   A mass vote on an issue rather than for a candidate; a type of direct democracy.

seized power in a 1999 military coup—had himself confirmed in office by a 2002 referendum. Few were fooled. Direct democracy is difficult to carry out because of the size factor. As the Englishman John Selden noted in arguing for a Parliament in London: "The room will not hold all." A national government that submitted each decision to millions of voters would be too unwieldy to function. **Representative democracy** evolved as the only workable system.

REPRESENTATIVE DEMOCRACY

Modern democracy is not the actual setting of policy by the people. Instead, the people play a more general role. Democracy today is, in Lipset's words, "a political system which supplies regular constitutional opportunities for changing the governing officials, and a social mechanism which permits the largest possible part of the population to influence major decisions by choosing among contenders for political office." *Constitutional* means that the government is limited and can wield its authority only in specific ways. Representative democracy has several essential characteristics. Notice that it is not a simple system or one that falls into place automatically. It must be carefully constructed over many years. Attempts to thrust it onto unprepared countries like Russia or Iraq often do not work as planned.

Popular Accountability of Government   In a democracy the policymakers must obtain the support of a majority or a plurality of votes cast. Leaders are accountable to citizens. Elected leaders who govern badly can be voted out. No one has an inherent right to occupy a position of political power; he or she must be freely, fairly, and periodically elected by fellow citizens, either at regular intervals (as in the United States) or at certain maximum time spans (as in Britain). Most systems permit reelection, although some specify term limits. Reelection is the people's means both of expressing support and of controlling the general direction of government policy.

Political Competition   Voters must have a choice, either of candidates or parties. That means a minimum of two distinct alternatives. In Europe, voters have a choice among several parties, each of which tries to distinguish its ideology and policies. One-party or one-candidate elections are fake. Americans are supposed to have a choice of two candidates, one for each major party, but many congresspersons run with little or no opposition, as campaign costs dissuade challengers from even trying. Gerrymandering by state legislatures guarantees most incumbents' reelection. Even the United States is less than fully democratic.

The parties must have time and freedom to organize and present their case well before elections. A regime that permits no opposition activity until shortly before election day has rigged the election. Likewise, denying media access—for example, by controlling television—stunts any opposition. Much of democracy depends on the political freedoms in the months and years before the actual balloting

---

representative democracy   One in which the people do not rule directly but through elected and accountable representatives.

KEY CONCEPTS

THE "TWO-TURNOVER TEST"

Harvard political scientist Samuel Huntington proposes a "two-turnover test" to mark a stable democracy. That is, two electoral alternations of government indicate that democracy is firmly rooted. Poland, for example, overthrew its Communist regime in 1989 and held free and fair elections (called "founding elections"), won by the Solidarity coalition of Lech Walesa. Some Poles, however, hurt by rapid economic change, in 1995 voted in a president from the Socialists, a party formed out of the old Communist party. But after a while they did not like the Socialists either and in 1997 voted in a right-of-center party. Poland has thus had two turnovers and has established its democratic credentials. Russia has never had a turnover.

takes place. Physical balloting can still be a problem. In some countries (as in old Chicago), reliable people "vote early and often," and votes can be miscounted. Defective voting systems, such as Florida's punch-card ballots, may negate the popular will. Elections by themselves do not equal democracy.

Alternation in Power　The reins of power must occasionally change hands, with the "ins" becoming the "outs" in a peaceful, legitimate way. No party or individual should get a lock on power. A system in which the ruling party stays in power many decades cannot really be democratic. Such parties say they win on popularity but often tilt the rules. In 2001 Singapore's People's Action party won its ninth election in a row; it allowed only nine days for campaigning and redrew constituency boundaries. Mexico's Institutional Revolutionary Party (PRI) won fourteen straight elections since the 1920s. In 2000, however, Vicente Fox of the National Action party (PAN) won the presidency, and Mexico started looking democratic. Likewise Kenya in 2002 voted out the party that had ruled for 39 years. Other African countries are also getting alternation in power, a good sign.

One unstated but important role of alternation in power is control of corruption. An opposition party that hammers incumbents for corruption is a powerful corrective to the human tendency to misuse public office. Systems without alternation are invariably corrupt.

Popular Representation　In representative democracies, the voters elect representatives to act as legislators and, as such, to voice and protect their general interest. Each legislator usually acts for a given district or group of people. But how should he or she act? Some theorists claim legislators must treat elections as **mandates** to carry out constituents' wishes. What the voters want is what they should get, says this theory. Other theorists disagree; constituents often have no opinion on issues. Therefore representatives must act as **trustees**, carrying out the

---

mandate　A representative carrying out the specific wishes of the public.

trustee　A representative deciding what is the public good without a specific mandate.

wishes of constituents when feasible but acting for the best interests of the community as a whole. Joseph Schumpeter puts the argument against the mandate theory as follows: "Our chief problems about the classical (democratic) theory centered in the proposition that 'the people' hold a definite and rational opinion about every individual question and that they give effect to this opinion—in a democracy—by choosing 'representatives' who will see to it that the opinion is carried out."

Of course, few people hold definite opinions on every subject. If they were asked to vote on car fuel economy or depreciation rules for taxes, few would vote. Representative democracy, therefore, does not mean that the representative must become a cipher for constituents; rather, it means that the people as a body must be able to control the *general* direction of government policy. For example, the people may have a general desire to improve education, but they leave the means and details of achieving this goal to their legislators. It is this partnership between the people and the lawmakers that is the essence of modern democracy. E. E. Schattschneider summarizes the case succinctly:

> The beginning of wisdom in democratic theory is to distinguish between the things that the people can do and the things the people cannot do. The worst possible disservice that can be done to the democratic cause is to attribute to the people a mystical, magical omnipotence which takes no cognizance of what very large numbers of people cannot do by the sheer weight of numbers. At this point the common definition of democracy has invited us to make fools of ourselves.

Majority Decision   In any important government decision there is rarely agreement. Usually one faction favors something and another group opposes it. How then shall the popular will be determined? The simple answer is that the majority should decide: In any controversy, the policy that has the support of the greatest number should generally become the policy of government. This is the procedure that was used in the democracies of ancient Greece. However, our more modern and practical concept of democracy is that the majority decides but with respect for minority rights. To uphold such rights, an independent judiciary, one not under the thumb of the regime, is a necessity.

Minority views are important. Probably every view now widely held was once a minority view. Most of what is now public policy became law as a result of conflict between majority and minority groups. Furthermore, just as it is true that a minority view may grow over time until it is widely accepted, so may a majority view eventually prove to be unwise, unworkable, or unwanted. Just as minorities may be right, so, too, may majorities be wrong. If minority views are silenced, the will of the majority becomes the "tyranny of the majority," which is just as foreboding as executive tyranny.

Right of Dissent and Disobedience   Related to minority rights, people must have the right to resist the commands of government they deem wrong or unreasonable. This right was invoked in 1776 by Thomas Jefferson in the Declaration of Independence. Henry Thoreau, in his opposition to the war with Mexico, made probably the most profound American defense of **civil disobedience** when he declared, "All men recognize the right of revolution; that is, the right to refuse allegiance to, and to resist, the government, when its tyranny or its inefficiency are great and unendurable." The most celebrated advocate of civil disobedience was Indian independence leader Mahatma Gandhi, who was strongly influenced by Thoreau. Both considered their method of resistance to be "civil"; that is, it was disobedience but it was nonviolent and did not exceed the general legal structure of the state. It was an attention-getting device that forced the authorities to rethink. Ultimately, Gandhi and his followers forced the British to leave India.

Some look on civil disobedience as an individual act of conscience, but others seek to organize it and mobilize it. The most prominent American organizer was Reverend Martin Luther King, Jr., whose 1960s nonviolent civil-rights campaigns deliberately challenged racist local laws. He and others in his Southern Christian Leadership Conference were often arrested, but once the charges were brought before a federal court, the discriminatory law itself was usually declared unconstitutional. The long-range consequence of their actions changed both the laws and the psychology of America. Without civil disobedience, minority claims would have gone unheard.

Political Equality   In a democracy, all adults (usually now age eighteen and over) are equally able to participate in politics: "one person, one vote." In theory, all are able to run for public office, but critics point out that it takes a great deal of money—and often specific racial and religious ties—to really enter public life. Under the pressure of minority claims and civil disobedience, however, systems tend to open up over time and become less elite in nature.

Popular Consultation   Most leaders realize that to govern effectively they must know what the people want and must be responsive to these needs and demands. Are citizens disturbed—and, if so, *how* disturbed—about foreign policy, taxes, unemployment, the cost of living? Intelligent leaders realize that they must not get too far ahead of—nor fall too far behind—public opinion. Therefore, a range of techniques has evolved to test opinion. Public opinion polls are taken on many issues. The media can create a dialogue between the people and their leaders. At press conferences and interviews with elected officials, reporters will ask questions they believe people want answered. Editorials and letters to the editor also indicate citizens' moods and feelings.

In recent years, several critics have noted that U.S. officials often rely heavily on the opinions of small segments of their constituencies because they are well-organized and highly vocal. Most Americans favor at least some gun control, but the National Rifle Association often blocks firearms legislation.

---

civil disobedience   The nonviolent breaking of an unjust law to serve a higher law.

Free Press   Dictatorships cannot tolerate free and critical **mass media**; democracies cannot do without them. One of the clearest ways to determine the degree of democracy in a country is to see how free its press is. The mass media provide citizens with facts, raise public awareness, and keep rulers responsive to mass demands. Without a free and critical press, rulers can disguise wrongdoing and corruption and lull the population into passive support. As China permitted a "democracy movement" in the late 1980s, the Chinese media became freer, more honest, and more critical. As part of the crushing of this movement, outspoken journalists are fired or arrested.

Some Americans argue that the U.S. media go too far, that they take an automatic adversarial stance that undermines government authority and weakens the nation. In some cases this may be true, but in a democracy there is no mechanism to decide what "too far" is. The checks on reckless reporting are competing journals and channels that can criticize and refute unfair commentary. Then citizens, with no government supervision, can decide for themselves if charges are accurate. Only half in jest has the U.S. press been called "the fourth branch of government."

■ DEMOCRACY IN PRACTICE: ELITISM OR PLURALISM?

Even if all these democratic criteria are met—no easy feat—political power will still not be evenly distributed; few will have a lot, and many will have little. Political scientists see this unevenness of power as normal and unavoidable: **Elites** make the actual decisions, and ordinary citizens, the *masses*, generally go along with these decisions. The key dispute is how much elites are accountable to masses. Those who argue that elites are little accountable are *elite theorists*; those who argue that elites are ultimately accountable are **pluralists**.

One of the early thinkers on elites, Italian political scientist Gaetano Mosca, argued that government always falls into the hands of a few.

> In all societies—from societies that are very undeveloped and have largely attained the dawnings of civilization, down to the most advanced and powerful societies— two classes of people appear—a class that rules and a class that is ruled. The first class, always the less numerous, performs all of the political functions, monopolizes power, and enjoys the advantages that power brings, whereas the second, the more numerous class, is directed and controlled by the first, in a manner that is now more or less legal, now more or less arbitrary and violent.

The German thinker Robert Michels argued that any organization, no matter how democratic its intent, ends up run by a small elite; he called this the "Iron

---

mass media   The means of communication that quickly reach large audiences.

elites   The "top" or most influential people in a political system.

pluralism   Theory that politics is the interaction of many groups.

HOW TO . . .

REFERENCES

Whoever reads your paper should be able to look up your sources, to make sure they are valid and in context. References are now usually put at the end. Shown here is the standard urged by the American Political Science Association, but this is not sacred. It is derivative from that of the American Psychological Association ("psych style") and a variation of the *Chicago Manual of Style*. Your instructor may prefer the similar style of the Modern Language Association. And some may prefer the old-fashioned footnote style, which at least was consistent across disciplines. There is some variation in what is considered standard, especially with Web sites. In general, references give the reader a road map to your sources.

At the end of your paper, under the subhead "References" or "Works Cited," with hanging indents and in alphabetical order, give the author (last name first), the year, the article in quotation marks, the journal or book title underlined or italicized, and, if a book, the city and publishing house. If a journal, give the month and day at the end. Separate these elements with periods. If there is no listed author, use the article's title or, especially with Web sites, the sponsoring agency's name. Referring to the "Sources" box on page 67, here is what they look like:

Works Cited

Adams, Jonathan. 2005. *Development and the Environment*. Washington, D.C.: National Ecology Association.

Berry, Nicholas O. 2004. "Wrong Turns in Iraq." *Foreign Policy Forum*. April 21. foreignpolicyforum @msn.com

Jones, Robert. 2006. "Bush Announces Environment Program." *New York Press*. 4 March.

Smith, Paul. 1996. "Bush Against the Environment." *New Departure*. June 20.

Thompson, Earl. 1991. *George Bush and the Environment*. New York: Simple & Simon.

Williams, Charles. 2003. "The EPA Budget under Bush." *Ecology Quarterly* 17:417. [These are volume and page numbers.]

World Bank. 2003. *World Development Report 2002/2003*. New York: Oxford University Press.

Law of Oligarchy." More recently, Yale political scientist Robert Dahl held that "participatory democracy is not possible in large modern societies; government is too big and the issues are too complex . . . The key political, economic, and social decisions . . . are made by tiny minorities. . . . It is difficult—nay, impossible—to see how it could be otherwise in large political systems." These three agree on the inevitability of elites, but Mosca and Michels, elite theorists, see elites as unaccountable whereas Dahl, a pluralist, sees them as accountable.

Contrary to what one might suppose, modern elite theorists are generally not conservatives but radicals; they decry rule by elites as unfair and undemocratic. Columbia sociologist C. Wright Mills denounced the "Power Elite" in which big business gave money to politicians, politicians voted massive defense spending, and top generals gave lush contracts to big business. This interlocking conspiracy was driving the United States to war, Mills predicted.

Interest groups such as these trade unionists are a key element in the pluralistic makeup of this country. (Laima E. Druskis)

Money and connections give elites access to political power, emphasize elite theorists. In 2004 both Bush ('68) and Kerry ('66) were Yale graduates and members of the secretive Skull and Bones, the elite of the elite. Few rich people run for office but instead use contributions to get laws, subsidies, and tax breaks to favor themselves. The Bush administration gave the biggest of its 2001 tax cuts to the richest 1 percent and boosted the oil industry, in which both Bush and Vice President Cheney had been executives. Big corporation money controls both major parties, charged independent presidential candidate Ralph Nader. Massive campaign contributions make sure no important industry gets seriously harmed; witness the tobacco companies' ability to block laws and lawsuits. Elite theorists make their case with items like these.

Look again, argue pluralists. The Cold War, not a power elite, drove defense spending, which declined sharply after the Soviet threat disappeared. Most politicians are of modest origins; few are from wealthy families (exceptions: both Roosevelts, JFK, and both Bushes). Politicians may take big contributions, but they are usually attuned to what wins votes. Big companies do get leaned on. The entire asbestos industry was closed down as a health hazard. Tobacco firms have had to pay millions in lawsuits and face continual government pressure.

Politics functions, say pluralists, through **interest groups**, which we will explore more fully in Chapter 9. Just about any group of citizens can organize a group to protest or demand something, and politicians generally listen. To be sure, if the group is wealthy and well-placed, it gets listened to more, but nobody has a hammerlock on the political system. U.S. oil companies are among the richest firms in

---

interest groups   Associations that pressure government for policies they favor.

the world, and they are pro-Arab. Why then does U.S. policy permanently tilt toward Israel? Because most American Jews and fundamentalist Christians are pro-Israel, and politicians listen to them more than to the oil companies. According to pluralists, interest groups are the great avenues of democracy, making sure government listens to the people. Many argue that only a pluralist society can be democratic. Efforts to found democracies in societies without traditions of pluralism are like trying to plant trees without soil, as we have seen in Russia, where the long Communist rule erased most naturally occurring interest groups.

The pure elite theorist views society as a single pyramid, with a tiny elite at the top. The pure pluralist views society as a collection of billiard balls colliding with each other and with government to produce policy. Both views are overdrawn. A synthesis that more accurately reflects reality might be a series of small pyramids, each capped by an elite. There is interaction of many units, as the pluralists would have it, but there is also stratification of leaders and followers, as elitist thinkers would have it. (See Figure 5.1.) Robert Dahl called this a "polyarchy," the rule of the leaders of several groups who have reached stable understandings with each other. Arend Lijphart called it "consociational democracy." The elites of each important group strike a bargain to play by the rules of a constitutional game and to restrain their followers from violence. In return, each group gets something; no one gets everything. Lijphart's example of where this has worked successfully is the Netherlands, where the elites of the Catholic, Calvinist, and secular blocs have reached an "elite accommodation" with each other. In Lebanon, by contrast, elite accommodation broke down, resulting in a horrible civil war. Most stable countries have "conflict management" by elites. The United States shows an interplay of business, labor, ethnic, regional, and other elites, each delivering enough to keep their people in line, each cooperating to varying degrees with other elites. When elite consensus broke down, the United States, too, experienced a bloody civil war.

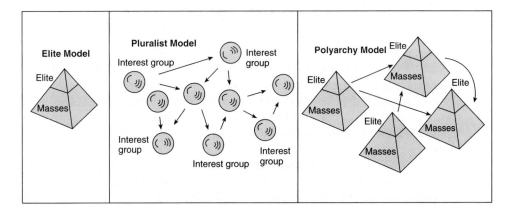

Figure 5.1

Elite, pluralist, and polyarchy models.

■ TOTALITARIANISM

In **totalitarian** systems, elites are almost completely unaccountable; they lock themselves into power and are very difficult to oust, short of regime collapse, which we saw in Eastern Europe in 1989 and in the Soviet Union in 1991. There is now little totalitarianism left. Its emphasis on total control, brainwashing, and worship of the state and its leaders has proven mistaken and inefficient. Few people are now attracted to such political models. Now, only North Korea remains as a pristine example of totalitarianism, while China and Vietnam have opened up economically if not politically. Earlier in the twentieth century, though, with the regimes of Stalin, Mussolini, and Hitler, it looked like totalitarianism was riding high and might even be the wave of the future. Now it is more likely that it will prove to be a disease of the twentieth century. Most of our examples are historical, not current.

WHAT IS TOTALITARIANISM?

The twentieth-century phenomenon of totalitarianism is far removed from the autocracies of the past. Peter the Great and Louis XIV were powerful despots, but the scope and extent of their power and authority were severely limited by the poor means of communication and transportation of the time. Until the twentieth century, communications were so slow and difficult that it was impossible for the most autocratic rulers to control effectively or completely all the territory in their domain. Even Louis XIV, a kind of royal dictator, did not try to control everything in France; average citizens lived their private lives. In contrast, totalitarian states of the twentieth century attempted to remold and transform the people under their control and to regulate every aspect of human life and activity.

Totalitarianism starts only after World War I and was made possible by modern technology. It is essentially a system of government in which one party holds all political, economic, military, and judicial power. This party attempts to restructure society in accordance with party values and interferes massively in the personal lives of individual citizens. Freedom disappears. The old autocratic rulers kept their subjects out of political participation, but the totalitarian state insists on mass participation and tries to generate enthusiasm. With modern electronic devices, the state is able to control communications and private activities and to coordinate and centralize economic life.

Carl J. Friedrich and Zbigniew Brzezinski identified six basic features common to totalitarian states. Four of them would have been impossible to achieve in preindustrial societies and are central to the system.

An All-Encompassing Ideology   Totalitarian ideology is an official body of doctrine that includes theories of history, economics, and future political and social development. The ideology portrays the world in black-and-white terms, and citizens

---

totalitarian   Political system in which state attempts total control of citizens.

The "People's Palace" in Bucharest, huge, outrageously expensive, and unfinished, was to be the personal palace of Romanian dictator Nicolae Ceausescu, who was deposed and shot in late 1989. With no checks or controls, dictators can launch insane projects. (Michael Roskin)

are judged to be either for the state or against it. The ideology usually points toward a perfect society, which humankind will attain in the future (such as Marx's prediction that the classless society would lead to an eventual withering away of the state). All citizens are supposed to believe and study the official ideology. Courses on Marxist-Leninist thought were required in the schools of all Communist states.

A Single Party   Only one party legally exists, usually led by one man who establishes a cult of personality around himself. Mussolini, Hitler, Stalin, and Mao had themselves worshipped. Entrance into the party is controlled (official membership is usually less than 10 percent of the population) and is supposed to be an honor. Membership brings privileges, and in return the members give their dedication and support to the party. **Hierarchically** organized and oligarchically controlled, the party is either superior to or tied in with the formal institutions of government. The party leader wields considerable power in the government, and party functionaries hold all important posts in the bureaucracy. Party officials impose at least outward conformity at all levels of society.

Organized Terror   A security police, using both physical and psychological methods, keeps citizens cowed. The Nazi Gestapo, the Soviet NKVD under Stalin, and Mussolini's OVRA were immune from judicial restraints. Constitutional guarantees either did not exist or were ignored, thus making possible secret arrests, jailing, and torture. The security forces—sometimes called "secret police"—are

---

hierarchy   Organized in a ranking of power from top to bottom, as if on a ladder.

Before the breakup of the Soviet Union, long lines waited to file past Lenin's tomb in Red Square.
(Charles Gatewood)

Now, hardly anyone waits in line to see Lenin's tomb. Lenin's ideas and system became irrelevant with the collapse of communism.
(Michael Roskin)

often directed against whole classes of people, such as Jews, landlords, capitalists, socialists, or clergy. The threat of the "knock at the door" terrorizes most of the population into acquiescence. Mass arrest and execution shows the state's power and the individual's helplessness. Not counting deaths in war, the Soviet Union killed an estimated 62 million civilians, Communist China 35 million, and Nazi Germany 21 million. Such terror doesn't work over the long run, however, and the Soviet Union abandoned the more ruthless tactics of Stalin. The purges and mass executions were replaced by more subtle forms of control and intimidation, such as loss of job or exile to a remote city.

Monopoly of Communications The primary function of the mass media in totalitarian states is to indoctrinate the people with the official ideology and promote a feeling that the system is working well under wise leaders. Sinister outside forces, however, are trying to harm the system and must be stopped.

Monopoly of Weapons Governments of totalitarian nations have a complete monopoly on weapons, thus eliminating armed resistance.

CASE STUDIES

IMAGE AND REALITY OF TOTAL CONTROL

Just as there is no perfect democracy, neither is there perfect totalitarian dictatorship. Often outsiders are overly influenced by the image of total control projected by these states. Visitors to fascist Italy were impressed by the seeming law, order, cleanliness, and purposefulness of what they thought was one-man rule. We know now that many Italians disliked Mussolini, that his organizations and economic plans were mostly for show, and that he wasn't even in firm command of the country. In 1943, as the British and Americans overran the southern part of Italy, Mussolini's own generals—who had been disobeying and lying to him for years—overthrew him in a coup. Then the king of Italy—Italy was technically a kingdom until 1946—fired Mussolini as prime minister. What kind of total control is that?

Since Stalin's death, every Soviet party chief denounced the bureaucracy, the deadening hand of routine, and the economic irregularities that impeded Soviet growth. But neither Khrushchev, Brezhnev, nor Gorbachev touched the problem. Much of Soviet economic life ran by means of under-the-table deals and influence that defied centralized planning. Soviet workers stole everything from radios to locomotives and often showed up to work drunk or not at all. Where was the total control? The pages of *Pravda* and *Izvestia* thundered against these problems, but the government seemed unable to fix them.

We should bear in mind that the model of totalitarianism presented above never precisely matched reality. The model describes an *attempt* to impose total control, not the achievement of it.

Controlled Economy   Totalitarian regimes control the economy, Stalin directly by means of state ownership and Hitler indirectly by means of party "coordination" of private industry. Either way, it makes the state powerful, for resources can be allocated to heavy industry, weapons production, or whatever the party wishes. Workers can be moved wherever labor is needed, and incentives can stimulate production. The needs or wants of the consumer are unimportant. The Soviet Union was the first to send men to outer space, for example, but non-Communist countries always had vastly more and better consumer products. Economic backwardness proved to be the great weakness of the Soviet Union.

Starting in late 1989, as one country in Eastern Europe after another cast off its Communist system, we beheld how weak the system was. As to ideology, most citizens, even former party members, detested communism. The single ruling parties collapsed and handed power over to non-Communists. Organized terror lost its punch. The official mass media, widely ignored for years, was simply discarded in favor of a free press. The controlled economies were turned, with much pain, into market economies. We now realize that these Communist regimes had never exercised total control. In addition, we must be aware that there is more than one type of totalitarianism.

Right-Wing Totalitarianism   Right-wing totalitarianism, as exemplified in Italian Fascism and German National Socialism, developed in industrialized nations that were plagued by economic depression, social upheaval, and political confusion and weakness, and in which democratic roots and traditions were shallow and weak. Germany in the late 1920s and early 1930s was in turmoil. The nation was saddled with an enormous reparations debt following World War I; unemployment was widespread; labor disputes were frequent and violent; and a runaway inflation had wiped out the savings of the middle classes—the shopkeepers, the petty bureaucrats, and the skilled workers. In his rise to power, Hitler promised to discipline the labor unions, to restore order, to renounce the humiliating Versailles Treaty, and to protect private property from the Communist menace to the east. His program appealed to industrialists, militarists, and middle-class people, who typically constitute the backbone of a fascist state's support.

Right-wing totalitarianism does not want revolution, rather it aims to strengthen the existing social order and to glorify the state. It attempts to get rid of those deemed foreign or inferior, as Hitler strove to annihilate Jews and Gypsies. Citizens are also directed toward national glory and war. Private ownership is generally permitted, but obedient cartels and national trade associations carry out party wishes.

■ AUTHORITARIANISM

The terms *authoritarianism* and *totalitarianism* are often confused but have different meanings. **Authoritarian** regimes are governed by a small group—a party, a dictator, or the army—that minimizes popular input. They do not attempt to control everything. Many economic, social, religious, cultural, and familial matters are left up to individuals. Most of the six points of totalitarianism discussed earlier are diluted or absent. Authoritarian regimes, for example, rarely have a firm ideology to sell. Some called the Saddam regime in Iraq totalitarian, but it was more properly authoritarian.

Authoritarian regimes oppose individual freedoms in favor of command, obedience, and order. They view society as a hierarchical organization with a chain of command under the leadership of one ruler or group. Citizens are expected to obey laws and pay taxes that they have no voice in establishing. Some trappings of democracy may exist but have little function. The legislature is usually little more than a "rubber stamp" to approve the dictator's laws. Likewise, puppet prime ministers and cabinets carry out the dictator's wishes. Louis XIV of France showed an early form of authoritarianism with his famous phrase: *"L'état c'est moi"* (The state—that's me).

Spain under Franco (1939–1975) was "traditional authoritarian" rather than totalitarian, as the *caudillo* (leader) sought political passivity and obedience rather than enthusiastic participation and mobilization. Franco and his supporters had no single ideology to promote, and the economy and press were pluralistic within limits. Jeane J. Kirkpatrick, a political scientist and President Reagan's ambassador to the United Nations, argued that there is a difference between authoritarian

---

authoritarian   Nondemocratic government but not necessarily totalitarian.

and totalitarian regimes. The former (such as Argentina, Chile, and Brazil) can reform, but once a totalitarian system (such as communism) takes over, the system
cannot reform itself. Argentina, Chile, and Brazil did return to democracy in the
1980s. Kirkpatrick's thesis was borne out in the fact that the Communist regimes
of the Soviet bloc never did reform themselves; they collapsed while trying reform. In contrast, China illustrated the nature of totalitarian regimes by bloodily
crushing its democracy movement in 1989. Chinese can get rich in private business but are arrested for demanding democracy.

AUTHORITARIANISM AND THE DEVELOPING NATIONS

One of the great political movements since World War II has been the breakup of
colonial empires into independent nations. For the most part, the ideological struggle for national independence in these states followed the "self-determination" argument of the American Declaration of Independence and the French Declaration
of the Rights of Man and Citizen. Yet once national independence was won, democracy did not last long. A democratic political culture had always been discouraged.
Democracy in the Western tradition grew out of individualism and a competitive
market economy. The developing societies have preindustrial, traditional peasant
economies that stress families and tribes. Levels of education and income are often
low, and most people are absorbed in the struggle to survive. The leadership often
believes that political and economic survival and growth need centralized power
to make what is really needed rather than according to what people want. The
leaders think they know what is really needed.

In this way, much of the Third World fell into authoritarianism with single-party
dominance. Zimbabwe started with a two-party system in 1980 but found that
some parties opposed the dominant party and its leader, Robert Mugabe, who
cracked down harshly with soldiers of his dominant tribe and created a single-
party system, arguing that this was the only way to build unity and a socialist economy. Zimbabwe slid into authoritarian dictatorship. Such systems are usually
terrible. Government officials push wasteful, unrealistic projects, stifle individual
initiative by regulations and taxes, and crush critical viewpoints. Corruption becomes massive. In this way have such countries as Tanzania and Myanmar (Burma)
impoverished themselves, ending up with neither democracy nor economic growth.

■ THE DEMOCRATIZATION OF AUTHORITARIAN REGIMES

Since 1974, dozens of countries have abandoned authoritarian or totalitarian systems in favor of democratic systems. Now, about half of the world's nations are at
least approximately democratic. The expansion of democracy from the previous two
dozen countries—mostly in Western Europe and North America, where it had earlier taken root—became a major scholarly topic. An excellent new quarterly appeared in 1989, *Journal of Democracy*, devoted to explaining and encouraging the
spread of democracy.

KEY CONCEPTS

WHY DEMOCRACIES FAIL

Democracy can actually come too soon in the political life of a nation. As we discussed in "modernization theory" in Chapter 2, stable democracy tends to come in at least medium-income countries, because they have large, educated middle classes. People in poor countries care more about survival than democracy. In a 2004 UN survey of Latin America, a majority said they preferred a dictator who puts food on the table to an elected leader who does not. Middle classes bring with them moderation, tolerance, and the realization that not everything can be fixed at once. Without that, elections can undermine democracy, as seen recently in Haiti, Russia, and Zimbabwe.

The transition to democracy is delicate and happens best slowly and gradually, as it did in Britain with a series of Reform Acts during the nineteenth century. Typically, during the first decades of democracy only the better-off can participate, a pattern called **whig democracy**. (In the United States, this ended with Jackson's election in 1828.) When the broad masses of citizens suddenly get the vote, the system can break down. Newly enfranchised and unsophisticated voters often fall for the extravagant or extremist promises of **demagogues**, who offer simple solutions aimed at getting the votes of the gullible. They may vow to "share the wealth" or advocate aggressive nationalism or religious fundamentalism. Perón of Argentina, Milosevic of Serbia, and currently Chávez of Venezuela are examples. Military coup often ends their rule. If Saudi Arabia had free elections, many Saudis would vote for Osama bin Laden. Attempting democracy too soon can lead to rule by demagogues, generals, or fanatics.

There seem to be two types of regimes that contributed to the latest wave of democracy: authoritarian regimes that enjoyed strong economic growth and collapsed Communist regimes whose economic growth lagged. The fast-growth systems—such as Chile, South Korea, and Taiwan—were politically authoritarian but developed a market economy largely in private hands. It was as if the dictator said, "I'll take care of politics; you just work on your various businesses." The probusiness regimes set macroeconomic policy (sound currency, low inflation, sufficient capital for loans) and plugged into the world market. After a time, the growing economy transformed the whole society in the direction of democracy. As countries improve from poor to middle-income, they become ready for stable democracy. (See "modernization theory" in Chapter 2.) Democracy seldom lasts in poor countries—India is the massive exception—but it almost always works in middle-income and higher countries.

Why should this happen? First, economic growth creates a large middle class, one of the bases for democracy. Middle classes are inherently democratic. They have a stake in the system; they may wish to modify it but not overthrow it. Second, and related to the size of the middle class, education levels have risen. Most people are high-school graduates, and many are college graduates. They are no longer ignorant and do not fall for demagogues or extremist ideas. Third, and related to both the

---

whig democracy   Democracy for the few; typical of early stages of democracy.
demagogue   Politician who whips up masses with extreme and misleading issues.

previous points, people increasingly recognize their interests and express them: pluralism. They express business, professional, regional, and religious demands. They can spot cruel, corrupt, or inefficient governments and do not like being treated like children. Finally, the market itself teaches citizens about self-reliance, pluralism, tolerance, and not expecting too much, all attitudes that sustain democracy. Gradually, the regime eases up, permitting a critical press, the formation of political parties, and finally free elections. Taiwan is an excellent example of this transition.

How about the other trend that has led to newly democratic systems, the collapse of Communist regimes? Here, too, the economy has a great deal to do with the process, but in a negative sense. It was poor economic performance and slow growth, especially in comparison with the West and with the rapid-growth countries, that persuaded relatively liberal Communists, such as Mikhail Gorbachev, to attempt to reform the system. They knew they were falling behind, especially in crucial high-tech areas, and thought they could energize the system by bringing elements of the free market into an otherwise socialist economy. But communism, like other brands of totalitarianism, doesn't tolerate reform. By attempting to control everything, as in the six points outlined earlier by Friedrich and Brzezinski, they have created a brittle system that can break but not bend. Once they started admitting that the system needed to be fixed, they admitted that they were wrong. The ideology was wrong; single-party control was wrong; the centralized economy was wrong; and so on. The attempt at reform turns into system collapse.

Will the countries that emerged from the wreckage of dictatorship be able to establish lasting democracies? Will Iraq? So far, the ex-Communist lands of Central Europe (Poland, Czech Republic, Hungary, and others) have done so. As you go farther east and south, however, democracy is still incomplete. Market systems are strange and rather frightening to Russians, Ukrainians, Uzbeks and others, and indeed the transition from a controlled to a market economy inflicts terrible hardships. Some voters, never having known democracy, turn to authoritarian figures, who promise to restore stability and paychecks. President Vladimir Putin cowed or jailed opposition, and most Russians supported him. Russian political culture favors rule by one strong leader. The president is extremely powerful and can rule by decree; the State Duma (parliament) is weak and obeys the president; privatization favored a few who have made themselves tremendously rich while others starved; and much of the mass media is again controlled by the state. Some called this a **kleptocracy**, and it is found in much of the world.

Democracy is not easy. It is a complex, finely balanced system that depends on a political culture that grows best under a market economy with a large, educated middle class and a tradition of pluralism. Centuries of religious and philosophical evolution prepare democratic attitudes. Iraq lacked all these. Eventually Iraq or any other country can turn democratic, but it may take some time. Most scholars look forward to it, as there is strong support for the theory of the **democratic peace**, that no two democracies have ever fought each other. If this is true, a more democratic world means a more peaceful world.

---

kleptocracy   Rule by thieves, used in derision and jest.
democratic peace   Theory that democracies do not fight each other.

CASE STUDIES

DEMOCRACY IN IRAQ?

Iraq was a new and artificial country the British put together in 1922 from three former Ottoman provinces. Its population groups do not like each other. Sixty percent of Iraqis are Shia Muslims, a repressed and suspect minority throughout the Arab world. Saddam Hussein had ruled through his Sunni Arabs (20 percent of the population) and murdered hundreds of thousands of Shia. Freed in 2003, Shia immediately demanded elections, which they won in early 2005. Many fear the Shia will now fight the Sunnis; civil war could break out. In the north of Iraq, Kurds (about 20 percent) who are Sunnis but not Arabs, want to rule themselves in a strongly federal system. Only the Kurds have any experience with democracy.

Whoever rules Iraq must be willing and able to crush the armed ethnic and religious groups that wish to take over or break away. If rulers really implement human rights and democracy, they are soon overthrown. Note that most of Iraq's neighbors are dictatorships, some more brutal than others. Saddam was not an accident but a product of a rebellious country that is ready to fall apart. Nice guys do not rule countries like Iraq.

Ironically, the successful Iraqi elections of 2005 could lead to repressive rule, this time by Shias. Many Sunnis, angered over the U.S. crushing of their terrorist headquarters in Falluja, refused to participate in the elections. The real purpose of elections is to calm things down by producing a legitimate regime that most citizens feel represents them. Did elections calm things in Iraq? Elections do not work everywhere; they require stable countries with much economic, educational, and political development. Democracy imposed on an unready country tends to turn into dictatorship.

KEY TERMS

authoritarian (p. 86)
civil disobedience (p. 77)
demagogue (p. 88)
democratic peace (p. 89)
democracy (p. 73)
elites (p. 78)
hierarchy (p. 83)
interest groups (p. 80)
kleptocracy (p. 89)

mandate (p. 75)
mass media (p. 78)
pluralism (p. 78)
referendums (p. 73)
representative democracy (p. 74)
totalitarian (p. 82)
trustee (p. 75)
whig democracy (p. 88)

KEY WEB SITES

Parties and their orientation to democracy
www.agora.stem.it/elections/parties.htm

Journal of Democracy
www.press.jhu.edu/journals.jod/

Iraq

www.megastories.com/iraq/

Hitler

www.historyplace.com/worldwar2/riseofhitler/index.htm

Freedom House ranking of democracies
www.freedomhouse.org/

Civil disobedience
www.kids-right.org/philosop.htm

FURTHER REFERENCE

Carothers, Thomas. *Critical Mission: Essays on Democracy Promotion*. Washington, D.C.: Carnegie Endowment, 2004.

Colomer, Josep M. *Political Institutions: Democracy and Social Choice*. New York: Oxford University Press, 2001.

Crick, Bernard. *Democracy: A Very Short Introduction*. New York: Oxford University Press, 2003.

Crotty, William J., ed. *The State of Democracy in America*. Washington, D.C.: Georgetown University Press, 2001.

Dahl, Robert A., Ian Shapiro, and José Antonio Cheibub, eds. *The Democracy Sourcebook*. Cambridge, Ma: MIT Press, 2003.

Gerard, Alexander. *The Sources of Democratic Consolidation*. Ithaca, NY: Cornell University Press, 2002.

Gill, Graeme. *The Dynamics of Democratization: Elites, Civil Society and the Transition Process*. New York: Palgrave, 2000.

Grugel, Jean. *Democratization: A Critical Introduction*. New York: Palgrave, 2002.

Linz, Juan. *Totalitarian and Authoritarian Regimes*. Boulder, CO: Lynne Rienner, 2000.

Lipset, Seymour Martin, and Jason M. Lakin. *The Democratic Century*. Norman, OK: University of Oklahoma Press, 2004.

Olson, Mancur. *Power and Prosperity: Outgrowing Communist and Capitalist Dictatorships*. New York: Basic Books, 2000.

Overy, Richard. *The Dictators: Hitler's Germany, Stalin's Russia*. New York: Norton, 2004.

Rabb, Theodore K., and Ezra N. Suleiman, eds. *The Making and Unmaking of Democracy: Lessons from History and World Politics*. New York: Routledge, 2002.

Sharansky, Natan. *The Case for Democracy: The Power of Freedom to Overcome Tyranny and Terror*. Boulder, CO: Public Affairs, 2004.

Shlapentokh, Vladimir. *A Normal Totalitarian Society: How the Soviet Union Functioned and How It Collapsed*. Armonk, NY: M.E. Sharpe, 2001.

POLITICAL IDEOLOGIES

CHAPTER

6

QUESTIONS TO CONSIDER

- Is it possible to be totally pragmatic, with no ideology?
- How did classic liberalism turn into U.S. conservatism?
- How close are modern liberalism and social democracy?
- What changes did Lenin make to Marxism?
- Why is nationalism the strongest ideology?
- What are the main elements of fascism?
- Do any ideologies attract today's students?
- Could ideological politics die out?

The appointments and policies of the (younger) Bush administration remind us that political **ideology** is still alive in the United States. Some Republicans prescribed what they called conservatism to solve problems from the economy to energy supplies. Probably few of them knew it, but they were actually classic *liberals,* harkening back to Adam Smith's two-century-old admonition to get government out of the economy. Others in the Bush administration were a new breed, "neo-conservatives," who advocated expanding federal powers: "big-government conservatism." They were especially influential in foreign policy, advocating muscular and unilateral U.S. intervention to make the country safe and spread democracy. Iraq was a neocon policy. Older Republican conservatives disliked the neocons. **Pragmatic** America is still quite ideological.

---

ideology   Belief system that society can be improved by following certain doctrines; usually ends in *ism.*

pragmatic   Attitude of using whatever works without theory or ideology.

■ WHAT IS IDEOLOGY?

An ideology begins with the belief that things can be better than they are; it is basically a plan to improve society. As Anthony Downs put it, ideology is "a verbal image of the good society, and of the chief means of constructing such a society." Political ideologies are not political science; they are not calm, rational attempts to understand political systems. They are, rather, commitments to *change* political systems. (One exception here might be classic conservatism, which aims to keep things from changing too much.) **Ideologues** make poor political scientists, for they confuse the "should" or "ought" of ideology with the "is" of political science.

In politics, ideology cements together movements, parties, or revolutionary groups. To fight and endure sacrifices, people need ideological motivation, something to believe in. Americans have sometimes not grasped this point. With their emphasis on moderation and pragmatism they fail to understand the energizing effect of ideology in the world today. "Our" Vietnamese, the South Vietnamese, were physically no different from the Vietcong and North Vietnamese, and they were better armed. But in the crunch, the Vietnamese who had a doctrine to believe in—a mixture of Marx, Lenin, and Mao with heavy doses of nationalism and anticolonialism—won against the Vietnamese who didn't have much to believe in. We tend to forget that more than two centuries ago Americans were quite ideological, too, and—imbued with a passion for freedom and self-rule, via the pens of John Locke and Thomas Paine—beat a larger and better equipped army of Englishmen and Hessians who had no good reason to fight. Now we are bewildered at the fanatics of a new ideology, Islamism. It pays to learn.

Ideologies never work precisely the way their advocates claim. Some are hideous failures. All ideologies contain a certain amount of wishful thinking, which frequently collapses in the face of reality. Ideologues claim they can perfect the world; reality is highly imperfect. The classic liberalism of Adam Smith did contribute to the nineteenth century's economic growth, but it also led to great inequalities of wealth and recurring depressions; it was modified into modern liberalism. Communism led to brutal tyrannies, economic failures, and collapse. All ideologies, when measured against their actual performance, are to greater or lesser degrees defective. They should all be taken with a grain of salt.

■ THE MAJOR IDEOLOGIES

CLASSIC LIBERALISM

According to the late Frederick Watkins of Yale, 1776 could be called "the Year One of the Age of Ideology," and not just for the American Revolution. In that same year, Scottish economist Adam Smith published *The Wealth of Nations*, thereby

---

ideologue   Someone who believes passionately in an ideology.

CLASSIC WORKS

THE ORIGINS OF IDEOLOGIES

Many ideologies stem from the political theories discussed in Chapter 2. Classical liberalism traces back to the seventeenth-century English philosopher John Locke, who emphasized individual rights, property, and reason. Communism traces back to the late eighteenth-century German philosopher G. W. F. Hegel, who emphasized that all facets of a society—art, music, architecture, statecraft, law, and so on—hang together as a package, the expression of an underlying cause.

The philosophers' ideas, however, become simplified and popularized. Ideologists want plans for action, not abstract ideas. Marx, for example, "stood Hegel on his head" to make economics the great underlying cause for everything else. Most ideologies have a large economic component, for it is economics that will improve society. Lenin later stood Marx on *his* head to make his ideas apply to a backward country where Marx doubted they should. Mao Zedong then applied Lenin's ideas to an even more backward country, where they did not fit at all.

One ideology gives rise to others (see figure below). Starting with the classic liberalism of Adam Smith, we see how it branched leftward into radical, socialist, and communist directions. Meanwhile, on the conservative side, it branched rightward.

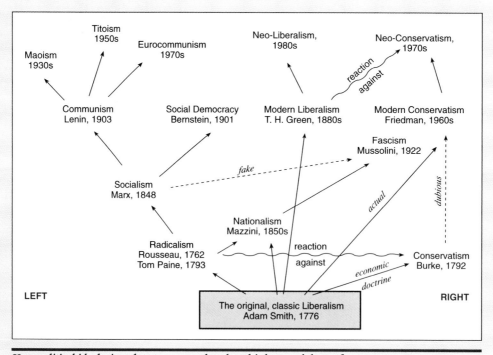

How political ideologies relate to one another: key thinkers and dates of emergence.

CLASSIFYING IDEOLOGIES

Ideologies can be classified—with some oversimplification—on a left-to-right spectrum that dates back to the meeting of the French National Assembly in 1789. To allow delegates of similar views to caucus and to keep apart strong partisans who might fight, members were seated as follows in a semicircular chamber: Conservatives (who favored continuation of the monarchy) were on the speaker's right; radicals (who favored sweeping away the old system altogether in favor of a republic of freedom and equality) were seated to his left; and moderates (who wanted some change) were seated in the center.

We have been calling their ideological descendants left, right, and center ever since, even though the content of their views has changed. The left now favors equality, welfare programs, and sometimes government intervention in the economy. The right stresses individual initiative and private economic activity. Centrists try to synthesize and moderate the views of both. People a little to one side or the other are called center-left or center-right. Sweden's political parties form a rather neat left-to-right spectrum: a small Communist party; a large Social Democratic party; and medium-sized Center (formerly Farmers'), Liberal, Christian, and Conservative parties.

founding classic laissez-faire economics. The true wealth of nations, Smith argued, is not in the amount of gold and silver they amass but in the amount of goods and services their people produce. Smith was refuting an earlier notion, called *mercantilism,* that the bullion in a nation's treasury determined whether it was a rich country. Spain had pursued this in looting the New World but actually grew poorer. The French, too, since at least Louis XIV in the previous century, had followed mercantilist policies by means of government supervision of the economy with plans, grants of monopoly, subsidies, tariffs, and other restraints on trade.

Smith reasoned that this was not the path to prosperity. Government interference retards growth. If you give one firm a monopoly to manufacture something, you banish competition and with it efforts to produce new products and lower prices. The economy stagnates. If you protect domestic industry by tariffs, you take away incentives for better or cheaper products. By getting the government out of the economy, by letting the economy alone (*laissez-faire,* in French), you will promote prosperity.

But won't free competition unsupervised by government lead to chaos? No, said Smith; the market itself will regulate the economy. Efficient producers will prosper and inefficient ones go under. Supply and demand determine prices better than any government official. In the free marketplace, an "unseen hand" regulates and self-corrects the economy. If people want more of something, producers increase output, new producers enter the field, foreign producers bring in their wares, or there is a combination of all three. The unseen hand—actually, the rational calculations of myriad individuals and firms all pursuing their self-interest—micro-adjusts the economy with no government help.

This ideology took the name **liberalism** from the Latin word for "free," *liber*: Society should be as free as possible from government interference. As aptly summarized by Thomas Jefferson, "That government is best that governs least." Americans took to classic liberalism like a duck takes to water. It fit the needs of a vigorous, freedom-loving population with plenty of room to expand. Noneconomic liberty also suited Americans. Government should also not supervise religion, the press, or free speech.

But, you say, what you're calling liberalism here is actually what Americans today call conservatism. True. In the late nineteenth century, liberalism changed and split into modern liberalism and what we now call conservatism, which we will discuss next. To keep our terminology straight, we call the original ideas of Adam Smith "classic liberalism" to distinguish it from the modern variety.

CLASSIC CONSERVATISM

By the same token, we should call the ideas of Edmund Burke, published in the late eighteenth century, "classic conservatism," for his conservatism diverges in many ways from modern conservatism. Burke knew Adam Smith and agreed that a free market was the best economic system. Burke also opposed crushing the rebellious American colonists; after all, they were only trying to regain the ancient freedoms of Englishmen, said Burke. So far, Burke sounds like a liberal.

But Burke strongly objected to the way liberal ideas were applied in France by revolutionists. There, liberalism turned into radicalism, influenced by philosopher Jean-Jacques Rousseau and, fresh from the U.S. revolution, Thomas Paine. As is often the case, an ideology devised in one place becomes warped when applied to different circumstances. Liberalism in America was easy; once the English and their Tory sympathizers cleared out, it fell into place without resistance. But in France, a large aristocratic class and a state-supported Roman Catholic church had a lot to lose. The revolutionaries tried to solve the problem with the guillotine and swept away all established institutions.

This, warned Burke, was a terrible mistake. Liberals place too much confidence in human reason. People are only partly rational; they also have irrational passions. To contain them, society over the years has evolved traditions, institutions, and standards of morality, such as the monarchy and an established church. Sweep these aside, said Burke, and man's irrational impulses lead to chaos, which in turn ends in tyranny far worse than the old system. Burke, in his 1792 *Reflexions on the Revolution in France,* predicted that France would fall into military dictatorship. In 1799, Napoleon took over.

Institutions and traditions that currently exist cannot be all bad, Burke reasoned, for they are the products of hundreds of years of trial and error. People have become used to them. The best should be preserved or "conserved" (hence

---

liberalism   Ideology founded by Adam Smith to keep government out of economy; became U.S. conservatism.

the name **conservatism**). They are not perfect, but they work. This is not to say that things should never change. Of course they should change, said Burke, but only gradually, giving people time to adjust. "A state without the means of some change is without the means of its conservation," he wrote.

Burke was an important thinker for several reasons. He helped discover the *irrational* in human behavior. He saw that institutions are like living things; they grow and adapt over time. And most important, he saw that revolutions end badly, for society cannot be instantly remade according to human reason. Although Burke's ideas have been called an *anti-ideology*—for they aimed to shoot down the radicalism then engulfing France—they have considerable staying power. Burke's emphasis on religion, traditions, and morality has been taken over by modern conservatives. His doubts about applying reason to solve social problems were echoed by political scientist Jeane Kirkpatrick, President Reagan's UN ambassador, who found that leftists always suppose that things can be much better when in fact violent upheaval always makes things worse. In these ways, classic conservatism is very much alive.

MODERN LIBERALISM

What happened to the original, classic liberalism of Adam Smith? By the late nineteenth century, it was clear that the free market was not as self-regulating as Smith had thought. Competition was imperfect. Manufacturers rigged the market—a point Smith himself had warned about. There was a drift to bigness and fewness: monopoly. The system produced a large underclass of the terribly poor (which Dickens depicted). Class positions were largely inherited; children of better-off families got a good education and the right connections to stay on top. Recurring economic depressions especially hurt the poor and the working class. The laissez-faire society created some problems.

The Englishman Thomas Hill Green rethought liberalism in the 1880s. The goal of liberalism, reasoned Green, was a free society. But what happens when economic developments take away freedom? The classic liberals placed great store in contracts (agreements between consenting parties with no government supervision): If you don't like the deal, don't take it. But what if the bargaining power of the two parties is greatly unequal, as between a rich employer and a poor person desperate for a job? Does the latter really have a free choice in accepting or rejecting a job with very low wages? Classic liberalism said let it be; wages will find their own level. But what if the wage is below starvation level? Here, Green said, it was time for government to step in. In such a case it would not be a question of government infringing on freedoms but of government protecting them. Instead of the purely negative "freedom from," there had to be a certain amount of the positive "freedom to." Green called this *positive freedom*. Government was to step in to guarantee the freedom to live at an adequate level.

---

conservatism Ideology of keeping system largely unchanged.

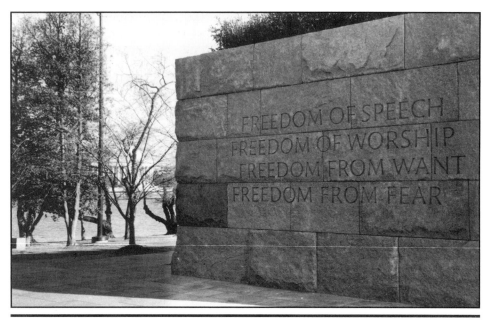

Here are FDR's "Four Freedoms" at his D.C. memorial; in the background is the Jefferson memorial. Jefferson would have understood the first two of Roosevelt's freedoms—of speech and worship—because they are classic liberalism. He might not have grasped the second two freedoms—from want and fear—because they are modern liberalism. (Michael Roskin)

Classic liberalism had expelled government from the marketplace; **modern liberalism** brought it back in, this time to protect people from a sometimes unfair economic system. Modern liberals championed wage and hour laws, the right to form unions, unemployment and health insurance, and improved educational opportunities. To do this, they placed heavier taxes on the rich than on the working class. This is the liberalism of the twentieth-century United States, the liberalism of Woodrow Wilson, Franklin D. Roosevelt, and Ted Kennedy. One strand of the old liberalism remains in the new, however: the emphasis on freedom of speech and press.

MODERN CONSERVATISM

What happened to the other branch of liberalism, the people who stayed true to Adam Smith's original doctrine of minimal government? They are still very important, only we call them conservatives. (In Europe, they still call them liberals or neoliberals, much to the confusion of Americans.) American conservatives got

---

modern liberalism   Ideology favoring government intervention to correct economic and social ills; U.S. liberalism today.

a big boost from Milton Friedman, the Nobel Prize-winning economist. Friedman argued that the free market is still the best, that Adam Smith was right, that wherever government intervenes it messes things up. Margaret Thatcher in Britain and Ronald Reagan in the United States applied this revival of classic liberalism in the 1980s with mixed but generally positive results.

Modern conservatism also borrows from Edmund Burke a concern for tradition, especially in religion. American conservatives would get prayer into public schools, outlaw abortion, and support private and church-related schools. Modern conservatives are also traditional in opposing special rights for women and homosexuals. Modern conservatism is thus a blend of the economic ideas of Adam Smith and the traditionalist ideas of Edmund Burke.

MARXIST SOCIALISM

Although liberalism (classic variety) dominated the nineteenth century, a strand of critical opinion arose in reaction to the obvious excesses of the capitalist system. Unlike T. H. Green, some critics did not believe that just a few reforms would suffice; they wanted to overthrow the capitalist system. They were the socialists, and their leading thinker was Karl Marx, whose complex theory we discussed in Chapter 2. Marx wrote not as a scholar but to promote revolution. He hated the "bourgeoisie" long before he developed his elaborate theories that they were doomed. The initial outline of his ideas appeared in his 1848 pamphlet,

Karl Marx glares down at the citizens of Tashkent, Uzbekistan, now an independent ex-Soviet republic. The communists built such statues—more of Lenin than of Marx—all over the Soviet Union. (Michael Roskin)

CASE STUDIES

WHY DID CAPITALISM NOT COLLAPSE?

One of the enduring problems and weaknesses of Marx is that capitalism, contrary to his pre-diction, has not collapsed. Marx thought the Paris Commune of 1870–1871 was the first pro-letarian uprising. (It was not.) True, capitalism has gone through some major depressions, in the 1890s and 1930s, but it has always bounced back. Now it is stronger than ever.

Marx erred in at least a couple of ways. First, he failed to understand the flexible, adaptive na-ture of capitalism. Old industries fade, and new ones rise. Imagine trying to explain Bill Gates and the computer software industry to someone in the 1960s. They wouldn't believe you. Capitalism rarely gets stuck at one stage; it is the system of constant change. Second, Marx failed to under-stand that capitalism is not just one system; it is many. U.S., French, Singaporean, and Japanese capitalisms are distinct from each other. Marx's simplified notions of capitalism illustrate what happens when theory is placed in the service of ideology: Unquestioning followers believe it too literally.

The Communist Manifesto, which concluded with the ringing words: "The prole-tarians have nothing to lose but their chains. They have a world to win. Work-ers of all countries, unite!" Marx participated in organizing Europe's first socialist parties.

Marx's *Capital* was a gigantic analysis of why capitalism would be over-thrown by the proletariat. Then would come socialism, a just, productive soci-ety without class distinctions. Later, at a certain stage when industrial production was very high, this socialist society will turn into communism, a perfect society without police, money, or even government. Goods will be in such plenty that people will just take what they need. There will be no private property, so there will be no need for police. Since government is simply an instrument of class domination, with the abolition of distinct classes there will be no need for gov-ernment; it will "wither away." Communism, then, was the predicted utopia beyond socialism.

Marx focused on the ills and malfunctions of capitalism and never specified what socialism would be like. He only said that socialism would be much better than capitalism; its precise workings he left vague. This has enabled a wide va-riety of socialist thinkers to put forward their own vision of socialism and say it is what Marx really meant. This has ranged from the mild "welfarism" of social-democratic parties, to anarcho-syndicalism (unions running everything), to Lenin's and Stalin's hypercentralized tyranny, to Trotsky's denunciation of same, to Mao's self-destructive permanent revolution, to Tito's experimental decentralized system. All, and a few more, claim to espouse "real" socialism. These different interpre-tations of socialism caused first the socialist and then the communist movement to splinter.

SOCIAL DEMOCRACY

By the beginning of the twentieth century the German Social Democrats (SPD), espousing Marxism, had become Germany's biggest party. Marx had disparaged conventional parties and labor unions; bourgeois governments would simply crush them, he believed. At most, they could be training grounds for serious revolutionary action. But the German Social Democrats started having success. Their members got elected to the Reichstag and local offices; their unions won higher wages and better working conditions. Some began to think that the working class could accomplish its aims without revolution. Why use bullets when there are ballots?

Eduard Bernstein developed this viewpoint. In his *Evolutionary Socialism* (1901), he pointed out the very real gains the working class was making and concluded that Marx had been wrong about the collapse of capitalism and revolution. Reforms that won concrete benefits for the working class could also lead to socialism, he argued. In revising Marxism, Bernstein earned the name **revisionist**, originally a pejorative hurled at him by orthodox Marxists. By the time of the ill-fated Weimar Republic in Germany (1919–1933), the Social Democrats had greatly toned down their militancy and worked together with Liberals and Catholics to try to save democracy. Persecuted by the Nazis, the SPD revived after World War II, and in 1959 they dropped Marxism altogether, as did virtually all **social democratic** parties. As social democrats in many countries moderated their positions, they got elected more and more. They transformed themselves into center-left parties with no trace of revolution.

What, then, do social democrats stand for? They have abandoned the state ownership of industry. Only about 10 percent of Sweden's industry is state-owned, and much of that conservatives did long ago to keep firms from going under and creating unemployment. Said the late Olof Palme, Sweden's Social Democratic prime minister, "If industry's primary purpose is to expand its production, to succeed in new markets, to provide good jobs for their employees, they need have no fears. Swedish industry has never expanded so rapidly as during these years of Social Democratic rule." Instead of state ownership of industry, social democrats have used *welfare* measures to improve living conditions: unemployment and medical insurance, generous pensions, and subsidized food and housing. Social democracies have become welfare states: *Welfarism* would be a more accurate term than *socialism*.

There's one catch—there's always at least one catch—and that is that welfare states are terribly expensive. To pay for welfare measures, taxes climb. In Denmark and Sweden, taxes consume a majority of the gross domestic product, exactly the kind of thing conservative economist Milton Friedman warned about. With those kinds of taxes, soon you are not free to choose how you live. U.S. liberalism is tinged with social-democratic ideas on welfare. The left wing of our Democratic party resembles ideologically the moderate wings of European social democratic parties.

---

revisionist   Changing an ideology or view of history.

social democracy   Mildest form of socialism, stressing welfare measures but not state ownership of industry.

COMMUNISM

While the social democrats evolved into reformists and welfarists, a smaller wing of the original socialists stayed Marxist and became the Communists. The key figure in this transformation was a Russian intellectual, Vladimir I. Lenin. He made several changes in Marxism, producing Marxism-Leninism, another name for **communism**.

Imperialism   Many Russian intellectuals of the late nineteenth century hated the tsarist system and embraced Marxism as a way to overthrow tsarism. Ironically, Marx meant his theory to apply in the most *advanced* capitalist countries, not in backward Russia, where capitalism was just beginning. Lenin, mostly in exile in Switzerland, remade Marxism to fit backward Russia. He offered a theory of economic **imperialism**, one borrowed from German revolutionary Rosa Luxemburg and English economist J. A. Hobson, who wondered why the proletarian revolutions Marx had foreseen had not broken out in the advanced industrialized lands. They concluded that capitalism had transformed itself, expanding overseas into colonies to exploit their raw materials, cheap labor, and new markets. Capitalism had won a temporary new lease on life by turning into imperialism. The domestic market could not absorb what the capitalist system was producing, so it found overseas markets. With enormous profits from its colonies, the mother imperialist country could also pay off its working class a bit to render it reformist rather than revolutionary.

While imperialism was expanding, Lenin noted, it was growing unevenly. Some countries, such as Britain and Germany, were highly developed, but where capitalism was just starting, as in Spain and Russia, it was weak. The newly industrializing countries were exploited as a whole by the international capitalist system. It was in them that revolutionary fever burned brightest; they were imperialism's "weakest link." Accordingly, a revolution could break out in a poor country, reasoned Lenin, and then spread into advanced countries. The imperialist countries were highly dependent on their empires; once cut off from exploiting them, the imperialists would fall. World War I, wrote Lenin, was the collision of imperialist powers trying to dominate the globe.

Lenin shifted the Marxian focus from the situation *within* capitalist countries to the situation *among* countries. The focus went from Marx's proletariat rising up against the bourgeoisie to exploited nations rising up against imperialist powers. Marx would probably not have approved of such a shift.

Organization   Lenin's real contribution lay in his attention to *organization*. With the tsarist secret police always on their trail, Lenin argued, the Russian socialist party could not be like other parties—large, open, and trying to win votes. Instead, it had to be small, secretive, made up of professional revolutionaries, and

---

communism   Marxist theory merged with Leninist organization into a totalitarian party.
imperialism   Amassing of colonial empires, mostly by European powers; pejorative in Marxist terms.

HOW TO . . .

TIGHT WRITING

Hemingway urged writers "to strip language clean, to lay it bare down to the bone." If you make your written work half as long, typically you make it twice as clear. Throw out unnecessary words. Ripest targets: adverbs, adjectives, and specialized jargon. Combine sentences that have the same subject. Ask yourself, "By making it shorter, have I really left anything out?" Use active voice rather than passive. Whenever possible, use verbs instead of nouns. Stanley Walker, city editor of the old *New York Herald Tribune*, told budding journalists to learn "to avoid adjectives and to swear by the little verbs that bounce and leap and swim and cut."

Loose

Persistent governmental indifference and bureaucratic obstructionism over a long period of time tend to foster a political culture of apathy and nonparticipation.

Tight

Distant government and do-nothing bureaucrats turn people away from politics.

Uses Nouns

German elections show a marked tendency to the casting of ballots along confessional lines, with Catholic *Länder* favoring the Christian Democratic party and Protestant *Länder* favoring the Social Democratic party.

take a leadership role

achieve success

Uses Verbs

German Catholics tend to vote Christian Democrat, Protestants Social Democrat.

lead

succeed

Same Subject, Two Sentences

The Federal Election Commission figures showed Gore with a small (half a percent) lead in the popular vote nationwide. But the same commission showed that Bush had won in the electoral college by four votes.

Combined Sentence

The Federal Election Commission gave Gore a small lead in the popular vote but found Bush had won in the electoral college.

Passive Voice

The popular vote was won by Gore.

Active Voice

Bush won the electoral vote.

tightly organized under central command. In 1903 the Russian Social Democratic Labor party split over this issue. Lenin had enough supporters at their party's Brussels meeting to win the votes of thirty-three of the fifty-one delegates present. Lenin called his faction *bolshevik* (Russian for "majority"). The losers, who advocated a more moderate line and a more open party, took the name *menshevik* ("minority"). In 1918 the Bolsheviks changed the party name to Communist.

Lenin's attention to organization paid off. Russia was in chaos from World War I. In March 1917, a group of moderates seized power from the tsar, but they were unable to govern the country. In November, the Bolsheviks shrewdly manipulated councils (*soviets* in Russian) that had sprung up in the leading cities and seized control from the moderates. After winning a desperate civil war, Lenin called on all true socialists around the world to join in a new international movement under Moscow's control. It was called the Communist International, or Comintern. Almost all socialist parties in the world split; their left wings went into the Comintern and became Communist parties in 1920–1921. The resultant social democratic and Communist parties have been hostile to each other ever since.

How much Marxism-Leninism did the rulers of the Soviet Union really believe? They constantly used Marxist rhetoric, but many observers argued they were cynical about ideology and just used it as window dressing. The Soviets never defined their society as Communist—that was yet to come; it was what they were working on. It is we in the West who called these countries "Communist." In 1961, party chief Nikita Khrushchev rashly predicted "communism in our generation," indicating that utopia would be reached by 1980. Instead, it declined, and in late 1991 the Soviet system collapsed.

Maoism and Titoism   In the 1930s, Mao Zedong concluded that the Chinese Communist Party (CCP) had to be based on poor peasants and guerrilla warfare. This was a break with Stalin's leadership, and after decades of fighting, the CCP took over mainland China in 1949. Mao pursued a radical course that included a failed attempt at overnight industrialization (the Great Leap Forward of 1958), the destruction of bureaucratic authority (the Proletarian Cultural Revolution in 1966–1976), and even border fighting with the Soviet Union in 1969. After Mao's death in 1976, calmer leaders moved China away from his extremism, which had severely damaged China's economic progress. A few revolutionary groups stayed Maoist: Pol Pot's murderous Khmer Rouge and Peru's Shining Path. **Maoism** is a form of ultraradical communism.

Yugoslav party chief Josip Tito went the other way, developing a more moderate and liberal form of communism. Even though Tito's partisans fought the Germans in Stalin's name, Stalin did not fully control Tito, and in 1948 had Yugoslavia kicked out of the Communist camp. During the 1950s, the Yugoslav Communists radically reformed their system, basing it on decentralization, debureaucratization, and worker self-management. Trying to find a middle ground between a market and a controlled economy, Yugoslavia suffered severe economic problems in the 1980s. **Titoism** might have served as a warning to Communist rulers who wanted to experiment with "middle ways" between capitalism and socialism. The combination is unstable and worked only because Tito ran it; when he died in 1980, Yugoslavia started coming apart until by the early 1990s it was a bloodbath.

---

maoism   Extreme form of communism, featuring guerrilla warfare and periodic upheavals.
titoism   Mild, decentralized form of Communism.

NATIONALISM

The real winner among ideologies—that still dominates today—is nationalism, the exaggerated belief in the greatness and unity of one's country. Nationalism is often born out of occupation and repression by foreigners. "We won't be pushed around by foreigners any more!" shout Cuban, Palestinian, Iraqi, Vietnamese, and many other nationalists. Nationalism has triumphed over and influenced all other ideologies, so that in the United States conservatism is combined with American nationalism, and in China communism is intertwined with Chinese nationalism.

The first seeds of nationalism came with the Renaissance monarchs who proclaimed their absolute power and the unity and greatness of their kingdoms. *Nationality* was born out of sovereignty. *Nationalism,* however, appeared only with the French Revolution, which was based on the "people" and heightened French feelings about themselves as a special, leading people destined to free the rest of Europe. When conservatives tried to invade France in 1792, the "nation in arms" stopped them; enthusiastic volunteers beat professional soldiers. The stirring "Marseillaise," France's national anthem, appeared that same year. Napoleon's legions were ostensibly spreading the radical liberalism of the French Revolution, but were really spreading nationalism. The conquered nations of Europe quickly grew to hate the arrogant French occupiers. Spaniards, Germans, and Russians soon became nationalistic themselves as they struggled to expel the French. Basic to nationalism is resentment of foreign domination, be it by British redcoats, Napoleon's legions, or European colonialists. Nationalism awoke in Europe in the nineteenth century and by the twentieth century had spread to Europe's colonies throughout the world. It is in the Third World that nationalism is now most intense.

By the mid-nineteenth century, thinkers all over Europe—especially in Germany and Italy—defined the nation as the ultimate human value, the source of all things good. Italian writer Giuseppe Mazzini espoused freedom not for individuals—that was mere liberalism—but for nations instead. One achieved true freedom by subordinating oneself to the nation. Education, for example, had to inculcate a sense of nationalism that blotted out individualism, argued Mazzini.

Nationalism generally arises when a population, invariably led by intellectuals, perceives an enemy or "other" to despise and struggle against. In the twentieth century, this has often been a colonial power such as Britain, France, or the Netherlands, against whom, respectively, Indians, Algerians, and Indonesians could rally in their fight for independence. Nationalism holds that it is terribly wrong to be ruled by others. Thus, Bosnian Serbs do not consent to be ruled by Bosnian Muslims, Palestinians by Israelis, and Chechens by Russians. Some Chinese and Iranians, feeling they have been repressed and controlled by outside powers, lash out with highly nationalistic military and diplomatic policies. Even some Canadians, fearful of U.S. economic and cultural dominance, turn nationalistic.

The big problem with nationalism is that it tends to economic isolation. "We won't let foreigners take over our economy!" say nationalists, but rapid economic growth needs foreign investment and world trade. More than any of the previous ideologies, nationalism depends on emotional appeals. The feeling of belonging to a nation seems to go to our psychological center. What other human organization would we fight and kill for?

Work makes you free, proclaims the sign over the gate at the notorious concentration camp of Auschwitz. The Nazis' aim was to make prisoners think they were headed for work rather than for the gas chambers. (Michael Roskin)

Regional Nationalism   In recent decades the world has seen the rise of another kind of nationalism: regional nationalism, which aims at breaking up existing nations into what its proponents argue are the true nations. Militant Québécois want to separate from Canada, Basques from Spain, Corsicans from France, and Tamils from Sri Lanka. It too is based on hatred of being ruled by unlike peoples.

FASCISM

In Italy and Germany nationalism grew into **fascism**, one of the great catastrophes of the twentieth century. One sign of a fascist movement is uniformed members. Before World War I, Italian journalist Benito Mussolini was a fire-breathing socialist; military service changed him into an ardent nationalist. Italy was full of discontented people after World War I. Maximalist socialists threatened revolution. In those chaotic times, Mussolini assembled a strange collection of people in black shirts who dreamed of getting rid of democracy and political parties and imposing stern central authority and discipline. These Fascists—a word taken from the ancient Roman symbol of authority, a bundle of sticks bound around an ax (the *fasces*)—hated disorder and wanted strong leadership to end it.

Amid growing disorder in 1922, the king of Italy handed power to Mussolini, and by 1924 he had turned Italy into a one-party state with himself as *Duce* (leader). The Fascists ran the economy by having their men in all key positions. Italy looked impressive: There was little crime, much monumental construction, stable prices, and as they used to say, "The trains ran on time." Behind the scenes, however, fascism was a mess, with hidden unemployment, poor economic performance, and corruption.

---

fascism   An extreme form of nationalism with elements of socialism and militarism.

With the collapse of the world economy in 1929, however, some thought fascism was the wave of the future. Adolf Hitler in Germany copied Mussolini's fascism but had his followers wear brown shirts and added racism. For Hitler, it was not just Germans as a nation who were rising up against the punitive and unfair Versailles Treaty and chaos of the Weimar Republic; it was Germans as a distinct and superior race. Hitler did not invent German racism, which went back generations, but he hyped it. The racist line held that a special branch of the white race, the Aryans, were the bearers of all civilization. A subbranch, the Nordics, which included Germans, were even better. (Actually, Germans are of very mixed genealogy.) Hitler argued that the superior Nordics were being subjugated to the sinister forces of Judaism, communism, world capitalism, and even Roman Catholicism. This doctrine was the basis for the death camps.

Hitler was named chancellor (prime minister) in 1933 in a situation of turmoil and, like Mussolini, within two years had perfected a dictatorship. Probably a majority of Germans supported Hitler. With Nazis "coordinating" the economy, unemployment ended and many working people felt they were getting a good deal with the jobs, vacations, and welfare the regime provided. The Nazis' full name was the National Socialist German Workers Party, but the socialism was fake. Hitler's true aim was war, as war builds heroes. For a few years Hitler dominated Europe and started turning the Slavic lands of Eastern Europe into colonies for Germans—*Lebensraum* (living space). Nazi death camps killed some 6 million Jews and a similar number of Christians who were in the way. Was Hitler mad? Many of his views were widely held among Germans, and he had millions of enthusiastic helpers. Rather than insanity, the Nazis demonstrate the danger of nationalism run amok.

The word *fascist* has been overused and misused. Some leftists hurl it at everything they dislike. Spanish dictator Francisco Franco, for example, was long considered a fascist, but he was actually a "traditional authoritarian," for he tried to minimize mass political involvement rather than stir it up the way Mussolini and Hitler did. Brazilian President Getúlio Vargas decreed a fascist-sounding "New State" in 1937, but he was merely borrowing some fascist rhetoric at a time when the movement was having its heyday in Europe. The Ku Klux Klan in the United States is sometimes called fascist, and its members wear uniforms. The Klan's populist racism is similar to the Nazis', but the Klan strongly opposes the power of the national government, whereas the Nazis and Fascists worshipped it. A kind of neo-fascism has appeared in the anti-immigrant parties in Britain, France, Germany, and Austria.

◼ IDEOLOGY IN OUR DAY

THE COLLAPSE OF COMMUNISM

By the 1980s, communism the world over was ideologically exhausted. Few people in China, Eastern Europe, and even the Soviet Union believed in it any longer. In the non-Communist world, leftists deserted Marxism in droves. Several West

European Communist parties embraced "Euro-communism," a greatly watered-down ideology that renounced dictatorship and state ownership of industry. Capitalism was supposed to have collapsed; instead, it was thriving in the United States, Western Europe, and East Asia. Many Communist leaders admitted that their economies were too rigid and centralized and that the cure lay in cutting back state controls and giving free enterprise a bigger role. Reform-minded Soviet President Mikhail Gorbachev (1985–1991) offered a three-pronged approach to revitalizing Soviet communism: *glasnost* (openness, or publicizing problems), *perestroika* (economic restructuring), and *demokratizatzia* (democratization). Applied haltingly and half-heartedly, the reforms only heightened discontent, for now Soviets could voice their complaints. Starting in Eastern Europe in 1989, non-Communist parties took over. In the Soviet Union, a partially free parliament was elected and began debating change. Non-Communist parties and movements appeared. Gorbachev still could not make up his mind how far and fast reforms should go, and the economy, barely re-formed, turned wildly inflationary. A 1991 coup failed, and by the end of the year the Soviet Union had ceased to exist.

NEOCONSERVATISM

In the 1970s, a new ideology emerged in the United States: **neoconservatism**, much of it from disillusioned liberals and leftists. As neoconservative writer Irving Kristol put it, "A neo-conservative is a liberal who's been mugged by reality." Neo-conservatives charged that the Democratic party had moved too far left with unrealistic ideas on domestic reforms and a pacifist foreign policy. Neoconservatives reacted against the Great Society programs introduced by Lyndon Johnson in the mid-1960s that aimed to wipe out poverty and discrimination. Some liberals said the Great Society was never given a chance because funds for it were siphoned away by the Vietnam war. But neocons said it worked badly, that many of the programs achieved nothing. The cities grew worse; educational standards declined; medical aid became extremely costly; and a class of welfare-dependent poor emerged, people who had little incentive to work. Neocons spoke of negative "unforeseen conse-quences" of well-intentioned liberal programs. One point especially bothered neo-cons: Affirmative action gave racial minorities preferential treatment in hiring, sometimes ahead of better-qualified whites. This really hit home when affirmative action quotas were applied to academic hiring; liberal, white, male professors some-times had to taste their own medicine in getting turned down for teaching jobs that went to blacks, Hispanics, and women.

Many neoconservatives were horrified at the extreme relativism that had grown in the 1960s. Simplistic ideas—such as "It's all right if it feels good" and "It just depends on your point of view" and "multiculturalism"—drove many liberals to neoconservatism. Ironically, some neocons were college professors

---

neoconservatism   U.S. ideology of former liberals turning to conservative causes and methods.

who had earlier tried to broaden their students' views by stressing the relativity of all viewpoints and cultures. Instead, students became vacuous rather than enlightened. In the Bush 43 administration, highly placed neocons promoted war with Iraq both to protect the United States and to pull the Muslim world into democracy so that it would no longer spawn terrorism. Many old-fashioned Republican conservatives, who dislike overseas crusades, parted company with the neocons.

LIBERTARIANISM

Slowly growing since the 1960s is an ideology so liberal that it became conservative—or vice versa. **Libertarians** would return to the original Adam Smith, with essentially no government interference in anything. They would deliver what Ronald Reagan only talked about. They note that modern liberals want a controlled economy but personal freedom while modern conservatives want a free economy but constraints on personal freedom. Why not freedom in both areas? Libertarians oppose subsidies, bureaucracies, taxes, intervention overseas, and big government itself. As such, they plugged into a very old American tradition and gained respectability. Although no Libertarian candidates won elections, their Cato Institute in Washington became a lively think tank whose ideas could not be ignored.

FEMINISM

Springing to new life in the 1960s with a handful of female writers, by the 1970s the women's movement had become a political force in the United States and Western Europe. **Feminist** writers pointed out that women were paid less than men, were not promoted, were psychologically and physically abused by men, were denied loans and insurance, and were in general second-class citizens.

The root problem was psychological, argued feminists. Women and men were forced into "gender roles" that had little to do with biology. Boys were conditioned to be tough, domineering, competitive, and "macho," but girls were taught to be meek, submissive, unsure of themselves, and "feminine." Gender differences are almost entirely learned behavior, taught by parents and schools of a "patriarchal" society, but this could be changed. With proper child rearing and education, males could become gentler and females more assertive and self-confident.

Feminists started "consciousness-raising" groups and railed against "male chauvinist pigs." Feminism started having an impact. Many employers gave women a fairer chance, sometimes hiring them over men. Women moved up to higher management positions (although seldom to the corporate top). Working wives became the norm. Husbands shared in homemaking and child rearing.

---

libertarianism   U.S. ideology in favor of shrinking all government power in favor of individual freedom.

feminism   Ideology of psychological, political, and economic equality for women.

Politically, however, feminists did not achieve all they wished. The Equal Rights Amendment (ERA) to the Constitution failed to win ratification by enough state legislatures. It would have guaranteed equality of treatment regardless of gender. Antifeminists, some of them conservative women, argued that the ERA would take away women's privileges and protections under the law, would make women eligible for the draft, and would even lead to unisex lavatories. Despite this setback, women learned that there was one way they could count for a lot politically—by voting. In the 1980 election a significant "gender gap" appeared, and now women generally vote more Democratic than do men.

ENVIRONMENTALISM

Also during the 1960s **environmentalism** began to ripple through the advanced industrialized countries. Economic development paid little heed to the damage it did to the environment. Any growth was good growth: "We'll never run out of nature." Mining, factories, and even farms poisoned streams; industries and automobiles polluted the air; chemical wastes made areas uninhabitable, and nuclear power leaked radioactivity. To the credo of "growth" ecologists responded with "limits." They argued, "We can't go on like this without producing environmental catastrophe." Love Canal, Three Mile Island, and Chernobyl seemed to prove them right. The burning of fossil fuels and rain forests may be creating a "greenhouse effect," trapping heat inside the earth's atmosphere and changing the planet's weather.

The ecologists' demands were only partly satisfied with the founding of the Environmental Protection Agency (EPA) in 1970. Industrial groups found that EPA regulations restricted growth and ate into profits; under President Reagan, the EPA was rendered ineffective.

Regulation was only part of the environmental credo. Many argued that consumption patterns and lifestyles in the advanced countries should change to conserve the earth's resources, natural beauty, and clean air and water. Americans, only about 6 percent of the world's population, consume close to half the world's manufactured goods and a third of its energy. In addition to being out of balance with the poor nations of the world, this profligate lifestyle is unnecessary and unhealthy, they argued. Ecologists urged public transportation and bicycles instead of cars, whole-grain foods and vegetables instead of meat, and decentralized, renewable energy sources, such as wind and solar energy, instead of fossil- or nuclear-fueled power plants.

Some environmentalists formed political parties, first the Citizens party, then the Greens, but their main impact was within the two big parties, neither of which could ignore the environmental vote. In Western Europe in the 1980s, especially in Germany and Sweden, Green parties were elected to parliament, determined to end nuclear power, toxic waste, and war. Many young Europeans found the Greens an attractive alternative to the old and stodgy conventional parties.

---

environmentalism   Ideology that environment is endangered and must be preserved through regulation and lifestyle changes.

CASE STUDIES

ISLAMISM: A NEW IDEOLOGY

Islamism—sometimes called "Islamic fundamentalism"—illustrates how a new ideology can suddenly arise by combining elements of pre-existing ideologies. Although it has existed for decades, Islamism exploded with the Iranian revolution of 1979 (see Chapter 19), an angry blend of religion, nationalism, socialism, and a "rage against modernity" that had long been brewing in the Muslim world. With America in the lead, Islamists argue, the West erodes Islamic morals and culture, subjugates the region economically (oil), and steals Islamic holy land (Israel). Some of this traces back to centuries of antipathy between Christendom and Islam, some to the frustrations of modernization. Islamism grows with rapid population increases and high unemployment and in reaction to corruption and misrule in Muslim countries.

Islamism resembles nationalism, but in Islam the political was always intertwined with the religious. Mosque and state are to be one. The Prophet Muhammad founded Islam as one giant community, the *umma*, that disdains nations as forms of idolatry. Accordingly, Osama bin Laden and his followers were uninterested in Palestinian or Iraqi nationalism except to use it on their march to a Muslim empire. Islamists seek to oust U.S. influence, destroy Israel, and take over all Muslim countries and eventually the world. Then a purified Islam will share the wealth now concentrated in the hands of a few corrupt rulers, a sort of socialism. Fanatic and uncompromising, Islamists jolted the world with terrorism. Several Muslim countries—Pakistan and Saudi Arabia among them—fearing Islamist overthrow, attempted to buy them off. Islamists could take over several Muslim countries, but they have no solution to economic problems, especially unemployment. With the harsh Taliban rule of Afghanistan that the United States ousted in 2001 as a negative example, many Muslims oppose Islamism.

■ IS IDEOLOGY FINISHED?

In 1960, Harvard sociologist Daniel Bell argued that the century-long ideological debates were coming to a close. The failure of tyrannical communism and the rise of the welfare state were producing what Bell called the "end of ideology": There simply was not much to quarrel about. Henceforth political debate would focus on almost technical questions of how to run the welfare state, said Bell, such as what to include under national health insurance. In 1989, political scientist Francis Fukuyama went even farther: Not only had the great ideological debate ended with the victory of capitalist democracy but also history itself could be ending. Widely misunderstood, Fukuyama did not mean that time would stand still but rather that the human endpoint propounded by Hegel—free people living in free societies—was now coming into view. Not only had we beaten communism, suggested Fukuyama, there would not likely be any other ideologies to challenge ours. With the end of ideology would come the end of history in the sense of the struggle of great ideas. (Life could get boring, sighed the puckish Fukuyama.)

Islamism   Islam turned into a political ideology.

Is either the Bell or the Fukuyama thesis accurate? There are grounds for doubt. First, the collapse of communism in Europe by itself does not disprove Marx's original ideas, although those now propounding them must carefully distance themselves from the Soviet type of socialism. (We use *socialism* here to mean state control of industry, not *welfarism*, which is but a variation on capitalist democracy.) Socialist thought is still alive with debates over the possibility of a benign socialism. New and dangerous ideological challenges emerged just as communism collapsed: neofascism, breakaway nationalism, and Islamic fundamentalism. And within free democracy itself there are numerous ideological viewpoints: free market or government intervention, more welfare or less, a secular or religious state, and spreading democracy abroad or avoiding overseas involvement. Fukuyama need not worry about boredom.

KEY TERMS

communism (p. 102)

conservatism (p. 97)

environmentalism (p. 110)

fascism (p. 106)

feminism (p. 109)

ideologue (p. 93)

ideology (p. 92)

imperialism (p. 102)

Islamism (p. 111)

liberalism (p. 96)

libertarianism (p. 109)

maoism (p. 104)

modern liberalism (p. 98)

neoconservatism (p. 108)

pragmatic (p. 92)

revisionist (p. 101)

social democracy (p. 101)

titoism (p. 104)

KEY WEB SITES

Yahoo
dir.yahoo.com/Social_Science/Political_Science/Political_Theory/

Democratic Socialists of America
www.dsausa.org

Heritage Foundation (conservative)
www.heritage.org

Cato Institute (libertarian)
www.cato.org

Communist Party of America
www.cpusa.org

Liberal Party of Canada
www.liberal.ca

National Organization for Women
www.now.org

Environmentalism
www.envirolink.org

American Conservative Union
www.conservative.org

FURTHER REFERENCE

Baradat, Leon P. *Political Ideologies: Their Origins and Impact,* 9th ed. Upper Saddle River, NJ: Prentice Hall, 2005.

Boaz, David. *Libertarianism: A Primer.* New York: Free Press, 1997.

Freeden, Michael. *Ideology: A Very Short Introduction.* New York: Oxford University Press, 2003.

Gregor, A. James, and Alessandro Campi. *Phoenix: Fascism in Our Time.* Piscataway, NJ: Transaction, 2001.

Marx, Anthony W. *Faith in Nation: Exclusionary Origins of Nationalism.* New York: Oxford University Press, 2003.

Micklethwait, John, and Adrian Wooldridge. *The Right Nation: Conservative Power in America.* New York: Penguin, 2004.

Nisbet, Robert A. *Conservatism: Dream and Reality.* New Brunswick, NJ: Transaction, 2002.

Rawls, John. *Political Liberalism,* 2nd ed. New York: Columbia University Press, 2005.

Reich, Robert B. *Reason: Why Liberals Will Win the Battle for America.* New York: Knopf, 2004.

Shutkin, William. *The Land That Could Be: Environmentalism and Democracy in the Twenty-First Century.* Cambridge, MA: MIT Press, 2000.

Snyder, Louis L. *The New Nationalism.* New Brunswick, NJ: Transaction, 2003.

Walzer, Michael. *Politics and Passion: Toward a More Egalitarian Liberalism.* New Haven, CT: Yale University Press, 2004.

White, Stephen. *Communism and Its Collapse.* New York: Routledge, 2001.

POLITICAL CULTURE

CHAPTER 7

QUESTIONS TO CONSIDER

- What is political culture?
- How does political culture differ from public opinion?
- How are Russia and Iraq problems of political culture?
- Explain the three types of political culture found by Almond and Verba.
- If Americans are participatory, why do they vote so little?
- What happened to U.S. attitudes starting in the 1960s?
- How do elite and mass political cultures differ?
- Why do some cultures lead to economic growth?
- How can you tell if a group forms a distinct subculture?
- What are the most potent agents of political socialization?

Americans and Canadians appear so similar in clothing and cars that some people think they are nearly the same. But culturally they are distinct. Americans are optimists and winners; Canadians are pessimists and just try to survive. In politics, Americans are more insistent about individual rights and limits on government authority than are Canadians. Canadians are more law-abiding and willing to let government guide the economy and society. Americans find Canadians too obedient; Canadians think Americans are too wild and lawless. Canadians are becoming more like Europeans, less religious and more tolerant on drugs and gay marriage. Canada's **political culture** differs—but not totally—from America's.

---

political culture   The psychology of the nation in regard to politics.

■ WHAT IS POLITICAL CULTURE?

Each society imparts its norms and values to its people, and the people in turn have distinct notions about how the political system is supposed to work, about what the government may do to them and for them, and about their claims and obligations. These beliefs, symbols, and values about the political system are the political culture of a nation—and it varies considerably from one nation to another.

The political culture of a nation is determined by its history, economy, religion, and folkways. Basic values, laid down early, may endure for centuries. Political culture is a sort of collective political memory. America was founded on the basis of "competitive individualism," a spirit of hustle and looking out for oneself, which is still very much alive. The millennia-old Hindu emphasis on caste persists in present-day India despite government efforts to abolish it. The French, after centuries of *étatisme,* still expect a big state to supervise the economy. Iraq, an artificial country constructed by Britain only in 1921, has known only autocracy, recently under the brutal Saddam Hussein. Democracy has an uphill struggle in Iraq.

As defined by political scientist Sidney Verba, political culture is "the system of empirical beliefs, expressive symbols, and values, which defines the situation in which political action takes place." What are these beliefs, symbols, and values that determine how a people interprets the proper role of government and how that government operates? Much of this goes far back. Americans always liked minimal government. In Japan, where the vestiges of a traditional feudal class system still exist, those who bow lower indicate they are of inferior status. The Japanese still tend to submit to the authority of those in office, even when they dislike their corruption and incompetence. Americans, who traditionally do not defer to anyone, consider it their democratic birthright to have a say in the way the country is governed, even if they know little about the issues. In political culture, Japan and the United States are vastly different.

POLITICAL CULTURE AND PUBLIC OPINION

What is the difference between political culture and public opinion? Obviously the two overlap, for both look at attitudes toward politics. Political culture looks for basic, general values on politics and government. Public opinion, on the other hand, looks for views about specific leaders and policies. Political culture looks for the underpinnings of legitimacy, the gut attitudes that sustain a political system, whereas public opinion seeks responses to current questions.

The methodologies of political culture and public opinion also overlap: Random samples of the population are asked questions, and the responses are correlated with subgroups in the population. The questions, however, will be different. A political culture survey might ask how much you trust government; a public opinion survey might ask if you think the current president is doing a good job.

KEY CONCEPTS

CIVIL SOCIETY

The concept of "civil society" is closely related to political culture. Hobbes used the term to indicate humans after becoming civilized; Hegel used it to designate associations bigger than the family but smaller than the state—churches, clubs, businesses, and so on. Edmund Burke called these the "little platoons of society" that form the basis of political life. They encourage cooperating with others, rule of law, restraint, and moderation, what Tocqueville called "habits of the heart." Without them, politics becomes a murderous grab for power.

With the fall of communism in Eastern Europe and the Soviet Union, the concept attracted new interest to explain the growth of democracy—or the lack of it. The Communist regimes had attempted to stomp out civil society and control nearly everything. When a totalitarian (see Chapter 5) regime collapses, it leaves a vacuum where there should be a civil society. Nothing works right; lawlessness sweeps the land. Americans supposed that after Communism, Russia would quickly become like us, but Russia had no civil society and soon reverted to authoritarianism. Likewise we supposed that after Saddam Hussein, Iraq would become a stable democracy, but with little civil society Iraq degenerated into chaos.

A vibrant and developed civil society is the bedrock of democracy. Central Europe—especially Poland's strong Catholic Church, which has always taught Poles to ignore communism—had some civil society and moved quickly to democracy. Without a civil society, democracy may not take root.

A political culture study may ask the same questions in several countries in order to gain a comparative perspective. Both may want to keep track of responses over time to see, in the case of political culture, if legitimacy is gaining or declining or, in the case of public opinion, how a president's popular support changes.

Political culture studies often go beyond surveys, however. Some use the methods of anthropology and psychology in the close observation of daily life and in the deep questioning of individuals about their feelings. Public opinion studies rarely go beyond quantified data, whereas political culture studies can use history and literature to gain insights. For instance, the observations of nineteenth-century European visitors show continuity in American political and social values. Indeed, the brilliant comments of Frenchman Alexis de Tocqueville, who traveled through the United States in the 1830s, still generally apply today. Tocqueville was one of the founders of the political culture approach in political science.

It used to be widely assumed that political culture was nearly permanent or changed only slowly, whereas public opinion was fickle and changed quickly. Recent studies, however, have shown that political culture is rather changeable, too. Periods of stable, efficient government and economic growth solidify feelings of legitimacy; periods of indecisive, chaotic government and economic downturn are reflected in weakening legitimacy. Public opinion, if held long enough, eventually turns into political culture. In the 1960s, public opinion on Vietnam showed declining support for the war. Over precisely the same time, confidence in the U.S.

government also declined. Public opinion on a given question was infecting the general political culture, making it more **cynical** about the political system.

To be sure, a country's political culture changes more slowly than its public opinions, and certain underlying elements of political culture persist for generations, perhaps for centuries. One can easily recognize the America of Tocqueville in the America of today; basic values are largely unchanged. The French still take to the streets of Paris to protest perceived injustice, just as their ancestors did. Italians continue their centuries-old cynicism toward anything governmental. Russians, who have never experienced free democracy, still favor strong leaders and shrug off democracy. Although not as firm as bedrock, political culture is an underlying layer of attitudes that can support—or fail to support—the rest of the political system. This is one reason why Russia's attempt at democracy faded.

PARTICIPATION IN AMERICA

Even in America, not all actively participate in politics. How, then, can Almond and Verba (see box on page 118) offer the United States as their model of a "civic culture"? One of their key findings was that for democracy to work, participation need only be "intermittent and potential." In effect, they offer a "sleeping dogs" theory of democratic political culture. Leaders in a democracy know that most of the time most people are not paying close attention to politics. But they also know that if aroused—because of scandal, high unemployment, inflation, or unpopular war—the public can vote them out of office at the next election. Accordingly, leaders usually work to keep the public unaroused and quiet. Following the **rule of anticipated reactions**, leaders in democracies constantly ask themselves how the public will likely react to any of their decisions. They are quite happy to have the public *not* react at all; they wish to let sleeping dogs lie.

This theory helps explain an embarrassing fact about U.S. political life, namely, its low voter **turnout**, the lowest of all the industrialized democracies. Until 2004, only about half of U.S. voters bothered to cast a ballot in presidential elections, even fewer in state and local contests. In Western Europe, voter turnout has been about three-quarters of the electorate (but is declining there too). How, then, can the United States boast of its democracy? Theorists reply that a democratic culture does not necessarily require heavy voter turnout. Rather, it requires an attitude that, if aroused, the people will participate—vote, contribute time and money, organize groups, and circulate petitions—and that elected officials know this. Democracy in this view is a psychological connection between leaders and led that restrains officials from foolishness. It is the attitudes of the people, and not their actual participation, that makes a democratic culture. The 9/11 attacks and Iraq War aroused Americans.

---

cynical   Untrusting and suspicious, especially of government.

rule of anticipated reactions   Politicians form policies based on how they think public will react.

turnout   Percent of eligible who vote in a given election.

CLASSIC WORKS

THE CIVIC CULTURE

Gabriel Almond and Sidney Verba did the pioneering study of cross-national differences in political beliefs, symbols, and values. The researchers interviewed some 1,000 people each in five countries in 1959 and 1960, to measure national political attitudes. From the data, Almond and Verba discerned three general political cultures: participant, subject, and parochial. Every country, they emphasize, is a varied mixture of all three of these ideal types.

Participant

In a **participant** political culture, such as the United States and Britain, people understand that they are citizens and pay attention to politics. They are proud of their country's political system and are willing to discuss it. They believe they can influence politics and claim they would organize a group to protest something unfair. Accordingly, they show a high degree of **political competence** and **political efficacy**. They say they take pride in voting and believe people should participate in politics. They are active in their communities and often belong to voluntary organizations. They are likely to trust other people and to recall participating in family discussions as children. A participant political culture is clearly the ideal soil to sustain a democracy.

Subject

A notch lower than the participant political culture is the **subject** political culture, predominant at that time in West Germany and Italy, in which people still understand that they are citizens and pay attention to politics, but more passively. They follow political news but are not proud of their country's political system and feel little emotional commitment toward it. They feel uncomfortable speaking about politics. They feel they can influence politics only to the extent of speaking with a local official. It does not ordinarily occur to them to organize a group. Their sense of political competence and efficacy is lower; some feel powerless. They say they vote, but many vote without enthusiasm. They are less likely to trust other people and to recall voicing their views as children. Democracy has more difficulty sinking roots in a culture where people are used to thinking of themselves as obedient subjects rather than as active participants.

Parochial

Still lower is the parochial political culture, as in Mexico, where many people do not much care that they are citizens of a nation. They identify with the immediate locality, hence the term **parochial** (of a parish). They take no pride in their country's political system and expect little of it. They pay no attention to politics, have little knowledge of it, and seldom speak about it. They have neither the desire nor the ability to participate in politics. They have no sense of political competence or efficacy and feel powerless in the face of existing institutions. Attempting to grow a democracy in a parochial political culture is very difficult, requiring not only new institutions but also a new sense of citizenship.

---

participatory   Interest or willingness in taking part in politics.

political competence   Knowing how to accomplish something politically.

political efficacy   Feeling that one has at least a little political input (opposite: feeling powerless).

subject   Feeling among citizens that they should obey authority but not participate much in politics.

parochial   Narrow, having little or no interest in politics.

Another of Almond and Verba's key findings was the response to the question of what citizens of five countries would do to influence local government regarding an unjust ordinance. Far more Americans said that they would "try to enlist the aid of others." Americans seem to be natural "group formers" when faced with a political problem, and this trait could be an important foundation of U.S. democracy. In more "subject" countries, this group-forming attitude was weaker.

Other studies show that Americans are prouder of their system and more satisfied with the way democracy works in their country compared to the citizens of other lands. A 1995 Gallup survey found that 64 percent of the Americans polled expressed some degree of satisfaction. Sixty-two percent of Canadians responded likewise, as did 55 percent of Germans, 43 percent of French, 40 percent of Britons, 35 percent of Japanese, and only 17 percent of Mexicans and Hungarians. Americans may complain about government, but their faith in democracy is still the strongest in the world.

■ THE DECAY OF POLITICAL CULTURE

In the late twentieth century, the political cultures of most of the advanced democracies grew more cynical and voter turnout declined. More citizens saw politicians as corrupt and government institutions as ineffective. Only the Netherlands showed growing trust, probably related to its strong economy. The steepest drop was in Japan—where the economy was stagnant for more than a decade. In the 1960s and 1970s—the years of the Vietnam war, Watergate, and inflation—U.S. surveys showed a sharp decline in trust in government (see Figure 7.1 on page 120). In the 1980s, under the "feel-good" presidency of Ronald Reagan, the trusting responses went up but never recovered the levels of the early 1960s. The dip in 2004 may reflect unhappiness over the U.S. war in Iraq. The growth in cynicism made America harder to govern and is reflected in an electorate that seems to be permanently split and unhappy with Washington. American political culture is not as unified and legitimate as it used to be.

A related development is America's "culture wars," a nasty polarization between conservatives and liberals, who dislike and vote against each other. For two centuries one spoke of the "Two Spains" because it was badly split by region and religiosity. Now America seems to be two countries. One is conservative, evangelical, small-town, and living in middle of the country; it votes Republican (the "red states" on news maps). The other is liberal, **secular**, urban, and living on both coasts; it votes Democrat (the "blue states"). Conservatives hate gay and women's rights, taxes, and Bill Clinton (example: Fox TV). Liberals hate big corporations, the Iraq War, and George Bush (example: Michael Moore). The causes of this polarization are several and disputed. One is between religious and

---

secular Not connected to religion.

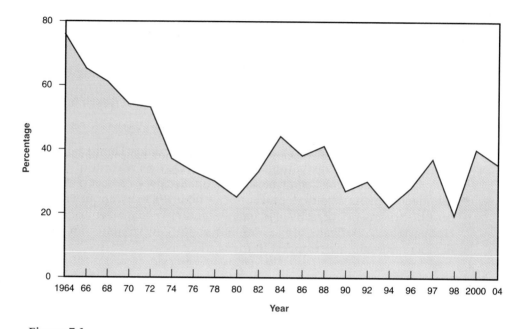

Figure 7.1

Americans' Trust in Government, 1964–2004 (Sources: 1964–1996, American National Election Studies of the University of Michigan; 1997–2004, Pew Research Center for People and the Press.)

secular America (see box on page 121). Another possibility is that America never psychologically recovered from the Vietnam War, leaving angers that awoke with the Iraq War. Economically and demographically, the coasts of America grew while the center stagnated. Economic change means lost jobs and farms, and the losers get angry. If polarization keeps growing, some fear for U.S. political stability. Dialogue between the Two Americas fails, as their views are visceral, not rational.

One factor much discussed is the decline of the American tendency to form associations, anything from volunteer fire departments to labor unions. In the 1830s, Tocqueville noted: "Americans of all ages, all conditions, and all dispositions constantly form associations." He was impressed by this tendency, for it was (and still is) largely absent in France, and he held it was the basis of American democracy, a point supported much later by the *Civic Culture* study. Some observers claim that these grassroots associations are fading. Harvard political scientist Robert Putnam noted, for example, that the number of people bowling has increased, but league bowling has declined. His article, "Bowling Alone," caught much attention and controversy. Putnam noted the membership loss of many associations—unions, PTAs, Boy Scouts, and fraternal orders—and feared it meant decline of our "social capital" and decay of civil society.

Others argue that Americans volunteer and join as much as ever, but they now join newer associations that may have escaped Putnam's count. Old associations, such as the Scouts and Elks, may be shrinking, but new ones, such as Habitat for

CASE STUDIES

AMERICA THE RELIGIOUS

The United States has long been known as a religious nation. A 2002 Pew survey found that 59 percent of Americans said religion plays a very important role in their lives, far higher than Britons (33 percent), Canadians (30), Italians (27), Germans (21), Japanese (12), or French (11), even higher than Poles (36). Among the advanced, industrialized nations, the United States is an "outlier" (see page 303). In general, poorer countries are the most religious—India (92 percent), Brazil (77), and Mexico (57)—as well as Muslim lands—Indonesia (95) and Pakistan (91).

American religiosity is also one of the points of cultural divergence between Americans and Europeans, many of whom think the United States is dominated by Christian fundamentalists. Polls find that nearly half of Americans believe in creationism and two-thirds in the devil. A majority believes the Book of Revelation will come true. Americans' favorite reading: the "Left Behind" books, of which more than 40 million have been sold. President Bush 43, himself an evangelical Christian, enjoyed strong electoral support from conservative Christians. This would not work in Europe or Japan.

Humanity and Meals on Wheels, may be growing. Forty percent of American college students volunteer to help the homeless, feed the needy, tutor, participate in religious life, clean up the environment, and other altruistic activities. The American volunteer spirit is not necessarily dead.

Those who see the decline of America's voluntary associations, however, fear political and economic repercussions. With individuals demanding their "rights" without a corresponding sense of having to contribute something, demands on government become impossible. Democracy becomes less a matter of concerned citizens meeting face-to-face to discuss a community problem than disgruntled citizens demanding "Gimme!" Furthermore, argued Francis Fukuyama (who earlier brought us the "end of history" theory), trust or "spontaneous sociability" underpins economic growth and stability. If you can trust others, you can do more and better business with them. Hence "high trust" societies lead to prosperous countries.

Another school of thought sees the growth of distrust in government as a natural thing and not necessarily bad. Politicians worldwide have for decades promised citizens more and more, promises governments could not possibly deliver; there is simply not enough money. But citizens meantime had been growing more educated and aware of this gap and more willing to criticize. What some see as the growth of cynicism others see as the growth of "critical citizens" who are actually improving democracy by telling politicians what voters think of them.

Political culture changes. It is a combination of long-remembered and deeply held attitudes plus reactions to current situations. These changes are responses to government performance, which almost always fall short of promises. Political cultures do not fall from heaven; they are created by government actions and inactions.

HOW TO . . .

QUOTATIONS

Do not quote everything. Quote only important statements from key figures. You might quote the secretary of state on a major foreign policy but do not normally quote a journalist or an academic. Their precise words are rarely that important. Instead, if you want to borrow their ideas, paraphrase them in your own words, but still cite them. Occasionally, a scholar says something so clear and provocative that it's worth quoting: "Islam has bloody borders" (Huntington 1993).

Quote

"Iraq has weapons of mass destruction," said Secretary of Defense Donald Rumsfeld as he readied the country for war (Sinclair 2003). [Capitalize titles when used directly before names, otherwise lowercase.]

Paraphrase

Washington pundits grew critical when they learned that Iraq had no weapons of mass destruction (Sinclair 2003). [Summarizes rather than quotes directly.]

Use partial quotes instead of long quotes. Pick out the interesting or operative phrase and quote it: Pentagon officials said they had "not anticipated" chaos in Iraq (Sinclair 2003). If you must include a long quote—more than three lines—make it an indented block quote. Use ellipses (. . .) to indicate you have omitted unnecessary words. Use brackets ([ ]) to indicate you have inserted a clarification of words not in the original.

To slow down the tempo means to lag behind. And those who lag behind are beaten. The history of Old Russia shows . . . that because of her backwardness she was constantly defeated . . . We [the Russians] are behind the leading countries by fifty to one hundred years. We must make up this distance in ten years. Either we do it or we go under. (Stalin 1931)

ELITE AND MASS CULTURES

The political culture of a country is not uniform and monolithic. One can usually find within it differences between the mainstream culture and subcultures (discussion following) and differences between elite and mass attitudes. Elites, used here more broadly than the "governing elites" discussed in Chapter 5 (a tiny fraction of 1 percent), in political-culture studies means those with better education, higher income, and more influence (several percent). Elites are much more interested in politics and more participatory. They are more inclined to vote, to protest injustice, to form groups, and to run for office. One consistent finding of the *Civic Culture* study has been confirmed over and over again: The more education a person has, the more likely he or she is to participate in politics.

Delegates to both Democratic and Republican conventions—who are clearly very interested in politics—illustrate the differences between elite and mass culture. Usually half the delegates have some postgraduate education (often law school), far more than average voters. Most convention delegates come from households with annual incomes much higher than average voters. Delegates are also more ideological than average voters, the Democrats more liberal and the Republicans more conservative. In other words, the people representing parties at conventions are not closely representative of typical voters. People with more education, money, and ideological convictions take the leading roles. There is nothing wrong with this; it is standard worldwide.

Why should this be so? Here we return to the concepts mentioned earlier: *political competence* and *political efficacy.* Better-educated people know how to participate in political activity. They have greater self-confidence in writing letters, speaking at meetings, and organizing groups. They feel that what they do has at least some political impact. The uneducated and the poor lack the knowledge and confidence to do these kinds of things. Many of them feel powerless. "What I do doesn't matter, so why bother?" they think. Those at the bottom of the social ladder thus become apathetic.

The differences in participation in politics between elites and masses are one of the great ironies of democracy. In theory and in law, a democracy is open to all. In practice, some participate much more than others. Because the better-educated and better-off people (more education usually leads to higher income) participate in politics far more, they are in a much stronger position to look out for their interests. It is not surprising that the 2001 tax cut favored the wealthiest, who speak up and donate money; those lower on the socioeconomic ladder do not. There is no quick fix for this. The right to vote is a mere starting point for political participation; it does not guarantee equal access to decision making. A mass political culture of apathy and indifference toward politics effectively negates the potential of a mass vote. An elite political culture of competence and efficacy amplifies their influence.

POLITICAL SUBCULTURES

The 2000 census showed that over 30 percent of those who live in the United States are nonwhite. They might be black, Latino, Asian, Native American, or Pacific Islander. In California, whites are a minority. Even among white Americans there are differences among ethnic, religious, and regional groups. When the differentiating qualities are strong enough in a particular group, we say that the group forms a **subculture**. Defining subculture is tricky, as not every group is a subculture. The Norwegian-Americans of "Lake Wobegon," Minnesota, do not form a subculture because their culture and politics are **mainstream**.

But African Americans are on average poorer and less educated than white Americans, and the black vote is solidly Democratic. In attitudes toward the criminal justice system, blacks sharply diverge from whites, as the 1995 murder trial of O. J. Simpson dramatically illustrated. Most blacks, convinced the police and courts are racist and rig evidence, were glad to see Simpson acquitted. Most whites, convinced the police and courts are just and fair, thought the jury (with its black

---

subculture   A minority culture within the *mainstream* culture.
mainstream   Sharing the average or standard political culture.

Integration came hard to Little Rock, Arkansas, in 1957. Black students needed a National Guard escort to get past jeering white students at Central High School. The problem was not confined to the South or to the 1950s, however. (AP/Wide World Photos)

majority) ignored the evidence. Many whites had naively believed that U.S. society had made great strides since the 1950s in **integrating** African Americans; the Simpson trial and the reactions to it showed how great a gap remained. Accordingly, African Americans form a political subculture.

Groups with a different language who dislike being ruled by the dominant culture constitute subcultures. Many of the French-speakers of Quebec would like to withdraw from Canada and become a separate country. The Bengalis of East Pakistan, ethnically and linguistically distinct from the peoples of West Pakistan, did secede in 1971. The Basques of northern Spain and the Roman Catholics of Northern Ireland are sufficiently different to constitute political subcultures. The Scots and Welsh of Britain harbor the resentments of the "Celtic fringe" against the dominant English: They vote heavily Labour, whereas the English vote heavily Conservative. They, too, constitute subcultures.

Where subcultures are very distinct, the political system itself may be threatened. The Soviet Union and Yugoslavia ceased to exist because citizens were more loyal to their ethnic groups than to the nation. Ethnic Albanians in Serbia and Macedonia, by religion (Muslim) and language very distinct from their Serbian and Macedonian rulers, fought for independence. In India, some Sikhs seek independence for the Punjab, their home province, and resort to arms. Prime Minister Indira Gandhi's Sikh bodyguards assassinated her in 1985. Recalling a term we used earlier, such countries as Lebanon and India are still undergoing crises of identification.

---

integration   Merging subcultures into the *mainstream* culture.

QUEBEC: "MAÎTRES CHEZ NOUS"

The French arrived in North America about the same time the English did, but France was more interested in the lucrative fur trade than in colonization and sent few French settlers; as a result the population of New France stayed tiny compared to that of the English colonies to the south. The two empires collided in the French and Indian War, which essentially ended when the British conquered Quebec City in 1759. After the historic battle on the Plains of Abraham—which was actually quite small with only a handful killed, including both commanders—the English let the French Canadians keep their language and Roman Catholic religion. It was a magnanimous gesture, but it meant that two centuries later Canada faced an angry and defiant Quebec separatist movement.

Culturally and politically, Quebec province fell asleep for two centuries, an island of tradition in an otherwise dynamic North America. Quebec missed the French Revolution and thus stayed far more conservative than France. Quebec has been called "France without the Revolution." Economic leadership moved into the hands of English-speakers, and Montreal became a mostly English-speaking city. Many **francophones** became **marginalized**, living as poor and isolated farmers with little education. An unstated deal was struck: **Anglophones** would run the economy while francophones, a majority of the population, would obey local politicians and the Catholic Church.

In the 1960s, Quebec woke up with its "Quiet Revolution." Francophone attitudes shifted dramatically, away from traditional politicians and the priests. It was almost as if a new generation of Québécois said, "You have held us down and backward long enough. We want to be modern, rich, and *maîtres chez nous* (masters in our own house)." Out of this massive shift in attitudes emerged the Parti Québécois (PQ) of René Levesque (pronounced Leveck) with its demand to separate Quebec from Canada. The PQ argues that Quebec really is a different culture and is tired of being under the thumb of English-speaking Canada.

The PQ and related Bloc Québécois became the province's largest parties. A 1980 referendum on separation failed 60–40 percent, but a 1995 referendum failed only by a whisker. Since then, Quebec separatism has subsided, and the PQ's vote has declined. Quebeckers simply got tired of the issue. For Americans, Quebec served as an example of what goes wrong with bilingualism and multiculturalism: They can lead to national fragmentation.

Should a nation attempt to integrate its subcultures into the mainstream? Such efforts are bound to be difficult, but if left undone the subculture in later years may seek independence, as do the Tamils of Sri Lanka. The Spaniards in Peru who conquered the Incas let them retain their language and culture. But now the Spanish-speaking Peruvians of the cities know little of the Quechua-speaking Peruvians of the mountains. Thirty percent of Peruvians speak no Spanish. Any nonintegrated subculture poses at least a problem and at worst a threat to the national political system.

---

francophone   A French speaker.
marginalized   Pushed to the edge of society and the economy, often said of the poor and of subcultures.
anglophone   An English speaker.

Starting in the 1870s, France deliberately pursued national integration through its centralized school system. Many regions were backwaters and spoke strange dialects. The French education ministry sent schoolteachers into the villages almost like missionaries. The teachers followed an absolutely standard curriculum—the education ministry could tell what was being taught across France at any given minute—that was heavy on rote learning and on the glory and unity of France. Gradually, in the phrase of Eugen Weber, they turned "peasants into Frenchmen." After some decades, a much more unified and integrated France emerged, an example of *overt political socialization* (see discussion following).

The United States has relied largely on voluntary integration to create a mainstream culture in which most Americans feel at home. Immigrants found they had to learn English to get ahead. The achievement-oriented consumer society standardized tastes and career patterns. The melting pot worked—and, with nearly one in ten U.S. residents an immigrant, is still working—but not perfectly. Many Americans retain small subculture distinctions—often in the areas of religion and cuisine—but these may not be politically important. Italian Americans did not rally behind Geraldine Ferraro, the first Italian American to run for national office as the vice-presidential candidate on the Democratic ticket in 1984. Their failure to do so pointed out how well Italian Americans had become integrated into the mainstream: They really did not care that one of their own was at last on the ballot. Asian Americans integrated rapidly into the U.S. mainstream. Now some 4 percent of the total U.S. population, they hold several of the 535 elected seats on Capitol Hill.

Not all American groups have been so fortunate. Blacks and Hispanics are not fully integrated into the American mainstream. Should they be better integrated? This has been one of the great questions of post–World War II U.S. politics. With the 1954 *Brown v. Board of Education of Topeka* decision, the Supreme Court began a major federal government effort to integrate U.S. schools. It encountered massive resistance. In some instances federal judges had to take control of local school systems to enforce integration by busing. The integrationist Kennedy and Johnson administrations argued that America, in its struggle against communism, could not field a good army and offer an example of freedom and justice to the rest of the world if some Americans were oppressed and poor. Integration was portrayed as a matter of national security.

Should integration be forced in the area of language? Should African Americans abandon their black dialect in favor of standard English, and should Hispanics learn English? If they do not, they will be severely handicapped their whole lives, especially in employment prospects. But some blacks, Hispanics, and Native Americans cling to their language as a statement of ethnic identity and pride. The U.S. Constitution does not specify any national language, nor does it outlaw languages other than English. In some areas of the United States, signs and official documents are in both English and Spanish. In 1986, California voters approved a measure making English the state's official language by a wide margin. People could, of course, continue to speak what they wished, but official documents and ballots would be in English only. In 1998, California voted to end bilingual education in order to speed the assimilation of subcultures. California is often an indicator of nationwide trends, and other states passed similar laws.

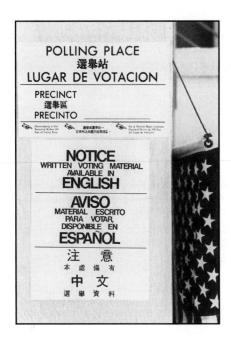

A trilingual sign in California emphasizes the multicultural character of the population of that state. In an effort to promote cultural unity, Californians voted in 1986 to make English the state's only official language. (Michael Roskin)

■ POLITICAL SOCIALIZATION

In the **socializing** process, children acquire manners and speech patterns that often last lifelong. Although some is formally taught, most is absorbed by imitating others. In the same way, political socialization teaches political values and specific usages. Learning to pledge allegiance to the flag, to sing the national anthem, and to obey authority figures, from presidents to police officers, is imparted by families, friends, schoolteachers, and television. Children raised in cultural ghettoes, such as minorities in America's inner cities, pick up their subcultures, which are sometimes at odds with mainstream culture. Political socialization is thus crucial to stable government.

THE AGENTS OF SOCIALIZATION

The Family What children encounter earliest—the family—usually outweighs all others factors. Attempts at **overt socialization** by government and schools generally fail if their values are at odds with family orientations. Communist countries, such as Poland, had this problem: The regime tried to inculcate socialist values in a child, but the family taught the child to ignore these messages. Where family and government values are generally congruent, as in the United States, the two modes of socialization reinforce one another.

---

socialization   The learning of culture.
overt socialization   Deliberate government policy to teach culture.

KEY CONCEPTS

CULTURE AND DEVELOPMENT

The recent economic growth of East Asia brought cultural explanations of why some poor countries stay poor while others get rich. Japan, South Korea, Taiwan, Hong Kong, and Singapore have no natural resources, but they do have disciplined people who work hard, save their money, and trust each other. (Most also turned into democracies.) Some point to their common Confucian heritage, which promotes such values. The Middle East, on the other hand, has rigidly Islamic people who do not trust each other. Its oil wealth has brought only superficial modernization and no democracy.

A century ago, Max Weber argued that Protestantism laid down the cultural basis of capitalism. A "Protestant work ethic" pushed people to work hard and amass capital. The countries of northwest Europe, mostly Protestant, were the first capitalist and democratic nations. Even today, these countries are rich, have high levels of trust and rule of law, and little corruption. Countries lacking this culture, such as Rwanda or Egypt, do not take quickly to economic growth or democracy.

If the cultural theory of prosperity is accurate, countries will stay poor until they rid themselves of traditionalism, mistrust, and fatalism, all prominent in the Middle East. Without a shift of values, outside aid and advice often disappear into corruption. Critics of the cultural theory point out that decades ago Confucianism was blamed for keeping East Asia *backward*, and that values often change *after* economic growth has taken hold. No one has been able to predict which countries will grow rapidly based on their culture or anything else; it's always a surprise.

Parents influence our political behavior for decades. Most people vote as their parents did. More basically, the family forms the psychological makeup of individuals, which in turn determines many of their political attitudes. It imparts a set of norms and values, including political aspects, and it transmits beliefs and attitudes such as party loyalty and trust or cynicism about government.

Conditioning and training in the early years have the strongest effect, especially from ages three to thirteen. Children accept many parental norms, values, and attitudes unconsciously and uncritically and retain them all their lives. People often give back to the world as adults what they got from it as children. One study found that people with authoritarian personalities had been treated roughly as children. Parental overprotection may also harm, causing children to fear leaving the family, a fear that may later be expressed as distrust and dislike of public figures. Almond and Verba found that those who remembered having had a voice in family decisions when they were children had a greater adult sense of political efficacy. Those who took part in family decisions were, on average, more inclined to feel that expression of their political beliefs could influence the government.

Most of the political socialization that takes place in the family is informal, as when the father "lays down the law" and refuses to hear any argument, or when the mother complains about the burdens of housework. And parental attitudes and actions about political matters—for instance, their interest in elections or their readiness to seek special favors—probably are more important in shaping the child's future political behavior than specific ideas about government and politics that the parents try to impart.

The School　　More deliberate socialization occurs in school. Most governments use schools to teach their citizens that they are a national community. Many African nations try to unify their tribes, usually with different languages and histories, by teaching in French or English about a mythical past when they were a great and united nation. It often does not work, as seen recently in the Congo (formerly Zaire). Communist nations also used schools for systematic inculcation to support the regime. As we saw in 1989, though, this effort failed; family and church overrode the attempts of schools to make East Europeans into believing Communists. U.S. schools did a brilliant job of turning immigrants from many lands into one nation, something critics of bilingual education say must be restored.

The amount of schooling a person receives also affects political attitudes. Uniformly, people with many years of education show a stronger sense of responsibility to their community and feel more able to influence public policy than do less-educated citizens. Persons with more schooling are more participatory. College graduates are more tolerant and open-minded, especially on questions of race, than high-school dropouts, who are often parochial in outlook. This is because education imparts more open-minded attitudes and because educated people generally enjoy higher incomes and status, which by themselves encourage interest and participation.

Japanese schoolchildren learn about their democracy by visiting the Diet (parliament) in Tokyo. (Michael Roskin)

CLASSIC WORKS

THE AUTHORITARIAN PERSONALITY

One of the boldest attempts to link individual character traits with political attitudes was a 1950 book, *The Authoritarian Personality* by Theodore Adorno and others, mostly refugees from Nazi Germany. Based heavily on the Freudian theory that personality is laid down in early childhood, Adorno and his colleagues devised a twenty-nine-item questionnaire that allegedly showed pre-fascist political views; hence its name, the F-Scale. Persons who scored high on it were conventional in lifestyle to the point of rigidity; were intolerant, prejudiced, and aggressive toward outsiders and minorities; submitted to and liked power; and were superstitious and mystical. The Adorno study attracted great interest but was soon criticized over its methodology and its direct connection of personality and politics. Many people have all or some of the F-Scale's characteristics but are good democrats. Although it has faded from view, some still find the study accurate and insightful.

Peer Groups   Friends and playmates also form political values. For example, working-class children in Jamaica who went to school with children of higher social classes tended to take on the political attitudes of those classes, but when they attended school with working-class peers, their attitudes did not change. The relative strength of peer-group influence appears to be growing. With both parents working, children may be socialized more by peers than by families. Upholders of "family values" see this as the underlying cause of youthful drug-taking and violence.

The Mass Media   The mass media, especially television, are a fourth important socializing force and probably gaining in influence. Many fear the influence is negative. Harvard political scientist Robert Putnam argues that heavy TV watching makes people passive and uninterested in community or group activities. As American children watch thousands of hours of television (the "plug-in babysitter") a year, they witness myriad crimes and murders. Some critics charge this tends to make them heartless and violent, a point that has not been proven. TV reaches kids early; even three-year-olds can recognize the president on television and understand that he is a sort of "boss" of the nation. Senators and members of Congress, who receive much less coverage, are treated with relative indifference, a view the children may hold the rest of their lives.

As with schools, the mass media may be unsuccessful if the messages they beam are at odds with what family and religion teach. Even Soviet researchers found that families were much bigger influences on individuals' political views than the Soviet mass media. Iran's mass media, all firmly controlled by the shah, tried to inculcate loyalty to him, but believing Muslims took the word of their local *mullahs* in the mosques and hated the shah. Now, ironically, with Iran's media controlled by Islamist conservatives, most Iranians believe the opposite of what the press feeds them. Mass media alone cannot do everything.

The Government   The government itself is an agent of socialization. Virtually everything that the government does takes into account its citizens' reactions, and many government activities are intended to explain or display the government to the public, always designed to build public support and loyalty. Great spectacles of state, such as the crowning of a British king or queen, have a strengthening effect, as do parades with flags and soldiers, and proclamations of top leaders. The power of government to control political attitudes is limited, however, because messages and experiences reach individuals through conversations with primary groups of kin or peers, who put their own spin on messages. Alienated groups may socialize their children to dislike the government and ignore its messages.

KEY TERMS

anglophone (p. 125)
cynical (p. 117)
francophone (p. 125)
integration (p. 124)
mainstream (p. 123)
marginalized (p. 125)
overt socialization (p. 127)
parochial (p. 118)
participatory (p. 118)

political competence (p. 118)
political culture (p. 114)
political efficacy (p. 118)
rule of anticipated reactions (p. 117)
secular (p. 119)
socialization (p. 127)
subculture (p. 123)
subject (p. 118)
turnout (p. 117)

KEY WEB SITES

Pew Research Center
www.people-press.org/

Civil society
www.civsoc.com/index.htm

National Civic League
www.ncl.org/

Activist groups
www.webactive.com/

Tocqueville
www.tocqueville.org/

Further Reference

Codevilla, Angelo M. *The Character of Nations: How Politics Makes and Breaks Prosperity, Family, and Civility.* New York: Basic Books, 1997.

Huntington, Samuel P. *Who Are We?: The Challenge to America's National Identity.* New York: Simon & Schuster, 2004.

———— and Lawrence E. Harrison, eds. *Culture Matters: How Values Shape Human Progress.* New York: Basic Books, 2000.

Jung, Hwa Yol, ed. *Comparative Political Culture in the Age of Globalization: An Introductory Anthology.* Lanham, MD: Lexington, 2002.

Lipset, Seymour Martin. *Continental Divide: The Values and Institutions of the United States and Canada.* New York: Routledge, 1990.

————. *American Exceptionalism: A Double-Edged Sword.* New York: Norton, 1996.

Norris, Pippa, ed. *Critical Citizens: Global Support for Democratic Governance.* New York: Oxford University Press, 1999.

Putnam, Robert D. *Bowling Alone: The Collapse and Revival of American Community.* New York: Simon & Schuster, 2001.

————, ed. *Democracies in Flux.* New York: Oxford University Press, 2004.

Rimmerman, Craig A. *The New Citizenship: Unconventional Politics, Activism, and Service,* 3rd ed. Boulder, CO: Westview, 2005.

Seabright, Paul. *Company of Strangers: A Natural History of Economic Life.* Princeton, NJ: Princeton University Press, 2004.

Sperling, John. *The Great Divide: Retro vs. Metro America.* Phoenix, AZ: Polipoint, 2004.

Warren, Mark E., ed. *Democracy and Trust.* New York: Cambridge University Press, 1999.

PUBLIC OPINION

QUESTIONS TO CONSIDER

- Does government follow or create public opinion?
- How important is religion in forming U.S. opinion?
- What is the theory of political generations?
- Explain the three classic opinion curves.
- Why did the *Literary Digest* miscall the 1936 election?
- Why did the polls miscall the 1948 election?
- What is a random sample?
- What does presidential "popularity" really measure?
- What is intensity and volatility?

Widely reported, eagerly watched, and a multibillion dollar industry, **public opinion** clearly plays a major role in modern democracy. But can or should it play a leading role? Few political scientists would wish it to, and for good reasons.

Public opinion is important in a democracy, as elections provide only a crude expression of the public's will. An election generally indicates what voters think of an official's overall performance; they rarely focus on specific issues. Public-opinion surveys fill in the details so officials know what people think about specific problems, such as Medicare or a war. Public opinion can thus be seen as a backup and detailing device for inputting mass views into politics, a way to fine tune elections.

Executives often try to create the public opinion they desire. They spend a lot of time addressing the nation through the media. When Richard Nixon announced in late 1971 that he would be the first president to visit China, Americans quickly

---

public opinion   Citizens' reactions to current, specific issues and events.

KEY CONCEPTS

WHAT PUBLIC OPINION IS AND ISN'T

Political culture and public opinion are linked but are not the same. Political culture focuses on long-standing values, attitudes, and ideas that people learn deeply. Most Americans firmly believe that government power is potentially tyrannical and must be controlled and that democracy is the only just form of government. Public opinion concerns people's reactions to specific and immediate policies and problems, such as sending troops overseas or voting intentions.

Public opinion is not the same as individual opinion. A woman's opinion of her neighbor's religion would not be part of public opinion, but her feeling on prayer in public schools would. Public opinion refers to political and social issues, not private matters. **Anecdotal** evidence is a poor indication of public opinion, as we have no way of knowing if it is representative. Beware of the journalistic "one-person cross-section" of opinion.

Public opinion does not necessarily imply that citizens have strong, clear, or united convictions; such unity is rare. So-called public opinion often involves several small, conflicting groups, plus many who are undecided, plus an even larger number with no interest or opinion on the matter. On most subjects, public opinion is an array of diverse attitudes that can change quickly.

Public opinion sometimes shows widespread ignorance. A 2000 poll found that 71 percent of Americans were unaware there was a federal budget surplus, and 56 percent had no idea who Alan Greenspan was. (The influential chairman of the Federal Reserve Board. You knew that.) Some respondents manufacture answers in order to sound well-informed. A 1948 poll found that 59 percent of Americans said the (fake) "Metallic Metals Act" would be a good thing but should be left up to the states. Many people are poorly informed. Months after the 2003 Iraq War, one American in five thought weapons of mass destruction had indeed been found.

So, do numbers make right? Most Americans are opposed to raising taxes on gasoline. Does that mean government should never do it? Should elected leaders always bow to public opinion? President Truman shrugged off public opinion and was vilified for it. Decades later, many celebrated him as a leader who did the right thing without fear of disapproval. Some say current politicians pay too much attention to public opinion. If you are always following, how can you lead?

became more favorable toward China. Spanish Prime Minister Felipe González, head of a party that opposed NATO, changed his mind and supported Spain's affiliation, although polls showed that most Spaniards did not want Spain in NATO. González urged support for NATO in a 1986 referendum, and Spaniards swung around to support him. British socialist Beatrice Webb long ago said: "There is no such thing as spontaneous public opinion. It all has to be manufactured from a center of conviction and energy."

Public opinion is often led or manipulated by interest groups. Bringing grievances to public attention, especially when the media watches, can generate widespread sympathy. The televised brutality of sheriffs' deputies in Selma, Alabama, toward blacks demanding the right to vote turned public opinion in favor of the Voting Rights Act of 1965.

---

anecdotal   Recounting the views of a few respondents.

Tibetan-Americans in New York City protest Chinese rule of their country. Hundreds of them gathered outside the UN building, trying to generate interest. (Michael Roskin)

Any government is vulnerable to public opinion. Mahatma Gandhi, by simple dramas of nonviolent protest, used public opinion to win independence for India. A gaunt, bespectacled old man in a loincloth, he led protests, wove his own cloth, and threatened to starve himself to death if the British did not pull out of India. So powerful was the support he generated that the British gave India independence in 1947.

Government by sheer violence and coercion cannot last long. Even Stalin's Soviet Union, with all its brutal apparatus for suppressing dissent, depended first on the dream of a classless utopia and on Russian patriotism to repel the Nazi invader, and only secondly on night raids by the security police. After Stalin died in 1953, something had to give, and the regime turned to incentives and propaganda to keep up a veneer of legitimacy, which collapsed quickly in 1989 in Eastern Europe and then in the Soviet Union itself in late 1991. Ultimately, lack of public support ended these regimes.

■ THE SHAPE OF PUBLIC OPINION

Social scientists have found roughly who thinks what about politics. No social category, of course, is ever 100 percent for or against something. Indeed, 60 or 70 percent is often quite high. What we look for are *differences* among social categories, the significance of which can be tested by the rules of statistics. We look for shades of gray, not for black and white. Once we have found significant differences, we may be able to say something about **salience**, the degree to which

---

salience   Literally, that which jumps out; the importance of given issues in public opinion or the characteristics of publics holding various opinions.

categories and issues affect the public opinion of a country. In Scandinavia, for example, social class is salient in structuring party preferences: The working class tends to vote Social Democratic, and the middle class votes for the more conservative parties. In Latin Europe, social class is weakly salient, with the working class scattering its vote among parties of the left, right, and center. In Latin Europe, religion and region are typically most salient. In the United States, religion and urban-rural differences are salient.

SOCIAL CLASS

Karl Marx saw **social class** as massively salient. Workers, he predicted, would become socialists. Actually, only some of them did, but social class does matter, even in the relatively classless United States. Over the decades, the American manual worker has tended to vote Democratic; the better-off or professional person has tended to vote Republican. But these are only tendencies, and they are often muddied by other factors. Poor people are often very conservative on religious and social issues, and affluent people can be liberal or even radical. During hard times, when bread-and-butter issues, such as jobs, become salient, the American working class tends to rediscover the Democratic party, as it did in 1992. When these issues lose their salience, however, the working class often focuses on noneconomic issues, such as gun control, morality (abortion, gay rights), or leadership in war.

Social class can be hard to measure. There are two general ways, the objective and the subjective. An objective determination involves asking people their annual income or judging the quality of the neighborhood. The subjective determination involves simply asking respondents what their social class is, which sometimes diverges from objective criteria. A majority of Americans call themselves middle class even if they are not. Sometimes even wealthy people, thinking of their modest origins, call themselves middle class. The way a person earns a living may matter more than the amount he or she makes. Typically, American farmers are conservative, and miners and steelworkers are not. Different political attitudes grow up around different jobs.

Sometimes social class works in precisely the opposite way envisioned by Marx. Highly educated professionals make some affluent U.S. suburbs quite liberal compared to the conservatism of poorer country dwellers. Spanish researchers found an *inverse* relationship between social class and preferring the left; that is, better-off persons were more leftist than poorer Spaniards. In the Spanish study, education was most salient.

Class matters, especially in combination with other factors, such as region or religion. In Britain, class plus region structures much of the vote; in France, it is class plus region plus religiosity (practicing Catholic vs. nonpracticing); in Germany, it is class plus region plus denomination (Catholic or Protestant). As Yale's Joseph La-Palombara put it, the question is "Class plus what?"

---

social class   A broad layer of society, usually based on income and often labeled lower, middle, and upper.

EDUCATION

Educational level is related to social class; that is, children of better-off families usually get more education, and education in turn leads to better-paying jobs. Education in the United States often has a split impact, making people more liberal on **noneconomic issues** but more conservative on **economic issues**. Abundant survey data show that college-educated people are more tolerant, favor civil rights, and understand different viewpoints. But on economic issues, many of them are skeptical of efforts to redistribute income by higher taxes on the upper brackets—which happen to be them—and welfare measures for the nonworking. There are, to be sure, some educated people who are consistently liberal on both economic and noneconomic questions, but in the United States the categories sometimes diverge. The same is often true of the American working class: Its members want higher wages but can be intolerant in the areas of race, lifestyle, and patriotism. Middle-class college youths protesting the Vietnam War ran into the snarls and fists of unionized construction workers, an illustration of the split between economic and noneconomic liberalism.

REGION

Every country has a south, goes an old saw, and this is true in politics. It is uncertain, however, whether a country's south is more conservative or more leftist than its north. France south of the Loire River and Spain south of the Tagus have for generations gone left. The south of Italy, though, is conservative, as is Bavaria in Germany's south. In Great Britain, England is heavily conservative, whereas Scotland and Wales go for Labour. And of course the U.S. South was famous for decades as the "solid South," which went automatically Democratic but now goes Republican.

A country's outlying **regions** usually harbor resentment against the capital, creating what are called **center-periphery tensions**. Often an outlying region was conquered or forcibly assimilated into the nation and has never been happy about it. Regional memories can last for centuries. This is true of the south of the United States, France, and Italy, as well as all of Quebec and Scotland. Often the region feels economically disadvantaged by the central area. The region may have a different language, as in Spain's Catalonia and the Basque country, Wallonia in Belgium (the French-speaking south), Quebec, Slovenia in ex-Yugoslavia, and several parts of India.

Once a region gets set in its politics, it stays that way for a long time. Region plays a big role in the politics of Britain, France, Germany, and the United States.

---

noneconomic issues   Questions relating to patriotism, religion, race, sexuality, and personal choice.

economic issues   Questions relating to jobs, income, taxes, and welfare benefits.

regions   Portions of a country with a sense of self and sometimes subcultural differences.

center-periphery tensions   Resentment by outlying regions of rule by the nation's core area and/or capital.

Most "sunbelt" states in the U.S. South and West (but not California) are conservative on both economic and noneconomic issues and jealous of states' rights. The "frostbelt" of northern and eastern states, where industry has declined, tends to be liberal, especially on questions of government spending programs. In 2001, when President Bush cut taxes, some conservative, southern Democrats supported him, and some liberal, northern Republicans opposed him, illustrating the effects of region on U.S. politics. In the United States, region can trump party, as we saw with the departure of Vermont Sen. Jim Jeffords from the Republicans in 2001.

RELIGION

Religion is often the most explosive issue in politics and contributes a great deal to the structuring of opinion. Religion can mean either denomination or religiosity. In Germany, Catholics tend to vote Christian Democrat, Protestants Social Democrat. In Germany, it is a question of denomination. In France, where most citizens were baptized Catholic, it is a question of religiosity, as most French are indifferent to religion. The more often a French person goes to Mass, the more likely he or she is to vote for a conservative party. Few Communist voters are practicing Catholics. In Poland, the Roman Catholic Church encouraged Poles to oust the Communist regime and support pro-Church parties. One of the biggest divisions in Catholic countries is between clericalists and **anticlericalists**. France, Italy, and Spain have long been split over this issue, with the conservative parties pro-Church and the parties of the left hostile to church influence.

Religion plays a great role in the United States, where Protestants tend to vote Republican. Religion overlaps with ethnicity. Catholics, especially Polish Catholics, were once among the most loyal Democrats of all. In the great immigrations of a century ago, big-city Democratic machines welcomed and helped immigrants from Catholic countries, and their descendants stayed mostly Democratic, a connection that eroded as the Democratic party endorsed "pro-choice" positions. For a long time it was believed that no Catholic could be elected president of the United States; John F. Kennedy in 1960 put that view to rest. In 2004, however, Catholic John F. Kerry lost many Catholic votes when the clergy denounced him for being pro-choice. Many Catholics and fundamentalist Protestants now have a common cause in fighting abortion. The 2000 vice-presidential candidacy of Sen. Joseph Lieberman (D-Conn.), an observant Jew, aroused little attention or opposition, a measure of the increased tolerance of Americans.

The rise of the "religious right" in the 1980s was important to U.S. politics. Roughly one American in seven can be counted as religious right, and fundamentalist groups became highly political. Ministers such as Jerry Falwell mobilized their television flocks against pornography, abortion, and gay rights and for the Republican party. Bush 43, himself an evangelical, connected closely to them. The Christian Coalition is a major conservative force inside the Republican party.

---

anticlericalism   Movement in Catholic countries to get Church out of politics.

American candidates, especially for the presidency, like to be known as church-goers, but since the rise of fundamentalism many also wish to be known as "born-again" Christians. Jimmy Carter, Ronald Reagan and both Bushes claimed to have been born again in Christ. Former Senator Eugene McCarthy, who tried for the Democratic nomination in 1968, reflected that he was the last presidential contender who had been born only once. Bill and Hillary Clinton attended church most Sundays with the president clutching a family bible. There are few avowed atheists in U.S. politics.

AGE

There are two theories on how age impacts political opinions, the **life cycle** and generation theories. The first, widely accepted, holds that people change as they age. Thus young people are naturally radical and older people moderate or even conservative. With few responsibilities, young people can be idealistic and rebellious, but with the burdens of home, job, and children of their own, people tend to become conservative.

This life-cycle theory does not always work because sometimes whole generations are marked for life by the great events of their young adulthood. Survivors of wars and depressions remember them for decades, and they color their views on war, economics, and politics. Sociologist Karl Mannheim called this phenomenon **political generations**. Many who lived through the Vietnam War were instinctively critical about U.S. troops in Iraq. Those who personally experienced the Depression of the 1930s were more supportive of federal welfare measures than younger people who had been raised in postwar prosperity. In the 2004 elections, those 75 and older were the strongest age group for Kerry, who vowed to maintain their Social Security and Medicare. Age does not necessarily make you conservative.

GENDER

Even before the women's movement, gender made a difference in politics. Traditionally, and especially in Catholic areas, women were more conservative, more concerned with home, family, and morality. This still applies in Catholic Spain and Portugal. But as a society modernizes, men's and women's views change. Women leave home to work, become more aware of social and economic problems, and do not necessarily adopt their husbands' political views. In the United States, an interesting **gender gap** appeared in the 1980s as women became several percentage points more liberal and Democratic than men. And this was precisely because

---

life cycle   Theory that opinions change as people age.

political generations   Theory that great events of young adulthood permanently color political views.

gender gap   Tendency of American women to vote more Democratic than do men.

KEY CONCEPTS

CLASSIC OPINION CURVES

The ways people feel about issues are summarized statistically in curves that show the distribution of opinions on a range from one extreme position to the other. A matter on which there are few doubters shows opinions **skewed** to one side, a "J-curve." Few Americans, for example, did not wish to destroy Islamist terrorists after September 11 (see chart at top of right column).

On many issues, public opinion forms the familiar "bell-shaped curve" or **unimodal** distribution, which shows few people at the extremes and most in the moderate center. All industrialized democracies show ideological distributions with few extreme leftists or rightists and a big bulge in the center (see chart at middle of right column).

A third characteristic pattern is a **bimodal** distribution or "U-curve," where the extremes are bigger than the center. Catholic and Protestant opinion in Northern Ireland forms a U-curve, leading to decades of violent civil conflict (see chart at bottom of right column).

Bell-shaped opinion curves are the basis of democracy. If many citizens take extreme positions and form a U-curve, the political system is breaking down. This can lead to extremist takeovers as in Germany in 1933, to civil war as in Spain in 1936, or to military coup as in Chile in 1973. Almost all democratic countries have unimodal distributions of opinion on basic issues; that is, people cluster in the center. Democracy is a centrist thing.

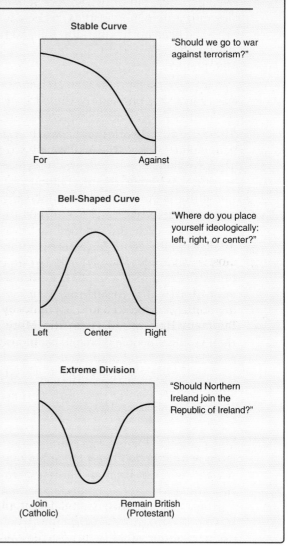

Stable Curve

"Should we go to war against terrorism?"

For   Against

Bell-Shaped Curve

"Where do you place yourself ideologically: left, right, or center?"

Left   Center   Right

Extreme Division

"Should Northern Ireland join the Republic of Ireland?"

Join   Remain British
(Catholic)   (Protestant)

---

skewed   A distribution with its peak well to one side.

unimodal   A single, center-peaked distribution, a bell-shaped curve.

bimodal   A distribution with two large clusters at the extremes and a small center.

women had found the federal government necessary to support home and family. Further, many women disliked the Republican emphasis on war. In 1996 and 2000, women were about 11 percentage points more likely to vote Democrat for president than were men (declining to 4 percentage points in 2004). It may be that in the modern political world, women will be the natural liberals.

ETHNIC GROUP

Ethnicity is related to region and religion but sometimes plays a distinct role of its own, especially in the multiethnic United States, where some ethnic groups form political subcultures (see previous chapter). America was long touted as a "melting pot" of immigrant groups, but ethnic consciousness lasts many generations. American politics is often described in ethnic terms, with WASPs (white Anglo-Saxon Protestants) and other northern Europeans generally conservative and Republican, and people of southern and eastern European origin, blacks, Hispanics, and Asian Americans more liberal and Democratic. This sometimes oversimplifies the complexity of individuals and of politics, but some working politicians still use it as a guide.

Ethnic politics changes over the decades. After the Civil War, most blacks were Republican, the party of Lincoln. With Franklin D. Roosevelt and the New Deal, most African Americans became Democrats and stayed that way. In the nineteenth century, American Jews were mostly Republican, for the Republicans criticized the anti-Semitic repression of tsarist Russia. The Jewish immigrants of the turn of the century, introduced to U.S. politics by Democratic machines such as New York's Tammany Hall, went Democratic. More recently, many Jews, influenced by neo-conservatism (see Chapter 6), swung to the Republicans. Ethnic politics is not fixed in concrete.

■ PUBLIC OPINION POLLS

People can be for, against, or undecided about an issue. But the factors of uncertainty and changeability are so prominent in many areas that we cannot always be confident that the polls tell us a dependable story when they report percent for and against.

Often opinion distribution does not fall into well-defined patterns, mainly because most people most of the time pay little attention to politics. They have weak interest in issues that do not directly touch their lives and acquire no information about most issues. Most surveys, for example, find that nearly half of those questioned cannot name their representative in Congress.

Thus, on most issues, only a small portion of the total public is attentive enough to news reports and editorials to hold a clear opinion. And in many situations, a general public opinion curve will be a rather dim reflection of the opinion pattern within this "attentive public." With all of the uncertainties, personality quirks, and just plain ignorance involved in public opinion, how are surveys able to reflect an accurate picture of what people are thinking?

CASE STUDIES

A SHORT HISTORY OF POLLING

In 1824, the *Harrisburg Pennsylvanian* asked passersby whether they would vote for John Quincy Adams or Andrew Jackson. The tally was printed on the theory that these "straws in the wind" foresaw the election results. Many other newspapers, using a variety of both careful and haphazard methods, conducted "straw polls" in various elections thereafter. The popular magazine *Literary Digest* developed a prestigious survey that predicted the 1924, 1928, and 1932 presidential elections. The *Literary Digest,* using a huge sample on the theory that it was more reliable, mailed questionnaires to nearly 10 million of its subscribers, car owners, and people in phone books. In 1936, the magazine predicted Republican Alfred M. Landon would win with 59.1 percent of the vote. Roosevelt's landslide—with over 60 percent of the vote—signaled the demise of both casual methods of sampling and of *Literary Digest* itself.

But 1936 was also the first year of the newly developed "scientific polling," a branch of another new field, market research. George H. Gallup's survey results, syndicated in newspapers, forecast Roosevelt's victory. Gallup predicted that the *Digest* poll was far off because its sample was drawn heavily from higher-income people, many of whom were angered by Roosevelt's social and economic policies. The new technique used by Gallup was to select a **sample** as *representative*, rather than as large, as possible.

This scientific sampling method has dominated the field since then, with a generally successful record. But even it failed in the 1948 election, when almost every poll predicted that Thomas E. Dewey would defeat Harry S. Truman by a landslide. Truman won with 49 percent in a four-way contest. The error was in assuming that respondents who said they were undecided would wind up voting in the same ratio as those who had made up their minds. In fact, the undecideds went much more heavily for Truman—close to 75 percent. The major polls have further refined their methods since that time and today make special efforts to detect late swings to one candidate or the other. They do not claim to be able to predict divisions within closer than 2 to 3 percentage points. The margin of victory in several presidential elections has been less than 1 percent, so polls cannot confidently predict close elections. Elections such as those of 2000 are called "too close to call."

Any effort to gauge the attitude of the public by means of a representative sample is called a **survey**. Published polls, particularly in election years, are carefully watched. Almost daily we see statistics and percentages on what Americans think of war, unemployment, abortion, and candidates. This is useful for policymakers and candidates. But debate has developed over some of their political side effects. For example, do the polls give undue attention and influence to uncertain opinions? Do journalists create self-fulfilling prophecies by treating the polls as authoritative verdicts, which people read about and then follow? And should public-opinion surveys be treated, as some propose, as a fair and democratic method of deciding public policies? Are polls reliable enough to determine policy? Who uses surveys, what purpose do they serve, and can we trust them?

---

sample   Those persons to be interviewed in a survey, a small fraction of a population.
survey   A public-opinion poll.

POLLING TECHNIQUES

How can a sample of 1,000 people depict the opinions of two hundred million? The answer is complex, but it revolves around a technique that can be summarized as follows.

Selecting the Sample   In deciding whom to sample, the pollster has two major approaches. One, the stratified-**quota** sampling, tries to include a proportionally representative cross section of the society. This is very difficult to carry out because interviewers must question precisely *x* number of blue-collar workers, *y* number of older women, and *z* number of Republicans. If they query too many or too few of various groups, they lose proportionality.

The second major approach is a random sample with no picking and choosing among dozens of categories. In a truly random sample, the number of blue-collar workers (or any other category) interviewed will be very close to their percentage of the population. **Randomization**, aided now by computers, produces more dependable results than the quota system.

The method most often used, "area sampling," has one hundred to two hundred regular interviewers in different areas around the country each interview fifteen to twenty persons in a designated locality. The sample, which is both random and highly representative, involves selecting which geographic districts to sample, their population characteristics, and random selection of which people to question from various categories. The resulting sample is quite close to that which a completely random selection would obtain and is considerably less expensive.

Reaching the Sample   Polling is expensive, and pollsters try to economize. Unfortunately, the least expensive methods tend to be the least accurate. The cheapest is to mail out ballots to a sample, but people who are involved enough to reply will not be representative, the *Literary Digest* error. Telephone polling tries to avoid this problem, but it rarely establishes rapport to obtain candid replies. For telephone surveys, a computer actually dials the numbers nationwide at random, even unlisted ones. There are at least two problems with this method: (1) Many people ignore telephone solicitations; and (2) women, old, and unemployed people are the most likely to be home, making the sample nonrandom. The most dependable method is still the costly face-to-face interview, which requires interviewers to be carefully selected and trained. To cover costs, political questions are often appended to commercial or product questions: "Do you eat Krunchy Flakes?"

Asking the Questions   The unbiased wording of questions to avoid slanting responses is also important. In 1999, for example, a Washington Post/ABC poll asked half its sample whether President Clinton should resign if impeached or "fight the charges in the Senate." Fifty-nine percent said resign rather than fight. The other half was asked essentially the same question but worded with

---

quota   Drawing a sample to match categories of the population.
randomization   Drawing a sample at random, with everyone having an equal chance of inclusion.

HOW TO . . .

VARIABLES

A variable is a factor that varies; it shows some change. If you can, you like to quantify these factors. Variables come in two basic types, **independent** and **dependent**. The former is what you think influences or perhaps causes the change, but you cannot always be sure. You might hypothesize, for example, that increases in a country's per capita GDP lead it to democracy. The per cap is your independent variable, and democracy is your dependent variable, the one that literally depends on the impact of the other variable.

You might switch the two and make democracy your independent variable to see how it impacts on wealth. Causality is hard to prove, and the causal flow can go both ways. Some argue that democracy promotes prosperity. In some cases, of course, causality can flow only one way. We can posit "white Protestant male" as the independent variable causing a Republican vote, but we cannot say that voting Republican will turn people into white Protestant males.

If you have two variables with reliable numbers to measure them, you can follow them over time and put two lines on the same graph or colors on a map to show positive **covariance**—as one changes, so does the other—which may go a long way to supporting your thesis. Sometimes you see negative or inverse covariance—as one goes up, the other goes down—but this may still prove your thesis. If there is little or no covariance—if the two lines on a graph wobble around with no relation to each other—you should go back and change your thesis. Sometimes covariance happens with a time lag, giving you a more interesting thesis. For example, the president makes foreign-policy decisions, but public opinion reacts to them about six months later.

---

the alternative of resign or "remain in office and face trial in the Senate." To this, only 43 percent said resign. A slight difference in wording—"fight" sounds nastier than "face trial"—greatly shifted responses. In 1992, answers to a badly worded question (it had a double negative) suggested that one in five Americans doubted the Nazi Holocaust had really happened. When the question was worded clearly in 1994, only 2 percent denied the Holocaust had happened. The pollster must also avoid tones of voice or sympathetic looks that might encourage one response over another and skew the results.

HOW RELIABLE ARE THE POLLS?

Public-opinion surveys are generally reliable, providing we recognize their limits. Overall, the U.S. opinion-research business takes in several billion dollars a year, and candidates commission thousands of private polls in primary and general elections. Unpredictability of voter turnout is a major limitation of pre-election polls. Many respondents who say they intend to vote actually do not. These voters and the undecideds are likely not to divide the same way as those who do vote and those

---

independent variable   The factor you think influences or causes something to happen.

dependent variable   The factor that changes under the impact of the *independent variable*.

covariance   How much two factors change together, indicating how strongly they are related.

already decided. This underlay the mistaken predictions of Truman's defeat in 1948. A heavy turnout may shift election results. Pollsters must adjust raw findings for this factor, but no one can be certain of how high turnout will be or the effects of events such as weather or terrorist strikes.

Public opinion is **volatile**, able to change quickly under the impact of events. In 1965, as Lyndon Johnson escalated the war in Vietnam, an aide told him that "we have overwhelming public opinion on our side." Johnson, a crafty political pro who closely followed the polls, replied, "Yes, but for a very underwhelming period of time." He was right; two-thirds support for the war in 1965 turned into two-thirds opposition in 1968. Majority support for the war in Iraq in 2003 turned negative in 2004. Nothing is permanent in public opinion; change is the norm.

A new problem calls into question all telephone surveys: the high "no response" rate. Americans, harassed by telemarketers, decline or just hang up on callers asking anything. Some estimate that telephone response rates have fallen to around 50 percent. If only half respond, the survey is likely not random or representative. This may be the main reason the surveys done for the 2000 and 2004 elections differed from one another and did not predict well. Surveys over the Internet have the same problem, because respondents are "self-selected" and of above-average income and education. Any survey that records only those who want to participate is invalid.

■ AMERICAN OPINION

PRESIDENTIAL RATINGS

One of the oldest and most important items in U.S. public-opinion polls asks how the president is handling his job, not how much the respondent likes the president. In practice, however, the respondent who likes the president will approve of the president's job performance, so the term "popularity" is often used for this poll. The correct terms are "support" or "approval."

Typically, presidents start with high support and then decline. During their first year they enjoy a **honeymoon** with the press and the public. The high point of their support often comes early in their term of office. After some years, however, problems accumulate—the economy sours or foreign policies fail. This brings a popularity low point. Presidents seldom leave office as popular as they were during their first year.

When a president comes under intense pressure or takes a major action, his support enjoys a temporary upturn. Americans rally to a president who faces a difficult decision, and they like decisive responses. Political scientist John Mueller called these **rally events**. President Carter gained 13 percentage points over the

---

volatility   Tendency of public opinion to change quickly.

honeymoon   High support for presidents early in their terms.

rally event   Occurrence that temporarily boosts president's support.

seizure of American hostages in Iran, but he was soon blamed for helplessness and lost reelection the next year. Bush 41 enjoyed an 18-point gain when he began the Gulf war in 1991, but he lost reelection a year and a half later, the casualty of a lingering recession. Bush 43 gained a massive 35 percentage points after 9/11, support that continued through the U.S. conquest of Iraq in 2003 but weakened as chaos in Iraq continued. No rally event has lasted a year.

Some suspect that presidents, especially later in their terms of office, deliberately try to appear decisive in a dramatic way to boost their sagging popularity. Foreign policy provides the natural arena for such dramatic moves and (as we will consider in the next chapter) the best television coverage. A meeting with foreign leaders, a bold strike against terrorists, or the rescue of American hostages provides a welcome lift in support for a president. The highest support ratings of Presidents Truman, Kennedy, Nixon, Carter, Reagan, and both Bushes came with a dramatic foreign-policy event. Even a failure, the 1961 Bay of Pigs invasion to overthrow Castro, rallied Americans around President Kennedy. When a humiliating situation lasts a long time, however, presidential popularity sinks, as Carter and Reagan both found in dealing with Iran. Similarly, a war that drags on a long time destroys popularity; Truman experienced this in Korea, Johnson in Vietnam, and Bush 43 in Iraq. Economic recession is also bad for popularity; four Republican presidents (Eisenhower, Ford, Reagan, and the first Bush) were rated low during economic downturns. A good economy is great for presidents; Clinton's approval stayed high in the prosperous late 1990s, even during his impeachment.

Presidential approval based on one situation tends to spill over into other areas of presidential activity. As might be expected, President Reagan's support jumped several points in the wake of the successful 1983 U.S. takeover of Communist Grenada and the rescue of American students there. At that same time, approval of Reagan's economic policies also climbed, although little in the economy had actually changed.

LIBERALS AND CONSERVATIVES

Republican presidents do not necessarily mean Americans have become more conservative. For decades, about twice as many Americans have been calling themselves conservative as call themselves liberal, but many still call themselves moderates. Such unimodal distributions—variations on a bell-shaped curve—are standard in all industrialized democracies, a fact that makes democracy possible. During the Reagan and Bush (both 41 and 43) years, the percentage of Americans identifying themselves as conservatives increased little, and more Americans expressed support for environmental and welfare legislation, typically liberal causes. The percentage who think the poverty programs of the 1960s—one of the Republicans' favorite targets—make things better is stable. Americans may like Republican presidents and even call themselves conservative, but they have not repudiated the moderate welfare state.

To explain this seeming inconsistency we return to the difference between economic and noneconomic liberalism discussed earlier. Americans are not very clear about what they mean by "liberal" or "conservative." All retired people, for example, support Social Security and Medicare—the programs of economic liberals—but many call themselves conservatives because they like traditional values. They use "conservative" in the noneconomic sense. On economic issues, however, such as federal aid for prescription drugs, they (often unwittingly) assume ultra-liberal positions. The problem is self-identification, which often diverges from people's views on specific issues. People who say they are conservative—because where they live it is fashionable to do so—may actually be economic liberals when it comes to getting more federal dollars for themselves.

WHO PAYS ATTENTION?

Public opinion is fragmented; groups are interested in different questions. Farmers are concerned about produce prices, steel and auto workers about imports, women about wage equality, and minorities about job opportunities. In 1998, for example, amid news of a federal budget surplus, younger people said spend it on education and other social problems, and older people said spend it to fix Social Security, but few wanted a tax cut. A time when some groups are satisfied may be a time when others are dissatisfied. Blacks and poor people did not much notice the good economic times of the late 1990s; better-off Americans praised the economy.

The **attentive public** (see box on page 148), although fewer in number, has more political impact because they have ideas and articulate them, demonstrating political competence. Sometimes they can rouse the general public. Opposition to the Vietnam and Iraq wars and to South Africa's apartheid started with a few critics who wrote and spoke in churches, newspapers, and classrooms. In the early 1990s, while few people were paying attention, some of the attentive public were raising questions about atrocities in the Balkans and Africa. The attentive public can act as "spark plugs" for the apathetic and slow-reacting general public. This is why all regimes treat intellectuals with caution and sometimes with suspicion. Communist regimes expended great effort to ferret out a handful of dissident intellectuals. In Washington, administration officials devote much time and energy to win over the attentive public to minimize criticism that might influence the general public and the next election. As we will consider in Chapter 9, relations between the White House and the news media often resemble a cat-and-mouse game. Political elites, aware of the ignorance and low interest of the general public, may convince themselves to not pay much attention to public opinion. A 1998 Pew study found that members of Congress, presidential appointees, and senior civil servants believed most Americans do not know enough to form sound opinions on vital issues of the day. Elites, in other words, believe elites have to decide many questions because they are the only ones following them. Unfortunately for democracy, they may be right.

The general public's indifference and fragmentation mean that their views are often hard to discern and may have little impact on decision making. Elected leaders are apt to pay attention to the group with the most intensely held views.

---

attentive public   Those citizens who follow politics, especially national and international affairs.

CLASSIC WORKS

ALMOND'S THREE PUBLICS

In his 1950 *The American People and Foreign Policy,* political scientist Gabriel Almond proposed that there were three American public opinions, not just one:

1. A *general public* of a majority that does not know or care about much beyond their immediate concerns. For example, they show little interest in foreign policy unless the country is in a war or international crisis.
2. An *attentive public* of a minority who are among the better-educated and who follow more abstract political concerns, such as foreign policy. They are the audience the elite plays to; and, in turn, this attentive public passes on views that mobilize the general public.
3. A *policy and opinion elite* of a few highly influential people who are involved in politics, often professionally. These members of Congress, appointed officials, and top journalists devise foreign and domestic policies and articulate them to the attentive and general publics.

Especially regarding foreign affairs, Almond makes a strong case. The number of Americans who follow the news is decreasing, and surveys show ignorance of world affairs. Attentive and elite opinion—such as business, media, and religious leaders and academics—favored NAFTA, trade expansion, and U.S. missions in the Balkans far more than did the general public.

Polls show that most Americans would permit abortion, but few strongly support it. The "pro-life" foes of abortion, although a minority nationwide, feel such great **intensity** about the subject that they often drown out the greater numbers who are not passionately concerned. Jews make up less than 3 percent of the U.S. population, but among them are such intense supporters of Israel that most elected officials take a pro-Israel stance. Most Americans favor some form of gun control, but they are mostly lukewarm about the issue. The opponents to gun control are red hot and thus quite influential. Intensely held views of a few often override large numbers of indifferent people.

The disproportionate influence of the attentive public and passionate opinion holders underscores one of the problems of public opinion. Often there is little "public" opinion, just the opinions of scattered and small groups who pay attention to issues and care intensely about them. Should their views be excluded as unrepresentative of the public, or should they take on added weight as the only people who really care about the issues? Which is the more democratic approach? Most people would be inclined to say democracy means going with the greatest numbers, even if their views are lukewarm. When it comes to a question that deeply concerns them, however, many people do not wish to have a simple head count, arguing that the majority view is ignorant or mistaken and should not be heeded. We will consider some of these questions when we discuss interest groups in Chapter 10.

---

intensity   The firmness and enthusiasm with which an opinion is held.

■ IS POLLING FAIR?

Polls do not merely monitor public opinion; they also help make it. Critics charge that published or broadcast poll results can distort an election. For example, the news media may highlight polls showing one candidate leading another by a wide margin. Such publicity, claim underdog candidates, devastate their campaigns by making supporters and contributors lose interest. Poor poll showings, especially early in the campaign, are a self-fulfilling prophecy of defeat for some candidates. Those who lead in the early polls get more donations, more news coverage, and thus more supporters.

One current controversy is the effect of "exit polls," in which voters are questioned just as they leave the balloting area. With the three-hour time difference between the East and West Coasts, exit polls enable television to predict winners in the East while westerners still have hours in which to cast a ballot. Does the early prediction in the East persuade westerners to not bother to vote? Even if the early prediction is accurate, what about the state and local candidates in the West who might have won if more people had voted? Some urge a delay in broadcasting the results of exit polls, which were unusually bad in 2000; the television networks predicted Gore's victory at first. No evidence has been found that exit polls influence the presidential vote, but they might influence other contests for the House, Senate, or state legislature. Polls, especially when broadcast so quickly, are not neutral in their impact, but no constitutionally legal way has been found to control them.

SHOULD AMERICA BE GOVERNED BY POLLS?

Considering the preceding discussion, it would seem in most cases that America should not be governed by polls. First, public attention varies widely. On many issues, the general public has no knowledge or opinion, which lets the intensity of a minority dominate poll results. Leaders, especially with modern means of communication, influence public opinion in their direction and encourage them to create the kind of feedback they want to hear. Typically, public opinion follows executive decisions.

The wording of the questions and the selection of the sample can seriously skew results. The survey must be done by reliable professionals with standardized questions and a random sample. Polls by partisans of a cause or a candidate can seriously mislead and should be ignored. The low rate of response to telephone surveys undermines their reliability. Equally serious is the problem of volatility. What the public likes one year it may dislike the next year. Decisions made on the basis of a survey may turn sour when the consequences sink in. Bush advisor Karl Rove thought that war with Iraq would play well with voters. It did, for a while. Top officials who "go with the polls" may be trapping themselves. Polls, if done well, are useful snapshots of public opinion at a given moment but are no substitute for careful analyses and prudent anticipation.

KEY TERMS

anecdotal (p. 134)

anticlericalism (p. 138)

attentive public (p. 147)

bimodal (p. 140)

center-periphery tensions (p. 137)

covariance (p. 144)

dependent variable (p. 144)

economic issues (p. 137)

gender gap (p. 139)

honeymoon (p. 145)

independent variable (p. 144)

intensity (p. 148)

life cycle (p. 139)

noneconomic issues (p. 137)

political generations (p. 139)

public opinion (p. 133)

quota (p. 143)

rally event (p. 145)

randomization (p. 143)

regions (p. 137)

salience (p. 135)

sample (p. 142)

skewed (p. 140)

social class (p. 136)

survey (p. 142)

unimodal (p. 140)

volatility (p. 145)

KEY WEB SITES

National Election Studies
www.umich.edu/~nes/

Votelink
www.votelink.com/

Gallup
www.gallup.com/poll

Polling Report
pollingreport.com

Quiz your political identity
www.self-gov.org/quiz.html

Internet in politics
www.polsci.ucsb.edu/~bimber/research/

Race and ethnicity
www.providence.edu/polisci/rep/

Rankings of surveys
www.ukans.edu/cwis/units/coms2/po/index.html

World issues
www.americans-world.org/

FURTHER REFERENCE

Alvarez, R. Michael, and John Brehm. *Hard Choices, Easy Answers: Values, Information, and American Public Opinion.* Princeton, NJ: Princeton University Press, 2002.

Aronowitz, Stanley. *How Class Works: Power and Social Movement.* New Haven, CT: Yale University Press, 2003.

Asher, Herbert. *Polling and the Public: What Every Citizen Should Know,* 6th ed. Washington, D.C.: CQ Press, 2004.

Dalton, Russell J. *Citizen Politics: Public Opinion and Political Parties in Advanced Industrial Democracies,* 3rd ed. New York: Chatham House, 2002.

Elazar, Daniel J. *The American Mosaic: The Impact of Space, Time, and Culture on American Politics.* Boulder, CO: Westview Press, 1994.

Lavrakas, Paul J., and Michael W. Traugott, eds. *Election Polls, the News Media, and Democracy.* New York: Chatham House, 2000.

MacManus, Susan A., with Patricia A. Turner. *Young v. Old: Generational Combat in the 21st Century.* Boulder, CO: Westview, 1996.

Mueller, John. *War, Presidents and Public Opinion.* New York: Wiley, 1973.

Sobel, Richard. *The Impact of Public Opinion on U.S. Foreign Policy Since Vietnam.* New York: Oxford University Press, 2001.

Stimson, James A. *Public Opinion in America: Moods, Cycles, and Swings.* Boulder, CO: Westview Press, 1991.

Stonecash, Jeffrey M. *Class and Party in American Politics.* Boulder, CO: Westview, 2000.

Wald, Kenneth D. *Religion and Politics in the United States.* Washington, D.C.: CQ Press, 1996.

Weissberg, Robert. *Polling, Policy, and Public Opinion: The Case Against Heeding the "Voice of the People."* New York: Palgrave, 2002.

POLITICAL COMMUNICATION AND THE MEDIA

CHAPTER

9

QUESTIONS TO CONSIDER

- How do mass media and face-to-face have different impacts?
- What journals constitute the "elite media"?
- Has the Web become an important medium? Will it?
- What are the weaknesses of television news coverage?
- Can money buy television time and hence buy elections?
- Has television created political apathy?
- Which country has the freest mass media?
- How can you stay well informed?
- Is it good that media and government are adversaries?

The **mass media** have always loomed large in American politics. In the 1780s, the *Federalist Papers* were published in daily newspapers throughout the colonies to win support for the new constitution. Andrew Jackson's victory in 1828 over John Quincy Adams marked one of the dirtiest "media campaigns" in America's history, in which some papers accused Jackson and his wife of moral irregularities. In 1904, Teddy Roosevelt was a "media candidate," who tailored his rough-and-ready image to win press coverage and the election. And Franklin D. Roosevelt used his famous "fireside chats" on radio, along with hundreds of press conferences, to win support for his policies. Today, the mass media are a recognized component of politics worldwide, and modern campaigns depend on television so much that many critics complain that candidates no longer run for office on issues; instead, professional marketing consultants package them and sell them like products.

---

mass media   Modern means of communication that reach very wide audiences. (Note that media is plural; singular is medium.)

■ COMMUNICATION IN POLITICS

Political scientists have long recognized the dependence of politics on communications. Karl W. Deutsch showed how modernization and nationalism can be measured from patterns and flow of mail, telephone calls, and newspapers. The political system and the communication system precisely parallel one another, and it is doubtful that one could exist without the other.

All political action is a reaction to communication of one kind or another. There are, however, different levels and types of communication. **Face-to-face** communication is the most basic and most effective for altering or reinforcing political opinions because it allows for dialogue where mass media cannot. Until the early 1930s, face-to-face communication was the main method of political campaigning. Candidates **stumped** (in the old days, many spoke from tree stumps) their districts and addressed small groups of voters, appealing for their support with the help of ward bosses, precinct captains, and political organizers. However, the rise of television and the complexity of modern society have today largely bypassed grassroots stumping, except as a means of getting free media coverage.

The mass media reach an infinitely larger audience, and therefore yield a greater voter or public-opinion return than face-to-face communication. A speech that gets on television can reach millions of people, but a speech at even the largest rally may be heard by only a few thousand. Even a small percentage of television viewers responding positively can yield tens of thousands of votes, perhaps enough to swing an election.

But the mass media are one-way communication. If viewers dislike the president, they can change channels. If they disagree with his message, he cannot counter with custom-made responses. Mass media generally reinforce existing political opinions but rarely convert anyone. Radio and television do have stronger persuasive power than the printed word because they mimic face-to-face communication, but their impact still depends partly on the influence of chats with friends afterwards.

Television may have eroded the role of opinion leaders as television newscasters become opinion leaders on a grand scale. Television not only transmits direct political messages but also indirectly changes society by bringing news and ideas into the homes of all. Most observers agree that the 1960s civil-rights movement would not have succeeded without television. Racial discrimination in the South was largely unnoticed—perhaps deliberately unnoticed—in the print media and radio. But television news showing fire hoses and police dogs attacking peaceful marchers turned most Americans in favor of equal rights for black people. Some believe that television coverage of the Vietnam war—the world's first television war—turned many against the war and against President Johnson. Photos of the mistreatment of Iraqi prisoners had a similar impact in 2004.

---

face-to-face   Pre-mass media communication by personal contact.
stump   Verb, to campaign by personally speaking to audiences.

CLASSIC WORKS

THE TWO-STEP FLOW OF MASS COMMUNICATIONS

How do the mass media penetrate an audience? Paul Lazarsfeld and Elihu Katz were among the first to perceive a two-step pattern in this process. They found that every community has respected **opinion leaders**—teachers, ministers, community and civic leaders, outstanding business and professional persons—what Almond called the "attentive public" (see Chapter 8). These people get political ideas from the mass media and pass them on to their less-attentive friends in normal daily contact. Mass-media effectiveness depends on these opinion leaders, and it is they whom successful politicians must reach, influence, and convince. The few influence the many.

Fewer Americans are interested in news than they were one and especially two generations ago. Fewer watch television news or read a newspaper. And news is shifting from politics and world affairs to human interest and "news you can use" about health, business, and lifestyles. This shift parallels the decline in Americans' interest in politics in general, confirming the close connection between communications and politics. The causes of this decline are debated. Some see a shift in values, especially among a new and **introspective** generation addicted to entertainment. Only terrorist attacks, involvement in war, or high gasoline prices can jolt them into paying attention to the real world.

The various modern media appeal to different audiences who can be distinguished by education, income, and age. The more educated individuals are, the more media they consume. College graduates and better-off people tend to read newspapers, magazines, and books as well as follow radio and television. But grammar and high-school graduates, who use the mass media largely for entertainment, favor television and motion pictures more than the print media. Ninety percent of the people in high-income brackets are regular magazine and book readers, but only half of low-income people are.

Age also affects mass-media usage. People between the ages of thirty and fifty pay far more attention to the editorial and news content of newspapers and magazines than do teenagers and young adults, who tend to use newspapers for entertainment. Young readers follow sports, rock stars, and feature articles rather than hard news. The college student who keeps up on the news and editorial opinion is rare.

MODERN MASS MEDIA

Newspapers In 1910, the United States had more than 2,600 daily newspapers, and 57 percent of all American cities had two or more competing papers. Today, about half that number remain, and few U.S. cities have two separately

---

opinion leaders Locally respected people who influence the views of others.
introspective Looking within oneself.

KEY CONCEPTS

THE TENDENCY TO MEDIA MONOPOLY

If many competing media voices are good, America has some concerns, for media ownership has moved toward **oligopoly**. Some twenty corporations control most of what Americans read, hear, and view, as they own newspapers and radio and television stations. The five biggest:

Murdoch, an Australian-born press baron, owns FoxTV, HarperCollins (books), the *Weekly Standard* (influential neocon magazine), the *New York Post*, the *London Times*, and DirecTV.

General Electric owns NBC and Universal-Vivendi, itself a major conglomerate.

Time-Warner was the merger of a big magazine publisher and major studio that now includes CNN and AOL.

Disney owns ABC and ESPN.

Comcast, the biggest cable company, has tried to take over Disney.

Clear Channel owns a large fraction of U.S. radio stations and programs them centrally, eliminating local content.

What happens to free speech and multiple sources of information? Media critics worry that we receive bland uniformity and unquestioning acceptance of White House pronouncements. The president says it, so it must be true. Some feel there is still adequate diversity and criticism, now bolstered by the Internet with its innumerable sources and viewpoints. The Federal Communications Commission is supposed to guard against oligopoly but in recent years has seen no problem with bigness and fewness.

owned daily papers. Does this decline in competition mean that citizens do not get a variety of political and editorial opinion? The "free press" is also a business. Big corporations, seeking profits and not controversy, own some 75 percent of U.S. newspapers, giving them a **status-quo** orientation. Few newspapers present the news in an obviously partisan manner, for both practical and idealistic reasons. Most newspaper revenue comes from advertising, and ad rates depend on the papers' circulation. Thus high circulation is the main concern, which usually leads to a middle-of-the-road news policy that is calculated to not antagonize and that makes newspapers bland.

Journalism has a long tradition of objectivity in news reporting (not so the editorial page). The profession's own standards influence newspeople to present the news fairly and honestly. Further, most news in U.S. newspapers is from a service, The Associated Press, which takes special pains to be objective and to refrain from editorializing.

How much political impact, then, do U.S. newspapers have? Not as much as they used to. Fewer households take newspapers now than half a century ago,

---

oligopoly   Market dominated by a few big firms.
status quo   Keeping the present situation.

KEY CONCEPTS

THE ELITE MEDIA

The *New York Times,* the *Washington Post,* and the *Wall Street Journal* are read by a small fraction of the U.S. population, but they carry by far the most clout. Decision makers in Washington and indeed across the country read them and take both their news stories and their editorials seriously. Leading thinkers fight battles on their "op-ed" pages (opposite the editorial page) or in their letters to the editor. That is why these papers have influence out of all proportion to their circulation. They are the **elite media** because the people who read them are generally wealthier and better educated and have more influence than readers of hometown papers.

The elite press pursues "investigative reporting," looking for government and partisan wrongdoing, something the average paper usually shuns. The *New York Times* jolted the nation when it published the Pentagon Papers on the Vietnam War in 1971. The dogged pursuit of the 1972 Watergate burglary by the *Washington Post* brought down the Nixon administration in 1974. The editorials of the *Wall Street Journal* influence economic decisions in Washington.

Some small-circulation magazines of opinion are also among the elite press. The conservative *National Review,* the liberal *New Republic,* the leftist *Nation,* and the neoconservative *Commentary* have considerable impact on opinion leaders, the sorts of people who influence others. President Reagan named Jeane Kirkpatrick ambassador to the United Nations on the strength of an article of hers that he had read in *Commentary.* Students often ignore the elite press, but those who aspire to leadership should follow one or more of these journals.

and fewer than half of adult Americans read a daily paper. One limiting factor: Americans, raised on television, do not read much. The content of newspapers is mostly advertisements (one important reason people read them) and wire-service copy. The editorials of most newspapers carry little weight. The exceptions are the "elite" media.

Radio   Like newspapers, radio is not what it used to be. Now three companies own half of America's radio stations. Clear Channel Communications alone controls more than 1,200 stations, programmed from its headquarters with homogenized news and no local content, not even tornado warnings. Between the two world wars, however, radio was popular, and radio news, comments, and political addresses—such as Franklin D. Roosevelt's famous "fireside chats," which served as models for both Jimmy Carter and Ronald Reagan—were quite influential. With the rise of television in the 1950s, radio became less important, with two exceptions. Popular "talk radio" shows, often hosted by angry right-wingers, reinforce conservative views. Reinforcing liberal views, the radio magazine "All Things Considered" on National Public Radio offers world events, economics, politics, and critical opinions.

---

elite media   Highly influential newspapers and magazines read by elites and the attentive public.

The News Services   Most hard news in newspapers and on radio, and even a good deal of television's news, is not produced in-house but comes from a printer hooked up to the New York offices of The Associated Press (AP), hence the old-fashioned name **wire service**. The elite newspapers disdain wire-service copy, as it is a matter of pride for them to have their own reporters cover the story. But most papers in America are little more than local outlets for The Associated Press, which provides them with photos, sports coverage, even recipes, as well as news. Often, editors on small-town papers read just the first two paragraphs, so that they can write a headline, and slap the stories into their papers nearly at random.

The AP is a cooperative, with members paying assessments based on their circulation. They also contribute copies of local stories to the AP, which may rewrite them for nationwide transmission. The AP is one of the few news services not owned, subsidized, controlled, or supervised by a government. It is free of government influence and proud of it. Britain's Reuters gets discreet government subsidies; France's AFP has government supervision, as does Germany's DPA; and China's Xin Hua is wholly a creature of Beijing. United Press International (UPI) used to compete with AP, but now Rev. Sun Myung Moon, a conservative and eccentric Korean millionaire, owns UPI, which is a shadow of its former self.

No government controls the AP, but it has other problems that limit its quality and influence. First, it moves fast; every minute is a deadline. This means it does no digging; its stories are superficial. Second, the wire services' definition of news is something from an official **source**. Wire-service stories are carefully attributed to police, the White House, the State Department or Pentagon, and so on. If it's not official, it's not news. This causes the wire services to miss many explosive situations in the world because they do not report on opposition people, average citizens in the street, or merchants in the bazaar, who might have a completely different—and sometimes more accurate—perspective than official spokespersons. The American news media failed to notice the coming of the Iranian revolution for this reason. Often the best news stories are not about a key event or statement but about what people are saying and thinking, which is rarely covered.

■ THE GIANT: TELEVISION

When Americans say "the media," they mean television, for television towers over everything else in terms of impact. Some 90 percent of Americans get their news from television—more from cable channels than from broadcast networks nowadays—and most accord it higher credibility than newspapers. Television has touched and changed almost everything in U.S. politics. Election campaigns now revolve around the acquisition of television time; winners are usually those who

---

wire service   News agency that sells to all media.
source   Who or where a news reporter gets information from.

KEY CONCEPTS

THE WEB: NEWEST MASS MEDIUM?

The political impact of the Internet is not yet clear. You can look up whatever you want on it—such as a candidate's proposals—but that often "preaches to the converted," to people who already like the candidate. Fewer Americans follow news on TV and in newspapers, but news on the Web has grown. Now over one-third of Americans go on-line for news at least once a week, and many do it daily. It is especially popular among the younger and better educated. The advantages of news on the Web: You can grab news any time and focus only on what interests you. Most prefer financial to political. Howard Dean's 2004 bid for the Democratic presidential nomination featured on-line fundraising for the first time. It was quite successful and was copied by John Kerry.

The Internet can cover stories the conventional media leave untouched and catch their errors and omissions. The on-line magazine *Salon* broke the story of Rev. Moon's coronation in the U.S. Capitol as the messiah. This jolted the conventional media into covering the embarrassing incident months later. Will the Web overall make well-informed citizens? Likely not. With the rise of "blogs" (short for Web logs), everyone can put out their own magazine, and tens of thousands do, most highly partisan. Most of the regular news on the net is simply digests of TV and newspapers, brief stories without depth or insight. (And you have to *read* it!) You can get all manner of detailed information on the Web, but you have to *want* to do it. You can read Japan's top daily at www.asahi.com/english, but how many will?

The Web may help overthrow undemocratic regimes. For the sake of economic growth, most countries allow the Web, but with the economic and technical come the political and critical, cracking the regime's information monopoly. With chat rooms come dissident chat. Iran and China censor their Web systems, just as they muzzle their conventional media, but it is harder when anyone with a computer and modem is a potential critical newspaper. This is not always positive. Because it is cheap, all manner of strange and unhealthy viewpoints can spread their poison on the net. Pornography, racism, and bomb-making are standard fare and impossible to control.

---

raise the most money to hire the best media consultants. Television has become a suspect in the decline of both U.S. election turnout and political parties. Some observers see television, which focuses on "sound bites" of a few seconds, as contributing to the trivialization of U.S. politics. Calm analysis is out; the catchy phrase is in.

TELEVISION NEWS

Television, by very definition, favors the visual. "Talking heads" provide no more news than does radio. (Talking heads do provide a sense of personality and hence credibility, an imitation face-to-face communication.) News producers therefore devote more attention to a news story with "good visuals" than without. As with the wire services, abstract, deeper topics go by with little coverage, but dramatic action—if there was a camera crew on hand to catch it—gets played up. Television, like most of the rest of the U.S. news media, ignored the hatred that was brewing against the shah of Iran for years but caught the dramatic return of the Ayatollah Khomeini.

AP photographer Eddie Adams snapped the summary execution of a captured Vietcong assassin in 1968. Adams later said he was sorry he took the history-making photo, which made the Vietcong look heroic. In truth, the Vietcong assassin had just murdered the family of one of the assistants to South Vietnam's police chief, who took speedy revenge. Images can mislead. (Eddie Adams, AP/Wide World Photos)

Television never did explain what the Vietnam War was about, but a brief film clip of a Saigon general shooting a Vietcong assassin in 1968 helped sicken Americans and turn them against the war. Just as the wire services are hooked on official sources, television news is hooked on the eye-catching. The 2004 Abu Ghraib photos underscored this. Television is inherently a more emotional medium than the others; its coverage can go straight to the heart, bypassing the brain altogether; that is its great power.

Unfortunately, television camera crews are expensive to maintain in the field, especially overseas, so they usually arrive where the action is only *after* having been notified by the wire services. Television needs to know in advance what's going to happen; then it can schedule a camera crew. This makes television news lopsided with press conferences, speeches, committee hearings, and official statements. Some critics characterize these happenings as **media events**, things that would not have occurred without television coverage. A media event is not fake, but it is planned in advance with an eye to catching TV coverage. Officials understand this, and so do protest groups, who stage marches, sit-ins, and mass arrests

media event   News happening planned to get media coverage.

Television cameras and reporters camped out in front of the D.C. federal court building awaiting the verdict in an important Microsoft antitrust case, news of which flashed around the world in minutes. (Michael Roskin)

to get television exposure for their cause. Chanted protesters at the 1968 Democratic convention in Chicago: "The whole world is watching!" The number of film clips of events that were obviously scheduled in advance greatly outnumber those that were not.

Deep analysis is also not television's strong point. An average news story runs one minute; a four-minute story is considered an in-depth report. Walter Cronkite, long the dean of television anchors, emphasized that television news was just a "headline service," meaning that if viewers wanted detail and depth they would have to go elsewhere. Many Americans, of course, look no deeper and are left with the tardy, the eye-catching, and the media event as their daily diet of information. Thus it is not surprising when polls repeatedly discover that Americans are poorly informed about the great issues of the day.

TELEVISION AND POLITICS

Television has changed politics in several ways. Incumbency, especially in the White House, has always brought recognition. Television has enhanced this recognition, but not always to the **incumbent's** satisfaction. Television news is heavily focused on the president and, to a lesser extent, on the rest of the executive

---

incumbent   Official who already occupies the office.

HOW TO . . .

DEFINITIONS

You must define the variables you use so clearly that neither you nor the reader can mistake them for anything else. This means deliberate narrowing. For example, it is difficult to use the term "democracy" in all the complexity of the description on pages 74–78. There are just too many things to keep track of. You would find countries have some of the characteristics but not all. A good definition allows you to easily put items into categories. You might define a flat or falling economy in presidential election years as "bad times" and see if incumbents lose.

Even something like "voting" needs to be narrowed. Do we mean voting in primary, local, presidential, or congressional elections? We cannot compare turnout in the 2004 presidential election with turnout in the congressional 2006 elections; presidential elections bring higher turnout. We must compare like elections, such as the presidential elections every four years.

Especially difficult are broad and unclear terms that carry emotional baggage, such as "isolationism." How would you demonstrate that senators of certain regions or parties are more isolationist? If you ask them, all will deny being isolationists, as the term connotes ignorance. You might come up with a narrower term, such as "non-interventionist," and define it as willingness to send U.S. troops overseas. Then, by surveying senators' voting records, you might discern patterns of noninterventionism.

branch. Congress gets much less coverage, the courts even less. This deepens a long-term American tendency to president-worship. The president—especially with the way television socializes small children—is seen as an omnipotent parental figure, a person who can fix all problems. That should make a president very happy. But then things go wrong; the president fails to fix the problems; ultracritical media imply he is making them worse. The flip side of being treated as all-powerful is catching all the blame. The media, especially television, whips up president-worship and then whips up mass dissatisfaction with the president's performance. Expectations, heightened by the media, are too high, and disappointments are correspondingly bitter. Some critics charge that the media are wrecking the U.S. political system with that kind of coverage, making the country unstable and ungovernable.

Nomination by Television   Television does much to nominate presidential candidates. With all eyes focused on the early presidential primaries—especially New Hampshire—commentators grandly proclaim who is the "real winner" and has "momentum." The candidate thus designated as front-runner goes into the remaining primaries and the national convention with a **bandwagon** effect, enhanced recognition, and lots of television coverage. In the nominating process,

---

bandwagon   Tendency of front-runners to gain additional supporters.

In the 1960 election campaign, Richard Nixon debated John Kennedy live and nationwide, a televised first. Kennedy's more relaxed performance helped him win. (UPI/Corbis/Bettmann)

television has become a kind of kingmaker. It is no wonder that candidates arrange their schedules and strategies to capture as much television exposure as possible.

Television coverage of candidates focuses on their personalities, not on issues. Television, with its sharp close-ups and seeming spontaneity, gives viewers what they think is a true glimpse of the candidate's character. Actually, this may not be so; some candidates play the medium like professionals (Ronald Reagan), and others tense up and hide their normal personalities (Robert Dole). How candidates perform on television is a poor indicator of how they will perform in office, but it is the one most American voters use.

While television is playing this major role in nominating and electing candidates, political parties are bypassed. Party organizations and bosses are no longer important, as candidates on television go right over their heads to the voters. Since the leading contender or two have already picked up their "momentum" going into the convention, they do not need party professionals to broker a nominating deal. Politics has come out of the proverbial smoke-filled back room and into the glare of television lights, not always for the better. The party and its chiefs used to know a thing or two about politics and were often capable of putting forward tried and tested candidates. With television, a candidate can come out of nearly nowhere and win the top national office with little political experience.

We must be careful, though, in blaming television for the weakening of the parties. American parties, with the exception of a few urban machines, were never as strongly organized as most European parties. Moreover, American parties began declining a long time ago, not just with the advent of television. Other factors, such as special-interest groups, political action committees, and direct-mail solicitation, have also undermined party strength. Television is not the sole culprit.

   Television and Apathy   Observers long suspected that television induces passivity and apathy. Harvard political scientist Robert D. Putnam (see his discussion of "bowling alone" on page 120) believes "the culprit is television." Reviewing possible causes of the decline of "civic engagement" in the United States, Putnam found older people, those born before World War II, are more trusting and more inclined to join groups and participate in politics. The reason: They were raised before the television age began in the 1950s. Younger people, raised on television, lack these qualities. Says Putnam: "Each hour spent viewing television is associated with less social trust and less group membership, while each hour reading a newspaper is associated with more."

   A related charge is that television has lowered election-day turnouts. There is a close coincidence in time; turnout dropped 13 percentage points from 1960, when television first established itself as the top means of campaigning, to 1988, then stayed at the same low level. Television saturates viewers so far in advance that they lose interest. The top two candidates usually sound so similar that many voters see little difference. Negative campaigning also disgusts many voters. Charges and countercharges in political spots come so thick and fast that the voter is **cross-pressured** into indecision and apathy. In Western Europe, where paid-for political television spots are generally prohibited and campaigns are much shorter—usually about a month instead of the year and more in the United States—voter turnout is higher. Only America does not regulate TV political ads.

   One thing U.S. television does for sure: It costs a bundle. Spending on political TV ads alone zoomed from $24.5 million in 1972 to $606 million in 2000. (Total spending on the 2004 U.S. elections: some $1 billion.) Depending on the time of day and locale, a one-minute spot can go for $100,000. The cost factor has transformed American politics. Members of Congress can sometimes get by with little television advertising, but virtually all senatorial and presidential candidates need it. About half of presidential campaign chests now go for television. Political consulting—the right themes, slogans, and speeches presented in scripted television spots—has become a big business. In most contests, the winner is the one who spent the most money, most of it on television. This heightens the importance of special-interest groups and political action committees, which in turn has weakened the role of the parties and perhaps deepened feelings of powerlessness among average voters.

   Many Americans ignore party labels, either calling themselves "independents," splitting tickets, or voting against their party registration. The trend, alarming to some political scientists, is called voter "dealignment," citizens *not* lining up with a party (explored in Chapter 12). Lacking party identification, these voters are

---

cross-pressured   Pulled between opposing political forces; said to produce apathy.

open to persuasion via the media, especially television. In 2004 most Americans believed that Bush had sent three million jobs overseas and that Kerry voted for higher taxes 350 times. Voters believed absurd TV ads.

TELEVISION: OWNERSHIP AND CONTROL

The U.S. government exercises the *least* control of communications of any industrialized country. Since the invention of the telegraph, the American government has stood back and let private industry operate communications for profit. In Europe, in contrast, telegraphy was soon taken over by the postal service, as were telephones. The U.S. government—partly because of First Amendment guarantees of free speech and partly because of the U.S. ethos of free enterprise—simply does not like to butt in. For European nations, with traditions of centralized power and government paternalism, national control of electronic communications is as normal as state ownership of the railroads. Now European TV is partly still state-run and partly private, and both of them face continual charges of politically partisan coverage.

The U.S. attitude of **nonpaternalism** has led to the freest airwaves in the world, but it has also brought some problems. With the rapid growth of radio in the 1920s, the **electromagnetic spectrum** was soon jammed with stations trying to drown each other out. To bring some order out of the chaos, the Radio Act of 1927 set up a five-member Federal Radio Commission (FRC) appointed by the president to assign frequencies, call letters, and maximum power. Stations had to get licenses and could lose them. Most important, the 1927 act put the government on record for the first time as recognizing that the airwaves were public property and should serve "the public interest, convenience and necessity." The Communications Act of 1934 superseded the FRC and created the Federal Communications Commission (FCC), which monitors broadcasting to this day. The 1934 act recognizes the danger of partisanship and now provides for five FCC commissioners appointed by the president and approved by the Senate. The commissioners serve staggered seven-year terms, and no more than three can be members of the same party.

The FCC does not supervise the content of programs, but it does have a political impact. Section 315 of the 1934 act, known as the "equal-time provision," tells broadcasters that if they give or sell air time to one candidate, they must do the same for others. Station owners, of course, don't like to give away air time. They also fear that public interest programs featuring the candidates of the two big parties will lead to a demand for equal time by minor or frivolous candidates. News broadcasts are exempt from the equal-time rule, so debates between the two leading presidential contenders are conducted by a panel of newspeople to get around the equal-time

---

nonpaternalism   Not taking a supervisory or guiding role.
electromagnetic spectrum   The airwaves over which signals are broadcast.

THE TELEVISION WASTELAND

In 1961 FCC Commissioner Newton Minow despaired that television was culturally a "vast waste-land," and the phrase stuck. In theory, the FCC licenses radio and television stations to serve "the public interest," but in practice no station has its license revoked for broadcasting junk. The FCC lays down no rules about program content except against obscenity on the air. (Cable, because it is not broadcast through the air, can use obscenities.) Programs can be as trashy or as lofty as the owners want. Most owners, in their appraisals of the audience, emphasize the former. The FCC claims it can do nothing to make programs more cultural, educational, or morally uplifting.

Most broadcasting in America is private and profit-oriented. Profits derive from advertising, which depends on audience size. Station owners argue that they automatically serve the public interest in offering the programs most people want. They are also, of course, serving their own interests. If most people in a given area want twenty-four hours of rock and roll, that must be the public interest. If most people like violent and sexy detective shows, television should provide them. Thus do self-interest and altruism happily merge.

Critics bemoan this kind of reasoning, pointing out that broadcasters are not merely *following* public tastes but *setting* them by offering only competing junk. One sitcom about adorable singles brings several; one "reality" show breeds another. Cable and public broadcasting offer some escape from junk. During the 1950s, noncommercial FM and television stations, financed by universities and community donations, began to offer programming at higher cultural and educational levels. The Ford Foundation and Congress added support. In 1967, Congress set up the Corporation for Public Broadcasting (CPB), with National Public Radio (NPR) and the Public Broadcasting Service (PBS) under it. Government funding of them has almost disappeared. This is as close as the United States has come to establishing a link between government and broadcasting, and it's not very close.

U.S. broadcast media are free but expensive. They are not under government control, but listeners and viewers pay a price in programming skewed to earn broadcasters the maximum amount of money. The price is junk programming that does indeed leave America culturally, educationally, and informationally underdeveloped.

provision. Broadcasters also dislike selling air time to candidates, for it must go at the lowest rate, which in turn must be offered to the opponents. Broadcasters long fought the equal-time provision.

Another FCC power, more vague than "equal time," is the "fairness doctrine" first published in 1949 by the commission. Recognizing that broadcast editorials are part of the public interest, the fairness doctrine requires broadcasters to offer air time for those with opposing views to respond. Enforcement, though, is left to the broadcasters, and many public-spirited interest groups feel that broadcasters simply try to avoid all controversy so that they will not have to make air time available to anyone. The Reagan-appointed members of the FCC abolished both the equal-time and fairness provisions, arguing that they tended to limit political debate on the airwaves.

■ Are We Poorly Served?

The U.S. mass media do not serve Americans very well. First, news coverage is highly selective, overconcentrating on some areas while ignoring others. This is called "structural bias." The president and staff occupy over half the news time given to the federal government. The president is inherently more dramatic and eye-catching than the other branches of government. Reporters, editors, and producers are afraid that if they devote more than a little time to Congress and the courts, readers and viewers will become bored. What the president does is also visually more exciting than what Congress or the courts do. The president gets in and out of helicopters, greets foreign leaders, travels overseas, or gets involved in scandals; all provide good television footage. Congress may get some attention when one of its committees faces a tense, controversial, or hostile witness. Then the committee members hurl accusatory questions, the witness stammers back denials, and sometimes shouting erupts. That's good drama; the rest of Congress is pretty dull. And the courts face the biggest obstacle of all: No cameras are allowed in most courtrooms. Accordingly, Americans grow up with the notion that the White House does most of the work and has most of the power, whereas Congress and the courts hardly matter.

Especially undercovered are the civil service and state governments. The myriad departments, agencies, and bureaus govern America, but bureaucrats give boring interviews and federal regulations are unintelligible. Still, many of next year's news stories are buried in the federal bureaucracy. What agency using what criteria allowed a nuclear power plant to operate? The media pay no attention until a Three Mile Island occurs. What department gave millions in contracts to presidential-campaign contributors? The wrongdoings of federally insured savings and loan associations went on for years unnoticed by the media. What federal agency decides whether commercial airlines have adequate safety standards? The news media rarely try to cover such things; they wait until something goes wrong and then evince shocked surprise. The very stuff of politics is there in the federal agencies, but few pay attention.

Coverage of state governments may be even worse. Much of the problem here is that there are national media—the big networks and elite newspapers—and there are local media—your town's local stations and paper. But there are no state media, partly because states are not "market areas" (population centers) that advertisers try to reach. Accordingly, outside of state capitals, there is little news about state politics, even important items.

On the world scene, the news media wait for something to blow up before they cover it. Except for the elite media, there is little background coverage of likely trouble spots. Thus, when terror hits America or an East Asian economy crashes, most Americans are surprised. They shouldn't be; even moderate news coverage of these threats over the years would have kept Americans informed about the increasing problems. But the U.S. media send few reporters overseas. Latin America, with all its implications for the United States, is largely uncovered.

We live in a revolutionary world, but the U.S. media pay little attention until the violence erupts. Providers of "good visuals" rather than analysis and early warning is the way they define their role, and this sets up Americans to become startled and confused.

The biggest problem with the U.S. media is that they do not try to give a coherent, comprehensive picture of what is happening in the world. Operating under tight deadlines, flashing the best action footage, and basing reports heavily on official sources, the media bombard us with many little stories but seldom weave them together into a big story. They give us only pieces of a jigsaw puzzle. Part of this problem is the nature of any news medium that comes out daily: Newspapers and television take events one day at a time. Such news is usually incomplete and often misleading. We see people shooting, but we do not know why. The media world is, in Shakespeare's phrase, "full of sound and fury, signifying nothing."

WHAT CAN BE DONE?

The mass media—except for the elite media—do not provide *meaning*. Some, such as the wire services, deliberately shun analysis and interpretation in their stories; that would be unobjective or editorializing. Reporters are typically unequipped to explain the historical background or long-term consequences of the stories they cover. Reporters are expected to be generalists, to be able to cover everything and anything. All you have to do is write down what the official source says. It is for this reason that editorials and columns of opinion often contain more "news" than the straight news stories, for the former set the news into a meaningful context, while the latter just give scattered bits and pieces. Unfortunately, most Americans make do with the bits and pieces as they make decisions on candidates, economic matters, and sending troops abroad.

Can anything be done? Professional newspeople generally agree that the public is ill-informed, and some will even admit that their coverage could be wider and deeper. But the limiting factor, they emphasize, is the public itself. Few people want to be well-informed, especially about things that are distant or complicated. Audience surveys find that people care least about foreign news and most about local news. Newspapers can go broke pushing world news; color photos and local human interest is what works. Few people are intellectuals and most dislike complicated, in-depth analyses. They notice the shooting but do not care about the reasons behind it. Do the media have any responsibility in educating the mass public so that citizens can comprehend our complicated world? Some idealists in the media do feel a responsibility, but these idealists are offset by the hardheaded business types, who have the last word. After a while, the idealists become cynical. We cannot expect any major improvements any time soon. For you, however, the student of political science who is already among the more attentive, the answer is the elite media. Use the mass media for sports coverage.

■ THE ADVERSARIES: MEDIA AND GOVERNMENT

The role of the press as critic in a democracy has long been recognized. Thomas Jefferson wrote in 1787, "Were it left to me to decide [between government without] newspapers and newspapers without government, I should not hesitate a moment to prefer the latter." In Russia, Ukraine, and Colombia, journalists who investigate corruption and abuse of power are routinely killed, and no suspects are caught. Many news organizations there now practice "self-censorship" to stay open and alive.

Over the centuries, the press has criticized government. In the late 1960s and early 1970s, however, a new **adversarial** relationship between media and government emerged that is still with us. To be sure, not all the media entered into the fray; most newspapers with their wire-service stories continued to quote official sources. But the elite media and television often adopted hostile stances toward the executive branch.

The causes are not hard to see: Vietnam and Watergate. In both episodes the executive branch lied to the media in order to soothe public opinion. Many media people resented being used and struck back with sharp questioning in press conferences and investigative reporting. Nixon's presidency made things worse; he had long feared and hated the press. On losing the governor's race in California in 1962, he slouched off muttering that the press "won't have Nixon to kick around any more." Before presidential press conferences, Nixon used to calm his nerves by relaxing in a darkened room. He liked to operate in secrecy and then spring his decisions on the public in direct telecasts without any newspeople getting in the way. In turn, the press resented him all the more.

In Saigon, the U.S. military held afternoon press briefings, dubbed the "five o'-clock follies," in which upbeat spokesmen tried to show progress in the war. Journalists soon tired of the repetitive, misleading, and irrelevant briefings and took to snooping around for themselves. They found a corrupt, inept Saigon regime that was not winning the hearts and minds of its people; a Vietcong able to roam and strike at will; and tactics and morale inadequate to stop them. One young *New York Times* reporter was so critical of the Diem regime that his stories undermined American confidence in Diem and paved the way for Diem's 1963 ouster and murder by his own generals. Such is the influence of the elite media.

Vietnam is described as the first television war: bloody bodies of young GIs in full color. We should be careful of the widely accepted charge that television coverage turned Americans against the Vietnam war. The Korean War (1950–1953) had essentially no television coverage, but U.S. public opinion turned against it precisely the same way: As the toll of U.S. casualties mounted, support dropped. It was combat deaths, not television coverage, that changed Americans' minds on both wars. Vietnam also brought the *Pentagon Papers,* first in the *New York Times,* then in the *Washington Post.* (See the box in Chapter 4.) The nicknamed Pentagon

---

adversarial   Inclined to criticize and oppose, to treat with enmity.

THE MEDIA AND WATERGATE

In 1972 a news story began that brought the fall of the Nixon administration and, for at least portions of the media, a new self-image as guardians of public morality. Persons connected to the White House were caught burglarizing and planting telephone "bugs" in the Democratic campaign headquarters in the Watergate office and apartment complex. Dogged investigation by two young *Washington Post* reporters, who later wrote the book *All the President's Men,* revealed a massive cover-up led by the Oval Office. The more Nixon promised to come clean, the guiltier he looked. Nixon was never impeached. A House special committee voted to recommend impeachment; then Nixon resigned. The House certainly would have voted impeachment, and the Senate probably would have convicted.

Would the same have happened without media coverage? Ultimately, the legal moves came through the courts and Congress, but the media made sure these branches of government would not ignore or delay their duties. Did the media bring Nixon down? The Nixon people thought so, but then they always loathed the press. Others have argued that the same would have happened without the investigative reporting, but more slowly and with less drama. The point is that media and government are so intertwined that they are part of the same process and hard to separate.

Since Watergate, some branches of the media, namely the elite press and the national television networks, have adopted generally adversarial stances toward the executive branch. Criticism of later presidencies of both parties was immoderate and sometimes unreasonable. Typically, presidents now claim the press is out to get them. Presidential policies are almost automatically doubted and criticized. The media see scandal everywhere in Washington and then descend in a "feeding frenzy" that leaves no reputation untarnished.

Papers were a multivolume, top-secret study commissioned by former Secretary of Defense Robert McNamara to document decision making on the Vietnam War. Daniel Ellsberg, a former Pentagon official who had turned against the war, made photocopies and delivered them to the newspapers. In the Xerox age, there are no more total secrets. The Nixon administration was outraged—although the Papers made the Johnson officials the chief culprits—and ordered their publication halted, the first time the U.S. government ever censored newspapers. The Supreme Court immediately threw out the government's case, and the presses ran again. By this time, there was open warfare between government and the media.

Has the press gone too far? Some people are fed up at the high-handedness with which the media impugn all authority. The media seem to think they are always right, the government always wrong. Republicans charge that the media are strongly liberal and automatically opposed to their politicians and policies. There is some truth to the charge, but one should note that Democratic politicians and policies also come under hefty media scrutiny. The press washed President Clinton's dirty laundry in prime time. It is as if the media is out to "get" all politicians. Studies show that news reporters and writers indeed tend to be liberals and Democrats, and this sometimes shows up in their coverage. Owners of stations and newspapers, though,

CASE STUDIES

THE MEDIA AND THE IRAQ WAR

The 2003 Iraq War had strong media support both going into it and during it. 9/11 was a huge "rally event" (see page 145) that produced emotional and uncritical support for President Bush, including from the press. The media accepted without questioning administration claims that it had evidence of Iraq building weapons of mass destruction (WMD). After the war, however, we found no WMD, and implanting a stable democracy amid deadly chaos was difficult. As if in revenge for having been misled before the war, much of the media turned critical, and the administration again fumed that the press was out to get them.

The U.S. military still blames television for declining public support in Vietnam. The charge has never been proved—casualties rather than film clips are a more likely cause—but the military tries to keep the media under close control. In 2003 journalists could cover the Iraq War only "embedded" into combat units. This generally brought positive coverage, as the newspeople quickly bonded with the soldiers. It also showed Iraqis the speed of the U.S. advance and persuaded many to give up rather than fight.

But it was narrow-angle coverage, the view from one Humvee, that did not explain what was happening overall. And it did not extend into the looting and resistance that erupted after the fall of Baghdad. Public support for the occupation declined as news coverage showed how difficult it was. It was impossible to say which caused which. A major moral shift—comparable to the impact of the Mylai massacre in Vietnam—came with the TV and newspaper publication of photos of U.S. soldiers sexually humiliating Iraqi prisoners. In the digital age, images travel worldwide in seconds.

In unusual apologies, the *New York Times* and *Washington Post* in 2004 regretted having gone along with administration claims leading up to the 2003 war. They had not been sufficiently skeptical, editors said, and should have asked more questions. The *Times* had been burned by a too-close relationship with the administration before. In 1961 the paper delayed stories of the upcoming Bay of Pigs invasion of Cuba at White House request. If they had published, officials would have understood that Castro too knew about the invasion. Withholding the news did Kennedy no favor. The media function best when not too close to government.

By 2004 the rally event was clearly over, and columnists of all sorts—including conservative Republicans—denounced the administration. Neither the White House nor the Pentagon can suppress bad news for long. There is no sure way to "manage" news coverage; reality eventually emerges, often angrily. The media seem to follow a "bounce-back" pattern. Initially the media accept administration claims but then, discovering that they have been misled, turn angry and negative.

tend to be conservative and Republican, and they curb the liberal impulses of their employees. Radio talk shows tend to the angry right, documentary films to the radically liberal. (Any ideas why the two media are so different?) Charges of media bias are hard to prove, because you can usually show that the media mistreats all politicians, Republican and Democrat. The Bush 43 White House tried to keep a tight rein on information, which the media resented. Bush disliked the media and held the fewest press conferences of all presidents.

What is the proper role of the media in a democracy? That they can and should criticize is clear: This keeps government on its toes. But how much should they criticize? Should they presume wrongdoing and cover-up everywhere? Should many reporters model themselves after Woodward and Bernstein of Watergate fame and try to ferret out scandals at every level of government? The press is largely protected from charges of libel, for under the Supreme Court's **Sullivan** rule, "public" persons are presumed to be open to media scrutiny. This has left some public figures feeling helpless and bitter at the hands of an all-powerful press and has increased cynical attitudes about politics in general. Public opinion has grown critical of the too critical media. Perhaps the United States can find some happy middle ground.

KEY TERMS

adversarial (p. 168)
bandwagon (p. 161)
cross-pressured (p. 163)
electromagnetic spectrum (p. 164)
elite media (p. 156)
face-to-face (p. 153)
incumbent (p. 160)
introspective (p. 154)
mass media (p. 152)

media event (p. 159)
nonpaternalism (p. 164)
oligopoly (p. 155)
opinion leaders (p. 154)
source (p. 157)
status quo (p. 155)
stump (p. 153)
Sullivan (p. 171)
wire service (p. 157)

KEY WEB SITES

Associated Press
www.ap.org/

Atlantic Monthly
www.theatlantic.com/atlantic/

National Public Radio
www.npr.org/

National Review
www.nationalreview.com/

New York Times
www.nytimes.com/

Public Broadcasting System
www.pbs.org/

Sullivan   Short for *New York Times v. Sullivan,* 1964 Supreme Court decision protecting media against public officials' libel suits.

USA Today
www.usatoday.com/

Wall Street Journal
www.wsj.com/

Washington Post
www.washingtonpost.com/

Cable News Network
www.cnn.com/

FURTHER REFERENCE

Alterman, Eric. *What Liberal Media?: The Truth About Bias and the News.* New York: Basic Books, 2004.

Auletta, Ken. *Backstory: Inside the Business of News.* New York: Penguin, 2004.

Cappella, Joseph N., and Kathleen Hall Jamieson. *Spiral of Cynicism: The Press and the Public Good.* New York: Oxford University Press, 1997.

Dautrich, Kenneth, and Thomas H. Hartley. *How the News Media Fail American Voters: Causes, Consequences, and Remedies.* New York: Columbia University Press, 1999.

Gans, Herbert J. *Democracy and the News.* New York: Oxford University Press, 2003.

Graber, Doris A. *Mass Media and American Politics*, 7th ed. Washington, D.C.: CQ Press, 2005.

Han, Lori Cox. *Governing from Center Stage: White House Communication Strategies During the Television Age of Politics.* Cresskill, NJ: Hampton Press, 2001.

Kuypers, Jim A. *Press Bias and Politics: How the Media Frame Controversial Issues.* Westport, CT: Praeger, 2002.

Liebovich, Louis W. *Richard Nixon, Watergate, and the Press: A Historical Retrospective.* Westport, CT: Praeger, 2003.

Norris, Pippa. *A Virtuous Circle: Political Communications in Postindustrial Societies.* New York: Cambridge University Press, 2000.

Seib, Philip. *Beyond the Front Lines: How the News Media Cover a World Shaped by War.* New York: Palgrave, 2004.

Shogan, Robert. *Bad News? Where the Press Goes Wrong in the Making of the President.* Chicago IL: Ivan Dee, 2001.

Starr, Paul. *The Creation of the Media: Political Origins of Modern Communications.* New York: Basic Books, 2004.

West, Darrell M. *Air Wars: Television Advertising in Election Campaigns, 1952–2004*, 4th ed. Washington, D.C.: CQ Press, 2005.

INTEREST GROUPS

CHAPTER

10

QUESTIONS TO CONSIDER

- Can democracy exist without interest groups?
- Are all citizens equal in organizing interest groups?
- Does government create interest groups?
- Are interest groups and their money too powerful?
- What are PACs, 527s, and "soft money"?
- Why are the French antipluralist?
- Which is more effective, lobbying Congress or the administration?
- Can interest groups bypass democracy?

On your own, even in the finest democracy, you can do little. The solution: Form a group of like-minded individuals. After hard work organizing, fundraising, and lobbying, you can start having an impact. In this view—a pluralist view (see Chapter 5)—the crux of politics is groups. Interest-group activity is especially strong in the pluralistic United States but is found everywhere, even in dictatorships, where groups quietly try to win the favor of the dictator. In a democracy, if you dislike something, do as union organizer Joe Hill urged a century ago: "Don't mourn me, organize!"

■ WHAT IS AN INTEREST GROUP?

The term **interest group** covers just about any collection of people trying to influence government. In *The Governmental Process,* David B. Truman defines an interest group as "a shared-attitude group that makes certain claims upon other

---

interest group   Association that tries to influence policy.

KEY CONCEPTS

How Interest Groups Differ from Political Parties

Interest groups are a bit like political parties. Both try to influence public policy, but interest groups do it outside the electoral process and are not responsible to the public. A party must win elections. Interest groups may influence the nomination of candidates who are sympathetic to their cause, but the candidates run under the party banner—not the interest group banner.

Goals

Parties try to acquire power though elections. Interest groups usually focus on specific programs and issues and are rarely represented in the formal structure of government. Instead, they try to influence legislators and executives. They often seek the favor of all political parties. Industry groups want the support of both the Republicans and the Democrats. Some interest groups favor one party. The National Rifle Association, for example, strongly supports Republican candidates.

Nature of Memberships

Political parties seek broad support to win elections and draw many interests into their ranks. Their membership is much broader than that of an interest group. Even the conservative Republican party includes people in all income brackets and occupations, and some of its members are more liberal than many Democrats. The Democratic party, on the other hand, billing itself as the party of the common person, welcomes all walks of life among its supporters, including wealthy people.

Interest groups generally have a narrower membership. Members of a labor union are likely to share similar living and working conditions and to have comparable educational and cultural backgrounds. Idealistic interest groups, such as those for ecology or gender equality, may draw their members from a wider spectrum. Some interest groups link people who have previously stayed apart, as when Roman Catholics and fundamentalist Protestants unite to oppose abortion.

Almost Unlimited Number

For several reasons, including the length of a ballot, there are rarely more than ten or twelve political parties. But there is no limit on interest groups, and some countries, such as the United States, foster their growth. As Tocqueville observed in the 1830s, "In no country of the world has the principle of association been more successfully used or applied to a greater multitude of objects than in America." Tocqueville is still accurate. Just open a Washington, D.C., phone book to "National . . ." and count the hundreds of national associations, federations, and committees. Washington's prosperity is based on its attraction as a headquarters for more than 20,000 interest groups.

---

groups" by acting through the institutions of government. Some interest groups are transient, others permanent. Some focus on influencing a particular policy, others on broad changes. Some work through the executive or administrative agencies, others through the judicial or legislative sectors, still others through public opinion. But all are nonpublicly accountable organizations that attempt to promote shared private interests by influencing public-policy outcomes.

WHO BELONGS TO INTEREST GROUPS?

Every advanced society is pluralistic (see Chapter 5) with many industrial, cultural, economic, educational, ethnic, and religious groups. David Truman argued that divergent interests lead almost automatically to group formation. In a pluralist democracy, a multiplicity of interest groups push their own claims and viewpoints, creating a balance of opposing interests that, in theory, prevents any one group from dominating the political system. In this optimistic view, government policy is the outcome of competition among many groups, which represent the varied interests of the people.

Interest groups, however, tend to overrepresent middle-class, upper-class, and business interests. Because some groups are richer and better-connected, the democratic playing field is not level. Elite theorists argue that if group theory really operated, the poor would organize groups to get a bigger piece of the economic pie. But the poor, who have less education, are slow in forming groups to promote their interests. Better-off and better-educated people are much more likely to participate in politics, and this includes organizing and running interest groups. In this area, too, the poor get shortchanged.

With few organizations to represent their interests, the lower classes may act explosively rather than as groups working within the political system. Their grievances can burst out, as in the storming of the Bastille at the start of the French Revolution. In recent U.S. history, inner-city riots reflected the anger that race-related poverty produced among many African Americans. The ghetto riots, while publicizing grievances, did little to challenge the power of business, labor unions, or other groups that keep things as they are. Not all sectors of society can effectively form and use interest groups.

INTEREST GROUPS AND GOVERNMENT

Interest groups try to influence government. But what if there is no government? To take an extreme example, consider Afghanistan, where in the early 2000s near-anarchy prevailed. The government's writ did not extend much outside of the capital, Kabul. There were plenty of groups: dozens of tribes, clans, warlords, and opium growers, each with its own militia. Would we call these "interest groups"? Probably not. Although some interest groups engage in occasional violence, they do so in a context of trying to influence government. In Afghanistan, there was little government to influence; the groups fought to guard their respective "turfs" and opium trade. Not all clashes of groups automatically qualify as "interest-group activity."

Interest groups presuppose an existing government that is worth trying to influence. Government, in fact, virtually calls many interest groups into life, for they are intimately associated with government programs. There are farm lobbies because there are farm programs, education lobbies because there are education programs, and veterans' lobbies because in years past the government went to war.

CASE STUDIES

NDEA: HOW GOVERNMENT CREATED AN INTEREST GROUP

In 1957, the launch of the Soviets' *Sputnik,* the first earth-orbiting satellite, jolted Americans and their Congress, because it seemed to prove the Soviets were ahead of us (actually, they were not). Congress passed the 1958 National Defense Education Act (NDEA) that put millions of dollars into university science, engineering, and foreign-area and language programs.

A decade later, as enthusiasm for the last two subject areas waned (partly because of the Vietnam war), a vigorous lobby dedicated to "world education" and funded by universities that received NDEA grants tried to persuade Congress to continue the program. Congress had created a program, the program created an interest group, and then the interest group worked on Congress to keep the money flowing. U.S. farm subsidies, originally to help struggling farmers during the Depression, now cost billions a year, much of it to "agri-business," and few try to curb it. Programs, once set up, are hard to terminate due to interest-group influence.

Once government is funding something, the groups that benefit develop constituencies with a strong pecuniary interest in continuing the programs. As government has become bigger and sponsored more programs, interest groups have proliferated. By now, virtually every branch and subdivision of the U.S. government has one or more interest groups watching over its shoulder, demanding more grants, a change in regulations, or their own agency. The Departments of Education and Energy were created under these circumstances, and Ronald Reagan vowed to abolish them. He was unable to: The interests associated with them—in part created by them—were too powerful.

Sometimes interest groups participate in government legislation and implementation. In Britain, "interested members" of Parliament are those who openly acknowledge that they represent industries or labor unions. This is not frowned on and is considered quite normal. (Quietly selling government influence to British interest groups, however, is considered "sleaze" and has produced scandals.) In Sweden, interest groups are especially large and powerful. Swedish "royal commissions," which initiate most new legislation, are composed of legislators, government officials, and interest-group representatives. After a proposal has been drafted, it is circulated for comments to all relevant interest groups. Some Swedish benefits for farmers and workers are administered by their respective farm organizations and labor unions. Some call this **corporatism**, meaning interest groups taking on government functions. Top representatives of business, labor, and the cabinet meet regularly in Sweden to decide a great deal of public policy. Critics charge that this too-cozy relationship bypasses parliamentary democracy altogether.

---

corporatism   The direct participation of interest groups in government.

KEY CONCEPTS

COUNTERVAILING POWER

One of the theories of pluralists is that no interest group can monopolize power because there is always one or more groups working against it. The theory of countervailing power argues that business associations are offset by labor unions, the Jewish lobby by the Muslim lobby, industries fearful of imports by industries eager to export, and drug companies by retiree associations. It is such balances that keep us free and democratic, argue pluralists.

But do things always balance? As in most of the world, U.S. unions have been declining in membership and are now much weaker than business associations. Producers of electric power and gasoline form powerful lobbies that face no countervailing lobby of 295 million consumers. The battle over patients' rights is fought by giant health insurers, hospital and physician organizations, employers, and trial lawyers, all spending millions of dollars in "a lobbying war of near-epic proportions," in the words of one Washington observer. People who use managed health care are weakly represented by consumer groups. Just because there theoretically could be countervailing power does not mean that it actually exists.

BUREAUCRATS AS AN INTEREST GROUP

Government and interest groups are related in another important but sometimes overlooked way: The bureaucracy has become one of the biggest and most powerful interest groups of all. Civil servants are not merely passive implementers of laws; they also have much input in the making and application of those laws. Much legislation originates in specialized agencies. Many of the data and witnesses before legislative committees are from the executive departments and agencies. In Japan, the powerful bureaucrats of the finance and international trade **(MITI)** ministries are used to telling the **Diet** what to legislate.

Bureaucracies develop interests of their own. They see their tasks as terribly important and demand bigger budgets and more employees every year. When was the last time a civil servant recommended abolishing his or her agency or bureau? Bureaucrats have a lot of knowledge at their fingertips, and knowledge is power. The Reagan administration said it would abolish the Department of Energy (DOE). One of the authors of this book asked a friend, an official of the department, why he wasn't worried. "They won't abolish us," he asserted knowingly. "They can't. DOE manufactures nuclear bombs, and the administration needs the DOE budget to disguise how big the nuclear-bomb budget is." He was right; Reagan did not abolish the Department of Energy.

It was earlier proposed that interest groups are offshoots of society and the economy. That is only partly true, for they are also offshoots of government.

MITI   Japan's Ministry of International Trade and Industry (now called *METI*).
Diet   Japan's national legislature.

FRENCH ANTIPLURALISM

The United States and Britain are highly pluralistic, for interest group activity is acceptable and desirable, and lobbying is normal for a healthy democracy. In France, on the other hand, interest-group activity, although it does exist, is frowned on and considered dirty. France is heir to centuries of centralized and paternalistic government. The French are used to Paris ministries setting national goals and supervising much of the nation's economy. Further, the philosopher Jean-Jacques Rousseau still has a powerful hold on the French mind. Rousseau argued that there must be no "particular wills" to muddy and distort the "general will," that which the whole community wants. Rousseau presumed there was such a thing as a general will, something pluralists deny. Accordingly, interest groups are seen as trying to pervert the good of the whole community. The French bureaucratic elites pay little attention to interest groups, considering them "unobjective." French interest groups operate in a more constrained atmosphere than their American or British counterparts.

Government and interest groups, to paraphrase Thomas Hobbes, were born twins. The more government, the more interest groups.

To say that every political system has interest groups says little, for interest groups in different systems operate quite differently. One key determinant in the way interest groups operate is the government. Here we can refine our definition of pluralism discussed in Chapter 5. Pluralism is determined not by the mere existence of groups, each trying to influence government, but by the degree to which government permits or encourages the open interplay of groups. Pluralism has a normative component, an "ought" or a "should."

■ EFFECTIVE INTEREST GROUPS

POLITICAL CULTURE

Interest groups flourish in pluralistic societies with traditions of local self-governance and of forming associations. Where this is weak (see box on France above), interest groups have tough going. In their study of political cultures, Almond and Verba noted that Americans, Britons, and Germans were more likely to participate in voluntary associations than were Italians and Mexicans. Civic participation in every country increased with educational level, and in all except the United States, more men than women were participants. Not all of the groups were political, but even nonpolitical groups, by discussion among members, have some political influence. Members of a bicycle club become involved in politics when they support rails-to-trails bicycle paths. One key finding of the study was that in societies where many join groups, people have a greater sense of political competence and efficacy. Some worry that the U.S. tendency to form groups has declined (see Chapter 7 on political culture).

CASE STUDIES

THE ENRON SCANDAL

The crooked Houston-based energy-trading firm of Enron was briefly the seventh-largest U.S. corporation, but in 2001, even after robbing California of billions in manipulated electricity prices, it collapsed amid massive, hidden debts. Enron executives walked away with over $1 billion while employees and investors lost everything. Enron was also a **scandal**, as its managers had given $5.9 million in political contributions, mostly to Republicans. Enron was the twelfth-largest contributor to Texas governor and 2000 presidential candidate George Bush. Seventy-one of the hundred senators and nineteen of the twenty-three members of the House energy committee got Enron money. The important chairman of the Federal Energy Regulatory Commission got his job on the recommendation of Enron chief Ken Lay. Enron thus reached into both Congress and the administration.

When Enron fell, though, its former friends stood clear. They did not wish to be tarnished. Several Enron executives were convicted, and the blue-chip accounting firm of Arthur Andersen (also a major Bush contributor), was found to have rigged audits and was forced to close. Congress itself, by deregulating Enron's freewheeling deals, bears much responsibility. The scandal embarrassed Congress into passing the McCain-Feingold reform act in 2002. In Europe, such scandals are frequent and worse.

THE RISE OF BIG MONEY

Money is probably the single most important factor in interest group success. With enough money, interests hardly need a group. Money is especially important for elections, and groups help candidates who favor their cause. Most democracies have recognized the danger in too close a connection between interests and candidates, the danger that we will have the "best Congress money can buy." It is but a very short step from influence-buying to **corruption**. U.S. peanut, sugar, corn, and cotton growers give generously to candidates and get federal subsidies. Said California political boss Jesse Unruh: "Money is the mother's milk of politics."

Many countries have tried reforms. Japanese reformers tried to break "money politics," the extreme dependence of politicians on interest groups—business conglomerates, banks, farmers, even gangsters—but have not yet succeeded. Germany and Sweden provide for almost complete **public financing** of the major parties in national elections. Spain, which rejoined the democracies only in 1977, subsidizes parties after the election according to how many votes they received and parliamentary seats they won. Some countries—Britain, France, and Germany, among others—try to limit campaign spending.

The United States has been reluctant to go to public financing of or spending on campaigns for several reasons. First, there is the strong emphasis on freedom.

---

scandal   Corruption made public.

corruption   Use of public office for private gain.

public financing   Using tax dollars to fund something, such as election-campaign expenses.

THE RISE OF POLITICAL ACTION COMMITTEES

In 1971 and 1974 (following Watergate), Congress, thinking it was instituting important reforms, sharply limited the amount of money that individuals and corporations could contribute directly to candidates in an effort to curb the influence of "big money" in politics. But there was no prohibition on individuals and businesses organizing committees and donating money in ways that favor desirable candidates.

Political action committees (PACs) grew like mushrooms, from 600 in 1974 to over 5,000 now. During presidential elections, they now give in total a billion or so dollars to candidates and parties (less when only Congress is up for election). Incumbent U.S. representatives receive on average some quarter of a million dollars from PACs, perhaps half their total campaign expenses. Challengers get perhaps a tenth of that. Incumbent senators get on average some $2 million from PACs, again about half their total campaign expenses. (The rest comes from individuals, corporations, and foundations.)

Although PACs were originally an idea of labor unions, business PACs now greatly outspend labor PACs. Large corporations, many with defense contracts, are heavy PAC contributors. The bulk of contributions go to incumbents, which enables members of Congress to lock themselves into power nearly permanently. Especially favored by PACs are incumbents on committees relevant to the PACs interests (for example, farm PACs give to members of the House Agricultural Committee). The rise of PACs illustrate how interests "work around" whatever reforms are put into place.

The U.S. Supreme Court has interpreted the First Amendment to include dollars as a form of free speech. When a person gives money to a candidate or a candidate spends it, those are political statements. Second, U.S. campaigns are much longer and more expensive than in other democracies, the result of our weak, decentralized parties and nominating system. In Western Europe, elections can be short and cheap because the parties are already in place with their candidates and platforms. And third, given these two previous conditions, American legislators have not been able to find a formula for public financing that really works in the manner intended. Some efforts turn out to have negative **unforeseen consequences**.

Some individuals and political action committees (see box above) contribute to parties and interest groups not directly working for a candidate's election campaign. This **soft money** funds groups to produce "issue ads" aimed *against* the

---

political action committee   U.S. interest group set up specifically to contribute money to election campaigns.

unforeseen consequence   Bad or counterproductive result when laws or policies do not work as expected.

soft money   Campaign contributions to parties and issue groups so as to skirt federal limits on contributions to candidates.

other side without mentioning their own candidate's name, a big loophole in federal campaign laws. Soft money thus contributes to the trend toward negative advertising in political campaigns. In 2004, for example, a committee called MoveOn.org (a "527," see below), clearly Democratic, spent without limit on anti-Bush ads accusing him of incompetence.

In 2002, after a hard struggle, the McCain-Feingold Campaign Reform Act passed. In 2003, the Supreme Court ruled it constitutional. Many cheered, but by 2004 it was irrelevant, skirted in three ways. First, limits are not very limiting; individuals may give up to $2,000 directly to a presidential candidate, $25,000 to a national party, and much more to state and local parties and candidates. Second, many presidential hopefuls simply walked away from public campaign financing—which imposed spending ceilings—in favor of funds they raised on their own (now often gathered online), which have no limit. Third, well-funded groups with no formal ties to candidates—called "527 committees" after a section of the tax code—spent prodigiously on "issues" that clearly favored one side. 527s operate under looser rules than PACs.

It is now apparent that parties and candidates will work around whatever reforms or laws attempt to curb big money in politics. In 1907 Teddy Roosevelt, reacting to the big-money politics of his predecessor McKinley, supported the first reform, the Tillman Act, prohibiting corporations from giving funds. It looked good but was ineffective.

Some critics fear money politics is out of control. Defenders say this is just the workings of pluralist democracy, and the amounts are peanuts compared to the overall U.S. economy. Can or should anything be done about interest groups and money? Some suggest we go to a European-type system in which the parties are well-organized and campaigns are short and relatively cheap. But that is simply not the U.S. nominating and electoral system, which is complex and long. And Europe's interest groups still give plenty (sometimes under the table) to their favored candidates.

Another solution might be to limit the amount that any company or individual could give to a PAC or a 527. At a certain point, though, that becomes restriction on free speech, and the Supreme Court rejected such limits in 1985. Public financing of all candidates—presidential nominees who gain at least 5 percent of the national vote are already entitled to federal financing—would be terribly expensive. Many U.S. taxpayers do not check off the option on their tax returns to contribute a few dollars to presidential campaigns, even though it costs them nothing. For the foreseeable future, it will not be possible to break the tie between interest groups and candidates in the United States.

THE RISE OF SINGLE-ISSUE GROUPS

Perhaps the second greatest factor in the influence of interest groups (after money) is the intensity of the issue involved. The right issue can mobilize millions, give the group cohesion and commitment, and boost donations. There have always been American interest groups pursuing one or another idealistic objective, but since

The abortion battle is being fought on the streets of this nation as well as in the courts. Abortion is a highly emotional issue that activates strongly committed interest groups on both sides. (U.S. Department of Health and Human Services)

the 1970s the rise of **single-issue interest groups** have changed U.S. politics. Typically, interest groups have several things to say about issues, for their interests encompass several programs and departments. Organized labor tries to persuade government on questions of Social Security, medical insurance, education, imports and tariffs, and the way unemployment statistics are calculated. The **AFL-CIO** has a long-term, across-the-board interest in Washington. The same can be said for many business groups, such as the **NAM**.

But to the single-issue groups only one issue matters, and it matters intensely. Typically, their issues are moral—and therefore hard to compromise—rather than material. The most prominent of them is the right to life, or antiabortion, movement. In 1973 the Supreme Court ruled that states could not arbitrarily restrict a woman's right to an abortion. Many Roman Catholics and Protestant fundamentalists were shocked, for they believe that human life begins at the moment of conception and that aborting a fetus is therefore murder. "Pro-life" people oppose, for a start, allowing any state or federal medical funds to be used for abortion. They would also like to amend the Constitution to outlaw abortion. Opposing them are "pro-choice" forces, many linked to the women's movement. Feminists argue that abortion is a matter for the individual woman to decide and no one else; the right to choose gives women control over their lives and is part of their liberation from second-class status.

The antiabortionists make life miserable for many senators and representatives. They care about nothing else—where officials stand on taxes, jobs, defense, and so on. They want to know where they stand on abortion, and a compromise middle ground—the refuge of many politicians faced with controversial issues—is

---

single-issue interest group   Interest association devoted to one cause only.

AFL-CIO   American Federation of Labor-Congress of Industrial Organizations, largest U.S. union federation.

NAM   National Association of Manufacturers, major federation of industrial executives.

not good enough. How can you be a "moderate" on abortion? Some elections turn on the abortion issue. Meanwhile, the pro-choice forces organize and grow militant to offset the pro-life forces. The 2005 Terri Schiavo case reiterated the conflict.

Other single-issue causes appear, such as prayer in public school and homosexual rights. Taken together, these two and the abortion question are sometimes referred to as the "morality issue." Gun control grew into a major issue, fanned by the assassinations of John and Robert Kennedy and Martin Luther King, Jr. The powerful National Rifle Association (NRA) opposes such groups as Handgun Control. None of these issues makes elected representatives any happier. They like to be judged on a wide range of positions they have taken, not on one narrow issue on which it is hard to compromise.

SIZE AND MEMBERSHIP

Their size and members' intensity give groups clout. The biggest and fastest growing U.S. interest group is the American Association of Retired Persons, with 35 million members (one American in nine), many of them educated, forceful, and strongly committed to their cause of preserving and enhancing Social Security and Medicare. Both parties proclaim that they want to preserve the two vast programs. When AARP speaks, Congress trembles.

Size alone, however, is not necessarily the most important element in interest-group strength. Money and intensity often offset size. Groups that claim to speak for large numbers are not appreciated if only a small fraction of the group are committed members. The National Association for the Advancement of Colored People (NAACP) claims to speak for millions of African Americans, but its actual membership is much smaller. All things being equal, a large group has more clout than a small one—but things are never equal.

The **socioeconomic status** of members gives groups clout. Better-off, well-educated people with influence in their professions and communities can form groups that get more respect. The socioeconomic status of American Jews boosted the impact of the American-Israel Public Affairs Committee (AIPAC) and other Jewish groups. As Japanese Americans climbed educationally and professionally, their Japanese American Citizens' League (JACL) started having an impact and won apologies for the unconstitutional internment in World War II; JACL then worked on getting compensation. Respect leads to clout. This means, paradoxically and unfairly, that disadvantaged groups with the biggest grievances are among the least likely to be listened to.

ACCESS

Money, issue, and size may not count for much unless people in government are willing to listen. The careful cultivation of members of Congress and civil servants over the years makes sure doors are open. When a group has established a stable

---

socioeconomic status   Combination of income and prestige criteria in the ranking of groups.

HOW POWERFUL ARE U.S. UNIONS?

Labor unions in the United States are not very powerful, at least in comparative perspective. Since the 1950s, the percent of American workers in labor unions has dropped by more than half. Approximate percentages of the workforce that is unionized:

Sweden	50%
Germany	22
Britain	20
Japan	20
United States	15
France	10

U.S. unions seem powerful because they attract much attention when they strike at major firms, but their biggest numbers are actually among government employees at all levels, including schoolteachers, who are often prohibited from striking. Business in the United States has far more clout than unions. U.S. unions are now striving for new members to get back some of their former strength.

The sign in a union hall reminds a Democratic candidate for the Senate where his support comes from. Many interest groups support candidates in the expectation of future consideration. (Michael Roskin)

and receptive relationship with a branch of government, it is said to enjoy, in the words of Joseph LaPalombara, **structured access**. Greek-American members of Congress are, quite naturally, receptive to Greek arguments on questions concerning Turkey, Macedonia, and Cyprus. Michigan legislators likewise heed the complaints of the automobile industry. Arab Americans complained bitterly that Jews enjoyed too much access on Capitol Hill and organized their own groups to gain such access. There is nothing wrong with access as such; it is part and parcel of a working democracy.

But what happens when groups are shut out and have no access? Pluralists think this cannot happen in a democracy, but it does. Black and Native American militants argued that no one was listening to them or taking their demands seriously. Only violence in urban ghettos and on Indian reservations got Washington to listen. When the wealthy and powerful have a great deal of access, the poor and unorganized may have none. The consequences sometimes lead to violence.

STRATEGIES OF INTEREST GROUPS

Approaching Lawmakers   **Lobbying** receives the most attention. The campaign contributions and favors to legislators given by corporations persuade many that lobbyists buy Congress. Indeed, any major interest threatened by new laws spares no expense to make sure they are not passed, and they are usually successful. Senator John McCain (R-Ariz.), a critic of big money, said sadly, "Money buys access." He referred to a 2003 energy bill as "no lobbyist left behind." Big tobacco, which is especially generous to incumbent Republican candidates, routinely blocks or dilutes antismoking legislation. One favor big companies provide cooperative congresspersons: trips in the corporate jet. The average lobbying group, however, lacks large sums of money to give, so most see themselves as providers of information.

Approaching the Administration   Depending on the issue, the executive branch of government may be a better target for interest-group pressure and persuasion. The interest group may not need or want a new law, merely favorable interpretation of existing rules and regulations. For this, they turn to administrators. Antipollution groups, for instance, seek tighter definitions of clean air; industry groups seek looser definitions. Interest groups concentrate their attention on the department that specializes in their area. Farm groups deal with the Department of Agriculture, public service companies with the Federal Power Commission, and so forth. As a rule, each department pays careful heed to the demands and arguments of groups in its area. In fact, at one time or another, many government bureaucracies have been "captured" or "colonized" by the groups they deal with. The

---

structured access   Long-term friendly connection of interest group to officials.
lobbying   Interest-group contact with legislators.

HOW TO . . .

TABLES

A table is a list of the things you are studying—counties, countries, years, voters, legislators, interest groups—with numerical measures attached to each thing. Later, you may use some of these as "variables" (see page 144). Measures are whatever is relevant to the case you wish to make—dollars, population, or how many listings in a phone book. You list these things in some order—the biggest, most, or latest. Alphabetical order is often useless. In the current chapter, we might list which PACs gave the most money, with biggest givers first.

To take another example, the relative wealth of countries can be measured in several ways. The most basic is Gross Domestic Product (GDP, see page 31), now usually corrected for cost of living (purchasing-power parity, PPP), the first column. Dividing that by population (the second column) gives per capita GDP (GDPpc) at PPP, the third column, the best comparison of relative wealth. Note how the table goes from richest to poorest.

Country	GDP ($ Billion)	Population (Million)	Per Capita GDP at PPP
United States	$10,990	293	$37,800
France	1,661	60	27,600
Mexico	941	105	9,000
Russia	1,282	144	8,900
Colombia	263	42	6,300
China	6,449	1,299	5,000
Syria	58	18	3,300
India	3,003	1,065	2,900
Kenya	33	32	1,000

Source: www.cia.gov/cia/publications/factbook/indexgeo.html

flow goes the other way, too. Many top officials of a former administration stay in Washington—with offices on famous K Street—as highly paid lobbyists, some billing clients $500 an hour.

Interest groups employ many of the same tactics on executive departments that they use on legislators, including personal contacts, supplying research, and public relations. Some provide money; in most of the world corruption of public officials is the norm. The U.S. federal bureaucracy is one of the least corrupt in the world—state and local is something else. Federal officials caught on the take are usually political appointees and not career civil servants. Interest groups really make their influence felt in nominations to top-level government posts, including positions in the president's cabinet. Then interest groups may secure an appointee who truly serves their interests.

CASE STUDIES

HOW THE NAACP USED THE COURTS

Aware of the importance of the U.S. judicial system, especially of the Supreme Court, the National Association for the Advancement of Colored People (NAACP) focused much of its fight against racial segregation on the courts. It paid off. The legal staff of the NAACP, whose chief attorney was Thurgood Marshall (later a U.S. Supreme Court justice), successfully challenged the constitutionality of all state laws requiring racial segregation in public schools in the famous *Brown* decision of 1954. Then it went on to challenge the legality of state laws on segregation in public transportation, restaurants, lodging, and other areas. The vast changes in U.S. civil rights happened more through the courts than through legislation.

Approaching the Judiciary   Interest groups may also use the courts, especially in the United States, for the U.S. judicial system has far more power than most judiciaries, which are merely part of the executive branch. In countries where rule of law is strong, the courts become an arena of interest-group contention, as in Germany, where groups have taken cases on abortion and worker rights before the Federal Constitutional Court.

Every year in the United States the state and federal courts hear cases filed or supported by such interest groups as the American Civil Liberties Union, Sierra Club, and NAACP. In recent years the U.S. Supreme Court has dealt with several social issues brought to it by interest groups, including women's rights, the death penalty, abortion, and school prayer. Interest groups use two judicial methods to pursue their goals. First, they may initiate suits directly on behalf of a group or class of people whose interests they represent (such suits are commonly referred to as **class actions**). The second is for the interest group to file a "friend of the court" brief (**amicus curiae**) in support of a person whose cause they share.

Appeals to the Public   Organized interests often take their case to the public with peaceful—or not so peaceful—appeals. Even powerful interest groups realize the importance of their public image, and many invest in public-relations campaigns to explain how they contribute to the general welfare and why their interests are good for the country. For example, railroads used television to explain their case for "fair" government policies so they could stay alive and compete with trucking. The gasoline lobby explained why environmental restrictions work against building new refineries.

Some interest groups maintain a low profile by promoting their objectives without advertising themselves. Such groups may plant news stories that promote their

---

class action   Lawsuit on behalf of a group.
amicus curiae   Statement to a court by persons not party to a case.

cause and quietly work against the publication of stories detrimental to them. The Tobacco Institute, for example, discreetly funds research that casts doubt on findings that smoking is bad for your health. The American Petroleum Institute seeks no news coverage but has its officers quoted as unbiased experts above the political fray.

Demonstrations   Certain organizations, such as the American Cancer Society and the Heart Fund, may get free advertising space and time, but most interest groups do not, and many cannot afford to purchase such publicity. Such a disadvantaged group may try nonviolent demonstrations to publicize their cause. Mahatma Gandhi used this tactic to get the British to leave India in 1947. Gandhi learned about nonviolent protest from an influential essay on "civil disobedience" by American Henry David Thoreau, who protested the war with Mexico in 1846–1848. Thoreau's idea was also adopted by the Rev. Martin Luther King, Jr. to push for African American civil rights in the 1950s and 1960s.

Some protesters against nuclear plants, facing the financial and political resources of power companies, felt that marching, picketing, and sometimes blocking plant entrances were their only options. News media coverage of their protests brought them adherents, contributors, and sometimes access in Washington. Their

Citizens protest plans for a toxic-waste incinerator, claiming it would bring poisonous fumes to nearby towns. In this case, well-organized local citizens beat a well-heeled corporation, which was forced to drop its plans. (Michael Roskin)

A leftist union of Japanese schoolteachers protests peacefully in Tokyo park against Japanese rearmament, NATO, and the United States, and for socialism and higher salaries. (Michael Roskin)

powerful opponents, of course, often prevailed, leading some protesters to become frustrated and bitter.

    Violent Protest A group that loses faith in conventional political channels may see violent protest as its only alternative. Clearly, the United States is no stranger to violent protests, which require a psychological buildup nurtured by poverty, discrimination, frustration, and a sense of personal or social injustice. An incident may spark the pent-up anger of a frustrated group, and mob behavior may escalate. Shootings and arrests of African Americans have sparked riots in U.S. cities. The more articulate rioters claim they are simply *opposing* the violence they suffered daily at the hands of police, all levels of government, and an economy that keeps them underpaid or unemployed. Does violent protest work? Perhaps it was no coincidence that the Great Society was passed during a period of U.S. urban riots. The British got out of India and Palestine when outbursts of violence made the areas difficult to govern. The white government of South Africa started offering reforms only when blacks turned to violence. In certain circumstances, violence works. As black radical H. "Rap" Brown put it, "Violence is as American as cherry pie." (He is now in prison for murder.)

■ INTEREST GROUPS: AN EVALUATION

Interest groups are part of every democracy. Yet how well do they serve the needs of citizens? Interest groups help represent a wider range of interests in the legislative process, a good thing. Many smaller organizations, however, have neither the members nor the money to have any input. Unless they are able to form coalitions, they cannot defend their interests from larger, more powerful groups. The mere fact that interest groups can articulate demands does not mean that the demands will be heeded. Resources are highly unequal among interest groups. Some are rich and powerful and have a lot of influence. Others are ignored.

    There is a further problem: What about individuals who are not organized into groups? Who speaks for them? Many citizens are not members or beneficiaries of interest groups. They vote for elected leaders, but the leaders pay more attention to group demands than to ordinary voters. If legislators and executives are attuned to interest groups, who is considering the interests of the whole country? At times, it seems as if no one is. Then we may begin to appreciate Rousseau's emphasis on the "general will" over and above the "particular wills" that make up society.

    For this reason, the "citizens' lobby" Common Cause was formed in 1970. Supported by donations, it won public funding of presidential campaigns, an end to the congressional seniority system, and disclosure of lobbying activities. In a similar vein, Ralph Nader set up several public-interest lobbies related to law, nuclear energy, tax reform, and medical care. Although groups such as these have done much good work, they raise an interesting question: Can a society as big and complex as America's possibly be represented as a whole, or is it inherently a mosaic of groups with no common voice?

OLSON'S THEORY OF INTEREST GROUPS

American economist Mancur Olson's 1968 *Logic of Collective Action* is widely accepted and cited. He noted that small and well-organized groups, especially with money, often override the broader public interest. The reason: The former have much to gain from favorable but narrow laws and rulings, so they lobby intensely. The latter see nothing to gain, are not organized or intense, and lobby little. The public does not care if the price of shoelaces jumps up, but shoelace manufacturers do. The few trump the many.

Related to this is Olson's "free-rider syndrome": Why buy a ticket when you can ride for free? People will not invest their time and money in a cause when they get the same results anyway. Why pay union dues when you are already under a union contract? Why should Europeans contribute much to NATO when the Americans provide them with free security?

Olson also warned against what happens when interest groups become too strong: They choke off change and growth, leading to national stagnation. Politicians, responding to one or more powerful interests, do not consider the wider public good. A prime example: Britain, with highly organized interests and politicians listening closely to them, went into economic decline until Margaret Thatcher blasted policy loose from both unions and owners.

Germany and Japan, their organized interests destroyed in World War II, were free for spectacular growth in the decades after the war. By the late twentieth century, however, both were so gunked up with labor, industry, and farming associations that their growth slowed to a trickle. Japan has an "iron triangle" of economic interest groups, politicians, and bureaucrats that defies reform. Some followers of Olson fear that such "sclerosis" is the fate of all countries. Has the United States fallen victim to or has it been able to periodically shake loose from overstrong interests?

Another problem is whether interest groups really speak for all their members or represent the views of a small but vocal minority. Most interest-group leaders, like leaders of political parties, have stronger views than followers. Leaders are often red-hot, simple members lukewarm.

STALEMATING POLITICAL POWER

Interest groups compete with one another, and in so doing limit the influence that any group can have on Congress or a government agency. Interest groups may stalemate government action. Certain issues are "hot potatoes" because government action either way arouses an outcry from one group or another. Typically, such issues are ardently supported and vehemently opposed by competing groups with enough voting power and influence to drive politicians to equivocation. Government may get stuck, trapped between powerful interests and unable to move on important problems. Italy has been called a "stalemate society" for this reason.

In two-party systems especially, issues tend to be muted by political candidates who try to appeal to as broad a segment of the voting public as possible. The result is a gap between the narrow interest of the individual voter and the general promises of an electoral campaign—a gap that interest groups attempt to fill by pressing for firm political actions on certain issues. But how well do interest groups serve the needs of the average citizen? The small businessperson, the uninformed citizen, and minority groups with little money tend to get lost in the push and pull of larger interests and government. The successful interest groups, too, tend to be dominated by a vocal minority of well-educated, middle- and upper-class political activists. In some cases interest groups have become so effective that they over-shadow parties and paralyze policymaking with their conflicting demands. The precise balance between the good of all and the good of particular groups has not yet been found.

KEY TERMS

AFL-CIO (p. 182)
amicus curiae (p. 187)
class action (p. 187)
corporatism (p. 176)
corruption (p. 179)
Diet (p. 177)
interest group (p. 173)
lobbying (p. 185)
MITI (p. 177)

NAM (p. 182)
political action committee (p. 180)
public financing (p. 179)
scandal (p. 179)
single-issue interest group (p. 182)
socioeconomic status (p. 183)
soft money (p. 180)
structured access (p. 185)
unforeseen consequence (p. 180)

KEY WEB SITES

American Association of Retired Persons
www.aarp.org/

American Civil Liberties Union
www.aclu.org/

Common Cause
www.commoncause.org/

National Association for the Advancement of Colored People
www.naacp.org/

National Organization for Women
www.now.org/

National Association of Manufacturers
www.nam.org/

American Federation of Labor-Congress of Industrial Organizations
www.aflcio.org/

National Rifle Association
www.nra.org/

FURTHER REFERENCE

Berry, Jeffrey M. *The New Liberalism: The Rising Power of Citizen Groups.* Washington, D.C.: Brookings, 2000.

Biersack, Robert, Paul S. Herrnson, and Clyde Wilcox, eds. *After the Revolution: PACs, Lobbies, and the Republican Congress.* Needham Heights, MA: Allyn & Bacon, 1999.

Browne, William P. *Groups, Interests, and U.S. Public Policy.* Washington, D.C.: Georgetown University Press, 1998.

Cigler, Allan J., and Burdett A. Loomis, eds. *Interest Group Politics,* 5th ed. Washington, D.C.: CQ Press, 1998.

Graziano, Luigi. *Lobbying, Pluralism and Democracy.* New York: Palgrave, 2001.

Grossman, Gene M., and Elhanan Helpman. *Special Interest Politics.* Cambridge, MA: MIT Press, 2002.

Johnson, Haynes, and David S. Broder. *The System: The American Way of Politics at the Breaking Point.* Boston, MA: Little, Brown, 1996.

Rauch, Jonathan. *Government's End: Why Washington Stopped Working.* New York: PublicAffairs, 1999.

Sabato, Larry J., and Glenn R. Simpson. *Dirty Little Secrets: The Persistence of Corruption in American Politics.* New York: Times Books/Random House, 1996.

Smith, Bradley A. *Unfree Speech: The Folly of Campaign Finance Reform.* Princeton, NJ: Princeton University Press, 2001.

Thomas, Clive S., ed. *Political Parties and Interest Groups: Shaping Democratic Governance.* Boulder, CO: Lynne Rienner, 2001.

POLITICAL PARTIES AND PARTY SYSTEMS

CHAPTER

11

QUESTIONS TO CONSIDER

- Can you have a democracy without competing parties?
- What is "interest aggregation" and how do parties do it?
- What good is party centralization, as in Britain?
- How can a party seemingly commit electoral suicide?
- How did Communist parties differ from democratic parties?
- How may parties be classified on an ideological spectrum?
- What is a "catchall" party?
- What are the several types of party systems?
- How do competitive party systems handle corruption?

To many Americans, a **political party** means little. The two major U.S. parties often appear alike; their basic values and proposals often overlap. In elections, candidate personality is usually more important than party. Many American political scientists worried that U.S. parties were becoming so weak that they could not do what parties are supposed to do.

This weakness of American parties is curious, for the United States was the first country to develop mass political parties, which appeared with the presidential election of 1800, decades before parties developed in Europe. Europeans, however, may have developed political parties more fully. Americans have tended to forget that parties are the great tools of democracy. As E. E. Schattschneider put it, "The rise of political parties is indubitably one of the principal distinguishing marks of modern government. Political parties created democracy; modern democracy is unthinkable save in terms of parties."

political party   Group seeking to elect office-holders under a given label.

Almost all present-day societies, democratic or not, have parties that link citizens to government. In much of the twentieth century, military dictators—such as Franco in Spain, Pinochet in Chile, or generals in Brazil—tried to dispense with parties, blaming them for the country's political ills. But even these dictators set up tame parties to bolster their rule, and after the dictators departed free parties appeared almost immediately. Love them or hate them, countries seem unable to do without political parties.

■ FUNCTIONS OF PARTIES

In both democracies and authoritarian systems, parties perform several important functions that help hold the political system together and keep it working.

A BRIDGE BETWEEN PEOPLE AND GOVERNMENT

To use a systems phrase, political parties are a major "inputting" device, allowing citizens to get their needs and wishes heard by government. Without parties, individuals would stand alone and be ignored by government. By working in or voting for a party, citizens can have some impact on political decisions. At a minimum, parties give people the feeling that they are not utterly powerless, and this belief helps maintain government legitimacy, one reason even dictatorships have a party.

AGGREGATION OF INTERESTS

If interest groups were the highest form of political organization, government would be terribly chaotic and unstable. One interest group would slug it out with another, trying to sway government officials this way and that. There would be few overarching values, goals, or ideologies that could command nationwide support. (Some worry that the United States already resembles this situation.) Parties help tame and calm interest group conflicts by **interest aggregation**—pulling together their separate interests into a larger organization. The interest groups then find that they must moderate their demands, cooperate, and work for the good of the party. In return, they achieve at least some of their goals. Parties, especially large parties, are often coalitions of interest groups.

INTEGRATION INTO THE POLITICAL SYSTEM

As the aggregation of interest groups goes on, parties pull groups that had previously been left out into the political system. Parties usually welcome new groups into their ranks, giving them a say or input into the formation of party platforms.

---

interest aggregation   Melding separate interests into general demands put forward by a political party.

CASE STUDIES

FDR's COALITION PARTY

A classic example of a party as interest aggregator was the Democratic party that Franklin D. Roosevelt built in the 1930s, a coalition that got him elected four times. It consisted of workers, farmers, Catholics, Jews, and blacks. Labor unions, for example, working with the Democrats, got labor legislation they could never have won on their own. As long as this coalition held together, the Democrats were unbeatable; since then the coalition has badly decayed. In the 1980s, Ronald Reagan aggregated economic and noneconomic conservative groups into the Republican party, a coalition revived by Bush in 2000.

This gives the groups both a pragmatic and a psychological stake in supporting the overall political system. Members of the group feel represented and develop a sense of efficacy and loyalty to the system. The British Labour party and the U.S. Democratic party, for example, enrolled workers by demanding union rights, fair labor practices, welfare benefits, and educational opportunities. Gradually, a potentially radical labor movement learned to play by democratic rules and support the system. Now, ironically, British and American workers are so successfully integrated into the political systems that many vote Conservative or Republican. In countries where parties were unable to integrate workers into the political system, labor movements turned radical and sometimes revolutionary. In the United States, parties also integrate successive waves of immigrants and minorities into American political life.

POLITICAL SOCIALIZATION

As parties integrate groups into society, they also teach their members how to play the political game. Parties introduce citizens to candidates or elected officials and show members how to speak in public, to conduct meetings, and to compromise, thus deepening their political competence and building among them legitimacy for the system as a whole. Parties are also the training grounds for leaders. Historically, some European parties attempted to set up distinct political subcultures—with party youth groups, soccer leagues, newspapers, women's sections, and so on. The effort was self-defeating, however, for as these parties socialized their members to participate in politics, the members emerged from their subcultures. The fading remnants of this effort can still be found in Italy both in the renamed Christian Democrats, now the Popular party, and the renamed Communists, now the Democratic Party of the Left. Some American parties provided social services. New York's Tammany Hall served as a welcome wagon for European immigrants, helping them find jobs and housing, while enrolling them as Democrats.

MOBILIZATION OF VOTERS

Parties get out the vote. In campaigning for their candidates, parties are **mobilizing** voters—whipping up interest and boosting turnout. The 2004 U.S. election is an example of this. Without party advertising, many citizens would ignore elections. Most political scientists believe there is a causal connection between weak U.S. political parties and low voter turnout. In Sweden, strong and well-organized parties have produced voter turnouts of 90 percent (recently lower). Some critics object that party electoral propaganda trivializes politics, but simplifying and clarifying issues enables voters to choose among complex alternatives.

ORGANIZATION OF GOVERNMENT

The winning party gets government jobs and power and tries to shift policy its way. The party with the most seats in the U.S. House of Representatives or Senate appoints the chamber's leaders and committee chairpersons. A new president can appoint some 3,000 people to executive departments and agencies, allowing the party to steer policy for at least four years. Party control of government in Britain is tighter than in the United States because Britain's parliamentary system gives simultaneous control of both the legislative and executive branches to the winning party. What a prime minister wants, he or she usually gets, and with minimal delay, because party discipline is much stronger. In no system, however, does a party completely control government, for bureaucrats are also quite powerful (see Chapter 16). Parties *attempt* to control government; they do not always succeed.

■ PARTIES IN DEMOCRACIES

In democracies, three points of party organization are important: the degree of **centralization**, the extent to which a party participates in policy, and how parties finance themselves.

CENTRALIZATION

The control party leadership can exert on its people elected to office varies widely. Israel has highly centralized candidate selection; each party draws up a national list of 120 nominees to the Knesset (parliament). Under proportional representation (see pages 239–240) only those listed at the top can be expected to win seats. Party chiefs can place tried and trusted people higher on the list and newcomers lower. This helps ensure centralized party discipline. Britain is a little less centralized. British parties select candidates by bargaining between national headquarters and

---

mobilization   Rousing people to participate in politics.
centralization   Degree of control exercised by national headquarters.

HOW TO . . .

CROSS-TABULATION

Across-tabulation is a table that shows two variables, arrayed so the reader can see a relationship between the two. When one is high, for example, so is the other. Let's take two variables, per capita GDP (page 186) and Freedom House's ranking of countries on a scale from 1 to 7, with 1 to 2.5 as "free," 3 to 5 as "partly free," and 5.5 to 7 as "not free."

Country	2003 Per Capita GDP at PPP	Freedom House 2005 Ranking
United States	$37,800	1 (free)
France	27,600	1 (free)
Mexico	9,000	2 (free)
Russia	8,900	5.5 (not free)
Colombia	6,300	4 (partly free)
China	5,000	6.5 (not free)
Syria	3,300	7 (not free)
India	2,900	2.5 (free)
Kenya	1,000	3 (partly free)

Sources: www.cia.gov/cia/publications/factbook/indexgeo.html and www.freedomhouse.org/ratings/index.htm

Readers quickly see that rich countries (the United States and France) and a middle-income country (Mexico) are democracies (what FH calls "free") but poorer countries generally are not. A cross-tab is not your whole paper; it is just a starting point and may raise questions. Here, for example, two countries, India and Russia do not fit. Why is poor India a democracy? We might study the long development of India's Congress party and how it set India on the course (sometimes unsteady) to democracy. And Russia, whose oil industry boosted its economic ranking, is not free. Kenya for a long time was unfree, but recently held reasonably free and fair elections. Economic level tells part of the story, but you must get into each country's history, institutions, and culture as well.

local constituency organizations. The national headquarters may suggest a candidate who is not from that district—often the case in Britain—and the local party will look the person over to approve or disapprove the candidate. The local party may also run its own candidate after clearing the nomination with national headquarters. Germany, like Israel, uses party lists but is divided into sixteen states where parties have the dominant say, thus partly decentralizing national party control. The varying degrees of centralization of these systems

KEY CONCEPTS

PARTIES THAT IGNORE VOTERS

Can a political party in a democracy ignore voters? According to democratic theory, no, for they will soon lose elections and have to change their tune. But according to **neo-institutional theory** (pages 33–34), they can be so self-absorbed that they rumble on with little regard to what voters want. An old, established party with strong traditions and leadership patterns may be so focused on struggles *inside* the party that they neglect voter opinion *outside* the party. The party as institution can take on a life of its own apart from trying to win elections. The British Labour party, talking mostly to itself and assuming positions too far left for most voters, lost four elections in a row. Finally getting sensible and centrist, they won in 1997, 2001, and 2005.

The Canadian Progressive Conservatives (PC) in 1983, under Brian Mulroney, won a majority of the House of Commons's 295 seats. Mulroney and the PC adopted Thatcherite free-market policies and stayed with them even though unemployment climbed and their popularity declined. The PC and Mulroney campaigned on the new free trade agreement (NAFTA) and won again in 1988, but with a reduced majority. A worsening economy, the Quebec question, and favoritism to certain firms brought the PC into public disrepute. Why didn't the PC change? Why didn't Mulroney resign? Eventually he did, but late in his second five-year term; he passed power to Kim Campbell, Canada's first woman prime minister, a short-lived sacrificial lamb. In the 1993 elections, the PC almost disappeared, winning only two (2!) seats out of 295. The Liberals took over Ottawa, and a new (but short-lived) Reform party displaced the PC in Canada's west.

Japan's Liberal Democratic party (LDP), which governed Japan for decades, also ignored voters. In 1990, however, Japan entered a long economic slump. Inept LDP leaders talked about financial reforms but delivered little. Factions inside the LDP blocked each other. LDP chiefs figured they would always be reelected because Japanese voters dislike change, but the voters grew fed up with the LDP and in a series of elections brought it down to less than half of the Diet seats. Many LDP politicians left the party to start new parties. (The LDP still governed, but in a coalition with other parties.)

The result in Canada and Japan: new parties. How could ruling parties shoot themselves in the foot? Do they read the polls? They do, but politics inside the parties and payoffs from interest groups mattered more to them than voters. They forgot their original purpose, to win elections. Actually, every time a major party loses big, it is a sign that they are too self-absorbed: the U.S. Republicans under Goldwater in 1964, the British Conservatives under Major in 1997, and the German Social Democrats under Kohl in 1998.

gives their parties **coherence**, discipline, and ideological consistency. When you vote for a party in Israel, Britain, or Germany you know what it stands for and what it will implement if elected. Once elected, members of these parliaments do not go their separate ways but vote according to party decisions.

Party discipline in the United States, where parties have historically been decentralized, is weaker. In most cases, candidates rely on themselves to raise funds

---

neo-institutional theory   Institutions take on lives of their own, sometimes disconnected from electorates.
coherence   Sticking together to make a rational whole.

and campaign. Candidates for the House and the Senate, in effect, create a new local party organization every time they run. Between elections, U.S. parties lie dormant. The Republican National Committee and Democratic National Committee may not have many resources to distribute to candidates. Candidates appeal directly to voters through television and other media. Increasingly, television advertisements do not even mention the candidate's party affiliation. Candidates are thus in a position to tell their national parties, "I owe you very little. I didn't get much party help to win, and I won't necessarily obey you now that I'm in office." This makes U.S. parties radically decentralized and often incoherent. Elected officials answer to their conscience, to their constituents, and to their PACs, and not to their political parties. President Reagan made the Republican party more coherent and cohesive. The Democrats, as usual, were not.

SETTING GOVERNMENT POLICY

To what extent can the winning party enact its legislative program? Here, the American party system faces its severest criticism. In parliamentary systems, the majority party must resign when it can no longer muster the votes to carry on its legislative program. The U.S. problem is often identifying where the majority lies. Some Democrats on certain measures vote with Republicans. Some change parties, as Sen. Jim Jeffords of Vermont did in 2001. The platform the president won on is not binding on congressional members of the party. Often the president's party is not the majority party in one or both houses. And who determines a party's legislative program? The president? The Speaker of the House? The Senate majority leader?

The U.S. president may present a legislative program, but it must be acted on by 535 individual senators and representatives, all ultimately responsible for their own vote, as they are for their own reelection. Is the president, then, to be blamed for failing to fulfill campaign promises, or does the fault lie with too-loose party discipline? Schattschneider argued that because U.S. national parties are so decentralized, they cannot agree on a strong national platform, making Washington "a punching bag for every special and local interest in the nation." Most Americans, however, prefer our senators and representatives to vote their consciences rather than the dictates of party leadership as is the case in Europe.

PARTY PARTICIPATION IN GOVERNMENT

A European type of parliamentary system is more conducive to what Schattschneider regards as responsible party government. The U.S. system, with its checks and balances, makes it difficult for parties to bridge the separation of powers to enact platforms. Occasionally, when a powerful president controls both the White House and Congress, party platforms turn into law, as when Lyndon Johnson got his **Great Society** program through the Democratic Congress of 1965–1966. No European parliamentary system had ever passed so many sweeping reforms so quickly.

Great Society   President Johnson's ambitious program of social reforms.

CLASSIC WORKS

DUVERGER'S THREE TYPES OF PARTIES

One of the first scholars to formulate a scheme for classifying political parties was French politi-cal scientist Maurice Duverger, who developed three descriptive categories: mass, cadre, or devotee. The **mass parties** are well organized and strive for a large and ideologically committed membrship, such as West European Socialist parties. They fund themselves with members' dues. In contrast, **cadre parties**, such as the U.S. Democratic and Republican parties, are weakly organized and based on a politically active elite. Duverger uses the term **devotee** for parties such as the Nazis under Hitler, where the party's formal structure is built around one person. Latin American strong-men, such as Peron of Argentina and Vargas of Brazil, built **personalistic parties** to keep themselves in power. One such recent party was Saddam Hussein's Ba'ath (Arab Renaissance) party in Iraq. Personalistic parties, however, have trouble outliving their founder.

In West European parliamentary systems, the winning party is the govern-ment, or more precisely, the party's leadership team becomes the cabinet. This sys-tem allows for more clear-cut accountability and voter choice than in the decentralized American party system. In both systems, parties participate in gov-ernment by providing jobs for party activists in departments and agencies. In Britain, about 100 members of the winning party's parliamentary faction take on cabinet and subcabinet positions, compared to the 3,000 Americans who can receive **political appointments** when a new president takes office.

FINANCING THE PARTY

Parties must finance their activities, and these are increasingly expensive, deepening the parties' dependence on rich interest groups. There is little **transparency** in these relationships. As one political scientist put it: "Whole books could remain unwritten if we just knew how parties got their money." Japan's Liberal Democ-rats were notorious for the sums they received from businesses, banks, farmer fed-erations, and even *yakuza* gangsters. The traditional European style of small membership dues does not provide nearly enough, and parties have become des-perate to raise money. Some do it crookedly. Almost every democratic country has recently suffered scandals related to party fund-raising: the United States, Britain,

---

mass party   One that attempts to gain committed adherents; usually has formal membership.

cadre party   One run by a few political professionals and only intermittently active.

devotee party   One based on a single personality.

personalistic party   Based on personality of strong ruler.

political appointment   Government job given to non–civil servant, often as reward for support.

transparency   Political money and transactions open to public scrutiny.

France, Germany, and Japan. The problem may be incurable, related to the political competition that is the crux of democracy. In 1976, an estimated $500 million was spent on U.S. political campaigns. In 2004, an estimated $4 billion was spent for presidential and congressional campaigns. In contrast, total spending in the 2001 British general elections was only $100 million, but it too is growing rapidly.

As we discussed in the previous chapter, many democracies have laws to restrict or regulate political contributions. Germany, Spain, Sweden, and Finland use government funds to subsidize political parties in proportion to each party's electoral strength. This obviously discriminates against new parties. The U.S. Congress in 1974 passed a similar plan (the Presidential Campaign Fund), which allowed taxpayers to authorize the Internal Revenue Service to designate $3 of their income tax payment for the fund, which subsidized presidential nominees in proportion to the votes they received, provided they got a minimum of 5 percent nationwide. But only one taxpayer in four authorizes the checkoff, far too little to cover campaign expenses. PACs and 527s (discussed in Chapter 10) have filled the vacuum with a vengeance.

CLASSIFYING POLITICAL PARTIES

One basic way to classify parties is on a left-to-right spectrum, according to party ideology (see Chapter 6). Left-wing parties, such as Communists, propose leveling of class differences by **nationalizing** major industries. Center-left parties, such as the Socialist parties of Western Europe, favor welfare states but not nationalizing industry. Centrist parties, such as the German and Italian Liberals, are generally liberal on social questions but conservative (that is, free market) on economics. Center-right parties, such as the German Christian Democrats, want to rein in (but not dismantle) the welfare state in favor of free enterprise. Right-wing parties, such as the British Conservatives under Thatcher, want to dismantle the welfare state, break the power of unions, and promote vigorous capitalist growth. Sweden has a rather complete political spectrum (see Figure 11.1 on page 202).

■ THE PARTY IN COMMUNIST STATES

Communist systems—that is, countries ruled by Communist parties—have become rare. In Eastern Europe and the Soviet Union, Communist parties were voted out of power. China, Vietnam, North Korea, and Cuba tried to preserve the party-controlled state, but they too appeared ripe for change.

The "classic" Communist system founded by Lenin and developed by Stalin in the Soviet Union featured the interlocking of a single party with government and the economy. The Communist party did not rule directly; instead it supervised, monitored, and controlled the personnel of the state and economic structures.

---

nationalization   Putting major industries under government ownership.

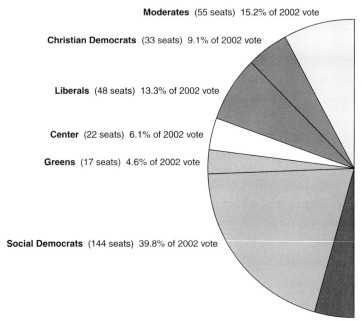

Moderates (55 seats) 15.2% of 2002 vote

Christian Democrats (33 seats) 9.1% of 2002 vote

Liberals (48 seats) 13.3% of 2002 vote

Center (22 seats) 6.1% of 2002 vote

Greens (17 seats) 4.6% of 2002 vote

Social Democrats (144 seats) 39.8% of 2002 vote

Party of the Left (30 seats) 8.3% of 2002 vote

Figure 11.1

The parties in Sweden's unicameral Riksdag (parliament) show a left-right ideological spectrum, with percent and number of seats (out of 349) each won in the 2002 elections. Swedish elections use proportional representation (see Chapter 13). Needing a majority of Riksdag seats, the Social Democrats governed in a coalition with the Left and Green parties.

Members—perhaps 10 percent of the adult population—were hand-picked from among the most intelligent, energetic, and enthusiastic. Most Soviet officials wore two hats, one as government functionary and another as Communist party member. Every level of government, from local to national, had a corresponding party body that nominated its candidates and set its general lines of policy. At the top of the state structure, for example, was the legislature—the Supreme Soviet. Corresponding to it in the party system, the Central Committee oversaw the nomination of candidates to the Supreme Soviet, set its agenda, and guided its legislative outcomes. Supervising the Central Committee, the **Politburo** of a dozen or so top party leaders was the real heart of Soviet governance. Guiding the Politburo was the party's general secretary, who could appoint loyal followers to high positions and thus amass great power.

Why did Soviet President Mikhail Gorbachev deliberately undermine this structure? A single party that attempts to control everything important develops severe

---

Politburo   Russian for "political bureau"; the ruling committee of a Communist party.

CLASSIC WORKS

KIRCHHEIMER'S "CATCHALL" PARTY

Accompanying the tendency of most democracies to two-plus party systems has been the growth of big, sprawling parties that attempt to appeal to all manner of voters. Before World War II, many European parties were ideologically narrow and tried to win over only certain sectors of the population. Socialist parties were still at least partly Marxist and aimed their messages largely at the working class. Centrist and conservative parties aimed at the middle and upper classes, agrarian parties at farmers, Catholic parties at Catholics, and so on. These were called **Weltanschauung** parties because they tried not merely to win votes but also to promote their view of the world.

After World War II, Europe changed a lot. With prosperity, people began to reject the old ideological narrowness. In most of Western Europe big, ideologically loose parties that welcomed all voters either absorbed or drove out the *Weltanschauung* parties. German political scientist Otto Kirchheimer coined the term **catchall** to describe this new type of party. His model was the German Christian Democratic party, a party that sought to speak for all Germans: businesspersons, workers, farmers, Catholics, Protestants, women, you name it. The term now describes virtually all ruling parties in democratic lands; almost axiomatically, they must be catchall parties to win. The British Conservatives, Spanish and French Socialists, and Japanese Liberal Democrats are catchall parties. And, of course, the biggest and oldest catchall parties of all are the U.S. Republicans and Democrats.

Most political scientists welcome this move away from narrowness and rigidity, but with it comes another problem. Because catchall parties are big and contain many viewpoints, they are plagued by factional quarrels. Struggles within parties replace struggles between parties. Scholars counted many factions in the Italian Christian Democrats and Japanese Liberal Democrats, parties that resembled each other in their near-feudal division of power among the parties' leading personalities. A good deal of American politics also takes place within rather than between the major parties.

problems over the years. Because it gives members the best jobs, housing, and consumer goods, the party fills up with **opportunists**, many of them corrupt. The party **apparatchiks** also become highly conservative. The system favors them, and they have no desire to reform it. With such people supervising it, the Soviet economy ran down and fell farther behind the American, West European, and Japanese economies. A Communist party that was to lead the Soviet Union into a radiant future came to be seen as leading the country backwards. Gorbachev concluded that to save his country he had to break the Communist party's monopoly on power. Gorbachev failed to understand (as did many Western political scientists) how brittle the system was. Unable to reform, it collapsed.

Weltanschauung   German for "worldview"; parties that attempt to sell a particular ideology.

catchall   Large, ideologically loose parties that welcome all.

opportunists   Persons out for themselves.

apparatchik   Russian for "person of the apparatus"; full-time Communist party functionary.

The Soviet experience suggests that single parties that monopolize power are not workable over the long-term. Without the invigorating elements of debate, competition, and accountability, Communist-type parties become corrupt, inflexible, and unable to handle the new, complex tasks of a modern world. Study Communist systems while you can; soon there may be none left.

■ PARTY SYSTEMS

There is a logical distinction between "parties" and "party systems." Parties are organizations aimed at influencing government, usually by winning elections. **Party systems** are the interactions of parties with each other and with the overall political system. Much of the health of a political system depends on the party system, whether it is stable or unstable, whether it has too many parties, and whether they compete in a "center-seeking" or "center-fleeing" manner. An unstable party system can wreck an otherwise good constitution. Stable, moderate party systems made democracy possible in West Germany after Hitler and in Spain after Franco. In turn, much of the country's party system depends on its **electoral system**— whether it is based on single-member districts or on proportional representation.

CLASSIFYING PARTY SYSTEMS

The simplest way to classify party systems is to count the number of parties in them: one-party, dominant-party, two-party, two-plus, and multiparty. Theoretically, there can be a no-party system but, as we discussed, even dictators like obedient parties to support them. And some systems may be so messy we could call them fluid or **inchoate** party systems.

The One-Party System   Associated with totalitarian regimes of the left or right, this is a twentieth-century phenomenon. The Soviet Union, China, and many of the emerging nations of Africa and Asia are or were one-party states. These have a single party that controls every level of government and is the only legal party allowed in the country.

The leaders of such parties rationalize that they are still democratic because they represent what the people really want and need. No fair election or honest public-opinion poll can substantiate this claim. When allowed, as in East European countries, citizens repudiate one-party systems. Some developing lands, especially in Africa, argue that having several parties spells chaos and violence, for they form along tribal lines.

---

party system   How parties interact with each other.
electoral system   Laws for running elections; two general types: single-member district and proportional.
inchoate   Not yet formed.

WHAT IS A "RELEVANT" PARTY?

Columbia University political scientist Giovanni Sartori asks just what counts as a party? Every group that calls itself a party? Every group that wins a certain percentage of votes or at least one seat in parliament? We should count as "relevant parties," Sartori argues, those which the main parties have to take into account either in campaigning for votes or in forming coalitions. If a party is so small and weak that no major party needs to worry about trying to win over its adherents, it is irrelevant. Likewise, if it is unnecessary in forming a governing coalition, it is irrelevant. Thus, British Trotskyists and Irish Communists are ignored by all and do not count as parties, but Sweden's Liberals and Israel's small religious parties, each with only a few percent of the vote, may be necessary coalition partners and thus count as relevant parties.

Using Sartori's definition of "relevant" parties, would we include various American third-party efforts? Although the Democrats in 1948 denied the importance of the States' Rights party (Dixiecrats) and in 1968 the importance of Wallace's forces, in both elections they took them into account. In 1968, Democratic nominee Hubert Humphrey visited the South and emphasized that the Democratic party was a "very big house" that could accommodate many viewpoints, a lame attempt to make white southern voters forget the civil rights reforms of the Johnson administration. In 1980, the independent candidacy of John Anderson probably forced President Carter to emphasize foreign and ecological policies he might otherwise have minimized. In 1992, Ross Perot forced Bush and Clinton to pay more attention to the federal budget deficit. In 2004, John Kerry paid attention to Ralph Nader's effort, for it had cost the Democrats the 2000 election. In these cases, we could say the United States had relevant third parties. The tiny Communist, Socialist Worker, and Socialist Labor parties no one has to take into account, so under Sartori's definition we should not consider them relevant. Do the Republicans pay attention to the Libertarian party, an extreme free-market party that pledges the near dismantling of the federal government?

The Dominant-Party System In contrast to one-party systems, opposition parties in dominant-party systems are free to contest elections, but they rarely win. Some democratic nations had dominant-party systems, but they tend not to last because voters get fed up with the dominant party's corruption and ineptitude. India was long governed by the Congress party, Japan by the Liberal Democratic party, and Mexico by the Party of Institutional Revolution (PRI). In 2000 Mexico's conservative National Action party (PAN) overcame PRI's lock on the presidency with the election of Vicente Fox, thus moving Mexico from a dominant-party to a multiparty system (flanked on the left by the Revolutionary Democratic party).

The Two-Party System Most familiar to us is the two-party system of the United States and Britain. Here, two major parties have a fairly equal chance of winning. Although third parties, such as Ralph Nader's and Britain's Liberal Democrats, seldom win, they serve to remind the two big parties of voter discontent. Often one or both of the two main parties then offer policies calculated to win over the discontented. In this way, even small third parties can have an impact.

MULTIPARTY SYSTEMS ARE MORE FUN

In a multiparty system, you get to choose from a bigger menu. With several relevant parties, as in Sweden (see Figure 11.1 on page 202), you can find a party that matches your preferences much better than just the two big U.S. parties. In most of Europe, people concerned about the environment can vote for a Green party. Serious Christians can vote for a Christian Democratic party. Leftists can vote for a Socialist party and conservatives for a Conservative party.

True, U.S. ballots (depending on the state) may list more than a dozen parties, ranging from Green to Libertarian to Socialist Workers, but if you vote for them you know you are throwing your vote away. Such is the impact of our winner-take-all electoral system, so a vote for a third-party in the United States is simply a protest vote. Voters in much of Europe and in Israel know they are not throwing their votes away; if their party gets some minimum threshold (5 percent in Germany, 1.5 percent in Israel), the party wins some seats in parliament. The interesting choices on European ballots help explain Europe's higher voter turnout.

Some observers argue that new political ideas come mostly from third parties, as the big parties are too stuck in their ways.

The Multiparty System   These have several competing parties. The Swedish party system (as we saw in Figure 11.1 on page 202) shows how its parties, arrayed on a left-to-right spectrum, receive seats in parliament in proportion to their share of the vote. This system is often criticized as being unstable. Israel and Italy are examples of the shortcomings of having too many parties, as each has been unable to keep any government in power for a long time. A fragmented party system makes it harder for any one party to win a governing majority, but this is not always the case. The Netherlands, Sweden, and Norway generally manage to construct stable multiparty coalitions that govern effectively. The number of parties is not the only reason for cabinet **instability**. Much depends on the political culture, the degree of agreement on basic issues, and the rules for forming and dissolving a cabinet. Scholars have spent considerable effort debating which is better, two-party or multiparty systems. It's hard to say, for both have fallen prey to indecision and **immobilism**. In the meantime, there has been a drift in both systems toward a middle ground, "two-plus" party systems.

The Two-Plus Party System   Many democratic countries now have two large parties with one or more relevant smaller parties. Germany has large Christian Democratic and Social Democratic parties, but the Free Democratic and Green parties win enough votes to make them politically important. Austria was long

instability   Frequent changes of cabinet.
immobilism   Getting stuck over a major political issue.

dominated by two big parties, but now has a third party, the highly nationalistic and anti-immigrant Freedom party. Britain is often referred to as a two-party system, but it has long had third parties of some importance: the Liberal Democrats, the Scottish Nationalists, and Plaid Cymru (the Welsh nationalists). Even Spain, which has a history of multiparty fragmentation, now has a **two-plus party system**: a large Socialist party, a large center-right Popular party, and a scattering of smaller parties. The U.S. system is also really two-plus, for it too has long had third parties, some of which were mentioned earlier. Did a third party count in the 2004 U.S. election?

Fluid Party Systems   New and unstable democracies often have party systems so fluid and inchoate they change before your eyes and fit none of the above categories. "Mess" is the only way to describe them. In such countries, parties rise and fall quickly—sometimes existing just for one election—often personalistic vehicles to get leaders elected, but otherwise standing for no program or ideology. Poorly organized, many of them soon fall apart. Charismatic Latin American politicians often invent new parties, but they rarely last. In Poland, Czechoslovakia, and Hungary, broad catchalls ousted the Communists in 1989, won free elections, but soon fragmented. The Russian party system is fluid; President Putin founded his own Unity party just before the 1999 election and by 2004 turned it into Russia's largest, but it is personalistic, just a tool for Putin to govern with. The Japanese system broke down from a dominant-party system to an inchoate one in the 1990s. After some years, these systems may settle down into two-plus or multiparty systems.

As long as there are at least two parties, we call the system a "competitive party system," the essence of which is to impede corruption. A single party that locks itself in power, whatever its ideological rationale, inevitably becomes corrupt. Corruption can be kept in check only by the "out" party or parties hammering away at alleged corruption in the administration of the "in" party. The utility of a competitive party system was underscored in 1989 in East Germany, where Communist leaders were revealed to have skimmed millions from foreign-trade deals and stashed them in Swiss banks for personal use. When such antics are uncovered in competitive-party systems, the "ins" are soon out.

THE PARTY SYSTEM AND THE ELECTORAL SYSTEM

How a nation gets its party system is unclear. Much is rooted in historical developments. When and under what circumstances was the electoral franchise expanded? Some very different countries have similar party systems: Culturally segmented India produced a dominant party system (under the Congress party), as did culturally homogeneous Japan (under the Liberal Democrats). Single-factor explanations do not suffice, but political scientists generally agree on the importance of the electoral system, which we shall review in greater detail in Chapter 13.

---

two-plus party system   Country having two big and one or more small parties.

CLASSIC WORKS

SARTORI'S TYPES OF PARTY COMPETITION

Giovanni Sartori (see earlier box on page 205), among others, is not satisfied with simply count-ing the number of parties to classify party systems. Also important is the degree and manner in which the parties *compete*. The term *multiparty system* does not differentiate between those systems that are stable and those that are unstable. Sartori does; he delineates party systems of "moderate plu-ralism" from those of **polarized pluralism**.

In the former, there are usually five parties or fewer, and they compete in a **center-seeking** or centripetal manner; that is, their platforms and promises appeal to middle-of-the-road voters. Left-wing parties curb their radicalism and right-wing parties dampen their conservatism, for both know that the bulk of the voting public is in the center. Thus, political life in moderate pluralism tends to be calm and stable, with ideological considerations toned down.

When the number of parties is greater than five or six, Sartori finds, there is the danger of po-larized pluralism. Here, the parties compete in a **center-fleeing** or centrifugal manner, becoming ideologically extreme and engaging in a "politics of outbidding" with their rivals. Some parties offer more and more radical solutions, either radical left or radical right. Some are "antisystem" or revo-lutionary. Parties that try to stick to the center find themselves attacked from both sides. Such a sit-uation causes political instability, sometimes leading to civil war, as in Spain in the 1930s, or to military takeover, as in Chile in 1973.

Single-member election districts, such as U.S. congressional districts, where a simple plurality wins, tend to produce two-party or two-plus systems. The reason is clear: Small third parties are underrepresented in such systems and often give up trying. Such is the case in the United States and Britain, based on the original Eng-lish model. The British call this the "first past the post" (FPTP) system, as it re-sembles a horse race; even a nose better wins. There is a big premium in single-member districts on combining political forces to form the party with a ma-jority or at least a plurality. If one party splits, it often throws the election to the party that hangs together. The factions within a party may not love each other, but they know they must stay together to have any political future. This factor goes a long way toward explaining why the two big American parties remain in-tact despite considerable internal differences.

Proportional representation (PR) allows and perhaps even encourages parties to split. PR systems use multimember districts and assign parliamentary seats in pro-portion to the percentage of votes in that district. Accordingly, not such a big pre-mium is placed on holding parties together; a splinter group may decide that it can

---

polarized pluralism   System in which parties become more extremist.

center-seeking   Parties become moderate, aiming for large block of votes in center of political spectrum.

center-fleeing   Parties become extremist, ignoring voters in center.

get one or two people elected without having to compromise with other viewpoints. Israel's PR system put fifteen parties in the Knesset. Modification of electoral laws can change a country's party system, pushing a country from a multiparty to a two-plus system, as in Germany, from a multiparty system to a "two-bloc" system, as in France, or from an exceedingly fragmented multiparty system to a moderate one, as in Poland.

ARE PARTIES FADING?

Parties are not what they used to be. In most democracies, party membership is down, and voters are less loyal. The big ideological clashes of the twentieth century are over; most parties are centrist and similar. The mass media and interest groups have taken over some of the functions of parties. New policy ideas often come from specialists in think tanks. But what will take the place of parties? 527s? Television? Neither prospect is appealing.

U.S. parties may foreshadow the future of parties elsewhere. Dependent on big money, parties fall under special-interest influence. Because U.S. parties are weakly organized and decentralized—in effect, every congressional district and state has its own parties, little related to each other—the parties do not cohere well at the national level. Said one nineteenth-century politician: "I belong to no organized party, sir. I'm a Democrat." Because there are only two main parties, each aiming for the political center, they do not offer voters much to choose from. These characteristics are no longer just American but also found in Europe and Japan.

Can anything be done? Parties and party systems are rooted in their countries' history, society, and institutions. The U.S. Constitution never recognized parties, and the Founding Fathers warned against them. American society is not terribly fragmented; it may not need more than two parties to express the general divisions within the population. Single-member districts with simple plurality win favor a two-party system. Realistically, we can expect no major change in America's two-party system.

There has been some movement toward U.S. party centralization. Ronald Reagan made the Republicans a more coherent conservative party with a reasonably clear program, forcing the Democrats to get their act together. Information technology is helping to centralize the parties. Computerized mailing lists induce state and local party organizations to cooperate with national headquarters. The national party committees can also channel PAC money to loyal candidates. In the long run, this may make the two parties more cohesive and ideologically consistent.

And there may be an advantage in *not* having strong parties, which may fall into the hands of oligarchic leaders who control too much and stay too long, getting the party stuck in rigid and outmoded viewpoints. The U.S. system, by virtue of its very fluidity, may be better able to process demands from a wider range of citizens. The lack of programmatic coherence confers the benefit of flexibility.

KEY TERMS

apparatchik (p. 203)
cadre party (p. 200)
catchall (p. 203)
centralization (p. 196)
center-fleeing (p. 208)
center-seeking (p. 208)
coherence (p. 198)
devotee party (p. 200)
electoral system (p. 204)
Great Society (p. 199)
immobilism (p. 206)
inchoate (p. 204)
instability (p. 206)
interest aggregation (p. 194)

mass party (p. 200)
mobilization (p. 196)
nationalization (p. 201)
neo-institutional theory (p. 198)
opportunist (p. 203)
party system (p. 204)
personalistic party (p. 200)
polarized pluralism (p. 208)
Politburo (p. 202)
political appointment (p. 200)
political party (p. 193)
transparency (p. 200)
two-plus party system (p. 207)
Weltanschauung (p. 203)

KEY WEB SITES

Democratic National Committee
www.democrats.org/

Republican National Committee
www.rnc.org/

Green party
www.greens.org/

Libertarian party
www.lp.org/

Reform party
www.reformparty.org/

European socialist parties
www.pes.org/

FURTHER REFERENCE

Alexander, Herbert E. *Financing Politics: Money, Elections, and Political Reform,* 4th ed. Washington, D.C.: CQ Press, 1992.
Beck, Paul Allen, and Marjorie Randon Hershey. *Party Politics in America,* 10th ed. White Plains, NY: Longman, 2002.
Bibby, John F., and L. Sandy Maisel. *Two Parties—Or More?: The American Party System.* Boulder, CO: Westview, 1998.

Carty, R. Kenneth, William Cross, and Lisa Young. *Rebuilding Canadian Party Politics.* Vancouver, BC: University of British Columbia Press, 2000.

Cohen, Jeffrey E., Richard Fleisher, and Paul Kantor, eds. *American Political Parties: Decline or Resurgence?* Washington, D.C.: CQ Press, 2001.

Dalton, Russell J., and Martin P. Wattenberg, eds. *Parties without Partisans: Political Change in Advanced Industrial Democracies.* New York: Oxford University Press, 2001.

Duverger, Maurice. *Political Parties: Their Organization and Activities in the Modern State,* 3rd ed. London: Methuen, 1964.

Eldersveld, Samuel J., and Hanes Walton, Jr. *Political Parties in American Society,* 2nd ed. New York: St. Martin's, 2000.

Karvonen, Lauri, and Stein Kuhnle, eds. *Party Systems and Voter Alignments Revisited.* New York: Routledge, 2001.

Keefe, William J., and Marc J. Hetherington. *Parties, Politics, and Public Policy in America,* 9th ed. Washington, D.C.: CQ Press, 2003.

Mair, Peter. *Party System Change: Approaches and Interpretations.* New York: Oxford University Press, 1997.

Rosenstone, Steven J., and John Mark Hansen. *Mobilization, Participation, and Democracy in America.* White Plains, NY: Longman, 2002.

Ware, Alan. *Political Parties and Party Systems.* New York: Oxford University Press, 1996.

ELECTIONS

CHAPTER 12

QUESTIONS TO CONSIDER

- Why did U.S. voting turnout rise in 2004?
- What went wrong with the U.S. electoral system in 2000?
- Should we view U.S. nonvoting with alarm?
- How does party ID help decide elections?
- Why is there a "gender gap" in U.S. voting?
- Does income predict how a person votes?
- Are we seeing electoral realignment, dealignment, or neither?
- How does the economy influence elections?

In this chapter we ask three general questions about voting, each followed by a more specific question about voting in the United States. First, we ask why people vote. This leads us to the puzzle of why voting turnout in the United States is low. Second, we ask how people vote. This brings us to the question of whether party loyalties in the United States are shifting. Finally, we ask what wins elections. This takes us to some of the strategies used in U.S. elections.

■ WHY DO PEOPLE VOTE?

Although committed to democracy and participation, Americans vote less than citizens of other democracies. In the 2004 U.S. election, 55.3 percent of those eligible voted, a major improvement from previous years. Likely reason: Both parties worked hard to turn out their potential supporters. Historically, voter **turnout** in

---

turnout Percent of those eligible who vote.

the United States was never high; its peak in 1960 was 63 percent. Turnout in Sweden, Germany, and Italy has reached 90 percent. Black South Africans in 1994, allowed to vote for the first time, had a turnout of 86 percent, a measure of how much they appreciated the right to cast a ballot.

In nonpresidential elections, U.S. turnout is perhaps a quarter to a third. Why do Americans vote so little? Typically, more than half of U.S. nonvoters say they are uninterested in or dissatisfied with candidates. Many feel their vote makes no difference or that none of the candidates is really good. Another reason is the U.S. party system, in which the two large parties may not offer an interesting or clear-cut choice; both tend to centrist positions. Television saturates voters so long in advance—often with primitive, dirty political spots—that disgust many with both parties by election day. Fewer than one adult American in twenty is involved enough in politics to attend a political meeting, contribute money, or canvass a neighborhood.

U.S. nonvoting has brought major debate among political scientists. One school views the decline with alarm, arguing that low electoral participation means that many Americans are turning away from the political system, which loses legitimacy. Another school is unworried, arguing that the decline means Americans most of the time are basically satisfied with the system, or not sufficiently dissatisfied to go to register and vote. Countries with very high voter turnouts may have a sort of political fever in which partisan politics has become too intense. The United States experienced some of this intensity in 2004, when emotional issues and a divided electorate brought out more voters.

Unusually high turnout in 2004 saw voters line up early in a rural polling station where there is usually no line. (Michael Roskin)

CASE STUDIES

IS THE U.S. ELECTORAL SYSTEM DEFECTIVE?

The 2000 U.S. presidential election was a double train wreck, and both train wrecks were waiting to happen: (1) An anachronistic **Electoral College** was eventually going to deny victory to the popular-vote winner; and (2) a defective balloting mechanism was eventually going to really matter. Gore, with a nontrivial half-a-million more votes (0.51 percent more), lost in electoral votes to Bush, 271–266. Similar situations had happened three times in the nineteenth century.

States and counties use whatever balloting system they wish, including defective ones. Some still use paper ballots, some hand-lever voting machines designed in 1892, and some light-scanned ballots. Counties are slow to upgrade to electronic and touch-screen systems because of cost. The worst type of system was in Palm Beach County, Florida, which had a widely used and cheap forty-year-old technology: Voters put an IBM-type card into a metal frame and punched out a rectangle by their choice. Some of the little "chads"—as high as 6 percent—were not completely punched out, so counting machines read them as "no vote." The system was long known to be defective and had spawned court cases in several states; Massachusetts had outlawed it.

Making things worse in Palm Beach was a two-page "butterfly ballot" that confused voters, many of whom accidentally voted for rightwing populist Pat Buchanan instead of the intended Al Gore. Those who tried to fix the error by making another punch invalidated their ballot. This strongly Democratic county lost some 20,000 votes for Gore, several times more than were needed to win Florida and to win in the Electoral College.

The Electoral College was designed to overrepresent states with fewer voters, especially the Southern states, where slave-owning elites rejected notions of "one person, one vote." Each state gets as many electors as its senators and representatives, so even very small states get three electors. A vote for president in a thinly populated state has several times the power of a vote for president in a populous state. A vote in Wyoming is worth almost four times that of a vote in California. And small states, a huge swath of the middle of America, tend to go Republican. States with big cities, clustered in the Northeast and on the Great Lakes and West Coast, tend to go Democrat.

The Electoral College is widely thought to be an **anachronism** but can't be seriously reformed because nineteen small states with three or fewer representatives like being overrepresented.

Why the difference between European and American turnout? One obvious reason is that in Europe registration is automatic, upon reaching eighteen local authorities register you. Americans must register personally, months before the election and before campaign excitement mounts. U.S. elections are held on Tuesdays, in much of Europe on Sundays. The U.S. long ballot with many local, state, and national candidates plus referendums baffles voters. European (and Canadian)

Electoral College   U.S. system of weighting popular presidential vote to favor smaller states.

anachronism   Something out of the past.

These states can block constitutional change, which requires two-thirds of each house plus three-fourths of the state legislatures. Is the U.S. system unreformable?

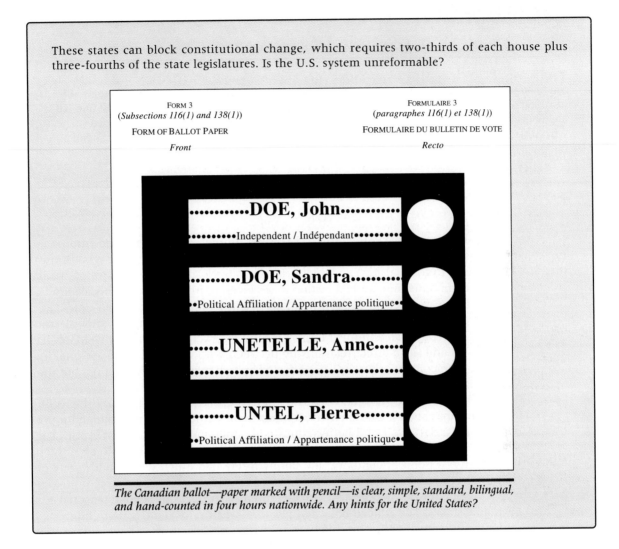

FORM 3
(Subsections 116(1) and 138(1))

FORM OF BALLOT PAPER

Front

FORMULAIRE 3
(paragraphes 116(1) et 138(1))

FORMULAIRE DU BULLETIN DE VOTE

Recto

DOE, John
Independent / Indépendant

DOE, Sandra
Political Affiliation / Appartenance politique

UNETELLE, Anne

UNTEL, Pierre
Political Affiliation / Appartenance politique

The Canadian ballot—paper marked with pencil—is clear, simple, standard, bilingual, and hand-counted in four hours nationwide. Any hints for the United States?

ballots are simple, usually just a choice of party, and most countries control and limit television political advertising; some allow none. America might take a hint.

■ WHO VOTES?

Voters in most democracies tend to be middle-aged and better educated with white-collar jobs, more urban and suburban than rural. They are also more likely to identify with a political party. Nonvoters show the reverse of these characteristics: young, lacking education, and with blue-collar or no jobs. Income and education, race, age, gender, and area of residence are key factors in who votes.

DOWN'S THEORY OF VOTING

In a landmark 1957 work, *An Economic Theory of Democracy,* Anthony Downs theorized that people vote if the returns outweigh the costs. That is, if the stakes seem important, citizens will go to the trouble of voting. Property owners fearing tax hikes are much more likely to vote than renters not immediately hurt by the tax. The cost of political information, both financial and personal, also determines whether a person will vote. Not all have the energy or interest to follow political news or attend political meetings. Accordingly, the poor and uneducated in every society are the least likely to vote.

INCOME AND EDUCATION

High-income people vote more than the less affluent, the well-educated more than high-school dropouts. These two characteristics often come together (good education leads to good salaries) and reinforce each other. High income gives people a stake in election outcomes, and education raises levels of interest and sophistication.

Factory workers in small towns may see little difference between candidates. They pay taxes, follow rules, make a living, and see little difference under Democratic or Republican administrations. In contrast, executives and professionals feel involved and see a direct relationship between who wins and their personal fortune. Blue-collar workers are also affected by a change in administration, but they are less likely to know it.

The difference between voters and nonvoters is a feeling of *efficacy,* the feeling that one has at least a little power. It tends to be low for workers and high for professionals. Better-off and better-educated people have seen interest groups succeed in changing policy. Blue-collar workers likely see political life as a "silent majority." Friends, neighbors, and family rarely had much wealth and rarely organized to pressure the government.

Well-educated people have broader interests in elections beyond personal economic stakes. The college-educated person—wealthy or not—is more interested, better informed, and more likely to participate in elections. As we discussed in Chapter 7, education provides a sense of participation and an abstract intellectual curiosity, which makes people more likely to follow political news and feel involved. Much research shows that education is the strongest determinant of who votes.

RACE

Despite federal laws and black organizations, black voting rates are lower than white. The gap may eventually close as black income and education levels rise. The 1965 Voting Rights Act overcame some of the barriers placed in the way of black registration, chiefly in the South. Many blacks have gone through political consciousness-raising and learned the value of participation and voting. Some previously racist white politicians got the message and became respectful toward their

Black voter registration in recent decades has enfranchised a group of citizens who previously had little political clout but who are now courted by candidates of both parties. (Laima E. Druskis)

black constituents. Latinos faced similar problems and also showed low turnouts. Race, accordingly, is still a factor in U.S. election turnout.

AGE

Young people—those under twenty-five—typically feel less politically involved, and they vote less. About half of U.S. citizens eighteen to twenty-five are currently not registered to vote. Young people, with little income and property, also feel economically uninvolved with election outcomes. When they start paying taxes, they become more interested. Focused on the concerns of youth, many have no time or interest in political questions, which seem abstract and distant.

In 1971 the Twenty-sixth Amendment lowered the U.S. voting age from twenty-one to eighteen at almost the same time that most other democracies did. The results were similar: The newly **enfranchised** young people did not vote as much as their elders, and when they did, their votes were little different. Middle-aged and older people are more likely to vote than the young, probably because the middle-aged person is at peak earning power, and the old person is concerned about Social Security and Medicare. In recent U.S. elections, those over seventy show the highest turnout.

GENDER

Traditionally, men were more likely to vote than women in almost every society. Women had only comparatively recently won the right to vote. (Switzerland enfranchised women only in 1971.) Since 1920, when female **suffrage** was granted

---

franchise   Right to vote.
suffrage   Right to vote.

CASE STUDIES

The Puzzle of Education and Voting

All studies agree that education makes people more participatory. But declining U.S. turnout happened precisely as U.S. educational levels *grew*. America has the highest percentage of both young people in college and college-educated citizens. That should make us very participatory and should lead to rising voter turnouts.

No one has cracked this puzzle. Education may not mean what it used to. The sheer numbers of U.S. college graduates have diluted its former elite status. A college degree, in terms of getting a job nowadays, is more like a high-school diploma before World War II. Many majors are vocational or career-related and do not awaken curiosity or knowledge of the nation and world.

And perhaps voting does not mean what it used to. Even well-educated citizens may not see a great choice between parties and candidates. Potential voters may be turned off by negative campaigning and conclude that all politicians are dirty. (In 2004, however, negative ads seemed to have boosted turnout.) As we considered in Chapter 9, some blame television for a decline in political participation.

Postmaterialism offers another explanation. According to this cultural theory, in all the industrialized nations the economy has moved away from manufacturing and into knowledge and information industries. With this has come a shift of values, away from society and toward self. Only personal things matter in the New Age: relationships, correct diet, outdoor activities, and music. Social and political questions no longer interest many. If the postmaterialism theory is accurate, we might see less political involvement, and education will incline people to avoid politics. If true, this does not bode well for democracy.

in the United States, the gap between men's and women's voter turnout narrowed and then even reversed; in recent U.S. elections women have voted more than men, a reflection of women's higher educational levels.

PLACE OF RESIDENCE

City dwellers are more likely to vote than rural residents. Polling stations are nearer in cities. People who have lived in the same place for a long time are more likely to vote than are transients or newcomers, for longtime residents feel more involved in local affairs and are more likely to participate in groups and activities in the community.

Voter turnout in the U.S. South is somewhat lighter than in the North and West, a reflection of lower living standards and a lack of party competition. But the South and its politics have changed, and now turnout in the South is approaching that of other areas. Other nations are also characterized by regional differences in voter participation. In France, the areas south of the Loire River have a lower voter turnout than the northern areas of the country.

---

postmaterialism   Theory that modern culture has moved beyond getting and spending.

Voters in a village school use old hand-lever voting machines. Elections are also a chance to socialize.
(Michael Roskin)

■ HOW DO PEOPLE VOTE?

The reasons that people vote as they do are many and complex. Factors can be divided into *long-term* and *short-term* variables. Loyalty to a political party is a long-term influence and can affect a person's votes for his or her lifetime. Short-term variables may cause a person to vote one way for one election but not four years later. Margaret Thatcher shrewdly called British elections in 1983 to catch the glow of military victory in the Falklands and again in 1987 during an economic upswing and disarray in Labour's ranks. Her Conservatives won both times. Similarly, in 1976 in the United States, Jimmy Carter benefited from a "morality factor" awakened by the Watergate scandal. Economic conditions matter; the 1992 downturn hurt incumbent President Bush. Such short-term variables rarely mean a permanent shift in party loyalty.

PARTY IDENTIFICATION

Party identification—party ID, for short—is a mental attachment many feel toward one party over many years. Strong party identifiers habitually vote for that party; weak identifiers can be swayed to vote for another party. People with no party ID are up for grabs and may shift their votes every election. Remember, party ID is something that people carry around in their heads; it is not something that parties carry around.

party identification   Long-term voter attachment to a given party.

Party ID is heavily influenced by parents early in life. Some children proclaim they are Democrats or Republicans and may never change what they learned from their parents, like the early learning of a religion. It is also easier to vote along party lines, especially important with complicated U.S. ballots. Party ID is a "standing decision" on how to vote. Strong identifiers feel good about their party's candidates and view other candidates with suspicion.

Party ID is important to electoral stability. People who stick largely to one party allow politicians to anticipate what people want and to try to deliver it. Weak party ID produces great volatility in voting, as citizens shift their votes too easily, often in response to clever TV ads. Political scientists worry that declining party ID in the United States bodes ill for democracy.

Party identification in much of Europe and Japan used to be stronger than in the United States, but the difference may be fading. Britain, Germany, Sweden, Japan, and other countries were long characterized by consistent splits between their two biggest parties. Typically, the **swing** from one major party to another ranged from only about 1 percent to 5 percent, as most voters stuck with the same party. The reason: Strong party ID anchored voters to parties. With the decline in **class voting** (see below) and rise of postmaterialism, party ID has been fading and volatility increasing, sometimes to U.S. levels. French voters, on the other hand, were even less likely than Americans to have a party ID, partly the result of the splitting, merging, and renaming that French parties engage in. Such changes do not give party IDs time to take root. Result: French voting is and always has been volatile.

■ WHO VOTES HOW?

Using the social categories discussed in Chapter 8 (on public opinion) and earlier in this chapter (on voting turnout), political scientists can generally describe what kinds of people tend to identify with the various parties. No social category votes 100 percent for a given party; people often disregard group norms. This fact accounts for poor Republicans and rich Democrats. If more than half of a given social category votes for one party, there is probably a significant relationship between the social category and the party. If three-quarters votes for a party, there is a strong relationship. We are making statements here that indicate a tendency, not an absolute relationship.

Practicing politicians and political scientists call a tendency in a group to identify with a certain party a **voting bloc**. The candidates' strategy is then to secure enough blocs to deliver a plurality of the electorate, and they tailor their campaign to win over the blocs most likely to vote for them. The concept of voting blocs is an oversimplification; there is no such thing as a solid bloc.

---

swing   Percentage of voters switching parties from one election to the next.
class voting   Tendency of a given social class to vote for a party that claims to represent its interests.
voting bloc   Group with a marked tendency.

TENDENCY STATEMENTS

It is hard to show that one thing causes another, especially in the social sciences. Often the best we can do is show how one thing correlates or covaries with another. For example, we have noted how rich countries are democracies and poor not, but this is only approximately true. There are many exceptions, so instead of saying "is," we say "tends to." Further, which causes which? Does being rich make countries democratic? Or does being democratic make countries rich?

Most social scientists are cautious about causal statements—X causes Y—and say that causality is indirect and complex. X might give rise to Q, which in turn influences Z to move in the direction of Y. In our example, wealth creates a large middle class, which likes education and articulates its interests, which in turn undermines authoritarian rule. Simple it ain't.

Much of what we study is **multicausal**: P, Q, and R working together lead to Z. Which matters more—per capita GDP, education, or interest-group formation—to the founding of democracy? They all matter and are hard to disentangle. They tend to come as a package. Instead of making causal statements, we learn to make **if-then statements**, where we find X so also do we find Y. We also learn that this connection is rarely one-to-one: Where we find X, two-thirds of the time we find Y. This is called a **tendency** statement, the standard fare of the social sciences. For example: "Poor countries tend to not be democracies, but several are." And remember, individuals often defy the tendency of their group: "African Americans tend strongly to vote Democratic, but some vote Republican."

CLASS VOTING

Social class is one determinant of party identification and voting behavior. Even in the United States, where class distinctions are blurred, blue-collar workers tend to register and vote Democratic, especially in families in which breadwinners are union members. Notice in Table 12.1 on page 222 how voters with family incomes under $30,000 tended to go to Kerry in the 2004 election; higher brackets went to Bush. In most European countries, this tendency is stronger, for unions are often connected to social-democratic or labor parties. The big Swedish and German unions, respectively the LO and DGB, persuade most of their members to vote Social Democrat. Better-off Britons, French, German, and Swedes are likely to support their respective conservative parties.

Two things muddy class voting. Some working-class people—because they consider themselves middle class, have a family tradition, or have individual convictions—vote for conservative parties. Sometimes a majority of the U.S. and British working class vote, respectively, Republican and Conservative. Conversely, some middle- and even upper-class people—because they are of working-class origins, have a family tradition, or picked up liberal views in college—vote for parties on

---

multicausal   Several factors making something happen.
if-then statement   Says that two things are linked: Where this happens so does that.
tendency   Finding that two things are linked, but not perfectly.

Table 12.1   Survey of Voting Intentions, 2004

	Bush	Kerry
Total	48%	45%
Male	52	43
Female	44	48
White	54	40
Black	7	86
Hispanic	47	49
18–24	45	50
25–34	58	39
35–44	49	45
45–54	48	46
55–64	49	46
65–74	48	42
75+	39	51
East	38	56
Midwest	51	43
South	55	38
West	44	51
Postgraduate study	41	54
College graduate	49	45
Some college	54	41
High-school graduate	49	44
Less than high school	38	55
Family income		
$100,000+	55	39
$75,000–100,000	56	41
$50,000–74,999	52	44
$30,000–49,999	51	45
$20,000–29,999	38	56
less than $20,000	39	53
White Protestant Evangelical	75	20
White Catholic	49	46
Secular	24	67
Urban	34	59
Suburban	52	42
Rural	56	37
Married	56	39
Unmarried	36	56
Republican	93	4
Democrat	6	90
Right decision in Iraq	83	12
Wrong decision in Iraq	7	89
Union household	34	62

Source: Pew Research Center, telephone survey of 1,925 likely voters, October 27–30, 2004.

the left. Such people are especially important in providing working-class parties with educated leadership. This two-way crossover—working class going conservative and middle class going left—dilutes class voting. Class voting has receded everywhere; it just happened first in the United States.

REGIONAL VOTING

Some regions identify strongly with certain parties. Often these are areas that were conquered and subjugated centuries ago, and the inhabitants still harbor resentments. South of the Loire River, the French tend to vote Socialist. Scotland and Wales go Labour. The southern United States used to be solidly Democratic, but since the 1980s has been the strongest Republican region, and the Northeast—which following the Civil War had been a Republican bastion—is now the strongest for the Democrats.

RELIGIOUS BLOCS

Religious vs. secular is the single strongest predictor in U.S. voting. In 2004, Bush won three-fourths of white Protestant evangelicals; Kerry won two-thirds of the "seculars" (nonreligious). In France, devout Catholics vote mostly conservative; secular people vote mostly left. In Italy, the Popular party was founded by and is still linked to the Roman Catholic church. Catholic areas of Germany vote more Christian Democrat than do Protestant areas.

AGE GROUPS

Younger people are not necessarily more radical than their elders. Rather, they tend to catch the tide that is flowing in their youth and stay with it. Young people socialized to politics during the Depression tended to vote Democratic all their lives. Republicans now think that the enthusiasm for Reagan among young voters in the 1980s gives them a permanent sense of identification with the Republican party. Age groups react in part to the economic situation. Some young voters feel that Republican policies of growth lead to jobs, but old voters fear Republican cuts in Social Security and Medicare. In recent elections this has made oldsters more Democrat than youngsters.

GENDER GAP

It also used to be assumed that women were more traditional and conservative than men, but that has been reversed in the United States and several other countries. Women now vote Democrat by several percentage points more than men. Women tend to like the Democrats' support for welfare measures and for abortion rights and to dislike the Republicans' opposition to such views.

MARRIAGE GAP

Starting in 2000, observers noticed a "marriage gap." (It had probably existed earlier but had not been included among survey questions.) Unmarried people are several percentage points more Democrat than are married. The responsibilities of raising a family make voters conservative, and Republicans stress "family values."

RACIAL MINORITIES

Blacks are the most loyal Democrats by far; over 80 percent of those who vote generally vote for Democrats. Hispanic voters have shifted from Democrat to a nearly even split in 2004. The affinity of racial minorities for the Democrats may cost the party white votes. Republicans are delighted to portray the Democrats as the party of minorities, feminists, and labor unions—and themselves as the party of everyone else.

URBAN VOTING

Big cities worldwide tend strongly to vote liberal or left. The working-class vote is concentrated in cities. Cities are also centers of education and sophistication, places where intellectuals are often liberal and leftist. Country and suburban dwellers tend to embrace conservative values and vote for conservative parties. England votes overwhelmingly Tory, but the city of London does not. Germany's Bavaria is a conservative stronghold, but not Munich. Italy was long dominated by the Christian Democrats, but not Italy's cities, most of which had leftist mayors.

A map of U.S. elections shows a major urban-rural split. Bush 43 represented rural values—religion, Texas twang, anti-abortion, anti–gun control, anti-government, and pro-defense—that won him almost all thinly populated states. These states—because they have two senators and at least one representative—are overrepresented in the Electoral College, and that is what won the 2000 election for Bush.

■ ELECTORAL REALIGNMENT

Political scientists have long debated a theory of **critical** or **realigning elections**. Typically, people retain their party identification for a long time, sometimes all their lives. But, according to this theory, in several watershed presidential elections, the party loyalties of many voters dissolved, and they established new, durable party identities. These "critical elections" do not determine how every election will go, but they set the terms of debate and the main topics. They give one party

critical election   One showing a realignment.
realignment   Major, long-term shift in party ID.

dominance but not absolute control. The critical or realigning elections in U.S. history are usually seen as the following:

1800, the emergence of Jeffersonian Democratic Republicans

1828, the emergence of Jacksonian populist Democrats

1860, the emergence of Lincoln Republicans

1896, the emergence of business Republicanism

1932, the emergence of Roosevelt's New Deal Democrats

Between these critical elections, party identifications are stable and most people vote according to them. This is called the "normal vote" or "maintaining elections." Occasionally, enough voters disregard their party identification to elect the weaker party: Democrat Grover Cleveland in 1884 and 1892, Democrat Woodrow Wilson in 1912 and 1916, and Republican Dwight Eisenhower in 1952 and 1956. These are called "deviating elections" because the party shift was only temporary; afterward voters went back to their long-term party ID.

A REAGAN REALIGNMENT?

Republicans anticipated that the Reagan sweeps of 1980 and 1984 marked a realignment in their favor. Party registration rose for Republicans and declined for Democrats until the parties were about equal in size. Young people in particular registered and voted Republican. Even more important, Reaganite thinkers restructured the ideological debate in a conservative direction (see Chapter 6). Using government to fix social ills and provide welfare were less fashionable than cutting taxes, government spending, regulation, and the federal deficit. Before Reagan, even Republicans went along with the welfare state, and some of the biggest expansions of welfare programs occurred under Nixon. After Reagan, even the Democrats demanded fiscal responsibility. Said President Clinton: "The era of big government is over."

But realignments come without name tags. It might not be possible to tell if there has been a realignment until some decades later. Furthermore, it may be difficult to spot the precise election in which realignment occurred. Looking at the results of the 1968 election, which brought Nixon to the White House, and carefully dissecting regional trends, Kevin Phillips concluded in 1969 that a Republican majority was emerging. Which, then, was the critical election, 1968 or 1980? If it was 1968, it would mark Carter's election in 1976 as a "deviating election," and, indeed, Carter's victory was largely the result of the Watergate scandal. The Nixon administration, however, lacked the ideological conservatism that came with Reagan. Perhaps the ingredients for a Republican realignment came with the 1968 election but did not coalesce until 1980 and was confirmed and deepened in 2004. Instead of a single "critical" election, it occurred over many years. Instead of national realignment, some researchers think we are seeing *regional* realignment: the South and Plains states more purely Republican, the Northeast and West more purely Democrat.

There are problems with realignment theory. Many argue that it applies only to voting for president, which is often out of synch with voting for Congress. Americans sometimes vote for "divided government"—legislative and executive under different parties—to deadlock them and limit the damage they can do. (French voters often do the same.) The Clinton victories in 1992 and 1996, both based on the economy, undermine the theory of electoral realignment. If voters react mostly to current situations and candidates' personalities, the basic supposition of party identification will have to be reconsidered. Perhaps party ID is not as important as it once was.

Instead of realignment, some suggest we experienced **dealignment**. Since the mid-1960s, the number of voters committed to neither major U.S. party increased. In 1948, fewer than 20 percent of U.S. voters called themselves independents. Polls now show about equal thirds of the electorate calling themselves independent, Democrat, and Republican. Independents tend to be young and college-educated. Many came of age in turbulent times. In 1964 they heard Lyndon Johnson promise not to send Americans to fight in Vietnam. In 1974 they saw Nixon resign in shame. After the 2003 war they learned that Iraq had no weapons of mass destruction. Their faith in conventional party politics was shaken; both major parties appeared to be dishonest. Scandals did not improve their image.

Some political scientists noted that this process—which proceeded during both bad and good economic times—coincided with three trends: (1) declining voter turnout, (2) declining party ID, and (3) declining trust in Washington. Do the three items hang together? Which causes which? Declining trust is probably the underlying cause, giving rise to the other two.

Some researchers doubt there is much dealignment and independent voting. Many voters who call themselves "independent" actually lean to one party or the other, and they vote for that party rather reliably. Instead of the third of the electorate that says they are independent, claim these researchers, only 15 percent are genuine neutrals, and this amounts to only 11 percent who actually cast ballots (because genuine independents tend to vote less). By the time you count the weak identifiers, they say, party ID in the United States is largely unchanged. The 2004 elections suggested a Republican realignment rather than a dealignment.

■ WHAT WINS ELECTIONS?

In theory, elections enable citizens to choose and guide their government. In modern elections, however, the element of rational choice is heavily manipulated by the twin factors of personality and the mass media. People vote without clearly realizing what they are voting for or why, and this could become a threat to democracy.

Modern parties showcase their leaders' personalities. Especially in the advanced industrialized world, ideology is seldom emphasized. Ads and TV spots feature the

---

dealignment   Major, long-term decline in party ID.

KEY CONCEPTS

PARTISAN POLARIZATION

Political scientists note growing **polarization** in the U.S. electorate. Party identifications have become stronger, as have dislikes and slurs against the other party. Although the trend was underway for some time, by the 1990s Republicans despised Clinton even when the economy boomed. In the 2004 election, Republicans and Democrats were passionately either for or against Bush 43. Reason and consistency were not in command. There were few fence-sitters. Most voters were committed months in advance and few shifted. The swing vote was small but still critical.

Several factors contributed to the polarization tendency:

1. Under Reagan (1981–1989) the Republican party had become more consistently conservative, with fewer and fewer moderates. In turn, the Democrats had to become more consistently liberal, until there were few conservative Democrats.

2. Elites articulated more strongly ideological agendas than previously. New think tanks, magazines, and Web sites, especially on the conservative side, took positions that the big parties, always seeking the centrist vote, had usually avoided.

3. The Supreme Court's 1972 "one person, one vote" rule (see page 330) required states to make their congressional districts equal in population. Now some states redistrict after every census. Computers gerrymander with great accuracy, so that congressional districts now contain many like-minded voters. Candidates running in them can now be more ideologically pure and less concerned about votes in the center.

4. Whole regions of the country became purer ideologically, the South conservative and the Northeast liberal. What the media designated as "red" (the Republican states) and "blue" (the Democratic states) did not speak nicely to each other.

5. The trend reflects America's "culture wars" (see page 119), based heavily on **religiosity**. Religious Americans rallied to the "moral values" espoused by the Republican party. Less-religious Americans focused on the economy, Iraq, and health care and rallied to the Democrats. The two cultures, interested in totally different issues, disdain and vote against each other.

Some historians and political scientists say U.S. politics has always been like this; regional and cultural politics have always loomed large in U.S. elections. Polarization is not all bad. In 2004 it markedly boosted voter turnout.

leaders' images, sometimes without even mentioning their parties. The leader is presented as **charismatic** and decisive but calm and caring. Ronald Reagan was an excellent example of a winning political personality, and leaders in other countries have adopted similar approaches. British Prime Minister Tony Blair won in part

---

polarization   Opinion fleeing the center to form two hostile camps.
religiosity   Depth of religious conviction (not same as choice of denomination).
charismatic   Having strong personal drawing power.

Bill Clinton and running mate Al Gore took their show on the road in the 1992 election campaign, crossing parts of the country by bus and stopping for speeches every day, a technique reminiscent of the old "whistle stop" campaigns conducted by rail in earlier decades. (Wilfredo Lee, AP/Wide World Photos)

by copying the style of Bill Clinton. French presidential candidates project an image of a caring, fatherlike intellectual who is above the political fray, almost nonpartisan. German candidates for chancellor project a tried-and-true, reliable and upbeat image but also say little about what policies they will pursue. The pattern worldwide: Keep it general, keep it happy, don't mention parties, and smile a lot.

U.S. presidential candidates who present the most upbeat image of America almost always win. Pessimistic candidates, who worry about things going wrong, tend to lose. The leaders' personalities are sold through the mass media, especially through television, where the candidate's image is controlled; even physical appearance can be altered. "Photo opportunities" instead of question-and-answer sessions avoid embarrassing probes by journalists. The "photo op" shows seemingly spontaneous candidate activity; words explaining the activity can be added later. The "photo op" itself is largely wordless. The candidates' professional "handlers" worry that their candidate could say something foolish and ruin a carefully built-up image. Journalists must be kept distant.

And this is happening worldwide. One British observer argued that "television very largely *is* the campaign." In France, journalists complain about the *hypermédiatisation* of French politics. On television everything is professionally controlled: set, lighting, music, makeup, narration—a mini-drama more perfect (and often more expensive) than many regular programs. The television spot, developed in America, now blankets Europe. The French call it *le clip politique*. French political scientist Jean-Paul Gourevitch saw three types: (1) the "jingle clip," a simple attention-getting device; (2) the "ideological clip," which sets an idea in images; and (3) the "allegorical clip," which portrays the hero-candidate in an epic. Increasingly, elections are won by the candidate with the sunniest personality and best ads. This generally means the

THE 9/11 ELECTION

Events often govern politics. The 2001 terrorist attacks brought out American emotion and patriotism that favored President Bush for reelection, and his strategists played it well. A nation under attack rallies around a strong leader. Bush's actions on Afghanistan, Iraq, and homeland security let the Republicans portray Bush as the one who would keep America safe and portray Sen. John Kerry as an indecisive "flip-flopper." Voters concerned with terrorism went heavily for Bush. An effective Bush TV ad showed a pack of wolves ready to strike again.

Many voters were unhappy over Iraq but accepted Bush's claim that we were fighting terrorism there. Besides, Kerry had supported the war in 2002 and offered no plan for a speedy exit. The danger of the Bush strategy is that it commits us to staying in Iraq for years and could ignite a series of Islamic Wars. Americans hate long wars, and if Iraq is not settled well before the 2008 elections, events could play into the Democrats' hands.

candidate with the most money, for television is terribly expensive. Candidates, desperate for money, sell themselves to interests groups. Parties become little more than fund-raising organizations. This is not just an American problem; it started in the United States but has since spread to Europe.

RETROSPECTIVE VOTING

Few voters carefully evaluate issues in a presidential election, but they do form an overall evaluation of the performance of an incumbent president. That is, they feel the president has done a good job or a poor one, especially on the economy. Morris P. Fiorina called the accumulated or package views of voters toward incumbent presidents **retrospective voting** because it views in retrospect a whole four years of performance in office. When voters think the government in general is doing a good job they reward the incumbent's party: Johnson in 1964, Nixon in 1972, Reagan in 1984, Bush in 1988, and Clinton in 1996. When they think the government in general is doing a poor job they punish the incumbent's party: Humphrey in 1968, Ford in 1976, Carter in 1980, and Bush in 1992. The Index of Consumer Confidence—a measure of how economically secure Americans feel—predicts most presidential elections. When they feel good about jobs, they generally vote for the incumbent's party.

Retrospective voting is colored, naturally, by party identification, issues, and the candidate's personality. For weak party identifiers plus independents, the feeling of overall performance determines much of their vote. A strong positive retrospective view could even turn into party ID. Voting behavior is complex. When people say they "like" candidates, it could mean they like the candidates' party

---

retrospective voting   Voters choosing based on overall incumbent performance.

KEY CONCEPTS

CHANGING POSITIONS

Candidates are endlessly opportunistic and modify their positions on issues to win the most votes. Many call this "slippery" or "unprincipled," but it is really just democracy in action. Elected officials who support discredited or unpopular policies get voted out. Those who urge politicians to stand by their principles and "do the right thing" meet the hard-nosed reply: "But if I'm not reelected, all the good and just things I'm trying to accomplish will be thrown away. So I've got to bend on this issue." Soon pure expediency reigns.

The 1994 Republican "Contract with America" included a ten-year phaseout of farm subsidies, something the GOP had long championed. By 2002 Republicans were shoveling more money into farm subsidies than ever. To do otherwise, said President Bush, would be "political suicide" for his 2004 reelection. Democrats, seeking those same farm-state votes, supported the subsidies.

In 2002, Sen. John Kerry (and most Democrats) denounced the Saddam regime and supported a joint congressional resolution authorizing a U.S. invasion of Iraq. By 2004, with voters unhappy over Iraq, Kerry changed his tune, offering criticism and a plan to get out. Indeed, so did President Bush. Looking to reelection, Bush emphasized a major UN role and a handover of "sovereignty" to Iraq four months before the November elections. By then, there was little difference on Iraq policy between the two candidates, as both played for the maximum vote. It is for this reason that issues seldom dominate an American political campaign: By election day, both candidates have adjusted their positions toward the center.

Can it be otherwise in a democracy? Should politicians go against the mass will for the sake of "consistency" or "principle"? Their changes are frequently held up to ridicule by the media and their opponents, but they are really adjusting to new realities on a continuous basis. Asked what drove his policies, British Prime Minister Harold Macmillan (1957–1963) replied, "Events, dear boy, events." Much of political life is the opportunistic reaction to events.

affiliation, their stand on issues, their personal images, or the performance of the economy. Unraveling such puzzles is the crux of campaign strategy.

CANDIDATE STRATEGIES AND VOTER GROUPS

Campaign strategies have two goals: keeping "one foot on home base" by not alienating the normal party supporters and trying to win over votes from the undecided and from the opposition. Presidential candidates focus on states with more electoral votes and close to 50–50 voting, considered "up for grabs." Candidates concentrate on such "battleground" states as Florida and Pennsylvania. States lopsided for one party—such as California (Democrat) and Texas (Republican)—are considered "not in play" and get less time and money. Campaign strategy is highly rational.

Most campaigns are designed to fit the opinions and needs of the **constituency**, often determined by public-opinion polls. Candidates must be aware of pockets of party strength and resistance, what various groups are thinking about,

---

constituency   The people or district that elects an official.

what districts have the lowest turnouts (and therefore merit less candidate time), and which issues anger constituents. Aware of the direction and intensity of voter opinion, candidates then typically try to assemble enough "voting blocs" to win.

Voting blocs parallel the public-opinion blocs discussed in Chapter 8. Religion, geography, and class—probably in that order—are the most important influences in opinion formation, and these partially predict voting. Urban and rural voters will oppose each other on a mass-transit bond, blacks and whites on school busing. Coalitions of several smaller blocs of voters often win. On a national scale, the Democrats used to represent a coalition of labor, blacks, Catholics, Jews, and urban voters; the Republicans received their support from a coalition of rural and farm voters, the remaining Protestants, and nonunion workers. By the 1960s, though, these traditional blocs had begun to break up, and neither party has managed to reconstruct them in a durable way. The breakup of the blocs, it should be noted, coincides with the declining voter turnout and party loyalty discussed earlier.

The "blocs" are not what they used to be, and many Americans do not fit demographic, ethnic, or religious pigeonholes. Instead, attitudes on religion, free enterprise, welfare, patriotism, civil rights, and other issues cut across the old voting blocs. "Liberal" and "conservative" are tricky categories because people are often liberal on some things and conservative on others. Neither does party ID matter much in an era of dealignment and rapid shifts between parties. Clusters of *values* may now count for more than social categories. Thus candidates strive to align themselves with their constituents' values.

KEY TERMS

anachronism (p. 214)
charismatic (p. 227)
class voting (p. 220)
constituency (p. 230)
critical election (p. 224)
dealignment (p. 226)
Electoral College (p. 214)
franchise (p. 217)
if-then statement (p. 221)
multicausal (p. 221)
party identification (p. 219)

polarization (p. 227)
postmaterialism (p. 218)
realignment (p. 224)
religiosity (p. 227)
retrospective voting (p. 229)
suffrage (p. 217)
swing (p. 220)
tendency (p. 221)
turnout (p. 212)
voting bloc (p. 220)

KEY WEB SITES

Worldwide elections
cnn.com/WORLD/election.watch/
www.klipsan.com/
www.electionworld.org.

Federal Election Commission
www.fec.gov/

British elections
politics.guardian.co.uk/election/

U.S. election campaigns
livingroomcandidate.movingimage.us/index.php
www.vote-smart.org/

History of televised presidential debates
www.mbcnet.org/debateweb/

FURTHER REFERENCE

Abramson, Paul R., John H. Aldrich, and David W. Rohde. *Change and Continuity in the 2004 Elections.* Washington, D.C.: CQ Press, 2005.

Farrell, David M. *Electoral Systems: A Comparative Introduction.* New York: Palgrave, 2001.

Flanigan, William H., and Nancy H. Zingale. *Political Behavior of the American Electorate,* 10th ed. Washington, D.C.: CQ Press, 2002.

Green, Donald, Bradley Palmquist, and Eric Schickler. *Partisan Hearts and Minds: Political Parties and the Social Identities of Voters.* New Haven, CT: Yale University Press, 2002.

Hill, Steven. *Fixing Elections: The Failure of America's Winner Take All Politics.* New York: Routledge, 2003.

Lewis, Charles. *The Buying of the President 2004.* New York: HarperCollins, 2004.

Mayhew, David R. *Electoral Realignments: A Critique of an American Genre.* New Haven, CT: Yale University Press, 2002.

Patterson, Thomas E. *The Vanishing Voter: Public Involvement in an Age of Uncertainty.* New York: Knopf, 2003.

Polsby, Nelson W., and Aaron Wildavsky. *Presidential Elections: Strategies and Structures of American Politics,* 10th ed. New York: Chatham House, 2000.

Powell, C. Bingham. *Elections as Instruments of Democracy: Majoritarian and Proportional Versions.* New Haven, CT: Yale University Press, 2000.

Rosenof, Theodore. *Realignment: The Theory That Changed the Way We Think about American Politics.* Lanham, MD: Rowman & Littlefield, 2003.

Schier, Steven E. *You Call This an Election?: America's Peculiar Democracy.* Washington, D.C.: Georgetown University Press, 2003.

THE BASIC INSTITUTIONS OF GOVERNMENT

CHAPTER 13

QUESTIONS TO CONSIDER

- What is the crux of a political institution?
- How do institutions structure political behavior?
- How does "Who's got the power?" help locate institutions?
- Why are Europe's monarchies among the most democratic countries?
- What are the two main electoral systems?
- What are the problems of territorially unitary systems?
- Why do some federal systems fall apart?
- In what ways is U.S. government extremely complex?
- What was Mark Twain's story of "burden shifting"?

Political institutions are the working structures of government, such as legislatures and executive departments. Parties, if they are important and stable, may also count as institutions. Institutions may or may not be housed in impressive buildings, although that helps bolster their authority. The U.S. Supreme Court, even if it met in a tent, would be an important institution as long as its decisions were obeyed. As we will consider later, it was not clear what the powers of the Supreme Court were to be when it began, but forceful personalities and important cases slowly gave it power. Like most institutions, the Supreme Court **evolved** into importance.

As we considered in Chapter 1, authority is a fluid thing, which requires continual maintenance. A political institution is congealed or partly solidified

---

political institution   Established and durable authority relationship.
evolve   To slowly develop.

authority. Over time, people have become used to looking to political institutions to solve problems, decide controversies, and set directions. Institutions, because they are composed of many persons and (if they are effective) last many generations, take on lives of their own apart from the people temporarily associated with them. This gives the political system stability; citizens know who is in charge.

Institutions are bigger than individual leaders. When President Nixon resigned under a cloud of scandal in 1974, the institution of the presidency was scarcely touched. If there had been a series of such presidents, and if they had refused to resign, the institution itself would have been damaged. Sometimes dictators try to make themselves into "institutions," but it fails; no matter how powerful dictators are during their lifetimes, the institutions they tried to build unravel upon their deaths. Josip Tito ruled Yugoslavia for thirty-five years and attempted to ensure his system would survive him, but it was too much based on himself. Eleven years after his death, Yugoslavia split apart in bloody fighting. Dictators seldom build lastingly; they rarely **institutionalize** their personal power.

As noted in Chapters 1 and 11, "neo-institutionalists" see politics as games played inside one institution or another. Typically, politicians internalize the rules of their particular institution and then try rationally to maximize their advantage within the institution. This makes their behaviors at least partly logical and predictable. U.S. congresspersons will try to get on the committees that most benefit their reelection and then deliver what pleases their constituents or major donors. British members of Parliament (MPs) will pay less attention to committee assignments because traditionally committees of the House of Commons have brought little payoff. An MP in opposition, however, may heckle cabinet ministers on the floor of the House of Commons, interrupting them with impolite language. If the MP heckles well—really gets the minister's goat on television—the heckler is regarded as a clever fellow and marked for promotion within his or her party. In Britain, heckling is part of the game, a test of a speaker's ability and cool. It is out of bounds on the floor of the U.S. House of Representatives. Different institutions, different rules, different behavior.

By the same token, interest groups operate among institutions and are generally rational in trying to influence them. Campaigns cost a lot of money. Elected officials know this and so spend much of their time fund-raising. Interest groups know it and so pass out contributions to officials who can do them the most good. Given the institutions they work in and with, their respective behaviors are rational (although sometimes also illegal). The Republicans derided President Clinton as "fund-raiser in chief," but President Bush broke records in raising funds for the Republicans. They really had little choice; the system requires them to raise maximum money. Do not get angry at individuals when institutions make them do things.

---

institutionalize   To make a political relationship permanent.

Powerful inhabitants of an office can sometimes put their personal stamp on the institution. George Washington retired after two terms, and until FDR no president tried to serve longer. Washington institutionalized term limits into the presidency that were not codified into law until the Twenty-second Amendment in 1951. In another example, the first chancellor of the Federal Republic of Germany, Konrad Adenauer, offered such decisive leadership that the chancellorship has been powerful ever since.

One way to begin the study of institutions is to locate the most powerful offices of a political system: Who's got the power? Constitutions may help locate power but do not tell the whole story. The U.S. Constitution indicates the executive and the legislative powers are equals and in balance. This is what the Founding Fathers intended, but over two centuries power has gravitated to the presidency.

The French constitution, set up by Charles de Gaulle in 1958, seems to give the presidency near-dictatorial powers. But French legislative elections have produced parliaments of one party facing a president of another. Before this first occurred in 1986, it was hard to predict how French institutions would handle the "deadlock" problem, common in the U.S. system. The French constitution was unclear on this point, but Socialist President Mitterrand solved it by trimming his role and letting Gaullist Prime Minister Chirac take a bigger role. When the same situation, called "cohabitation," occurred again, French institutions took it in stride; they had evolved to accommodate a different power relationship. Ironically, later President Chirac had to cohabit with Socialist Prime Minister Jospin. Constitutions are themselves institutions, gradually evolving in practice if not in wording.

■ THE FORM OF STATE

An example of such evolution is the modern constitutional **monarchy**. Calling a country a monarchy or a republic is to describe its "form of state." A **republic** is simply a form of state without a monarch. Republic does not necessarily mean "good" or "democratic." All but a few countries in the world are republics. Most of the remaining monarchies are figurehead constitutional monarchies such as those of northwestern Europe—Britain, Norway, Sweden, Denmark, Holland, and Belgium. Most of them see no reason to change. Australia, which still accepts Queen Elizabeth as its monarch, in 1999 voted 45–55 percent against becoming a republic. The traditional, working monarchies still found in the Arab world—Morocco, Saudi Arabia, Jordan, Kuwait—are probably doomed unless they can turn themselves into limited constitutional monarchies. Failure to do so has in recent decades led to the overthrow of traditional monarchies and their replacement by revolutionary regimes in Egypt, Iraq, Libya, Ethiopia, and Iran.

---

monarchy   Hereditary rule by one person.
republic   A political system without a monarch.

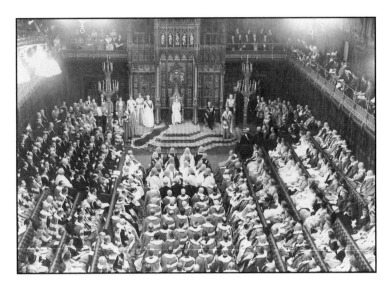

The constitutional monarchy of Great Britain, with its colorful ceremonies and pageantry, gives the appearance of a traditional monarchy, but the monarch is a figurehead and the real power is in the hands of the Parliament and the prime minister. (British Information Services)

■ ELECTORAL SYSTEMS

Electoral systems are important institutional choices; they help determine the number of parties, the ease of forming a stable government, and the degree of citizen interest in politics. There are two general types of electoral systems with many variations.

SINGLE-MEMBER DISTRICTS

The simplest electoral system is the Anglo-American **single-member district**, wherein one member of Parliament or of Congress is chosen to represent the entire district by winning a plurality (not necessarily a majority) of the votes. Called "single-member districts with plurality win" or "first past the post" (FPTP), this system pushes interest groups and political factions to coalesce into two big parties. If there were, say, four parties who received 25, 25, 24, and 26 percent of the vote respectively, the last would win. Losing parties that are not far apart ideologically quickly recognize their advantage is to combine for the next election. Then this new party wins, forcing other small parties to combine. The message: merge or lose. Woodrow Wilson won in 1912 only because Theodore Roosevelt split the Republican party. FPTP countries tend to have two-party systems.

Third parties can and do exist in such systems, but without much hope of winning. They may have an impact as protest groups or as pressure groups on the big

---

single-member districts   Electoral system that elects one person per district, as in the United States and Britain.

LEGITIMACY AND MONARCHY

How can the limited constitutional monarchies of northwestern Europe combine an old form of state with modern democracy? Indeed, these countries are some of the freest and most democratic in the world. Monarchies perform an integrative function, holding together divergent social groups during the delicate modernization phase. The traditional sectors of society—the clergy, army officers, and great landowners—usually oppose democracy and may be tempted to carry out coups to stop democratization. But these sectors are also monarchist, and if the king or queen goes along with democratization, the traditional sectors will probably support it also. The monarch thus serves as a bridge between the traditional political system of the Middle Ages and the modern participatory system, easing the way from one to the other.

Consider the histories of countries that retained their kings and queens but gradually limited their powers until they were figureheads. Then consider those countries that deposed their monarchs. Britain temporarily deposed its monarchy in the seventeenth century, but it was soon reestablished. Since then Britain's political evolution has been peaceful and gradual. The French Revolution guillotined the king and alienated French conservatives, producing a nasty tug of war between conservative and radical forces with rare periods of stability. Sweden retained its monarchy and evolved into a modern social-welfare state. Germany lost its monarchy after World War I, when the kaiser abdicated and fled to Holland; after the shaky fourteen years of the Weimar Republic, Hitler took over with his Nazis. Monarchs can confer legitimacy on new democratic institutions. When King Juan Carlos of Spain blocked a military coup in 1981, the head of the Spanish Communist party announced his support for monarchy. The king had thus bridged most sectors of Spanish society, even those that had previously been antimonarchist.

parties. The British Liberal Democrats win nearly one vote in five, but because they are dispersed rather evenly throughout the country, they win few seats. Single-member systems are unkind to third parties except in situations like Canada, where provincial concentration of parties permits many to exist.

Advantages of Single-Member Districts Politics in FPTP systems tend to the center of the political spectrum, for this is where the votes are. This inhibits the growth of extremism. If leaders out of touch with mainstream views control the party, it will lose, and the losing leaders will likely be replaced. This is what happened with the Republicans after the conservative Goldwater in 1964, the Democrats after the liberal McGovern in 1972, and the British Conservatives after ineffective William Hague in 2001. As was mentioned in Chapter 8, public opinion in most democracies arrays itself as a bell-shaped curve. Parties that depart too far from the center penalize themselves.

FPTP systems also generally give a clear parliamentary majority to one party—thus it is called a **majoritarian** system—so coalitions are rarely necessary. Victories

---

majoritarian   Electoral system that gives over half of seats to one party.

CASE STUDIES

FRENCH AND GERMAN VARIATIONS

France uses single-member districts but with runoffs. Few candidates win a **majority** (over 50 percent, not the same as the simple plurality in the Anglo-American system) on the first round, so those with at least an eighth of the vote go to a runoff a week later. Then a simple **plurality** suffices to win. By previous agreement between parties, some candidates withdraw and urge their supporters to vote for the candidate closest to them ideologically, so in most second-round contests there are only two or three candidates. The first round in France is somewhat like U.S. primaries.

The German system is basically half FPTP and half **proportional representation**. On a split ballot, Germans vote for both an individual to represent their district and a party to represent their *Land* (state) in proportion to the votes received. Overall strength in the Bundestag is set by the second vote, the one for parties, so seats are always proportional to votes. Half of the seats, though, are reserved for the 328 winners of the district contests. The net effect of Germany's split representation system has been to produce a two-plus party system (discussed in Chapter 11) and great governing stability. The German system is a modification of the PR system and was designed after World War II to prevent a repetition of the weak and unstable Weimar system, which had proportional representation that treated the country as one big district. In the 1990s, Russia, Italy, New Zealand, and Japan adopted German-style **mixed-member** systems that combine single-member districts with PR for their parliamentary elections.

are magnified in single-member systems. In 2005, for example, Labour won only 36 percent of the votes (down from 41 percent) but still took a majority of the seats in Parliament. Remember, seats in FPTP systems are not supposed to be proportional to votes. A relatively small swing of votes from one party to another can translate into many parliamentary seats, perhaps enough to form a parliamentary majority and a new government. The United States, with its constitutionally mandated separation of powers, muddies the advantage of this system by frequently giving the White House to one party and the Congress to another.

Disadvantages of Single-Member Districts   FPTP creates a somewhat artificial majority in parliament, which makes governing easier but does not fairly or accurately reflect public opinion or voting strength. In each district the winner takes all. The losing party, even if it received 49 percent of the vote, gets no representation. Thanks to computers, most U.S. states are now so perfectly gerrymandered—some of the districts have bizarre shapes—that close to 400 out of 435 House seats are "safe" for one party or the other with few close or unpredictable races.

majority   More than half.

plurality   The most, even if less than half.

proportional representation   Elects representatives by party's percent of vote.

mixed-member   Hybrid electoral system that uses both single-member districts and proportional representation.

Single-member districts teach parties a sort of golden rule about sticking to the political center, which makes politics safe but dull. The two big parties often sound somewhat alike. The resulting voter boredom helps to explain the low voter turnout in U.S. elections. The European multiparty systems have higher voter turnouts, partly because voters can choose from a more interesting menu of parties.

PROPORTIONAL REPRESENTATION

Proportional representation (PR) systems are based on multimember districts; that is, each district sends several representatives to parliament, not just one. In the small countries of the Netherlands and Israel, the entire country is one big district. In Sweden the district is a county, in Spain a province. If the district is entitled to ten seats, each party offers voters a *party list* of ten candidates. Each voter picks one list, and the party gets seats in proportion to the votes it receives. If the party won 30 percent of the votes in a ten-member district, it would send the first three names on its party list to parliament. A party with 20 percent would send its first two names.

Rarely does the vote divide so neatly; one party might win 42 percent of eleven seats. Would it get 4.62 seats? How do you send a fraction of a person to parliament? The most common way to handle this is the d'Hondt mathematical formula, which slightly overrepresents the larger parties at the expense of smaller ones. Sweden "tops off" numerical discrepancies by using nationwide seats. Sweden's twenty-eight districts elect only 310 of the Riksdag's 349 seats; the remaining thirty-nine seats are parceled out to rectify variances from the parties' national percentages.

To minimize the problem of splinter, nuisance, or extremist parties, PR systems require parties to win a certain percentage of the vote in order to obtain any seats at all. These are called "threshold clauses." Germany and Poland require a party to get at least 5 percent of the vote nationwide; Sweden and Italy require 4 percent.

Advantages of Proportional Representation   PR means that the country's legislature accurately reflects public opinion and party strength. Parties do not have to capture the big middle of the electoral spectrum as in Anglo-American systems and can thus articulate ideologies and principles more clearly because they do not try to please everybody. If a small part of the population—as low as 1.5 percent in Israel—really believes in something, they can run as a party and win a seat or two. They are not forced to amalgamate into bigger parties and dilute their views, as in FPTP systems.

Disadvantages of Proportional Representation   PR systems do little to fight party splintering, so they often lead to multiparty systems. This tendency, however, is waning, and two-plus party systems have emerged even in PR systems. Sweden and Spain have one or two large parties plus a few smaller ones. Their political systems are not terribly splintered. Israel, on the other hand, is plagued

CASE STUDIES

THE SHAKY LIVES OF CONFEDERATIONS

Theoretically, a third alternative to unitary and federal systems is the **confederation**. In a unitary system, power tilts to the national capital. In a federal system, power is balanced between the **center** and the components. In confederations, the component parts can override the center. Confederations tend to have short lives; they either fall apart or become federations. This was the fate of the United States under the Articles of Confederation. Similarly, in the Confederate States of America each state had such independence that they could not effectively wage the Civil War. Switzerland still calls itself a confederation (Confederatio Helvetia)—which the Swiss proudly date to 1291—but it is now a federal system. The European Union (EU) started as a confederation but with the growth of the powers of Brussels (its headquarters), especially with economic and monetary union (the new euro currency), it is becoming a federal system.

by splinter parties; as many as fifteen parties are elected to the Knesset. If the chief party falls short of half the seats in PR systems it must form a coalition with other parties. These coalitions are often unstable and unable to decide important issues. Some Israelis protest their country's PR system and urge reforms that would reduce the number of parties. It is not true that multiparty systems are always unstable. Where one party is big enough to govern alone, the system is quite stable. The Anglo-American systems confer an almost automatic majority and thus stability.

■ UNITARY OR FEDERAL SYSTEMS

Another basic institutional choice is the territorial structure of the nation. There are really only two choices: unitary or federal. A unitary system accords its component areas little or no autonomy; most governance radiates from the capital city. The **first-order civil divisions**—departments in France, provinces in Italy, counties in Sweden, prefectures in Japan—are largely administered by national authorities with only small local inputs. The first-order civil divisions of federal systems—U.S. and Brazilian states, German *Länder,* and Swiss cantons—have considerable political lives of their own and cannot be legally erased or easily altered by the central power.

---

confederation   Political system in which components override *center.*

center   Nation's capital and its powers.

first-order civil divisions   Countries' main territorial components, such as U.S. states or Spanish provinces.

UNITARY SYSTEMS

Unitary governments generally control local authorities and touch people's daily lives in more ways than a federal government would. France's education ministry in Paris draws up school curricula in order to reduce regional differences in language and culture, which at one time were very strong. Many decades ago, a French education minister looked at his watch and proudly told an interviewer which Latin verbs were being conjugated all over France. Unitary states have a national police force and one court system, whose judicial officers are appointed by the national government. In Britain, counties and cities elect councils that control policing, education, and health and welfare matters

Center-periphery tensions grew in some unitary systems during the 1970s, and for several reasons. Economics was one. Local nationalists usually claim that their region is poorer and shortchanged by the central government. The region may have a distinct language or culture that its people want to preserve. Many feel that important political decisions are not under local control, that they are made by distant bureaucrats. Often regions harbor historical resentments at having long ago been conquered and forcibly merged with the larger nation. Iraqi Kurds feel this way about rule by Baghdad. Several unitary systems grope for solutions to the regional problem.

Devolution in Britain   The Celtic Scots and Welsh, pushed to the peripheries of Britain centuries ago by the invading Angles and Saxons, retain a lively sense of their differences from England. Many Scots and Welsh resent being ruled by London. During the 1970s, the Scottish and Welsh nationalist parties grew until they won several seats in Parliament. In 1997 the new Labour government of Tony Blair passed **devolution** bills that gave home-rule powers to Scotland, Wales, and Northern Ireland. The Scottish parliament, first elected in 1999, has the power to raise taxes and run Scotland's education, medical services, judicial system, and local government, somewhat like a U.S. state. Some say this makes Britain **quasi-**federal, but officially Britain is still unitary.

Decentralization in France   France was historically a much more unitary system than Britain. Everything is—or, until recently, was—run from Paris, a pattern that began with the absolutist (see page 254) moves of Louis XI in the fifteenth century. In the seventeenth century Cardinal Richelieu centralized power in Paris by a system of provincial administrators, *intendants,* who reported back to him. The French Revolution, Napoleon, and republics that followed increased centralization. Now **prefects** report back from the **departments** to the interior ministry.

---

center-periphery tension   Resentment of outlying areas at rule by nation's capital.

devolution   Shifting some powers from central government to component units.

quasi-   Nearly or almost.

prefect   Administrator of a French department.

department   French first-order civil division.

Most of France's ninety-six *départements* were named after rivers to try to erase the historical memories of the old provinces. But France, like Britain, has distinctive regional subcultures: the Celtic Bretons (who fled from Britain centuries ago to escape the Saxons); the southerners of the Midi, whose speech is still flavored with the ancient *langue d'oc;* and the Corsicans, who still speak an Italian dialect. Breton and Corsican separatists sometimes promote their cause with violence.

In 1960, to better coordinate economic development, President de Gaulle decreed twenty-two regions consisting of two to eight departments each. Starting in 1981, President Mitterrand instituted genuine **decentralization** that gave the regions certain economic-planning powers. The Paris-appointed prefects lost some of their powers to hitherto powerless departmental legislatures. France thus reversed five centuries of centralization.

Autonomy in Spain   Spain, too, decentralized. Here the problem was more urgent, for regional resentments, long buried under the dictatorial rule of Francisco Franco (1939–1975), came out with anger. Spain's regional problems were among the most difficult in Europe, second only to Yugoslavia (see following). Basques and Catalans, in the north of Spain, have non-Castilian languages and distinctive cultures. Basques, for example, speak a language related to no other and are intensely proud of it. In addition, many areas of Spain were granted *fueros* (local rights) in medieval times, which they treasured for centuries. On top of great regional diversity, Spanish centralizers attempted to plant a unitary system on the French model. The result was great resentment that appeared whenever Spain experimented with democracy. Breakaway movements appeared in 1874 and in the 1930s, only to be crushed by the Spanish army, which regards the unity of the country as sacred.

With this background, Spain held its breath in the late 1970s and 1980s as the post-Franco Spanish democracy instituted seventeen regional governments called **autonomías**. The big problem is still the Basque country in the northwest, where the terrorist ETA strives for complete Basque independence with murder and bombing. To appease regionalist feeling, which also appeared in more moderate forms in Catalonia, Galicia, Andalusia, and other areas, Madrid allowed regions to become autonomous, with regional parliaments, taxation power, language rights, and control over local matters. Most Spaniards approve of the *autonomías,* which go much further than French decentralization. Considering what could have happened in Spain after Franco and comparing it to Yugoslavia after Tito, Spain's *autonomías* worked.

Pros and Cons of Unitary Systems   Authority in unitary states may be absurdly overconcentrated. Local government may not be able to install a traffic light or bus stop without permission from the capital. This leads citizens to ignore local

---

decentralization   Shifting some administrative functions from central government to lower levels; less than *devolution.*

autonomías   Spanish regions with devolved powers.

HOW TO . . .

PERCENTAGES

Percent is also a device for comparing two things. It says that one item is a fraction the size of another. A **percent** is just a decimal fraction with the point moved two digits to the right. Thus ¼ = .25 = 25%. In a text, you spell it out, 25 percent; use the "%" sign in tables. For those who are a little rusty, just enter the smaller number in your calculator, press "divide by" (÷), enter the larger number, and then equal (=). Then move the decimal point two digits to the right. If 187 out of 232 House Republicans voted for a bill, then 80.6 percent did. For most purposes, you can round that off to 81 percent. This facilitates comparisons. If 109 out of 203 House Democrats voted for the bill (57 percent), then we can say Republicans showed greater discipline and cohesion.

There is a difference between percent and **percentage points**. If the British Labour party moves up from 41 percent of the vote in one election to 47 percent in the next, they have gained 6 percentage points. However, they have scored a thumping 14.6 percent increase (6 divided by 41). In calculating percent change, first subtract the earlier number from the later one, and divide that by the earlier number. In the example, subtract 41 from 47 and divide the result (6) by 41 to get 14.6 percent.

affairs and may lead to political alienation. Centralization of power, however, can be an advantage in facing modern problems. Clear lines of authority without excess bickering among units of government can be useful. In unitary systems, the capital can marshal economic resources and coordinate planning and development. Taxation is the same nationwide, so firms and individuals cannot flee to low-tax states, as in the United States. Education standards can be high and uniform, as in Japan.

Japan gives a certain amount of autonomy to its subunits, but they, too, tug in a quasi-federal direction. An 1871 copy of the French system, Japan has forty-three **prefectures** plus its three largest cities and the thinly populated northernmost island, each with its elected governor and unicameral assembly. Their activities are still overseen and limited by the home affairs ministry in Tokyo, and they collect only about 30 percent of the taxes they need, what Japanese call "30 percent autonomy." Colorful and outspoken prefectural governors have recently been demanding more autonomy.

FEDERAL SYSTEMS

Federalism gives first-order civil divisions considerable autonomy while the central government runs what is inherently national in scope. It is a difficult balancing act that varies among federal nations. Americans, with one of the first federal

---

percent   Decimal fraction with point moved two digits to the right.
percentage point   One-hundredth of a given quantity.
prefecture   Japanese first-order civil division.

systems, sometimes urge federalism on other nations, but it does not always work. (Iraq is a current test case.) The ex-Soviet Union and Mexico became so central- ized that some wondered if they were still federal. The crux of a federal system is that the component states have some powers that cannot be easily overridden by the central government.

The components are typically represented in an upper house such as the U.S. Senate or German Bundesrat. (Unitary systems do not really need upper houses, but most have them.) In federal systems, the central government has exclusive control over foreign, defense, and monetary policy. The states typically control ed- ucation, police, highways, and other close-to-home affairs. Because the division of these powers is seldom clear or permanent, a federal government rests on a deli- cate balance between central power and local autonomy.

There are several reasons for starting a federal union. The first is national se- curity; small and weak states cannot defend themselves against powerful aggressors. (This was one of the main arguments of the *Federalist* writers.) The pooling of diplo- matic and military resources of the states made Bismarck's Germany a major power. Federal unions serve economic purposes. U.S. prosperity is based in large part on its continent-wide market without trade barriers, a feat the European Union is now copying. Federalism is often the only way to protect national unity. As Britain freed India in 1947, New Delhi set up a federal system that allowed such states as Ben- gal and Punjab to maintain their own cultures while joining the Indian nation. In- dian states were jealous of their identities and would not have entered the federal union without a guarantee of local autonomy. Much of Latin America—especially the large countries of Argentina, Brazil, and Mexico—saw federalism as the only way to control their vast territories. Belgium in 1993 switched from a unitary to a fed- eral system to give its two languages (French and Flemish) their own turf.

Pros and Cons of Federal Systems   Citizens are closest to their state govern- ment; they may influence officials and see how decisions are made. U.S. states have been called "laboratories of democracy" because they can experiment with new programs. If they work they can be copied nationwide; if they fail not much harm is done. On the other hand, local governments may lack the money to finance pro- grams, and their officials are sometimes incompetent and corrupt. Local decision- making can lead to duplication of services and poor coordination.

The relationship of the states or provinces to other levels of government varies among federal systems. In Germany, each of the sixteen Länder has its own con- stitution and government for **Land** affairs. The Landtag (state legislature) can even affect the national policy, because it elects members of the Bundesrat (the upper house of the national legislature). States in the Indian federation likewise have control over such items as education, agriculture, and public health, but share au- thority with New Delhi in judicial matters. India is unique among federal states be- cause New Delhi can proclaim a state of emergency, suspend the constitution, and

---

Land   German federal first-order civil division; plural *Länder.*

take over the government of any state. "President's rule" is sometimes declared after disorders in India's states.

Each of America's fifty states can legislate in any area not delegated to the federal government or to the people. Usually, education, welfare, civil law, property taxes, and licensing of professions are all state functions. However, in the twentieth century, the federal government expanded in the areas of civil law, welfare, and economic regulation. Bush 43 moved education standards up to the federal level with his No Child Left Behind Act. Many states and traditional Republicans did not like this shift. Dependent on federal grants and revenue sharing, the states must meet federal standards in many areas. Washington, for example, threatened to withhold federal highway funds if states did not make twenty-one the legal drinking age. They did.

From the beginning, the United States has debated the proper role of the federal government and worried that "sectionalism" could pull the Union apart, which it did. Southern insistence on "states' rights" led to a clash with President Lincoln over slavery and then to civil war. In the 1960s, controversial U.S. Supreme Court decisions prompted a campaign to curb the power of federal courts. Some insist that the concentration of power in Washington perverts American federalism and encroaches on individual freedoms. At the same time, local governments and citizens continue to rely on federal help in solving complex—and expensive—problems. Federalism is not an easy system to maintain and does not necessarily solve the problems of large and diverse countries. Consider the following.

Ex-Soviet Federalism   On paper, the Soviet Union was a highly decentralized federation: Its fifteen **republics** were supposed to have the right to secede. In practice, under the tight control of the Communist party—although usually staffed by local talent (Georgians ran Georgia, Uzbeks ran Uzbekistan, and so on)—they followed Moscow's orders. Few understood that beneath a centralized veneer lurked disunion. Gorbachev totally underestimated the strength of local nationalism, and when he allowed **glasnost** in the late 1980s, many Soviet republics clamored for independence, especially the Baltic states of Lithuania, Latvia, and Estonia, which Stalin had brutally annexed in 1940. With the collapse of the Soviet Union at the end of 1991, all fifteen republics proclaimed themselves sovereign and independent, and many countries, including the United States, granted each of them diplomatic recognition.

Twelve of the old Soviet republics—all but the three Baltic states—enrolled in the "Commonwealth of Independent States" (CIS), a weak and uncertain entity with headquarters in Minsk, capital of Belarus. The CIS was supposed to promote trade among members. Fighting between two CIS members (Armenia and Azerbaijan) over disputed territory took thousands of lives, and the CIS was unable to settle their quarrel. Some observers suspect the CIS is merely a cover

---

republic   In Communist Soviet Union and Yugoslavia, federal first-order civil division.

glasnost   Gorbachev's policy of media openness.

Nationality and Citizenship

We think of nationality and citizenship as one and the same, but Communist and some other countries split the two terms, using "nationality" to designate what we call "ethnic group." You could have Uzbek nationality but Soviet citizenship, Macedonian nationality but Yugoslav citizenship, or Slovak nationality but Czechoslovak citizenship, and this was marked in your internal passport, which everyone had to carry. This system—devised by Stalin as "national in form, socialist in content"—was supposed to satisfy the "national question." Instead, it asked for trouble by locking people into a nationality and reminding them of it. Actually, the old tsarist system was better; it listed everybody as Russian. Legally, we have only one nationality, American, a point that helps cement us together.

for the eventual take-back of the old Soviet territory by Russia, which Russian nationalists openly advocate.

The bulk of the old Soviet Union continued as the Russian Federation, which is composed of eighty-nine autonomous republics, districts, regions, and even cities, most of which have signed a federation treaty with Moscow. Several areas, home to some of the hundred-plus ethnic groups within Russia, refused to sign and billed themselves as independent. In the Caucasus, Chechen terrorists still fight to break away from Russia. The Muslim Chechens, like many Muslims in Russia, never liked being ruled by Moscow. Moscow in turn fears that granting independence to Chechnya would encourage such demands elsewhere. President Putin reinstituted central control over unruly governors by creating seven super-regions, most headed by former colleagues from the security police.

Could the three Communist federations—the Soviet Union, Yugoslavia, and Czechoslovakia—have devised a more genuine federalism that would not have fallen apart? Or were these federations of unlike components doomed from the start? The Communists, by pretending to have solved the "national question," merely suppressed it until it came out later.

Ex-Yugoslav Federalism Yugoslavia, founded only in 1918, was a new and somewhat artificial country whose components were rarely content. It fell apart once before, in World War II, when its German conquerors set up an independent Croatia with expanded territories. Croatian fascists murdered some third of a million Serbs and others who had lived among them for centuries, thus sowing the hatred that erupted in the 1990s. The Communist Partisans who fought the Nazis thought federalism was the answer. Under the maverick Communist Tito, Yugoslav federalism went farther than the Soviet variety. Each of Yugoslavia's six republics really did run local affairs and sent equal numbers of representatives to both houses of parliament. Yugoslavia's collective presidency had one member from each republic.

This ultrafederal setup, however, did not calm local nationalism; it inflamed it. Each republic wanted its own railroads, steel mills, and control of its economy.

Under Tito, the Communist party and security police could hold Yugoslavia to-gether, but after he died in 1980 the republics started going their separate ways. Tito deserves blame for much of the horror of ex-Yugoslavia, for he designed an unworkable confederal system that had to fall apart. Yugoslavia is an example of poor institutional choices.

The most advanced republics, Slovenia and Croatia, resented being governed and taxed by a regime they disliked in Belgrade, which is also the capital of Ser-bia. Slovenia and Croatia were the biggest money-earners and rejected subsidiz-ing the poorer republics further south. (The north of Italy has the same resentment toward the south of Italy.) Ljubljana and Zagreb (their respective capitals) de-clared their independence in 1991, and fighting broke out as ethnic Serbs set up a minirepublic inside Croatia. The bloodshed was much worse after Bosnia, with a Muslim plurality (but not a majority), declared its independence in 1992. The problem was that 3 million ethnic Serbs lived outside of Serbia in areas where Serbs were massacred in World War II. Feeling endangered, Serbs felt entitled to take whatever lands they were living on for an eventual **Greater** Serbia. Serbian forces brutally practiced "ethnic cleansing" and murdered thousands. Serbia and Montenegro continue as a rump federation, and even it could split apart. A 1995 U.S.-brokered and NATO-enforced peace calmed Bosnia, but ethnic Albanians in Kosovo, a Serb province, moved for independence. In 1999 a U.S.-led bombing campaign prevented Serbia from wholesale massacre of Kosovars. Bosnia and Kosovo are in effect NATO protectorates.

Canadian Federalism   Canada is another federation with **centrifugal** ten-dencies. Quebec is not alone in seeking independence; so do some of the western provinces. As we considered in Chapter 7, the British allowed the French-speaking Québécois to keep their language, and francophones became second-class citizens, poorer than other Canadians and discriminated against because almost all private and government business was conducted in English.

In the 1960s the Parti Québécois (PQ) sprang up, dedicated to Quebec's inde-pendence from Canada. To appease them, the federal government in Ottawa in 1969 made Canada bilingual, with French and English having equal rights. The PQ wanted more and made French the only official language of Quebec, turning the English-speaking minority into second-class citizens. Trying to hold the federation—which came to look a bit like a confederation as the provinces overruled the center—together, Ottawa and the provincial governments laboriously developed two new federal accords (Meech Lake in 1987 and Charlottetown in 1992), which were then rejected. The stumbling block was a separate status for Quebec as a "distinct society." Quebeckers said it did not go far enough; other Canadians said it went too far. Quebec independence would be disastrous for all of Canada, splitting off the Atlantic provinces, breaking the flow of trade, and making Canada even more

---

Greater   Indicates desire to gather into one nation all areas of given ethnic group.
centrifugal   Pulling apart.

Linguistic nationalism shows in Quebec, where now all shop signs must be in French. Here a Montreal greengrocer had to paint over his fruit market sign with "marché de fruits," but was allowed to keep "Simcha's" in English, as it is an established business name. (Michael Roskin)

dependent on the United States. Quebec's drive for sovereignty is now receding, and Canada will likely hang together even as Canadians quarrel over federalism.

Federalism is difficult. These three cases remind us that federalism cannot cure everything. If the components are too different from one another—culturally, economically, linguistically, or historically—a federal system may not hold together. A shared political culture, as in the United States, Australia, Brazil, and Germany, is a big help. With that as a foundation, the right balance must be found between central and state governments. The United States is still searching for its correct balance.

■ THE UNITED STATES: BALKANIZATION OF GOVERNMENT

There are approximately 80,000 local governments in the United States—including 3,141 counties and thousands of school districts—plus fifty state governments and the national government. These governments often get in each other's way, a situation called, half in jest, **balkanization**, after the many little countries that emerged in the Balkans when the Turks were pushed out. The United States is plagued by immoderate jurisdictional conflicts over whose rules apply in which situation and to **burden shifting** as different levels of government try to dump expenses on other levels.

---

balkanization   Broken up into unreasonably small units.
burden shifting   Moving expenditures to other levels of government.

KEY CONCEPTS

BURDEN SHIFTING

The Founding Fathers feared the concentration of power that might come with a big army, so they divided defense responsibilities between a small (often microscopic) standing army and each state's militia, which we now call the National Guard. The Constitution mentions militias in Article I Section 8, but the Militia Act of 1792 got more specific, calling on the states to enroll all able-bodied men into militias. Funding, training, and officer selection were left up to the states, which promptly neglected their responsibilities because they cost money. In America's wars of the nineteenth century, state militias were nearly useless. Only a series of reforms in the twentieth century gradually created the modern National Guard, effective because it is federally funded and must meet federal standards.

We have here a **paradigm** of federal-state burden shifting. In principle and in the Constitution, the states are to do the bulk of governing. In practice, states tend to evade their tasks because they hate raising taxes to pay for them. This leads to uneven standards in education, health, welfare, highways, environmental protection, voting rights and balloting mechanisms, you name it. Some states do a good job; many do not. When standards get too lax, Washington feels it must step in with federal laws and federal money. Thus policies and programs keep getting bumped up from the state to the federal level, concentrating more power in Washington. This happens somewhat more under Democrats than under Republicans. Then, about once a generation, Washington (usually under Republicans) rediscovers a **New Federalism** to return power to the states where it belongs. The states are initially delighted, until they see how much this costs them; then they turn back to Washington for funds.

Another type of burden shifting is the **unfunded mandate**, a law passed by a higher level of government requiring lower levels to do something but providing no funds. President Bush's No Child Left Behind Act had bipartisan support for raising standards and making schools accountable. Soon, however, most states—including Republican ones—complained that they would have to pay most of the costs and that Washington was telling states what to do in education, which is unmentioned in the Constitution. States and local governments hate unfunded mandates. Burden shifting is as American as Mark Twain, who showed how Tom Sawyer tricked other boys into painting a fence for him.

The Growth of Federal Power   The Founding Fathers expected that the amount of governance would be small and that most of it would be done by the states under their "reserved" powers. For most of the nation's history this was so, and Washington was a small town. States and localities raised their own revenues and spent them on modest programs; federal help was minor. As late as 1932, federal grants were less than 3 percent of state and local revenue.

But things changed in 1913 with the passage of the Sixteenth Amendment, which allowed the federal government to tax income. It meant that Washington gained an extractive power much stronger than the states'. Soon small federally funded programs for highways, education, and public health appeared. With the

---

paradigm   (from the Greek "example") Model or pattern for other cases.
New Federalism   Nixon's and Reagan's program of returning powers to states.
unfunded mandate   Law requiring a lower level of government to pay for its implementation.

New Deal in the 1930s, federal programs increased in number and funding. With Lyndon Johnson's Great Society in the 1960s (Johnson was a great admirer of Roosevelt), federal programs expanded, and Richard Nixon greatly increased the funding for them. Now, many billions of dollars flow from Washington to state and local governments, which have come to depend on them for a portion of their revenues.

State and local governments often dislike being dependent on Washington, but they need the money. It's easier for the federal government to collect taxes through its progressive income tax (the richer you are, the bigger percentage you pay) than it is for states and cities through their income, sales, and property taxes. Public demand for services has outstripped the financial ability of most states and localities. Theoretically, states and cities could decline federal grants, but no one likes to turn down money, even if there is some red tape involved.

The net impact is the growth of federal power. Because it provides money, it sets standards. School effectiveness; the design and construction of hospitals, highways, and airports; and women's collegiate athletics (Title IX) come under federal supervision. Some suggest that this development makes the United States less federal than it used to be. Perhaps so, but reversing the process is difficult. Should toxic and nuclear waste disposal be left to state discretion? Is education a purely local concern? Standards and dollar support vary wildly across the fifty states, leaving many young Americans poorly educated. The growth of federal power is not a plot but a series of responses to changing times.

THE UNITARY-FEDERAL MIXTURE

No country is perfectly unitary, nor is any perfectly federated. Even strongly unitary systems have certain elements of local input and control, and federal systems keep considerable power for the center. The interesting trend of our time is the tugging of unitary systems in a federal direction. Britain, France, and Spain are examples of highly centralized governments moving to quasi-federalism. Japan's governors would like to do the same. It would be premature to say that eventually unitary systems will resemble federal systems, for both systems carry with them centuries of institutional and cultural baggage. Our task is not simply to classify countries as "unitary" or "federal," but to see how they actually operate in practice. Then we will find all manner of interesting deviations from the model, borrowings, and attempts to modify systems.

■ CHOOSING INSTITUTIONS

Political institutions are, in large measure, artificial creations. Most of them, of course, have evolved over time, but at key points in a nation's history, people have had the opportunity to choose their institutions. This brings an element of

---

New Deal   FDR's mild welfare programs during Depression.

creativity into politics. Institutions neither fall from heaven nor rise from earth. They are crafted by a handful of people who can do a good job or a poor one. They are guided both by past experience and by reason. Often they are taking a leap in the dark. The Founding Fathers had little in the way of precedent when they constructed a presidential federal republic. Modified by time, usage, amendments, statutes, and court decisions, their handiwork has endured. The drafters of Germany's Weimar constitution in 1919 were less fortunate. On paper, the Weimar constitution looked like a perfect democracy, but some of the institutional choices were poor: no monarch, a weak president, a PR electoral system that encouraged splinter parties and cabinet instability, and a provision for emergency powers that could be misused. One wishes we could have warned them of their fateful choices.

When political science was young, it focused heavily on constitutions, as if selecting the right institutions could confer moderation and stability on a political system. Well, often the right choices can structure behavior for centuries. Much political behavior is how people, especially politicians, react to the institutions they live in. The institutions of Tito's Yugoslavia seem almost calculated to wreck the system. We may wonder if political science, in trying to imitate the natural sciences, has strayed too far from its origins. There was something noble and challenging about trying to devise workable, durable constitutions. In a tumultuous world, there can be few higher tasks than the development of effective political institutions.

KEY TERMS

autonomías (p. 242)
balkanization (p. 248)
burden shifting (p. 248)
center (p. 240)
center-periphery tension (p. 241)
centrifugal (p. 247)
confederation (p. 240)
decentralization (p. 242)
department (p. 241)
devolution (p. 241)
evolve (p. 233)
first-order civil division (p. 240)
glasnost (p. 245)
Greater (p. 247)
institutionalize (p. 234)
Land (p. 244)
majoritarian (p. 237)

majority (p. 238)
mixed-member (p. 238)
monarchy (p. 235)
New Deal (p. 250)
New Federalism (p. 249)
paradigm (p. 249)
percent (p. 243)
percentage point (p. 243)
plurality (p. 238)
political institution (p. 233)
prefect (p. 241)
prefecture (p. 243)
proportional representation (p. 238)
quasi- (p. 241)
republic (pp. 235, 245)
single-member district (p. 236)
unfunded mandate (p. 249)

KEY WEB SITES

Local governments
world.localgov.org/

U.S. governors
www.nga.org/

State budget officers
www.nasbo.org/

Center for the Study of Federalism
www.temple.edu/federalism/

Publius: Journal of Federalism
www.lafayette.edu/publius/

New Federalism
newfederalism.urban.org/

Canada
www.ccu-cuc.ca/

Forum of Federations
www.forumfed.org

FURTHER REFERENCE

Donahue, John D. *Disunited States.* New York: Basic Books, 1997.

Doran, Charles. *Why Canadian Unity Matters and Why Americans Care: Democratic Pluralism at Risk.* Toronto: University of Toronto Press, 2001.

Duchacek, Ivo D. *Comparative Federalism: The Territorial Dimension of Politics,* rev. ed. Lanham, MD: University Press of America, 1987.

Lijphart, Arend. *Patterns of Democracy: Government Forms and Performance in Thirty-Six Countries.* New Haven, CT: Yale University Press, 1999.

McCabe, Neil Colman, ed. *Comparative Federalism in the Devolution Era.* Lanham, MD: Lexington, 2002.

Moreno, Luis. *The Federalization of Spain.* Portland, OR: F. Cass, 2001.

Redish, Martin H. *The Constitution as Political Structure.* New York: Oxford, 1995.

Sartori, Giovanni. *Comparative Constitutional Engineering: An Inquiry into Structures, Incentives and Outcomes.* New York: New York University Press, 1994.

Shapiro, David. *Federalism: A Dialogue.* Evanston, IL: Northwestern University Press, 1995.

Siegan, Bernard H. *Drafting a Constitution for a Nation or Republic Emerging into Freedom,* 2nd ed. Fairfax, VA: George Mason University Press, 1994.

Walker, David B. *The Rebirth of Federalism,* 2nd ed. New York: Chatham House, 2000.

CHAPTER 14

LEGISLATURES

QUESTIONS TO CONSIDER

- How did parliaments first come to be?
- What is the difference between presidential and parliamentary systems?
- Why does the U.S. Congress overspend?
- What is executive-legislative "deadlock"?
- What good is a bicameral legislature in a unitary system?
- Do legislatures originate the laws they pass?
- Is the U.S. "pork barrel" necessary to make the system work?
- Have legislatures declined in importance? Why?

Political institutions, it is theorized, become more specialized, complex, and differentiated as they become more modern. Primitive hunting bands had nothing more than a single leader who decided most things. Tribes added councils of elders to debate major problems and adjudicate disputes. City-states such as Athens had assemblies that combined legislative, executive, and judicial functions. The Romans developed a senate, but it too combined several roles, and its powers declined as Rome went from republic to empire. In the Middle Ages, the prevailing feudal system was a balance among a monarch, nobles, and leading churchmen, and it is in **feudalism** that we first glimpse the "balance of power."

Countries with limits on government have usually had feudal pasts, which teach that dispersion of power is good and concentration of power is bad. Countries with mostly absolutist traditions have trouble founding democracies. An example of this balancing of power is the oath the nobles of medieval Aragon (in

---

feudalism   System of political power dispersed among layers.

On the banks of the Thames river in London, Westminster, mother of Parliaments, represents the slow, gradual march to democracy over many centuries. (British Department of the Environment, Transport, and the Regions)

northeast Spain) pledged to a new king, "We, who are as good as you, swear to you, who are no better than we, to accept you as our king and sovereign lord provided you observe all our statutes and laws; and if not, no."

Ambitious monarchs, who were often at war, desperately needed revenues. Some of them started calling assemblies of notables to levy taxes. In return for their "power of the purse," these assemblies got a modest input into royal policies. Such were the beginnings of the British **Parliament**, which had two houses (Lords for peers and church leaders and Commons for knights and burghers), and the Swedish **Riksdag**, which originally had four chambers (for nobles, clerics, burghers, and farmers). The French **Estates General**, with three houses (for nobles, clerics, and commoners), got off to a weak start and was soon forgotten as French monarchs gathered more and more personal power in what became known as **absolutism**.

In Britain, Sweden, and some other European countries, though, legislatures slowly grew in power and were able to resist monarchs' absolutist demands. In Britain in the sixteenth century, Henry VIII, who broke with Rome because he

parliament   National legislature; when capitalized, British Parliament, specifically House of Commons.
Riksdag   Sweden's parliament.
Estates General   Old, unused French parliament.
absolutism   Post-feudal concentration of power in monarch.

wanted a divorce, developed a partnership with Parliament because he needed its support in passing laws to get England out of the Catholic church and the church out of England. By the seventeenth century, Parliament considered itself coequal with the monarch and even supreme in the area of taxes. The English Civil War was a quarrel between royalists and parliamentarians over who had top power. In 1649, Parliament decided the issue by trying and beheading Charles I.

John Locke, the English philosopher who lived through this momentous period, extolled the power of the "legislative" as the most basic and important. During the Age of Enlightenment in the eighteenth century, political theorists such as Montesquieu and Jefferson declared that liberty could be secured only if government were divided into two distinct branches, the legislative and the executive, with the ability to check and balance the other. Modern governments still have these two branches, but only in the United States do they check and balance each other. Theoretically at least, the legislature enacts laws that allocate values for society, and the executive branch enforces the statutes passed by the legislature. (A coequal judicial branch is rare; it is a U.S. invention found in few other systems.) But these responsibilities often overlap, and the separation of powers is rarely clear-cut.

■ PRESIDENTIAL AND PARLIAMENTARY SYSTEMS

Presidential systems most clearly show the separation of power between the executive and legislative branches. These systems, a minority of the world's governments, have a **president** who combines the offices of head of state with chief of government. He or she is elected more or less directly by the people (in the United States the quaint electoral college mediates between the people and the actual election), is invested with considerable powers and cannot be easily ousted by the legislative body. In **parliamentary systems**, the head of state (figurehead monarch or weak president) is an office distinct from the chief of government (**prime minister**, premier, or chancellor). In this system, the prime minister is the important figure.

Notice that in parliamentary systems voters elect only a legislature (see Figure 14.1 on page 256); they cannot split their tickets between the legislature and executive. The legislature then elects an executive from its own ranks. If the electoral system is based on proportional representation (see Chapter 13), there will likely be several parties in parliament. If no one party has a majority of seats, two or more parties will have to form a **coalition**. Whether one party or several, a majority of parliament must support the cabinet. Usually a monarch (as in Britain

---

presidential systems   Those with separate election of executive (as opposed to symbolic) president.

president   In U.S.-type systems, chief political official; in many other systems a symbolic official.

parliamentary systems   Those with election of parliament only, which in turn elects prime minister.

prime minister   Chief political official in parliamentary systems.

coalition   Multiparty alliance to form a government.

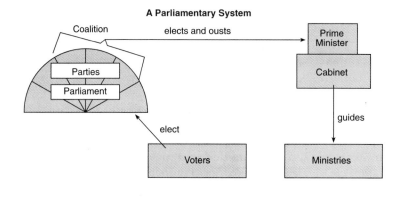

Figure 14.1

Parliamentary versus presidential systems.

and Spain) or weak president (as in Germany or Israel) "asks"—there's no real choice in the matter—the head of the largest party to become prime minister and "form a government." **Cabinet** and **government**, used interchangeably, are what Americans call an **administration** (the Blair government but the Bush administration). The prime minister, after consulting with the parties likely to support him or her, names a team of ministers for the cabinet who are themselves members of the parliament. These ministers then guide the various ministries or departments of government that form the executive branch. The prime minister and cabinet are "responsible" (in the original sense of the word, "answerable") to the parliament. (Prior to democratization in the nineteenth century, ministers were responsible only to the monarch.)

---

cabinet   Top executives who head major ministries or departments.
government   In Europe, a given cabinet, equivalent to U.S. "administration."
administration   Executives appointed by U.S. president, equivalent to European "government."

KEY CONCEPTS

HEAD OF STATE VERSUS HEAD OF GOVERNMENT

Two terms that sound almost alike often confuse students, especially Americans. A *head of state* is theoretically the top leader but often has only symbolic duties, such as the queen of England or king of Sweden. These monarchs represent their nations by receiving foreign ambassadors and giving restrained speeches on patriotic occasions. In republics, their analogues are presidents, some of whom are also little more than figureheads. The republics of Germany, Hungary, and Israel, for example, have presidents as heads of state, but they do little in the way of practical politics. (They are also not well known. Can you name them?)

The *head (or chief) of government* is the real working executive, called prime minister, premier, or chancellor. They typically also head their parties, run election campaigns, and run government. In Britain, this is Prime Minister Tony Blair, in Germany Chancellor Gerhard Schröder. The United States combines the two offices, for our president is both head of state and head of government.

Presidents in presidential systems are not responsible to legislatures. The close connection between the legislative and executive is broken. Presidents are elected on their own and choose cabinet ministers or department secretaries from *outside* the ranks of the legislative body. In the United States, of course, top executive and judicial officers must be confirmed by the Senate. The two branches of government cannot control, dissolve, or oust the other, as happens in parliamentary systems. This gives presidential systems great stability. Presidents may be unpopular and face a hostile Congress, but they can still govern with the constitutional and statutory powers they already have.

SEPARATION AND FUSION OF POWERS

The United States takes great pride in its **separation of powers**, the famous "checks and balances" that the Founding Fathers insisted on. Having just won independence from George III and his executive dictatorship, they set one branch of government as a check against the power of another. It was an extremely clever arrangement and has preserved America from tyranny. But it is terribly slow and cumbersome, what political scientist Edward S. Corwin called an "invitation to struggle" between the executive and legislative branches. The two branches often stymie each other. Congress can fail to pass something the president wants, and the president can veto something Congress wants. Some scholars think such an executive-legislative *deadlock* (see page 257) is common for the U.S. presidential system.

Important questions, such as campaign-funding reform, can get stuck for years between the two branches of government. The president cannot dissolve Congress and hold new elections, which are set by the calendar. Congress cannot oust a

---

separation of powers　Legislative and executive branches checking and balancing each other.

CLASSIC WORKS

WHERE DID THE U.S. SYSTEM ORIGINATE?

The U.S. system of checks and balances originated with a French nobleman, the Baron de Montesquieu (1689–1755), who traveled all over Europe to gather material for one of the classics of political science, *The Spirit of the Laws.* In trouble with the king of France, Montesquieu spent some years in England and admired its liberties, which he thought came from the mutual balancing of the king (the executive) and Parliament (the legislative). The French parliament, the Estates General, was unused for generations; French kings ran everything on an absolutist basis. Actually, by the time Montesquieu wrote about English checks and balances they had been overturned, and Parliament was supreme over king. Montesquieu was describing an idealized version of the English mixed monarchy that had slid into the past. The U.S. Founding Fathers, however, read Montesquieu literally and attempted to construct his theory of checks and balances. Few other countries have done this.

president except by the impeachment procedure. Only two presidents, Andrew Johnson and Bill Clinton, have ever been impeached, and the Senate did not convict them. Richard Nixon resigned before the House of Representatives could vote to impeach him. The repeated showdowns between the Clinton administration and the Republican-dominated Congress are standard in U.S. history.

West Europeans consider the American system inefficient and unintelligible, and they actually have more modern systems that evolved after the U.S. Constitution was devised. Their parliamentary systems have a **fusion of power** that does not set the branches against each other. In fact, it's hard to distinguish between legislative and executive branches, for the top executives are themselves usually members of parliament. In the British, German, Japanese, and Dutch systems, prime ministers must be elected to parliament, just like ordinary legislators, before they can become chief of government. As leaders of the biggest parties, they are formally called on (by the monarch or figurehead president) to form a government. The individuals forming this government or cabinet have both their seats in parliament and offices in the executive departments. They report back often to parliament. At any time, about a hundred British **MPs** (members of Parliament) also serve at various levels in the executive ministries and departments. Thus legislators are also executives. The cabinet, in effect, is a committee of parliament sent over to supervise the administration of the executive branches of government.

When Britain's parliament is in session, the cabinet members show up to answer questions from their fellow MPs. Britain's House of Commons holds a Question Hour most afternoons at the beginning of the session. The members of the

fusion of power   Executive as leading offshoot of legislature.
MP   British for member of Parliament, namely, the House of Commons.

two main parties sit facing each other across an aisle on, respectively, the "government benches" and "**opposition** benches." The front bench of the former is reserved for cabinet ministers, the front bench of the latter for the opposition's "shadow cabinet," the MPs who would become ministers if their party wins the next election. MPs with no executive responsibilities sit behind the cabinets and are called **backbenchers**. Most questions to the prime minister and his or her cabinet come from the opposition benches—first written questions and then oral follow-ups. The answers are criticized, and the opposition tries to embarrass the government with an eye to winning the next election. Most parliamentary systems operate in a similar fashion.

In the U.S. system, with its separation of powers, committees of the Senate or House can summon cabinet members and other officials of the executive branch to committee hearings. But appearing before a committee is not the same as a grilling before the entire legislative body. The president, of course, as equal to and separate from Congress, cannot be called to testify.

ADVANTAGES OF PARLIAMENTARY SYSTEMS

There are several advantages to a parliamentary system. The executive-legislative deadlock, which happens frequently in the American system, cannot occur because both the executive and legislative branches are governed by the same party. If the British Labour party wins a majority of the seats in the House of Commons, the leaders of the party are automatically the country's executives. When the Labour cabinet drafts a new law, it is sent to the House of Commons to be passed. There is rarely difficulty or delay in getting the law passed because the Labour MPs almost invariably obey the wishes of the party's leaders.

If members of the governing party disagree with their own leaders in the cabinet, they can withdraw their support and vote "no confidence" in the government. This is rare. The government then "falls" and must be replaced by a new leadership team that commands the support of a majority of the House of Commons. If a new election gives the opposition party the numerical edge in parliament, the cabinet resigns and is replaced by the leaders of the newly victorious party, formerly known as the "shadow cabinet." Either way, there cannot be a long disagreement between executive and legislative branches; they are fused into one.

The prime minister and cabinet can be speedily ousted in parliamentary systems. Any important vote in parliament can be designated a **vote of confidence**. If the prime minister loses, he or she takes it as a lack of parliamentary support and resigns. There is no agony of impending impeachment of the sort that paralyzed Washington under Presidents Nixon and Clinton. A new prime minister is voted in immediately. If the government makes a major policy blunder, parliament can

---

opposition   Those parties in parliament not supporting the government.

backbencher   Ordinary member of parliament with no leadership or executive responsibilities.

vote of confidence   Vote in parliament to oust government.

get rid of the cabinet without waiting for its term to expire. When Americans become unhappy with presidents' policies, there is little the system can do to remove them from the White House early. Parliamentary systems do not get stuck with unpopular prime ministers.

Parliamentary systems have other difficulties, however. First, because members of parliament—supervised by their parties' **whips**—generally obey their party leaders, votes in parliament can be closely predicted. The parties supporting the government vote for any bill the cabinet has drafted. Parties opposing the government vote against it. Floor speeches and corridor persuasion have no impact; the legislators vote the way their party instructs. MPs in such systems have lost their independence, and their parliaments have become little more than rubber stamps for the cabinet. The passage of legislation is more rational, speedy, and efficient, but parliament cannot "talk back" to the executive or make independent inputs. This makes European parliaments rather dull and less important than **Capitol Hill** in Washington, where legislators often oppose the president, even when of their own party. Many European legislators are jealous of the spunky independence and separate resources that American representatives and senators enjoy.

Second, depending on the party system and electoral system, parliamentary democracies often have many parties, with no single party controlling a majority of seats in parliament. This means the largest party must form a coalition with smaller parties in order to command more than half the seats. In Canada's 2004 elections, Liberals emerged as the largest party but still lacked a majority of seats, so they sought the support of the small New Democratic party to form a government. In parliamentary systems the head of the largest party usually becomes prime minister, and the head of the second largest party becomes foreign minister. Other cabinet positions, or **portfolios**, are assigned by bargaining. Italy and Israel are examples of coalition governments, and they illustrate what can go wrong: The coalition partners quarrel over policy, and one or more parties withdraws from the coalition, bringing it below the required majority in parliament. The government then "falls" for lack of parliamentary support, with or without a formal vote of no confidence. This leads to instability, frequent cabinet changes, and loss of executive authority. Italy, for example, has had some sixty governments since World War II.

This is not as bad as it sounds—remember, the "government" simply means "cabinet"—and the cabinets are often put back together again after bargaining among the same coalition partners. The trouble is that prime ministers must concentrate on not letting the coalition fall apart, and thus they hesitate to launch new policies that might alienate one of the member parties. The problem here is not one of too much change but of too little: the same parties in the same coalitions getting stuck over the same issues. **Immobilism**, the inability to decide major

---

whip   Legislator who instructs other party members when and how to vote.

Capitol Hill   Home of U.S. Congress. (Note spelling: -ol.)

portfolio   Minister's assigned ministry.

immobilism   Inability of coalition governments to solve major questions.

BICAMERAL OR UNICAMERAL?

Some two-thirds of parliaments in the world have two chambers, an upper house (the U.S. Senate, British House of Lords, French Sénat, German Bundesrat) plus a lower house (the U.S. House of Representatives, British House of Commons, French **National Assembly**, or German **Bundestag**). These are called **bicameral** (two chambers) legislatures. Despite its name, the upper house usually has much less power than the lower house. Typically if the upper house objects to something passed by the lower house, the lower house can override their objections, often by a simple majority. Only the two houses of the U.S. Congress are coequal and must pass identically worded versions of a bill.

A smaller number of parliaments are **unicameral** (one chamber), such as China's National Peoples Congress, Sweden's Riksdag, and Israel's Knesset. Yugoslavia once experimented with a five-chambered parliament. South Africa had a curious and short-lived three-chambered parliament with one house each for whites, mixed-race peoples, and East Indians. The majority black population was unrepresented. (Since 1994, South Africa has had a bicameral parliament with a black majority.)

The reason for two chambers is clear in federal systems (see Chapter 13). The upper house represents the component parts, and the lower house represents districts based on population. This was the great compromise solution incorporated in the U.S. Constitution: The Senate represented the states and the House the people. A federal system requires an upper chamber. Germany's **Bundesrat**, for example, represents the sixteen *Länder* and is coequal to the lower house on constitutional questions. On other issues, however, it can be overridden by the Bundestag.

The utility of an upper house in unitary systems is unclear. Britain's House of **Lords**—reformed in 1999 by keeping **life peers** and excluding most hereditary peers—is still mostly an elderly debating society that sometimes catches errors in laws passed too quickly and obediently by Commons. Otherwise, the Commons overrides any objection from the House of Lords with a simple majority vote. This is also true of the French Sénat, an indirectly elected body that largely expresses farming interests. New Zealanders, Danes, and Swedes—all with unitary systems—concluded that their upper houses served no purpose and abolished them in recent decades.

questions, is the danger of multiparty parliamentary systems. Notice how this parallels the problem of deadlock in presidential systems.

Not all parliamentary systems, to be sure, suffer from immobilism. Britain, Germany, New Zealand, and Sweden have cohesive and effective cabinets because they have to share little or no power in coalition governments. The largest parties

---

National Assembly   Lower, more important chamber of French parliament.

Bundestag   Lower, more important chamber of German parliament.

bicameral   Parliament having two chambers, upper and lower.

unicameral   Parliament with one chamber.

Bundesrat   Upper, weaker chamber of German parliament.

Lords   Upper, weaker chamber of British parliament.

life peer   Distinguished Briton named to House of Lords for his or her life only, not hereditary.

The Finnish parliament is unicameral—with no upper chamber—and consists of 200 seats arrayed in a semi-circle, the standard layout for parliaments. Also standard are the buttons on each member's desk to register his or her vote, which is then electronically tabulated and displayed instantly. (Michael Roskin)

in these countries are big enough to govern either alone or with only a little help from like-minded parties. German and British governments have fallen on votes of no-confidence only once each since World War II. In general, the more parties in a coalition, the less stable it is. Israel's multiparty cabinet is often immobilized.

■ WHAT LEGISLATURES DO

Consider the old high-school civics question: How does a bill become law? They may have told you that individual members introduce proposals, but they usually cover small matters, such as getting a tax break for a constituent. Most important bills originate in the government or administration. Typically, an executive agency develops an idea, the cabinet drafts a proposal, and the largest party introduces it to the legislature, which then debates and modifies it.

THE COMMITTEE SYSTEM

Much power in modern legislatures resides in their committees, which can make or break proposals. Democratic parliaments often hold public hearings to get expert testimony and input from interest groups. If the bill is reported favorably out of committee, it goes to "the floor," the full chamber, where it needs a majority vote to pass.

A Senate subcommittee hearing chaired by Senator Joseph Biden (D-Delaware) hears testimony from experts and interest groups on the situation of East European minorities. Much legislative work is done in such committees, often with little notice by the press or public. (Michael Roskin)

Virtually every legislature has a number of standing or permanent committees and may from time to time create special ad hoc committees to study urgent matters. The British House of Commons has five standing committees plus several specialized committees. These committees are less important than their U.S. counterparts, for the fusion of powers of the British system means that Parliament is not supposed to criticize or reject bills the cabinet has submitted. It may, however, modify them. With separation of powers, the committees of the U.S. Congress are most fully developed. The House of Representatives has twenty-seven standing committees—the Senate, twenty-one—and they often make the news. Assignment to the more prestigious of these committees, such as the House Ways and Means Committee or Armed Services Committee, can help members' careers, for they give members media exposure.

U.S. congressional committees screen the thousands of bills that are introduced at every session and pick out the few that merit serious study and consideration. A government bill in a parliamentary system is automatically important; "private members' bills" may be quickly weeded out in committee. Second, legislatures are so large that bills cannot be drafted by the entire membership; to work out an agreement on the precise wording and scope of legislation, proposals must be referred to relatively small groups of lawmakers. It should not be surprising, therefore, that the bulk of legislative work is not performed on the floor but in committee rooms.

In the United States, each committee has several specialized subcommittees; the two houses have a total of about 250 subcommittees. Changes in the 1970s weakened the sometimes tyrannical powers of committee chairpersons by making it

PORK-BARREL POLITICS

Legislators everywhere ensure their reelection by looking after their districts. Projects that bring improvements to or spend money in their district are called **pork barrel**, after the gifts of plantation owners to their slaves of a barrel of pickled pork parts. Modern pork-barrel programs include highways, bridges, flood control, military contracts, and farm subsidies. The U.S. pork barrel may take second place to the Japanese, whose legislators are famous for delivering massive (and often unneeded) public-works projects to their districts and shielding farmers from competition.

Individual legislators support others' pork projects so their projects will get support, a process called **log rolling**: "You help roll my log, and I'll help roll yours." Republicans long denounced Democrat pork but could not resist it when they won control of Congress. Legislators do whatever gets them reelected, and that usually means pork projects. If the United States and Japan wish to reduce their pork intake, they will have to break the close connection between elected representatives and home districts. But this connection is precisely what these democracies prize. Would you want a system in which congresspersons are distant and uncaring about their districts?

Besides, much good and important legislation would not pass if leaders could not use pork as inducements to vote for it. The 2004 budget included 6,000 pork projects, little bribes for every state and congressional district to get legislators to support the White House budget. Even Republicans use pork to get things done. Returning to a theme of Chapter 1, do not get angry at a fact like the pork barrel; instead, analyze it. Why does it exist? What functions does it serve? You may find that it is built into the system.

easier to establish subcommittees. Chairpersons are now weaker than they used to be, but now subcommittees and *their* chairpersons have decentralized and fragmented power too much, weakening Congress as an institution. A cure for one problem produced new problems, the story of many political reforms.

These same reforms of the 1970s broke the power of appointment of the senior House and Senate leaders of both parties. Committee chairs and membership were generally assigned on the basis of seniority. Now, when the parties caucus at the beginning of a session in each house, members vote for committee chairpersons by secret ballot, effectively breaking the seniority system. Party committees in each house make committee assignments and usually try to take members' interests and expertise into account. On the Hill, specialization is the name of the game. The larger committees, such as the Senate Foreign Relations Committee, may have a dozen subcommittees. Capitol Hill is now more open and democratic than it used to be, but this has not enhanced its power vis-à-vis the executive branch.

---

pork barrel   Government projects aimed at legislators' constituencies.
log rolling   Legislators mutually supporting each other to get *pork-barrel* bills passed.

Standing committees in the U.S. Congress are balanced so that they will represent both political parties and the states or geographic regions with the greatest interest in the committee's area of specialization. A Nebraskan is often on the Agricultural Committee and a New Yorker on the Education and Labor Committee. Each standing committee is bipartisan, made up of Democrats and Republicans in proportion to each party's seats in that house of Congress.

A CLOSER LOOK AT LEGISLATURES

The main purpose of legislative bodies, in theory, is to formulate laws. This, however, varies among political systems and is generally in decline. Ideally, legislatures initiate laws, propose constitutional amendments, ratify treaties, control tax revenues, and scrutinize government activities. In authoritarian systems, however, legislatures are usually just rubber stamps for the dictator.

Lawmaking   Although legislatures *pass* laws, few of them *originate* laws—which is why we must take their "rule-initiation function" with a grain of salt. As we noted, much legislation originates in government departments and agencies, comes to the attention of cabinet officers, and is sent on to the legislature, which may alter it somewhat. In parliamentary systems, especially where one party has a majority of seats, the cabinet gets what it wants. Party discipline makes sure that members of the ruling parties will automatically vote the way party leaders instruct. Votes in such legislatures are highly predictable along party lines; some observers say such parliaments have become rubber stamps for the executive. In the U.S. Congress, where party discipline is more lax, members sometimes buck their own party. But even there, notice how much of the legislative agenda is set by the White House: economic initiatives, invading another country, expanding or cutting domestic programs, and setting criteria for education. Even the budget, the original "power of the purse" that gave legislatures their importance, is now an annual congressional *reaction* to the budget produced by the White House budget office. Typically, Congress takes the president's budget, adds their own pork spending, and passes it. Accordingly, "lawmaking" is not the only or perhaps even the most important thing that legislatures do.

Constituency Work   Legislators spend much time helping constituents. Most have staffs to answer letters, make sure people get their government checks, and generally show that the elected representatives really care. Often "lawmakers" are so busy with **constituency casework** that they pay little attention to making laws. In effect, elected representatives have partly transformed themselves into **ombudsmen**, specialists who intervene with government on behalf of people with

---

constituency casework   Attention legislators pay to complaints of people who elect them.
ombudsman   Swedish for "agent"; lawyer employed by parliament to help citizens wronged by government.

complaints. (Standard complaint: "Where's my check?") Is there anything wrong with this? Is it not a perfectly valid and necessary role for legislators to play? It is, but something gets lost: the wider view that a representative should have in looking out for the common good of the whole country. A legislator immersed in constituency casework has no time for or interest in bigger questions, so the initiative goes more and more to the executive branch, and democracy grows a little weaker.

Constituency service is one main way elected representatives keep getting re-elected. Legislators are in a position to do favors. They frequently visit their home districts to listen to local problems and arrange for government help, something an out-of-office challenger cannot do. Thus, legislators in systems as different as the United States and Japan can lock themselves into power.

Supervision and Criticism of Government   Potentially the most important role of modern legislatures is keeping a sharp and critical eye on the executive branch. Even if they originate little legislation, legislatures can powerfully affect the work of government by monitoring government activity to make sure it is in the nation's interest, incorrupt, and effective.

Virtually every U.S. administration must modify its policies because Congress raises difficult and sometimes embarrassing questions, even though it may have passed little legislation on these matters.

In Britain, the **Question Hour** allows members of Parliament to grill ministers, sometimes with devastating results. Even if the British cabinet knows that it is almost immune to a vote of no confidence—because it controls the largest party in Commons—its members must be careful in answering these questions. A bad, unconvincing answer or lie can hurt the ruling party in the next election.

Members of both parties on Capitol Hill criticized the Bush administration for failing to anticipate terrorism, for saying Iraq had dangerous weapons, and for getting U.S. forces bogged down in Iraq. No Child Left Behind and seniors' drug benefits also came in for Hill criticism. The Bush administration had to change its tune in several policy areas because of congressional criticism. Keeping the government on its toes is one of the best things a legislature can do, even if it passes few laws.

Education   Legislatures also inform and instruct the citizenry on the affairs of government; they create mass demands by calling public attention to problems. In the mid-1960s, Senator J. William Fulbright (D-Arkansas), chair of the Senate Foreign Relations Committee, educated Americans about the Vietnam War by televising his committee's hearings. All democratic countries carry extensive press reports on parliamentary debate, and many now televise them.

Representation   The most elemental function of a legislature is to represent people. Although legislators are more elite than the people they represent, most legislators in democracies consider the interests of all their constituents; it helps get

---

Question Hour   Time reserved in Commons for opposition to challenge cabinet.

HOW TO . . .

LONGITUDINAL STUDY

One good way to study something is to see how it changes over time, a **longitudinal** study. For example, suppose you want to see if interest groups located in Washington have grown in number. You would probably find a reliable secondary source (perhaps Common Cause) that keeps track of these things. You might also count the numbers of "National" and "Associations" in D.C. phone books over several years. Then you would list the numbers, probably with most recent first, looking something like this:

2001	1,827
2000	1,779
1999	1,654
1998	1,628
1997	1,607
1996	1,592

For a longer-range study, you might take every fifth or tenth year over many decades or a century. Other longitudinal studies might take a closer look at the behavior of one or several interest groups, campaign spending, laws initiated by Congress, or presidential votes by states. You may be able to display such numbers graphically, which helps readability. (See pages 286–287.)

Not all longitudinal studies need to be quantified. Some do not lend themselves to numbers. A longitudinal study of Sen. J. William Fulbright (D-Ark.), for example, might use quotes and paraphrases from his speeches and writings to show how he changed over time, from supporting the administration on foreign affairs to opposing it over the Vietnam War.

them reelected. Even in the U.S. South, now that African Americans are voting in considerable numbers, members of Congress take care not to offend them. A large part of representation is psychological; people need to *feel* they are represented. When they do not, they resent government power, and the government loses legitimacy. "No taxation without representation," chanted American colonials. The **apartheid** laws of South Africa, passed by a whites-only legislature, evoked no support and much disobedience from the black majority. Because of this, the apartheid system eventually cracked.

The foregoing are some of the roles performed by legislatures. Notice that only one of them is lawmaking, and that is usually just a follow-up on ideas initiated by bureaucrats and executives. Still, if legislatures carry out the other functions mentioned, they are doing a lot.

---

longitudinal   Studying how something changes over time.
apartheid   System of strict racial segregation formerly practiced in South Africa.

■ THE DECLINE OF LEGISLATURES

By the late nineteenth century, observers were noticing that parliaments were not working the way they were supposed to. Contrary to Locke's expectations, legislatures were losing power to the executive. Most political scientists would agree that the trend has continued and grown. Some, however, hold that the original Lockean expectations were too high and that parliaments provide useful checks on the executive even though they do not originate much legislation. For better or worse, a high-tech age has shifted power away from legislatures.

STRUCTURAL DISADVANTAGES

In parliamentary systems, party discipline is strong, and legislators obey party whips. In European parliaments we can usually predict within a vote or two how the issue will be decided: in favor of the government, because the government (or cabinet) commands a majority of seats. In such systems, individual members do little and there is no special excitement in the press and public about parliamentary affairs. Only when coalitions break up or when members of one party defect to another (a rare occurrence) do things get unpredictable and therefore interesting. The European parliaments really are more rational and efficient than the U.S. Congress, but they are also less powerful and less interesting. Efficiency has led to atrophy.

The U.S. Capitol Hill has no such problem with efficiency. Its near-feudal dispersion of power with weak party discipline and its tendency to deadlock with the executive has made it most inefficient. But this is why Congress is lively and important. In few other countries can the national legislature as a whole "talk back" to the executive and even override a presidential veto. On occasion, members change parties to show their displeasure, as Vermont's Jim Jeffords did in 2001. Nevertheless, even in the United States power has drifted to the executive. The president speaks with one voice, Congress with many. Congress is fragmented into committees and subcommittees—with chairpersons vying for media attention—and this delays and often prevents agreement. Congress expects and even demands presidential leadership and usually gives presidents most of what they want after some controversy and debate.

LACK OF EXPERTISE

Few legislators are experts on technical, military, economic, or social problems. Of the 535 senators and representatives in both houses of Congress, nearly half are lawyers. European parliaments have fewer lawyers and more schoolteachers, journalists, and full-time party people. But hardly anywhere are technical experts elected to legislatures, and few legislators are professionally equipped to deal with such technical matters as intelligence estimates, medical care, international currency fluctuations, and environmental pollution. Accordingly, legislators must rely chiefly

CASE STUDIES

CONGRESSIONAL OVERSPENDING

The tendency of Congress to overspend is built into the situation of congresspersons. In the abstract, they are all for a balanced budget. When it comes to their pet interests—usually linked to getting reelected—they like spending increases. New dams and highways, military hardware, and farm subsidies often directly benefit their constituents (see box on "Pork-Barrel Politics" on page 264). Paying for prescription drugs under Medicare shows they hear the cries of senior citizens. Rationally, individual self-interests drive the system as a whole to overspend, something allegedly nobody wants. What's good for the individual is not necessarily good for the **aggregate**.

At various times, Congress tries to restrain itself. In 1985, Congress attempted to hand the power to limit spending to an appointed congressional official. The Supreme Court threw it out as unconstitutional. Congress then attempted to hand the power to the White House with the 1996 "line-item" veto, a major shift in power from the legislative to the executive. The Supreme Court threw it out; the Constitution does not permit the veto of part of a bill. It was almost as if Congress said, "We give up; we're too divided. So here, Mr. President, you take over our constitutional duties." The astonishing thing about the U.S. Congress, the last Mohican of independent parliaments, is that it *wants* to surrender power to the executive.

The Republicans who took over both houses in 1994 were determined to end deficits (see page 343) by setting "spending caps." The caps were evaded almost immediately, but an economic boom provided unforeseen tax revenues and budget surpluses by the turn of the millennium. Quickly, the limits were forgotten as both Republicans and Democrats put forward their pet spending projects. With the end of the boom and the 2001 tax cut, revenues shrank and record deficits loomed, but federal spending was higher than ever. As the baby boom generation retires, spending will only go up. Is Congress inherently unable to limit spending?

on experts from the executive departments. Much legislation originates with these specialists, and they are often called as witnesses to committee hearings. The ensuing legislation usually grants these executive specialists considerable discretion in applying the law.

Most parliaments have little or nothing in the way of independent research support; their data come either from the government or from private interest groups. Only the U.S. Congress—again, based on the idea of separation of powers—can generate its own data. The Government Accountability Office (GAO, formerly the General Accounting Office), Congressional Research Service (CRS), and Congressional Budget Office (CBO) are all part of the legislative branch. They provide independent evaluations and data to lessen Congress's dependence on the executive. No other legislature in the world has a fraction of this research capability, which still cannot counterbalance the massive information advantage of the executive branch.

---

aggregate   Thing or population considered as a whole.

PSYCHOLOGICAL DISADVANTAGES

Citizens everywhere are more impressed with presidents or prime ministers than with parliaments. There may be a deep human need to respond to a single chief. A president can have charisma but a legislature cannot. American children are socialized to revere the president but to disdain members of Congress. As was mentioned in Chapter 12, even in parliamentary systems voters now respond to the personalities of the candidates for prime minister. Television, by giving much more air time to chief executives than to any other political figure, heightens this tendency. People come to see their president or prime minister as a parental figure, calmly guiding the country toward safety while the silly parliamentarians squabble among themselves. This leads to what some political scientists fear is "president worship."

THE ABSENTEE PROBLEM

If you visit a legislature in session you might be disappointed, for usually the chamber is nearly empty. Most of the time, most members need not be present, and they aren't. They have many other things to do: helping and visiting constituents, talking with interest groups, and sitting on committees. Why bother listening to speeches? They will not change anyone's mind, and everyone knows their content in advance. The speeches are for the mass media.

Absent most of the time, the member is really needed only to vote, and sometimes not even then. British party whips can get a high turnout for an important vote. In Sweden, an electronic system summons members from all over the Riksdag after the speeches are over. They press their *ja* or *nej* button according to their parties' wishes, glance up at the electronic tabulation (which was never in doubt), and then leave. The Riksdag chamber has been full for only five to ten minutes.

Most systems have ways of recording members' votes without their presence. When the French National Assembly votes, a few members of each party move down the rows of absent fellow party members' desks and flick their voting switches to a *pour* or *contre* position, as the party has specified. The press then reports that the measure passed by a vote of around 300 to 200, but that count is deceptive, as often only three dozen members were present for the vote. Theoretically, the French system could function with just one member present from each party.

The U.S. House and Senate require members to be present to vote, but even if absent they can arrange to have their votes "paired against" that of another absent legislator with the opposite viewpoint. The yes vote cancels out the no vote, so the passage of the measure is unaffected, and the member can still claim to have voted for or against something.

What is the impact of legislative absenteeism? It may indicate that the legislator is busy doing other important things of the sort discussed earlier. It may also indicate just plain laziness. But it surely means that legislators no longer regard legislating as their chief function. By their absence they admit that they are not important, at least not in the way originally intended. Is there any way to fix the problem? Only by weakening party discipline and party-line voting so that no one could predict how a floor vote would go. If bills were up for grabs, some excitement and tension would return to floor debate, and members would have an interest and incentive to show up and participate. The trade-off would be that the passage of legislation would be more chaotic and unpredictable.

LACK OF TURNOVER

In democratic parliaments, members tend to become career, lifetime legislators. Once elected, they usually get reelected as long as they wish to serve. This means little fresh, young blood enters parliament with new ideas, and on average parliamentarians are rather old, in their fifties. In U.S. House contests, over 90 percent of incumbents win. Incumbency brings terrific advantages: gerrymandered districts, name recognition, favors done for constituents, media coverage, and plentiful campaign funds from PACs and interest groups. Unless representatives are tarred by scandal, they almost cannot lose. Challengers are so discouraged that several dozen House incumbents run unopposed. In many other contests opposition is only token. Why waste time and money in a hopeless race?

What happens to democracy when elected representatives stay until death or retirement? It loses some of its ability to innovate and respond to new currents in public opinion. It gets stodgy. The Founding Fathers made the House term deliberately short, just two years, to let popular views wash freely into the chamber. Alexander Hamilton described the frequent elections to the House in this way: "Here, sir, the people govern. Here they act by their immediate representatives." He could not imagine that turnover is actually higher in the Senate, a chamber that was designed to be insulated from mass passions. All this raised the question of limits on congressional terms, which some promised but few practiced. Once in power, they discovered they were the only ones who could serve their constituents.

Parliamentary systems have similar problems. Few legislators are replaced by elections and most consider their membership in parliament a career. If the system is proportional representation (discussed in Chapter 12), the more senior party people are higher up on the party list, ensuring their election. Young newcomers may be entered at the bottom of their party lists with scant chance of winning. However, PR systems do have the advantage of letting new, small parties into parliament with fresh faces and new ideas. In the 1980s, the Greens (ecology parties) entered several West European parliaments, forcing the big, established parties to pay attention to environmental problems.

THE DILEMMA OF PARLIAMENTS

What Russia has gone through recently illustrates the dilemma of parliaments. In the 1990s Russia experienced a deadlock between President Boris Yeltsin and the Russian legislature, the **State Duma**. To get things done, power must be concentrated in the hands of a powerful executive. To keep things democratic, however,

---

State Duma   Lower, more important chamber of Russian parliament.

power must be dispersed, that is, divided between an executive and a legislature. Russia urgently needed vast reforms—the economy teetered on the brink of collapse—but the Duma, dominated by Communists and nationalists who opposed Yeltsin, disputed and blocked reforms. Putin solved the problem by founding his own party, which now controls two-thirds of the Duma's seats. Putin owns parliament, but Russia is no longer a democracy.

Even in the United States, Congress works as intended only when dominated by the party opposed to the president, what is called "divided government," something many voters prefer. Locke was right: Parliaments are the foundation of democracy. But worldwide their functions have atrophied and power is flowing to chief executives.

KEY TERMS

absolutism (p. 254)

administration (p. 256)

aggregate (p. 269)

apartheid (p. 267)

backbencher (p. 259)

bicameral (p. 261)

Bundesrat (p. 261)

Bundestag (p. 261)

cabinet (p. 256)

Capitol Hill (p. 260)

coalition (p. 255)

constituency casework (p. 265)

Estates General (p. 254)

feudalism (p. 253)

fusion of power (p. 258)

government (p. 256)

immobilism (p. 260)

life peer (p. 261)

log rolling (p. 264)

longitudinal (p. 267)

Lords (p. 261)

MP (p. 258)

National Assembly (p. 261)

ombudsman (p. 265)

opposition (p. 259)

parliament (p. 254)

parliamentary systems (p. 255)

pork barrel (p. 264)

portfolio (p. 260)

president (p. 255)

presidential systems (p. 255)

prime minister (p. 255)

Question Hour (p. 266)

Riksdag (p. 254)

separation of powers (p. 257)

State Duma (p. 271)

unicameral (p. 261)

vote of confidence (p. 259)

whip (p. 260)

KEY WEB SITES

U.S. House of Representatives
www.house.gov/

U.S. Senate
www.senate.gov/

Congressional activities
thomas.loc.gov/home/thomas2.html

British House of Commons
www.parliament.uk/commons/cminfo.htm

German Bundestag
www.bundestag.de/

Legislatures around the world
www.soc.umn.edu/~sssmith/Parliaments.html
www.agora.stm.it/elections/parlemen.htm

FURTHER REFERENCE

Baldwin, Nicholas D. J., and Donald Shell, eds. *Second Chambers.* Portland, OR: Frank Cass, 2001.

Copeland, Gary W., and Samuel C. Patterson, eds. *Parliaments in the Modern World: Changing Institutions.* Ann Arbor, MI: University of Michigan Press, 1994.

Davidson, Roger H., and Walter J. Oleszek. *Congress and Its Members,* 9th ed. Washington, D.C.: CQ Press, 2003.

Deering, Christopher J., and Steven S. Smith. *Committees in Congress,* 3rd ed. Washington, D.C.: CQ Press, 1997.

Dodd, Lawrence C., and Bruce I. Oppenheimer, eds. *Congress Reconsidered,* 7th ed. Washington, D.C.: CQ Press, 2001.

Hayes, Michael T., and Lou Frey, Jr., eds. *Inside the House: Former Members Reveal How Congress Really Works.* Lanham, MD: University Press of America, 2001.

King, Anthony. *Running Scared: Why America's Politicians Campaign Too Much and Govern Too Little.* New York: Free Press, 1997.

Laver, Michael and Norman Schofield. *Multiparty Government: The Politics of Coalition in Europe.* New York: Oxford University Press, 1990.

Lijphart, Arend, ed. *Parliamentary versus Presidential Government.* New York: Oxford University Press, 1992.

Mayhew, David R. *Congress: The Electoral Connection,* 2nd ed. New Haven, CT: Yale University Press, 2004.

Suleiman, Ezra N., ed. *Parliaments and Parliamentarians in Democratic Politics.* New York: Holmes & Meier, 1986.

Wolfensberger, Donald R. *Congress and the People: Deliberative Democracy on Trial.* Baltimore, MD: Johns Hopkins University Press, 2000.

EXECUTIVES

CHAPTER

15

There have been executives a lot longer than there have been legislatures. Tribal chiefs, kings, and emperors appeared with the dawn of civilization, and most of the time they had no legislatures to worry about. Parliaments are relatively new. Even today, powerful executives seem more natural to us than divided and contentious parliaments. Executives have a built-in psychological advantage over legislatures.

Indeed, the word *government* in much of the world means the executive branch. In Europe, *government* equals *cabinet*. The "Blair government" is just another way of saying Prime Minister Blair's cabinet plus some additional subcabinet assistants. In the United States (and nowhere else), this is called the *administration*. What Americans call the government, meaning all the bureaus and bureaucrats, is known in Europe as the **state**.

---

state   In Europe, all branches of the national political system; what Americans call "the government."

■ PRESIDENTS AND PRIME MINISTERS

As discussed in Chapter 14, in parliamentary systems, a national legislature indirectly elects a chief executive from its own ranks, a prime (originally meaning "first") minister. Such parliaments serve as electoral colleges that stay in session to consider legislation. They can also oust a prime minister and cabinet by a vote of no confidence, although this is now rare. Still, prime ministers are responsible to parliament. If they represent a party with a majority of seats, they are secure in office and can get legislative programs passed quickly and with little backtalk. A British prime minister with a sizable and disciplined majority in the Commons wields powers that might make a U.S. president jealous.

If no party has a majority, however, a government is formed by a *coalition* of parties, each of whom gets one or more ministries to run. Sometimes the coalition partners quarrel over policy and threaten to split up. This weakens the hand of the prime minister, as he or she knows that any major policy shift could lead to new quarrels. It is not quite right to say that prime ministers are "weaker" than presidents; it depends on whether prime ministers have a stable majority in parliament.

A presidential system bypasses this problem by having a strong president not dependent on or responsible to a parliament but elected on his or her own for a fixed term. The U.S. Congress may not like the president's policies and may vote them down, but it may not vote out the president. The U.S. president and Capitol Hill stand side by side, sometimes glaring at each other, knowing there is nothing they can do to get rid of one another. It is sometimes said that presidents are "stronger" than prime ministers, and in terms of being able to run the executive branch for a fixed term, they are. But they may not be able to get vital new legislation or budgeting out of their legislatures. This **"deadlock** of democracy," the curse of the U.S. political system, parallels parliamentary *immobilism* (see page 260). Neither system can guarantee cooperation between legislative and executive. Any system that could would be a dictatorship.

"FORMING A GOVERNMENT" IN BRITAIN

Great Britain is the classic of parliamentary systems, one in which we still see its historical roots. The monarch, currently Queen Elizabeth II, initiates a new government (in the European sense) by formally inviting the leader of the largest party in the House of Commons to become prime minister and "form a government." As such, the prime minister appoints two dozen **ministers** and a greater number of sub-cabinet officials. All are MPs and in the prime minister's party, usually chosen to represent significant groups within the party. Theoretically, the prime minister is *primus inter pares* (first among equals) and guides the cabinet to consensus. But the prime minister is really boss and can dismiss ministers. Ministers

---

deadlock   In presidential systems, executive and legislative branches blocking each other.
minister   Head of ministry, equivalent to U.S. departmental secretary.

who oppose government policy are expected to not go public but to resign and return to their seats in Commons. Under Tony Blair, the British cabinet merely concurred on decisions he had reached earlier with a small group of close advisors, on the American pattern.

"CONSTRUCTIVE NO CONFIDENCE" IN GERMANY

The **chancellor** of Germany is as strong as a British prime minister. The chancellor, too, is head of the largest party in the lower house (Bundestag). Once in the office the chancellor can be ousted only if the Bundestag votes in a replacement cabinet. This is called "constructive no confidence," and it has contributed to the stability of Germany's governments. It is much harder to replace a cabinet than just oust it; as a result, constructive no confidence has succeeded only once, in 1982, when the small Free Democratic party defected from the Social Democrat-led coalition to the opposition Christian Democrats. A prime minister with constructive no confidence is more powerful than one without it, as one might see in a comparison of the average tenures of Italian and German cabinets (several months as compared to several years).

"COHABITATION" IN FRANCE

President Charles de Gaulle of France (1958–1969) designed a semipresidential system that has both a working president and a prime minister. The president was elected directly for seven years (recently reduced to five) and a parliament elected for five years. If both are of the same party, there is no problem. The president names a like-minded **premier**, who is the link between president and parliament. In 1986 and again in 1993, though, a Socialist president, François Mitterrand, with two years left in his term, faced a newly elected parliament dominated by conservatives. The constitution gave no guidance in such a case. Mitterrand solved the problem by naming opposition Gaullists as premiers and letting them dismantle many Socialist measures. Mitterrand reserved for himself the high ground of foreign policy. The French called the arrangement "cohabitation," an unmarried couple living together. In 1997, the reverse happened: Gaullist President Jacques Chirac called parliamentary elections early, lost them, and had to face a Socialist-dominated National Assembly. The solution was cohabitation again; Chirac named Socialist chief Lionel Jospin as premier. Cohabitation works, and the French accept it. France thus handled the problem of deadlock that is common in the United States. The 1993 Russian constitution incorporated a French-style system with both president and premier, and it produced executive-legislative deadlock, no longer the case under President Putin, who controls two-thirds of the Duma.

---

chancellor   Germany's prime minister.
premier   France's and Italy's prime minister.

CASE STUDIES

ISRAEL'S DIRECTLY ELECTED PRIME MINISTERS

In 1996 Israelis, under a new law, elected a parliament and a prime minister *separately and directly,* something never before done in the world. Each Israeli voter had two votes, one for a party in the legislature and one for prime minister. By definition, parliamentary systems elect prime ministers indirectly, usually the head of the largest party in parliament, while presidential systems directly elect their chief executives, so Israel turned from purely parliamentary to presidentialism, but not all the way. The **Knesset** could still vote out the prime minister on a motion of confidence, and coalition cabinets were as hard to form as ever.

Even worse, Israeli voters, figuring that selection of prime minister was taken care of by one ballot, used the other to scatter their votes among a dozen small parties, making the Knesset even more fractionated. After two unhappy tries of the unique hybrid system, the Knesset repealed it in 2001. The experiment showed that halfway borrowings from one system (presidentialism) into another (parliamentary) do not work. If you want stability, go all the way to presidentialism.

THE "PRESIDENTIALIZATION" OF PRIME MINISTERS

Parliamentary systems tend to "presidentialize" themselves. Prime ministers with stable majorities supporting them in parliament start acting like presidents, powerful chiefs only dimly accountable to legislators. They know they will not be ousted in a vote of no confidence, so the only thing they have to worry about is the next election, just like a president. This tendency is strong in Britain and Germany.

Increasingly, elections in parliamentary systems resemble presidential elections. Technically, there is no "candidate for prime minister" in parliamentary elections. Citizens vote for a party or a member of parliament, not for a prime minister. But everybody knows that the next prime minister will be the head of the largest party, so indirectly they are electing a prime minister. For these reasons, virtually all European elections feature posters and televised spots of party chiefs as if they were running for president. As in U.S. elections, personality increasingly matters more than policy, party, or ideology.

EXECUTIVE TERMS

Presidents have fixed terms, ranging from four years for U.S., Brazilian, and Russian presidents (they can be reelected once) to a single six-year term for Mexican presidents. French and many other presidents can be reelected without limit. When presidents are in office a long time, even if "elected," they become corrupt and dictatorial, as President Suharto did in thirty-two years at Indonesia's helm. He was forced out after Indonesia's economy, looted by Suharto's friends and family, collapsed in 1997.

Knesset   Israel's 120-member unicameral parliament.

CASE STUDIES

AUTHORITARIANISM RETURNS TO RUSSIA

President Vladimir Putin is consolidating authoritarian power. The new Russian constitution—which set up a de Gaulle-type semipresidential system (see page 276)—tilted power to the presidency. Putin made the Russian presidency even stronger. Putin had been a **KGB** colonel and headed the post-Soviet equivalent, the Federal Security Service (FSB in Russian). Unstable President Yeltsin plucked Putin from obscurity and named him his fifth prime minister in seventeen months. Some thought Putin would be another temporary, but he used police sources—he knows who has robbed what—to keep and expand his power. With Russia in steep decline, the unpopular Yeltsin in late 1999 handed over the presidency to Putin, who was easily elected to it in 2000 and reelected in 2004. He set up his own United Russia party and used it to control the Duma.

In a climate of despair and mistrust, Putin became immediately popular. Russians like a strong hand at the top, and Putin showed his. He waged war against the rebellious Chechens and cracked down on corruption, uncooperative regional governors, the independent mass media, and the "oligarchs"—people who had gotten rich fast through insider privatization deals. Putin called it "managed democracy," staffed it with old KGB hands, and paid little attention to the State Duma; he ruled by decree. Some who criticized Putin were harassed and silenced, but few Russians worry about encroachments on democracy; food on the table matters more. Putin's rule was earlier called "quasi-authoritarian," but many now drop the "quasi-."

In parliamentary systems, prime ministers have no limits on their tenure in office, providing their party wins elections. As noted, increasingly their winning depends on the personality of their leader, almost as if they were presidential candidates. Britain's Margaret Thatcher was elected for a third time in 1987, but by 1990 her mounting political problems persuaded her to resign after a total of eleven and a half years in office. Jean Chrétien was prime minister of Canada for a decade; in 2003 he handed over the post to his fellow Liberal Paul Martin, who then held new elections, which the Liberals won. Most prime ministers can **dissolve** parliament when they wish, namely, when they believe they'll do best in elections. A good economy, sunny weather, and high ratings persuade prime ministers to call elections a year or two early. Powers such as these might make an American president jealous.

On the other hand, British prime ministers can get ousted quickly if they lose the support of a majority of parliament. When Labour Prime Minister James Callaghan lost the support of just eleven Scottish Nationalist MPs in 1979, he slipped below a majority in Commons and was replaced overnight by **Tory** chief Thatcher. Some Italian premiers have held office only briefly as their coalitions disintegrated.

KGB   Soviet Committee on State Security, powerful intelligence and security agency.

dissolve   Send a parliament home for new elections.

Tory   Nickname for British Conservative.

Japanese prime ministers, the playthings of powerful faction chiefs within the ruling Liberal Democratic party, average less than two and a half years in office, some just a few months. Theoretically, prime ministers can serve a long time; in practice their tenure depends on political conditions such as elections, coalition breakups, and scandals. Parliamentary systems practice a kind of easy-come, easy-go with their prime ministers, something an American president would dislike. Presidents in presidential systems are partially insulated from the ups and downs of politics.

A U.S. president can face **impeachment**, but this is a lengthy and uncertain procedure that has been attempted only three times. Andrew Johnson was impeached by the House in 1868 but acquitted in the Senate by one vote. Richard Nixon was about to be impeached by the House but resigned just before the vote. Clinton was impeached but not convicted. When faced with a problem character as chief executive, parliamentary systems have a big advantage over the U.S. system. A simple vote of no confidence in parliament, and the rascal is out. This helps explain why, even though there are many scandals in parliamentary systems, few become as big and paralyzing as Watergate: It's much easier to get rid of the chief.

■ THE ROLES OF THE EXECUTIVE

Richard E. Neustadt wrote that "a President is 'many men' or one man wearing many 'hats,' or playing many roles." Most modern chief executives wear more than one hat, but U.S. presidents are uncommonly strong. Elected independently of the legislature, they are the people's choice (well, not quite, in 2000). They are head of state, chief of government, party leader, commander in chief of the armed forces, top diplomat, chief executive, and even leading legislator. There is no one presidents can blame for mismanaged affairs. As the sign on Harry Truman's desk put it, "The buck stops here." Since 1789, the powers of the president have grown enormously, as have those of the chief executives of all other nations.

HEAD OF STATE

Presidents are the visible symbol of the nation and perform public ceremonies that monarchs and figurehead presidents do in other nations: greet and meet visiting heads of government, receive ambassadors, represent the country to the world, and report to Congress on the state of the nation.

CHIEF OF GOVERNMENT

Chiefs of government—presidents, prime ministers, or chancellors—are responsible for making and carrying out policy decisions. They supervise the bureaucratic machinery at the national level, a staggering job. The U.S. president is responsible

---

impeachment   Indictment by the House for the Senate to try the president.

CASE STUDIES

LIMITING THE PRESIDENT'S WAR POWERS

The U.S. Constitution specifies—and the Supreme Court has upheld—the right of presidents to deploy the country's armed forces as they see fit. Congress has long been exasperated with this power and has tried, never successfully, to curb it. Congress fears that the president's power as commander in chief infringes on its power to declare war. In the late 1930s, Congress passed a series of Neutrality Acts designed to keep the country out of the coming war, but FDR circumvented them.

In 1973 Congress, which was too timid to move when the Vietnam War was at its height, passed (over President Nixon's veto) the War Powers Act, which is supposed to limit the president's use of troops in overseas combat to ninety days unless Congress approves an extension. This law did not prevent President Reagan from sending U.S. troops to Lebanon, Grenada, and Central America; Bush senior from sending troops to Panama, the Persian Gulf, and Somalia; Clinton from sending forces to Haiti, Bosnia, and Kosovo; or Bush junior from sending forces to Afghanistan and Iraq. The president says, in effect, "I don't need a declaration of war." It is likely that no law will seriously check presidential war powers and that the War Powers Act is an unconstitutional legislative veto.

for fifteen major departments of government, more than 100 executive bureaus, 500 administrative offices, and 600 divisions employing 2.8 million civil servants. One American worker in fifty is a federal employee (compared to one in 2,000 in Washington's day). The Executive Office of the President, with some 1,700 full-time workers, was formed in 1939 to guide the administration on a daily basis.

PARTY CHIEF

U.S. presidents are also leaders of their political party, as are the British, French, and German heads of government. As such, they are also "fundraisers-in-chief" and spend much time and effort at it. They endorse and campaign for the party's candidates and formulate much of the party's legislative program. The president is not as powerful a party leader as the prime minister in a parliamentary government because of the lack of centralization and discipline in the American party system.

COMMANDER IN CHIEF

Virtually all heads of government are commanders in chief of their country's military establishment. In nations new to democracy, this is a problem, as presidents or prime ministers may use the military in extralegal ways, to crush political opponents or lock themselves into power. Most countries have, at least on paper, procedures and command structures to make sure that all orders are constitutional and legal. Presidential systems often make it too easy to go to war. Both U.S. and Russian presidents have used troops in ways their respective parliaments did not approve, and nothing could be done about it. The power of commander in chief is one of the most dangerous in any political system.

CHIEF DIPLOMAT

Likewise, presidents and prime ministers largely run diplomacy without parliamentary approval. They can grant diplomatic recognition to foreign countries, negotiate trade deals, and conclude "executive agreements" that are almost treaties. Treaties themselves, important international contracts, generally must be ratified by the countries' legislatures. In the United States, that means a two-thirds assent from the Senate. The Supreme Court has upheld presidential preeminence in foreign relations, and Congress has gone along with it.

DISPENSER OF APPOINTMENTS

Since the introduction of the merit system into the U.S. Civil Service a century ago, the power of patronage has been considerably diminished. However, all federal judges and legal officers are appointed by the president, as are top diplomats and upperechelon management personnel in the federal departments, agencies, offices, bureaus, and divisions. All in all, a new president has some 3,000 jobs to dispense. One key way a president can enforce party discipline in Congress is through patronage appointments. The president says in effect: "I'll appoint your nominee to a federal office if you support my program." Politics is very much a part of appointments.

CHIEF LEGISLATOR

Heads of government are not only responsible for executing the laws but also initiate most legislation. In Washington, the State of the Union message and national budget indicate the policies, programs, and laws the president wants. Further, most parliaments draft general laws and give the chief executive broad discretionary powers in interpreting and implementing them.

■ EXECUTIVE LEADERSHIP

Back to back, America was treated to two distinct leadership styles. President Carter (1977–1981) was a hands-on, detail person; he tried to supervise nearly all parts of his administration. With intelligence and energy, he put in long hours and memorized much data. Critics, including management experts, say this is the wrong approach, that chief executives only scatter and exhaust themselves if they try to run everything.

President Reagan (1981–1989) was a hands-off person; he supervised little and left most administration to trusted subordinates. He took afternoon naps and frequent vacations. Critics say Reagan paid no attention to crucial matters, letting things slide until they turned into serious problems. The Iran-contra fiasco showed what happens when subordinates get only general directions and go off on their own. The National Security Council staff thought it was doing what the president wanted when it illegally sold arms to Iran and illegally transferred the profits to the Nicaraguan contras.

KEY CONCEPTS

AN IMPERIAL PRESIDENCY?

"The accumulation of all powers, legislative, executive, and judiciary, in the same hands," James Madison wrote in *The Federalist* no. 47, "may justly be pronounced the very definition of tyranny." Checks and balances, John Adams declared, are like "setting a thief to catch a thief." In recent years, however, some fear that the modern presidency has become too powerful.

Congress and the presidency no longer balance (maybe they never did). Samuel P. Huntington noted that from 1882 to 1909, Congress initiated 55 percent of significant legislation; between 1910 and 1932, the figure dropped to 46 percent; and from 1933 to 1940, Congress initiated only 8 percent of all major laws. The legislative function, said Huntington, "has clearly shifted to the executive branch."

As the Vietnam War wound down and Watergate boiled up, historian Arthur Schlesinger, Jr. captured the worried feeling of the time in his book, *The Imperial Presidency.* Lyndon Johnson had taken the country to war without a congressional declaration of war. Richard Nixon had expanded that war into Laos and Cambodia, again with no declaration. Nixon also "impounded" appropriations made by Congress; he simply refused to spend funds in certain areas, in effect exercising an illegal item veto. Was the president overstepping constitutional bounds? Were we becoming an imperial presidency, going the way of ancient Rome, from republic to rule by Caesars?

Congress attempted to reassert some of its authority, passing the War Powers Act in 1973 (see earlier box on page 280) and moving toward impeachment of Nixon the following year. It looked like the beginning of a new era, with Congress and the president once again in balance. But this failed to happen, for the U.S. system *needs* a strong president to function properly.

When Jimmy Carter took office in 1977, he attempted to deimperialize the presidency, but this simply led to an ineffective White House. As an outsider, Carter was ignorant of the ways of Washington and quickly alienated a Congress that was dominated by his own party. His important legislation stalled on Capitol Hill and was diluted by amendments, especially his energy proposals. By the 1980 election, much of the American electorate and Congress wished for a more forceful and experienced chief executive.

Congress's reassertion of independent authority in the 1970s proved brief, for with the arrival of Ronald Reagan in the White House in 1981, the president once again had a fair degree of command over Capitol Hill. In 1986 it was revealed that officials of the president's National Security Council bypassed Congress in selling arms to Iran and using the money to fund the overthrow of the Nicaraguan government. Even Reagan's supporters in Congress turned angry and grilled his appointees in committee hearings. Once again, a Congress disappointed with executive misuse of power tried to check the executive branch it had repeatedly invested with enormous powers. With the terrorist attacks of 2001, Congress gave even more powers to the executive branch. Is the march of executive power inexorable?

Can there be a happy middle ground between hands on and hands off? Some say President Eisenhower (1953–1961) achieved this middle ground without letting it show. He appeared to be a hands-off president who was too busy golfing to run the affairs of state, and the press made fun of Eisenhower's relaxed style. Princeton political scientist Fred Greenstein, however, analyzed Eisenhower's schedule and calendar and concluded that he was in fact a very active and busy president who made important and complex decisions. He did not like to show it, preferring to let others take the credit (and sometimes the blame). Greenstein called Eisenhower's style the "hidden-hand presidency." Greenstein's findings at least partially refute those of Barber (see box on page 284), who saw Eisenhower as a passive character.

Instead of grandstanding, Eisenhower quietly manipulated things to go his way. It fooled most observers at the time, but it was an effective style. In 1954, for example, faced with the question of whether to commit U.S. forces to help the French in the Indochina war, Eisenhower called top senators to the White House. He knew they would be cautious, for we had just ended the unpopular Korean War. The senators did not favor sending U.S. forces, and Eisenhower went along with their view. Actually, he never wanted to send troops, but he made it look as if the senators had decided the issue.

President Franklin D. Roosevelt (1933–1945) used a style that some call deliberate chaos. Setting up numerous agencies and advisers, some of them working at cross-purposes, Roosevelt would let them clash. The really difficult and important decisions would reach his desk; the others would be settled without him. This, too, was a kind of middle ground between hands on and hands off. The Clinton White House borrowed this spontaneous and creative approach, but Clinton participated personally in many policy deliberations in a more hands-on manner.

■ DISABLED PRESIDENTS

Presidential systems have another problem that parliamentary systems do not. If a prime minister becomes disabled or insane in office, he or she can be replaced overnight. Presidential systems don't know quite what to do with a seriously ill chief executive. Ecuador, for example, had difficulty legally replacing a president—known as "El Loco"—who showed serious mental problems. The U.S. Constitution says that a president unable "to discharge the powers and duties" of office should be replaced by the vice-president, but it never defined inability. As a result, several presidents have stayed in office even though seriously infirm. In France, President Mitterrand was slowly dying of cancer for most of his two terms (fourteen years) in office, but his physicians went public with it only after his death in 1996.

Woodrow Wilson (1913–1921) had suffered strokes even before he went to **Versailles** in 1918. His poor health weakened his diplomatic bargaining power there. He collapsed while on a U.S. speaking tour to drum up support for the Versailles Treaty and the attached League of Nations Covenant. After that, his wife ran things, saying she was just conveying the president's wishes. When Franklin Roosevelt was elected for a fourth term in 1944 he was suffering from heart

---

Versailles   Conference and treaty ending World War I.

BARBER'S PRESIDENTIAL CHARACTER

Can you foresee how a president will act in office? Political scientist James David Barber in 1969 virtually predicted how Richard Nixon would handle a major crisis. Barber focused on "presidential character," divined from psychological studies of individuals' earlier lives, especially of how they reacted to problems. Virtually all presidents had been in college politics (often student body president), and the way they handled their campaigns and student offices then was pretty much how they would handle them later. Character is laid down early, by college years, Barber argued.

Barber posited variables: (1) how much presidents like political office and (2) how much energy they put into it. The first has two types. Someone who really likes the job, relishes the power and perquisites, Barber called "positive." A person who does not especially enjoy the job but is ambitious and driven to achieve it, Barber called "negative." The second variable also has two types. Someone with a lot of energy for the job is called "active"; one with little energy is called "passive." This produced a fourfold table for four types of presidential character.

	Active	Passive
Positive	Roosevelt Kennedy Bush ?	Taft Harding Reagan
Negative	Johnson Nixon	Coolidge Eisenhower

Active-positives enjoy being president and put a lot of energy into it. They are flexible, have a sense of humor, and learn and change in office. Passive-positives like being president but do not do it with great energy. They prefer to delegate matters to subordinates. They are friendly and want to be liked. Passive-negatives are rarer: They are politicians who have been drafted for the job, do not relish it, and have little energy for it. Active-negatives are the real "meanies" in office. They have plenty of energy but do not enjoy power in a relaxed, happy way. The office is a heavy burden on them, and they take political opposition personally, as if numerous foes are "out to get them." Johnson and Nixon indeed got themselves into deeper and deeper trouble.

Many objected that a fourfold classification is too simple; people are more complicated. Moreover, few presidents have not actively sought the position—they have to work very hard to win it. How can a "passive" person advance so high? Can a person who does not relish the office want it? Barber argues that people can be driven to win the presidency and then discover they are unhappy in it.

Barber, long before Watergate, predicted Nixon would be devious, would dig in his heels and refuse to confess, and would make things worse for himself, precisely how Nixon behaved. Chronically insecure, Nixon worried about reelection, even though he was certain to win in 1972. Barber urges political scientists and journalists to search the lifelong character of presidential candidates for such general patterns.

There is a problem with this method, however: How many investigators have the ability and time to do a fair study of each major candidate? "Character" is a tricky area, open to many interpretations. If several journalists, political scientists, and psychologists come up with different analyses, whom do we believe? Whose insight is the correct one? Such studies could be one-sided partisan electioneering.

President Reagan came close to death in a 1981 assassination attempt. The ability of a young, unbalanced man to purchase a gun, get close to the president, and fire off six shots demonstrated how vulnerable the chief executive is. (Michael Evans, The White House Photo Office)

failure and hypertension. Near death's door, he went to **Yalta** in early 1945; perhaps that is why he conceded too much there to Stalin. Kennedy had Addison's disease, a failure of the adrenal glands, and was on steroids. He also took painkillers for his back and sleeping pills. Could medications have affected his judgment in risky situations?

Why didn't White House physicians speak out? They protected the president, both because the doctor-patient relationship is privileged and because they genuinely liked the president and did not want him to lose power. Their motivation was impeccable, but they may have done their country a disservice by keeping a sick president in power when he should have stepped down.

The Twenty-fifth Amendment, ratified in 1967, tried to define presidential inability, but it has not solved the problem. In 1981 President Reagan was severely wounded in an assassination attempt; he lost half his blood and was in surgery more than two hours. A lung infection and fever kept him bedridden the following week, yet at no time was the amendment invoked to let Vice-President Bush (41) take over. Presidential advisers decided not to alarm the public. The tendency is to close ranks around an ill president, even if that is not what the Constitution specifies or the public interest requires.

Even more difficult, what can be done if a president suffers a nervous breakdown or mental disability in office? It may have happened in the 1960s. Richard

---

Yalta   Early 1945 agreement by FDR, Churchill, and Stalin on postwar Germany and Eastern Europe.

Graphs

Thanks to computers, graphs are easy and colorful but sometimes misused. A bunch of numbers does not necessarily make a good graph. The numbers should display some pattern. If upward, you would show the growth of something; if up and down, you would show cycles. Let's expand the longitudinal study of the growth of Washington-based interest groups we discussed on page 267, taking them back twenty years, from 1980 to 2000. Our hypothesis is that they tend to grow over time.

We can either have the computer set up a graph or do it with paper and ruler. First, draw a big "L." The upright leg is the **Y axis**, on which you draw a scale, usually from zero to a little more than the highest number we have, in this case, 1,827 plus a little more to make it 2,000. Divide that scale into increments of, say, 100 or whatever interval fits the study. It might be every 5 percent or every $5,000 per capita GDP. A metric ruler can make drawing scales easier.

Now take the horizontal leg, the **X axis**, and mark off twenty steps from 1980 to 2000. Measuring rightward from the Y axis, mark with a dot the number of interest groups above the year on the X axis. For easier readability, you may connect the dots (or have the computer do it), thus making a **line graph**:

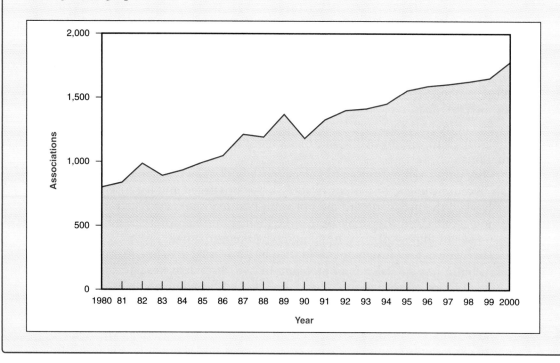

Y axis   The up-and-down leg of a graph.

X axis   The left-to-right leg of a graph.

line graph   Connection of data points showing change over time.

If the line generally rises (and it will always have some ups and downs), you have demonstrated your thesis, that interest groups keep growing in Washington. If the line trends downward, you go back and alter your thesis, now stating a decline of D.C.-based interest groups (unlikely). And if the line is generally flat, neither trending up nor down, you change your thesis to match your findings.

If you want to compare how two or more things change over time (covariance), you could use different colored lines, say blue for the percent Democratic vote in Altoona, PA, and red for size of the railroad workforce in Altoona, to show how both decline at about the same rate. (Unionized workers tend to vote Democrat.) Pie charts are not very useful; use them to show popular preferences in pies.

Not every graph should be a line graph. The zig-zags of line graphs show change over time but are meaningless for comparing categories at the same time. For that, use a **bar graph**. A line graph indicates that one data point sets the stage for the next; a bar graph does not. If you want to show change over time, say, percent voting Republican over several elections, use a line graph. If you want to show differences between items at the same time, say, voting differences among income levels in the 2004 election, use a bar graph. Our GDP data from page 197 would go on a bar graph, not a line graph:

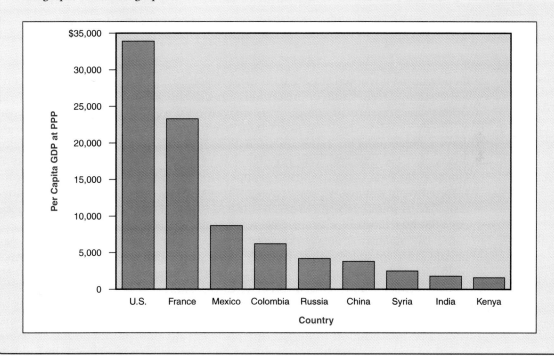

bar graph   Stand-alone data points comparing categories.

CLASSIC WORKS

LASSWELL'S PSYCHOLOGY OF POWER

The mental problems of presidents lead us back to a classic work by Harold Lasswell of Yale, who introduced concepts from Freudian psychology into political science. In his 1936 *Politics: Who Gets What* and other works, Lasswell held that politicians start out mentally unbalanced, that they have unusual needs for power and dominance, which is why they go into politics. Normal people find politics uninteresting. If Lasswell is right, many executives should be removed from office, and only people who don't want the job should be elected. This is the kind of analysis that cannot be applied in practice; it is fascinating but useless.

It was Plato who first wrote that even sane people who become too powerful in high office go crazy. They've got to, for they can trust no one. They imagine, probably accurately, that they have many enemies, and they amass more and more power to crush these real and imaginary foes, thus creating even more enemies. It's an insightful description of Hitler and Stalin. According to Plato, tyrants must go insane in office; there's no such thing as a sane tyrant. The problem is not personal psychology but the nature of a political office that has grown too powerful. The solution, if Plato is right (and we think he is), is to limit power and have mechanisms to remove officeholders who abuse it. In the U.S. system, the threats of electoral defeat and impeachment tend to keep the presidency and its occupants healthy.

Goodwin, who worked closely with Lyndon Johnson (1963–1969) as a presidential assistant, argues that Johnson took on the appearance of clinical **paranoia** under the pressure of Vietnam. In private, Johnson thundered that "those Kennedy people" were "out to get him." Goodwin suspects that Johnson was always a bit paranoid but hid it and used its energizing effect to climb politically. He always got his way and took revenge if he thought someone had crossed him. Once in the Oval Office, Johnson snapped under the strain of Vietnam, a war he feared but did not know how to avoid. Tapes of Nixon's private discussions show a similar paranoia. Nixon reacted to the 1971 leak of the "Pentagon papers" (see page 68) by telling his assistant, "We're up against an enemy, a conspiracy. They're using any means. *We are going to use any means.* Is that clear?" The Pentagon papers led to a "plumbers unit" (to stop leaks), which led to the Watergate break-in, which led to the destruction of the Nixon administration. Paranoids keep making things worse for themselves.

But how can you tell if such behavior is an illness, the temporary effects of difficult decisions, or just the president's normal (if overbearing) personality? Who should be in a position to declare the president psychologically disabled? There was then and is now nothing to be done about a president who gets a "little funny"; you just have to wait until the term is up.

---

paranoia   Unreasonable suspicion of others.

■ CABINETS

Chief executives are assisted by cabinets. A cabinet member heads one of the major executive divisions of government called a *department* in the United States and a **ministry** in most of the rest of the world. The former is headed by a *secretary* and the latter by a *minister.* Cabinets range in size from a compact fifteen in the United States to twenty or more in Europe.

The United States enlarges its cabinet only slowly and with much discussion, for it takes an act of Congress and the provision for its own budget. For most of its history, the United States had fewer than ten departments. Health and Human Services, Housing and Urban Development, Transportation, Energy, Education, Veterans Affairs, and Homeland Security were added only since the 1960s. In Western Europe, chief executives add, delete, combine, and rename ministries at will; their parliaments routinely regard this as an executive right. In the 1980s, for example, most West European governments added environmental ministries. The U.S. Environmental Protection Agency stayed at the sub-cabinet level, and environmental responsibilities were divided between it and several departments.

What is the right size for a cabinet? It depends on how the system is set up and on what citizens expect of it. The United States has been dedicated to keeping government small and letting the marketplace make decisions. When this led to imbalances—for example, bankrupt farmers, unemployed workers, and business collapses—the U.S. system added the Departments of Agriculture, Labor, and Commerce. The Department of Energy was added after the "energy shocks" of the 1970s. Slowly, U.S. cabinets have been creeping up to European size.

WHO SERVES IN A CABINET?

In parliamentary systems like Britain and Germany, ministers are drawn from parliament and keep their parliamentary seats. They are both legislators and executives. Usually they have had years of political experience in winning elections and serving on parliamentary committees. The chair of Germany's Bundestag defense committee, for example, is a good choice to become defense minister. In a presidential system like the United States or Brazil, secretaries or ministers are generally not working politicians but businesspersons, lawyers, and academics. They may have some background in their department's subject area, but few have won elective office. President Bush Sr. named four members of Congress to his cabinet, Clinton named three. This made U.S. cabinets look a bit European, but the secretaries had to first resign their seats in Congress.

Which is better, a cabinet member who is a working politician or one from outside government? The elected members of European parliaments who become ministers have a great deal of both political and subject-area knowledge. They

---

ministry   Major division of executive branch; equivalent to U.S. *department.*

know the relevant members of parliament personally and have worked closely with them. Ministers and parliament do not view each other with suspicion, as enemies. The ministers are criticized in parliament, but from the opposition benches; their own party generally supports them.

Outsiders appointed to the cabinet, the traditional U.S. style, may bring with them fresh perspectives, but they may also be politically naive, given to brash statements and unrealistic programs that get them in trouble with Congress, where members of their own party do not necessarily support them. Their lack of political experience in the nation's capital leads to another problem.

In the United States especially, the cabinet counts for less and less. A cabinet meeting serves little purpose and takes place rarely. Few Americans can name three or more cabinet members. Why has the cabinet fallen into neglect? Part of the problem is that few cabinet secretaries are well-known political figures. And their jobs are rather routine: Get more money from Congress to spend on their department's programs. Cabinet secretaries are in charge of administering established programs with established budgets, "vice-presidents in charge of spending," as Coolidge's vice-president Charles G. Dawes called them. As such, they are not apt to be consulted on much. They are largely administrators, not generators of ideas.

THE RISE OF NONCABINET ADVISERS

A basic problem of government in modern times is that it moves fast and combines several subject areas. The president typically wants people close at hand who can produce new ideas and a quick estimate of what's happening. Thus Washington, and to a growing extent other capitals, have seen the rise of noncabinet advisers who are often more important than cabinet secretaries. These people make up the Executive Office of the President (EOP), and few of them have to be confirmed by Congress or answer to Congress, unlike secretaries. Most answer only to the president and are located either in the White House; the adjacent, ornate Executive Office Building; or the New Executive Office Building across Pennsylvania Avenue from the White House. The EOP keeps getting bigger.

In recent years, for example, great attention has focused on the "White House chief of staff," an office mentioned nowhere in the Constitution or in statutes. The chief of staff, however, is the president's gatekeeper, possibly the president's brains. No one, not even a cabinet secretary, gets in to see the president without approval by the chief of staff, and most of the president's activities and agenda are determined by this person. Information flows to the president as the chief of staff deems necessary. Invariably, the White House chief of staff is a long-term and close associate of the president who knows—or thinks he knows—exactly what the president wishes.

In foreign affairs, a "national security adviser" holds sway. In 1947 Congress provided for a National Security Council (NSC), consisting of the president, the secretaries of state and defense, and a few others. They were to meet to coordinate foreign policies. There was no mention of a staff for the NSC, but over the years a large and powerful staff grew, supervised by a national security adviser. The NSC staff gets all the relevant State, Defense, and CIA cables and reports and structures them into policy alternatives for the president. In some cases, the national security adviser, who is in the White House and can preserve secrecy better, has become more important than the secretary of state or defense, the case with Henry Kissinger in the Nixon White House. Bush 43 named a brilliant political scientist, Condoleeza Rice—who also happened to be black and a woman—to the position (and in 2005 to secretary of state). In 2004 she testified in public before the 9/11 commission, but only because President Bush ordered her to; otherwise she could not be called upon.

There are other White House offices that wield more power than departments. The Office of Management and Budget (OMB) commands compliance from all departments because it decides whose budgets will be cut and whose will grow. This office often knows as much about specific programs as the departments who run them and is better able to initiate new policies because it can see the whole picture of government activity. Those who control the budget control policy. (This is also the case with the British Treasury Ministry, but it is a full-fledged ministry.) The chair of the president's National Economic Council, founded by President Clinton, is the architect of economic policy, more so than the secretaries of treasury, commerce, or labor. Most presidents have political advisors to help them raise funds and win elections. Karl Rove reputedly advised Bush 43 on just about everything, including his speaking engagements and how to handle terrorism and Iraq, but no one could say for sure, as Rove could not be called to testify.

There is no plot here. There is a gradual drift of power away from official departments and into the hands of the chief executive's personal staff. It is a tendency in many governments. British Prime Minister Blair was criticized for ignoring his cabinet. The culprit is the complexity of modern government and the speed with which decisions have to be made. Chief executives must have advisors and assistants close at hand, and they become powerful, secretive, and unaccountable to parliaments.

■ THE DANGER OF EXPECTING TOO MUCH

In both presidential and parliamentary systems, attention focuses on the chief executive. Presidents or prime ministers are expected to deliver economic growth with low unemployment and low inflation. They are expected to keep taxes low but government benefits high. They are held responsible for anything that goes wrong but told to adopt a hands-off management approach and delegate matters to subordinates. The more problems and pressure, the more they have to delegate.

How can they do it all? How can they run the government, economy, subordinates, and policies? They cannot, and increasingly they do not. Instead, the clever ones project a mood of calm, progress, and good feeling, and this makes most citizens happy. President Reagan was a master of this tactic. The precise details of governance matter little; they are in the hands of advisers and career civil servants, and few citizens care about them. What matters is getting reelected, and for this personality counts for more than policy, symbols more than performance.

Worldwide, power has been flowing to the executive, and legislatures have been in decline. The U.S. Congress has put up some good rear-guard actions, but it, too, has been in a slow retreat. Some observers have argued that this cannot be helped, that several factors make this shift of power inevitable. If true, what can we do to safeguard democracy? Democracies still have a trump card, and some say it is enough: electoral punishment. As long as the chief executive, whether president or prime minister, has to face the electorate at periodic intervals, democracy will be preserved. The "rule of anticipated reactions," of which we spoke in Chapter 5, will keep them on their toes. Perhaps the concept of checks and balances was a great idea of the eighteenth century that does not fit the twenty-first. Maybe we will just have to learn to live with executive dominance.

KEY TERMS

bar graph (p. 287)
chancellor (p. 276)
deadlock (p. 275)
dissolve (p. 278)
impeachment (p. 279)
KGB (p. 278)
Knesset (p. 277)
line graph (p. 286)
minister (p. 275)

ministry (p. 289)
paranoia (p. 288)
premier (p. 276)
state (p. 274)
Tory (p. 278)
Versailles (p. 283)
X axis (p. 286)
Yalta (p. 285)
Y axis (p. 286)

KEY WEB SITES

World leaders
www.odci.gov/cia/publications/chiefs

U.S. presidents
www.ipl.org/ref/POTUS/

White House
www.whitehouse.gov/

U.S. cabinet
www.whitehouse.gov/government/cabinet-link.html

British government
www.open.gov.uk/

Canada's prime minister
pm.gc.ca/

Germany's chancellor
www.bundeskanzler.de/

FURTHER REFERENCE

Blondel, Jean, and Ferdinand Müller-Rommel, eds. *Cabinets in Western Europe,* 2nd ed. New York: St. Martin's, 1997.

Burke, John P. *The Institutional Presidency: Organizing and Managing the White House from FDR to Clinton,* 2nd ed. Baltimore, MD: Johns Hopkins University Press, 2000.

Elgie, Robert, ed. *Semi-Presidentialism in Europe.* New York: Oxford University Press, 1999.

Gilbert, Robert E. *The Mortal Presidency: Illness and Anguish in the White House.* New York: Fordham University Press, 1998.

Greenstein, Fred. *The Presidential Difference: Leadership Style from Roosevelt to Clinton.* New York: Free Press, 2000.

Jones, Charles O. *Passages to the Presidency: From Campaigning to Governing.* Washington, D.C.: Brookings, 1998.

Klein, Joe. *The Natural: The Misunderstood Presidency of Bill Clinton.* New York: Doubleday, 2002.

Kowert, Paul A. *Groupthink or Deadlock: When Do Leaders Learn from Their Advisors?* Albany, NY: SUNY Press, 2002.

Nelson, Michael, ed. *The Evolving Presidency.* Washington, D.C.: CQ Press, 1999.

Neustadt, Richard E. *Presidential Power and the Modern Presidents: The Politics of Leadership from Roosevelt to Reagan.* New York: Free Press, 1991.

Pika, Joseph A., and John Anthony Matese. *The Politics of the Presidency,* 6th ed. Washington, D.C.: CQ Press, 2004.

Posner, Richard A. *An Affair of State: The Investigation, Impeachment, and Trial of President Clinton.* Cambridge, MA: Harvard University Press, 1999.

Shapiro, Robert Y., Martha Joynt Kumar, and Lawrence R. Jacobs, eds. *Presidential Power: Forging the Presidency for the Twenty-First Century.* New York: Columbia University Press, 2000.

ADMINISTRATION AND BUREAUCRACY

QUESTIONS TO CONSIDER

- Must every large organization be bureaucratic?
- At which level—federal, state, or local—do most American civil servants work?
- How do agencies get "captured" or "colonized"?
- Must communist countries be heavily bureaucratic?
- Describe the higher ranks of the French bureaucracy.
- How did Max Weber characterize bureaucracy?
- Why is it hard for a government to control bureaucrats?
- What was Djilas's theory of the "new class"?
- How did smoking get on the U.S. political agenda?

The term **bureaucracy** has negative connotations: the inefficiency and delays citizens face in dealing with government. Actually, the great German sociologist Max Weber, who coined the term, disliked bureaucracy but saw no way to avoid it. Basically, a bureaucracy is any large organization of appointed officials who implement laws and policies. Ideally, it operates under rules and procedures with a chain of command (or **hierarchy** of authority) and applies policy to particular situations. It lets government operate with some rationality, uniformity, predictability, and supervision. No bureaucracy, no government.

Another definition of bureaucracy—a nicer name is "civil service"—is that it is the *permanent* government. Much of what we have studied might be called the

---

bureaucracy   The *career* civil service that staffs government executive agencies.
hierarchy   Arrayed as on a ladder of command.

"temporary government" of elected officials who come and go. The **career** civil servants stay, often making a career with one government agency. They may take orders from the elected officials, but they also must follow the law and do things "by the book." They usually know a lot more about their specialized areas than the new political appointee who has been placed above them. There is often friction between elected officials and career bureaucrats. The former sometimes want to redo the system with bold, new ideas; the bureaucrats, who have seen bold, new ideas come and go, move with caution. A bureaucracy, once set up, is inherently conservative, and trying to move it is one of the hardest tasks of politicians.

Almost any large organization will have a bureaucracy. In the Middle Ages, when Europe was composed of loose confederations of feudal powers, the Roman Catholic Church had a complex and effective administrative system. Through a hierarchy of trained people who spent their life in the Church, authority flowed from the pope down to parish priest. Until they developed their own administrators in the Renaissance, kings depended on clerics, who were among the few who could read and write. Armies also have bureaucratic structures, based on the military chain of command and myriad regulations. Bureaucracy is pervasive in schools, hospitals, and large corporations, such as Exxon and General Motors. In the modern world, you cannot escape bureaucracy.

■ THE U.S. FEDERAL BUREAUCRACY

Fewer than 15 percent of the civil servants in the United States are federal. Of our 21.5 million civil servants, some 15 million are employed by local governments, 4 million by state governments, and fewer than 3 million (not counting military personnel) by the federal government. Remember, most government services—schools, police, and fire protection—are provided by local governments.

THE CABINET DEPARTMENTS

In the United States, the fifteen cabinet departments—employing between 85 and 90 percent of all federal civil servants—share a common anatomy, even though they differ in size and scope of operations. Each is funded by Congressional **appropriations** and headed by a secretary who is appointed by the president (with the consent of the Senate) and serves at the president's pleasure. The undersecretaries and assistant secretaries are also political appointees. This differs from most other systems, where officials up through the equivalent of our undersecretaries are permanent civil service.

---

career   Professional civil servant, not political appointee.
appropriation   Government funds voted by legislature.

The departments carry out legislative and executive policies, but this is no simple matter, for the intent of Congress is often unclear. Most laws are couched in general terms that leave the bureaucracy to establish specific working policy. Neither legislators nor executives can supervise everything a bureaucracy does. Departments are subdivided into bureaus headed by career civil servants rather than political appointees. The Bureau of Labor Statistics is part of the Department of Labor, and the Bureau of the Census is part of the Department of Commerce. They do the day-to-day work of the departments, and bureau chiefs have discretionary authority, even though they work under statutes and executive policy. The departments maintain local offices in each state to keep policies uniform.

FEDERAL AGENCIES

Some independent agencies of the federal government, like the departments, are accountable to the president. Each is headed by a single administrator whom the president appoints and can remove. Sometimes created in response to a particular lobby, the agency performs a single, highly complex function that may be more political than administrative. The Environmental Protection Agency (EPA) was set up in response to growing public concern over pollution. The National Aeronautics and Space Administration (NASA) was established to put Americans into space ahead of the Soviets.

INDEPENDENT REGULATORY AGENCIES

Some agencies regulate private businesses that affect the public welfare. Congress gives them quasi-judicial and quasi-legislative authority. The Nuclear Regulatory Commission (NRC) can shut down unsafe nuclear power plants. Such decisions are enforceable in court. These agencies are often criticized as overly influenced by the very industries they should be controlling. Many commissioners are appointed from private industries that have given to presidential campaigns. Critics say they are more concerned with preserving vested interests than with protecting the public. The Federal Power Commission, for example, is heavy with representatives of the power industry. In defense of such appointments, commissioners need the technical expertise that comes from years working in those industries. In these ways, many big industries "capture" or "colonize" regulatory agencies.

■ BUREAUCRACIES IN OTHER NATIONS

Believe it or not, U.S. bureaucracy is relatively small and light compared to many other countries. Europe and Latin America, with their strong statist traditions (see page 47), have much more bureaucracy and regulation than the United States.

COMMUNIST COUNTRIES

The Soviet Union was one of the world's most bureaucratic nations, and that was one of the causes of its collapse. Tied to the Communist party, the Soviet civil service was corrupt, inefficient, and unreformable. According to Marxist theory, a dictatorship of the proletariat had no need for Western-style bureaucracy, but immediately after the 1917 revolution the Soviets instituted strict bureaucratic management, and Stalin increased it with his **Five-Year Plans** in the 1930s.

Top Soviet bureaucrats were a privileged elite. They got higher pay, nice apartments, special shops, and country houses. To rise in the hierarchy, one had to be a party member, for the party interlocked with the bureaucracy. Most Soviet bureaucrats were university graduates, who in return for their free education had to work in a state agency for three years. After that, many stayed. Those the party named energetic and effective could be rapidly moved and promoted.

At the top of each ministry was a minister, who was a member of the Council of Ministers (roughly equivalent to a Western cabinet), the highest executive authority. It was made up of high-ranking party members, some of whom were also members of the Politburo. Trusted party members were placed strategically in subordinate positions to carry out party policy. This made the Soviet bureaucracy extremely conservative, an obstacle no Soviet president could overcome. Still guarding their perks, Russian bureaucrats undermine reforms.

FRANCE

In the seventeenth and eighteenth centuries, France dominated Europe, and most European countries patterned their bureaucracies on the French model. Most of Europe has code or Roman law (see next chapter) and centralized rule. After the French Revolution destroyed the monarchy, Napoleon restored central control of the bureaucracy and, by making it more rational and effective, increased its power. Napoleon, with the *intendants* of Richelieu as his model, created the *prefects* to carry out government policy at the local level.

Top French civil servants are graduates of one of the "Great Schools," such as the Ecole Polytechnique, an engineering school, or, since World War II, the Ecole Nationale d'Administration, created to train government officials. The instability of the Third (1871–1940) and Fourth (1947–1958) Republics increased the bureaucracy's power because it had to run France with little legislative or executive guidance. In many cases, *directeurs* (roughly equivalent to American bureau chiefs), had to operate independently. The Fifth Republic brought greater stability and stronger ministerial control, but France is still heavily bureaucratic.

Decentralization has only recently come to France; Paris viewed local levels of government as administrative conveniences and still centrally controls the country's bureaucratic network. From the American viewpoint, centralization is often extreme. Local conditions, problems, or initiatives were secondary considerations

---

Five-Year Plans   Stalin's plans for rapid, centrally administered Soviet industrial growth.

CASE STUDIES

JAPAN: BUREAUCRATS IN COMMAND

Critics of Japan charge that it is run by bureaucrats, not democrats. Increasingly, even Japanese accept this view. Modeled on the French civil service by the Meiji modernizers in the 1870s, Tokyo's ministries were powerful and Japanese were taught to obey them. Before, during, and after World War II, essentially the same bureaucrats were in charge, imbued with the mission of boosting economic growth by guided capitalism rather than the free market. Japan's bureaucrats view elected officials as clowns who should be ignored.

The key Tokyo ministries are finance, international trade and industry, agriculture, and construction. They guide their respective economic sectors by arranging loans and subsidies, wining and dining, and (for construction) government contracts. Top Japanese bureaucrats are often graduates of Tokyo University (nicknamed "Todai"), Japan's most selective. Many civil servants retire young to go into lush jobs in the industries they supervised.

Tokyo's ministries are self-contained and do not cooperate with each other or seek the good of the whole, provoking some to say that in Japan "no one is in charge." The ministry supervises its economic sector, which mostly obeys the ministry. The minister is a political appointee, usually a member of the Diet, but the **vice minister**, who really runs things, is a career civil servant, much like a British "permanent secretary" (see page 299).

The most famous ministry is **MITI** (renamed METI, ministry of economy, trade and industry), the brains of Japan's export mania, which encouraged designated businesses (such as cameras) to grow until they owned the world market. Some think that MITI helped Japan set economic growth records after World War II and suggested Japanese guided capitalism as a model for others. In the 1990s, however, the Japanese economy stayed flat, and bureaucratic supervision was blamed for industrial overexpansion, money-losing investments, bankrupt banks, and the world's highest consumer prices. A new generation of Japanese politicians is now trying to reform their bureaucracies and bring them under democratic control.

in bureaucratic decisions. The Socialists, who won the 1981 elections, however, began the decentralization of France. A 1982 law reduced the powers of the prefects, and elected councils in the ninety-six *départements* and twenty-two regions got policy and taxation powers in education and economic development. Decentralization reversed five centuries of centralized French administration.

GERMANY

Prussia and its ruling class, the **Junkers**, put their stamp on German administration. Obedient, efficient, and hard-working, the aristocratic Junkers were a state nobility, dependent on Berlin, and controlling all its higher civil service positions.

---

vice minister   Top bureaucrat in a Japanese ministry.

MITI   Japan's Ministry of International Trade and Industry.

Junker   (Pronounced: YOON-care) Prussian state nobility.

Frederick the Great of Prussia, who ruled from 1740 to 1786, had a passion for effective administration and established universities to train administrators. When Germany united in 1871 under Prussia's leadership, Prussian administrative styles permeated the new nation. Democracy was suspect among German administrators; loyalty to nation and emperor was all that counted. One of the reasons the short-lived Weimar Republic (1919–1933) failed was because the civil-servant class had only contempt for democracy. With the Third Reich, they eagerly flocked to Hitler.

The current German government has a strongly federal structure that puts most administration at the *Land* level and leaves relatively little for Berlin, which handles foreign affairs, collecting taxes, defense, and other programs that are inherently national in scope. Today's German civil servants are committed to democracy. A section of Berlin's interior ministry, for example, in cooperation with *Land* agencies, does educational programs to fight political extremism. Generally trained in law—throughout Europe law is at the undergraduate level—German bureaucrats tend to bring with them the mentality of Roman law, that is, law neatly organized into fixed codes rather than the more flexible U.S. and British common law (see next chapter).

GREAT BRITAIN

Britain, unlike France, has strong traditions of local self-government and dispersion of authority. This pattern of administration is an outgrowth of the Anglo-American emphasis on representative government, which encourages legislative control of administrative authorities. During the nineteenth century, the growth of British government at the local level also encouraged the dispersion of administrative authority; it was not until the twentieth century that the central government began to participate in local affairs.

Great Britain was rather late in developing a modern bureaucracy. Until the Northcote-Trevelyan Report calling for major reform was issued in 1854, the bureaucracy was rife with corruption and nepotism. Positions in the bureaucracy (for instance, military commissions) were openly bought and sold. By 1870, however, a **merit civil service** based on competitive examinations had been established.

British ministers are accountable to Parliament for the conduct of their departments and, along with their cabinet colleagues, make departmental policy. However, real bureaucratic power is in the hands of the career "permanent secretary" and the career deputy secretaries, undersecretaries, and assistant secretaries who serve at lower ranks. Thus, even though the British and American bureaucracies share the same tradition of decentralized authority, control over the bureaucracy is tighter in Britain than in America. British bureaucrats pride themselves on being **apolitical**, so they faithfully carry out the ministry's policies whatever government is in power.

---

merit civil service   One based on competitive exams rather than patronage.
apolitical   Not interested or participating in politics.

WEBER'S CHARACTERISTICS OF BUREAUCRACIES

Weber's analysis was based on the German bureaucratic model, but his principles can be applied worldwide. Weber's criteria for defining bureaucracy were the following:

1. Administrative offices are organized hierarchically.
2. Each office has its own area of competence.
3. Civil servants are appointed, not elected, on the basis of technical qualifications as determined by diplomas or examinations.
4. Civil servants receive fixed salaries according to rank.
5. The job is a career and the sole employment of the civil servant.
6. The official does not own his or her office.
7. The official is subject to control and discipline.
8. Promotion is based on superiors' judgment.

Weber felt he was studying a relatively new phenomenon. Some of the above characteristics could be found in classic China, but not all. Like the nation-state, bureaucracies started in Western Europe around the sixteenth century but were reaching their full powers—which Weber distrusted—only in the twentieth century.

■ CHARACTERISTICS OF BUREAUCRACIES

Max Weber (1864–1920) was the first scholar to analyze bureaucracy. His classic study (see box above) provides the starting point for a current examination of bureaucracy.

At the start of the twentieth century, Woodrow Wilson and Frank J. Goodnow studied the American administrative system, which, they noted, must work within the framework of a democratic society. But how can professional civil servants, who are not directly accountable to the electorate, fit the goals of democracy? Wilson and Goodnow argued that they could combine democracy and professional efficiency by separating the political (policy making) from the administrative (enforcement). Elected political officials must always control the administrative officials. Administrators never initiate policy; they merely follow the laws and policies laid down by the political leaders.

Political scientists today feel that these distinctions do not match reality. Administrative officials, often given only broad policy guidelines by Congress and the president, make policy decisions all the time. Many of these decisions are made on the basis of the administrators' expertise in their fields, which because of our highly specialized government, political leaders do not always have. Bureaucrats make a lot of policy.

The overlapping of administrative and political functions flow from the demands of modern government and not from a bureaucratic power grab. The United States in the twenty-first century can no longer look to Weber or Wilson and Goodnow for an analysis of modern bureaucracy. Weber's bureaucracy served a highly stratified, authoritarian society—one in which the average citizen did not "talk back" to bureaucrats. America today is a far different place, and private citizens and legislators do not hesitate to criticize bureaucrats or demand that they explain their actions. Some investigations, however, can be carried to extremes, as the excesses of Senator Joseph McCarthy in the 1950s illustrate. McCarthy's witch hunt against alleged Communists in government eliminated, among others, an entire generation of experts on China. Bureaucrats in sensitive political posts try to keep themselves attuned to prevailing public and congressional opinion. They cannot function solely on the basis of precedent and paper rules and procedures.

Further, anyone who has dealt with a bureaucracy knows that it is not as impersonal, predictable, and precise as the Weberian ideal. Bureaucrats are psychological beings and seldom act in the sterile manner implied by Weber. In a bureaucracy, as in other organizations, friendship, improvisation, informality, and entrepreneurship are common. In a word, bureaucracies are political.

Additionally, some political scientists have noted the tendency for government agencies to become interest groups themselves. Far from being neutral and passive administrators, bureaucrats are active participants in the formation of laws and policies. Elected and appointed executives are often entirely dependent on the data and ideas that career civil servants provide. Civil servants frequently lobby legislators to get the programs and funds they want. The danger here is government of the bureaucrats, by the bureaucrats, and for the bureaucrats. It is startling to realize that no government, East or West, democratic or dictatorial, civilian or military, has managed fully to control its bureaucracy.

■ Bureaucracy in Modern Governments

Modern bureaucracies administer, service, regulate, license, and gather information, in varying combinations.

ADMINISTRATION

Most bureaus execute and enforce the laws enacted by the legislature, steered somewhat by the policies of the current executive. The United States, for example, channels federal funds to the states to pay for various welfare programs. The Department of Health and Human Services administers this policy by deciding how much federal money each state is entitled to and seeing to it that the money is used for its intended purpose. Britain provides free medical care to citizens; its National Health Service administers this policy by overseeing medical training, assigning patients to doctors, and running the hospitals.

How to . . .

Scattergram

To make clear that your numbers form a pattern, you can move beyond a cross-tab (Chapter 11) and build a **scattergram** or scatterplot, which turns items into dots on a graph and makes your argument clearer. If you have found something worthwhile, these dots will form a pattern—never perfect—showing more clearly than a cross-tab a relationship between two variables. If, on the other hand, the dots scatter randomly over the graph, you demonstrate that there is no pattern or relationship.

Country	Per Capita GDP at PPP	Transparency International 2004 CPI
Finland	$27,400	9.7
Britain	27,700	8.6
Canada	29,800	8.5
Germany	27,600	8.2
United States	37,800	7.5
Chile	9,900	7.4
France	27,600	7.1
Japan	28,200	6.9
Uruguay	12,800	6.2
Malaysia	9,000	5.0
Italy	26,700	4.8
South Africa	10,700	4.6
Greece	20,000	4.3
Czech Republic	15,700	4.2
Brazil	7,600	3.9
Colombia	6,300	3.8
Mexico	9,000	3.6
Peru	5,100	3.5
China	5,000	3.4
Iran	7,000	2.9
Russia	8,900	2.8
India	2,900	2.8
Kenya	1,000	2.1
Nigeria	900	1.6
Haiti	1,600	1.5

Sources: www.cia.gov/cia/publications/factbook/indexgeo.html and www.transparency.de/documents/cpi/index.html

scattergram   Graph showing position of items on two axes.

Let's take country per capita GDP plus the Corruption Perception Index (CPI) from Transparency International, a Berlin research group. The CPI is a compilation of surveys, mainly of international business people, asking how much corruption they encounter. It is subjective and imperfect, but objective measures of corruption are impossible, as few officials admit to taking bribes. TI ranks countries from 10 (squeaky clean) to 1 (totally corrupt). The table (on page 302) shows a cross-tab, ranking CPI from highest to lowest. Then we look up each countries' economic level.

We see from the cross-tab that richer countries are generally less corrupt, but with many discrepancies. Graphing them tells us more. If we display the per caps on the X (horizontal) axis and the CPIs on the Y (vertical) axis, it looks like the graph below.

The graph emphasizes that while richer countries are mostly less corrupt, several countries do not fit the pattern. Countries with nearly the same per cap differ greatly in their degree of perceived corruption. Poor countries, with wide variation, tend to be the most corrupt; they cluster in the lower left of the graph. But some medium-income countries show the same (fairly bad) CPI.

A "line of best fit" (which a computer package such as SPSS and Excel can calculate) runs about from Haiti to Finland. Most dots are not too far from it, demonstrating that, very generally, the wealthier a country, the less corrupt it tends to be. However, there are some **outliers**, countries far from the line. Chile, with a third the per cap of rich countries, is unusually clean. Italy, Japan, and France—where scandals are frequent and standard—are more corrupt than their wealth suggests they ought to be. And the biggest outlier of all, the richest country but not the cleanest, is the United States. To explain the outliers, you would study their histories, institutions, and political cultures. For example, how does the extreme localness of U.S. government—as in the powers of counties and school boards—contribute to corruption in America? (Lots.) The outliers frequently tell the most interesting stories.

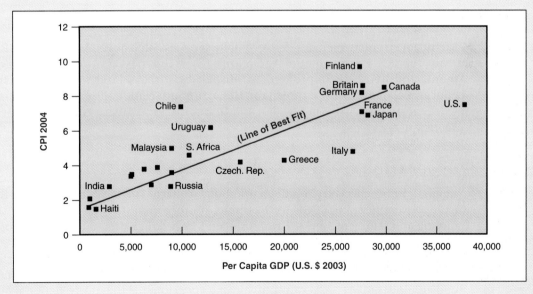

outlier Item that deviates from its expected position.

Administration is the implementation of public policy, and because it involves policy decisions, it also entails rule making. In conjunction with their administrative duties, departments often initiate campaigns to publicize their work and to educate the public about a program's benefits and purposes. Some agencies do educational programs covering everything from democracy and the environment to the ills of tobacco.

Patterns of administration vary from country to country. In China, for example, the party watches over the bureaucratic network. Virtually all Chinese officials are party members, and all offices have party people in them. What the party calls its control function keeps Chinese bureaucrats on their toes. If their unit runs poorly or if they are egregiously crooked (and many are), they can be fired, demoted, or transferred to a remote area. This tends to make them extremely cautious and to go by the book. China's bureaucracy is huge, partly because it also runs state industries. If China goes all the way to a market economy, the number of Chinese administrators may shrink. Party control is probably indispensable for the present system. Note that the West does not have a comparable party mechanism for supervising and checking its bureaucracies.

Administrators oversee the day-to-day operations of their departments, and higher civil servants draft legislation and prep their ministers to field questions from parliament. Many countries have nationalized industries—steel, oil, railroads, telecoms—run by government-controlled corporations, whose civil-servant chiefs make business-type decisions. These industries are endless sources of corruption.

SERVICES

Many government agencies deliver public services, such as the U.S. Weather Bureau. The U.S. Department of Agriculture researches pest control, land management, and livestock improvement; dispenses surplus food to the poor; and educates about nutrition. In Britain, the mammoth National Health Service provides most health care. In Sweden and Germany, government runs employment agencies.

REGULATION

Regulatory functions try to safeguard public welfare. The U.S. Securities and Exchange Commission (SEC), for example, protects investors by supervising the buying and selling of stocks. Britain since 1819 has regulated factory conditions. The U.S. Department of Labor oversees union elections and can throw out crooked union bosses. In Germany, the Bundesrat (the upper house of parliament), supervises enforcement of federal law by the *Land* governments, and federal administrative courts can compel *Land* governments to enforce national law. In some countries, regulation is backed by potential use of force. U.S. agencies can issue "cease and desist" orders with force of law. Although offenders may challenge these orders in court, most comply.

KEY CONCEPTS

BUREAUCRATIC POLITICS

Some political scientists argue that struggles—often behind the scenes—among and within bureaucracies contribute to or even control policy decisions. Bureaucrats provide information, which top officials depend on in deciding policy. He who controls information controls policy, goes the theory. America's balkanized bureaucracies gather, analyze, and disseminate information in different ways, often quarreling among themselves.

Harvard's Graham Allison found that the 1962 Cuban missile crisis turned on when the photographic evidence arrived at the White House. It had been delayed because the Air Force and Central Intelligence Agency quarreled over who should pilot the U2 spy plane. Competition among agencies and "standard procedures" created the informational world in which Kennedy and his advisors operated. With this noted 1969 article, Allison founded the **bureaucratic politics** model, which political science briefly embraced.

Control of information became a hot issue with 9/11 and the 2003 U.S. invasion of Iraq. Before 9/11, the FBI and CIA did not share information, partly due to legal restrictions. It was not clear that the new Department of Homeland Security will solve the problem, as the FBI and CIA were not part of it. Department of Defense (DoD) analysts claimed to have solid evidence that Iraq had weapons of mass destruction (WMD) and was sponsoring terrorism. State and CIA analysts were cautious, saying evidence was unclear. DoD prevailed, making war a certainty. No WMD were found after the war. Furthermore, State, claiming that it had the expertise, drew up elaborate plans for the occupation of Iraq after the war. DoD ignored State and its plans. The result was a chaotic occupation and great anger in the State Department.

The bureaucratic politics model is still not persuasive because the president really is in charge. He often has strong personal preferences in advance and decides which agency to listen to. In 2003 President Bush had long hated Iraq, and DoD told him that Iraq was guilty. DoD even had a special staff to make the case for an attack on Iraq; it excluded evidence to the contrary. By structuring bureaucracies, the White House created the informational world it preferred. Washington bureaucracies played a blame game for 9/11 and Iraq's WMD—several of the CIA's top people resigned—but it was more a question of how these agencies were used. Bureaucrats mostly obey.

LICENSING

Licensing is part of regulation, enabling governments to impose minimum standards. If you want to drive a car, practice medicine or law, teach school, or work as a barber, you must meet certain government standards. In the United States, these standards are set by the states. In unitary countries such as France or Britain, the national government sets standards and administers tests. The European Union is increasingly taking on and standardizing such criteria.

---

bureaucratic politics   Infighting among and within agencies to set policy.

DJILAS'S "NEW CLASS"

Milovan Djilas (pronounced *jee-lass*) was until 1954 a dedicated Communist and right-hand man to Yugoslav Communist chief Tito. After World War II when the Yugoslav Communists took over the country, however, Djilas noticed that it was not becoming their envisioned happy society of equals. The Communists had eliminated capitalists as a class, he wrote, but they created a "new class" of bureaucrats, party officials, secret police, and army officers, who quickly became rich, powerful, and corrupt.

Socialism brought no improvement over capitalism, Djilas concluded; both were ruled by a social class out for its own interests. Bureaucrats had replaced capitalists. Worse, communism brought tyranny over the mind and economic stupidity. For his candor, Djilas spent ten years in Yugoslav prisons. Djilas's 1957 book *The New Class* became a classic analysis of why Communist parties do not lead societies into communism. Once the New Class is in power, it preserves its position and becomes conservative. Communism is bureaucracy to an extreme degree, and that is why it fails.

INFORMATION GATHERING

Administration needs information to catch law violations and make policy decisions. For example, the U.S. Civil Rights Division of the Justice Department investigates citizen complaints of civil-rights violations. The Environmental Protection Agency must gather data on air and water pollution to catch excesses and devise new policies. The French government made an extensive study of the nation's energy needs and concluded that France needed nuclear energy. France gets three-fourths of its electricity from nuclear plants, run by the nationalized Electricité de France.

■ THE TROUBLE WITH BUREAUCRACY

The world does not love bureaucracy. The very word is pejorative. In France and Italy, hatred of the official on the other side of the counter is part of the political culture. Americans like to hear candidates denounce the bureaucracy. Even American civil servants complain about "those damn bureaucrats." The paradox of the modern state is that bureaucratic administration is a necessity but is also often an impediment to the fulfillment of national goals.

Incoming U.S. administrations, particularly Republican, usually vow to bring business-type efficiency to public administration. They rarely make a dent in the problem and sometimes make things worse. "Efficiency" is hard to apply in public affairs. Businesses can calculate profits and productivity; bureaus don't make any profits and **productivity** is hard to measure. Government offices are sometimes overstaffed, but it is hard to tell which workers are redundant.

---

productivity   The efficiency with which goods or services are produced.

At its worst, bureaucracy can show signs of "Eichmannism," named after the Nazi official who organized the death trains for Europe's Jews and later calmly assured his Israeli judges that he was just doing his job. Nazi bureaucracy treated people like things, a problem not limited to Germany. On the humorous side, bureaucracy can resemble Parkinson's Law: Work expands to fill the staff time available for it. Parkinson never called himself a humorist, and many who have worked in featherbedded, purposeless, paper-shuffling agencies say Parkinson's Law is accurate.

Bureaucracy and **corruption** are intertwined. Wherever officials carry out rules, some are bent for friends and benefactors. The more regulations, the more bureaucrats, the more corruption. A few countries with a strong ethos of public service—Denmark and Singapore, for example—have been able to maintain incorrupt public administration. Most countries are corrupt, some a little and some egregiously (see box on pages 302–303). Chile became the least corrupt Latin American country by cutting the amount of administration and number of bureaucrats. Corruption grows at the interface of public and private sectors. Shrink that interface and you shrink corruption. Perhaps the most serious problem with bureaucracy, alluded to previously, occurs when it becomes interlocked with and sometimes replaces other branches of government.

ADMINISTRATOR OR POLICYMAKER?

Early theorists of bureaucracy (Weber, Wilson, and Goodnow) assumed that professional bureaucrats would never make public policy but merely carry out the will of elected officials. Indeed, nonpartisan administration was the original motivation behind merit civil services. However, as Guy S. Claire warned decades ago, most Western nations have developed "administocracies" (an aristocracy of administrators), whose personnel are not publicly accountable but who nevertheless make policy. Japan (see box on page 298) shows this to an extreme degree. A return to the nineteenth-century spoils system is neither possible nor desirable, but the question of whether a democracy can afford to allow nonelected and non-responsible administrators to make decisions that affect people's lives must be considered. Following are some of the ways.

ADJUDICATION

Many regulatory agencies maintain administrative courts that operate much like regular courts and whose decisions are enforceable in regular courts. Most U.S. states, for example, have separate courts to **adjudicate** workers' compensation cases; in these courts, claimants have legal counsel and offer evidence. Similar FDA tribunals can order a drug off the market, and the SEC can ban trading in a particular stock. Some critics maintain that these tribunals' orders should be made

---

corruption　　Use of public office for private gain.
adjudication　　Settling problems through courts of law.

by the regular courts. If a cosmetic is harmful, should not the courts—and not the FDA—make this decision? Proponents of the administrative courts answer by pointing out that the courts lack expertise on technical matters. Others feel that even though the law empowers agencies to "regulate in the public interest, convenience, or necessity," administrative courts give administrators too much power, and unaccountable power at that.

DISCRETIONARY IMPLEMENTATION

When a statute is specific, enforcement is relatively simple, but this is rarely the case. For example, the U.S. Congress passed a law to clean up toxic dump sites. It enabled EPA to do whatever necessary to achieve this goal. The EPA had to set priorities because every dump cannot be cleaned up at once, and each one has different problems. In deciding such matters, the EPA has **discretionary** power and in effect makes laws. No law can anticipate all circumstances, so administrators must have leeway. Furthermore, administrators can always be overruled by public or legislative pressure or by executive edict.

RULE MAKING

The rule-making authority of regulatory agencies is related to discretionary implementation. For example, higher rates for telephone use must be approved by the Public Service Commission (PSC).

ADVISORY ROLES

The complexity of modern life leads legislators and executives to rely more and more on the technical expertise of bureaucrats. Congress may decide that unsafe mines should be shut down, but only mining experts can determine what makes a mine unsafe. Many laws require administrative interpretation. For example, Congress may outlaw deceptive advertising, but the determination of what *is* deceptive is made by the FTC. Law-makers need the technical assistance of specialists, another way bureaucrats make policy.

Conflicts can arise, however. For example, Kennedy's Secretary of Defense Robert McNamara, a political appointee, was intent on cutting costs but ran into angry opposition from generals, who claimed that they alone knew the technical side of security needs. Similarly, in 1948, President Truman was under intense pressure from State Department experts not to recognize the new state of Israel. Truman ignored them and was heard to remark, "There ain't many Arab voters in this country." Both McNamara and Truman realized that some decisions are inherently political and can be made only by a politically responsible official.

---

discretionary   Ability of officials to decide questions on their own without adjudication or higher authority.

CASE STUDIES

BUREAUCRATS AND SMOKING

One of the best examples of bureaucratic rule-making was the fight to force cigarette manufacturers to place health hazard warnings on cigarette packages and in advertisements. Congress would never have moved by itself because the tobacco industry is generous to candidates. Change came via a branch of the bureaucracy—public-health specialists and statisticians equipped with computers. In 1965 the Advisory Committee on Smoking and Health and the surgeon general (the nation's chief public health officer) presented solid data that heavy cigarette smoking increased lung cancer and shortened lives. The report disturbed the public, and public pressure on Congress increased. Since 1966 cigarette manufacturers have been required to print warnings on all packs.

Meanwhile, the tobacco industry tried unsuccessfully to discredit the surgeon general's report, but organizations such as the American Cancer Society agitated for still firmer antitobacco legislation. In 1967 the FCC, citing the fairness doctrine, ordered all radio and television stations accepting cigarette commercials to make free time available for antismoking commercials.

In 1969 the FCC banned cigarette advertising on radio and television. And in 1971 President Nixon signed an FTC-sponsored bill requiring cigarette companies to print health warnings on all advertising copy. Political scientist A. Lee Fritschler, in his *Smoking and Politics,* reached the following conclusion:

> The initiation and continuation of the cigarette controversy were possible because of both the political power and delegated authority possessed by bureaucratic agencies. Had the decision on cigarettes and health been left to Congress alone, it is safe to assume that the manufacturers would have triumphed, and no health warnings of any kind would have been required. The cigarette-labeling controversy is a clear example of agencies' power to influence and even formulate public policy.

Here was a vivid case of federal agencies openly practicing "rule initiation."

The bureaucracy's role of adviser is a feature of all modern industrial states. In France, laws and presidential decrees are drawn up and promulgated by the bureaucracy (particularly the Council of State), and career executives thus can shape policy. Bureaucrats play a large role in the framing of legislation in Germany. Since top bureaucrats rarely supervise field or branch offices, they can devote their energies to policy matters and often win over the ministers appointed over them.

■ WHAT TO DO WITH BUREAUCRACY?

Bureaucracy has become big, powerful, rigid, unresponsive, intrusive, and corrupt. Some contend it has taken on a life of its own, divorced from the needs of the citizens and governments that gave it birth. Can anything be done about this? As Joseph LaPalombara has observed, most of the ideas offered to cure bureaucracy entail *adding* more bureaucrats. An example came with the 2005 creation of a new chief over all U.S. intelligence agencies, to get them to coordinate and communicate with each other. Here are some suggested remedies for bureaucracies.

OMBUDSMEN

As we discussed briefly in Chapter 14, the ombudsman is Sweden's contribution to the art of governance. Established by the 1809 Swedish constitution, the *Justitieombudsman* (literally, agent of justice) is appointed and paid by the parliament, not the executive. This is important, for no government agency can be its own ombudsman; that must come from outside. An official who says, "Bring all complaints to me. I'm my own ombudsman," doesn't understand the concept. Absolute independence is necessary for an ombudsman to work effectively. The ombudsman is a legislative-branch lawyer who intervenes on behalf of citizens treated wrongly by the bureaucracy. The ombudsman has subpoena power, and a reprimand to errant officials is usually enough to set things right. Denmark, Norway, Britain, and New Zealand have set up similar institutions.

Some have suggested the ombudsman concept for the United States. In a sense, we already have it: members of Congress, whose constituency work is much like that of ombudsmen. Furthermore, the United States is already overrun with lawyers, so no citizen has far to go to find one. Poor people can often obtain free legal assistance. The ombudsman idea works in countries with a tradition of respect for law and a political and moral climate in which a simple reprimand is enough. The American context is not precisely that law-abiding.

LEGISLATIVE CHECKS

The United States has other mechanisms to oversee the bureaucracy. Congress has the Government Accountability Office (GAO), Congressional Research Service (CRS), and Congressional Budget Office (CBO). The GAO looks to see that federal funds are spent correctly and effectively; the CRS gives Congress the expertise needed to check on the executive branch specialists; and the CBO, established in 1974, consolidates Congress's budget-making functions to reply to the White House's powerful Office of Management and Budget. In effect, the United States has set up competing bureaucracies—one executive, the other legislative. This does not save money or reduce the number of bureaucrats; it does keep the executive side tied to the national purpose as represented on Capitol Hill.

CUTTING

Americans dream of some golden yesteryear when there were no bureaucrats on their backs. Politicians often promise to cut the bureaucracy, but they rarely succeed. Cutting bureaucrats means cutting programs, and most citizens soon find their favorite programs getting the ax. They meant to cut other people's wasteful programs, not the necessary and prudent expenditures they benefit from. Once a welfare state has been built, it is terribly difficult to dismantle because so many people have a stake in its bounties.

In the 1980s, the Reagan administration tried a different tack: Keep the programs on the books but fail to fund or staff them adequately. Many federal offices, especially those providing services the president and his supporters disliked, operated with reduced budgets and personnel and were unable to carry out their legislated mandates. At a time of massive federal budget deficits, Congress found it difficult to restore these cuts. In highly public areas such as education and environmental pollution, however, irate citizens and their interest groups demanded attention, and President Reagan had to partially back down. In recent years the "cutting" of federal bureaucracies often means farming out government functions to private contractors and consultants, often leading to worse results and no cost savings. The meat-ax approach to bureaucracy is tempting but hard to carry out in practice.

DECENTRALIZATION

For highly centralized systems, as in France and Italy, decentralization offers some improvement. Decisions can be made closer to home, in consultation with the people they will affect. Decentralization can solve some problems but create others. It brings bureaucratic decision-making closer to the local level, but this can *increase* corruption and inefficiency. Without Paris or Rome looking over their shoulders, who knows what those bureaucrats in the provinces will do? For most of its history, the United States has had a decentralized education system. The result has been a great deal of freedom and local control but also extreme unevenness of quality and blatant racial segregation. Bush's No Child Left Behind Act brought greater centralization. Many Americans wish they could go back to strict local control, but they also want federal dollars. True decentralization means localities have to raise their own taxes, something they dislike doing.

Decentralization may entail widely varying standards and problems of coordination. With Germany's strongly decentralized federal system, it took years to get the different *Länder* to agree on a program and standards to clear up the polluted Rhine River. Each state saw its environmental responsibilities differently and didn't want its authority eroded. Further, decentralization does not mean reducing the number of bureaucrats, just placing them at different levels, *burden shifting*. As such, it may actually seem to put more bureaucrats on the people's backs, not fewer.

POLITICIZE THE BUREAUCRACY

Most governments are proud that they have moved to nonpolitical, neutral, professional civil services. In the United States, we disdain the corrupt "spoils system" of the nineteenth century in which political bosses would place their people in choice jobs. But maybe we've gone too far with the career, neutral, detached bureaucrat. Perhaps it's time to reinject a certain amount of political control into the system. Political appointees bring fresh approaches, innovative plans, and a mandate from the people and elected officials for change. Bureaucrats live by routine and hate to rock the boat; they are not capable of changing their own system. Only outsiders, appointed from other walks of life for a few years, can do that.

The old U.S. urban machines, such as that of the late Mayor Daley in Chicago, were decried for their corruption, but they responded to citizens' needs and often worked better than the reform administrations that followed. A new American president has some 3,000 appointive positions to fill, a very high number compared to other countries. Some say this is too many, that we should use career civil servants to fill some of these slots. But it is this appointive power that gives presidents what little leverage they have over the U.S. bureaucracy. Decrease it and the civil service will be less responsive.

The negative side to political appointments is the corruption that often comes with them. Because the political appointees are often from the very branches of industry their bureaus are supposed to be monitoring, they tend to see things the industry's way, to overlook irregularities, and sometimes to dispense favors to friends and party contributors. Almost all cases of corruption in U.S. federal offices are those of political appointees, not career civil servants. Career civil servants in the Federal Home Loan Bank Board in the 1980s tried early to signal irregularities with Lincoln Savings and Loan in California. Their politically appointed bosses and five senators, recipients of $1.3 million in campaign donations by Lincoln's owner, overrode the civil servants and delayed action against the firm.

The Iran-contra fiasco occurred precisely because the White House insisted on bypassing State and Defense Department bureaucrats, who would have told them that the plan to arm the Nicaraguan contras was an illegal **slush fund**—all federal receipts of money must be turned over immediately to the Treasury Department—and unworkable to boot. Political guidance of bureaucracy, yes; bypassing bureaucracy, no.

■ BUREAUCRACY AND SOCIETY

For all our dislike of bureaucracy, we must remember that it was not visited on us from an alien planet. It was set up, funded, and given its duties by Congress. To be sure, agencies sometimes take on lives of their own, but the initial reasons for them still apply. Is there a lot of red tape to get a driver's license? Imagine if drivers weren't required to be licensed. Do bureaucrats interfere too much with private industry? What would happen if we rolled back our standards on foodstuffs, drugs, and product safety? Do Title IX bureaucrats harm male athletics by paying too much attention to women's sports? No bureaucrat set up these laws; it was Congress. Congress, to be sure, was vague and sloppy, leaving administrators great leeway in drawing up guidelines and then dropping the whole thing on the courts. But the bureaucrats themselves are only the results of what Congress has done.

---

slush fund   Unaccountable money in hands of government officials; illegal under U.S. law.

We live in a complex society. We may try from time to time to make it simpler, to do away with what appear to be burdensome regulations and officious bureaucrats. But when we do, we discover anew that the regulations and civil servants were put there for a purpose. We may—indeed must—attempt to improve our rules and the agencies that implement them, but we are unlikely to eliminate them unless we are prepared to return to a simpler age, a time without terrorism, cars, telecommunications, or employment security. Until then, we are stuck with our unlovely bureaucrats, for in the final analysis, they are us.

KEY TERMS

adjudication (p. 307)
apolitical (p. 299)
appropriation (p. 295)
bureaucracy (p. 294)
bureaucratic politics (p. 305)
career (p. 295)
corruption (p. 307)
discretionary (p. 308)
Five-Year Plans (p. 297)

hierarchy (p. 294)
Junker (p. 298)
merit civil service (p. 299)
MITI (p. 298)
outlier (p. 303)
productivity (p. 306)
scattergram (p. 302)
slush fund (p. 312)
vice-minister (p. 298)

KEY WEB SITES

U.S. departments
www.nttc.edu/resources/government/exec.asp

U.S. non-departmental agencies
www.nttc.edu/resources/government/independents.asp

Securities and Exchange Commission
www.sec.gov/

Tennessee Valley Authority
www.tva.gov/

Internal Revenue Service
www.irs.ustreas.gov/

FURTHER REFERENCE

Adams, Guy B., and Danny L. Balfour. *Unmasking Administrative Evil*. Thousand Oaks, CA: Sage, 1998.
Crozier, Michel. *The Bureaucratic Phenomenon*. Chicago, IL: University of Chicago Press, 1964.

Fry, Brian R. *Mastering Public Administration: From Max Weber to Dwight Waldo.* Chatham, NJ: Chatham House, 1989.

Golden, Marissa Martino. *What Motivates Bureaucrats?: Politics and Administration during the Reagan Years.* New York: Columbia University Press, 2000.

Heady, Ferrel. *Public Administration: A Comparative Perspective,* 6th ed. New York: Marcel Dekker, 2001.

Hodess, Robin, ed. *Global Corruption Report.* Berlin: Transparency International, 2002.

Jreisat, Jamil E. *Comparative Public Administration and Policy.* Boulder, CO: Westview, 2002.

Kerwin, Cornelius M. *Rulemaking: How Government Agencies Write Law and Make Policy.* Washington, D.C.: CQ Press, 1994.

Light, Paul C. *The True Size of Government.* Washington, D.C.: Brookings, 1999.

Lindblom, Charles E. *The Policy-Making Process,* 3rd ed. Englewood Cliffs, NJ: Prentice Hall, 1992.

Selden, Sally Coleman. *The Promise of Representative Bureaucracy: Diversity and Responsiveness in a Government Agency.* Armonk, NY: M.E. Sharpe, 1997.

West, William F. *Controlling the Bureaucracy: Institutional Constraints in Theory and Practice.* Armonk, NY: M.E. Sharpe, 1995.

Wilson, James Q. *Bureaucracy: What Government Agencies Do and Why They Do It.* New York: Basic Books, 1990.

LEGAL SYSTEMS AND THE COURTS

- Why is the U.S. political system so dependent on the courts?
- Contrast natural and positive law.
- What are the differences between common and code law?
- Describe the U.S. court system.
- How are European trials quite different from ours?
- What does Germany have that resembles the U.S. Supreme Court?
- How did an 1803 case give the Supreme Court vast powers?
- In what major cases did the Warren Court make new law?
- Have subsequent courts reversed Warren Court decisions?

The United States prides itself on "rule of law." One indication of this is the number of American lawyers—281 for every 100,000 people, as compared to ninety-four in England, thirty-three in France, and only seven in Japan. Law plays very different roles in these systems. America's legions of lawyers express its ethos of freedom and competitive individualism. In few other countries does the "little person" have our ability to sue the powerful. Many Americans complain that we have too many lawsuits, but few would accept a Japanese system where citizens are expected to simply obey government and corporations. Law without lawyers means law administered by bureaucrats. If you want freedom under **law**, you must have lots of lawyers.

---

law   That which must be obeyed under penalties.

THE ROOTS OF LAW

Higher law is an old concept that grew out of the Christian melding of Greek philosophy with Judeo-Christian thought. Attributed to God or the Creator, it was thus higher than laws made by humans. It is behind the idea that people are "endowed by their Creator" with the rights to life, liberty, and the pursuit of happiness and the right to own property and enjoy the fruits of their labor—rights that no just government can take away. Many argue that higher law takes precedence over laws enacted by humans, and some justify their defiance of ordinary laws by citing it. Mahatma Gandhi in India and Martin Luther King, Jr. in the United States claimed that their actions, which violated human-made laws, were moral because they conformed to higher law.

Natural law, developed by medieval Catholic theologians, argues that some law is basic to human nature and can be understood just by thinking about it. You need no law books to tell you that murder is wrong, for example. Israel's attorney general, in prosecuting Nazi official Adolph Eichmann, argued from natural law that Eichmann had to know that mass murder is wrong.

■ TYPES OF LAW

We focus on **positive law**, that which is written and compiled by humans over the centuries. Unlike natural law, positive law does use law books to discover right and wrong. Our complex society requires many types of law, of which there are five major branches.

CRIMINAL LAW

With some 2 million people in U.S. jails, the criminal law system is the one we hear most about. Modern criminal law is largely statutory law and covers a specific category of wrongs that are considered social evils and threats to the community. Consequently the state, rather than the victim, is the prosecutor **(plaintiff)**. Offenses are usually divided into three categories. *Petty offenses*, such as traffic violations, are normally punished by a fine. Serious but not major offenses such as gambling and prostitution are *misdemeanors* punishable by larger fines or short jail sentences. Major crimes, *felonies* such as rape, murder, robbery, and extortion are punished by imprisonment. In the United States, some criminal offenses such as kidnapping and interstate car theft are federal in nature; others, such as murder and robbery, are mainly state concerns; and a few, such as bank robbery and drug trafficking, violate both state and federal laws.

---

higher law   That which comes from God.

natural law   That which comes from nature, understood by reasoning.

positive law   That which is written by humans and accepted over time, the opposite of natural law.

plaintiff   The person who complains in a law case.

CIVIL LAW

Many statutes govern civil rather than criminal matters. Marriage and divorce, inheritance, contracts, and bankruptcy are civil concerns. In most English-speaking countries, statutory law is supplemented by **common law**. **Civil law** provides redress for private plaintiffs who can show they have been injured. The decisions are usually in dollars, not in jail time. Private individuals, not the state, conduct most civil litigation.

CONSTITUTIONAL LAW

Written constitutions are usually general documents. Subsequent legislation and court interpretation must fill in the details. An important role of U.S. courts, under our system of **judicial review**, is to make sure that statutory laws and administrative usages do not violate the constitution. Judicial review is America's great contribution to governance, and since World War II most democracies added some sort of judicial review.

In the United States the ultimate responsibility of interpreting the Constitution rests with the U.S. Supreme Court, and this means that laws change over time: "The Constitution is what the Supreme Court says it is." In 1896, for example, the Court ruled, in *Plessy v. Ferguson,* that state laws requiring racial segregation in public transportation did not necessarily violate the Fourteenth Amendment, which provides for equal protection under the laws, as long as the transportation facilities for whites and blacks were physically equal. In *Brown v. Board of Education of Topeka* (1954), the court reversed itself and ruled that separate public education facilities for whites and blacks are *inherently* unequal, even if physically alike. The Constitution had not changed, but society's conception of individual rights did. **Constitutional law** (indeed, law itself) is not static but a living, growing institution.

ADMINISTRATIVE LAW

A relatively recent development, administrative law covers regulatory orders by government agencies. It develops when agencies interpret statutes, as they must. For example, federal statute prohibits "unfair or deceptive acts" in commerce. But what business practices are "unfair"? The Federal Trade Commission must decide. As the agencies interpret the meaning of Congress's laws, they begin to build up a body of regulations and case law that guides the commission in its future decisions. These rulings may be appealed to the federal courts. The federal government now codifies administrative regulations, and they fill many volumes.

---

common law "Judge-made law," old decisions built up over the centuries.

civil law Noncriminal disputes among individuals.

judicial review Ability of courts to overturn laws.

constitutional law That which grows out of a country's basic documents.

KEY CONCEPTS

COMMON LAW VERSUS CODE LAW

The English common law started with the customary usages of Germanic tribal law of the Angles and Saxons who took over England from the third to the fifth centuries. This law stressed the rights of free and equal men and developed on the basis of **precedent** set by earlier judges; it is thus called "judge-made law." The Normans who conquered England decided the local, decentralized nature of this law hindered their governance of the country as a whole, so they set up central courts to systematize the local laws and produce a "common" law for all parts of England. They also added new features, such as trial by jury.

In administering justice, English judges and courts were forced to improvise. Most had a church education and were familiar with canon law. Accordingly, when royal law was inadequate, the judges applied canon law. If these were not applicable, they used common sense and the common practices of the English people. Over the centuries, a substantial body of common law developed— an amalgam of Roman law, Church law, and local English customs.

Common law has three distinctive features. First, it is *case* law; that is, it is based on individual legal decisions rather than on a comprehensive code of statutes. Second, common law was made by *judicial decision* and thus has great flexibility. Judges can easily reinterpret or modify previous rulings and principles to fit each case. Third, common law relies heavily on *stare decisis,* or precedent. Because no two cases are exactly alike, a judge can note points of difference to justify breaking precedent. In this way, common law retains a marvelous flexibility. With the rise of Parliament as a dominant institution in seventeenth-century England, statute (see page 55) law supplemented and then supplanted much of the common law. Today, when the two conflict, statute law always takes precedence.

Common law has declined in importance but still has influence in England (but not Scotland), the United States, Canada, Australia, New Zealand, and a number of former British colonies. In many instances, statute law is the formal enactment of old common-law provisions. Common law shaped the development of English society and politics and imparted distinctive political habits to America.

INTERNATIONAL LAW

International law (IL) consists of treaties and established customs recognized by most nations. It is different because it cannot be enforced in the same way as national law: It has no judges, courts, or police. IL, however, is generally observed, because it is in the interests of most countries not to break it. IL's key mechanisms are **reciprocity** and **consistency**. Countries generally like being treated nicely, so they must extend the courtesy to others. They also do not like being accused of applying different standards to various countries, so they try to keep their dealings consistent. Some IL is enforced by national courts. The U.S. Supreme Court has ruled that U.S. states have to observe international treaties. A U.S. business harmed abroad can seek redress in U.S. courts against the assets of the foreign firm that did the damage. We mostly

---

precedent   Legal decisions based on earlier decisions.
reciprocity   Mutual application of legal standards.
consistency   Applying the same standards to all.

The legal systems of continental Europe (France, in particular) developed very differently. As French kings were overturning feudalism in favor of absolutism (see Chapter 3), legal scholars revived Roman law to bolster central government and encourage commerce. French jurists saw the value of Roman law; it was universal, written, worked well for the ancient world, and was already known through canon law.

Codifying the law was Napoleon's lasting contribution to French justice and, eventually, to much of the world. His *Code Napoléon* (1804), the first modern codification of European law, discarded feudal laws and broke civil law away from religious influence. It preserved many of the gains of the French Revolution, such as elimination of torture and arbitrary arrest and imprisonment, civil liberty, and civil equality. Napoleon conquered most of Europe and brought the code with him; Europe's legal systems are still based on it. It is also in use in Louisiana and Asia, Africa, and Latin America. The centralization of French life even to this day is a reflection of its basic philosophy.

Today, much of the world lives under some form of the Code Napoleon. Most **code law** is detailed, precise, comprehensive, and understandable by laypersons. Judges are not expected to "make" law, merely to apply it. Precedent carries less weight. The judiciary is not independent of the executive as in the American system. Therefore, its powers of judicial review are limited—either shared with the legislative branch or assigned to a special constitutional court, which most European countries now have, a relatively new feature.

The differences between the common law and the Roman system are marked. The former is general and largely judge-made, and it relies on precedent and custom. The latter is specific and is largely the product of legislation. Both systems developed to serve the needs of modernizing and centralizing monarchs—Henry I and II in England and Louis XIII and Napoleon in France. The two systems, however, are becoming more and more alike. As the volume of statute law increases in the English-speaking nations, the importance and relevance of common law decreases. In both systems, administrative agencies increasingly fill in the details of legislative enactments, producing regulations that are now part of legal systems.

study international public law, but international private law is a rapidly growing field as more and more businesses operate globally (see Chapter 21).

Primitive legal systems are oral and consist of customs and beliefs. Modern legal systems are written and largely codified, that is, systematically arranged. Putting laws in writing makes them more precise and uniform. Codification began in ancient times and has been a major feature in the development of civilization. The Ten Commandments and the Code of Hammurabi were early law codes, but the great ancient code was **Roman law**. Its details, covering all aspects of social life and based on "right reason," were so universal, flexible, and logical that they are still in use in much of the world today. Roman law was incorporated by the Catholic Church in its **canon law**, and in the East by the Byzantine Emperor Justinian,

---

code law   Laws arranged in books, originally updated Roman law.

Roman law   System based on codes of ancient Rome.

canon law   Laws of the Roman Catholic Church, based on Roman law.

whose celebrated Code of Justinian (*Corpus Juris Civilis*) of A.D. 533, is the foundation of most of Europe's modern legal systems. Modern European law is largely an
amalgamation of Roman, feudal, and church law.

■ THE COURTS, THE BENCH, AND THE BAR

As legal systems developed, so did judicial systems, for they handle day-to-day administration of the law. Judicial systems are always hierarchical with different
courts having specific jurisdictions; that is, they hear different kinds of cases or
have authority in specific geographical areas.

THE U.S. COURT SYSTEM

Our court system is unique, consisting of fifty-one judicial structures: the national system, comprising the federal courts, and fifty state systems. The federal system
overlaps that of the states. The federal courts hear many cases in which the issue
is one of state laws but the parties are residents of different states, the so-called "diversity jurisdiction." Also, of course, they hear cases concerning federal laws. Conversely, issues of federal law (constitutional or statutory) may first arise in state
courts. The Supreme Court of the United States can review the state court's judgment on a federal question.

The National Court Structure   Ninety-four federal district courts are the base
of the national court system. They employ over 500 judges and serve as trial courts
in civil suits arising under federal law, criminal cases involving federal infractions,
and the diversity jurisdiction. Most criminal cases, however, even those involving
federal law, are tried in state courts.

Federal district court decisions can be appealed to a U.S. court of appeals. The
thirteen courts of appeals, presided over by 132 judges, may also review the rulings of administrative tribunals and commissions, such as the Federal Trade Commission, the Federal Aviation Administration, and the Food and Drug
Administration. Each court of appeals consists of three or more judges, depending
on need. Panels of three judges hear arguments but rarely question the facts of
the case; they consider only whether the law has been misinterpreted or misapplied.
The court of appeals bases its majority-vote verdict on the **appeal** primarily on
the **briefs** submitted by the attorneys for both parties; oral arguments are limited.

The pinnacle of the federal court system is the U.S. Supreme Court, consisting
of one chief justice and eight associate justices. Its jurisdiction is almost entirely ap-
pellate, from lower federal or state supreme courts. For example, if a state supreme
court declares a federal statute unconstitutional, it is almost certain that the Court

---

appeal   Taking a case to a higher court.
brief   Written summary submitted by one side giving relevant facts, laws, and precedents.

will hear the case. Unlike a court of appeals, however, it is not obliged to hear every case and accepts only a few of the petitions that it receives. The Court will generally not hear a case unless it involves a substantial constitutional question, a treaty, or some significant point of federal law. Because the U.S. system is based on precedent, the Court's ruling *is* national law.

The State Court System   Each of the fifty states has its own court systems, and they handle perhaps 90 percent of the nation's legal business. Most of their cases are civil, not criminal. Generally, state trial courts operate at the county level and have original jurisdiction in all civil and criminal cases. In rural areas, justices of the peace try minor matters. In urban areas, magistrate's or police courts do the same. These local courts operate without juries (serious cases go to state courts) and most of their penalties are fines or short jail terms.

JUDGES

Federal Judges   Federal judges are nominated by the president and must be approved by the Senate. They hold their positions during "good behavior," which generally means that they serve for life unless impeached. This is to free them from executive and political pressure. Some federal judges owe their appointments to political favors, but most are well qualified. The attorney general lists eligible candidates; as vacancies occur, the president selects a few names from that list. The president often considered the reputation-based ratings of prospective judges by the American Bar Association (ABA) until Bush 43 discontinued the practice, believing the ABA is too liberal. The FBI checks out each candidate. Senate approval used to be routine but is now highly political. The opposition party accuses the president of trying to fill the **bench** with incompetent partisans and often tries to block confirmation. Under Clinton, many federal judgeships went unfilled because Senate Republicans rejected nominees as too liberal. In reaction, Senate Democrats tried to block Bush's choices as too conservative.

Some presidents wanted a federal judiciary that was nonpartisan, or at least bipartisan. Eisenhower, for example, appointed some Democrats to the federal bench (including Supreme Court Justice William J. Brennan) and sought a kind of balance. Most presidents, however, appoint judges of their own political party who share their judicial philosophy. President Johnson, for example, appointed Thurgood Marshall—a liberal who believed that the Court should take an active role in promoting social justice—to the Supreme Court. President Nixon, in contrast, appointed four conservative justices who believed that the Warren Court of the 1950s and 1960s went too far in protecting the rights of individuals and hampered law enforcement. President Reagan followed the Nixon example with the appointment of conservative Sandra Day O'Connor, the first female on the Court. The five conservative justices really mattered when the Supreme Court refused five-to-four to

---

bench   The office of judge.

prolong Florida vote recounts and thus gave the 2000 presidential election to George Bush. Bush 43 also made it clear that he would appoint conservatives as several vacancies occurred on the Supreme Court. In this way, he hoped his conservative legacy would live long after his presidency.

State Judges   State judges are either popularly elected or appointed, for terms ranging up to fourteen years. Both parties often nominate the same slate of judges, so that the judicial elections have become largely nonpartisan affairs; only rarely do party fights for a judicial office take place. In a 1986 referendum, Californians ousted their state chief justice, Rose Bird, who had opposed the death penalty. California justices are appointed but later have to be confirmed by voters. Some argue that elected state judges turn into crowd-pleasing politicians with shaky judicial skills. Others counter that appointed state judges can be the governor's political pals.

COMPARING COURTS

What role should judges play? Should they act as umpires, passively watching the legal drama, just ruling on disputed points of procedure? Or should they actively direct the trial, question witnesses, elicit evidence, and comment on the proceedings? The second pattern strikes Americans as strange and dangerous, because we have been raised in the common-law tradition of passive judges. Yet in code-law countries, judges play just such an active role.

The Anglo-American Adversarial and Accusatorial Process   English and American courts are passive institutions that do not look for injustices to correct or lawbreakers to apprehend. Instead, they wait until a law is challenged or a defendant is brought before them. The system operates on an **adversarial** and **accusatorial** basis. In the adversary process, two sides (plaintiff and defendant) compete for a favorable decision from an impartial court. Courts do not accept a case that does not involve a real conflict of interest; the plaintiff must demonstrate how and in what ways the defendant has caused damage. During the trial, the judge acts as an umpire. Both parties present their evidence, call and cross-examine witnesses, and try to refute each other's arguments. The judge rules on the validity of evidence and testimony, on legal procedures, and on disputed points. After both sides have presented their cases, the judge rules on the basis of the facts and the relevant law. If a jury is hearing the case, the judge instructs the members on the weight of the evidence and relevant laws and then almost always accepts the jury's verdict.

In criminal cases, the police investigate and report to a public prosecutor, often a county's district attorney, who must decide whether to prosecute. The actual trial proceeds like a civil one, but the government is the plaintiff and the accused the defendant. Unless a jury has been waived, the jury determines guilt under instructions from the judge on laws and facts.

---

adversarial   System based on two opposing parties to a dispute.
accusatorial   Like adversarial, but with a prosecutor accusing a defendant of crimes.

THE BRITISH COURT SYSTEM

Britain's court system was established by the Judicature Act of 1873 and largely continues common-law traditions. It is divided into civil and criminal branches.

Selection and Tenure of Judges   British judges are nominally appointed by the monarch, but the choice is really the prime minister's, based on recommendations of the lord chancellor, who presides over the House of Lords and is usually a cabinet member. British judges have lifetime tenure and are above politics. Britain has lacked judicial review, something many Britons want and Prime Minister Blair vowed to introduce. This will be a major step, because Britain has no written constitution and whatever laws Parliament passes are automatically constitutional. The British judiciary—like most countries' judiciaries, a part of the executive—is not supposed to be a coequal branch of government.

The Lawyer's Role   The United States and Britain share a common legal heritage, but there are important differences. One is that in Britain the Crown—meaning the government—hires lawyers to prosecute crimes. There are no professional prosecutors like U.S. district attorneys. American lawyers may take on any type of legal work, in or out of the courtroom, but British *solicitors* handle all legal matters except representing clients in court. That is reserved for a few specialized lawyers called *barristers*.

THE EUROPEAN COURT SYSTEM

Based heavily on the French system—the pattern for much of the world because of the widespread usage of the Code Napoléon—European courts, unlike British courts, do not have separate criminal and civil divisions. Instead, most European countries maintain separate systems of regular and administrative courts. European judges sit as a panel to rule on points of law and procedure, but at the conclusion of the trial they retire *with* a jury to consider the verdict and the sentence. Obviously, the lay jurors often go along with the superior—or at least professional—knowledge and wisdom of the judges. In some systems, such as the German, a judge either sits alone or with two "lay judges."

The European Inquisitorial Process   In code law countries—most of the world—judges play a more active role than in common-law countries. The prosecutor (French *procureur,* German *Staatsanwalt*) is an official who forwards evidence to an **investigating judge** (*juge d'instruction, Ermittlungsrichter*), a representative of the justice ministry who conducts a thorough inquiry (*enquête*), gathering evidence and statements. Without parallel in the Anglo-American system, these European magistrates first make a preliminary determination of guilt *before* sending

---

investigating judge   In European legal systems, judicial officer who both gathers evidence and issues indictments.

the case to trial, something mind-boggling to Americans. French and Italian investigating judges have become heroes by going after corrupt officials. In European criminal procedure the decision to **indict** is made not by a district attorney but by a judge, and the weight of evidence is not controlled by the adversaries (plaintiff and defendant) but by the court, which can take the initiative in acquiring needed evidence.

In the U.S. system, the accused is presumed innocent until proven guilty; in Europe the assumptions are nearly reversed. In an American or British court, the burden of proof is on the prosecution, and the defendant need not say one word in his or her defense; the prosecutor must prove guilt "beyond a reasonable doubt." In code-law countries, the accused bears the burden of having to prove that the investigating judge is wrong.

The Lawyer's Role   Unlike a British or American trial lawyer, the French *avocat* or German *Rechtsanwalt* does not question witnesses; the court does that. Instead, he or she tries to show logical or factual mistakes in the opposition's argument or case and sway the lay jury in the summation argument. For the most part, the role of the European lawyer is not as vital or creative as that of the American lawyer, for the court takes the initiative in discovering the facts of the case.

■ THE ROLE OF THE COURTS

Judicial review is more highly developed in the United States than in any other country and Americans expect more of their courts than do other peoples. In no other country is the "courtroom drama" a television staple, because few other countries have our dramatic courtroom clashes.

Court structures in other Western democracies parallel the U.S. system, but they do not do as much. In Switzerland, for example, cases from the cantonal (state) courts come before the Federal Tribunal, which determines whether a cantonal law violates the Swiss constitution. However, the tribunal does not pass on the constitutionality of laws passed by the Swiss parliament. The German Constitutional Court reviews statutes to make sure they conform to the Basic Law (the German constitution). The court, located in Karlsruhe, was included in the Basic Law partly on American insistence after World War II; it was a new concept for Europe. It consists of sixteen judges, eight elected by each house of parliament, who serve for nonrenewable twelve-year terms. The court decides cases between states, protects civil liberties, and outlaws dangerous political parties. Its decisions have been important. In the 1950s it found that both neo-Nazi and Communist parties wanted to overthrow the constitutional order and declared them illegal. It found the 1974 abortion bill was in conflict with the strong right-to-life provisions of the Basic Law. Because Germany's Constitutional Court operates within the more rigid code law, its decisions do not have the impact of U.S. Supreme Court decisions, which under the common law are literally the law of the land.

---

indict   Pronounced *in-dite;* to formally charge someone with a crime.

CASE STUDIES

LAW IN RUSSIA

Russia's post-Communist legal system has continued much of the Soviet legal structure because virtually all personnel were trained under the Communists. Now Russia is struggling to build "rule of law," including "bourgeois" concepts, such as property law and civil rights. In 1991 a Constitutional Court with fifteen justices was established, the first independent tribunal in Russian history. It can theoretically rule on the constitutionality of the moves made by the president and the State Duma. In practice, Russian presidents have so much power—including power over selection of justices—that the court is no counterweight to the executive. Crime is rampant in Russia. Newly rich *biznesmeny* hire *keelers* to remove anyone in their way, including members of parliament, journalists, and the competition. "The only lawyer around here is a Kalashnikov," despaired one Russian, referring to the assault rifle.

The basic concepts of Soviet law and the workings of the Soviet judicial process were quite different from those of the Western democracies, even though they were similar in strictly criminal—as opposed to political—matters. Soviet law started with Marx's idea that law serves the ruling class. Capitalists naturally have bourgeois laws designed to protect private property. Proletarians, theoretically in power in the Soviet Union, had socialist law to protect state property, which belongs to all society. Especially after the relaxation of Stalin's climate of fear, monumental theft of state property became the norm for Soviet economic life and helped bring down the system. Almost nothing was said of private property, which scarcely existed. Another part of Soviet law dealt with sedition and subversion, areas of extremely minor importance in the West. Soviet citizens could receive harsh sentences to Siberia for "antistate activities" or "slandering the Soviet state."

Unpolitical cases were generally handled fairly under Soviet law. Prosecutors gathered evidence and brought cases to court but sometimes took into account mitigating social factors and asked for lighter sentences. Defense attorneys were permitted, but they merely advised their clients on legal points and did not challenge the prosecutor's evidence. There were no jury trials. Soviet judges had to be Communist party members.

Some political cases never came to trial. Obedient Soviet psychiatrists used to diagnose dissidents as "sluggish schizophrenic" and put them in prisonlike hospitals with no trial. Nobel Prize-winning writer Alexander Solzhenitsyn was simply bundled onto a plane for Germany in 1974 with no trial. Likewise, dissident physicist Andrei Sakharov was banished to a remote city in 1980 to get him away from Western reporters. The Committee on State Security (KGB) was powerful and often acted independently of courts. The KGB was succeeded by the Federal Security Service (FSB in Russian) and, staffed by old KGB officials, continues the KGB's primary aim: to make sure those in power stay in power. President Putin graduated in law, served as a KGB officer and head of the FSB, and appointed ex-KGB agents to top positions. Putin used legal-looking procedures to get rid of opponents, who could be charged with embezzlement or tax evasion. Many fear that if rule of law is not established in Russia, democracy will die. The two are closely connected.

THE U.S. SUPREME COURT

The U.S. Supreme Court's power to review the constitutionality of federal legislative enactments is not mentioned specifically in the Constitution and has been vehemently challenged. Judicial review was first considered and debated at the Constitutional Convention of 1787. Delegates suggested that when in doubt,

CASE STUDIES

MARBURY V. MADISON

President John Adams, a Federalist, appointed William Marbury, a Washington justice of the peace shortly before leaving office. For some unknown reason, however, Secretary of State John Marshall did not deliver the commission to Marbury. Marshall's successor, the Republican James Madison, refused to deliver the commission. Marbury brought suit in original jurisdiction before the Supreme Court, asking the Court to issue a writ of *mandamus* commanding Madison to deliver the commission.

This presented the Court with a dilemma. If Chief Justice Marshall and the Supreme Court issued the writ, and Madison refused to deliver the commission, the prestige and authority of the Court would be dealt a severe blow. If, however, Marshall refused to issue the writ, he would in effect call into question the legitimacy of the hasty judicial appointments given to Federalists in the final days of the Adams administration.

Marshall's solution was brilliant, for it not only criticized Madison and Jefferson but also established the principle of judicial review. On the one hand, Marshall ruled that Marbury was entitled to his commission and that Madison should have given it to him. On the other hand, he stated that the Supreme Court had no authority to issue a writ of *mandamus* in a case brought to it in original jurisdiction and that because Section 13 of the Judiciary Act of 1789 implied otherwise, that part of the act was unconstitutional. The decision infuriated President Jefferson, for he understood how cleverly Marshall had escaped the trap and asserted the authority of the Court. He realized that the precedent for judicial review had been laid and called it "both elitist and undemocratic."

---

legislators might call on the judges for an opinion on a proposed law's constitutionality. James Madison stated that a "law violating a constitution established by the people themselves would be considered by the judges as null and void." However, this position was challenged by those who believed that such a power would give the Court a double check and compromise its neutrality. Others felt it would violate the separation of powers. Elbridge Gerry stated that it would make "statesmen of judges," a prophetic remark. At the close of the convention, judicial review had not been explicitly provided for.

Alexander Hamilton, however, argued in *The Federalist* No. 78 that only the courts could limit legislative authority. John Marshall, chief justice of the Supreme Court from 1801 to 1835, agreed with this position; in fact, he went on record in favor of it nearly fifteen years before *Marbury v. Madison* (1803), the landmark decision establishing judicial review. The doctrine has never been universally popular, however. Strong-willed presidents have resisted the authority of the Court. Thomas Jefferson, Andrew Jackson, Abraham Lincoln, and Franklin D. Roosevelt differed sharply with equally strong-willed judges.

From 1803 to 1857, the Supreme Court did not invalidate any act of Congress. In 1857, it threw out the Missouri Compromise of 1820, which had barred slavery in the old Northwest Territory. This touched off a political storm that made Abraham Lincoln president. In the twentieth century, the doctrine was used extensively. The court itself, however, has always been divided on how it should be used. Judicial "activists," led by Hugo Black, William O. Douglas, and Earl Warren, have argued that the Supreme Court must be vigilant in protecting the Bill of Rights. Advocates of judicial "restraint," such as Oliver Wendell Holmes, Felix Frankfurter, and Warren Burger, have argued that only Congress should make public policy and that unless a legislative act clearly violates the Constitution, the law should stand. The Warren Court (1953–1969), named after its chief justice, was markedly activist, issuing decisions in the areas of racial segregation, reapportionment, and rights of the accused that had great impact on U.S. society. The courts that followed have been more cautious, reflecting the fact that most of its members were appointed by conservative Republicans.

THE SUPREME COURT'S POLITICAL ROLE

In this country, the Supreme Court's rulings often become political issues, rarely the case in other countries. When the Supreme Court of Franklin Roosevelt's day ruled that many New Deal laws were unconstitutional, FDR referred to the justices as "nine tired old men." Richard Nixon in the 1968 campaign charged that the Warren Court's liberal decisions had worsened crime and endangered society. The U.S. Supreme Court plays an important political role, and the appointment of just one new justice changes split decisions from five to four against to the same number for. It is important to know to what extent judges let their personal beliefs influence their decisions. Are their ideological views incompatible with the idea of the Court as an impartial dispenser of justice?

THE VIEWS OF JUDGES

Clearly, justices personal beliefs influence their decisions. Most Supreme Court justices have been **WASP** upper- or upper-middle-class males, and radical critics claim that such judges cannot appreciate the situation of the poor or racially oppressed. The relatively recent arrival of blacks and women to the high bench has not necessarily overturned conservative tendencies, for such justices can be conservative in their own right. Many liberals disliked the views of Justice Clarence Thomas, the second black ever on the Court, who said he reached conservative conclusions by thinking for himself.

   Other factors affect a judge's rulings. They are older, averaging 70 in 2005. Southern jurists have usually been more conservative on racial matters, but one of the strongest champions of civil rights was Alabama's Hugo L. Black, who had been a member of the Ku Klux Klan in his youth. Former corporation lawyers may be more sympathetic to business problems. Some justices, like Louis D. Brandeis (one of five Jewish justices) and Thurgood Marshall (the first black justice), were active in reform and civil rights causes and brought their liberalism to the bench. Others who have served on state courts believe that states' rights should be strengthened.

WASP   White, Anglo-Saxon, Protestant.

The two most important influences on voting, however, seem to be party affiliation and the justice's conception of the judicial role. Democratic justices are more likely to support liberal stands than are Republican justices. Democrats tend to be judicial activists and to see the Supreme Court as a defender of minorities and the poor. They are more likely to distrust states and to favor federal authority, while also seeking to protect individual rights under the Fourteenth Amendment. Republicans usually favor judicial restraint, are more likely to uphold state authority within the federal system, and are less likely to accept the Bill of Rights as a blanket guarantee. There are many exceptions. When President Eisenhower appointed California Governor Earl Warren in 1953, he thought he was picking a good Republican moderate as chief justice. Later, Eisenhower called the choice "the biggest damned-fool mistake I ever made."

Many justices see the Court's role as standing firm on certain constitutional principles, despite public opinion. Justice Jackson put it this way: "One's right to life, liberty and property, to free speech, a free press, freedom of worship and assembly, and other fundamental rights may not be submitted to vote; they depend upon the outcome of no election." But Supreme Court justices are influenced by changing public attitudes. In the 1936 election, after the Court had struck down several important laws designed to alleviate the Depression, President Roosevelt was given the greatest mandate in the nation's history. In 1937, he submitted legislation to expand the Supreme Court to fifteen members and encourage justices 70 or over to retire. The plan failed because many felt that FDR was attacking the constitutional principle of an independent judiciary, but it did force the Court to look beyond its narrow world and accept change. The election of 1936 and the controversy over "court packing" led to the Court's becoming more restrained in dealing with New Deal legislation. As one jokester put it, "A switch in time saves nine."

Another influence is colleagues' opinions. Both Chief Justices John Marshall (1801–1835) and Earl Warren (1953–1969) were able to convert some of their colleagues to their judicial philosophies by force of personality and their judicial reasoning. Many factors—not all of them knowable—influence decisions. The fact that Supreme Court justices are appointed for life may be the most important of all. They are independent and immune to congressional, White House, and private-interest pressures. This factor changes them, and in unpredictable ways. Liberals turn into conservatives, activists into restrainers, and vice versa. The seriousness of their position and the knowledge that their votes alter American life make justices think deeply and sometimes change views. The office in part makes its occupant.

THE POLITICAL IMPACT OF THE COURT

Our legal system poses a basic conflict. Justices are expected to be impartial, but the importance of the Court gives them political power. In the twentieth century this power increased. The **Warren Court** was active and controversial in three key

---

Warren Court   The liberal, activist, U.S. Supreme Court under Chief Justice Earl Warren, 1953–1969.

HOW TO . . .

FOURFOLD TABLE

One device political scientists love is the fourfold table, a cross-tab for two variables where each has only two possible positions, usually "high" and "low." On page 45, for example, we took two variables—amount of state ownership of industry (high or low) and amount of welfare benefits (high or low) a country might have. Each variable is simplified into just two possibilities (high and low). Since 2 + 2 = 4, we get a fourfold table. Thus we have socialist countries where both are high (Cuba), laissez-faire countries where both are low (the United States), statist countries where state ownership is high but welfare is low (Brazil), and welfare states where state ownership is low but welfare is high.

Barber did the same with "presidential character" (page 284), placing how much a president liked the job (positive or negative) as the Y axis and how much energy they had (active or negative) on the X axis. A fourfold table often oversimplifies reality but is useful in reminding us that if two variables interact, there are likely to be at least four possible outcomes. Two variables on Supreme Court justices might be party (Republican or Democrat) and judicial philosophy (activist or restrainer). Who then fits into which of the four categories?

---

areas—civil rights, criminal rights, and legislative reapportionment—where it rewrote constitutional law. In the opinion of some, as ninety-six southern members of Congress put it, the Court overturned "the established law of the land" and implemented its "personal political and social philosophy."

Civil Rights   The Supreme Court's decision in *Brown* (1954) triggered a revolution in American race relations, an area Congress had been unwilling to touch. In a unanimous ruling, the Court accepted the sociological argument of Thurgood Marshall (then attorney for the NAACP) that segregated public school facilities were "inherently unequal" because they stigmatized black children and deprived them of the Fourteenth Amendment's guarantee of equal protection. A year later, in *Brown II* (1955), desegregation of public schools was ordered "with all deliberate speed." Southern whites vowed massive resistance.

America's blacks, encouraged by this legal support, sought equal treatment in other areas and by 1963 engaged in confrontation with the white establishment. In *Lombard v. Louisiana* (1963), the Warren Court supported the **sit-in**, ruling that blacks who had refused to leave a segregated lunch counter could not be prosecuted where it appeared that the state was involved in unequal treatment of the races. The Court relied on the Fourteenth Amendment that no state may deny any person the equal protection of the laws. The sit-in became a major weapon in the civil rights struggle. In 1964, Congress followed the Court's lead and passed the Civil

---

sit-in   Tactic of overturning local laws by deliberately breaking them, as at segregated lunch counters.

Rights Act, which barred segregation in public accommodations such as hotels, motels, restaurants, and theaters. The Court led Congress.

Criminal Procedure   The Warren Court's rulings in criminal procedure were even more disturbing to many Americans. In *Mapp v. Ohio* (1961), the Court ruled that evidence police seized without a warrant was inadmissible in a state court. In 1963, in *Gideon v. Wainwright,* the Court held that **indigent** defendants must be provided with legal counsel. In *Escobedo v. Illinois* (1964), in a five-to-four decision, it ruled that a suspect could not be denied the right to have a lawyer during police questioning and that any confessions so obtained could not be used in court. One of the Court's most controversial rulings came in 1966 in *Miranda v. Arizona.* The majority (five to four) ruled that arrested persons must immediately be told of their right to remain silent and to have a lawyer present during police questioning.

Legislative Reapportionment   Equally important was the Warren Court's mandating of equal-population voting districts. Until 1962, many states had congressional districts that overrepresented rural areas and underrepresented cities. In a series of decisions in 1962 and 1964, the Court found that unequal representation denied citizens their Fourteenth Amendment (equal protection) rights. The Court ordered that state legislatures apply the principle of "one person, one vote" in redrawing electoral lines, which many now do after every census.

These decisions angered people who felt they had been hurt: segregationists who refused to share schools or accommodations with blacks, police who felt hampered in dealing with suspects, and rural people who wanted a more-than-equal vote. Billboards shouted "Impeach Earl Warren," and in 1968 Nixon ran as much against the Supreme Court as against Hubert Humphrey. The Warren Court overthrew **Jim Crow** laws, rewrote the rules for criminal procedure, and redrew legislative maps. With the possible exception of the Marshall Court, it was the most active, groundbreaking Court in U.S. history.

The Post-Warren Courts   The Burger Court (1969–1986) and the Rehnquist Court (1986–2005) were sometimes characterized as conservative, an effort to roll back the Warren Court. Actually, their decisions were not so clear-cut. Overall, there was a conservative drift, but an unpredictable one. The Burger Court in the 1978 *Bakke* case found that reserving quotas for black applicants to medical school violated equal protection for whites. The next year, however, in *Weber,* it found that quotas to help black workers attain skilled positions were constitutional. In criminal law, the Burger Court issued some hard-line decisions. In 1984 it added a "good faith exception" to the *Mapp* rule, which excluded wrongfully seized evidence. If the police, with a warrant to look for a particular piece of evidence, stumble on another, it may be used as evidence. This modified but did not overturn

---

indigent   Having no money.
Jim Crow   System of segregationist laws in U.S. South.

Mapp. In 1976, the Burger Court found that capital punishment was not necessarily "cruel and unusual" if the rules for applying it were fair.

The Rehnquist Court both pleased and alarmed conservatives. In 1988, in a move that stunned the Reagan administration, the Court upheld the constitutionality of independent federal prosecutors, something the White House said interfered with the powers of the executive branch. The Court also ruled that burning the American flag could not be outlawed because it is a form of free speech. This ruling brought a mass outcry and a new federal statute outlawing flag burning. In 2003 the court upheld campaign-finance reform, university affirmative-action programs to promote diversity, and other liberal causes. The post-Warren Courts modified rather than repudiated the Warren Court.

One of the problems with evaluating the thrust of Court decisions is the definition of *conservative*. The term may be applied to the substance of decisions, such as giving minorities special treatment, or it may be applied to the maintenance of existing institutions. Often the two coincide, as when the Court says states can pass laws limiting abortion. That would be both conservative concerning substance and conservative concerning the powers of states. But sometimes the two diverge, as when the Rehnquist Court unanimously overturned a $200,000 libel award for the Reverend Jerry Falwell. Some might call that a "liberal" ruling, but it really just upholds the First Amendment right to a free press. What the mass media and public opinion call "conservative" is irrelevant to the Court, which is intent only on constitutionality. Although labeled a staunch conservative, Justice Antonin Scalia at times sides with liberals. "Liberal" and "conservative" are simplified labels used by the mass media and politicians; they are not used by the Supreme Court.

The U.S. federal courts are an integral part of the policymaking apparatus—not just mechanical interpreters of law. Judicial decisions influence and are influenced by politics. Groups whose welfare depends on the court's decisions will try to influence the court to adopt their point of view; groups that do not succeed with the president or Congress hope that they will have better luck with the courts. Some have called the U.S. judicial system a back-up legislature or parliament of last resort, for it can take on issues the other branches fear. Without Supreme Court decisions leading the way, Congress would have not passed civil-rights bills and presidents would not have enforced them. An autonomous and coequal judicial branch is one of America's great contributions to governance. Very slowly, this approach to judicial power is growing worldwide, contributing to rule of law and stable democracy.

KEY TERMS

accusatorial (p. 322)	civil law (p. 317)
adversarial (p. 322)	code law (p. 319)
appeal (p. 320)	common law (p. 317)
bench (p. 321)	consistency (p. 318)
brief (p. 320)	constitutional law (p. 317)
canon law (p. 319)	higher law (p. 316)

indict (p. 324)
indigent (p. 330)
investigating judge (p. 323)
Jim Crow (p. 330)
judicial review (p. 317)
law (p. 315)
natural law (p. 316)
plaintiff (p. 316)

positive law (p. 316)
precedent (p. 318)
reciprocity (p. 318)
Roman Law (p. 319)
sit-in (p. 329)
Warren Court (p. 328)
WASP (p. 327)

KEY WEB SITES

U.S. Supreme Court decisions
supct.law.cornell.edu/supct/

Department of Justice
www.usdoj.gov/

American Bar Association
www.abanet.org/

Court TV
www.courttv.com/

Law in general
www.findlaw.com/

FURTHER REFERENCE

Abraham, Henry J. *The Judicial Process: An Introductory Analysis of the Courts of the United States, England, and France,* 7th ed. New York: Oxford University Press, 1998.

Baum, Lawrence. *The Supreme Court,* 8th ed. Washington, D.C.: CQ Press, 2003.

Belsky, Martin H., ed. *The Rehnquist Court: A Retrospective.* New York: Oxford University Press, 2002.

Calvi, James V., and Susan Coleman. *American Law and Legal Systems,* 4th ed. Upper Saddle River, NJ: Prentice Hall, 2000.

Carp, Robert A., Ronald Stidham, and Kenneth Manning. *Judicial Process in America,* 6th ed. Washington, D.C.: CQ Press, 2004.

Carter, Lief H., and Thomas F. Burke. *Reason in Law,* 6th ed. White Plains, NY: Longman, 2001.

Cushman, Clare, and Melvin I. Urofsky, eds. *Black, White and Brown: The Landmark School Desegregation Case in Retrospect.* Washington, D.C.: CQ Press, 2004.

Nelson, William E. *Marbury v. Madison: The Origins and Legacy of Judicial Review.* Lawrence, KS: University of Kansas Press, 2000.

Pacelle, Richard L. *The Role of the Supreme Court in American Politics: The Least Dangerous Branch?* Boulder, CO: Westview, 2002.

Powe, Lucas A. *The Warren Court and American Politics*. Cambridge, MA: Harvard University Press, 2000.

Rehnquist, William H. *The Supreme Court*. New York: Knopf, 2001.

Tate, C. Neal. *Comparative Judicial Systems*. Washington, D.C.: CQ Press, 2005.

Urofsky, Melvin I. *The Public Debate over Controversial Supreme Court Cases*. Washington, D.C.: CQ Press, 2005.

POLITICAL ECONOMY

- What policy choices do we now face that are not economic?
- What was Keynes's solution to the Depression?
- What started the U.S. inflationary spiral in the 1960s?
- Are U.S. taxes too high? Compared to what?
- What went right with the U.S. economy in the 1990s?
- Why has income inequality grown in the United States?
- How do entitlements differ from welfare?
- How does ideology influence our views on poverty?
- Which U.S. programs can realistically be cut?

Political economy is an old and flexible term. The classical economists of the late eighteenth and nineteenth centuries—Adam Smith, David Ricardo, John Stuart Mill, and Karl Marx—all wrote on what they called the **political economy**. In doing this they were taking a leaf from Aristotle, who viewed government, society, and the economy as one thing. The old political economists also had normative orientations, prescribing what government should do to promote prosperity. In the late nineteenth century, as economists became more scientific and numbers-based, they dropped "political" from the name of their discipline and shifted from "should" or "ought" prescription to empirical description and prediction.

Recently the term has revived, with partisan overtones. Radicals use the term "political economy" instead of Marxism (which is a hard sell these days) to describe their criticisms of capitalism and the unfair distribution of wealth among and within

---

political economy Influence of politics and economy on each other; what government should do in the economy.

nations. Conservatives use the term to try to get back to the pure market system advocated by Adam Smith. We will avoid taking ideological sides and use the term to mean the interface between politics and the economy. And it is a very big interface.

Economics undergirds almost everything in politics. Politicians get elected by promising prosperity and reelected by delivering it. Virtually all **public policy** choices have economic ramifications, and these can make or break the policy. A policy designed to protect the environment but that slows industry and costs jobs is unlikely to last long. An energy policy that subsidizes ethanol (alcohol from corn) by 50 cents a gallon can continue only because farmers demand it, even if it consumes more energy than it produces.

With a growing economy, a country can afford to play around with new welfare measures, as the United States did in the booming 1960s. With a stagnant economy, an administration has to cut back on welfare expenditures and devise policies to spur the economy into greater production. Whatever the issue—health care, environment, energy, or welfare—it will be connected to the economy. Some of the worst policy choices are made when decision makers forget this elementary point. Accordingly, economic policy takes priority and overshadows all other policies. Every political scientist should be to some degree an economist. As candidate Bill Clinton constantly reminded himself during the 1992 campaign, "It's the economy, stupid!" And he was right; the economy matters most. Good times buoyed his popularity even as he was impeached. Low inflation and low unemployment made most Americans reasonably content with the Clinton presidency.

■ GOVERNMENT AND THE ECONOMY

Nowadays, no one, not even conservatives, expects the government to keep its hands off the economy. Everyone wants the government to induce economic prosperity, and if it does not, voters may punish the administration at the next election, as happened in 1992. President Bush 41 had valid grounds for complaint; he was not to blame for the short, mild recession that preceded the election, but voters held him accountable. Earlier in the twentieth century this was not the case. Many European governments as well as Washington followed the "classic liberal" doctrines discussed in Chapter 6 and generally kept their hands off the economy. With the outbreak of the Great Depression in 1929, however, the hands-off policies tended to make things worse, and people demanded government intervention.

A 1936 book by the English economist John Maynard Keynes proposed to cure the depression by dampening the swings of the **business cycle**. During bad times, government would increase "aggregate demand" by "countercyclical spending" on public works and welfare to make **recessions** shorter and milder. An

---

public policy   What a government tries to do; the choices it makes among alternatives.
business cycle   Tendency of economy to alternate between growth and *recession* over several years.
recession   Period of economic decline; a shrinking GDP.

CASE STUDIES

POSTWAR U.S. RECESSIONS

Most agree that recessions are a normal phase of the business cycle, but no one can predict when they will hit, what will cause them, how long they will last, or how severe they will be. The one thing we can predict is that the current president will be (unfairly) blamed for them. The 2001 recession deflated some Wall Street suits, who had argued that the new high-tech economy and ten years of growth meant we could prevent economic downturns. No one has been able to repeal the business cycle.

Previous post–World War II recessions help put things in perspective: They do not last forever and do not shrink the nation's economy by much. For those who lose jobs, this brings little cheer. This table shows the years of U.S. recessions, how many months they lasted, and how much the GDP declined from its pre-recession peak to its bottom or "trough."

1948–49	11 months	down 3.6%
1953–54	10 months	down 2.6%
1957–58	8 months	down 3.2%
1960–61	10 months	down 0.5%
1969–70	11 months	down 0.1%
1973–75	16 months	down 3.4%
1980	6 months	down 2.2%
1981–82	16 months	down 2.8%
1990–91	8 months	down 1.3%
2001	8 months	down 0.3%

Source: National Bureau of Economic Research

economy growing too fast—with risks of speculative bubbles and inflation—should be cooled by raising taxes. Believers in the classic Adam Smith version of the free market were horrified at "deficit spending," but Keynes argued that we just owe the money to ourselves, and, "In the long run, we'll all be dead." Some say the "Keynesian revolution" brought us out of the Depression. Others say FDR's New Deal never fully applied Keynesianism; only the massive defense spending of World War II did that. Still others doubt that the New Deal achieved anything lasting except debt and **inflation**.

Now Keynesian ideas are standard, even among conservative Republicans. Worries that excess consumer demand could ignite inflation or that taxes should be cut to stave off recession are Keynesian economics. Because Congress is so slow,

---

inflation   A general, overall rise in prices.

the fight to smooth the business cycle shifted to the **Federal Reserve Board**, which, by controlling interest rates, can raise or lower economic activity. Fed chairman Alan Greenspan achieved heroic status for keeping the U.S. economy expanding during the 1990s.

What are some of our leading economic problems and government responses to them? Consider the approximate sequence of events the United States has gone through since the 1960s, and notice how the problems reoccur. Many are with us today.

INFLATION

Until 1965, the U.S. inflation rate was low, but as President Johnson escalated the Vietnam War in 1965, it kicked up. War spending pumped some $140 billion (now worth more than five times that, after adjusting for inflation) into the U.S. economy but not a corresponding amount of goods and services to buy with it. Too many dollars chased too few goods, the classic definition of demand-pull inflation. The Vietnam War brought an inflation that took on a life of its own and lasted into the 1980s. Johnson thought he could win in Vietnam quickly and cheaply, before the war made much economic impact. He failed. Many economists say that he could have avoided the worst of the inflation if he had been willing to raise taxes at the start of the war.

TAX HIKE

President Johnson was reluctant to ask for a tax increase to pay for Vietnam for two reasons. First, he had just gotten a tax cut through Congress in 1964; it would have been embarrassing to reverse course the following year. Second, he did not want to admit that he had gotten us into a long and costly war. By the time Johnson and Congress had changed their minds and introduced a 10 percent tax surcharge in 1968, it was too late; inflation had taken firm hold. The lesson was that in war you must increase taxes to mop up the increased government spending. Bush 43 ignored the lesson and, like LBJ, both cut taxes and took us to war. To head off inflation, the Fed had to boost interest rates.

BALANCE OF PAYMENTS

Starting in the late 1950s, the United States spent more abroad than it sold. With the war-induced prosperity of the 1960s, America sucked in growing imports without exporting enough to cover them. American industries outsourced, and Americans enjoyed bargain prices on imported goods. Large **balance-of-payments**

Federal Reserve Board   "The Fed"; U.S. central bank that can raise and lower interest rates.
balance of payments   The value of what a country exports compared to what it imports.

HOW TO . . .

MAPS

Maps are often underutilized, but they are essential for studies with territorial components. They are also easy for readers to understand. Like cross-tabs and scattergrams, maps can relate two variables, sometimes suggesting patterns you overlooked. A study of the Perot vote in Pennsylvania showed it was most pronounced in the rural counties along the state's northern border, a depressed region where voters have much resentment and low turnout. A map suggested that the Perot vote came from alienated people who typically do not vote.

The basic technique is to shade in territorial components (states, provinces, counties, or electoral districts) to show variation in, say, voting for a certain party. You might take the overall vote for the German Social Democratic party (SPD). In those German *Länder* (states) where the SPD got, say, 5 or more percent below the national average, leave them white. In those states where the SPD won from 5 percent under to 5 percent over the national average, color them light blue. In those states where

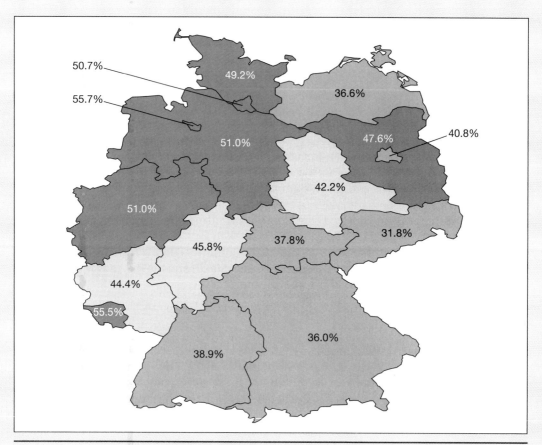

German Social Democratic Vote by State

the SPD got more than 5 percent over their national average, color them medium blue. At a glance, you'll have a picture of German voting by region. Most countries show regional voting patterns.

For your second variable, you might take religion, coloring in on the same basis in which states Protestants are either at, below, or above Germany's overall percentage of Protestants. You will likely notice that the two maps are similar, as German Catholics tend to vote Christian Democrat and Protestants SPD. Such maps show a rough fit between religion and voting.

U.S. Congressional and state legislative districts have an advantage in drawing up maps that show urban-rural voting differences. By law, U.S. districts for lower houses must have the same number of residents, adjusted after every census. Accordingly, territorially large districts are rural, small districts are urban. Districts of medium size suggest they are suburban. Coloring in Democratic districts in blue and Republican in red will likely show that rural districts went Republican, cities Democrat, particularly true of the 2000 and 2004 elections. States and counties, of course, were never designed to have equal numbers of residents.

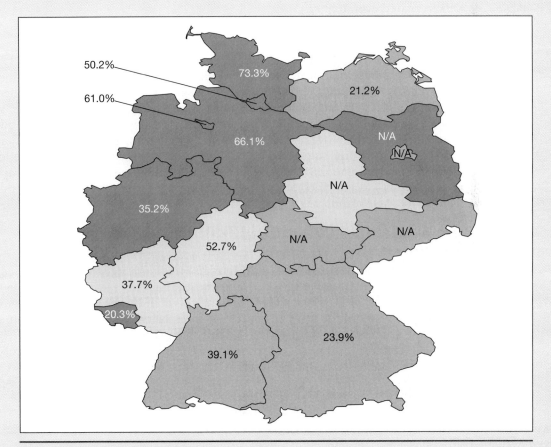

Percent Protestant by State

deficits grew. The too-high value of the dollar in relation to foreign currencies meant it was cheaper to buy foreign goods but harder to sell ours in foreign markets. Japanese and later Chinese products especially took a large share of the U.S. market. American dollars flooded the world; they were too plentiful.

GOLD STANDARD

In an effort to correct this imbalance, in 1971 President Nixon cut the link between the dollar and gold, a **fixed exchange rate** that had been in place since 1944. The Bretton Woods agreement—which fixed an ounce of gold at $35 and fixed other currencies in relation to the dollar—had been the basis of postwar recovery. But the inflation of U.S. dollars worldwide made our stock of gold way too cheap, so Nixon said no more gold and let the dollar "float" to a lower level in relation to other currencies. This **floating exchange rate** devalued the dollar by about one-fifth. The dollar went back up, however, and U.S. trade and payments deficits soared even higher.

WAGE-PRICE FREEZE

At the same time, Nixon froze wages and prices to try to knock out the inflationary psychology that had taken hold. The 1971 wage-price freeze was popular at first, but soon some complained that there was no corresponding freeze on profits, so that businesses benefited unduly. A bigger problem with wage-price freezes, however, is that when they are removed, pent-up pressures push inflation higher than ever. Many economists think Nixon's eighteen-month freeze just set the stage for greater inflation. Some (mostly liberal) economists supported the idea of wage and price controls—called "incomes policy"—but now few economists of any stripe want to try them again.

OIL SHOCKS

International oil deals, like most international trade arrangements, were made with U.S. dollars. The dollar's loss in value meant that the oil exporters were getting less and less for their black gold. The price of oil in the 1960s was ridiculously low. As a result of the 1973 Mideast war, the members of the Organization of Petroleum Exporting Countries (OPEC) were able to do what they had been itching to do: quadruple oil prices. In 1979, in response to the revolutionary turmoil in Iran, they increased prices again. Altogether during the 1970s, world oil prices soared from $2.50 to $34 a barrel, devastating economies around the world.

---

fixed exchange rate　　Dollar buys set amounts of foreign currencies.

floating exchange rate　　Dollar buys varying amounts of foreign currencies, depending on market for them.

*The oil shortages of the 1970s made the United States aware of its dependence on im-
ported oil.* (Irene Springer)

STAGFLATION

The manyfold increase in petroleum prices produced inflation everywhere while
simultaneously depressing the economy. During the 1970s a new word appeared—
stagflation—to describe inflation with stagnant economic growth. Previously, economists had seen a connection between economic growth and inflation; as one went
up, so did the other. In the 1970s, this connection was broken. Inflation hit double-
digit levels (10 percent or higher), but the economy shrank and joblessness increased.
Since 1973, average Americans have had stagnant living standards. The biggest single culprit is believed to be the massive increase in oil prices that affected every corner of the economy, from agriculture and transportation to manufacturing and
construction. The United States was especially hard hit, for Americans had gotten used
to cheap energy and had based their industry and lifestyle on it. Some feared similar results when oil topped $55 a barrel in 2004 and 2005.

INTEREST RATES

President Jimmy Carter attempted to stimulate the economy, but this made inflation worse than ever; in 1980 it was 13.5 percent and probably cost him reelection. The Fed, whose members are appointed by the president for four years

---

stagflation   Combination of slow growth plus inflation in the U.S. economy in the 1970s.

CASE STUDIES

HOW HIGH ARE U.S. TAXES?

Compared to other countries, not very. The Organization for Cooperation and Development (the "rich countries' club") figured that in 2002 countries paid the following percentages of their GDPs in total taxes (including state and local):

Sweden	51
France	44
Germany	36
Britain	36
Canada	34
United States	29
Japan	28
Mexico	18

Americans complain their taxes are too high—they would complain if taxes were zero—but among the advanced industrialized countries, we are at the low end. Most Europeans, figuring they get a lot from the system, complain little about taxes. The question is how much and what programs are Americans willing to cut to bring taxes even lower? Defense? Social Security? Medicare? Besides, some of the "cuts" in federal programs are just tax burdens shifted to the state and local level.

and cannot be fired, stemmed inflation by boosting interest rates to record levels; at one point they were over 20 percent. This brought slower economic growth and curbed inflation. But it was also painful medicine that brought the greatest rate of unemployment (over 10 percent) since the Depression. No one wants interest rates like that again. Americans became aware of how important the Fed is in our economic life.

TAX CUT

Again trying to stimulate the economy, President Reagan turned to an approach called "supply-side economics," which focuses on investment and production rather than on consumer demand, as Keynesian policy does. The inspiration of supply-siders was the Kennedy idea that lowering tax rates stimulates economic growth and ultimately generates more tax revenue. Too-high taxes discourage effort and investment. Congress bought the idea and cut income taxes 25 percent over three years. Actually, this scarcely offset the "bracket creep" that American taxpayers had suffered as a result of inflation; their purchasing power had stayed the same, but they found themselves in ever-higher tax brackets. The Reagan tax cut did stimulate the economy, but it also helped produce another problem.

UP AND DOWN PHASES OF THE U.S. BOOM

In the late 1990s, the U.S. economy was doing so well that some described it as a "virtuous circle" that other countries should learn from. Actually, it was just the up phase of the normal business cycle, which ended with the 2001 recession. While it was good, however, it was very good. Its interlocking components:

- Four years of Federal budget surpluses, which held down inflation and interest rates.
- Low inflation, which increased investor and business confidence and held down wage demands and interest rates.
- Low interest rates, which encouraged business expansion.
- Modest taxes, which left plenty of money for spending and business expansion.
- Slowly growing wages, which encouraged new hires and plunged unemployment to under 5 percent, half that of Europe's.
- Modest regulation, which encouraged the founding of new businesses and expansion of old ones.
- Plentiful imports, which held down wage demands and inflation.
- "Consumer-driven" prosperity fueled by households going deeply into debt.
- Low oil prices letting cheap energy fuel business growth.
- Massive investment in information technology. The dot.coms produced a speculative frenzy and instant millionaires.

As one element fed into another, the economy grew and generated unexpected tax revenues and budget surpluses, something not seen for decades. Nothing that good lasts forever. By 2000, the "high tech" bubble of computers and dot.coms burst when investors realized that the dot.coms had little to sell and made no profits.

At the same time, the stock market had soared beyond any reasonable value and then declined. Banking and currency collapses spread from East Asia to Latin America and Russia, slowing the world economy. The 9/11 terrorist attacks deepened the economic downturn. Those who thought the growth phase could last forever learned that the business cycle, although it cannot be closely predicted, still operates.

BUDGET DEFICITS

President Reagan presented Congress with budgets that featured both tax cuts and major increases in defense spending. He figured this would force Congress to cut domestic and welfare spending drastically. But Congress cut little, and the U.S. federal budget reached record **deficits**—$295 billion during the last year of President Bush 41. By issuing Treasury bills, the federal government borrowed the

---

deficit   Spending more in a given year than you take in.

money, and this "crowded out" commercial borrowing and raised interest rates. Because interest rates were high, foreigners found the United States a good place to invest, so in effect much of the U.S. budget deficit was covered by foreign investment. The deficits acted like a gigantic vacuum cleaner that swept in both goods and capital from around the world. The deficits of Bush 43 were even bigger—$413 billion in 2004—and made many worry that the dollar would lose value.

TRADE DEFICITS

America for several decades has consumed more than it produced and imported much more than it exported. U.S. imports topped exports by a staggering half-trillion dollars in 2004, about 5 percent of GDP. The foreign-trade deficit makes the United States the world's greatest debtor nation. This in turn leads to the buying up of American assets by foreigners. Americans often dislike this, but it is really no problem. If foreigners want to invest in America, it simply makes us more prosperous. By 2004, our trading partners bid down the value of the dollar and the value of the **euro** climbed. This in effect devalued the dollar and made U.S. products cheaper, something Europeans do not want. Some economists argue that the U.S. trade deficit is irrelevant because the U.S. economy is so strong that foreign creditors know they will be repaid. Others caution that too much hangs on confidence in the dollar; if it collapsed suddenly the world would have no standard "reserve" currency to do business with, leading to global recession.

BUDGET BALANCING

The 1994 Republican takeover of Capitol Hill brought a determined effort to trim government spending and end the chronic budget deficits, which every year are added to the national **debt**—the sum total owed by the federal government. This now totals over $7 trillion, which is covered by government borrowing. President Clinton went along with the effort, and the federal budget moved into surplus by the late 1990s. The surpluses were less the result of cuts—some of which simply shifted burdens to later years—than of the high-tech and stock boom, which boosted the wealth of the rich (in 1999, the richest one-fifth of U.S. households earned over half the country's income) and thus got more taxes from them. Then recession ended the surplus—both from lower tax revenues and from increased federal spending—and the federal budget returned to deficits. The Bush 43 administration projected a decade of surpluses, but they did not last a year, and the Republican administration and Congress spent faster than ever. Now it was the Democrats' turn to demand balanced budgets.

---

euro   Since 2002, common EU currency used in most of West Europe, worth about $1.30 in 2005.
debt   The sum total of deficits over many years.

CASE STUDIES

THE GROWTH OF INEQUALITY

Over roughly a third of a century Americans' incomes have grown less equal. The rich got a bigger piece of the nation's economic pie, the poor a little smaller piece. Much of the middle class stayed about the same, but some, especially those with a high-school education or less, had tough going.

What happened? Many economists believe that the industrial growth of other countries, especially in East Asia, cut the number and pay of American blue-collar manufacturing jobs as their factories moved overseas. Unions—during the early 1950s some 40 percent of the U.S. workforce was unionized—declined to under 15 percent of the workforce, much of it in government employees' and teachers' unions. U.S. manufacturers practiced **outsourcing**, buying parts and products either from abroad or from cheaper, nonunion U.S. producers, leaving workers vulnerable. By holding down U.S. wages and boosting **productivity** through constant technological improvements and reorganization—including "downsizing"—the United States regained its economic luster, but not all shared in it.

The real winners were not average workers or mid-level managers but top executives and investors. Chief executive officers are compensated extravagantly—many earn several million a year—and shareholders saw the value of their stocks increase. Fueling the 1990s **bull market** was the conviction of the **baby boom** generation that Social Security was unreliable so they had to save for retirement, and stocks were the best way. With more and more people shoveling money into the stock market—about a third of U.S. families, a record high, were in the market, most through mutual funds—many investors did well in the 1990s. The richest 5 percent of Americans became very rich; the extra taxes they paid made federal budget surpluses. Working-class Americans—with few funds to invest—did not do as well, but most accepted their situations because they had jobs. Most wives worked to make ends meet. The slower economic growth of the early 2000s brought resentments from those who had benefited little from the boom years.

■ WHO IS ENTITLED TO WHAT?

The federal budget is divided into two general categories, discretionary and mandatory. The former can be raised or lowered from year to year. Congress, for example, may decide to increase defense and cut highway spending. Mandatory spending—which now runs twice as much as discretionary—cannot be so easily changed; it is what the federal budget is stuck with from previous statutory commitments. Mandatory spending in turn is divided into interest payments on the national debt (12 percent of the budget in 2005) and **entitlements** (55 percent in

---

outsourcing   U.S. firms producing overseas.
productivity   The efficiency with which things are made.
bull market   A stock market that keeps rising.
baby boom   The big generation of Americans born from 1946 to 1964.
entitlement   U.S. federal expenditure mandated by law, such as Social Security and Medicare.

KEY CONCEPTS

WHAT IS POVERTY?

Defining poverty can be tricky. What's "poor" currently might have been "comfortable" in previous eras. Ask your grandparents how they fared during the Depression. A U.S. Labor Department statistician came up with a formula in 1963 that became standard, although many argue it is out of date. She found that families spent about one-third of their incomes on food, so a "poverty line" is three times a minimal food budget for nonfarm families of four. Using this definition, the percentage of Americans below the poverty line fell from 17.3 percent in 1965, when Johnson's War on Poverty started, to 11.7 percent in 1973. In 2003 it was 12.5 percent. Black and Hispanic rates are much higher, and one-sixth of America's children are below the poverty line.

Liberals complain that the poverty line—now nearly $19,000 for a family of four—is set much too low; it can take two to three times that to just get by in big cities, as rent and child care are now bigger items than food. Washington has considered updating the poverty line to include such items. Conservatives point out that poverty figures do not include *noncash* benefits transferred to the poor by government programs—food stamps, for example. Taking such benefits into account raises some poor families above the poverty line.

Before we conclude that the War on Poverty was a success or failure, we must look at the poverty rate in longer perspective. In 1950, some 30 percent of the U.S. population was classified as below the poverty line. Since then, the rate has dropped. One of the fastest decreases occurred between 1960 and 1965, *before* the War on Poverty programs were enacted. The U.S. economy expanded from 1950 to 1965, especially during the early 1960s. Jobs were plentiful. It is hard to tell if the further drop in the poverty rate from 1965 to 1973 was the result of government programs or of an economy heated by Vietnam War spending.

By the same token, when the poverty rate began to go up again in the mid-1970s, cutbacks in antipoverty spending were only partly to blame; also responsible were the recessions caused by the oil prices and high interest rates discussed earlier. Some blame the increase of poverty and homelessness on outsourcing, making many working-class Americans unemployed and pushing them down into the lower class. With the disappearance of modestly paying factory jobs, they faced either low-paid service jobs ("flipping hamburgers") or unemployment and welfare. Antipoverty programs cannot offset massive unemployment caused by long-term trends in the U.S. economy.

2005); together they are two-thirds of the federal budget. Interest payments are totally untouchable; if they were cut, future offerings of bonds and treasury notes would have no credibility or customers.

Entitlements are extremely difficult to cut because people are used to them and expect them as a right. They are payments to which one is automatically entitled by law: When you turn sixty-five (and a few months now) you are entitled to Social Security and Medicare; earn an income below a specified level and you get food stamps and Medicaid. There is no annual cap on entitlement spending; it grows as more people are entitled, what is called "uncontrollable" spending. The 2005 budget devotes 19 percent of all federal spending to Social Security. Medicare and Medicaid account for another 22 percent. Most of these entitlements go to seniors, who get seven times what children get from the federal budget. Children don't vote, and oldsters do.

A homeless man—one of a growing number of poor in the United States—camps out under a bridge in New York. (Michael Roskin)

Only a small fraction of federal payments is traditional "welfare" spending; more than 85 percent go to the middle and upper classes in the form of Social Security, Medicare, government retirement plans, and farm price supports. What goes to poor families includes Medicaid, food stamps, and Supplemental Security Income. With political realism in mind, what can be cut of the first category—middle-class entitlements? Some people argue that if we eliminated "welfare" spending we could cut taxes, but "welfare" is not the problem; entitlements are. Cuts in welfare spending save little and inflict hardship on society's most vulnerable members, especially children. How did the U.S. welfare system come about?

In the mid-1960s, President Lyndon B. Johnson launched his War on Poverty, aimed at creating a Great Society by eliminating poverty. Johnson, who had long been Senate majority leader, got Congress to deliver almost everything he wanted. Then the Vietnam War, with its rising costs and acrimony, seemed to cut down the War on Poverty in its infancy. There wasn't enough money for the growing programs, and the Great Society became discredited. Many of its programs were substantially dismantled or left to die on the vine. Some say the Great Society was never given a chance. Conservatives hold that the undertaking was inherently infeasible, a waste of money that often did more harm than good, locking recipients into **welfare dependency** and encouraging a subculture of drugs and crime. Some poverty specialists, however, say the Great Society programs generally did succeed and lowered the U.S. poverty rate. Conservatives, they say, have exaggerated the inefficiency and misuses that accompany any welfare program and have understated the very real accomplishments.

---

welfare dependency   Stuck on welfare with no incentive to get off.

KEY CONCEPTS

POVERTY AND IDEOLOGY

The U.S. debate about poverty is passionately ideological. Conservatives want to limit antipoverty programs, and liberals generally defend them. The policy analyst must cast ideology aside and gather factual answers to questions such as these:

Are we talking about welfare or entitlement?   The two categories overlap, but the essence of a welfare program is that it is "means tested," meaning recipients must demonstrate that they are poor according to certain criteria (typically, how much income and how many children). If the program is a pure entitlement, such as Social Security or Medicare, can it realistically be cut without incurring electoral wrath?

Do welfare programs have negative consequences?   Here is the great conservative attack: Welfare programs offer incentives for unemployment, illegitimacy, and drug use. Can this be proved or disproved? New York City, with its extensive welfare programs, has a high incidence of poverty. But so does Mississippi, with its weak and underfunded welfare programs. As usual, causality is terribly difficult to prove. Would a massive, nationwide cessation of all welfare programs force the indolent to work? This raises the next question.

Is poverty an unfortunate circumstance or a character defect?   Are people poor because they cannot find work or because they do not want to work? In other words, are the poor really different from you and me? Do they embody a "culture of poverty" that instills a "radical improvidence," an indifference to providing for their families and futures? If poverty is a character defect, as most conservatives maintain, then little can be done. If it is the product of unfortunate circumstances, as most liberals maintain, then programs that change those circumstances might get people out of poverty.

How much poverty is simply a lack of good jobs?   Do the jobs available to poor people pay enough for them to support their families? In most of America, people are willing to take jobs not

THE COSTS OF WELFARE

Food Stamps   Begun as a modest trial program under Kennedy in 1961, the Food Stamp program was made nationwide under Johnson in 1964. It has grown until now over 24 million Americans benefit. One does not dine royally on food stamps; cost per meal per person is figured at about a dollar. One-third of families headed by women receive food stamps.

The Carter administration simplified the program in 1977 by eliminating the provision that recipients *buy* the stamps at a discount with their own money. This policy had meant that the absolutely destitute, people with no money at all, could get no food stamps. Congress changed the law to eliminate the cash payment and much above minimum wage, even though a single mother earning that falls far below the poverty line. Good factory jobs are hard to find because many have moved overseas. Those who would drastically cut welfare should demonstrate there are sufficient jobs with adequate pay. But are poor people generally qualified for decent-paying jobs, or do they lack the skills?

Can we train people out of poverty? Job training and retraining have long been part of poverty-fighting programs. But do they work? Some who have completed job training still find no work. Can we take people with poor reading and math abilities and in a few months make them into skilled technicians? The deeper, underlying problem is the lack of proper education in grade schools, which creates an illiterate and innumerate workforce. But is the lack of proper education in America the fault of schools and teachers or of families and attitudes? Liberals like to blame schools, conservatives families. Either way, how do you fix the U.S. education system?

What is the international context of domestic poverty? How much poverty is due to the export of American jobs to low-wage countries? Note how many of your Christmas gifts were made in China or Central America. While lowering costs to consumers, outsourcing has closed thousands of American factories. Is U.S. poverty, then, the natural result of an open world economy in which many countries have much lower labor costs? Should we close our borders to such commerce in order to boost domestic employment? If we did, Americans would live a little less well—their clothing and electronic gadgets would cost more, so they would buy fewer of them—but other Americans would exit poverty through new factory jobs. Our trading partners in other lands would retaliate by keeping out U.S. products, so other U.S. factories would close. On balance, trade protectionism hurts more than helps.

These are some of the questions we must ask. Simple ideological approaches, either liberal or conservative, often deal with consequences rather than causes. Where ideology reigns, reason has difficulty making its voice heard.

the number of recipients expanded. Reagan, citing an apocryphal story of a young man who used food stamps to buy vodka, tightened eligibility requirements in an effort to eliminate fraud and misuse.

What should be done? The Food Stamp program became bigger than expected, but outright fraud and waste have not been major factors. Recipients selling food stamps at 50¢ on the dollar to buy liquor and drugs probably account for only a few percent of the program. (By 2004, all food stamps were debit cards, fixing some of the fraud problem.) There are poor people in America. Should they be helped? Outright cash grants, considered for a time by Carter as a replacement for food stamps, could easily be misused. Direct delivery of surplus commodities, as was done on a small scale in the 1950s and episodically in the 1980s to get rid of government cheese stocks (the result of price supports for dairy farmers), was clumsy and spotty. The food stamp program reached its peak in 1994 and declined, the result of both prosperity and of tightened eligibility.

Welfare Reform   In 1996, President Clinton signed the Personal Responsibility and Work Opportunity Act to "end welfare as we know it." This major welfare reform ended the old Aid to Families with Dependent Children (AFDC) that had begun as part of the 1935 Social Security Act. AFDC had provided federal matching funds to the states to help the poor; most of it went to single mothers. Many accused AFDC of promoting fatherless children and welfare dependency. Because many recipients were nonwhite, the issue became connected with the struggle for racial equality.

The 1996 reform replaced entitlement-type welfare payments with $16.5 billion a year in block grants to the states to spend fighting poverty as they saw fit. Recipients had five years to get off welfare. Many states developed **workfare** programs that required recipients to either take jobs or training. Workfare, which had been tried for years, does not always work and initially costs more than traditional welfare programs, because it must provide both welfare and training for a while. Some recipients who took jobs were still quite poor, because for every dollar they earned, they lost around 40 cents in "ancillary benefits," which include food stamps, child day care, and Medicaid. The federal earned income tax credit (EITC) helps low-paid workers cut their income taxes and may even give them supplemental cash. Some analysts call EITC the best welfare program of all, because it encourages people to work and climb out of poverty.

The 1996 reform came when the U.S. economy was excellent, and most people bumped off welfare found jobs. The unemployment rate for single mothers fell from around 48 percent during the 1980s and early 1990s to 28 percent in 1999. The total number of welfare recipients dropped from 12.2 million in 1996 to 5.8 million in 2000, a decline that does not necessarily mean they got out of poverty; they just got off welfare. The real test of welfare reform is how it holds up during recession.

Medicare and Medicaid   These two giants of entitlements, both enacted in 1965, serve different purposes. Medicare, a federally funded program for older people, now costs nearly $300 billion a year. Medicaid combines federal and state funds for poor people and costs a little less. Both grew so rapidly that benefits had to be limited and eligibility requirements tightened. As baby-boomers start to reach sixty-five in 2011, Medicare costs will soon double. Who will pay for it?

President Clinton arrived in Washington promising to revamp the nation's medical insurance programs. But a massive study chaired by his wife worked at cross-purposes: A new plan was to include all Americans—some 16 percent of

workfare   Programs limiting the duration of welfare payments and requiring recipients to work or get job training.

Americans, mostly people working for themselves or in small firms, have no insurance—but it was also to hold down soaring costs. Congress rejected the complex and expensive proposals out of hand. In 1995 Congressional Republicans proposed to hold down Medicare growth (not cut it) and heard an outcry from older Americans, who read it as a cut in a program they had come to depend on. Anything that looks like a cut in medical programs faces overwhelming resistance.

At least two factors induce exponential growth in medical assistance: More people become eligible and medical costs soar. Medicare is especially expensive, for all get it on reaching age sixty-five, even rich people. The proportion of older people in American society is increasing steadily, and they are by far the biggest consumers of medical care. Most Americans consume most of their lifetime medical expenses in the last year of life.

Hospitals and doctors, once they are assured of payment, have no incentive to economize. When in doubt, they put the patient in the hospital—often at $1,000 a day—and order expensive tests with the latest multimillion-dollar machines. Some hospitals expanded into medical palaces, and some physicians got rich from Medicare and Medicaid. (Ironically, the powerful American Medical Association had for years lobbied against such "socialized medicine.") Medical costs consume over 15 percent of the U.S. gross domestic product, most of it paid by government and private health insurance. Other countries paid less and had healthier populations (although their costs are growing too).

Washington tried various ways of tightening up, but medical costs continued to climb. Recipients were required to contribute more of the total payment to hold down overuse. Hospitals and doctors were monitored on costs and on how long they kept patients hospitalized. Hospices—nursing homes for the terminally ill—were made allowable under Medicare, as such care is cheaper than hospital care. Competitive bidding began in some states, and patients were assigned only to low-bid hospitals. Fees for each type of disorder were established, and overruns were not reimbursed. Recipients were encouraged to enter health-maintenance organizations (HMOs), whose efforts to cut costs through "managed care" created the resentment that led to the 2001 Patients Bill of Rights, which lets patients sue their HMOs. Every time the government tightens medical assistance, patients, doctors, and hospitals complain bitterly, and they form a powerful lobby. At the same time, not even conservatives could say no to a federal plan to help oldsters pay for prescription drugs. Congress trembles at the voting power of the retired.

■ How Big Should Government Be?

Americans have the funniest ideas about where their tax dollars go. Many think most of the federal budget goes for welfare, not at all the case. Television exposés suggest it goes to food-stamp and Medicaid fraudsters, but this percentage too is small. As noted on pages 345–346, the bulk of federal spending goes not for welfare for the poor but for entitlements to the middle class; it is impossible to repeal

Cut the federal government, say most citizens, but not programs that might help me, such as the Federal Emergency Management Agency (FEMA), here set up for one-stop disaster relief. (Michael Roskin)

or seriously cut most middle-class programs. A Congress dominated by Republicans had to add an expensive prescription-drug benefit to Medicare; otherwise they would cede the hot issue to Democrats. The complexity of the new program angered many elderly and pushed them to the Democrats in 2004. Few discuss holding down Social Security or Medicare expenditures. It's a sure vote-loser. If you want to cut taxes, just what programs are you prepared to cut?

As noted previously, the American welfare state is small compared to that of other countries. Should it get bigger? The American answer is to keep government small and to suspect and criticize the expansion of government power. But we also recognize that we need government intervention in the economy, education, energy planning, environmental protection, and so on. We have trouble making up our minds about how much government we want. Americans demand various forms of government intervention, but scarcely is the ink on new laws dry before we begin to criticize government bungling. Not understanding where Medicare comes from, one elderly American lady told an interviewer, "Don't let the government get its hands on Medicare!" Europeans and Canadians generally do not suffer from this kind of split personality; they mostly accept that government has a major role to play and do not complain much about their high taxes.

This reluctance to expand government's role may redound to America's long-term advantage. Government programs tend to expand, bureaucracy is inherently inefficient, and ending an entitlement program is all but impossible. Government programs become so sprawling and complex that officials don't even *know* what is in operation, much less how to control it. As political scientist Ira Sharkansky put it, "All modern states are welfare states, and all welfare states are incoherent." Accordingly, it is probably wise to act with caution in expanding government programs.

KEY TERMS

baby boom (p. 345)
balance of payments (p. 337)
bull market (p. 345)
business cycle (p. 335)
debt (p. 344)
deficit (p. 343)
entitlement (p. 345)
euro (p. 344)
Federal Reserve Board (p. 337)
fixed exchange rate (p. 340)

floating exchange rate (p. 340)
inflation (p. 336)
outsourcing (p. 345)
political economy (p. 334)
productivity (p. 345)
public policy (p. 335)
recession (p. 335)
stagflation (p. 341)
welfare dependency (p. 347)
workfare (p. 350)

KEY WEB SITES

Federal budget
www.whitehouse.gov/omb/budget/index.html

Economic data
www.clark.net/pub/lschank/web/econ.html

Economist magazine
www.economist.com/

World Bank
www.worldbank.org/

International political economy
www.pitt.edu/~ian/resource/ipe.htm

Economic policy
www.economic-policy.org/

Foundation for Economic Education
www.fee.org/

FURTHER REFERENCE

Adolino, Jessica R., and Charles H. Blake. *Comparing Public Policies: Issues and Choices in Six Industrialized Countries.* Washington, D.C.: CQ Press, 2001.

Altman, Daniel. *Neoconomy: George Bush's Revolutionary Gamble With America's Future.* New York: PublicAffairs, 2004.

Galbraith, James K. *Created Unequal: The Crisis in American Pay.* New York: Free Press, 1998.

Helsing, Jeffrey W. *Johnson's War/Johnson's Great Society: The Guns and Butter Trap.* Westport, CT: Praeger, 2000.

Kotlikoff, Laurence J., and Scott Burns. *The Coming Generational Storm: What You Need to Know about America's Economic Future.* Cambridge, MA: MIT Press, 2004.

Krugman, Paul. *The Great Unraveling: Losing Our Way in the New Century.* New York: Norton, 2004.

Neiman, Max. *Defending Government: Why Big Government Works.* Upper Saddle River, NJ: Prentice Hall, 2000.

Page, Benjamin I., and James R. Simmons. *What Government Can Do: Dealing with Poverty and Inequality.* Chicago, IL: University of Chicago Press, 2000.

Payne, James. L. *Overcoming Welfare: Expecting More from the Poor and from Ourselves.* New York: Basic Books, 1998.

Persson, Torsten, and Guido Tabellini. *Political Economics: Explaining Public Policy.* Cambridge, MA: MIT Press, 2000.

Rothstein, Bo, and Sven Steinmo, eds. *Restructuring the Welfare State: Political Institutions and Policy Change.* New York: Palgrave, 2002.

Weidenbaum, Murray. *One-Armed Economist: On the Interaction of Business and Government.* New Brunswick, NJ: Transaction, 2004.

Wilson, William Julius. *When Work Disappears.* New York: Knopf, 1996.

CHAPTER 19

VIOLENCE AND REVOLUTION

QUESTIONS TO CONSIDER

- What causes political systems to break down?
- What purposes can violence serve?
- Which types of violence are most prevalent today?
- How can modernization lead to unrest?
- How can you tell if there has been a revolution?
- Why are intellectuals prominent in revolutions?
- What are Brinton's stages of revolution?
- Do all revolutions end badly? Why?
- Why is revolution no longer fashionable?

Political scientists—under the influence of the "systems" approach discussed in Chapter 2—often talked about systems and stability; some even depicted political systems as well-oiled machines that never broke down. But in the late 1960s the media was filled with images of violence and revolution, and political scientists began criticizing the status-quo orientation of their discipline and directed their attention instead to breakdown and upheaval. Some had overlooked the tension and violence in their own backyards. With the black riots of 1965–1968, academics suddenly discovered violence in America. Formerly viewing violence as abnormal, many academics eventually suggested, along with black militant H. Rap Brown, that "violence is as American as cherry pie." By the same token, Europeans were shocked to learn, as the nationalities of ex-Yugoslavia slaughtered each other, that they were not immune to violence either.

■ SYSTEM BREAKDOWN

Political systems can and do break down. Indeed most countries have suffered or are suffering **system breakdown**, marked by major riots, civil wars, terrorism, military **coups**, and authoritarian governments of varying degrees of harshness. Dictatorships are rarely the work of small bands of conspirators alone; they are the result of system collapse, which permits small but well-organized groups—usually the military—to take over. This is why it does little good to denounce a cruel military regime. True, some governments commit acts of great evil; military regimes in Argentina, Chile, and Guatemala killed thousands on the slightest suspicion of leftism. But why did these coups happen? Why does system breakdown recur repeatedly in some countries? These are the deeper questions that must be asked if we are to begin to understand these horror stories.

Underlying breakdown is lack of legitimacy, the feeling among citizens that the regime's rule is rightful and should be generally obeyed. Where legitimacy is high, governments need few police officers; where it is low, they need many. In England, for example, people are mostly law-abiding; police are few and most carry no firearms. In Northern Ireland, until recently, terrorists killed with bombs and bullets, for a portion of the population saw the government as illegitimate. Here, the police are armed, and British troops until recently patrolled with automatic weapons and armored cars. The civil war in Northern Ireland cost some 3,600 lives.

One prominent reason for an erosion of legitimacy is the regime's loss of effectiveness in running the country. Uncontrollable inflation, blatant corruption, massive unemployment, or defeat in war demonstrate that the government is ineffective.

VIOLENCE AS A SYMPTOM

Violence—riots, mass strikes, terrorist bombings, and political assassinations—by itself does not indicate that revolution is nigh. Indeed, the most common response to serious domestic unrest is not revolution at all but military takeover. Violence can be seen as symptomatic of the erosion of the government's effectiveness and legitimacy. Perhaps nothing major will come of the unrest; new leadership may calm and encourage the nation and begin to deal with the problems that caused the unrest, as Franklin D. Roosevelt did in the 1930s. But if the government is clumsy, if it tries to simply crush and silence discontent, it can make things worse. In 1932, the "Bonus Army" of World War I veterans seeking benefits to help them in the Depression was dispersed by army troops under General Douglas MacArthur. Public revulsion at the veterans' rough treatment helped turn the country decisively against President Herbert Hoover in that fall's election.

---

system breakdown   Major political malfunction or instability.

coup   From French *coup d'état*, hit at the state; extralegal takeover of government, usually by military.

Domestic violence is both deplorable and informative. It tells that not all is going well, that there are certain groups that, out of desperation or conviction, are willing to break the law in order to bring change. A government's first impulse when faced with domestic unrest is to crush it and blame a handful of "radicals and troublemakers." To be sure, instigators may deliberately provoke incidents, but the fact that some people support anti-system groups should tell the authorities that something is wrong. At the 1968 Democratic convention, Chicago police went wild in attacking those who had come to protest the Vietnam war—as well as many who just happened to be passing by. The convention ignored the protesters and nominated President Johnson's vice-president, Hubert Humphrey, who lost, largely because of his equivocal position on the war. The riot showed that the Democratic party had drifted out of touch with important elements of its constituency, which only four years earlier had voted for Johnson because he vowed to keep the country out of war. The Democrats should have been listening to instead of ignoring the protesters.

As much as we deplore violence, we have to admit that in some cases it serves a purpose. The United States as a whole and Congress in particular paid little attention to the plight of inner-city blacks until a series of riots ripped U.S. cities in the late 1960s. The death and destruction were terrible, but there seemed to be no other way to get the media's, the public's, and the government's attention. The rioting in this case "worked"; that is, it brought a major—if not very successful—effort to improve America's decaying cities. When America "forgot" about its inner cities in the 1980s, new rioting reminded us of the problems still there.

The white minority government of South Africa used to pride itself on the capture or killing of black guerrillas. The South African security forces were proficient, but the fact that thousands of young black South Africans were willing to take up arms against the whites-only regime should have told the Pretoria government something. The ruling whites-only National party had imagined for decades that blacks (75 percent of the country's population) would simply keep their place (on 13 percent of the land). Pretoria engaged in no dialogue with the country's Africans; it expected them merely to obey. Finally, growing violence persuaded the government to begin a dialogue leading to the release of Nelson Mandela from prison, the political enfranchisement of the black majority, and a government elected by all citizens.

TYPES OF VIOLENCE

Not all violence is the same. Violence has been categorized in several ways. One of the best is that of political scientist Fred R. von der Mehden, who sees five general types of violence.

Primordial Primordial violence grows out of conflicts among the basic communities—ethnic, national, or religious—into which people are born. Fighting between Armenians and Azerbaijanis in the ex-Soviet Union, Christians and Muslims in ex-Yugoslavia, the multigroup war in Lebanon, and tribal war in Rwanda

TERRORISM

The attacks of September 11 remind us that terrorism is still alive. Basically, terrorism is a strategy to weaken a hated political authority. Related to guerrilla or underground warfare, it is not a new thing. The Irish Republican Army and Internal Macedonian Revolutionary Organization (IMRO) go back more than a century. Political, ethnic, nationalistic, religious, economic, and ideological grudges fuel terrorist activity. **Terrorism** is the product of groups with grudges.

Terrorism grows mostly in countries struggling to modernize. Typically these lands in Asia, the Middle East, and Latin America are undergoing rapid change that leaves many people rootless, confused, and unemployed. The governments terrorists hate are usually corrupt and repressive. Terrorists hate the United States for supporting these governments. Terrorists, because they are fighting a more powerful foe, use tactics calculated to surprise and horrify; they put bombs in cars, trucks, and boats, and strap them on their own bodies. Before September 11, few thought of using tons of jet fuel to bring down skyscrapers. The only advice that can be given: "Expect the unexpected."

Terrorists are not insane; they are highly calculating. They aim their acts to panic their enemies, to gain publicity and recruits, and to get the foe to overreact and drive more people to side with the terrorists. Osama bin Laden and his followers were calm and rational in their pursuit of political goals that strike outsiders as mistaken and evil. "One man's terrorist," an old saying goes, "is another man's freedom fighter." Basques, Kurds, Palestinians, and Tamils desire their own state. Spain, Turkey, Israel, and Sri Lanka, respectively, do not want them to have their own state and repress their movements. Thus were born, respectively, ETA, PKK, PLO, and the Tigers. There's always a reason behind every terrorist movement. In these cases, it's national liberation.

Terrorism is group activity, the work of committed believers in political causes. Lone gunmen such as John Hinkley, who shot President Reagan, are deranged. Currently, the Middle East is the breeding ground for much terrorist activity. The reasons are both material and psychological. High birth rates have produced many unemployed youth who are attracted to the simplistic lessons of Islamic fundamentalism, which has made the United States its number-one object of hate. Al Qaeda recruited Muslims everywhere and bonded them into a religious goal, to make all Muslim countries fundamentalist, remove U.S. influence from the Middle East, and destroy Israel. Bin Laden called his terrorists "the brothers," as if they were a religious order, which they nearly were. Ultimately, only modernization of Muslim lands—something many of them resist—can solve the problem of Islamist terrorism.

All nations officially denounce terrorism but some—such as Syria, North Korea, and Iran—engage in "state-sponsored terrorism." Although unproven, the 1981 attempt to kill Pope John Paul II clearly traces back to the Kremlin. The Turkish gunman, an escaped convict, got his money, forged passport, and gun from Bulgarian security police, who were supervised by the Soviet KGB. Terrorists

(which killed some 800,000 in the late 1990s) are examples of **primordial** violence. It is not necessarily confined to the developing areas of the world, though, for such antagonisms appear in Quebec, the Basque country of Spain, and Northern Ireland, where Protestants and Catholics conducted a nearly tribal feud.

---

terrorism   Political use of violence to weaken a hated authority.
primordial   Groups people are born into, such as religions and tribes.

need bases, money, arms, and bombs, usually supplied by the intelligence services of one country that wants to undermine another.

Does terrorism work? Rarely, and seldom alone. A touch of violence on top of massive political and economic pressures persuaded whites to abandon their power monopoly in South Africa in the early 1990s. In most cases, however, especially after civilians have been killed, terrorism just stiffens the resolve of the target country. Israelis, attacked by suicide bombers, grew less willing to compromise with Palestinians. The attacks of September 11 united most Americans behind the elimination of al Qaeda and the invasion of Afghanistan and Iraq. But the U.S. occupation of Iraq fostered more terrorism and taught Washington the difficulties of building stable democracy amid chaos.

The really scary next step comes when terrorists acquire weapons of mass destruction—nukes, bugs, or gas—which they would use without hesitation. U.S. agencies, even with the new Department of Homeland Security, are not well prepared to fight terrorism. The FBI and CIA still have trouble communicating with each other. Terrorism is tricky to fight because it falls between war and crime. Like war, it has big stakes, but like crime it is extremely diffuse, more like wisps of fog. Fighting it is often presented as a "war," but that is too simple. Terrorism is not a country and cannot be invaded like one. It requires something between an army and police, such as extremely mobile SWAT teams with language skills.

Smoke from the rubble of the World Trade Center drifted over the Brooklyn Bridge in wounded New York. New York recovered; al Qaeda is still hunted.
(Pamela Roskin)

Separatist   Separatist violence—sometimes an outgrowth of primordial conflict— aims at independence for the group in question. Tamils in northern Sri Lanka have been fighting since 1983 to break away; more than 60,000 have been killed. The Ibos tried to break away from Nigeria with their new state of Biafra in the late 1960s, but they were defeated in a long and costly war. But the Bengalis did break away from Pakistan with their new state of Bangladesh in 1971. Croatia and Slovenia successfully separated from Yugoslavia in 1991. Many Iraqi Kurds want their own state, which could fuel parallel efforts among the Kurds of Turkey, Syria, and Iran.

HOW TO . . .

THINKPIECE

Sometimes instructors want you to play with ideas rather than concentrate on theses, evidence, and endnotes. They may want you to consider how logically things might unfold, to anticipate events. This is called a **thinkpiece** and is quite useful in political science, where we often lack important data but still need an informed estimate of what is likely to happen.

Thinkpieces are often justifiable because we know that many data are flawed. Statistics from the Third World are mostly guesses. Some data are partly subjective, such as the Corruption Perception Index. Top decisions are made behind closed doors, even in democracies, leaving us with anecdotal evidence about who influenced whom. All data are historical; none come from the future. How then can we discuss the possibilities for democracy in Iraq, for authoritarianism in Russia, or for Iran developing nuclear weapons? Academics who worshipped evidence were unable to anticipate the collapse of the Soviet Union. Why? Because it hadn't happened yet, so there were no data.

To counteract this kind of learned helplessness, we turn to logic and construct an "if-then" (see page 221) essay: If A is repeatedly the case, then logically A will appear in similar situations. For example: An unruly Middle Eastern country like Egypt or Syria, where rebellious groups try to overthrow the regime, requires a tough dictator; others are soon overthrown and often killed. Iraq is such a country. America wants democracy for Iraq, but logically we must doubt the likelihood of it. We have no firm data for this, just an **analogy** drawn from the pattern of the entire region.

Reasoning by analogy, of course, is often dangerous, as no two things are exactly alike. We can get into trouble with false analogies. One infamous analogy compared the giveaway of Czechoslovakia to Hitler at Munich in 1938 to the challenge we faced in Vietnam in 1965. Intelligent Americans said "No more Munichs" in plunging us into the Vietnam war. But a good thinkpiece corrects for mistaken analogies by pointing out the **dysanalogy** between the two situations.

If political scientists are unwilling to do thinkpieces, what good are we on the great questions of the day, questions for which data are missing, mistaken, or incomplete? Do we have to wait until all the facts are in before making such statements as "Israel and Iran sincerely hate each other, and Iran is building nuclear weapons; nuclear war between them is possible"? A thinkpiece is not wild speculation; it is grounded on evidence but does not shy away from carrying it to a logical outcome. Some of the most interesting political-science articles are thinkpieces.

Revolutionary   Revolutionary violence is aimed at overthrowing or replacing an existing regime, such as the Islamists (see Chapter 6) who want to take over Muslim countries and make them fundamentalist. Countries such as Algeria, Egypt, Saudi Arabia, and Pakistan are threatened by violent underground Islamist movements. The Sandinistas' ouster of Somoza in Nicaragua, the fall of the shah of Iran, both in 1979, and continuing guerrilla warfare in

---

thinkpiece   Essay based on logic rather than on firm evidence.
analogy   Taking one thing as the model for another.
dysanalogy   Showing that one thing is a poor model for another.

Colombia are examples of revolutionary violence. Until recently, Central America and southern Africa were scenes of revolutionary violence. Von der Mehden includes under this category "counterrevolutionary" violence, the efforts of conservative groups to counteract revolutionary attempts—for instance, the killings carried out by Salvadoran rightists. The attempts to crush liberalizing movements in Hungary in 1956, Czechoslovakia in 1968, and Poland in 1970 and 1980 would also come under this heading, with the ironic twist that here the Communists were the counterrevolutionary force.

Coups   Coups are usually aimed against revolution, corruption, and chaos. Coups are almost always military, although the military usually has connections with and support from key civilian groups, as in the Brazilian coup of 1964. Most coups involve little violence, at least initially. Army tanks surround the presidential palace, forcing the president's resignation and usually exile, and a general takes over as president. When the military still senses opposition, though, it can go insane with legalized murder. Some 30,000 Argentines "disappeared" following the military takeover of 1976, many dumped alive at sea for the sharks. The Chilean military killed at least 3,000 people following its 1973 coup. Since the 1954 coup, the military in little Guatemala has murdered some 200,000 on suspicion of leftism. In Latin America, the counterrevolutionary terror that follows some coups is far bloodier than anything the revolutionaries have done. Once a country has had one coup, chances are it will have another. Some countries get stuck in **praetorianism**; Pakistan has had four coups since independence in 1947, the latest in 1999. Coups generally occur because the civilian institutions of government—parties, parliaments, and executives—are weak, corrupt, and ineffective, leaving the military the choice of taking over or chaos.

Issues   Some violence does not fit any of these categories. Violence oriented to particular issues is a catchall category and generally less deadly than the other kinds. Protests against globalization, student strikes at American and French universities in the late 1960s, and riots triggered by police beating black citizens are examples of issue-oriented violence. Unemployed and hungry Brazilians sometimes loot supermarkets. French farmers burn trucks of Spanish produce, which they perceive as undercutting their livelihood. In 1976, black students in South Africa's Soweto township protested against having to learn Afrikaans in school; police shot down several hundred of them. There may be a fine line between issue-oriented violence and revolutionary violence, for if the issue is serious and the police repression brutal, protests over an issue can turn revolutionary.

All these categories—and others one might think of—are arbitrary. Some situations fit more than one category. Some start in one category and escalate into another. The complaints of ethnic Albanians in Macedonia against their second-class

---

praetorianism   From the Praetorian Guard in ancient Rome; tendency of military takeovers.

status led successively to Albanian political parties, protests, underground groups, violence, and armed rebellion to break the Albanian-majority areas away from Macedonia. No country, even a highly developed one, is totally immune to some kind of violence.

CHANGE AS A CAUSE OF VIOLENCE

Many writers find the underlying cause of domestic unrest in the changes societies go through as they modernize. Purely traditional societies with old authority patterns and simple economies are relatively untroubled by violence. People live as their ancestors lived and expect little. Likewise, modern, advanced societies with rational types of authority and productive economies have relatively minor types of violence. It is the in-between stage, when modernization is stirring and upsetting traditional societies, when violence is most likely. Such societies have left one world, that of traditional stability, but have not yet arrived at the new world of modern stability. Everything is changing in such societies—the economy, religious attitudes, lifestyle, and the political system—leaving people worried, confused, and ripe for violent actions.

Economic change can be the most unsettling. The curious thing is that improvement can be as dangerous as impoverishment. The great French social scientist Alexis de Tocqueville observed that "though the reign of Louis XVI was the most prosperous period of the monarchy, this very prosperity hastened the outbreak of the Revolution of 1789." Why should this be? When people are permanently poor and beaten down, they have no hope for the future; they are miserable but quiet. When things improve, people start imagining a better future; their aspirations are awakened. No longer content with their lot, they want improvement fast, faster than even a growing economy can deliver. Worse, during times of prosperity, some people get richer faster than others, arousing jealousy. Certain groups feel bypassed by the economic changes and turn especially bitter; the Marxists call this "class antagonisms." Revolutionary feeling, however, typically does not arise among the poor but among what Crane Brinton called the "not unprosperous people who feel restraint, cramp, annoyance" at a government that impedes their right to even faster progress.

This is an extremely delicate time in the life of a nation. Rebellion and revolution can break out. The underlying problem, as Ted Robert Gurr emphasized, is not poverty itself but **relative deprivation**. The very poor seldom revolt; they're too busy feeding their families. But once people have a full belly they start looking around and notice that some people are living much better than they. This sense of relative deprivation may spur them to anger, violence, and occasionally revolution. Gurr's findings match those of Tocqueville and Brinton: Revolutions come when things are generally getting better, not when they're getting worse.

---

relative deprivation   Feeling of some groups that they are missing out on economic growth.

KEY CONCEPTS

RISING EXPECTATIONS

One way of looking at what economic growth does to a society is to represent it graphically (see pages 286–287). Here the solid line represents actual economic change in a modernizing society—generally upward. The broken line represents people's expectations. In a still-traditional society—at the graph's left—both actual performance and expectations are low. As growth takes hold, however, expectations start rising faster than actual improvement. Then may come a situation that produces a downturn in the economy—bad harvests, a drop in the price of the leading export commodity, or too much foreign indebtedness—and expectations are frustrated. A big gap suddenly opens between what people want and what they can get. In the words of Daniel Lerner, the "want:get ratio" becomes unhinged, producing a "revolution of rising frustrations."

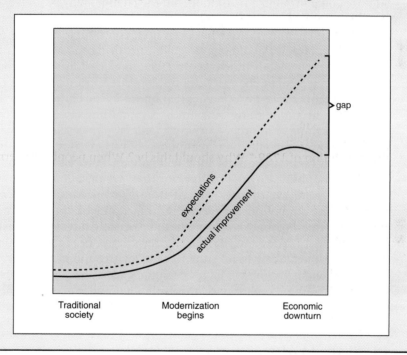

Other economic change can spur unrest. Anthropologist Eric R. Wolf argued that the shift from simple subsistence farming to cash crops dependent on markets, landlords, and bankers impoverishes many peasants and turns them from quietude to revolution. It was precisely the economic modernization of agriculture in Mexico, Russia, China, Vietnam, Algeria, and Cuba that paved the way for successful peasant-based revolutions in those countries, according to Wolf.

The political system may be out of date as well, based on inherited position with no opportunity for mass participation. As the economy improves, educational levels rise. People learn abstract ideas such as "freedom" and "democracy."

Especially among intellectuals, there is growing fury at the despotism that rules the land. Peasants may hate the system for squeezing them economically, but urban **intellectuals** hate it for suppressing rights and freedoms. It is the confluence of these two forces, argues Samuel P. Huntington—the "numbers" of the peasants and the "brains" of the intellectuals—that makes revolutions.

■ REVOLUTIONS

A **revolution** is a quick, dramatic system change that throws out the old system along with its elites. A small or moderate change that essentially leaves the system intact is reform, not revolution. Some regimes, to quiet mass discontent, claim they are going through a revolution, but the changes may be largely cosmetic. One test of whether a real revolution has occurred is to see if it has swept out old elites. If they are still in power, there has been no revolution. In a radical revolution, the new elite gets rid of the old one by guillotine, firing squad, and exile. Revolution is not necessarily bloody, however. In 1989, most East European countries underwent dramatic system change without bloodshed. (Romania was the bloody exception.) South Africa negotiated a revolution in the early 1990s.

Frustration is one thing; revolution is something else. People may be unhappy over one thing or another—peasants over crop prices, intellectuals over lack of freedom, businesspeople over corruption, and so on. But if there is no organization to focus their discontents, little will happen. Unrest and discontent by themselves will not bring down a regime; for that, organization is essential. In a study of Brazilian political attitudes, Peter McDonough and Antonio Lopez Pina found "a substantial amount of unchanneled dissatisfaction with the authoritarian regime," but it was "free-floating" resentment not especially directed against the military-run government. They suggest that "in the absence of organizational alternatives, resistance is most likely to take the form of apathy and indifference."

The previous factors we have considered may point to violence—rioting and strikes—but without organization they will not produce a revolution. Who provides the organization? For this we turn to the role of intellectuals.

INTELLECTUALS AND REVOLUTION

Intellectuals are nearly everywhere discontent with the existing state of affairs because they are highly educated and acquainted with a variety of ideas, some of them **utopian**. Preachers, teachers, lawyers, journalists, and others who deal with ideas often have a professional stake in criticizing the system. If everything were fine, there would be little to talk or write about. Intellectuals, although sometimes

---

intellectuals   Educated people who think deeply about things.
revolution   Sudden replacement of an old system by a new one.
utopia   An imagined and idealized perfect system.

REVOLUTIONARY POLITICAL WARFARE IN VIETNAM

Many people speak of "guerrilla warfare," but this is a misnomer and a redundancy, for *guerrilla* is simply Spanish for "little war," what Spaniards practiced against Napoleon. It is not really about ambushes and booby traps but the accompanying political action. The two combined equal revolutionary political warfare, which Bernard Fall described as the struggle "to establish a competitive system of control over the population." Fall, an expert on Vietnam who died when he stepped on a land mine there in 1967, emphasized *administration* as the crux of revolutionary warfare. "When a country is being subverted it is not being outfought; it is being outadministered. Subversion is literally administration with a minus sign in front."

Fall discovered, both under the French in North Vietnam during the early 1950s and under the Americans in South Vietnam during the early 1960s, that the Communists were collecting taxes throughout most of the country under the very noses of the regimes they were overthrowing. The occupying power, whether French or American, deceived itself by being able to drive through villages in armored convoys; this does not indicate administrative control, which may be in the hands of the insurgents. The emphasis on military hardware is a big mistake, argued Fall, for it detracts from the administrative element.

The Vietnamese insurgents were able to outadminister the regime for several reasons. In the first place, they were able to identify closely with the population, something the French and Americans could never do. Indeed, the fact that the anti-Communist side in both Vietnam wars was connected with white foreigners gave the kiss of death to the effort. There was no political package the French or Americans could sell to the locals. Even the Saigon rulers lacked legitimacy among their countrymen. The Diem and subsequent Saigon governments were run by Central and North Vietnamese urban Catholics who disliked the largely Buddhist rural South Vietnamese. The Saigon officials were city dwellers who disdained assignments in the provinces and working with the peasants, which was precisely the Communists' strong point.

Terror, to be sure, plays a role in revolutionary political warfare. The Vietcong murdered many Saigon officials and government-appointed village headmen. But the villagers were not uniformly horrified at such terror because it was selective and targeted at people who were outsiders anyway. To many peasants, the Vietcong executions seemed like extralegal punishment for collaborators. When the Americans made whole villages disappear, that was terror. There's nothing selective about napalm.

While the insurgent is patiently building a network to supplant the regime, the occupier or government is impatiently trying to substitute firepower for legitimacy. The killing of civilians produces more sympathizers and recruits for the guerrillas. The government's overreliance on firepower erodes its tenuous moral claims to leadership of the nation. Some critics wonder if the American people and leadership ever understood what we were up against in Vietnam. We fought a military war while our opponents fought a political war, and in the end the political mattered more than the military. Said one American officer as he surveyed the smoking ruins of a village, "Unfortunately, we had to destroy the village in order to save it."

better-off, are seldom wealthy. They may resent people who are richer but not as smart—businesspeople and government officials.

Such factors predispose some intellectuals—but by no means all or even a majority—to develop what James Billington called a "revolutionary faith" that the current system can be replaced with something much better. According to

Billington, revolution begins with this "fire in the minds of men." Common folk, ordinary workers and peasants, are seldom interested in abstract ideologies (see Chapter 6); they want improved material conditions. It is the intellectuals' idealistic convictions that provide revolutionary movements with the cement that holds them together, the goals they aim for, and a leadership stratum.

Most twentieth-century revolutionary movements were founded and led by educated people. Lenin, son of a provincial education official, was a brilliant law graduate. Mao Zedong helped found the Chinese Communist party while a library assistant at the Beijing National University. Fidel Castro and most of his original guerrilla fighters were law-school graduates. One of them, however—the famous Che Guevara, who was killed in 1967 while trying to foment revolution in Bolivia—was a medical doctor. The leader of Peru's Shining Path guerrillas was a philosophy professor. The leaders of Iran's revolution against the shah were either religious or academically trained intellectuals.

THE STAGES OF REVOLUTION

In his 1938 classic book, *The Anatomy of Revolution*, Harvard historian Crane Brinton developed a theory that all revolutions pass through similar stages, rather like a human body passing through the stages of an illness. In the English revolution of the 1640s, the American Revolution of 1776, the French Revolution of 1789, and the Russian Revolution of 1917, Brinton found the following rough uniformities.

The Old Regime Decays   Administration breaks down and taxes rise. People no longer believe in the government; in fact, the government doubts itself. Intellectuals transfer their allegiance from the regime to a proposed idealized system. All this is happening while the economy is generally on the upgrade, but this provokes discontent and jealousy.

The First Stage of Revolution   Committees, networks, cells, or conspiracies form, dedicated to overthrowing the old regime. People refuse to pay taxes. A political impasse arises that cannot be solved because the lines are too deeply drawn. The government calls in troops, which backfires because the troops desert and the people are further enraged. The initial seizure of power is easy, for the old regime has effectively put itself out of business. Popular exultation breaks out.

At First, the Moderates Take Over   People who opposed the old regime but were still connected with it by dint of background or training assume command. They initiate moderate, unradical reforms, which are not enough for extremists among the revolutionaries; they accuse the moderates of cowardice and of compromising with the forces of the old regime. The moderates are "nice guys" and not ruthless enough to crush the radicals, who exist side-by-side with the moderates in a sort of parallel government.

CASE STUDIES

THE IRANIAN REVOLUTIONARY CYCLE

The Iranian revolution closely followed Brinton's pattern. The Iranian economy boomed, especially with the quadrupling of oil prices in 1973–1974, but economic growth was uneven. Some people got rich fast, provoking jealousy. Corruption and inflation soared. Many educated Iranians opposed the shah's dictatorship; students especially hated the **shah** for his repression of freedoms. Networks of conspirators formed, rallying around the figure of exiled **Ayatollah** Khomeini and using mosques as their meeting places. Major riots broke out in 1978, but the use of troops to quell riots simply enraged more Iranians. Troops began to desert. Always disdainful of democracy and mass participation in politics, the shah had relied on his dreaded SAVAK secret police, but even they could no longer contain the revolution. In January 1979, the shah left and Khomeini returned to Iran.

Before he left, the shah named a moderate revolutionary, Bakhtiar, to head the government. But the very fact of being chosen by the shah ruined Bakhtiar, and the newly returned ayatollah, who instantly became the de facto power in Iran, replaced him with Bazargan, another moderate, but one never connected with the shah. Bazargan's government didn't count for much, though, because real power resided with Khomeini's Revolutionary Council. In November 1979, radical Islamic students, angered over the shah's admission into the United States, seized the U.S. Embassy and began the famous "hostage crisis" that lasted over a year. Bazargan, realizing he was powerless, resigned.

Muslim extremists devoted to Khomeini took over and purged anyone they did not control. Firing squads worked overtime to eliminate suspected "bad" people, including fellow revolutionaries who had deviated. Tens of thousands of young Iranians, promised instant admission to heaven, threw their lives away in repelling Iraqi invaders. Strict Islamic standards of morality were enforced—no alcohol or drugs, veils for women, and suppression of non-Islamic religions. After Khomeini died in 1989, the Iranian revolution gradually calmed and stabilized. There was not one single event to mark a Thermidor, but in 1997 a moderate, Mohammed Khatami, won the presidency in a landslide with promises of greater freedom and economic improvement. Khatami's reforms were blocked because real power stayed in the hands of the religious elite, which many Iranians now hate. We may not have seen the last upheaval in Iran.

The Extremists Take Over   More ruthless and better organized than the moderates, knowing exactly what they want, the extremists overthrow the moderates and drive the revolution to a frenzied high point. Everything old is thrown out. People are required to be "good" and obey the new, idealistic society the extremists construct. "Bad" people are punished in a reign of terror. Even revolutionary comrades who are deemed to have strayed from the true path are executed: "The revolution devours its children." The entire society appears to go mad in what Brinton likened to a high fever during an illness.

---

shah   Persian for king.
ayatollah   Top cleric in Shia Islam.

A "Thermidor" Ends the Reign of Terror   Eventually the society can take no more revolution. People, even revolutionaries, become exhausted from the frenzy and long to settle down, get the economy working again, and enjoy some personal security and pleasure. Then comes a **Thermidor**—so named after the French revolutionary month during which the extremist Robespierre was guillotined—which Brinton described as a convalescence after a fever. Often a dictator, who ends up resembling the tyrants of the old regime, takes over to restore order, something most people welcome.

■ AFTER THE REVOLUTION

Revolutions show a persistent tendency to overthrow one form of tyranny only to replace it with another. In little more than a decade, the French kings had been replaced by Napoleon, who crowned himself emperor and supervised a police state far more thorough than anything previous. The partial despotism of the tsars was replaced by the perfect despotism of Stalin. Russian life was freer and economic growth faster at the turn of the twentieth century under the inefficient tsarist system than under the Communists. Fidel Castro threw out the crooked Batista regime, and Cuban freedom and economic growth declined abruptly.

What good are revolutions? One is tempted to despair with Simon Bolivar, the liberator of South America, who said, "He who aids a revolution plows the sea." In general, revolutions end badly. (As soon as you can accept that statement, you have become to some degree a conservative.)

But what about the United States? We call our 1776–1781 struggle with Britain the Revolutionary War. Some say it was not really a revolution, for it did not remake American society. Indeed, some of its greatest leaders were wealthy and prominent figures in colonial society. They wanted simply to get rid of British rule but keep their elite positions. The American struggle was more a war of independence than a revolution, some argue, and extremists never seized control. Others point out that there was a great deal of revolutionary violence, directed especially at America's Tories, colonials who remained pro-British. Some 100,000 fled in fear to lands the Crown gave them in Canada.

The late, great Hannah Arendt also believed the American struggle was indeed a revolution, perhaps history's only complete revolution, for it alone ended with a new foundation of liberty instead of the tyranny of other revolutions. According to Arendt, American revolutionaries were fortunate in that they did not have to wrestle with the difficult "social question" that obsessed the French revolutionaries. America was prosperous, and wealth was distributed rather equally. The American struggle was not sidetracked by the poverty problem, so it could focus on establishing a just and durable constitution with balanced powers and political freedom. It was the genius—or, in part, luck—of the American Revolution that it was a purely *political* and not a social matter. America needed no guillotine, for

---

Thermidor   Summer month of French revolutionary calendar that marked end of revolutionary extremism.

"Albanians are revolutionary heroes" is the message of this mural facing Tirana's main square. The mural tries to foster the feeling that Albanian history is a steady march to communism. (Michael Roskin)

there was no aristocratic class to behead. It needed no demagogues of the Robespierre stripe because there was no rabble to rouse. The French Revolution, trying to correct social injustice, became a bloody mess that ended in dictatorship. In Arendt's terms, it was not a successful revolution because it did not end with the constituting of liberty, as the American Revolution did.

In France, the Revolution is controversial more than two centuries after it occurred. Few celebrate it uncritically, and many French conservatives hate it. Most French people are proud of its original idealistic impulses—"liberty, equality, fraternity"—but many admit that it went wrong, that it turned to bloodshed and dictatorship. The big question here is whether this was an accident—the Revolution fell into the hands of extremists and fanatics—or whether there was something built into the revolutionary process that made breakdown inevitable. Most serious scholars now argue for the inevitability thesis.

In Russia, this question is asked about the 1917 Bolshevik Revolution. Lenin, an intelligent and sophisticated man, died in 1924. Had he lived, would communism have taken a more humane and less brutal path? Stalin, in the view of some diehard socialists, was the culprit who betrayed the revolution by turning it into his personal dictatorship. More recent scholarship has shown that Lenin was ruthless and willing to exterminate all opposition; there was nothing moderate or humane about him. Many Russians are now willing to admit that Lenin was wrong from the start.

CASE STUDIES

ANTI-COMMUNIST REVOLUTIONS

One of the more interesting phenomena of the late twentieth century was the revolution *against* communism. Communist regimes long claimed for themselves the title "revolutionary" and denounced as "reactionary" anyone against them. But if, as we argued, revolution means sweeping system change, especially the ouster of the ruling elite, the overthrow of Communist regimes was also revolutionary.

The impulse to revolution in Communist systems is the same as in other systems: injustice and poverty. Promised a socialist utopia for generations, workers tired of the failure to deliver. Actually, Soviets generally enjoyed rising living standards, but their expectations, fanned by the party propaganda line, rose faster. A really explosive element was jealousy. Soviets were aware that the privileged party elite enjoyed special apartments, food shops, medical care, and vacation cottages. They were also aware that much of the consumer economy ran on the basis of corruption. Desirable products never made it to the store shelf; they were sold through the back door for big profits. The same resentments that smoldered in non-Communist countries smoldered in Communist countries.

As in earlier revolutions, the most dangerous time in the life of a Communist regime was when it tried to reform itself. Reform in Communist countries was as difficult as in non-Communist countries, for Communist elites also had a lot to lose in terms of power and privilege. In their system, the Communist party elite became the conservatives who lived well and were in a position to block reforms. When conditions so deteriorated that reform had to come, it was too late. Things were bad in the Soviet Union under Brezhnev, but mass unrest came only when Gorbachev instituted major reforms. By admitting that things were wrong, he gave the green light to restive workers and nationalities to demand more than any had dared mention a few years earlier. By asking for support and patience, Gorbachev also showed he was running scared, a further incitement to revolution. By letting in more Western media, he showed the Soviets how well Americans and West Europeans lived. Soon the pressure for massive change became explosive.

Halfway reform does not suffice and often makes things worse. The Communist regimes of Eastern Europe tried to calm their angry people by promising reform and bringing in fresh, new leadership. But most East European citizens were not fooled; they recognized that the reforms would basically leave defective systems intact and that the new leaders were simply party bigshots intent on staying in power. In Czechoslovakia in 1989, for example, the rapidly growing Civic Forum movement hooted down a new cabinet that the frightened Communist regime presented. The "new" cabinet, still dominated by Communists, looked pretty much like the old one. After massive street protest, Civic Forum won a cabinet of non-Communists, some of whom had been in jail only two weeks earlier. This was what Czech President Vaclav Havel called the "velvet revolution." When an unpopular regime begins by offering "reforms," it may end by putting itself out of business.

THE WANING OF REVOLUTION

Revolution, although popular in the 1960s, developed a bad reputation in the 1970s. By the 1980s, many radical countries were trying to back out of their revolutionary systems. There were simply no positive examples of revolutions that had worked out well. The Soviet Union and China, earlier the models for many

Faced with this prospect, some regimes attempt to crush mass demands with military force. An example is the bloody 1989 crackdown in China. Hundreds of protesting students were gunned down in Beijing's Tiananmen Square because an elderly party elite feared what they called a "counterrevolutionary revolt." Deng Xiaoping had attempted halfway reform only to find that it would not stay halfway. Partial reform of a corrupt dictatorship is impossible because as soon as you let people criticize it, they demand to replace it. Give them a free-speech inch and they want a democratic mile. That, of course, would mean ouster of the Communist elite, which then fights tenaciously for its power and privileges. But by digging in their heels and refusing to institute major reform, the party elite just builds up a head of steam for a later and greater explosion. They can crush political opponents, but they cannot produce the economic growth necessary to feed and house their people, who just get angrier. Ironically, Communist countries indeed led the way to revolution.

The secret police headquarters in Moscow was, until 1991, presided over by this statue of the KGB's founder, Felix Dzerdzinsky. Three months after this photo was taken, a mob tore down the statue. (Michael Roskin)

revolutionaries, admitted that they were in economic difficulty and tried to change to a more open, market system. In 1989 the Communist lands of Eastern Europe simply walked away from communism. Then communism collapsed in the Soviet Union in late 1991. In Africa, the revolutionary Communist lands of Angola, Mozambique, and Ethiopia liberalized and begged for aid from the capitalist West.

The worst revolutionary horror was Cambodia. In the late 1970s, the Khmer Rouge (Red Cambodia) murdered an estimated 1.7 million of their fellow citizens. The nonfiction movie about this bloodbath, *The Killing Fields,* shocked the world. And Vietnam, united by the Communists in 1975 after its fierce war with the United States, turned itself into one of the poorest countries in the world. Tens of thousands of Vietnamese "boat people" risked the open sea and Thai pirates to leave their starving land. Sadly, few countries wanted them. In 1995, Vietnam and the United States established diplomatic relations, and the Vietnamese economy turned to the world market. In Cuba, Fidel Castro continues to proclaim his regime revolutionary, but most Cubans have long since tired of the shortages and restrictions. And in Nicaragua, a free election in 1990 voted out the revolutionary Sandinistas and replaced them with a democratic coalition.

Currently, there are few major revolutionary movements in operation. In Colombia, Marxist armies, funded by the cocaine trade, wage guerrilla warfare and terrorism. In Algeria, Egypt, and Saudi Arabia, Islamists bomb and assassinate in an effort to overthrow corrupt authoritarian governments. Islamists are motivated by great passion and a burning sense of injustice but have only illusions about what is to come next.

Notice the difference between countries where revolution has triumphed and where it is still being fought. The former is characterized by disillusionment and bitterness; many people would like to get rid of the revolutionary regime. The latter movements are still idealistic and convinced they will bring a better society. Revolutions are based on the belief that by seizing state power, a truly committed regime can redo society, making it just, fair, and prosperous. This feeling grows in societies that are unjust and miserable. But after seizing power, the revolutionary regime discovers it's a lot harder to make an economy work than they thought. For decades they blame capitalist holdouts and imperialist saboteurs. To control these alleged plotters, they give themselves draconian police powers to stamp out private industry and criticism.

But things get worse. Farmers do not plant unless they get a decent price for their crops. Workers do not work without something to buy. Reluctant to admit they are mistaken after having killed so many people, the revolutionary regime locks itself into power through police controls. After some time of hardship and poor growth, a new generation may come to power and admit that the system needs to loosen up. Embarrassment may be a factor here. Comparing themselves with free countries, the revolutionary country sees itself falling behind. The Chinese could note with regret that on China's rim—in Singapore, Hong Kong, and Taiwan—Chinese were prosperous, but not in China. Under Deng Xiaoping, China turned (incompletely) to capitalist industry and foreign investment. The great revolution had failed.

It takes large-scale revolutionary experiences to demonstrate that revolutions end badly. The revolutionary promise is golden; the revolutionary results are mud. If you don't see it, you don't believe it. With several revolutionary experiences to ponder, many would-be revolutionaries turned away from revolution. This helps explain why the 1980s was a conservative decade: It could look back and survey the results of the 1960s. By the 1990s, only groups like al Qaeda wanted revolution.

The crux of revolutionary thinking is that it is possible to remake society. Without that, few would make revolutions. With the discovery that remaking society leads to terrible difficulties and poor results, the revolutionary dream dies. Does this mean that we will not see another major wave of revolutions? Not necessarily. There is plenty of injustice in the world, and this brings rage. Rage, as Hannah Arendt pointed out, leads to revolution. The greatest rage is now found among Muslims.

What can be done to head off revolutions? The answer is simple but difficult to carry out: reforms to end the injustices that revolutions feed on. Land reform in Peru and the Philippines, elected parliaments in Persian Gulf lands, and jobs in Algeria and Egypt could dampen or even end revolutionary movements in these countries. But landowners are not about to give up their holdings, and they are politically powerful. The rulers around the Persian Gulf fear the loss of their wealth and power if they democratize, and they have a good argument that liberalizing at this time would just let radicals take over. If Saudi Arabia held free and fair elections, someone like Osama bin Laden would likely win. The solution: slow and gradual reform.

The "socialist" governments of North Africa hate to admit that corrupt bureaucracies strangle economic growth. In practice, reforms are hard to apply because there is strong resistance from the class in power that has much to lose. In South Vietnam, for example, the United States urged the Saigon regime to carry out sweeping land reform to win the peasants away from the Communist guerrillas. But landowners, many of whom collected exorbitant rents from tenant farmers, blocked land-reform bills. If they had given up their land, they might have saved their country; instead, they lost both. The message is to institute reforms before revolutionary feeling is implanted, to head off the problem before it becomes dangerous.

KEY TERMS

analogy (p. 360)

Ayatollah (p. 367)

coup (p. 356)

dysanalogy (p. 360)

intellectual (p. 364)

praetorianism (p. 361)

primordial (p. 358)

relative deprivation (p. 362)

revolution (p. 364)

shah (p. 367)

system breakdown (p. 356)

terrorism (p. 358)

Thermidor (p. 368)

thinkpiece (p. 360)

utopia (p. 364)

KEY WEB SITES

Terrorism
nsi.org/Terrorism.html

American Revolution
www.historyplace.com/unitedstates/revolution/index.html

South Africa
www.southafrica.net/government/history/default.html

Genocide
web.inter.nl.net/users/Paul.Treanor/genocide/html

FURTHER REFERENCE

Bell-Fialkoff, Andrew. *Ethnic Cleansing.* New York: St. Martin's, 1996.

Diamond, Larry, and Marc F. Plattner, eds. *Nationalism, Ethnic Conflict, and Democracy.* Baltimore, MD: Johns Hopkins University Press, 1994.

Goldstone, Jack, ed. *The Encyclopedia of Political Revolutions.* Washington, D.C.: CQ Press, 1998.

Greene, Thomas H. *Comparative Revolutionary Movements,* 3rd ed. Englewood Cliffs, NJ: Prentice Hall, 1990.

Halliday, Fred. *Revolution and World Politics: The Rise and Fall of the Sixth Great Power.* Durham, NC: Duke University Press, 1999.

Heymann, Philip B. *Terrorism, Freedom, and Security: Winning Without War.* New York: Cambridge University Press, 2003.

Katz, Mark N., ed. *Revolution: International Dimensions.* Washington, D.C.: CQ Press, 2000.

Laqueur, Walter. *No End to War: Terrorism in the Twenty-First Century.* New York: Continuum, 2004.

Linz, Juan J. and Alfred Stepan, eds. *The Breakdown of Democratic Regimes.* Baltimore, MD: Johns Hopkins University Press, 1978.

Parsa, Misagh. *States, Ideologies, and Social Revolutions: A Comparative Analysis of Iran, Nicaragua, and the Philippines.* New York: Cambridge University Press, 2000.

Rapoport, David C., and Leonard Weinberg, eds. *The Democratic Experience and Political Violence.* Portland, OR: Frank Cass, 2001.

Snow, Donald M. *Distant Thunder: Patterns of Conflict in the Developing World,* 2nd ed. Armonk, NY: M. E. Sharpe, 1997.

CHAPTER 20

INTERNATIONAL RELATIONS

QUESTIONS TO CONSIDER

- How do domestic and international politics differ?
- Why does "power" loom so large in international relations?
- What are the several types of national interest?
- Which theory of war is the most satisfactory?
- Are democracy and peace related? How?
- Is there any effective way to prevent war?
- What was the Cold War? Why did it begin and end?
- What is the crux of deterrence? Did it work?
- What is Paul Kennedy's theory of "imperial overstretch"?
- Which supranational organizations do the most good?

International politics differs from the domestic politics we have been studying, because there is no world sovereign power over the nations to get them to obey laws and preserve peace. Compared to **domestic politics**, **international politics** is wilder and more complex. Sovereignty, as considered in Chapter 1, means being boss on your own turf, the last legal word within a country. The concept grew up in the sixteenth century, when absolutist monarchs were strengthening their positions and sought legal justification for it. Sovereignty is the dominant force within a country. Criminals, rebels, and breakaway elements are, in theory, controlled or crushed by the sovereign, who now, of course, is no longer a king or queen but the national government. Sovereignty also means that foreign powers have no business intruding into your country's affairs; their reach—again in theory—stops at your borders.

---

domestic politics   Interactions within states.
international politics   Interactions among states.

So much for theory. In practice, nothing is so clear-cut. Just because a nation is legally sovereign does not necessarily mean it really controls its own turf. Witness Iraq recently: conquered in a quick 2003 war, then occupied by foreign troops (mostly U.S., some British and others), its weak government propped up by friendly forces, and unable to stop violence by terrorists and militias. It was a stretch to call Iraq "sovereign" after the official handover of sovereignty in the middle of 2004. The opposite of Iraq is Western Europe's peaceful coming together in what earlier had been known as the Common Market but is now the European Union (EU). Its members had agreed to give up some of their sovereignty in order to form an economic and political union, which, if fully implemented, will mean a transfer of sovereignty from individual members to the EU headquarters in Brussels. Sovereignty is not a simple yes or no but a question of degree.

Further, the idea that sovereignty precludes outside intervention doesn't hold up. Small, poor countries are routinely dominated and influenced by larger and more powerful countries. Afghanistan in the 1980s could scarcely be said to be sovereign under Soviet occupation, nor could the small countries of Central America under the watchful eye of the United States. Some Canadians claim U.S. economic and cultural penetration erodes their sovereignty. What meaning has sovereignty in a "failed state" that cannot govern anything?

Still, the term sovereignty has some utility. Where established, national sovereignty does indeed bring internal peace, and most countries can claim to have done this. In dealing with other nations, countries still mostly do what they want. When France resumed nuclear testing in the South Pacific in 1995, there was nothing Australia and New Zealand could do to stop it, although they protested strongly. France did what it wished on islands that were its sovereign territory. When the United States urged the economic isolation of Iran, most of the world ignored the call and made trade and oil deals with Tehran. Congress passed laws threatening legal trouble for foreign firms that did business with Cuba and Libya, but other governments pointed out that the U.S. Congress cannot pass laws for other countries; they ignored the U.S. prohibitions and traded with whom they pleased. Most countries signed treaties to combat global warming, land mines, germ warfare, and exporting weapons, but not the United States, which claimed the treaties were flawed and we had a sovereign right to ignore them. There was no way to make the big, powerful United States conform to these treaties.

Within a sovereign entity there is—or at least there is supposed to be—law. If you have a grievance against someone, you do not take the law into your own hands. You take the person to court. In international relations, nearly the opposite applies: Taking the law into your own hands—by the threat or use of military force—is quite normal. Often there is no other recourse.

This important difference between domestic and international politics sometimes exasperates skilled practitioners of one when they enter the realm of the other. President Johnson was a master of domestic politics; whatever he wanted from Congress he got. But he could not make skinny little Ho Chi Minh back down, for Ho was boss on *his* own turf, Vietnam. What worked domestically for Johnson— deals, threats, persuasion—flopped internationally. Some suggest that it was Nixon's use of the "dirty tricks" of international politics in domestic politics that launched the Watergate scandal and his resignation. Nixon was a clever statesman; he simultaneously improved ties with the Soviet Union and China. But his deviousness and penchant for secrecy tripped him up in a delicate domestic problem. International politics is not just domestic politics on a grander scale.

■ POWER AND NATIONAL INTEREST

Lacking the sovereignty that prevails in most domestic situations, international relations depend a lot on power. Hans Morgenthau held that power is the basic element of international politics and that idealists ignore it at their peril. Without sufficient power, a country cannot survive, let alone prevail, in a tumultuous world. Power is not necessarily evil or aggressive; it may be simply persuading an aggressor to "Leave me alone!"

Power is not the same as force. Force is the specific application of military might; power (recalling our definition from Chapter 1) is a country's more general ability to get its way. Power includes military, economic, political, and psychological factors. The best kind of power: rational persuasion. Power is tricky to calculate. Whole departments of the CIA spend millions trying to figure out how much power various countries have. Some elements of power—such as a country's geography, natural resources, population, and economy—are tangible or calculable. Some of the most important factors, however—such as a country's military capability, the quality of its political system, and its psychological determination—cannot be learned until it is involved in a war. The war then provides—at a terrible price—the answer about which side had more power.

In this situation, countries generally pursue their **national interest**. This makes international politics inherently selfish; nations rarely behave like saints. Countries may practice generosity and altruism, but often with an eye to enhancing their international power and prestige. The world did little to staunch the horrible bloodletting in Rwanda and the Congo in the 1990s; over two million died from gunshots, machetes, or starvation. The region was out of the way and had little strategic or economic value. Only France sent some peacekeeping forces, because France wishes to portray itself as the dominant and protecting power of Central Africa, where it has strong economic ties.

Anticipating how another country will define its national interest is often hard. They see things through different eyes. Hungary in the 1990s was very cooperative with the West and eager to join NATO. In 1994, however, when the United States and France proposed air strikes to curb Serbian artillery atrocities in Bosnia, Hungary stopped the U.S. use of its territory for observation flights. An American looking at this refusal is puzzled: "But don't they want to be on our team?" A Hungarian looking at the refusal says, "We'll have to live with the Serbs for centuries;

---

national interest   What's good for the nation as a whole in world affairs.

TYPES OF NATIONAL INTEREST

National interests may be divided into the following four categories (which are discussed at length below):

1. vital versus secondary;
2. temporary versus permanent;
3. specific versus general;
4. complementary versus conflicting.

A vital interest is one that potentially threatens the life of your nation, such as Soviet missiles in Cuba. When a country perceives a threat to its vital interests, it may go to war. A secondary interest is usually more distant and less urgent. The United States, for example, has an interest in an open world oil supply, with no nation restricting or controlling it. Nations are more inclined to negotiate and compromise over their secondary interests, although military action may become necessary, as against Iraq in 1991.

When nations have some important goals in common, their interests are "complementary." Many nations saw their national interests as complementary during the 1991 Gulf War; several Arab countries sided with the West. Complementary interests are what make alliances. When interests conflict, as when a new Madrid government saw no Spanish national interest in keeping its small peacekeeping force in Iraq in 2004, countries pull apart.

A temporary interest is one of fixed duration, as in U.S. support for Iraq during its 1980s war with Iran. U.S. diplomacy had trouble understanding that as soon as that war was over, their complementary interests receded. A permanent interest lasts over centuries, as in the U.S. interest in keeping hostile powers out of the Western hemisphere.

A specific interest focuses on a single problem, such as Japanese trade barriers to U.S. goods. A general interest might be universal respect for human rights.

Two countries, even allies, seldom have identical national interests. The best one can hope for is that their interests will be complementary. The United States and Albania, for instance, may have a common interest in opposing Serbian crushing of ethnic Albanians in neighboring lands, but the U.S. interest is a general, temporary, and secondary one concerning human rights and regional stability. The Albanian interest is a specific, permanent, and possibly vital one of forming a Greater Albania that would include Kosovo and parts of Macedonia. Our interests may run parallel for a time, but we must never mistake Albanian interests for U.S. interests.

that border is a vital, permanent interest for us. Some 400,000 ethnic Hungarians live under Serbian control in Voivodina as virtual hostages. The Americans offer no guarantees of protection, but they expect us to join them in an act of war. Sorry, not a good deal." (The flights were quickly restored as the crisis passed.)

The diplomat's work is in finding and developing complementary interests so that two or more countries can work together. (Better diplomatic spadework would have signaled in advance the difference between Hungarian and U.S. interests in 1994.) Often countries have some interests that are complementary and others that are conflicting, as when NATO members cooperated to block the Soviet threat but clashed over who was to lead the alliance. The French-U.S. relationship can be described in this way. Where interests totally conflict, of course, there can be no cooperation. Here it is the diplomat's duty to say so and find ways to minimize the damage. Do not despair in this situation; national interests can shift, and today's adversary may be tomorrow's ally. Few would have guessed in the 1960s that China would be a U.S. friend in the 1970s, a condition that did not last into the 1990s. The 2001 attacks on the United States showed Washington and Moscow that they had common interests in fighting Islamist terrorists, but this did not carry over into the 2003 Iraq War, which Moscow opposed. We cannot define other countries' national interests for them.

Defining the national interest in any given situation may be difficult. Intelligent, well-informed people may come up with opposite definitions of the national interest. Hawks in the 1960s, for example, claimed a Communist victory in Southeast Asia would destabilize U.S. strategic, economic, and political interests. Others claimed Vietnam was a distant swamp of no importance to us. Neoconservatives in the Bush 43 administration claimed taking out Saddam Hussein in Iraq was urgent, to prevent him from building **weapons of mass destruction (WMD)**. Critics countered that it was an unnecessary war. How can you tell when a genuine national interest is at stake?

Feasibility is linked to national interest; power is the connecting link. An infeasible strategy—where your power is insufficient to carry out your designs—is inherently a bad strategy. If the type of power is wrong for the setting (for example, helicopters and artillery to counter Iraqi terrorists; air power to stop a civil war), you are undertaking an infeasible strategy.

■ THE ROLE OF ELITES

Nowhere are elites (see Chapter 5) more important than in international relations. The foreign policy of a country is inherently an elite game, however much we may dislike it. Unless there's a war or major threat, most people pay little or no attention to foreign policy, which, until 9/11, was nearly absent in U.S. elections. In a democracy the masses may influence foreign policy—as angry Americans did over the Vietnam and Iraq wars—but only long after the basic decisions have been made, usually in secrecy. Some suggest that foreign-policy decisions, even in democratic nations, are made by not much more than a dozen people. Notice how even in the United States, presidents and a few advisors make foreign policy and then announce it to the American people and Congress, which usually goes along with it. In late 2001 President Bush decided to invade Iraq, but only a few knew.

---

weapons of mass destruction (WMD)   Nuclear, chemical, and bacteriological weapons.

KEY CONCEPTS

Why War?

Much has been written on why there is war. Most thinkers agree that war has many causes, not just one. Very broadly, though, theories on the cause of war are divided into two general camps, the micro and the macro—the little, close-up picture as opposed to the big, panoramic picture.

Micro Theories

Micro theories are rooted in biology and psychology. They might attempt to explain war as the result of genetic human aggressiveness. Millions of years of evolution have made people fighters—to obtain food, defend their families, and guard their territory. In this, humans are no different from many animals. Most anthropologists reject such biological determinism, arguing that primitive peoples exhibit a wide variety of behavior—some are aggressive and some not—that can be explained only by culture, learned behavior. Writers with a psychological orientation explore the personalities of leaders, what made them that way, and how they obtained their hold over the masses and brought them to war.

Biological and psychological theories offer some insights but fall far short of explaining wars. If humans are naturally aggressive, why aren't all nations constantly at war? How is it that countries can fight a long series of wars—the Russian-Turkish struggle around the Black Sea or the Arab-Israeli wars—under different leaders who surely must have been psychologically distinct? Biological and psychological approaches may offer insights into some of the *underlying* causes of war but not the immediate causes. There is a certain human aggressiveness, but under what circumstances does it come out? For this we turn to macro theories.

Macro Theories

Macro theories are rooted in history and political science. They concentrate on the power and ambitions of states. States, not individuals, are the key actors. Where they can, states expand, as in the Germans' medieval push to the east, the Americans' "manifest destiny," the growth of the British empire, and the Soviets' takeover of Eastern Europe. Only countervailing power may stop the drive to expand. One country, fearing the growth of a neighbor, will strengthen its defenses or form alliances to offset the neighbor's power. Much international behavior can be explained by the aphorisms *Si vis pacem para bellum* ("If you want peace, prepare for war") and "The enemy of my enemy is my friend." Political leaders have an almost automatic feel for national interest and power and move to enhance them. Does the pursuit of power lead to war or peace? Again, there are two broad theories.

Balance of Power   The oldest and most commonly held theory is that peace results when several states, improving their national power and forming alliances, balance one another. Would-be expansionists are blocked. According to balance-of-power theorists, the great periods of relative peace—between the Peace of Westphalia in 1648 and the wars that grew out of the French Revolution (1792–1814), and again from 1815 to the start of World War I in 1914—have been times when the European powers balanced each other. When the balances broke down, there was war.

---

micro theories   Focus on individuals.
macro theories   Focus on nations and history.

Fighting in Bosnia calmed in 1995 only after power there roughly balanced. When the Serbs were ahead, they had no motive to settle; when they were on the defensive, they decided to stop the fighting. Many thinkers consider the Cold War a big and durable balance-of-power system that explains why there was relative peace—at least no World War III—for more than four decades.

Hierarchy of Power   Other analysts reject the balance-of-power theory. First, because calculations of power are so problematic, it is impossible to know when power balances. Second, the periods of peace, some writers note, occurred when power was out of balance, when states were ranked hierarchically in terms of power. Then every nation knew where it stood on sort of a ladder of relative power. It is in times of transition, when the power hierarchy is blurred, that countries are tempted to go to war. After a big war with a definitive outcome, there is peace because then relative power is clearly known. If this theory is correct, then trying to achieve an accurate balance of power is the wrong thing to do; it will lead to war because the participating states will think they have a good chance to win.

Misperception

Weaving micro and macro approaches together, some thinkers focus on "image" or "perception" as the key to war. Both psychological and power approaches contribute something but are incomplete. It's not the real situation (which is hard to know) but what leaders perceive that makes them decide for war or peace. They often misperceive, seeing hostility and development of superior weaponry in another country, which sees itself as acting defensively and as just trying to catch up in weaponry.

John F. Kennedy portrayed the Soviets as enjoying a "missile gap" over us; he greatly increased the U.S. missile program. It turned out that the Soviets were actually behind us, and they perceived the American effort as a threat that they had to match. The misperceptions led to the 1962 Cuban missile crisis, the closest we came to World War III. Iraq built weapons of mass destruction (WMD), but they were dismantled under UN supervision in the 1990s. The Bush 43 administration was convinced Iraq had revived its WMD programs and went to war in 2003 to remove a nonexistent threat. In the emotional and patriotic climate after 9/11, America was angry and suspicious. Intelligence data were skewed to show what the administration wanted to show. Misperception can count for more than reality.

In misperception or image theory, the psychological and real worlds bounce against each other in the minds of political leaders. They think they are acting defensively, but their picture of the situation may be distorted. In our time, it is interesting to note, no country ever calls its actions anything but defensive. The Americans in Vietnam and Iraq saw themselves as defending freedom; the Russians in Chechnya see themselves as defending their country. In its own eyes, a nation is never aggressive. A country—under the guidance of its leaders, its ideology, and its mass media—may work itself into a state of fear and rationalize aggressive moves as defensive. Under rabidly nationalistic leadership, most Germans and Japanese in World War II saw themselves as defending their countries against hostile powers. Serbian dictator Slobodan Milosevic played the Serbian nationalist card and got most Serbs to believe they were surrounded by enemies. Once convinced that they are being attacked, normally peaceful people will commit all manner of atrocities.

"They"

Beware of collective pronouns like "they," which often paint with too broad a brush. When you use "they," always ask what it stands for. Grammatically, "they" refers to the previous plural noun. Many new students of international relations use "they" as if an entire national population is carrying out decisions and actions when in reality only a handful of top decision makers are. The leaders of France are often critical of U.S. policy. Some Americans then say that "the French" are against us. Actually 99.99 percent of French people either have no interest in or no input into foreign policy. And many like America.

To guard against the overgeneralization that comes with "they," either specify who is taking the action—President Chirac, Premier Raffarin, or the Quai d'Orsay (French foreign ministry)—or use the name of the capital to stand for the top decision makers—"Paris" for France's foreign-policy elite, "Moscow" for Russia's, and "Tehran" for Iran's.

There isn't even much of a "we" in U.S. foreign policy. Most Americans have no or weak views on foreign affairs. Some criticize administration policies. Even "inside the beltway" (around the District of Columbia), every policy provokes conflicting views. In such situations, instead of the term "Washington," use the person's name and/or organization espousing the viewpoint: "Secretary of State Condoleeza Rice sometimes found herself at odds with the White House and with Secretary of Defense Donald Rumsfeld." Specific is better.

Many argue that foreign policy must be decided by a handful of people because things move too fast in the modern age to allow for extensive popular and even congressional debate. A delay of a few weeks can be fatal. Furthermore, few citizens understand or even care about distant threats and problems. How many Americans really care about the genocide in Sudan? Or the global impact of loans to Indonesia from the International Monetary Fund? What the experts often lack, on the other hand, is the common sense of average citizens, who may have pretty clear ideas as to whether their sons should fight and die far from our shores. Pundits sometimes call these two perspectives "inside the beltway" (that loops around Washington) and "outside the beltway" (the rest of America). Too often the former engages in discussions only with other "inside" people and ignores average Americans. If foreign policy stayed attuned only to the interests of most Americans, however, it would tend to isolationism, so a certain amount of agenda-setting and leadership by the White House is required.

Conventional usage often neglects the fact of elite leadership in foreign policy, as when we say "the Iranians" or "the Russians" are up to such and such. Perhaps a dozen Iranians or Russians decide foreign policy (although a much bigger number carry it out), so it is wrong to impute volition or responsibility to all of them. Most Iranians, for example, welcome visiting Americans; the anti-U.S. views of some Iranian leaders are not widely shared. As in the United States, most Iranians and Russians do not care or are powerless to influence decisions made at the top.

KEY CONCEPTS

THE DEMOCRATIC PEACE

Scholars note that no two democracies have ever gone to war with each other. This may not be absolutely true—the U.S. Civil War and Peru-Ecuador border squabbles may be exceptions—but it is an overwhelming tendency. Can you name any other cases where two democracies have fought each other? Argentina against Britain over the Falklands in 1982? But Argentina was then a military dictatorship. India against Pakistan seems a likely candidate, but Pakistan is now ruled by a general and has never been a stable democracy.

Why, logically, should there be this happy coincidence between democracy and peace? Recalling our discussion of Chapter 5, democracy renders leaders accountable to the citizenry at large. When leaders know they may be voted out of office, they tend to be cautious and to follow Friedrich's famous "rule of anticipated reactions" (page 117). They think, "If I take the country to war, how will voters react? Hmm, I guess I better not." When President Johnson ignored such caution in Vietnam—because he thought voters would hold it against him if the Communists won—he suffered a dramatic fall in his popularity and could not stand for a second term. Bush 43 suffered similarly from the Iraq War and occupation. Dictators have no such inhibitions and may be inclined to reckless misadventures, as when Brezhnev invaded Afghanistan in 1979 or Saddam Hussein invaded Kuwait in 1990. The cause of peace is served by the spread of democracy.

■ KEEPING PEACE

Whatever its causes, what can be done to prevent or at least limit war? Many proposals have been advanced; none has really worked.

WORLD GOVERNMENT

The real culprit, many thinkers claim, is sovereignty itself. The solution is to have states give up at least some of their sovereignty—the ability to decide to go to war—to an international entity that would prevent war much as an individual country keeps the peace within its borders. But what country would give up its sovereignty? Certainly not the United States. Did Iraq heed UN calls to open possible WMD sites to international inspection? Without the teeth of sovereignty, the United Nations, or any organization like it, becomes a debating society, useful for diplomatic contact but little more.

COLLECTIVE SECURITY

The United Nations' predecessor, the League of Nations, tried to implement an idea that had been around for some time: **collective security**. Members of the League (which did not include the United States) pledged to join immediately in economic

---

collective security   An agreement among all nations to automatically counter an aggressor.

and military action against any aggressor state. If Japan, for example, invaded China, every other power would break trade relations and send forces to defend China. Aggressors, faced with the forces of the rest of the world, would back down. It was a great idea on paper, but it failed in practice. When Japan took Manchuria from China in 1931, the League merely sent a commission to study the situation. Japan claimed the Chinese started it (a lie), and the other powers saw no point in getting involved in a distant conflict where none of their interests was involved. Aggression went unpunished because the League had no mechanism to make the other countries respond. The same thing happened when Italy invaded Ethiopia in 1935. Japan, Italy, and Germany withdrew from the league to practice aggression on a larger scale, and the League collapsed with World War II.

FUNCTIONALISM

Another idea related to world organizations is to have countries cooperate first in specialized or "functional" areas so that they will see that they can accomplish more by cooperation than by conflict. Gradually they will work up to a stable peace as a result of being increasingly able to trust each other. **Functionalism** will produce a "spillover" effect. Dozens of UN-related agencies now promote international cooperation in disease control, food production, weather forecasting, civil aviation, nuclear energy, and other areas. Even hostile countries are sometimes able to sit together to solve a mutual problem in specialized areas. But there is no spillover; they remain hostile. Sometimes the specialized organization becomes a scene of conflict, as when the Third World group expelled Israel and South Africa from the UN Educational, Scientific, and Cultural Organization (UNESCO) and the United States quit UNESCO over alleged Soviet dominance. Even offers of the UN-related International Monetary Fund (IMF) to bail out distressed economies generates controversy, as the recipient country often claims that economic reforms mandated by the IMF interfere with its sovereignty. The functionalist approach has brought some help in world problems but has not touched the biggest problem, war.

THIRD-PARTY ASSISTANCE

One way to settle a dispute is to have a **third party** not involved in the conflict mediate between the contending parties to try to find a middle ground. Third parties carry messages back and forth, clarify the issues, and suggest compromises, as the UN's Ralph Bunche did between Arabs and Israelis in 1949, President Carter did with Begin and Sadat at Camp David in 1978, and Richard Holbrooke did at Dayton over Bosnia in 1995. Third parties can help calm a tense situation and find compromise solutions, but the contenders have to *want* to find a solution. If not, third-party help is futile.

---

functionalism   Theory that cooperation in specialized areas will encourage overall cooperation among nations.

third party   A nation not involved in a dispute helping to settle it.

DIPLOMACY

The oldest approach to preserving peace is through diplomatic contact, with envoys sent from one head of state to another. A good diplomat knows all the power factors and the interests of the countries involved and has suggestions for compromise that leaves both parties at least partly satisfied. This is crucial: There must be a willingness to compromise. This can be hard because countries often define their vital, nonnegotiable interests grandly and are unwilling to cut them down to compromisable size. After years of intensive negotiations, presided over by the United States, Israelis and Palestinians could not compromise on what they saw as their vital interests. If successful, diplomats draw up **treaties**, which must be ratified and observed. If one country feels a treaty harms it, there is nothing to stop it from opting out, as Bush did in 2002 with the 1972 Anti-Ballistic Missile Treaty with Russia. Countries enter into and observe treaties because it suits them. Some observers say the United States and Soviet Union, both relative newcomers to the world of great-power politics, were unskilled at diplomacy, too unwilling to compromise. The climate of mistrust between them was one of the hallmarks of the Cold War.

PEACEKEEPING

Related to diplomacy is the idea of using third-party military forces to support a cease-fire or truce to end fighting. Such forces, wearing the blue berets of the UN, helped calm and stabilize truce lines between Israel and its Arab neighbors and between Greeks and Turks on Cyprus. Such forces cannot "enforce peace" by stopping a conflict that is still in progress. The only way to do that would be to take sides in the war, and that would be the opposite of **peacekeeping**. It was therefore inherently unrealistic to expect **UNPROFOR** (the UN Protective Force) to separate and calm the warring parties in Bosnia. UNPROFOR, given an impossible mission, covered itself with shame. The **IFOR** (Implementation Force) that took over from UNPROFOR was different and successful because it came after the three sides—Bosnia, Croatia, and Serbia—agreed to a U.S.-brokered peace in Dayton. IFOR was also equipped and instructed to destroy attackers; these robust **rules of engagement** dissuaded rambunctious elements, something UNPROFOR was unable to do. Some propose the IFOR model for future peacekeeping, but such actions work only if a peace agreement has been reached beforehand.

---

treaty   A contract between nations.

peacekeeping   Outside military forces stabilizing a cease-fire agreement.

UNPROFOR   UN Protective Force; ineffective peacekeeping effort in Bosnia in early 1990s.

IFOR   Implementation Force; effective, NATO-sponsored peacekeeping effort in Bosnia following 1995 Dayton Accords.

rules of engagement   Specify when peacekeeping forces can shoot back.

■ THE COLD WAR

Starting in 1946 or 1947, the **Cold War** was both a cause and a result of profound mistrust between the Soviet Union and the United States. Each perceived the other as a hostile aggressor. The Cold War started shortly after and as a direct consequence of World War II. Stalin's Red Army had fought the Nazis back through Eastern Europe, and Stalin was not about to give up what his country had lost 26 million lives for. Stalin turned Eastern Europe into a protective barrier for the Soviet Union by setting up obedient Communist "satellites" in each land and stationing Soviet troops in Central Europe. This state of affairs lasted until the Berlin Wall fell in late 1989, an event that many regard as marking the end of the Cold War, for by that point most of the East-West tension was gone. The collapse of the Soviet Union at the end of 1991 confirmed that the Cold War was over.

During the height of the Cold War the West, led by the United States, viewed Stalin's takeovers of Eastern Europe with great alarm. Stalin looked like another Hitler, a dictator bent on world conquest, and the United States took steps to stop it. In the spring of 1947, Washington came up with three connected policies that formed the basis of U.S. foreign policy for decades—the **Truman Doctrine**, the **Marshall Plan**, and **containment**.

TRUMAN DOCTRINE

President Truman asked a joint session of Congress for military aid to prevent the Communist takeover of Greece and Turkey, which were then under Soviet pressure. The United States should come to the aid of "free peoples" anywhere in the world. This repudiated traditional American attitudes of isolationism and, some say, contained the seeds of a globalism that eventually wrecked itself in Vietnam.

MARSHALL PLAN

At Harvard's 1947 commencement, Secretary of State George C. Marshall proposed a multibillion-dollar U.S. aid package to lift up war-torn Europe and prevent its takeover either by local Communists or by the Red Army. The aid started flowing in 1948 and put Western Europe back on its feet.

Cold War   Armed tension and mistrust between U.S. and Soviet camps, 1946–1989.
Truman Doctrine   Truman's 1947 call to block expansion of communism.
Marshall Plan   U.S. aid to uplift war-torn Western Europe.
containment   Kennan's 1947 call to block expansion of Soviet power.

CONTAINMENT

At this time a State Department official, George F. Kennan, was drafting an influential memo that was soon published in the journal *Foreign Affairs* under the byline "X" (to conceal his identity). Republished many times since, "The Sources of Soviet Conduct" spelled out the Kremlin's expansionistic tendencies and called for a "policy of firm and vigilant containment" of them. Wherever the Soviets tried to expand, we would stop them.

The Berlin Airlift (1948–1949), the formation of the North Atlantic Treaty Organization (1949), and the Korean War (1950–1953) deepened the Cold War and the U.S. containment policy. The two major U.S. parties competed over which of them could best stop communism. A "red scare," fostered by the accusations of Senator Joseph McCarthy (R-Wisc.), persuaded most public figures to appear tough and hawkish; all feared appearing "soft on communism."

At the height of the Cold War, the world seemed divided into two camps, one led by Washington, the other by Moscow, with very little in between. The condition was called *bipolarity,* which we will explore in the next chapter. Some see a bipolar system as essentially stable and comforting: You know where you stand. Others argue that it was a dangerous system, for it induced a "zero-sum" mentality (whatever I win, you lose), which pushed the superpowers into dangerous positions in the Third World. Every place on earth seemed to be strategic and worth fighting for. The United States, for example, intervened in Iran, Guatemala, Indonesia, Lebanon, the Congo, the Dominican Republic, and elsewhere on the suspicion that if we did not secure these areas, the Soviets would take them. The "contingent necessity argument" usually prevailed: If we don't take it, someone else will. In this way, Cold War fears drove both superpowers to extreme and ill-advised interventions, the Americans in Vietnam and the Soviets in Afghanistan.

DETERRENCE

At no time did the superpowers—the only two countries with global warmaking powers, the United States and the Soviet Union—fight each other directly. Both were afraid of **escalation** leading to World War III. If U.S. and Soviet forces started even a little battle, say, over Berlin, it could grow, engaging conventional forces all over Europe. Then one side would use small tactical nuclear weapons. The other side would strike back with bigger nuclear weapons, and soon the superpowers would rain nuclear missiles on each other's homeland. The fear of such escalation is the basis for **deterrence**; both sides are so afraid of the results that they deter each other from major war.

---

escalation   Tendency of conflicts to enlarge and intensify.
deterrence   Preventing attack by threatening great harm to attacker.

THE SOVIET UNION AND "OVERSTRETCH"

We now realize that Soviet President Mikhail Gorbachev was willing to relinquish Eastern Europe and give up nuclear warheads because the Soviet economy was in terrible shape. He had to call off the Cold War because he was broke. The socialist economic system was defective and every decade fell farther behind the West's, especially in the crucial high-tech sectors. Soviet defense spending ate a quarter of its economy. The Soviets' far-flung empire cost billions in subsidies for Eastern Europe, Cuba, Vietnam, and several African countries.

The Soviet Union was going through what Yale historian Paul Kennedy called **imperial overstretch**. The crux of Kennedy's argument is economic, especially relative economic growth. Strong powers are constantly tempted to expand. They have the money and work force, and other areas seem ripe for domination. Their empires expand until they overexpand; then they decay. Gradually their economic base weakens, and their empires grow increasingly expensive to maintain and defend. Other powers, whose economies have not been drained by imperial expenses, grow faster and become richer and more powerful.

Kennedy's theory accounts for the rise and fall of the **Habsburg** and British empires. The Habsburg dynasty of the sixteenth century united Spain, the Netherlands, and Austria and had shiploads of gold and silver pouring in from the New World. The wars it fought were only partly wars of religion—Catholic versus Protestant—they were also a Habsburg attempt to dominate Europe. The Habsburgs overstretched themselves and went into bankruptcy and decline. Spain especially was economically ruined for centuries.

Britain, the world's first industrial country, used its sea power to construct an incredible empire with holdings on every continent. But Britain's economic growth lagged behind its imperial expenses. By the late nineteenth century, several powers, including Germany and the United States, had become economically more powerful. The two world wars finished off the British Empire. The theory also explained Soviet collapse beautifully—a military empire that the decaying Soviet economy could no longer afford. Empire is a wasting asset.

The crux of deterrence is not just having enough nuclear warheads and missiles to deliver them but also making sure that enough of them could survive a *first strike* by the other side. Then you can hit back in a *second strike*. If you have credible second-strike capability, the other superpower will not attack you, for it knows that it will be horribly mutilated in retaliation. Deterrence is based on both sides understanding that they will suffer mutual assured destruction (MAD).

Did deterrence work? Sure, say its proponents; there was no nuclear war. Skeptics wonder, though, what could have happened in times of great stress, when mistrust is especially high and fingers are on nuclear triggers. Supporters argue

---

imperial overstretch   Theory that empires expand until they overexpand.

Habsburg   Powerful Catholic dynasty that ruled much of Europe and waged the Thirty Years War.

that the deterrence system had "crisis stability," the ability to withstand even a major U.S.-Soviet confrontation. They point to the Cuban missile crisis of 1962 as an example, but we learned decades later that there were Soviet nuclear warheads in Cuba and that local commanders would have used them if attacked. We also learned decades later that Kennedy never intended to attack Cuba; he knew it could easily escalate into World War III. The missile crisis had a sobering effect on both superpowers, which soon began arms control talks to slow down and control the arms race. Perhaps the high point of arms control was the 1987 Intermediate-range Nuclear Forces **(INF)** treaty by which both sides eliminated hundreds of missiles and warheads. President Reagan left office as a man of peace. The fall of the Berlin Wall in late 1989 and the breakup of the Soviet Union in late 1991 ended the Cold War.

■ BEYOND SOVEREIGNTY?

The end of the Cold War and of the most violent century in history brought into question the basic point of international politics, sovereignty—namely, is sovereignty slipping? Increasingly, the world community is acting in ways that infringe on the internal workings of sovereign states. For some decades the International Monetary Fund has been able to tell countries that wanted loans to stop their inflationary economic policies. The recipients of such advice often fumed that the IMF was infringing on their sovereignty, but if they wanted the loan, they took the advice. With the end of the Cold War, now even former Communist countries are going along with this sort of infringement on their sovereignty.

Starting with the Nuremberg War Crimes Trials in 1945–1946, international law increasingly ignores sovereignty as a cover for mass murder. The Tokyo war crimes trials and Eichmann trial in Israel reinforced the Nuremburg precedent. Mass murderers in Bosnia and Rwanda are tried before international tribunals. (Saddam Hussein was tried before an Iraqi court but with strong international support.) Nothing like this happened before World War II. International law is slowly eating into sovereignty.

After a broad, U.S.-led coalition booted Iraq out of Kuwait in 1991, UN inspectors combed through Iraq looking for the capacity to build WMD. The Baghdad dictatorship screamed that Iraq's sovereignty was being infringed upon. Indeed it was, and most of the world was glad of it. Should the international community stand back while a tyrant develops the power to annihilate neighboring countries? By the same token, should the civilized world stand by while the Sudanese government sponsors genocide against its own people? Should the rest of Europe act as if Balkan massacres were none of its concern?

INF   Intermediate-range Nuclear Forces; 1987 U.S.-Soviet treaty that eliminated this class of weapons.

The world seems to be changing, willing to move beyond sovereignty and toward some kind of order. The trouble is, no one knows what kind of order. President Bush 41 used the term *new world order* in building a coalition against Iraq, but he dropped the expression just as debate on it was starting. What to do in the face of the disorder unleashed by the dissolution of Soviet power? Paradoxically, the world was more orderly during the Cold War, because the two superpowers controlled and restrained their respective allies and spheres of influence.

Few wanted the United States to play world cop, but most understood that if there was to be leadership, only America could provide it. Could **supranational** (above-national) entities be getting ready to take on some of the responsibilities previously associated with individual nations' sovereignty? A new class of "world-order" issues has emerged, such as global warming, that no country can handle on its own. Are any organizations able to play such a role?

THE UNITED NATIONS

The United Nations comes quickly to mind, and indeed the UN has been functioning far better after the Cold War than during it. But it still has problems. As permanent members of the Security Council, Russia and China have the power to veto anything they dislike. Russia, for example, did nothing against Serbia, long regarded as a Slavic little brother. The UN has sent many peacekeepers to observe truces, as in the Middle East and Balkans, but these few and lightly armed forces from small countries were in no position to enforce peace. The bloodthirsty Khmer Rouge in Cambodia repeatedly kidnapped UN peacekeepers, knowing they would do nothing. Without enforcement powers and fragmented into blocs, the UN remained largely a "talking shop."

THE NORTH ATLANTIC TREATY ORGANIZATION

NATO was arguably the best defensive alliance ever devised. The former Communist countries of Eastern Europe were happy to join in 1999 and 2004 as it assured their freedom and security. Since 1949 NATO coordinated Western Europe and North America to act as a single defender under unified command in the event of Soviet attack. But now its very reason for being has come into question. Why not use NATO for other security and stability tasks, badly needed in the Middle East? But the North Atlantic Treaty is extremely specific—that an attack on one member in Europe or North America be treated as an attack on all—and it has no validity anywhere else, not in the Middle East, the Balkans, or Africa. Anywhere else is "out of area." NATO members can, to be sure, cooperate out of area, but it's on a purely voluntary basis, as they did in Bosnia and Afghanistan. What worked there may not work elsewhere. Accordingly, NATO would not be a reliable force for keeping peace.

---

supranational   A governing body above individual nations (such as the UN).

There is no organization that can seriously calm and stabilize world trouble spots. Should there be one, or should the civilized world put together a series of ad hoc arrangements, as the United States did in Afghanistan in 2001? Either way, the United States will have to take a leading role if anything is to be done effectively. If we don't lead, no one else will.

KEY TERMS

Cold War (p. 386)
collective security (p. 383)
containment (p. 386)
deterrence (p. 387)
domestic politics (p. 375)
escalation (p. 387)
functionalism (p. 384)
Habsburg (p. 388)
IFOR (p. 385)
imperial overstretch (p. 388)
INF (p. 389)
international politics (p. 375)

macro theories (p. 380)
Marshall Plan (p. 386)
micro theories (p. 380)
national interest (p. 377)
peacekeeping (p. 385)
rules of engagement (p. 385)
supranational (p. 390)
third party (p. 384)
treaty (p. 385)
Truman Doctrine (p. 386)
UNPROFOR (p. 385)
weapons of mass destruction (p. 379)

KEY WEB SITES

United Nations
www.un.org/

Bosnia
www.dtic.mil/bosnia/

Kosovo
www.csis.org/kosovo/
www.kforonline.com/

Nuclear weapons
www.nrdc.org/nrdcpro/nuguide/guinx.html

U.S. State Department
www.state.gov/

American foreign policy
www.afpc.org/

Further Reference

Blainey, Geoffrey. *The Causes of War,* 3rd ed. New York: Free Press, 1988.

Bobbit, Philip. *The Shield of Achilles: War, Peace, and the Course of History.* New York: Knopf, 2002.

Brzezinski, Zbigniew. *The Choice: Domination or Leadership.* New York: Basic Books, 2004.

Clark, Gen. Wesley K. *Waging Modern War: Bosnia, Kosovo, and the Future of Combat.* New York: PublicAffairs, 2001.

Dougherty, James E., and Robert L. Pfaltzgraff, Jr. *Contending Theories of International Relations: A Comprehensive Survey,* 5th ed. New York: Longman, 2000.

Ehrenreich, Barbara. *Blood Rites: Origins and History of the Passions of War.* New York: Metropolitan Books, 1997.

Ikenberry, G. John, *After Victory: Institutions, Strategic Restraint, and the Rebuilding of Order after Major Wars.* Princeton, NJ: Princeton University Press, 2000.

Jervis, Robert. *Perception and Misperception in International Politics.* Princeton, NJ: Princeton University Press, 1976.

Kennedy, Paul. *The Rise and Fall of the Great Powers: Economic Change and Military Conflict from 1500 to 2000.* New York: Random House, 1987.

Kissinger, Henry. *Does America Need a Foreign Policy?* New York: Simon & Schuster, 2001.

Lukacs, John. *The End of the Twentieth Century and the End of the Modern Age.* New York: Ticknor & Fields, 1993.

McWilliams, Wayne C., and Harry Piotrowski. *The World Since 1945: A History of International Relations,* 5th ed. Boulder, CO: Lynne Rienner, 2001.

Morgenthau, Hans J., Kenneth W. Thompson, and David Clinton. *Politics among Nations,* 7th ed. New York: McGraw-Hill, 2005.

CHAPTER 21

THE GLOBAL SYSTEM

QUESTIONS TO CONSIDER

- Is the world too messy to constitute an international system?
- How did balance of power work? Why did it stop working?
- Was the Cold War bipolar system stable?
- What kind of global system seems to be emerging?
- What forces could bring globalization to an end?
- Is Huntington's clash-of-civilizations theory valid?
- Is there a U.S. consensus on our foreign policy?
- Can a case be made for U.S. noninterventionism?

The world has clearly moved beyond the Cold War bipolar system. Moscow gave up Eastern Europe and no longer poses any invasion threat beyond Russia's borders because it is too weak. Western Europe moves closer to unity in the European Union (EU) and new euro currency. In Asia, China, after a quarter century of incredible growth, is now the second largest economy in the world. Japan is in third place and Germany fourth, but their economies are stagnant. The United States is still the world's largest economy, but massive budget and trade deficits also make us the world's biggest debtor. The United States does not have the kind of dominance it once had to call the tune and get compliance from allies in Europe and Asia. Most ignored Washington's calls to assist us on Iraq.

Added together, observers agree that these changes produce a new **international system**, but they do not agree on what kind of system. Because of

---

international system   The pattern in which countries interact, a power map of the world.

INTERNATIONAL SYSTEMS AND MODELS

An "international system" is what's out there in the real world, a distribution of power around the world: Who has what kind of power and how do they use it? A "model" is what we construct from data and our own imaginations in the hope that it matches the real-world system. It is in effect a simplified map of the world's current power distribution. The better the model's fit with the real world—and it will never be perfect—the more we will be able to anticipate the unfolding of events and possible dangers and disruptions. Notice that we are not looking for a "perfect" system, for we are not in charge of anything and are not able to "design" a system. Systems come into being from natural causes rooted in power, economics, and history. The best we can do is construct a model that explains a good deal of the real working system. It will never explain everything.

A model is in effect a theory of how the world works. We construct them because without a model widely shared by our decision makers that approximates the real world, we will engage in mistaken and possibly self-destructive moves. If our foreign-policy elite settles on one model of the international system and it fits reality, they will generally make wise decisions that both aid the United States and contribute to world peace. If they embrace a model that does not fit reality, they will lead us into one mistake after another. Underlying assumptions—unfortunately, many of them unexamined—are the basis for a sound foreign policy. Or, as some thinkers have long understood: "There is nothing so practical as theory."

this, political leaders cannot devise a rational, coherent **foreign policy** for the United States. Phrases like Bush 41's "new world order" or Clinton's "enlargement of democracy" do not resonate. Only the 2004 election brought world affairs and foreign policy back onto the agenda. In the absence of a threat, most Americans simply do not care.

■ HISTORICAL SYSTEMS

International systems have many components (countries or groups of countries) that interact with each other (by means of trade, alliances, hostilities, diplomacy, and so on). These systems change over time, with the rise of new powers, technologies, economies, and alliances. Looking back over more than a century, scholars believe there have been at least three international systems, each operating with different numbers of major players and with a different logic. The models constructed at the time to explicate these systems were never fully accurate; most understated their economic components.

---

foreign policy   Interface of domestic and world politics; in Lippmann's phrase, the "shield of the Republic."

THE NINETEENTH-CENTURY BALANCE OF POWER SYSTEM

Relative peace prevailed after the fall of Napoleon and agreement among the major European powers to not try for supremacy. Instead, they agreed to carve up the globe into great empires. This agreement decayed after the rise of two new major players, unified Germany in 1871 and rapidly modernizing Japan after the Meiji Restoration of 1868. **Balance of power** requires flexible, shifting alliances, but by the beginning of the twentieth century, Europe was arrayed into two rigid, hostile blocs. The game had changed. The start of World War I in 1914 did not necessarily prove that balance of power does not work; it showed that the balance had already broken down.

THE INTERWAR SYSTEM

In World Wars I and II, the European powers destroyed themselves. Between the two wars, Britain and France, drained by the first conflict, refrained from trying to balance Germany's resurgent power under Hitler. The United States and Soviet Union stood aside. The Axis dictatorships—Germany, Italy, and Japan—sensing passivity, expanded to take what they could. The interwar system was inherently unstable, what E. H. Carr called "the twenty years' crisis." After World War II, the European powers were so weakened that they had to give up their empires, and they became dominated and in some cases occupied by two new giant empires, the United States and the Soviet Union.

THE BIPOLAR COLD WAR SYSTEM

After World War II, the world seemed to be divided between the two superpowers into what Stalin called *sotslager* and *kaplager,* the socialist camp and the capitalist camp, what we called Communism and the Free World. Most of the small- and medium-sized powers found themselves in alliance with a superpower, the United States or the Soviet Union, some voluntary, some coerced. Some neutrals aligned with neither camp. A "zero-sum" mentality dangerously exaggerated the importance of peripheral countries such as Cuba and Laos. The **bipolar** system contained the seeds of its own decay. The superpowers' arms race grew increasingly expensive and drained both economically. Third World nationalism burned both the Americans (in Vietnam) and the Soviets (in Afghanistan). The Soviet bloc split; China left it in the 1960s. Seeing his economy falling behind, Gorbachev attempted reform but merely succeeded in collapsing the regime. Central Europe turned westward as the Warsaw Pact dissolved.

The Cold War bipolar system could have blown up in nuclear war over a miscalculation, such as over Cuba in 1962. Said President Kennedy as the Cuban

---

balance of power　System in which major nations form and reform alliances to protect themselves.

bipolar　System of two large, hostile blocs, each led by a superpower, as in Cold War.

missile crisis eased: "We were lucky." Some argue that it was a rather stable system, "the long peace." Many Americans liked the Cold War because they knew where they stood and what kind of foreign policy they had to pursue: Stop the spread of communism. Kennan's famous "containment" doctrine lasted four decades with only nuanced change.

■ WHAT SYSTEM IS EMERGING?

Now things are not nearly so clear. Several new, emerging systems have been suggested, but so far none has established itself as the accepted paradigm. We therefore discuss the following as models, as imagined possibilities, rather than as real-world systems. We do not yet know which of these, if any, will fit the real world, so all are tentative. As one wag put it, "The model's not for marrying."

A UNIPOLAR MODEL

Just as the Cold War was ending, the 1991 Persian Gulf War seemed to show the United States in command, able to rally and lead much of the world against aggression. President Bush 41 called it a "new world order," and some envisaged an emerging **unipolar** system, with the United States as the single remaining superpower, but it failed to emerge and probably could not. As the United States attempted to lead, the rest of the world did not follow. The 1991 Gulf War happened under special circumstances—a threat to the flow of the world's main source of petroleum—that most countries agreed had to be dealt with. Other situations—Bosnia, the Middle East, Rwanda—brought much bickering and no agreement among the powers. Washington tried to lead in isolating Iran, but many of our allies said the policy was counterproductive and sought business ties with Iran. U.S. armed forces were cut, and Washington hung back from using them in risky situations. The death of nineteen U.S. soldiers in Somalia, for example, persuaded Washington to withdraw all troops. Washington hesitated for years, while some 200,000 Bosnians were being killed, before sending peacekeeping forces. This was hardly the behavior of a "superpower."

A COUNTERWEIGHT MODEL

The 2003 Iraq War found the United States largely alone. Few allies followed the U.S. lead, and many opposed us. The unipolar model did not match reality. Some proposed a **counterweight** model in which much of the rest of the world shows

---

unipolar   System dominated by one very powerful nation.
counterweight   System in which several countries attempt to offset U.S. power.

its resentments of U.S. domination by ignoring and criticizing Washington. France, Germany, Russia, and most of the Muslim world refused to help America in Iraq. Instead, they tended to band together to resist U.S. **hegemony**. This banding together will likely come to little, as the other countries disagree among themselves and cannot form an alliance. It is probably a weak tendency but one the United States must pay some attention to.

A MULTIPOLAR MODEL

The most commonly used word to describe the post–Cold War world is **multipolar**, but the term is vague and covers several patterns; no one can be sure how it will work or if it will last. Its main feature is the breakup of the old bipolar blocs into several blocs. Most prominent are the European Union and the Pacific Rim, both of which tend to ignore American leadership. The United States, Canada, and Mexico joined to form the North American Free Trade Agreement (**NAFTA**), which could spread southward and eventually link up with **Mercosur**, a free-trade area of the southern cone of South America, to form a giant Free Trade Area of the Americas (**FTAA**). Other, small blocs dotted the globe. Instead of military confrontation, in a multipolar world economic growth becomes an obsession as countries and blocs strive to hold down unemployment, develop trade advantages, and move ahead technologically. Fear of falling behind motivates all the players.

The good news about such a system, if it indeed develops, is that the chances of major war are much reduced. The world relaxes as Russian and U.S. troops and nuclear weapons pull out of Europe. The zero-sum mentality and struggle for Third World clients recedes: What good are they? Cuba and Laos diminish in importance; no one wants to fight over them. The two powers reach important arms control agreements and reduce the warheads they have aimed at each other.

The bad news about such a system—already visible—is the murderous quality of the economic competition. Some players are more efficient than others. They develop huge trade and capital surpluses and start buying up the weaker players. There is a constant temptation to turn protectionist, to keep out foreign products and limit foreign business takeovers. Nasty accusations of trade protectionism already flow both ways across the Atlantic and the Pacific. What will happen cannot be foreseen. Much depends on the abilities of politicians to keep the blocs open to foreign trade. Should they close, trade wars could disrupt the global economy and plunge the world into a new Great Depression. We are sobered to remember that economic closure contributed to the coming of World War II.

---

hegemony   Leading or dominating other nations.

multipolar   System divided among several power centers.

NAFTA   North American trade bloc.

Mercosur   South American trade bloc of Brazil, Argentina, and others.

FTAA   Proposed hemispheric trade bloc of Americas.

A STRATIFIED MODEL

A **stratified** model, which combines the features of unipolar and multipolar systems, may better fit the emerging reality. In a stratified system, the United States is still, relative to other nations, the premier military power, but it depends on other powers in undertaking important international moves. The United States has the best military technology, especially airlift capacity, to project its power around the world, but it can't do it alone. Other countries, with either moderate power-projection capabilities (Britain and France) or money (Japan and Saudi Arabia), form a "second tier" without which the United States cannot or will not intervene in world hot spots. When the top military power, the United States, can rally the second-tier powers, they can accomplish much, as in the 1991 Gulf War. But when Washington tried to rebuild the same alliance in 2003 to invade Iraq, only Britain offered support. The other former partners said no, and the enterprise evaporated.

A ZONES-OF-CHAOS MODEL

Another stratified model sees a top layer of rich, high-tech countries, Europe, Japan, and North America. The second layer consists of middle-income industrializing lands, such as South Korea and Brazil. The third layer is a zone of chaos dominated by crime, terrorism, warlords, and chronic instability. It is startling to realize that the world's biggest single industry is now crime, much of it connected to the flow of drugs from the poor countries to the rich countries.

The top-layer countries can devastate most military targets, but they can't control the chaos of the bottom-layer countries, whose guerrillas and drug cartels offer no good targets. West Africa, Colombia, and Afghanistan are examples of chaos that the top-layer countries would like to avoid, but they may not be able to. Afghanistan, home to al Qaeda, suddenly drew in America in 2001. Many of the world's natural resources—especially oil—are in these chaos zones, so the first layer is inevitably drawn into their difficulties. And the rich lands' appetite for illicit drugs means the bottom layer reaches into the top layer.

A GLOBALIZED MODEL

Especially since the Cold War ended, some thinkers believe **globalization** is a strong trend. In a globalized system most countries become economic players in the world market, a largely capitalistic competition where goods, money, and ideas flow easily to wherever there are customers. The motto of a globalized system: Make money, not war. The few countries that don't want to play, such as Cuba and North Korea, live in isolation and poverty. After some years, most countries want to play. As such, the rules of a globalized system are self-enforcing: Play capitalism or stay poor.

---

stratified   Forming layers.

globalization   Free flow of commerce across borders making the world one big market.

HOW TO . . .

THEORIES

Your study should show that you are aware of what previous thinkers have found; that is, you should relate your thesis to an existing **theory** of politics. You do not necessarily have to confirm a theory; you may have more fun refuting it. In this chapter, for example, we mention Samuel Huntington's "clash of civilizations" theory, which attempts to explain the main forces of international relations in the postwar world (pages 401–402). You might do a study on the Huntington model, tabulating violent incidents around the globe over the last six months to see if they are mostly between civilizations or within them. If the former, your study confirms Huntington. If the latter, you refute Huntington. Both findings are equally good, and, either way, you have related them to a theory.

Few political scientists stake out such grand claims as Huntington; most try for a smaller **empirical theory** that doesn't explain the world but only one facet of politics. For example, studies of differences between urban and rural voting generally find that city people vote liberal or left, country people conservative or right. Studies of the 2000 and 2004 U.S. elections found this trend especially strong. Was it always that way? In all countries? Are there interesting exceptions?

Whatever theory you relate your study to, do not reify it. **Reification**, a constant temptation, means uncritically accepting a theory as reality rather than as an attempt to get a handle on reality. Notice in this chapter we are presenting our models—which are a form of theory—as possibilities, not as reality. Marxists often worshipped Marx's theories, denying reality when it suggested Marx was wrong. A joke has it that Marx's dying words were: "Hey, it's only a theory." That is good advice for all.

Globalization can bring much good. With a largely free flow of trade, the world economy has grown as never before, especially in the Third World. Poor countries, some written off as basket cases, are stirring to life. More products, including previously expensive items, are produced in abundance at low cost, enabling most of the world to enjoy DVDs and computers. Big, transnational corporations design an item in one country, assemble it in a second country with components from a third, and market it in a fourth. For these corporations, borders are just nuisances that impede business efficiency. "Philosophers used to dream about one world," these corporations in effect say, "We are making it happen. We are more effective than the UN in promoting world peace and prosperity."

But there are many problems that may limit and even terminate a globalized system. The first problem: Is globalization a cause or a consequence of peace? Are the two intertwined? If so, what happens to one when the other is disrupted? Predictions that economic interdependency would prevent war (widely believed before World War I) have proved false. It is sobering to remember that there was an

---

theory   A big picture of how things supposedly work.

empirical theory   A medium-sized picture of how things work, based on evidence.

reification   Taking a theory as reality.

A McDonald's flag flying in old Prague, ancient capital of the Czech Republic, serves as a symbol of globalization. (Michael Roskin)

era of globalization during the nineteenth century, led by Britain, but it collapsed with World War I. It revived, led by the United States, after World War II. Prosperity does not necessarily bring peace. Indeed, newly affluent countries often demand respect, resources, and sometimes territory. As China got richer, for example, it defined its borders more grandly, reaching far out into the South and East China Seas to include Taiwan.

A second problem: Who are the key players in a globalized system: countries, blocs, or transnational corporations? Will the corporations become so rich and powerful that they challenge and override traditional nation-states and even trade blocs? A globalized system could be a paradise for giant corporations, who, if they don't like the costs, taxes, and restrictions of one place happily move to another continent. "Don't give us any grief," the corporations tell governments and workers, "or we'll move our operations to India." Countries and their workers naturally fight such behavior, and if they are successful will build barriers against the free flow of goods, capital, and jobs. Not everyone likes the transnational corporations. Will they pursue profits at the expense of the environment and social justice?

A third problem: Economic growth is highly uneven, and some countries, especially landlocked countries with few resources, fall further behind. Eventually, they may turn into a "zone of chaos." In a globalized world, do the rich countries get richer at a faster rate, opening a bigger gap between the have and have-not countries? Or is the advantage to the poorer countries, which, thanks to their lower labor costs, enjoy faster growth? Either way, there will be discontents.

A fourth problem: Will all play the globalization game by the rules? Most countries talk "privatization" and "free trade" but sometimes protect domestic industries and banks and erect trade barriers, undermining the basis of a globalized system. Several financial meltdowns reveal that many countries' banks are unregulated and sometimes crooked; they extend loans recklessly until the bad debts are too big to hide. Their economies look modern and global, but at their heart are informal networks of politicians, bankers, and businesspersons who do favors for each other. Some economists fear that someday such a meltdown will ripple out until it engulfs the world and triggers a new depression.

A fifth problem: As globalization spreads it tends to create resentments, especially in Muslim and other lands with proud and different cultural traditions, at the American and capitalist culture of a globalized system: "McWorld." These countries in effect say, "We'll become modern, but in our own way. Our culture is old and good, and we will not abandon it to imitate the Americans." The whole world does not wish to become America, as Huntington understands well with his clash-of-civilizations model. Taking all these problems together, we should not count on the stability or durability of a globalized system.

A RESOURCE-WARS MODEL

If a globalized system falls apart, it may do so over the scramble for natural resources, especially petroleum. Some speak of "the geopolitics of oil." As East Asia, particularly China, industrializes, it consumes much more energy, for industry and private use, such as motor vehicles. Asians want to live like Americans, who consume energy prodigiously. Much of the 2004 oil price runup is attributed to China's rapid economic growth. Where will the oil come from? Will the world stay open to the free flow of natural resources, or will nations seek to gain advantage by exclusive deals with and control over the oil-producing areas? This is why questions of who controls the oilfields and transportation corridors of the Persian Gulf and Central Asia loom larger and larger. We may have already had our first resource wars, the 1991 and 2003 wars with Iraq.

A "CLASH-OF-CIVILIZATIONS" MODEL

In 1993 Harvard political scientist Samuel Huntington advanced a controversial theory that the post–Cold War world would be dominated by clashes among eight **civilizations**, each based heavily on religion: Western (with European and North American branches), Slavic/Orthodox, Islamic, Hindu, Sinic (China and its

---

civilization   In Huntington's theory, a large cultural area based chiefly on religion.

offshoots), Japanese (unique to one country), Latin American, and African. Some of these civilizations get along with each other tolerably well (Western and Latin American), but Islamic civilization clashes with most of its neighbors. "Islam has bloody borders," wrote Huntington. Countries home to two or more civilizations Huntington calls "cleft" countries. Bosnia, home to three civilizations (Western, Slavic/Orthodox, and Islamic) was thus a natural candidate for civil war. Countries with a Westernized elite but traditional masses, such as Mexico and Turkey, Huntington calls "torn"; they are torn between becoming Western or staying in their old civilization.

Much of the real world matches Huntington's civilizational theory, which gained horrifying plausibility on September 11, 2001. Religion is a potent political force, as we see in Iran, India, and Israel. Many of the world's worst conflicts are where Islam meets other civilizations (Bosnia, Kosovo, Macedonia, Chechnya, and Israel). The Catholic countries of Central Europe (Poland, Czech Republic, Hungary) adapted to markets and democracy much more quickly than the Orthodox lands further east and south (such as Russia, Serbia, and Bulgaria). Likewise, the European Union welcomed Central European countries as new members in 2004, but not Turkey, which Europe stills sees as Muslim and Middle Eastern. Japan and China quarrel over minute islands.

But much does not fit. Huntington's theory cannot explain massive fighting within a given civilization (the horrifying massacres of Rwandans) or the cross-civilizational ties based on security (the U.S.-Afghani link to oust the Taliban) or commerce (Western oil interests in the Persian Gulf and Caspian areas). Most of Huntington's civilizations contain serious splits and hostilities. Europe and the United States, supposedly one civilization, are often at odds. Vietnam, whose history is essentially a long fight against China, still fears it. Islam may have bloody borders, but it is also internally bloody, with Muslim killing Muslim, as we see in Iraq.

A PROLIFERATION MODEL

What would happen in a **proliferation** model—if many countries had nuclear weapons? For some decades only five major powers openly had nukes—the United States, Britain, France, the Soviet Union, and China—and these were precisely the five permanent members of the UN Security Council. The 1968 Nuclear Nonproliferation Treaty (NPT) tried to block the further spread of nukes, but several countries quietly built nuclear weapons. The way they saw it, only nukes confer security and prestige. If you have nuclear weapons, you are treated with respect and can deter military threats. With such reasoning, Israel, South Africa, India, and Pakistan quietly developed their own nuclear bombs. (South Africa dismantled its few warheads, figuring they did no good.) India denied it had nukes but in 1998 dramatically tested them, and most Indians were proud of it; now no one would push India around. This type of reasoning is infectious, and Pakistan then

---

proliferation The acquisition of nuclear weapons by many countries.

THE IMPORTANCE OF ECONOMICS

One common thread among most of the models of an emerging international system is economics. In place of military might and alliances, economics now looms large in almost everyone's thinking, the biggest single factor in structuring the globe. Economics, of course, was always important in the international system, but many refuse to recognize its impact until too late. The big flaw in the Cold War bipolar model was that it all but left out economics, the very factor that doomed the Soviet Union. Adherents of bipolarity went on and on about containment, nukes, and falling dominoes, but could not comprehend—much less predict—the collapse of Soviet power, largely because it had fallen behind economically (exception: George Kennan). In the words of Columbia economist Jeffrey Sachs, "Markets won."

But will markets stay the winner? Historically, countries have shown a strong tendency to control, regulate, or own their industries. Overall, perhaps the most free-market economy is that of the United States, but it too has numerous government subsidies, tax breaks, and regulations. The European pattern has been to construct large and expensive welfare states whose controls and taxes work against starting new enterprises. The East Asian pattern has been for the state to guide and subsidize what are deemed key industries, aimed at rapid growth and dominance of certain markets. Many say Adam Smith's ideas on a free economy are just theories, and few totally practice them.

In recent years controlled economies got a jolt from British Prime Minister Margaret Thatcher's attack on the welfare state and her promotion of capitalism. "Thatcherism" spread to many countries, leading to cuts in public spending and freer markets. Some countries—in large part because domestic interest groups strongly objected—resisted the encroachments of free markets; they tended to hide behind **tariffs** or **quotas**. And a few countries simply prohibit certain foreign imports; Japan, for example, for decades allowed no imported rice. Many domestic interest groups have sufficient clout to block foreign goods.

Keeping world trade open by cutting tariffs and other barriers is the task of the World Trade Organization (WTO), aimed at freer trade and having some powers of judicial settlement of disputes. Its predecessor before 1995, the General Agreement on Tariffs and Trade (GATT) did the same thing, but without enforcement powers. GATT and WTO have done much good. Tariffs are at an all-time low, and most goods flow unhindered over the globe, but now nontariff barriers increasingly irritate international economic relations, many of them concerning nonindustrial products. Several countries (including Canada and France) limit U.S. movies and TV shows, arguing that they replace local productions and endanger cultural and national identities. Some countries (including Japan and China) keep out U.S. banks and insurance companies, arguing that such vital areas belong under national control. We argue that if TV and banking are what we do best, our products should flow wherever there are customers. Keeping world trade open is a never-ending task, for new industries are always developing, and countries continually come up with excuses to keep out the new foreign products.

If the WTO system breaks down and the world goes back to protected markets, we could see another depression. The very high Hawley-Smoot tariff, which the United States introduced in 1930 to protect U.S. farmers and manufacturers from foreign competition as the Great Depression began, brought retaliation from our trading partners, and this made the Depression deeper and longer and worldwide, which was the biggest factor that led to the rise of Hitler and thus to World War II.

tariff   A tax on an import.

quota   A numerical limit on an import.

had to test its nuclear devices, which had long been under development. Iran, Iraq, and North Korea, isolated and fearful, worked to build their own nukes. (Iraq's program was dismantled under UN inspection in the 1990s.)

Where will it stop? The more countries that possess nuclear weapons, the greater the chance they will be used. Eventually, some argue, a hermit dictatorship like North Korea will acquire nukes—North Korea claims it already has several warheads—and use them or sell some to terrorists. Or will the deterrence stalemate discussed in the previous chapter prevail, forcing even unstable dictators to behave cautiously? Paradoxically, there is a greater chance of nuclear war after the Cold War than during it. A world with ever-growing numbers of nuclear powers, including those with active grudges, will be a dangerous world. It may limit the amount of international cooperation or leadership anyone can exercise. Some countries might hunker behind their nuclear barriers rather than seek peace and trade.

One can construct other international models that might, to greater or lesser degrees, match reality. Some could be combinations of the above; others could not. One valid model might combine multipolar economic blocs with the passivity of the interwar system. One could not combine a globalized system with a clash-of-civilizations system, as Huntington emphasizes. We must also be aware that one system can decay into another. A failed globalized system might fragment into hostile trade blocs, which in turn could engage in resource wars, which could turn nuclear in certain circumstances.

Historical systems are of some help in constructing a new model. Notice how some of the possible models have an **isolationism** component of only limited U.S. interest and leadership. This suggests something of the interwar system, in which the democracies, who should have led, stayed passive until almost too late. This may be undesirable, but after the Cold War Americans minimized foreign affairs until jolted awake by 9/11.

■ FOREIGN POLICY: INVOLVED OR ISOLATED?

Unfortunately, in the absence of an agreed-upon model that explains the workings of the real-world system, we are left floundering. Neither Republicans nor Democrats, legislators nor executives offer a definitive and valid model of the current world system and how to handle it. Some attempt to carry on as if the Cold War had simply been replaced by a Global War on Terrorism. Instead of containing Soviet power, we would contain Islamic fundamentalism. Many saw this analogy as far too simple.

The end of the Cold War reawoke an old question that had been asleep during the long period of tension with the Soviet Union: Should the United States defend its interests on the near or far side of the oceans? For most of America's history, it was assumed that we should generally stay on our own shores, that little overseas

---

isolationism   U.S. tendency to minimize importance of outside world.

really concerned us. Americans, some say, are natural-born isolationists. With Pearl Harbor in 1941, however, isolationism was rejected in favor of massive involvement in world affairs, first in winning World War II and then in waging the Cold War. Isolationism was not an option. Suddenly, as the Berlin Wall opened in 1989 and the Soviet Union dissolved in 1991, it became an option.

With the Cold War over and with budgetary constraints, U.S. armed forces shrank to half or less what they had been during the Cold War. There was no clear mission for them. Presidents Bush 41 and Clinton both articulated idealistic new uses for U.S. forces overseas. President Bush 43 at first argued against "humanitarian intervention" and "nation building" but soon found he had to use U.S. forces and build nations in the vital Persian Gulf region.

The old question remains: Should the United States send forces overseas—especially where few U.S. national interests are involved? There is no clear, simple answer. If the United States turns its back on horror and aggression overseas, the emerging international system will resemble the unstable and chaotic interwar system, a system in which the democracies held back from involvement until they were plunged into World War II. U.S. involvement overseas that lasts years, though, tends to provoke a voter backlash that few presidents want to risk. Over 70 percent of Americans supported the 2003 Iraq War, but by 2004 a majority thought it had been a mistake. Public opinion, as we saw in Chapter 8, is volatile. Too much U.S. military intervention also provokes the resentment of other countries (the "counterweight" model we discussed earlier), making it hard for America to rally the world for a common cause.

Unable to settle on where and when to intervene, the United States usually does either too little or too much overseas, and this produces an alternation in the history of U.S. foreign policy. Why can't we get it "just right"? But who is to say, in a time of emotion and exaggeration, what just right is?

CYCLES OF U.S. FOREIGN POLICY

U.S. foreign policy tends to swing between extremes of interventionism and isolationism. Can we find a stable and moderate middle ground? Many scholars think not; they have suggested theories that U.S. foreign policy tends to swing like a pendulum between extremes of overinvolvement and underinvolvement. Stanley Hoffmann discerned "the two *tempi* of America's foreign relations," alternating "from phases of withdrawal (or, when complete withdrawal impossible, priority to domestic concerns) to phases of dynamic, almost messianic romping on the world stage." Hans Morgenthau saw U.S. policy moving "back and forth between extremes of indiscriminate isolationism and an equally indiscriminate internationalism or globalism." Getting more specific, historian Dexter Perkins divided American foreign relations in cycles of "relatively pacific feeling," followed by "rising bellicosity and war," followed by "postwar nationalism," and then back to "relatively pacific feeling." If Perkins is right, in which phase of the cycle are we now? Probably most thinkers would pick postwar nationalism, our sense of triumph after the Cold War that was heightened by 9/11.

INTERVENTIONS WITHOUT RISK?

The 2001 attacks on the World Trade Center and Pentagon blasted America out of a tendency to avoid the risk of overseas military **intervention**. Prior to that, the U.S. public and Congress had serious doubts about intervention; many preferred not getting involved. Not far under the surface was the fear that an intervention could turn into another Vietnam, an endless war that enrages U.S. public opinion. This fear led us to pursue a "risk-averse" strategy—punctuated by occasional interventions—for roughly the last quarter of the twentieth century. A risk-averse U.S. strategy does not mean that a president never sends troops overseas but that he does so cautiously and with an eye on the next election. Can America sustain long-term interventions? Americans like their wars quick and definitive and do not like playing imperial masters over strange and unruly peoples.

Gulf War, 1991   Iraqi dictator Saddam Hussein conquered Kuwait in August 1990. President Bush 41 hesitated, but soon sent U.S. forces to defend Saudi Arabia. Public and congressional opinion on going to war split evenly until Bush, with support from many allies, in early 1991 beat Iraq. We did not push on to Baghdad and oust the brutal Saddam, however. It was considered too risky: Iraq could fall apart; Iran could take its southern portion; and we would have to stay as occupiers. The reasoning in 1991 was valid but was ignored in 2003.

Somalia, 1992–1993   Bush 41 sent peacekeeping forces into chaotic Somalia, where the government had collapsed and people were starving as local warlords robbed everything. The mission continued under Clinton but underwent **mission creep**. A battle in the streets of Mogadishu with the warriors of an ambitious strongman left eighteen U.S. Rangers dead. The body of an American helicopter pilot being dragged through the streets was shown on television. Americans quickly lost their idealism, and Clinton withdrew U.S. forces. Again, risk-avoidance.

Haiti, 1994   A brutal dictatorship pushed desperate Haitians to flee in rickety boats to Florida, forcing President Clinton to use U.S. forces. Much of the country, including many in Congress, opposed intervention, fearing it could become another Vietnam. The arrogance of Haiti's dictator and arrival of thousands of Haitians in Florida finally forced Clinton to intervene, and it went well. U.S. forces first disarmed and then deposed the dictatorship with scarcely a shot fired. Democracy has a tough time in a country as poor as Haiti, but at least we gave democracy a chance.

Bosnia, 1995   In the early 1990s, massacres in Bosnia horrified American TV viewers, but few wanted any direct U.S. intervention, arguing that it was none of our business. Quietly, U.S. officials trained and armed Croatian and Bosnian forces until in 1995 they beat back the Serbs. Then U.S. diplomats mediated a peace agreement among the warring parties who met in Dayton, Ohio,

intervention   Use of military force in other lands.
mission creep   Tendency of modest peacekeeping goals to expand.

and contributed 20,000 U.S. troops to a 60,000-troop NATO peacekeeping force, IFOR (Implementation Force). Clinton made the decision even though U.S. public opinion was two to one against sending troops, and Congress nearly blocked the move. The operation went well, and the United States showed it could and would take a leadership role in the world.

Kosovo, 1999 Serbian dictator Milosevic, faced with an uprising of ethnic Albanians in his southern province, began to massacre them. He was undeterred by Western threats. In coordination with allies, President Clinton waged an air-only campaign, without U.S. ground forces or casualties, that changed Milosevic's mind. In a curious reversal, U.S. elites were more frightened of risking casualties than were average Americans.

Colombia, Ongoing With most of the cocaine and much of the heroin flowing from Colombia to the United States, President Bush 41 first committed U.S. military forces to eradicating and blocking the drugs. Presidents Clinton and Bush 43 continued the policy of training and equipping Colombian forces. Some wonder if it will do any good, as the drug trade simply moves to other countries. The jungled mountains of Colombia look a lot like those of Vietnam. We want to stop the flow of drugs but do not want to get involved in Colombia's long and bloody civil war.

Afghanistan, 2001 Osama bin Laden was closely allied with the fanatic Taliban regime, one hated by most of the world. When they refused to turn over bin Laden after 9/11, a few U.S. special forces assisted local chiefs and quickly beat the Taliban but never caught Osama. A U.S.-installed president ruled little more than Kabul, the capital. Warlords with private militias, opium growers, and regrouped al Qaeda and Taliban fighters held sway in most of Afghanistan. As in 1989, we helped oust one Afghan regime but did not replace it with a viable, stable government. Again, the job was half-done, and Afghanistan was as unruly and dangerous as ever, but Americans had little appetite to complete the job.

Iraq, Ongoing In a time of rage and patriotism after 9/11, President Bush 43 said the dictatorship of Saddam Hussein in Iraq was rebuilding its weapons of mass destruction that had been dismantled after the 1991 war. In March 2003 U.S. and British forces invaded from Kuwait and conquered Iraq in a month. At first Americans were proud and delighted, but Americans hate long wars, and by 2004 many thought the invasion of Iraq had been a mistake and doubted Bush's Iraq policy. The Bush administration had exaggerated and oversold Iraqi WMD and ties to al Qaeda. Concerned about growing U.S. criticism over Iraq, Bush pushed Baghdad to take on more responsibilities so we could depart. Bush used diplomacy rather than war on Iran and North Korea, both of which really are building nuclear weapons. U.S. public opinion was not keen on taking on new risks.

CLASSIC WORKS

KLINGBERG'S ALTERNATION THEORY

A behaviorally inclined political scientist, Frank L. Klingberg, using such indicators as naval expenditures, annexations, armed expeditions, diplomatic pressures, and attention paid to foreign matters in presidential speeches and party platforms, discovered alternating phases of "introversion" (averaging twenty-one years) and "extroversion" (averaging twenty-seven years). Klingberg added: "If America's fourth phase of extroversion (which began around 1940) should last as long as the previous extrovert phases, it would not end until well into the 1960s." Writing about 1950 and making no reference to Vietnam, Klingberg virtually predicted the impact of the Vietnam War, for it was precisely in the late 1960s (1940 plus 27 years) that the U.S. public and Congress tired of the Vietnam War and intervention in general, an amazingly accurate prediction. Are we now in a new period of extroversion, or are Americans still cautious about sending troops overseas?

Could the United States slide into a kind of isolationism? We have to be careful how we define that term, as it may connote rigidity and ignorance. Some argue that with the 2003 Iraq War we have practiced **unilateralism**, losing allies and rejecting treaties that most countries want (against global warming, germ warfare, land mines, missile defense, and other issues). The neoconservatives who were prominent in the Bush 43 administration despised most of our European allies as cowardly. If we practice unilateralism long enough, however, we may turn our allies against us and isolate ourselves. Exercising too much U.S. power could actually lose us the power to influence others. Remember that power is the ability of one country to get another to do something.

Rather than isolationism, some prefer the term **noninterventionism**, a reluctance to use U.S. forces overseas. From the birth of the Republic until the 1898 war with Spain, the United States intervened rarely overseas, focusing instead on its own continent. World War II and the Cold War brought massive U.S. overseas intervention. Post–Cold War, we have mostly used U.S. forces abroad with caution, mindful of the risk of casualties. This suggested that the United States was not completely happy about a world leadership role. Prior to 9/11, the United States was called "the reluctant sheriff." Should the United States intervene overseas to stop horrors that do not directly affect U.S. national interests? If we don't, the horrors may be visited on us. This is precisely what happened after we helped oust the Soviets from Afghanistan in 1989. We walked away from Afghanistan and let it become the headquarters of al Qaeda.

---

unilateralism   Doing things our way against the wishes of allies.
noninterventionism   A policy of not sending troops abroad.

CLASSIC WORKS

KENNAN'S DINOSAUR ANALOGY

In a famous and oft-reprinted 1950 speech at the University of Chicago, diplomat-historian George F. Kennan (see page 387) compared American democracy to a pea-brained dinosaur sitting contentedly in a swamp unmindful of potential threats around him. Once harmed by an adversary, though, he erupts into a violent rage that not only destroys the foe but wrecks his own habitat. "You wonder whether it would not have been wiser for him to have taken a little more interest in what was going on at an earlier date and to have seen whether he could not have prevented some of these situations from arising instead of proceeding from an undiscriminating indifference to a holy wrath equally undiscriminating." Kennan had U.S. entrance into World War I in mind, but his advice fits many more recent instances of blind American rage. Pay attention earlier. In 2002 at age 98, Kennan warned that the U.S. conquest of Iraq would have a difficult and chaotic aftermath. He died in 2005 at age 101.

THE UNITED STATES IN A DANGEROUS WORLD

Foreign policy is one of the most difficult areas of governance, because we have to take into account not only our own abilities and preferences but those of dozens of other states. We can make two opposite errors (and often do), both related to the problem of *misperception* (discussed on page 381). First, we can underestimate the dangers we face. In the late 1930s, as the clouds of World War II gathered, we supposed the oceans would serve as two great moats, shielding us from the war. It took the shock of Pearl Harbor to make Americans realize they could not stay isolated.

During the Cold War, however, we often overestimated the importance of a region, supposing that all areas of the globe were of equal and urgent importance to our national security. On this basis we plunged into Vietnam, with unhappy results. Ironically, a decade and a half after the Communists took over South Vietnam, we won the Cold War largely due to the economic inefficiency of communism. American firms, taking advantage of low Vietnamese wages, now manufacture athletic clothing and footwear there.

Thus the United States faces a twin problem: (1) a messy outside world that often defies our influence, and (2) an American people and government little interested in or equipped for putting this world in order. There is no simple solution. Wise practitioners of foreign policy such as George Kennan (see box above) urge calm, reason, and patience. Avoid emotion and extremes. Military might is sometimes necessary but should be used sparingly, as the aftermath of wars is often a power vacuum.

We have recently been in a time of emotion and anger in our foreign affairs. This has led to oversimplifications and unanticipated consequences. Whichever side you take in a foreign-policy debate, panic or despair are seldom justified. Our generation lived through the fears of the Cold War and sometimes overreacted.

THUCYDIDES ON WAR

The terrible Peloponnesian War (431–404 B.C.) destroyed Athens. A cashiered Athenian general, Thucydides, turned into a historian who reflected on what had gone wrong. "War became inevitable," he wrote, "with the growth of Athenian power and the fear this caused in Sparta." The long and brutal war deranged both sides. Greek civilization took a big step backward and never fully recovered. Political discourse became debased:

> What used to be described as a thoughtless act of aggression was now regarded as courage . . .; to think of the future and wait was merely another way of saying one was a coward; any idea of moderation was just an attempt to disguise one's unmanly character; ability to understand a question from all sides meant that one was totally unfitted for action. Fanatical enthusiasm was the mark of a real man . . . Anyone who held violent opinions could always be trusted . . . Society became divided into camps in which no man trusted his fellow.

Still think the ancient Greeks have nothing to teach us?

We now realize that we were always going to win, that communism was an unworkable system that was eventually going to collapse. Current threats are not trivial, but we must not panic over a form of Islamic extremism that was founded in the fourteenth century. It is likely to fade, however, because, like communism, it cannot put food on the table. Our generation made it through the Cold War; with calm and reason yours will make it through the current struggle. Anger and panic can only harm us.

KEY TERMS

balance of power (p. 395)
bipolar (p. 395)
civilization (p. 401)
counterweight (p. 396)
empirical theory (p. 399)
foreign policy (p. 394)
FTAA (p. 397)
globalization (p. 398)
hegemony (p. 397)
international system (p. 393)
intervention (p. 406)
isolationism (p. 404)
Mercosur (p. 397)

mission creep (p. 406)
multipolar (p. 397)
NAFTA (p. 397)
noninterventionism (p. 408)
proliferation (p. 402)
quota (p. 403)
reification (p. 399)
stratified (p. 398)
tariff (p. 403)
theory (p. 399)
unilateralism (p. 408)
unipolar (p. 396)

KEY WEB SITES

Global governance, British and Swiss sites
www.bath.ac.uk/htsearch/

www.cgg.ch/

Conflict resolution
www.fourthfreedom.org/

European Union
europa.eu.int/index.htm

Scholarly research on world affairs
www.vuw.ac.nz/atp/frmain08.html

World Trade Organization
www.wto.org/

International Monetary Fund
www.imf.org/

FURTHER REFERENCE

Barber, Benjamin R. *Jihad vs. McWorld*. New York: Random House, 1995.

Callahan, David. *Unwinnable Wars: American Power and Ethnic Conflict*. New York: Hill and Wang, 1998.

Crocker, Chester A., Fen Osler Hampson, and Pamela Aall, eds. *Turbulent Peace: The Challenges of Managing International Conflict*. Herndon, VA: U.S. Institutes of Peace, 2001.

Cyr, Arthur I. *After the Cold War: American Foreign Policy, Europe, and Asia*. New York: New York University, 1997.

Ferguson, Niall. *Empire: The Rise and Demise of the British World Order and the Lessons for Global Power*. New York: Basic Books, 2004.

Haass, Richard N. *The Reluctant Sheriff: The United States after the Cold War*. New York: Council on Foreign Relations, 1997.

Hirsh, Michael. *At War with Ourselves: Why America Is Squandering Its Chance to Build a Better World*. New York: Oxford University Press, 2004.

Holbrooke, Richard. *To End a War: From Sarajevo to Dayton—and Beyond*. New York: Random House, 1998.

Huntington, Samuel P. *The Clash of Civilizations and the Remaking of World Order*. New York: Simon & Schuster, 1996.

Scholte, Jan Aart. *Globalization: A Critical Introduction*. New York: St. Martin's, 2000.

Singer, Max, and Aaron Wildavsky. *The Real World Order: Zones of Peace/Zones of Turmoil*, rev. ed. Chatham, NJ: Chatham House, 1996.

Snow, Donald M. *When America Fights: The Uses of U.S. Military Force*. Washington, D.C.: CQ Press, 2000.

INDEX

A

Abraham, Henry, 332
Abramson, Paul, 232
Absenteeism, legislative, 270
Absolutism, 254
Access, 183, 185
Accusatorial systems, 322
Adams, Guy, 313
Adjudication, 307
Administration, U.S., 256
Adolino, Jessica, 354
Adorno, Theodore, 130
Adversarial systems, 168, 322
AFL-CIO, 182
Age, 139, 217, 223
Aldrich, John, 232
Alexander, Herbert, 210
Almond, Gabriel, 17, 35, 118, 148
Alterman, Eric, 172
Alternation in power, 75
Altman, Daniel, 354
Alvarez, R. Michael, 151
Amicus curiae, 187
Anachronism, 231
Analogies, 360
Anarchy, 40
Anecdotal evidence, 134
Anglophones, 125

Anthropology, 4
Anticipated reactions, 117
Anticlericalism, 138
Apartheid, 267
Apathy, 120, 163
Apparatchiks, Soviet, 203
Appeals, 320
Appropriations, 295
Arendt, Hannah, 368
Aristotle, 2, 20
  types of government, 46
Arkes, Hadley, 70
Aronowitz, Stanley, 151
Asher, Herbert, 151
Auletta, Ken, 172
Authoritarianism, 86–87, 278
Authoritarian Personality, The, 130
Authority, 6–7
Autonomías, Spanish, 242
Autonomy, 50
Axelrod, Alan, 70
Ayatollahs, 367

B

Baby boom, 345
Backbenchers, 259
Balance of payments, 337
Balance of power, 380–81, 395

Baldwin, Nicholas, 273
Balfour, Danny, 313
Balkanization, 248
Bandwagon effects, 161
Baradat, Leon, 113
Barber, Benjamin, 411
Barber, James D., 284
Basic Law, German, 58
Baum, Lawrence, 332
Beck, Paul, 210
Behavioralism, 26–28
Bell-Fialkoff, Andrew, 374
Belsky, Martin, 332
Bench, legal, 321
Berry, Jeffrey, 192
Biersack, Robert, 192
Bibby, John F., 210
Bicameral, 261
Biersack, Robert, 192
Bimodal distributions, 140
Biology, 5, 8
Bipolarity, 395
Blainey, Geoffrey, 392
Blake, Charles, 354
Blondel, Jean, 293
Boaz, David, 113
Bobbit, Philip, 392
Boesche, Roger, 35
Boulding, Kenneth, 17
Bourgeoisie, 24
Brehm, John, 151
Briefs, legal, 320
Brinton, Crane, 366
Broder, David, 192
Brown, 329
Browne, William, 192
Brzezinski, Zbigniew, 82, 392
Budgets, 269, 344
Bull markets, 337
Bundesrat, 261
Bundestag, 261
Burden shifting, 248, 249
Bureaucracies, 294–95
　British, 299
　Communist, 297
　French, 297–98
　German, 298–99
　Japanese, 298
　U.S. federal, 295–96

Bureaucratic politics, 305
Burke, Edmund, 96–97
Burke, John, 293
Burns, Scott, 354
Bush, George W., 222, 291
Business cycle, 335, 343

C

Cabinets, 256, 289–90
Cadre parties, 200
Callahan, David, 411
Calvi, James, 332
Campi, Alessandro, 113
Canada, 60, 198
　federalism, 247–48
Canon law, 319
Capitol Hill, 260
Cappella, Joseph, 172
Carothers, Thomas, 91
Carp, Robert, 332
Carter, Jimmy, 281
Carter, Lief, 332
Carty, R. Kenneth, 211
Catchall parties, 203
Center-fleeing tendencies, 208
Center-periphery tensions, 137, 241
Center-seeking tendencies, 208
Centrifugal tendencies, 247
Chancellor, German, 276
Charismatic leaders, 227
Cheibub, José, 91
Cigler, Allan, 192
Civic Culture, The, 118
Civil disobedience, 77
Civilizations, Clash of, 401
Civil law, 317
Civil rights, 62, 63, 329–30
Civil society, 22, 50, 116
Clark, Wesley, Gen., 392
Class action, 187
Class voting, 220
Clinton, David, 35, 392
Coalitions, 255
Code law, 318–19
Codevilla, Angelo, 132
Cohabitation, 276
Cohen, Jeffrey, 211

Cold War, 386–89
Coleman, James S., 35
Coleman, Susan, 332
Collective security, 383
Colomer, Josep, 91
Committees, legislative, 262–64
Common law, 317, 318–19
Communication, 152–54
Communism, 89, 102–104
    collapse of, 107–108
Communist parties, 201–204
Competence, political, 118
Competition, 74–75
Confederations, 240
Confucius, 21
Conservatism
    American, 146–47
    classic, 96–97
    modern, 98–99
    neo, 108–109
Constituencies, 230
Constituency casework, 265–66
Constituent assembly, 61
Constitution, U.S., 61–69
Constitutionalism, 58
Constitutional law, 57–58, 317
Constitutions, 54–59
Constructs, 63
Containment, 386, 387
Copeland, Gary, 273
Corporatism, 176
Corruption, 179, 307
Countervailing power, 177
Counterweight model, 396
Coups, 356, 361
Courts, 320–31
    European, 323–24
    U.S., 320–22
Covariance, 144
Crick, Bernard, 91
Critical elections, 231
Crocker, Chester, 411
Cross, William, 211
Cross-pressures, 163
Cross-tabulations, 197
Crotty, William, 91
Crozier, Michel, 313
Culture, 8–9

Culture wars, U.S., 119
Cushman, Clare, 332
Cynicism, 117
Cyr, Arthur, 411

D

Dahl, Robert, 49, 53, 70, 79, 81, 91
Dalton, Russell, 151, 211
Dautrich, Kenneth, 172
Davidson, Roger, 273
Deadlock, 275
Dealignment, 226
Debt, 344
Decentralization, 242, 311
Deering, Christopher, 273
Deficits, 343
Definitions, 161
Demagogues, 88
Democracy, 71–78
Democratic peace, 89, 383
Democratization, 87–90
Departments, French, 241
Dependent variables, 144
Descriptive theory, 20
Deterrence, 387–89
Developing nations, 44, 87, 128
Devolution, British, 241
Devotee parties, 200
Diamond, Larry, 374
Diet, Japanese, 177
Diplomatic recognition, 52
Discipline, 2
Discretionary implementation, 308
Dissent, 76–77
Dissolution of parliament, 278
Distribution, 42, 44
Djilas, Milovan, 306
Dodd, Lawrence, 273
Donahue, John, 252
Doran, Charles, 252
Dougherty, James, 392
Downs, Anthony, 216
Duchacek, Ivo, 252
Duverger, Maurice, 200, 211
Dysanalogy, 360

E

Eastland, Terry, 70
Easton, David, 28–30, 35
Economic rights, 63
Economics, 4, 85, 137, 334–44, 403
Edelman, Murray, 51, 53
Education, 122, 137, 216, 218
Efficacy, political, 118
Ehrenreich, Barbara, 392
Eisenhower, Dwight, 282
Elazar, Daniel, 70, 151
Eldersveld, Samuel, 211
Elections, 226–29
Electoral College, U.S., 214
Electoral systems, 204, 207–209, 214–15,
    236–40
  French, 238
  German, 238
Electromagnetic spectrum, 164
Elgie, Robert, 293
Elite media, 156
Elites, 78–80, 122–23
  and foreign affairs, 379, 382
Emerson, Rupert, 53
Empiricism, 12
Enron, 179
Entitlements, 345
Environmentalism, 110
Epstein, Richard, 70
Escalation, 387
Estates General, 254
Ethnic groups, 141
Euro currency, 344
Evolutionary change, 233
Exchange rates
  fixed, 340
  floating, 340
Executives, 274
Expression, freedom of, 65–69, 78

F

Face-to-face communication, 153
Failed states, 41
Falk, Richard, 70
Families, 127–29

Farrell, David, 232
Fascism, 106–107
Federalism, 52
  U.S., 248–51
Federal Reserve Board, 337
Federal systems, 243–48
Feminism, 112
Ferguson, Niall, 411
Feudalism, 253–54
Finer, S. E., 53
First-order civil divisions, 240
Five-Year Plans, 297
Flanigan, William, 232
Fleischer, Richard, 211
Foreign policy, 386–89, 394, 404–409
Fourfold tables, 329
Francophones, 125
Freeden, Michael, 113
Freedom House, 73, 197
Frey, Lou, 273
Friedman, Milton, 99
Friedrich, Carl, 17, 82
Fritschler, A. Lee, 309
Fry, Brian, 314
FTAA, 397
Fukuyama, Francis, 111–12, 121
Functionalism, 384
Fusion of power, 258

G

Galbraith, James, 354
Game theory, 33
Gans, Herbert, 172
Gender, 139–41, 217–18
  gap, 223
General will, 34
Geography, 4
Gerard, Alexander, 91
Giglio, Ernest, 70
Gilbert, Robert, 293
Gill, Graeme, 91
Glasnost, Soviet, 245
Globalization, 398–401
Golden, Marissa, 314
Goldstone, Jack, 374

Government, 40–41, 44–50, 131, 256
Graber, Doris, 172
Graphs, 286–87
   bar, 287
   line, 286
Graziano, Luigi, 192
Great Society, 199
Green, Donald, 232
Green, Thomas Hill, 97
Greene, Thomas, 374
Greenstein, Fred, 293
Gregor, A. James, 113
Gross Domestic Product, 31
Grossman, Gene, 192
Grugel, Jean, 91

H

Haass, Richard, 411
Habsburgs, 388
Halliday, Fred, 374
Han, Lori Cox, 172
Hanson, John, 211
Hartley, Thomas, 172
Hayes, Michael, 273
Heads of government, 257, 279
Heads of state, 257, 279–80
Heady, Ferrel, 314
Hegel, 3, 23
Hegemony, 397
Helsing, Jeffrey, 354
Herrnson, Paul, 192
Hershey, Marjorie, 210
Hetherington, Marc, 211
Heymann, Philip, 374
Hierarchy, 83, 294
Hill, Steven, 232
Hirsh, Michael, 411
History, 3
Hobbes, Thomas, 22
Hodess, Robin, 314
Holbrooke, Richard, 411
Honeymoons, 145
Human rights, 63
Huntington, Samuel, 75, 132, 401–402,
   411

Hutchinson, John, 53
Huysmans, Jeff, 17
Hypotheses, 16

I

Ibn Khaldun, 21
Identity, 41
Ideologies, 82–83, 92–93, 111–12
   classifying, 95
   origins, 94
Ideologues, 93
IFOR, 389
If-then statements, 221
Ikenberry, G. John, 392
Immobilism, 206, 260
Impeachment, 279
Imperialism, 102
Imperial Presidency, The, 282
Inchoate party systems, 204
Income, 216
Incumbency, 160
Independence, 39–40
Independent variables, 144
Inequality, 345
Inflation, 336, 337
Instability, 206
Institutionalization, 234
Institutions, 25–26, 33–34, 233–35,
   250–51
Integration, 124–26
Intellectuals, 364–66
Intensity, 148
Interest aggregation, 194
Interest groups, 80, 173–75
   and government, 175–76
   single-issue, 182
International law, 318–19
International relations, 375–77
International systems, 393–402
Internet, 158
Interventions, 406–407
Introspection, 154
Investigating judges, 323
Iran, 367
Iraq, 90, 145, 170

Irrationality, 10
Islamism, 111
Isolationism, 404
Israel, 277

J

Jacobs, Lawrence, 293
Jamieson, Kathleen, 172
Janis, Irving, 17
Japan, 198
Japanese Americans, 64
Jervis, Robert, 392
Jim Crow, 330
Johnson, Haynes, 192
Johnson, Lyndon, 288
Jones, Charles, 293
Jreisat, Jamil, 314
Judicial activism, 57
Judicial restraint, 58
Judicial review, 57, 317
Jung, Hwa Yol, 132
Junkers, 298

K

Kagan, Jerome, 17
Kantor, Paul, 211
Karvonen, Lauri, 211
Katz, Mark, 374
Kautilya, 21
Keefe, William, 211
Kleptocracy, 89
Kennan, George F., 387, 409
Kennedy, Paul, 392
Kerwin, Cornelius, 314
KGB, 278
King, Anthony, 273
Kirchheimer, Otto, 203
Kirkpatrick, Jeane, 86–87
Kissinger, Henry, 392
Klein, Joe, 293
Klingberg, Frank, 408
Knesset, Israeli, 277
Kotlikoff, Laurence, 354

Kowert, Paul, 293
Krugman, Paul, 354
Kuhnle, Stein, 211
Kumar, Martha, 293
Kuypers, Jim, 172

L

Laissez-faire, 45, 46
Lakin, Jason, 91
Land, German, 244
Lane, Ruth, 35
Laqueur, Walter, 374
Lasswell, Harold, 17, 288
Laver, Michael, 35, 273
Lavrakas, Paul, 151
Law, 315–20
    in Russia, 325
Lawmaking, 265
Leftism, 25
Legislatures, 253
    decline of, 268–72
Legitimacy, 6–7, 41, 61
Lenin, Vladimir, 102–104
Lewellen, Ted, 17
Lewis, Charles, 232
Liberalism
    American, 146–47
    classic, 93–96
    modern, 97–98
Libertarianism, 109
Liebovich, Louis, 172
Life cycles, 139
Life peer, British, 261
Light, Paul, 314
Lijphart, Arend, 252, 273
Lindblom, Charles, 53, 314
Linz, Juan, 91, 374
Lipset, Seymour, 35, 53, 74, 91, 132
Lobbying, 185
Locke, John, 23, 44, 255
Log rolling, 264
Longitudinal studies, 267
Lords, House of, 261
Losco, Joseph, 35
Lukacs, John, 392

M

Machiavelli, 22
MacManus, Susan, 151
Macro theories, 380
Maddex, Robert, 70
Mainstream culture, 123
Mair, Peter, 211
Maisel, L. Sandy, 210
Majority systems, 238
Mandate, 75
Maoism, 104
Maps, 338–39
Marbury v. Madison, 326
Marginalization, 125
Marriage gap, 234
Marshall Plan, 386
Marx, Anthony, 113
Marxism, 99–100
Marx, Karl, 23–25
Mass media, 78, 130, 152, 154–57
    and government, 168–71
Mass parties, 200
Mass political culture, 122–23
Matese, Anthony, 293
Mayhew, David, 232, 273
McCabe, Neil, 252
McWilliams, Wayne, 392
Media events, 159
Medicare, 350–51
Members of Parliament, 258
Mercosur, 397
Merit civil service, 299
Methodology, 5
Micklethwait, John, 113
Milgram, Stanley, 17
Mills, C. Wright, 79
Ministers, 275
Ministries, 289
Minogue, Kenneth, 17
Minorities, 55, 64
Minow, Newton, 165
Miranda, 330
Misperception, 381, 409
Mission creep, 406
MITI, 177, 298
Mixed-member electoral systems, 238
Mobilization, 210
Models, 19–20, 30

Modernization, 31–32, 47–49
Monarchy, 235, 236, 237, 254
Montesquieu, 258
Moon, J. Donald, 35
Moon, Richard, 70
Moreno, Luis, 252
Morgenthau, Hans, 35, 392, 405
Mosca, Gaetano, 78
Mueller, John, 151
Mueller-Rommel, Ferdinand, 293
Multicausality, 221
Multipolarity, 397

N

NAFTA, 397
NAM, 182
National Assembly, French, 261
National interest, 377–79
Nationalism, 38, 105–106
Nationality, 246
Nationalization, 201
Nation-building, 41–44
Nations, 36–41
NATO, 390
Natural law, 316
Neiman, Max, 354
Nelson, Michael, 293
Nelson, William, 332
Neoconservatism, 108–109
Neo-institutional theory, 198
Neustadt, Richard, 293
New Deal, 250
New Federalism, 249
News media, 166–67
Nisbet, Robert, 113
Noneconomic issues, 137
Noninterventionism, 408
Normative theory, 20
Norris, Pippa, 132, 172

O

O'Brien, Rory, 17
Oil shocks, 340
Oleszek, Walter, 273

Oligopoly, 155
Olson, Mancur, 91, 190
Ombudsman, 265
Opinion curves, 140
Opinion leaders, 154
Oppenheimer, Bruce, 273
Opportunism, 33, 203, 230
Opposition, 259
Orwell, George, 71
Outliers, 303
Outsourcing, 345
Overspending, Congressional, 269
Overy, Richard, 91

P

Pacelle, Richard, 333
Page, Benjamin, 354
Palmer, Monte, 53
Palmquist, Bradley, 232
Paradigms, 33, 249
Paranoia, 288
Parliamentary systems, 255–62
Parochialism, 118
Parsa, Misagh, 374
Participation, 42, 117–19
Parties, 83, 174, 193–96
    classification, 201, 202
Party identification, 219
Party systems, 204–208
Patterson, Samuel, 273
Patterson, Thomas, 232
Payne, James, 354
Peace efforts, 383–85
Peacekeeping, 385
Penetration, 41–42
Pentagon Papers, 68
Percentages, 243
Personalistic parties, 200
Persson, Torsten, 354
Pfaltzgraff, Robert, 392
Pika, Joseph, 293
Piotrowski, Harry, 392
Plaintiffs, 316
Plato, 20
Plattner, Marc, 374
Pluralism, 78, 80–81, 178

Plurality, 238
Polarization, 227
Polarized pluralism, 210
Policy, 50–52
Politburo, 202
Political action committees, 180
Political culture, 58, 114–15
    and interest groups, 178
    decay of, 119–21
Political economy, 334
Political generations, 139
Political science, 2, 15–16
Politics, 1–3, 15
Polling, 141–45
    history of, 142
Polsby, Nelson, 232
Population, 39
Porter, Bruce, 53
Positive law, 316
Positivism, 26
Posner, Richard, 293
Postbehavioralism, 28
Postmaterialism, 218
Poverty, 346
    and ideology, 348–49
Powe, Lucas, 333
Powell, C. Bingham, 232
Power, 5, 8–12
Praetorianism, 361
Pragmatism, 92
Precedent, legal, 318
Prefect, French, 241
Prefecture, Japanese, 243
Premiers, 276
Presidential character, 284
Presidential systems, 255–62
Presidents, 275–79
    disabled, 283
Prime ministers, 255–62, 275–79
Primordial violence, 358
Productivity, 306, 345
Proletariat, 24
Proliferation, 402
Proportional representation, 208, 238–40
Psychology, 5, 8
Public financing, 191
Public opinion, 115–17, 133–35
    American, 145–48
Putnam, Robert, 132

Q

Quantification, 16
Quebec, 125
Question Hour, 266
Quotas, 403
Quota sampling, 143
Quotations, 122

R

Rabb, Theodore, 91
Race, 216–17, 224
Raj, 37
Rally events, 145
Randomization, 143
Rapoport, David, 374
Rational choice, 32–33
Rationality, 3, 9–10, 14
Rauch, Jonathan, 192
Ravitch, Frank, 70
Rawls, John, 113
Reagan, Ronald, 281, 285, 291
Realignment, electoral, 224–26
Realism, 22
Recessions, 335, 336
Reciprocity, 318
Redish, Martin, 252
References, 79
Referendums, 90
Regionalism, 37, 137–38, 223
Rehnquist, William, 331, 333
Reich, Robert, 113
Reification, 399
Relative deprivation, 362
Religion, 121, 138–39, 223, 227
Representative democracy, 74–78
Republics, 235, 245
Residence, 218–19
Retrospective voting, 231
Revisionism, 101
Revolutions, 360–61, 364–73
    anti-Communist, 370–71
    stages of, 366–68
Riksdag, Swedish, 254
Rimmerman, Craig, 132
Rising expectations, 363
Rohde, David, 232

Roman Law, 319
Roosevelt, Franklin D., 98, 195, 283
Rosenof, Theodore, 232
Rosenstone, Steven, 211
Rothstein, Bo, 354
Rousseau, Jean-Jacques, 23
Rules of engagement, 385
Russia, 246

S

Sabato, Larry, 192
Salience, 135
Sampling, 142
Sartori, Giovanni, 205, 208, 252
Scandals, 191
Scattergrams, 302–303
Schattschneider, E. E., 76
Schickler, Eric, 232
Schier, Steven, 232
Schlesinger, Arthur, 282
Schofield, Norman, 273
Scholarship, 14
Scholte, Jan Aart, 411
Schools, 129
Schultz, David, 35
Science, 12, 14
Seabright, Paul, 132
Second Amendment, 62
Secularization, 119
Sedition, 66–69
Seib, Philip, 172
Selden, Sally, 314
Semipresidentialism, 276, 278
Separation of powers, 60, 257
Shah, Iranian, 367
Shapiro, David, 252
Shapiro, Robert, 293
Sharansky, Natan, 91
Shell, Donald, 273
Shively, W. Phillips, 17
Shlapentokh, Vladimir, 91
Shogan, Robert, 172
Shutkin, William, 113
Siegan, Bernard, 252
Simmons, James, 354
Simpson, Glenn, 192
Singer, Max, 411

Single-member districts, 236–39
Sit-ins, 329
Skewed distributions, 140
Slush funds, 312
Smith, Adam, 93–96
Smith, Bradley, 192
Snow, Donald, 374, 411
Snyder, Louis, 113
Sobel, Richard, 151
Social class, 24, 136
Social contract, 34
Social democracy, 101
Socialism, 45, 47, 99–101
Socialization, 127–31, 195
Socioeconomic status, 183
Sociology, 4
Soft money, 180
Sources, 67
Sovereignty, 6–7, 375–76, 389
Soviet Union, 85, 89, 245–46
Sperling, John, 132
Spitzer, Robert, 70
Stagflation, 341
Starr, Paul, 172
State Duma, Russian, 60, 271
State of nature, 22
States, 36–37, 38, 274
Statism, 45, 47
Statutes, 55
Steinmo, Sven, 354
Stepan, Alfred, 374
Stimson, James, 151
Stone, Geoffrey, 70
Stonecash, Jeffrey, 151
Stratification, 398
Stumping, 153
Subcultures, 123–26
Subject political culture, 118
Suleiman, Ezra, 91, 273
Sullivan, 171
Superstructure, 25
Supranationalism, 390
Surveys, public opinion, 141–45, 222
Sweden, 202
Swing vote, 231
Symbols, 51–52
Systems, 28–31
  breakdown, 356
  global, 393–402

T

Tabellini, Guido, 354
Tables, 186
Tannenbuam, Donald, 35
Tariffs, 403
Tate, C. Neal, 333
Taxes, 337, 342
Television, 157–65
Tendency statements, 221
Territory, 37–39
Terror, 83–84, 358–59
  9/11, 229
Theodoulou, Stella, 17
Theories, 18–20, 399
Thermidor, 368
Theses, 27, 48
Third-party assistance, 384
Thomas, Clive, 192
Thompson, Kenneth, 35, 392
Thinkpiece, 360
Thucydides, 410
Tilly, Charles, 53
Tinder, Glenn, 35
Titoism, 104
Tocqueville, Alexis de, 116
Tories, 278
Totalitarianism, 71, 72, 82–86
Trade deficits, 344
Transparency, 200
Traugott, Michael, 151
Treaties, 385
Truman Doctrine, 386
Trustee, 75
Trust in government, 120
Turner, Patricia, 151
Turnout, electoral, 117, 212–13
Two-plus party systems, 207
Two-step flow, 154

U

Unforeseen consequences, 180
Unfunded mandates, 249
Unicameral, 261
Unilateralism, 408
Unimodal distributions, 140
Unions, 184

Unipolar model, 396
Unitary state, 52
United Nations, 390
UNPROFOR, 385
Urban voting, 224
Urofsky, Melvin, 333
Utopia, 364

V

Van Creveld, Martin, 53
Variables, 144, 219
Verba, Sydney, 115
Versailles, 283
Vice-minister, 298
Vietnam, 365
Violence, 189, 355–64
Volatility, 145
Votes of confidence, 259
Voting, 212–18
   blocs, 220

W

Wald, Kenneth, 151
Walker, David, 252
Walton, Hanes, 211
Walzer, Michael, 113
War, 43
   causes of, 380–81
War Powers Act, 280
Ware, Alan, 211
Warren Court, 328–30
Warren, Mark, 132
WASPs, 327
Watergate, 169
Wattenberg, Martin, 211
Weak state, 52
Weapons of mass destruction, 379
Weber, Max, 14, 300

Weidenbaum, Murray, 354
Weinberg, Leonard, 374
Weissberg, Robert, 151
Welfare, U.S., 348–50, 352
   dependency, 347
Welfare states, 45, 46
Weltanschauung, 203
West, Darrell, 172
West, William, 314
Whig democracy, 88
Whips, 260
White, Stephen, 35, 113
Wilcox, Clyde, 192
Wildavsky, Aaron, 232, 411
Wilson, Edward O., 17
Wilson, James Q., 314
Wilson, William Julius, 354
Wilson, Woodrow, 98
Wire services, 157
Wolfensberger, Donald, 273
Wooldridge, Adrian, 113
Workfare, 350

X

X axis, 286

Y

Yalta, 285
Y axis, 286
Young, Lisa, 211
Yugoslavia, 246–47

Z

Zeitgeist, 24
Zijderveld, Anton, 53